MODERN ETHOLOGY

MODERN ETHOLOGY
THE SCIENCE OF ANIMAL BEHAVIOR

S.A. BARNETT

Australian National University

New York   Oxford
OXFORD UNIVERSITY PRESS
1981

Copyright © 1981 by Oxford University Press, Inc.

Library of Congress Cataloging in Publication Data

Barnett, Samuel Anthony.
Modern ethology.

Bibliography: p.
Includes index.
1.   Animals, Habits and behavior of.   I.   Title.
QL751.B1865   591.51   80-12473
ISBN 0-19-502780-9

Cover photo: N. Tinbergen

Printed in the United States of America

PREFACE

To write a book, . . . can be a "vital joy", but a joy which is inevitably united with the thorns of anxious care. It is not a contribution to perfection. . . . To write anything worth writing is to arouse opposition, controversy . . .

John Passmore
The Perfectibility of Man

More than a million species of animals have been named. The behavior of some thousands, from Protozoa to Primates, has been described in detail. The descriptions appear in tens of thousands of papers and monographs, of which most have been published since 1950. During this period the theories of ethology have gone through a complete upheaval.

In this book I try to give an orderly account of the most important findings in ethology. I define ethology as the science of animal behavior. The word has then the same status as "ecology" or "genetics": it denotes a major subdivision of biology. I do not limit ethology to study by a particular method, or to social interactions, or to the views of a single school; and four chapters on "learning" (part III) are largely based on the work of experimental psychologists. I hope the book will be used by undergraduates and young graduates, and by their teachers, in all kinds of study of behavioral science.

In parts II, III, and IV behavior is classified mainly by its functions. Within chapters or sections the examples are sometimes arranged taxonomically. Certain examples could have been put in any one of several chapters. For instance, reproductive behavior is described in chapter 9, but it also appears in chapters 17 and 18. Similarly, bird song is discussed in chapter 12, before the general topic of communication is reached in chapter 13. There is no long segment of the book on the physiology of behavior, despite its importance; instead, physiological topics appear in many chapters. Nor is there a separate discussion of ecology and behavior; but ecological relationships turn up throughout the book. Other arrangements could have been used, but this one seemed the most convenient.

Most recent writings on ethology contain echoes of theories or concepts that are going out of use. These, and the ideas that are replacing them, are mentioned in many places; but the theoretical foundation of ethology is discussed mainly in chapters 16 through 19. This involves some repetition, which is deliberate. The fragments of the history of ethology, given especially in chapters 17 and 18, will, I hope, help to guide readers through important writings that use concepts we are now giving up.

Among the many matters of debate, three are important in all branches of biology. No account of modern ethology is complete without them. First is the question of heredity and environment. This subject not only causes violent argument in its application to human beings: it is also a source of confusion even when no social implications arise. It presents severe conceptual difficulties that I try to meet especially in chapters 16 and 17: these chapters give an epigenetic account of the development of behavior, in which the interaction of nature and nurture is analyzed.

Second, there is the question of reductionism: should we expect eventually to reduce all behavior to physiology (and physiology, in turn, to chemistry . . .)? In this book I treat both analysis at the behavioral level and also "reduction" to physiology as essential: neither can replace the other.

Third and last, the fact of evolution and the theory of natural selection are part of the foundation of ethology. Emphasis on evolution is sometimes thought to be in conflict with an epigenetic interpretation, but in fact the two themes are complementary. At the same time, the role of evolutionary ideas in ethology needs to be examined critically. I try to meet this need in chapter 18.

There is much debate also on whether a "human ethology" is possible. Students are often confused about this, with good reason. Part V is therefore on the human species, and there I try to give clear statements on questions of method. Readers interested only in conventional ethology should skip this part; but those concerned with the relationships of ethology with other disciplines will probably concentrate on chapters 8 and 14–19. Human behavior is also mentioned in other places in the book, whenever ethological methods seem to bear on human problems.

When there are rapid changes of ideas, there are also alterations in the meanings of words. Terms such as territory, dominance, imprinting, and habituation are used in different ways in different publications. I have tried to provide unambiguous and convenient definitions of all key terms, and to stick to the definitions throughout the book. These terms, and some others in common use that I do not recommend, are listed in the glossary.

One result of emphasizing definitions is that one becomes an easy target for adverse comment. I have been taken to task for using words, such as concomitant, propensity, and even orientation, without defining them. But these words are used with their ordinary meanings, given in any dictionary. The object of carefully defining key terms is to avoid ambiguity and obscurity.

Most of the work cited has appeared since 1950, but few items dated later than 1978 have been included. Nearly every section has references to recent reviews that give full information on sources. But many passages describe single researches: a reference is then given to the primary source—usually, a paper in a journal. Whenever an author's name is mentioned in the text or in a caption, there is a corresponding entry in the bibliography. Dates are given only when an author has more than one entry.

A textbook can be treated as a source of facts. This one contains many facts, some very strange. But studying a new subject can also lead to new attitudes. Some readers will perhaps appreciate, more than before, the variety and fascination of the ways in which animals live, and will have their curiosity further aroused. They may then be led to apply for themselves the scientific methods used to learn about behavior.

ACKNOWLEDGMENTS

This book was made possible by my wife, Kate Munro; and my son Amos (born 1975) provided both an additional incentive and much stimulation. It is dedicated to them.

Sabbatical leave granted by the Australian National University allowed periods of uninterrupted work, for which I am most grateful.

In the mechanics of producing the book I had essential help from Anne F. Cook, Cathy E. McKay, and Marian Obenchain; and with the illustrations, especially photographs, from Ivan A. Fox. Others who kindly sent photographs or original drawings are acknowledged in the captions.

A number of altruistic friends and colleagues read and criticized substantial parts of the book: Valerie A. Brown, Hiram Caton, Marian Dawkins, J. Derek Freeman, John B. Gibson, Donald L. Gunn, Jeremy G. M. Robertson, Richard J. Wallace, Martin J. Wells. Among others who helped with special problems are: Michael V. Brian, Vincent G. Dethier, Robert M. W. Dixon, B. M. Fitzgerald, H. J. Frith, Madhav Gadgil, H. W. Levi, Geoffrey V. T. Matthews, Anne McLaren, Randolph Menzel, D. John Mulvaney, Philip J. Regal, Susan C. Wilson.

Canberra   S.A.B.
April 1980

CONTENTS

I should not like my writing to spare other people the trouble of thinking. But, if possible, to stimulate someone to thoughts of his own.

Ludwig Wittgenstein
Philosophical Investigations

INTRODUCTION

THE SCIENCE
OF BEHAVIOR

I try to act and think on the hypothesis that all happenings are in principle explicable, and that, in so far as they are not completely explicable, this is because they consist of too many details for a human mind to grasp, and not because either the details or their pattern are beyond the scope of human reason.

J. B. S. Haldane (1963)

The science of animal behavior has special attractions, but it also puts unusual demands on our understanding. Everyday speech includes presumptions about animals which, for scientific analysis, have to be discarded. It is natural to say of a captive animal that it wants freedom. Or, if an adult animal exposes itself to danger through caring for a young one, we may exclaim at such self-sacrifice or altruism. And when a pest contrives to remain alive, despite efforts to kill it, we may remark on its intelligence.

All such ways of speaking can hinder understanding. All are examples of anthropomorphism, or of assuming that animals may be adequately described as if they had human needs, feelings, or abilities. Here are some examples of behavior explicable only if we discard such presumptions.

1.1 QUESTIONS OF METHOD

1.1.1 Needs and Feelings

The first concerns a herd of roe deer, *Capreolus capreolus,* kept in a paddock in a Swiss zoological garden. H. Hediger describes how a gate was carelessly left open, and the deer disappeared into a nearby forest where others of their species already lived. They had therefore escaped into an environment in which they could easily survive. Yet, soon afterward, the herd returned to the paddock. In human terms, it was as though prisoners, after making their escape, voluntarily returned to captivity. How can we explain this odd behavior? Here are some suggestions. Many mammals live in a well-defined region to which they cling as long as it provides needs such as food, shelter, and companionship. The return of the deer may be classified as an example of an attachment to a particular (satisfactory) region. We may also suspect that the habit of feeding in the paddock had some influence. If so, what induced the herd to move out? A possible answer is that the animals were exploring. Despite their attachment to an area, many animals are also

3

exploratory: they range quite widely, even though they regularly return to a home or center.

A critical reader will notice that these "explanations" are all hypothetical: they suggest reasons for the behavior observed, but provide no evidence. Such a reader may also have thought of additional hypotheses. For example, the deer may have been driven from the forest by the herd already in occupation. (If so, this would be an example of territorial behavior.) To account fully for what happened, experiments would be needed. But in this case no appropriate experiments were carried out. Hence all we can do is to propose explanations that seem likely from our general knowledge of animals.

Any person interested in animals is likely to observe or to hear of similarly strange and unexpected acts. Fortunately, some have been quite fully analyzed. Of all species, the honey bee, *Apis mellifera*, is among the most intensively studied (C. G. Butler; K. von Frisch, 1967; M. Lindauer, 1961; C. R. Ribbands). This animal is elaborately social, and has inevitably been described in human terms. In each colony one bee is larger than the rest and is surrounded by a number of attendants (figure 1-1). It was accordingly called the king. In Shakespeare's *Henry V* an archbishop says:

> They have a king and officers of sorts;
> Where some, like magistrates, correct at home,
> Others, like merchants, venture trade abroad,
> Others, like soldiers, arméd in their stings,
> Make boot upon the summer's velvet buds.

But in the 17th century it was noticed that the king lays eggs. She therefore came to be called the queen. She is, however, not much like a human queen: she is the only fertile female, and all the other bees in the colony are her offspring.

This instance of anthropomorphic terminology is in itself harmless: nobody is misled by it. The

FIGURE 1-1 Queen bee, *Apis mellifera,* on a comb and surrounded by a group of workers. She secretes odorous substances that attract workers and impel them to feed her. (Courtesy Norman E. Gary)

same applies to a statement, published in 1823 and quoted by Frisch, that bees sometimes "indulge in certain pleasures and jollity, and . . . at times they even set about a certain dance after their fashion." But such statements imply presumptions that can interfere with understanding. If the queen is removed from her colony, the conduct of the others gradually becomes disorganized. The change can be detected by an altered buzzing sound. In the 19th century, one observer wrote of the "low, mournful lament" of the bees deprived of their monarch. In contrast, modern experimental methods have told us something of how the change comes about. If a queen is isolated in a miniature cage, inside the hive, and the workers can touch her with their antennae and mouth parts, no such

disturbance occurs. Further experiment reveals secretions from the queen bee that are passed on
among the workers and regulate their behavior.
The best known of these chemical agents, queen
substance, *trans*-9-keto-2-decenoic acid, not only
ensures ordered behavior by the workers but also
prevents the workers from developing ovaries. Only
queens and the males (drones) have functioning
gonads.

Accurate information on bee societies has been
gained by painstaking observation and the use of
quantitative methods from the physical sciences.
For some purposes, even when we are concerned
with behavior, it is convenient to treat an animal
as a chemical system. Many advances in the understanding of behavior have depended on applying
such methods. The result is an account often of
marvels, but one that is detached, objective, and
perhaps, to a newcomer to science, disconcerting.
A description in more familiar terms is often more
readable. Indeed, a leading entomologist, E. O.
Wilson (1975), describes the role of a queen bee
as a "gentle despotism"; and he writes of the "self-
less" contribution of the workers to the upkeep of
the colony. In another passage, on ants of the
genus *Pheidole,* in which there are several "castes"
(another well established anthropomorphism), he
contrasts "the brutish soldiers . . . distinguished
by an extremely limited repertoire of responses,
and their versatile, nimble nestmates of the minor
worker subcaste." Such expressions can make
scientific writing more readable. One hopes that
readers do not take them seriously.

Insects are so remote from ourselves that it is
easy to reject the notion of a queen bee as a bossy
female. Greater difficulties arise when we are dealing with domestic animals. Here, adopting a matter-of-fact attitude can produce unexpected conclusions. In Britain, under the law on "vivisection",

animals may not see other animals being killed.
The attribution of human feelings to laboratory
animals is obvious. It is also, at least for some
species, inappropriate. Nobody who has dealt with
laboratory rats or mice can suppose that the death
of a rat or mouse under an anesthetic would have
any significance for other rats or mice. (The dead
body, however, would have significance: given the
chance, the survivors would probably eat it.)

This is an example of the way in which good
intentions are ill directed in the absence of knowledge. But, when we face questions of animal welfare, there are great problems in acquiring the
necessary knowledge. We cannot ask an animal, as
we would a human being, what it likes or dislikes.
Or, at least, we cannot do so by verbal means. As
Marian Dawkins (1977) shows, there is at least
one kind of procedure by which we can, in effect,
ask questions of animals. She is concerned with the
confinement of hens in battery cages. Such cages
look cruel: the hens are shut up permanently in a
small space, and they can do little more than eat,
drink, sleep, and lay eggs. Some hens were therefore given continuous access both to a commercial
battery cage and to a large pen: the hens showed
no preference. But other hens, allowed access to an
outside hen run, preferred the run to a cage; this
preference, however, was much influenced by the
previous experience of the hens. In this rather unusual study the methods of experimental ethology
are applied to a question concerning humane treatment of domestic animals.

In general, the confinement of wild or domestic
animals in cages, pens, or other enclosures raises
many questions, some of which I mention above in
the account of the roe deer that escaped. To us a
cage is a prison—something from which to escape.
Yet for a captive animal it may be a home and a
refuge. When my colleagues and I were studying

confined colonies of wild rats, *Rattus norvegicus,* the members of one group gnawed their way through a concrete floor and escaped into a neighboring farm. There they caused us some embarrassment by killing and eating the chickens. But they regularly returned to their proper home; and, by choosing the right moment for blocking the escape tunnel, we were able to confine them all again. Many mammals and birds occupy well-defined regions, each of which constitutes in itself a kind of prison; but occupation is unforced, and removal may even be resisted. Our own preferences are not a reliable guide to what is good for other species.

1.1.2 Morals

Expressions such as "brutish soldiers", applied to ants, remind us that throughout history animals have been used as examples of moral rather than scientific laws. The fables of Aesop and the bestiaries of the Middle Ages (figure 1-2) are well-known. Modern writers have maintained the tradition. Rudyard Kipling (1860–1939) wrote an entertaining short story, "The Mother Hive", in which a colony of bees becomes infested with parasites. Although Kipling draws on his experience as a beekeeper, his story is presented as fiction. The parasites (which include the wax moth) are not put forward as examples of ecological relationships, but as agents of moral degeneracy.

Here, to compare with Kipling's fantasy, is an account of an actual nest parasite, studied by Bert Hölldobler (1969, 1970). Beetles of the genus *Atemeles* live in and on colonies of ants, *Formica* (figure 1-3). The beetles find the ants by moving around until they detect the odor of an ant colony. They then move upwind, and so reach their target. At the nest entrance a beetle must first present an ant worker with secretions from an "appeasement gland" at the tip of th′ abdomen. The ant feeds on the secretion, and seems to become tranquilized. The ant then refreshes itself from the "adoption glands" further forward on the abdomen, after which it usually carries the beetle into its nest. Inside the nest the beetle is fed by the ants; it stimulates them to regurgitate food, as if to a fellow ant, by providing tactile stimuli like those used by the ants among themselves. Such experimental findings make strange ways of living still more fascinating; at the same time, they leave moral issues where they belong, in human society.

Nonetheless, few of us can resist resemblances to man in other species. Figure 1-4 shows how a female hornbill, *Buceros rhinoceros,* is confined to her nest during the breeding season, while the male feeds her through a hole. In the past the wall has been assumed to be an analog of that surrounding a harem; hence the cock bird has seemed to be an extreme example of male chauvinism. But actual observation has shown the wall to be built by the female (Hugh Whistler). The reader is free to devise her or his own analogy for that.

People have a tendency to project not only their

FIGURE 1-2 Animals as a source of moral instruction. A white goose (*Anser?*) exhorts a black bird (species uncertain). (After the *Dialogus Creaturarum;* from W. Ley, *Dawn of Zoology,* 1968)

FIGURE 1-3 Above, the larva of a beetle, *Atemeles pubicollis,* feeds on the larvae of an ant, of the genus, *Formica,* in whose nest it lives. Below, an adult ant, instead of destroying the parasite, feeds it as if it were a larva of its own species. The beetle evidently has an odor which resembles that of an ant larva. (Turid Hölldobler)

them (he says) to kill every male Negro they meet and to abduct every woman (figure 1-5). Here, in contrast, is a terrifying incident recorded by a modern observer. A full-grown chimpanzee charged straight toward him; it came to within a few meters, suddenly stopped, picked up a young chimpanzee, and rushed off again.

Some writers give the impression that the moral principles that bind human societies apply directly to the social conduct of other species. Human beings are often altruistic: they choose to act in ways that benefit others even at a cost to themselves. To

FIGURE 1-4 The mating system of a hornbill, *Buceros rhinoceros:* the female is walled up in a tree while she lays her eggs, and the male feeds her through a narrow hole. Is this an analog of extreme male chauvinism? (Drawing copyright © 1974 by Turid Hölldobler. Reproduced from *Animal Architecture* by K. von Frisch by permission of Harcourt Brace Jovanovich, Inc.)

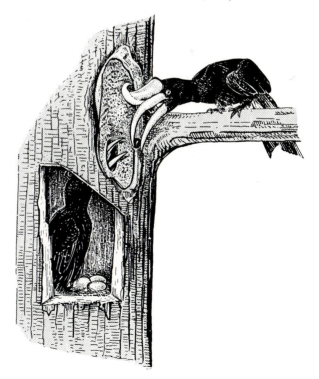

moral principles onto other species, but also human impulses which they dislike. As Vernon Reynolds (1967) shows, our nearest relatives, the Primates, are convenient for this purpose. G. L. Buffon (1717–1789) gives a dramatic account of the ferocity and passionate nature of apes, which lead

FIGURE 1-5 A 19th century image of the gorilla as a reflection of man. Today we know *Gorilla berengei* as a species threatened by human encroachment on its environment. (From Paul Du Chaillu, *Explorations and Adventures in Equatorial Africa,* London, 1861)

say this is to define *altruism* in terms of the intention of the actor. But the word altruism has recently been annexed, by writers on evolution, for another purpose. They ask how altruistic conduct can be favored by natural selection; but they define altruism as behavior that lowers the chances of survival of the actor and increases those of another member of the species. The definition is then in terms of the effects of the behavior, not of what motivates it. The question becomes one of population genetics. It is a real problem, because behavior of the kind described seems to be widespread in the animal kingdom.

At first sight, the theory of evolution by natural selection predicts that conduct which helps others at the expense of the performer must quickly be weeded out of any population. It seems to follow that natural selection always favors selfishness. A discussion of this sort of question is deferred to chapters 15 and 18. It is relevant in this chapter because it shows how easily a casual use of familiar words can lead to confusion. In this book we are concerned mainly with what is the case, not with statements about what conduct is right or wrong, desirable or undesirable. Such value judgments do not belong in a scientific account of bees or ants or even apes.

1.1.3 Intelligence

Biologists, then, have given a word—altruism—a new meaning without either warning the reader or acknowledging the theft. Such usage has to its credit only that it is objective. We can rarely say with any confidence that a monkey, let alone a bee, *intends* to help others; but the *effects* of certain types of behavior can be observed.

A similar objectivity has proved important in the study of animal intelligence. Early in the 20th century a horse owner attracted attention by declaring that "higher animals" are as intelligent as men, but rarely display their abilities owing to lack of training. His most celebrated horse, Clever Hans, could answer numerical questions correctly, by stamping, even if his owner were absent. Hence trickery by the owner could be ruled out. Clever Hans even responded correctly when shown pieces of cardboard on which questions had been written. David Katz describes how an investigator therefore took one from a number of such questions and showed it to the horse in such a way that nobody present knew which question it was. The horse duly began to stamp, and continued to do so as if awaiting a signal to stop. And so, in fact, he was. For when, on such an occasion, an observer knows the answer, and the correct number of stamps is reached, he often unknowingly makes an exceedingly small movement, usually of the head. It is to such movements that a "calculating" horse learns to respond. Today, experimenters take it for granted that they must avoid giving unintended information to the animals they observe.

Until well-designed experiments were carried out, the achievements of Clever Hans were both baffling and intriguing. The same applies to the performance of other "calculating" horses and dogs, accounts of which occasionally appear in the newspapers. Some people perhaps find the explanation a disappointing anticlimax. They may turn hopefully to dolphins, *Tursiops,* about which there is still a vigorous set of myths. These animals have brains similar in weight to those of man; they communicate by an apparently elaborate system of sounds; and they have a well-developed capacity for imitation. Few serious experiments have been done on them; but, as we see later, their abilities parallel those of other mammals with large brains, such as monkeys and elephants (8.2).

Sometimes a correct assessment of animal abilities is of practical importance. Of all pests, the brown or Norway rat, *Rattus norvegicus,* is among the most widespread. These animals have a long-standing reputation for intelligence. If traps are set, rats often refrain from going near them. If poison bait is put on their runways, the rats are liable to go elsewhere. It is as if they knew that they were in danger. In fact, however, these animals avoid anything novel in a familiar place, whether the object is injurious or not: they are indiscriminately neophobic. A harmless box, if strange, repels them as effectively as a trap or poison bait. We see later that neophobia combines with other features of behavior to protect wild rats from our efforts to kill them, unless those efforts are planned on the basis of knowledge of the rat's actual behavior. To call rats intelligent does not help at all: one needs to know exactly what they do in particular circumstances.

Probably the neophobia of rats that depend on man is a product of natural selection in man-made environments, which are liable to be littered with artificial hazards. In the same way, the ability of a horse to detect slight movements is important in a natural environment in which there is danger from large carnivores. Such statements about function, though speculative, make sense of the behavioral features peculiar to each species.

1.1.4 The Senses

Despite the admirers of horses and dolphins, we usually take it for granted that human beings are more intelligent than animals. Sensory abilities are a different matter. Many animals have senses that we lack, or that we have to a lesser degree. The danger here is in supposing an animal's "world" of sensations to be much like our own. The moray eel, *Gymnothorax mordax,* eats octopus, *Octopus,* and squid, *Sepia* (figure 1-6). An octopus, when attacked or pursued, throws off a black cloud called ink. To our eyes the ink is obviously a

"smoke screen" and interferes with pursuit. Yet an eel may fail to seize an octopus, even when its mouth is actually in contact with its prey, if ink has been released into the water. An explanation has been proposed by G. E. & N. McGinitie: evidently the eel hunts by smell, and eats only prey with a specific odor; and the ink-like secretion puts the eel's olfactory sense out of action.

The difference between the eel and ourselves is in the dominance of the eel's sense of smell. We are guided largely by sight. Sometimes, our difference from other species is merely in the range of a single sense: a dog can respond to sounds of a pitch beyond our range; hence it can be called by a whistle that produces a sound inaudible to us.

Another celebrated example is the ability of bats (Chiroptera) to avoid obstacles while flying in the dark. D. R. Griffin (1958) describes how the Italian genius, Lazzaro Spallanzani (1729–1799), largely solved this problem. He blinded bats and observed that their flight was unaffected. Next, by a brilliant stroke, he deafened them by blocking their ears. This rendered them helpless. As they fly around, bats squeak rapidly and at too high a pitch for our ears; the echoes of the squeaks enable them

FIGURE 1-6 An eel, *Gymnothorax,* and its prey, a squid, *Sepia.* How does the fish identify its prey?

FIGURE 1-7 Long-eared bat, *Plecotus auritis,* in flight. The large external ears are part of the equipment for hearing sounds of very high pitch. (E. Hosking)

to steer clear of obstacles and even to catch prey such as flying moths (figure 1-7). (Blind people develop a similar skill, for they can interpret the echoes produced by the tapping of a stick.)

Eels and bats provide examples of behavior not dominated by vision. Some animals can see features of their surroundings which we detect only by instruments. *Cataglyphis bicolor,* an ant of the north African desert, has been studied by P. Duelli & R. Wehner. These insects forage individually. The nests are underground. Outside, the habitat is virtually without visible landmarks. When an ant leaves the nest, it wanders around until it captures prey. It then returns to its nest on what might be called a beeline. The ants can also be trained to follow a particular course by rewarding them with food, such as a fragment of cheese. The sun need not be visible during these journeys. A human being, required to navigate in these conditions, would need at least a compass. The ants make use of the plane of polarization of light—a property that we detect only by means of instruments. The light reflected from the bowl of the sky—a bowl made of water and dust particles—varies in its degree of polarization according to a distinct pattern; and the pattern moves with the apparent movement of the sun. The desert ants, which run at about 20 m/min, can be followed by experimenters equipped with polarizers and other equipment. By altering the plane of polarization falling on them, one can change their direction of movement.

The detection by these animals of a feature of light invisible to us might be called extrasensory perception—a phrase associated with science fiction. But, although the ability falls outside the range of our senses, it has been successfully studied and explained by applying the laws of physics. As Haldane (1963) says, a scientist acts on the belief that the events he studies are explicable. The explanations he attempts are inevitably based on principles already established. (Very rarely a novel and revolutionary principle emerges.) To understand how such a method works, it is necessary to apply it to actual situations; and much of this book describes experiments that have given us new understanding of what animals do.

1.2 THE EVOLUTIONARY FRAMEWORK

In the preceding paragraphs ethology is presented as a science based on objective observation and experimental analysis. But the rational character of the science of behavior has another source, the theory of evolution by natural selection. Before the mid-19th century, the design of plants and animals was commonly seen as the work of an arbitrary creation. But geology had already vastly lengthened the time during which the world was supposed to have existed. Charles Darwin (1809–1882) proposed an orderly means by which, during hundreds of millions of years, the organisms we know today could have slowly evolved (Darwin, 1859). In every species we find genetically determined variation. If one type is more fertile or survives longer than another, its chances of leaving descendants are correspondingly greater. Darwin called this *natural selection,* and proposed it as an agent of change. And so any feature of a species—structural, chemical, or behavioral—may be thought of in terms of its *survival value.*

As an example, G. P. Bidder describes a peculiar feature of certain sponges (Porifera) common in western Europe between tide marks. These animals, of the genera *Halichondria, Grantia,* and *Sycon,* can squirt water for some distance. What function can this behavior have in the lives of these animals? When covered by the sea, they are in waters in continual motion. But occasionally a combination of low tides and heavy rain or hot weather kills all the sponges except those living in caves or other places where there is stagnant water. There the squirting of water removes waste products, and enables the cave dwellers to survive and to produce the next generation. It is assumed (but cannot be proved) that the squirting of water became a universal feature of these sponges by the action of natural selection on their ancestors in earlier periods.

The explanations suggested in the first part of this chapter concern the immediate causes of behavior: these include stimuli acting from outside, and also the animal's internal state. Evolutionary explanations refer to causes believed to have acted in the remote past. They are therefore speculative. But they have important implications. They lead us to attempt explanations of the behavior of each species as reflecting the adaptation of that species to a particular mode of life, or *niche.* Sometimes behavior is clearly related to quite specific needs, for water, food, shelter, and so on. In the next chapter we begin with movements of animals that are related to such needs, and that lend themselves to analysis in rather simple, mechanistic terms.

II

MAINTENANCE

In the first chapter of this part we ask what determines the direction of animals' movements. One answer could be in terms of function or survival value; another could be based on stimuli, sense organs, neural arrangements, and effector organs that produce the movements. It is sometimes easier to see the function of an activity than to discover how it is brought about. If the floating larva of a bivalve mollusk makes its way to the sea bottom and settles there, the descent puts it where it can metamorphose into the adult, sessile form. If a mosquito heads toward a warm, humid source of carbon dioxide, it has a good chance of landing on a supply of nourishing blood. These statements concern the survival value of the directed movement; but they say nothing about the sense organs or neural organization involved. Is the larva moving away from light, or is it responding to the pull of gravity? Is the mosquito guided by temperature, humidity, or carbon dioxide?

In the modern period, answers to such questions have been sought by treating animals as mechanisms, comparable in some respects to man-made machines. Today we are familiar with pilotless vehicles that can home on a radio beam. Chapter 2 describes some of the resulting findings, and indicates how this method can throw light on phenomena ranging from the settlement of larvae to the migration of birds.

The direction of an animal's movements is often determined by other animals of different species. Predators approach prey, and the prey flee. These and related topics are the subject of chapter 3. Like the orientations discussed in chapter 2 some of the movements can be described in a mechanistic way; but many—for example, exploratory searching—cannot. Moreover, predators adapt their behavior to circumstances: they develop new habits when they find new sources of food. They may also learn not to eat distasteful or poisonous prey. Such observations, superficially commonplace, raise many difficult (and often unanswered) questions. The behavior of prey species includes features that help them to avoid being eaten. In addition, examples are known of genetical changes that allow prey populations to remain protected in changed environments. This chapter, then, introduces themes, including those of learning new habits and of genetical change, which are more fully treated in part III and chapter 16, respectively.

In the last chapter of part II, behavior is related more consistently than before to physiology: respiration, temperature regulation, and especially feeding are used to illustrate the homeostatic functions of animal behavior. Yet another general concept is introduced—the concept of drive, which is illustrated by the question of what meaning, if any, we may give the expression "hunger drive".

2

MOVEMENT
AND ORIENTATION

Our nature is one of Movement; to
be completely still is to be dead.
                                    Pascal

Figure 2-1 shows woodlice collected in a characteristic group. It illustrates an aspect of animal conduct that we usually take for granted: members of a given species are neither uniformly nor randomly distributed in their habitat but are assembled (as a rule) in places that favor their survival. Correspondingly, animals rarely, if ever, move at random for long periods: their movements are directed in relation to other organisms or to inanimate features of their surroundings.

This chapter is mainly concerned with movements ordered by agencies such as the direction of light or the level of humidity. We sometimes say that animals select their environment. If this implies that they make a conscious choice, it is an unjustified anthropomorphism. As we shall find, to analyze their orientations it is often more convenient to treat the simpler animals as automata equipped with a small number of mechanisms that respond to measurable properties of their surroundings. At one time the movements generated by

these mechanisms were called tropisms, like the bendings of plants. But plant movements are due to differential growth. The movements of animals, usually brought about by muscles, are now classified differently (reviewed by G. S. Fraenkel & D. L. Gunn). In this book *orientation* signifies the determination of position or direction or rate of movement by an external agency.

2.1 PLACE AND TIME

2.1.1 Migration and Settlement: Zooplankton

Classifying and explaining movements depends on experiment, usually in the laboratory; but first it is useful to observe movements in natural conditions: such observation tells us more clearly what we have to explain.

We begin with marine zooplankton, the small animals that live in enormous numbers near the surface of the sea (figure 2-2). These creatures have been studied not only for their intrinsic interest but for economic reasons: herring, *Clupeus harengus,* cod, *Gadus morrhua,* and the whalebone whales (Mysticeti), all of great commercial im-

FIGURE 2-1 Woodlice, *Armadillidium,* grouped in a favorable environment. These terrestrial crustaceans assemble in damp places. (I. A. Fox)

portance, depend on them (reviewed by A. C. Hardy). One species of zooplankton, *Calanus finmarchicus,* a food of herring, has been observed in British waters. After dark these small crustaceans accumulate in the upper layers, but later they sink, and during much of the day are found mainly at greater depths. In the Clyde sea area of Scotland at 2200 hrs most of the *Calanus* are in the top 30 m, but at 1000 hrs nearly all are below 100 m. Vertical migration is a result of activity by the animals: with suitable equipment they can be observed, in the laboratory, swimming with or against gravity.

One of the factors in their movements is light. When put in a column of water lit from below, *Calanus* can be made to swim in a direction opposite to the normal. They can climb 15 m/h. They have been timed over periods of 2 min while swimming at their maximum speed. They then achieved

a rate of 66 m/h. When diving they go up to 10 m/h.

The function of vertical migration is often uncertain. It may be advantageous because it allows a continual change of environment and so, presumably, access to greater areas of sea.

Vertical migration may also be observed in freshwater. Another small crustacean, *Daphnia magna* (Cladocera), studied by E. R. Baylor & F. E. Smith, depends on an interaction of responses to gravity, light, temperature, and the composition of the water. As light or temperature increases, the tendency is to swim down. A high pH induces photopositive behavior, a low pH, photonegative. This animal also moves in an orderly way in the horizontal plane. In an experiment, a dish containing *D. magna* has above it a shallow tray divided into many compartments, some of which contain clear water and others water clouded with microscopic plants (phytoplankton). When the only source of light is above, the crustaceans gather below the phytoplankton in response to the difference in the quality of light that reaches them.

Calanus, Daphnia, and similar genera are permanent dwellers in surface waters. Also in the zooplankton are the larvae of species that spend their adult lives attached to rocks or buried in sand. The great majority die before they can metamorphose to the adult form. One might assume them to be nothing but drifters, borne passively by tide and current and dependent on chance for settlement on a suitable surface. But in fact they, too, are quite active, and in a directed way (reviewed by P. S. Meadows & J. I. Campbell; and by R. S. Scheltema).

When the larvae of such sessile animals are closely studied, they are often found capable of re-versing their responses to light or to gravity. The larvae of bristle worms (Polychaeta), such as *Owenia fusiformis,* are initially photopositive: they accumulate near the sea surface, where they feed on the phytoplankton. When ready to metamorphose, they become photonegative and sink to the bottom, over which they drift or swim. If no suitable surface is encountered, they rise, only to sink again later. The movements, though based on a simple alternation of responses, resemble a search. Metamorphosis may be deferred for many days if no suitable place is reached.

Sessile species are highly selective. A simple experiment is to suspend glass bottles in the sea at a chosen depth. Each holds a number of objects with different surface properties. A deposit accumulates in such bottles if they are left open at the top; and in this soft detritus are found a number of species,

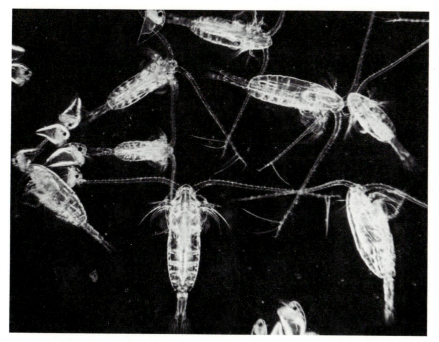

FIGURE 2-2 Zooplankton: *Calanus finmarchicus,* a common copepod of West European waters, which makes daily vertical migrations. Also present are examples of a smaller crustacean, a cladoceran of the genus *Evadne.* (Courtesy D. P. Wilson, Marine Biological Laboratory, Plymouth)

such as the cockle, *Cardium,* and the bristle star, *Ophiura.* One might assume that most, or all, larvae would settle, by gravity, in the detritus; but in fact only certain species accumulate there, and these species are never found elsewhere. If oblique glass surfaces covered by a thin film of mud are supplied, worms of the polychaete family Terebellidae settle on them, and only on them. Simple, smooth surfaces are colonized by worms, such as *Pomatoceros,* and barnacles, such as *Balanus.* If wood is supplied, the wood-boring mollusk, *Teredo,* appears in it.

Selection of the precise spot for attachment evidently depends on two properties, the texture of the rock or sand and its chemistry. The polychaete worm, *Ophelia bicornis,* in its adult state, is found in only a few localities on the coast of France and in an estuary on the southwest coast of England; but in a favored site, such as a particular English sandbank, there may be more than 200/m². At the age of five to eight days, the larvae readily settle on sand from this source, but not from others. They will burrow into other types of sand if the particles are not very small and sufficiently smooth, but will not metamorphose. A long series of experiments by D. P. Wilson suggests that sand coated with a layer of microorganisms is the target of these larvae.

Sometimes larvae attach themselves preferentially to sites where others of their species are or have been attached. The oyster, *Ostrea edulis,* settles more readily on surfaces already partly colonized. It is therefore a mistake to offer it a nicely clean and aseptic habitat. There should be a film of bacteria and diatoms, with some growth of small hydroids (Coelenterata, Hydrozoa). Such a population is the first to appear on a bare surface. Those who culture oysters for the market have learned to pay attention to zoologists who study the orientations of zooplankton.

Oysters in European waters have recently faced competition for sites from a barnacle, *Elminius modestus,* newly introduced from North America. The barnacles (Crustacea, Cirrepedia), are also of more general economic importance because they foul ships' bottoms. The orientations of the larvae of *Elminius, Balanus,* and others have been closely studied (reviewed by D. J. Crisp). In the first stage after leaving the egg, the larvae (called nauplii) are carried widely by tides and currents. In the final stage, the larvae (now called cyprides) drift near the bottom and descend at intervals to the surface over which they creep. This oscillation is due to an alternating positive and negative response to light.

Balanus balanoides, a common barnacle of European shores, is shown in figure 2-3, with cypris larvae about to settle. When larvae touch a surface, they attach themselves by their foremost appendages, the antennules; attachment is stimulated by movement of water over the surface. The larvae now walk over the surface on their heads, initially in a straight line with few pauses; but, if they remain on a surface for long, the pauses increase, and there are many changes of direction. Eventually, they settle.

In experiments, a panel has been used, with small depressions at regular intervals. On such a surface the pits are gradually occupied, each by a single barnacle, until all are used up; groups then form around the pits until finally the flat surface is colonized. Traces of occupation by the same species make a surface more attractive. When the animal settles on a natural surface, orientation tends to be along the axis of a groove; and, when possible, the anterior tends to be directed toward the light.

2.1.2 Movement on the Seashore

The seashore, with its regular but extreme fluctuations, provides an environment of special interest.

FIGURE 2-3 Adult shore barnacle, *Balanus balanoides,* with many grain-like cypris larvae about to metamorphose. (Courtesy P. S. Meadows)

I describe here movements of littoral species observed in nature.

Many mollusks move about feeding while the tide is at a certain level, but remain motionless on a rock at other times. The periwinkle, *Littorina littorea,* a snail common on British coasts, spends much time sitting still, often on vertical surfaces but sometimes on the flat tops of rocks (figure 2-4). As the tide rises or falls past them, the snails become active, and crawl about feeding on microscopic algae. G. E. Newell describes their movements when they set off from a horizontal surface. Typically, they first move toward the sun, but after a time they become photonegative: they turn round and follow a U-shaped track to a position near their starting point.

More precise homing is seen among other mollusks, the limpets. Each individual has its own position, marked by a scar on the rock, to which it has to find its way after each foray. *Siphonaria*

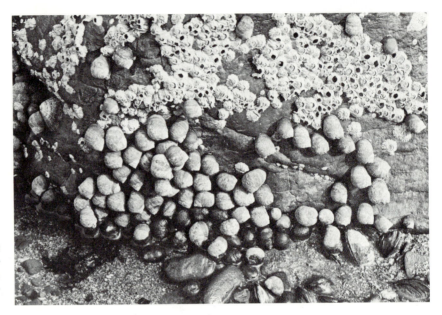

FIGURE 2-4 Periwinkles, *Littorina littorea*, common gastropods of European rocky shores. (Courtesy D. P. Wilson, Marine Biological Laboratory, Plymouth)

normalis, a pulmonate, lives on the Hawaiian Islands. It is most active as the tide rises and falls past its rock. Susan Cook rotated rocks bearing these animals, but the limpets still homed to their own scars. Hence distant clues, such as major landmarks, were not used; nor could navigation have been by the sun or moon. Some limpets were picked up while feeding and put elsewhere. Provided they were left in places in which they had previously been seen, they still got home safely; they were able to return directly and so were shown not to depend on a trace left during the outward journey.

Limpets of the common genus *Patella* have been similarly observed in England. *Patella vulgata* (figure 2-5) usually feeds while exposed and returns home before being covered by the tide. It evidently possesses a time sense that makes this possible. Homing can occur at any time of day, in any weather, and—once again—even if the rock has

been turned round. Limpets can also home without using the path followed on the outward journey. How do these enigmatic creatures find their way? In an experiment by A. Cook and others, the positions of two groups, each of nine limpets, were exchanged: group A was put on the rock of group B, and group B on the rock of group A. After a week, eight scars were occupied, and seven of the newcomers were in the same orientation as the original occupiers. Rocks over which these mollusks have moved evidently carry long-lasting chemical traces that allow homing. Such a finding is unexpected, and leaves many questions unanswered. The trace is probably an adsorbed protein, but its precise nature is not known. Nor is it understood how it can be directional or how the limpet detects it.

Another complexity is a social influence. Limpets of the Australian species, *Cellana tramoserica*, studied by D. A. Mackay & A. J. Underwood, home like other patellids, but not always: they may be deterred by the presence of conspecifics. If the microscopic algae, which are the food of these animals, are removed from an otherwise suitable rock surface, fewer limpets move into or remain in the denuded area. Hence homing is held to regulate density in relation to food supply. (See also 10.4.3.)

2.1.3 Biochronometry and Rhythms

In the preceding section I use the vague and rather anthropomorphic expression, "time sense", in a reference to the movements of limpets. A more precise (but long-winded) statement would have been this: the behavior of limpets in relation to the tide appears to be regulated by the passage of time; we may infer, or at least hypothesize, an internal process that reaches a threshold at intervals, alters the output of the nervous system to the muscles, and so changes behavior.

Such time-related processes are often called "internal clocks"; hence, like orientations, they are interpreted mechanistically. Biological rhythms are familiar to everyone: they include the cycle of sleep and wakefulness; the intermittent coming into "heat", or sexual receptiveness, of a female mammal; and the annual migrations of birds. Some rhythms have a much shorter time scale than any of these: examples are the contraction of heart muscle and—still briefer—the electroencephalogram or EEG (the "brain waves" that can be picked up by electrodes on the scalp or on the surface of the brain itself).

Biological rhythms, such as the estrous cycle, are referred to in many later passages in this book. Here it is convenient to give some definitions and one example (reviewed by E. Bünning; and by F. Halberg). The cycle of sleep and wakefulness usually has a natural period that corresponds to

FIGURE 2-5 Limpets, *Patella vulgata*, a common species of European shores. Scars on the rock mark resting sites of two others. Limpets home on these sites after foraging while covered by the tide. (Courtesy V. A. P. Harris)

that of the solar day. A 24-h rhythm is said to be *circadian*. Similarly, a rhythm with a natural period of about a year is called *circannual*. In some experiments, animals that display such rhythms have been isolated, as far as possible, from all external fluctuations. The rhythms continue. For example, a laboratory mammal can be kept in continuous light or continuous darkness; but its circadian rhythm is retained. Such rhythms are then said to be *endogenous:* they are evidently independent of external stimulation. Nonetheless, in such conditions, the animal's rhythm of sleep and wakefulness goes out of phase with the sun: it does not remain at exactly 24 h. For a circadian rhythm to remain in time with the solar day, there must be some external oscillation, such as the normal cycle of light and darkness. Such an environmental agent is a *Zeit-geber* (time-giver); and the synchronizing effect of a *Zeitgeber* on an endogenous oscillation is called *entrainment*.

As an example, I take the circadian rhythm of locomotor activity of cockroaches, such as *Periplaneta americana.* These insects usually move about only at night. Their circadian rhythm of activity has been experimentally studied in some detail (reviewed by J. Brady; and by S. K. Roberts and others). If the eyes are painted over, so that no light can enter, the activity rhythm becomes "free running": it drifts out of phase, so that activity occurs increasingly during the hours of light. If, after a number of days, the paint is removed, the rhythm quickly becomes entrained again.

Attempts have been made to find the pacemaker, that is, the internal source of the rhythm. A rather crude experiment is to cut off the head, and seal the neck. A headless cockroach lives for some days, but is inactive. If, however, an operation removes only the "brain", or supraesophageal gan-

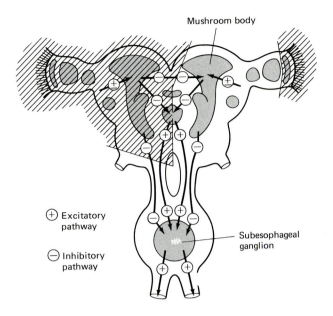

FIGURE 2-6 Diagram of brain of an insect such as the cockroach, *Periplaneta americana,* from above. The cross-hatched areas can be removed without stopping the circadian rhythm of activity. (After J. Brady, 1971)

glia (figure 2-6), the insect is quite active, but there is no rhythm. Further experiments suggest that the endogenous circadian rhythm depends especially on the optic lobes.

2.2 ORIENTATIONS CLASSIFIED

Zooplankton migrates or settles as a result of several interacting types of orientation. The same applies, as we shall see, to the movements of many land animals. Such a statement raises the question of classifying their movements or of analyzing them into their components. Classification can be by the relevant physical feature, such as light or gravity, and hence by the type of sense organ involved; but this section classifies postures and movements primarily according to the direction in which the body is pointing, or according to changes in the rate of movement (table 2–1). Such a system uses the findings of laboratory experiments in which all conditions are, as far as possible, very precisely controlled (reviewed by G. S. Fraenkel & D. L. Gunn; and, for insects, by H. Markl & M. Lindauer).

2.2.1 Stationary Orientations

2.2.1.1 Balance and Gravity: Although we are concerned with movement, it is convenient to begin with orientations that can be observed in a stationary animal. If we see a crustacean or a fish motionless in water, it is usually the right way up; if it is not, we suspect that it is sick or dead. In principle, an animal could keep itself upright by using its eyes; but the upright posture of a normal animal usually depends mainly on statocysts (figure 2-7). These organs are gravity receptors. In the vertebrates, including man, they are associated with the

TABLE 2-1   Orientations

TAXIS   Movement directly to or from a single source of stimulation

   Klinotaxis: Taxis dependent on lateral deviations of body or part of body and comparison and equalization of stimulation on the two sides. There may be only a single receptor

   Tropotaxis: Taxis dependent not on lateral deviations but on simultaneous comparison of stimulation intensity on the two sides. Unequal stimulation evokes turning. There must be paired receptors

   Telotaxis: Taxis not dependent on symmetrical stimulation; orientation is directly toward the source of stimulation even when one of a pair of receptors is out of action. Only phototelotaxis is known

TRANSVERSE ORIENTATION   Orientation (not necessarily movement) at an angle (which may be only temporarily fixed) to the direction of a stimulus. Includes dorsal or ventral light response, transverse gravity response, and light-compass reaction

KINESIS   Undirected movement of which the velocity or rate (or degree) of turning varies with the intensity of stimulation

   Orthokinesis: Kinesis in which the velocity of movement depends on the intensity of stimulation

   Klinokinesis: Kinesis in which the rate or degree of turning depends on the intensity of stimulation

---

(Modified from G. S. Fraenkel & D. L. Gunn)

FIGURE 2-7   Diagram of a statocyst. The cyst is a fluid-filled sac in which the statolith or weight rests on receptors (hair cells). The posture of the animal determines which hair cells are being stimulated. (After J. J. Gibson, 1966)

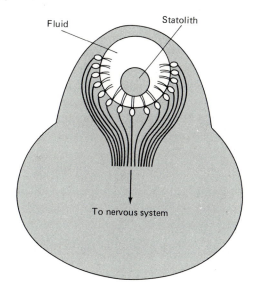

Fluid

Statolith

To nervous system

organs of hearing; and so they have been called otocysts, from the Greek word meaning an ear. Each consists of a chamber filled with fluid and lined in part with sensitive cells. In the fluid is a solid particle, the statolith, of which the position varies, under gravity, according to the animal's orientation. The statolith usually falls against or hangs from thread-like structures that project from the sensitive cells.

In the 19th century, statocysts were believed to be organs only of hearing and not of balance. But in 1892 A. Kreidl published the findings of remarkable and imaginative experiments on a crustacean, the prawn, *Palaemonetes*. When these animals molt, they replace the old statoliths with new ones—normally, grains of sand. Kreidl obliged his prawns to use iron filings instead. He then applied a magnetic field. The body position altered to one that represented a compromise or resultant of the two forces acting on the animal, the magnetic field and gravity. Other crustaceans with such a system include the lobsters (figure 2-8).

A prawn has two statocysts, just as a vertebrate has two organs of hearing and balance. In principle, an animal could maintain its position relative to gravity with only one such organ; and there are in fact animals that do so (G. S. Fraenkel & D. L. Gunn). The Ctenophora (figure 2-9) are radially symmetrical, and have a single, central statocyst. *Beroe,* which lives in the open sea, moves by means of groups of cilia, not muscles. Usually, the long axis is vertical, with the mouth pointing upward. The statolith can be drawn out of the animal with a pipette. There is then no response to

FIGURE 2-8 *Nephrops norvegicus,* an example of the decapod crustaceans. (H. Knudsen)

FIGURE 2-9 *Pleurobrachia pileus* (Ctenophora): these sea gooseberries have a single central statocyst. (D. P. Wilson, Marine Biological Laboratory, Plymouth)

gravity: the orientation of the animal is at the mercy of the movements of the water surrounding it.

Another example is provided by a turbellarian, *Convoluta roscoffensis*. If these small flatworms are put on a vertical wet glass plate, they move downward. The obvious assumption is that they are responding to gravity by means of their single statocyst. In this case the test was partly to nullify the effect of gravity by applying centrifugal force. A glass plate was rotated on the vertical axis of a centrifuge; and the flatworms, instead of moving vertically downward as usual, moved at an angle that represented the resultant of the centrifugal force and gravity. This resultant determines the movement of the statolith against the sensitive cells of the statocyst.

Further experiments have been done to demonstrate the functioning of paired statocysts. H. Schöne (1952, 1954, 1957), like Kreidl, used prawns, *Palaemonetes*. His experiments show still more clearly how the system that keeps these animals upright may be studied as a mechanism. The upright position represents a reference value or, in German, *Sollwert* ("should-be value"); departure from this position evokes compensatory movements of the limbs and also of the eyes, which are stalked. To test the functioning of the statocysts it is necessary to use animals of which the eyes have been covered, so that no visible information can contribute to the adjustment of movement. If one statocyst is removed, the animal adopts a tilted position. If a fine jet of water stimulates the sensory cells of one statocyst, the limbs and eyes move to correspond. Such movements, by an intact animal in natural conditions, would return it from a tilted position to normal.

In the intact animal, then, posture depends on the statocysts: but there is a fail-safe system that allows an animal to keep its balance if the statocysts are out of order. If the eyes are left uncovered and a statocyst is removed, posture is at first again disturbed; but after a time it returns to normal. Evidently, information through the visual system has made possible a compensatory adjustment. It may seem surprising that such compensation is possible. But in fact something of this sort is essential in natural conditions. When, after a molt, the statoliths are replaced, they must usually be of slightly different weight. Hence the input to the nervous system from the statocysts cannot be precisely symmetrical. Presumably, after each molt, there is a rapid adjustment to this slight asymmetry. We can therefore see that the existence of a compensatory mechanism has a function (that is, survival value) in natural conditions. We still, however, do not know anything of the physiology of the process.

2.2.1.2 Balance and Light: An orientation in which the reference value depends on gravity, and imposes movement in a straight line to or from the center of the earth, is a *geotaxis*—a positive geotaxis if downward, negative if up. But not all animals keep their balance by means of statocysts: some do so by using their eyes. If they hold themselves in the usual position with the dorsum upward, they are said to display the *dorsal light reaction.*

To identify this reaction, the animal should first be put in a dark room. A light is then shone from above. Most aquatic animals, in these conditions, swim with the dorsal surface upward. The light is now switched off, and another switched on below so that it shines on the animal through the aquarium floor. The question is whether the animal turns over and swims upside down. Some do.

An example is the fish louse, *Argulus.* If this crustacean is swimming normally, and is then illuminated from below, it could in principle either roll over or turn a somersault. In fact, it may do either; but it usually turns a somersault (figure 2-10). If one of its two eyes is destroyed, the movements of *Argulus* become abnormal in two respects. First, it circles in the horizontal plane toward the side with the intact eye. Second, it also makes rolling or spiraling movements. Hence the normal movements of this animal are maintained by balancing the input through the paired eyes. Another crusta-

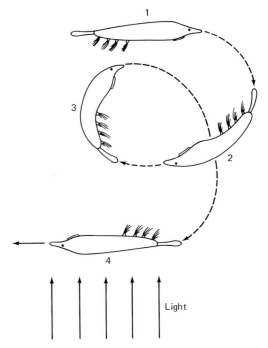

FIGURE 2-10 Dorsal light reaction. A carp louse, *Argulus foliaceus,* adjusts its position relative to light by pitching, not rolling. (After G. S. Fraenkel & D. L. Gunn, 1961)

cean, *Artemia salina,* when adult normally swims belly up (though not as a nauplius larva, when it possesses no compound eye): it may adjust its position by rolling or by somersaulting. Here then we have a ventral light reaction.

In describing the orientation of these crustaceans, only the eyes need to be considered. Many animals that show a dorsal light reaction also have functioning statocysts. Fish, like other vertebrates, have paired labyrinths (figure 2-11). The eighth cranial nerve carries information from the labyrinthine statocyst to the brain; and such information might be expected to maintain normal posture. But in fact, as E. von Holst has shown, some fish keep on an even keel partly by using their eyes. Certain tropical species, easily kept in aquaria, are laterally flattened: head on, they are remarkably linear; and the angle of inclination from the vertical can be readily recorded. The angel fish, *Pterophyllum,* (which might also be called an angle fish), was observed with the light shining only from the side (figure 2-12). It did not then turn through 90°, as it would if its position depended entirely on light, but through about 45°: once again, evidently, the position adopted is the resultant of two influences, the direction of light and that of gravity.

Such an interaction has also been studied by W. Braemer & H. Braemer; one of these experi-

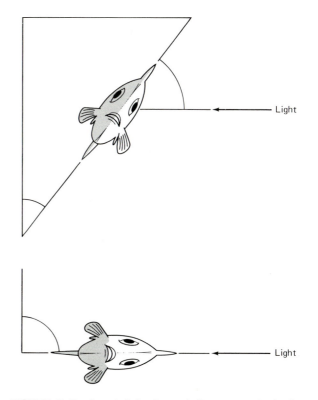

FIGURE 2-12 Angel fish, *Pterophyllum,* uses both the gravity receptors and eyes to stay upright. Above: light from the side makes an intact fish take an angle of 45° from the horizontal. Below: if the labyrinths are destroyed, the fish displays a full dorsal light reaction. (After E. von Holst, 1950)

menters joined their experimental subjects, the pencil fish, *Poecilobrycon eques,* in a vast centrifuge. In some experiments, diffuse light was used so that there was no directional effect from that source. Pencil fish are tailstanders: during the day, in their position of rest, they point upward, at an angle of around 60° to the horizontal; the statolith in the utriculus (statocyst) of the labyrinth is then tilted. This unusual position requires light from above: the effect of light is partly to counteract the input

FIGURE 2-11 Diagram of the membranous labyrinth of a vertebrate. The three semicircular canals and associated structures constitute the organ of balance, and allow response to movement in any direction. The cochlea is the organ of hearing. (After T. D. M. Roberts, 1967)

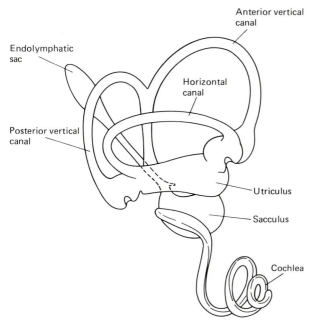

Endolymphatic sac

Anterior vertical canal

Horizontal canal

Posterior vertical canal

Utriculus

Sacculus

Cochlea

from the labyrinth. During active swimming and feeding, the visual input is dominant. At night, the labyrinth dominates: the fish rest in a nearly horizontal position.

Some fish swim belly upward. One, the upside-down catfish, *Synodontis nigriventris,* has been studied by D. L. Meyer and others. It illustrates further that the normal (that is, the most usual) posture is readily given up. This fish has a dark ventral surface, and so is camouflaged when in its usual position. Nonetheless, when it comes close to a surface, it turns over, and swims with its belly against it. It seems then to alter the "mechanism" that maintains posture to a new setting, and keeps it there, until it loses contact again. Once again, we see that, despite the apparently machine-like quality of orientations, they allow much adaptability of behavior.

2.2.2 Movement in a Straight Line

Despite the previous section, in this chapter we are mainly concerned with movement from place to place. Such movements, when related in a clear way to features such as light, gravity, an odor, or humidity, may be classified by the system given in table 2–1. The principal category is that of the *taxis,* in which an animal's long axis, during movement, is in line with a single source of stimulation.

The classification of taxes was initially designed to give an orderly account of responses to light, and all the examples given in this section are of phototaxes.

2.2.2.1 Klinotaxes: It is possible for an animal to be phototactic with only one light-sensitive organ, set in the midline. Examples come from the larvae (maggots) of flies (Diptera). These insects often breed in dung or other nutritious decaying organic mixtures. Their larvae are behaviorally equipped so that they surround themselves safely with their food. The larvae of common genera, such as the house fly, *Musca,* the blue bottle, *Calliphora,* and the green bottle, *Lucilia,* weave their way into their food by virtue of a negative response to light: if they are illuminated from a single source, they move away from it, swinging the front end as they go. For long it was inferred that there must be a single "eye" at the front end, but none could be found. Eventually a small cluster of cells above and behind the mouth was identified by Niels Bolwig as the light-sensitive structure.

A movement that depends on regularly swinging out of line is called a klinotaxis. A photoklinotaxis requires only a single eye, which must be partly shielded from light. The shield causes a shadow to fall on some of the light-sensitive cells; and as the animal moves the position of the shadow varies: hence every departure from a line directly away from light is corrected.

2.2.2.2 Tropotaxes: Photoklinotaxes are probably rare. More commonly, an animal has a pair of eyes (or several pairs), that make possible an equal input on the two sides. Movement can then be directly to or from a source of light, without swinging. G. S. Fraenkel & D. L. Gunn call such a movement a tropotaxis. In such a movement attainment of orientation is direct, by turning to the less-stimulated or the more-stimulated side, as a result of simultaneous comparison of intensities of stimulation on the two sides.

The definition, then, includes not only the direction of the movement but also the physiological mechanism by which orientation is achieved. Operationally, two tests should be satisfied for a movement to qualify. First, an animal is exposed to two light sources. It should then move on a line between them, equidistant if the two sources are of equal strength. Second, one eye may be put out of action. When the eye, as in an insect, has a hard covering of chitin, it may be conveniently painted over with black enamel without injury (figure 2-13). The animal is now put in diffuse light. So treated, it cannot balance the inputs from the two sides, and it makes continual circling movements toward the side with the ineffective eye. It is as if it were trying to achieve a balancing input on that side.

An example is provided by the photonegative larva of the meal moth, *Ephestia kuehniella*. Each of its two eyes consists of six units, the ocelli. In darkness, the larvae move without evident direction. Figure 2-14 illustrates the results of an experi-

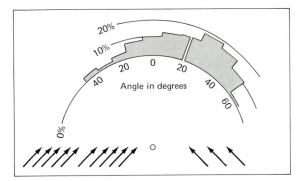

FIGURE 2-14 Photonegative *Ephestia* larvae were exposed to two beams of light at right angles to each other. Light intensity was stronger on the left. The histogram shows how the direction taken by the larvae, though varied, represents a resultant of two sources of stimulation. The percentages are of flies taking the directions shown. (After G. S. Fraenkel & D. L. Gunn, 1961)

FIGURE 2-13 An early experiment on the effect of covering one eye (the right) of an insect (a fly). The insect is shown on a rod held vertically. A normal fly would walk straight up; the treated fly walks in a spiral. (After J. Loeb, 1912)

ment in which two unequal lights were used. On the whole, the angle of movement between the lights corresponded to what one would expect in a tropotactic animal. The sensory and neural equipment of these larvae allows them to move away from light in natural conditions, when the light is usually rather diffuse. To quote Fraenkel & Gunn: "In nature, then, the meal-moth larva can . . . sum up the light and take a general direction away from it."

An example of positive phototropotaxis is provided by a woodlouse, *Armadillidium*, also known as a pillbug. Woodlice make the only group of Crustacea which are thoroughly terrestrial. They occur under rotten bark and beneath stones on damp soil, and would not be expected to be photopositive. Nor are they, most of the time. But *Armadillidium* has paired eyes and tends to move toward light if it has fasted for some time, or if its environment dries up or heats up. Exposed to two equal lights, it steers between them until it is on the line joining them, when it turns toward one. If one eye is put out of action, the animal tends to circle.

The dorsal light reaction (2.2.1 above) resembles phototropotaxis in important ways: as we saw, blinding on one side leads to continual movements similar to the circling of half-blind *Ephestia* larvae or *Armadillidium*. Hence the mechanisms of the dorsal light reaction and of phototropotaxis may be the same. A tropotaxis, however, is *defined* as a movement in a straight line to or from a source of stimulation. If I stipulate this as my definition in the present work, I am logically obliged to keep to it; and the dorsal light reaction does not fall within the definition: the animal may be stationary, and is in any case at an angle to the direction of the stimulus. If it were held to be more convenient to classify the dorsal light reaction in the same category as phototropotaxis, it would be necessary to use a different definition.

2.2.2.3 Telotaxes: Some animals move directly toward (or away from) a light even when there is another light shining with similar intensity. A small crustacean, *Hemimysis lamornei,* in a tank in the presence of one light, swims to and from the light; that is, it alternates between a positive and a negative response. Given two lights at right angles, it moves in relation to one or the other. If a number of these mysids are present, the result resembles an unregulated flow of traffic at a crossing. Here is an example of orientation without a balanced input on the two sides. Such telotaxes are known only as responses to light.

A further example is provided by the honey bee, *Apis mellifera.* A bee in a room usually flies straight to the window. In a dark room with two lights, a wingless bee usually walks straight to one light—the stronger, if the lights are not equal. But the behavior of bees toward light is not simple. If one eye is covered, in diffuse light the bee circles toward the seeing side: it behaves tropotactically. But in a beam of light a one-eyed bee, after a number of trials, moves straight toward the source. Such an ability is presumably important during foraging: a bee visiting flowers needs to fly directly to one flower, not to a point midway between two. (A critical reader will have noticed that, in the last sentence, I have turned from considering overt behavior, and the mechanisms that control it, to function—that is, to survival value. This reader will also have realized that an explanation in terms of survival value tells us nothing about the mechanism of the behavior.)

The statement on the probable function of telotactic behavior to the bee illustrates a special feature of telotaxis: it seems to be "goal-directed"—that is, determined by a particular target. Once again, a question of classification arises. Some ethologists have included, under telotaxis, orientations toward specific objects. For example, a nestling bird gapes toward its parent's head (figure 9-21) and so receives food (9.3.6). Such a response does not include locomotion and therefore formally does not come within the definition of a taxis. Moreover, the behavior is to a visible *pattern;* and there is no reason to believe that the physiological basis is the same. In this book, therefore, I keep to the narrower usage, on the grounds of convenience.

2.2.3 Transverse Orientations

We now turn to movements of which the direction is usually to or from a particular place, and not merely toward particular conditions. The movements are guided by the source of stimulation, which may be at an angle to the direction of movement.

When direction is determined by a source of light, we have the *light-compass orientation.* An example is provided by a mollusk, an attractive, green sea slug, *Elysia viridis* (Opisthobranchiata), which glides about among seaweeds in the Mediterranean. In the laboratory, offered a single beam of light, this animal moves at a steady angle to its direction; move the light, and the slug's direction alters accordingly. The angle made by the direction of movement with that of the light varies between 45° and 135°. Evidently the eyes are constructed so that only light from directions between these angles reaches the retina: the animal cannot see directly backward or forward. For *Elysia* the function of the behavior is not known. Perhaps it allows the animal to cover a large area instead of moving around in circles. Another possibility arises from the presence in the tissues of "symbiotic" chloroplasts, derived from plant food (R. Hinde & D. C. Smith); these contribute to the animal's metabolism, and for this they need light. One wonders just what course is steered in the animal's usual habitat, and what determines the different angles of movement of different individuals.

For other species the function of the light-compass orientation is quite clear. Vast numbers of animals settle in a home or nest, and range around it for food and other necessities. After each foray they must find their way back. In 2.1.2 above, I describe examples of such homing among mollusks of the seashore. Another example, from a similar habitat, is provided by the sand hoppers, crustaceans that are common on sandy beaches everywhere (reviewed by L. Pardi). One species, *Talitrus saltator,* spends much of its life in the sand just above the high water mark of European shores. At night, when the temperature is moderate, the tide low, and the humidity high, these amphipods move inland in vast numbers, sometimes as far as 100 m.

This movement may be a result of a general spreading out and not a directed migration. But they eventually return. The question now is how they find their way back.

If during the day sand hoppers are put in conditions much drier than their usual habitat, they move toward the sea. The movement is specifically seaward; hence its compass bearing depends on the local topography. If, however, the animals are accustomed to a shoreline facing west and are displaced to one facing east, they "home" in the wrong direction. If the sand hoppers are in their usual place but the sun is concealed from them by a screen, and if a mirror is arranged to reflect the sun from another angle, the animals change direction accordingly. When, for example, the mirror is placed to reflect the sun at an angle 180° from the normal, the sand hoppers move directly away from the sea. When the sky is overcast, there is no directional movement. Hence the return to the sea is guided by the sun.

The sun, of course, moves (or appears to move). Sand hoppers allow for this. They display the sun-compass orientation, which must depend on an "internal clock"—a rhythmical process synchronized with the 24-h cycle of the sun. Some sand hoppers were taken from Italy, in the northern hemisphere, to Argentina, in the southern; they then did not adjust to the different apparent movement of the sun: that is, they behaved as if the sun was due south at noon, and not due north, and so moved in exactly the wrong direction.

The return of sand hoppers toward the sea has been called "homing." More typical examples of animals that home by the sun are the ants. The direction of movement of a black ant, *Lasius niger,* like that of *Talitrus,* can be upset by the use of mirrors. Another celebrated experiment (described by T. C. Schneirla, 1953) is to trap an ant moving at, say, 90° to the sun's direction, under a box; after 150 min it is released; and, instead of remaining on its former path, it moves off at an angle of about 37° to the correct direction; this is the angle of the sun's apparent movement during the ant's imprisonment.

Such findings suggest that, unlike sand hoppers, these ants have no internal clock that allows for change in the sun's direction. If so, the direction of an ant's return journey would be regularly off course in proportion to the duration of its absence from the nest. In fact, however, ants usually return on a beeline. The apparent contradiction has been resolved by R. Jander, in a study of another common ant, *Formica rufa*. When workers of this species emerge either from the pupal stage or from hibernation, they cannot allow for the sun's movement. Evidently, they acquire the ability during forays outside the nest.

The most famous insect that uses sun navigation is the honey bee, *Apis mellifera*. In a celebrated series of experiments, bees were captured while feeding 150 m north of their hive and released in various positions on different bearings from the hive (figure 2-15). They nevertheless flew about 150 m due south, and then circled around, as if in search of their home. Only when the search failed did they successfully return, presumably by using landmarks. Such experiments are best carried out on a featureless plain. A disused airfield has sometimes been employed.

With the transverse orientations, we are dealing with movements of much greater complexity than the taxes. In the sun-compass response, the orientation is not a fixed feature common to a whole species, but has to be learnt by each individual, and for each journey. In addition, the orientation on return is (obviously) the obverse of that on the outward journey.

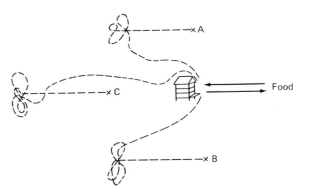

FIGURE 2-15 Beelines. Hive bees, *Apis mellifera,* were feeding at the point marked "food" and were then moved to A, B, or C. All flew from these points in what would have been the correct direction, evidently guided by the sun. After that, they searched and presumably found their way home by landmarks. (After E. Wolf, 1926)

2.2.4 Kineses

2.2.4.1 Orthokinesis: Under the heading of orientations it is usual to include certain nondirectional movements. Some animals change the *rate* of movement with the intensity of light, humidity, or other agency. Such movements are called kineses. The standard example is provided by those odd creatures, the woodlice or slaters (figure 2-1). *Porcellio scaber,* the most studied, occurs under rotten bark and beneath stones on damp soil; it soon dies if kept in dry air. Hence it is to its advantage to assemble in damp places. Woodlice do not, however, head directly for such places as soon as they find themselves in a dry area.

If woodlice are placed in a dish containing dry air, they move about, with no specific direction, until they begin to dry up. If they are put in a dish containing humid air, they move about at first, but most of them soon become still. In a dish with dry air at one end and moist at the other, the woodlice at the dry end are rather active, but those at the humid end rest. As a result, the animals collect at the humid end. Hence woodlice attain humid comfort, not by a directed movement but by increasing their rate of (apparently random) movement as aridity increases. Evidently, they have sense organs that act as humidity receptors, and that either stimulate the nervous system in dry air or inhibit it in humid air. Such organs may be quite simple, for they do not have to detect either the direction or the pattern of stimulation.

From this account, one might think that, when woodlice have around them food and other woodlice, they would hardly ever stir from their shelter. But they do break cover at intervals (P. J. den Boer). At night, a few of the members of a group move out to drier air. This is evidently not due to a change of conditions in the shelter, for others remain. Nor is it due to shortage of food. The probable cause is an internal change, resulting from the accumulation of too much water. Woodlice need to move in and out of cover to maintain their water balance. In other words, woodlice normally display a positive hygrokinesis; but at intervals they go into reverse and evidently become negatively hygrokinetic. We have seen that they also respond to light (2.2.2.2).

Woodlice, then, in laboratory experiments, exemplify orthokinesis, that is, the rate of their forward movement varies with the intensity of stimulation. The stimulation is due to something that varies quantitatively in the environment. Other variables that might evoke such an effect are temperature, light intensity, or the concentration of a substance such as carbon dioxide.

2.2.4.2 Klinokinesis: Another supposed undirected movement has caused difficulty and debate. Some animals change direction when they meet unfavorable conditions. A *klinokinesis* is defined as a change in the frequency or degree of turning in relation to an environmental variable. An example is the behavior of an inhabitant of human skin, the body louse, *Pediculus humanus,* described by V. B. Wigglesworth. If a louse enters a region of marked cold or dryness, or if it loses contact with the skin, there is an immediate increase, not in velocity of movement, but in rate of turning.

Turning often occurs at a boundary between favorable and unfavorable conditions. Unfortunately, some animals faced with a boundary behave in a different way, for which D. W. Ewer and E. Bursell have suggested the term "titubant responses", from a Latin word meaning "dithering" (*titubans*); but this proposal has not caught on. Nonetheless, such conduct is widespread in the animal kingdom. The propensity to vacillate shown by cattle (of the genus *Vaca*) is familiar. More seriously, the history of the concept of klinokinesis, reviewed by D. L. Gunn (1975), shows how difficult it is to fit the diversity of animal orientations into an orderly scheme.

2.3 THE SENSES AND ORIENTATION

It would be possible to classify the simple orientations and postures of animals solely by the physical or chemical factors that determine direction of movement or attitude. For most orientations, this would be equivalent to classifying them by the sense organs involved. By "simple" orientations I mean those explicable by only one factor. The present section illustrates further the range of physical properties that direct the movement of animals.

2.3.1 Light

2.3.1.1 The Ultraviolet: The first examples again concern light. Some animals can detect radiation of a shorter wavelength than the shortest visible to man. As so often, some of the best experiments have been on the honey bee, *Apis mellifera.* These insects were shown, early in this century, to be able to distinguish colors. (The survival value of such an ability, for insects that feed from flowers, is obvious.) The classical early work by K. von Frisch, and the many later findings, are described by Frisch himself (1967) and by E. O. Wilson (1971). Bees were trained to drink sugar solution from a dish on a blue card (figure 2-16). Next, many cards were offered, all without sugar solution, one blue as before, the others various shades of grey. The bees still visited only the blue card. Lastly, the same experiment was performed, but with a red card instead of a blue. The bees then did not distinguish the colored card from dark grey.

The main significance of this work for us now concerns the colors, that is the wavelengths, that bees can distinguish. Bees can detect, as a distinct color, wavelengths in the ultraviolet range (300–390μm) that we cannot; but they are not sensitive

to the longest wavelengths visible to us, that is, to red.

Sometimes the sensory abilities of a species are known from such experiments on behavior, but little can be said of the sense organs involved. In this case, however, much is known. The abilities of bees to discriminate colors, learned from training experiments, made it possible to infer the existence of three kinds of receptor in the bee eye, mainly sensitive to ultraviolet, blue-violet, or green. The compound eye of a bee consists of more than 6000 ommatidia, each of which is a complex, light-sensitive unit. It is possible to make electrical recordings from individual receptor cells in the ommatidia; and these cells prove to be of three kinds, corresponding in their maximum sensitivity to what was predicted.

2.3.1.2 Polarization: In color vision, then, bees differ in a minor way from man. But they can also distinguish a property of light that we identify only by instruments. Like the ants mentioned in 1.1.2, a bee can navigate by the sun, even when the sun is obscured by clouds or by a mountain. They do so, like the ants, by their perception of the polarization of light reflected from the water and dust particles in the sky. For this, they require a patch of blue sky that provides at least a visual angle of 10°.

The full story of bee navigation requires an account of their social interactions (13.3.2). There are, however, many other species, less social, which are sensitive to the polarization of light, for example, the shore-dwelling snails of the genus *Littorina* (figure 2-4). G. H. Charles describes how these winkles crawl on a line parallel to the plane of vibration when they are photonegative, but at right angles to it when they are photopositive. They can still do this even when blinded on one side.

FIGURE 2-16 A honey bee, *Apis mellifera,* feeding from a sugar solution. (J. B. Free)

2.3.2 Electricity and Magnetism

We owe to the elegant experiments of H. W. Liss-mann & K. E. Machin knowledge of animals that produce electrical pulses from special organs, and use the resulting field patterns to direct their movements. The animals are fish of two groups, both eel-like, the Gymnotidae and the Mormyridae, of which the members live in the muddy waters of large South American and African rivers. *Gymnarchus niloticus* is a slender creature with a finless, pointed tail and an undulating dorsal fin that allows movement forward or back. Even in murky water, the fish avoids obstacles with equal ease whether it is advancing or retreating. Crevices are entered tail first.

In the absence of any clues, such achievements are extremely mysterious. The most important clue in this case was the presence in the tail of an organ of unusual structure, which proved to produce pulses of up to 7 V at around 300 Hz. During a pulse, the tail is negatively charged (figure 2-17). At the head end the skin contains many microscopic organs, sometimes called mormyromasts, which are electric receptors. The afferent nerves from these structures go to expansions of the cerebellum found only in "electric" fish. The behavior of these fish can be altered or disorganized by changing the electrical properties of the water. The fish can also be trained to discriminate between objects of different electrical conductivity placed in identical pots.

The "electric" fish are further examples of animals, already mentioned in 1.1.4, which possess "extrasensory" powers: some of their receptors are without any counterpart in human sensory equipment. But their abilities are explicable within the framework of physical science.

The same applies to the final example in this

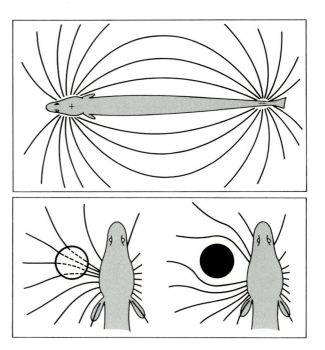

FIGURE 2-17 Above: diagram of electric fish, such as *Gymnarchus,* to show the electric field produced by the electric organ in the tail. The tail is negatively charged; the head, positively. Below: diagrams of the effects of objects in the water. The body of an animal, which is a good conductor, has the effect shown on the left; a poor conductor, such as a stone, has the effect shown on the right. (After A. H. Myrberg, 1976)

section, one that has caused considerable astonishment. It again concerns the honey bee, but not its general movement in the living space. The precision and economy with which bees build their combs has often been remarked. Domesticated bees in artificial hives build combs of which the arrangement is determined by the structure of the wood frames provided; but in natural conditions, in a hollow tree, no such framework exists. Moreover, the bees are in the dark. Nonetheless, the combs are precisely parallel. What determines this orientation? M. Lindauer and H. Martin used cardboard cylinders as hives; there were no frames to guide the bees in their building, and the entry was in the center of the floor. When a swarm was placed in such a hive, the bees still began to build the usual precisely parallel combs. Moreover, the orientation of the combs was almost exactly that of the combs in the hive from which the swarm had been taken. The bees seemed to be able to organize their building without any clue to guide them. The problem was solved by switching on a powerful magnet outside hives in which bees were building. The magnet was arranged so that it deflected the magnetic field of the earth by 40°. As a result, the orientation of combs built in the artificial magnetic field was at an angle of 40° to that of the combs previously built.

At first, this finding was still baffling, for no corresponding receptor was known. But magnetic material has now been identified in the abdomen (J. L. Gould and others). Here then is another sensory ability possessed by bees but not (as far as is known) by human beings.

2.3.3 Dynamics

Some orientations depend on mechanical effects. The responses to gravity, described in previous sections, are examples. In this section we are concerned with sensitivity, not to the earth's pull, but to air movements. In 1.1.2 I mention ants that move upwind in response to an odor. A movement directed by the flow of air is an *anemotaxis*.

Such a movement may be positive or negative. As an example, the locusts move about on foot, except when they are in the migratory phase, during which they assemble in their vast flying swarms. In experiments (reviewed by J. S. Kennedy, 1974), earthbound hoppers of the desert locust, *Schistocerca gregaria,* have been exposed to a current of air: they moved downwind. Then the odor of grass was added to the air. The insects turned around and went upwind. The function of this orientation is evident: it tends to bring the hoppers to where there is edible grass.

The common garden snail, *Helix aspersa,* can similarly find its way to food by an anemotaxis. In experiments by S. R. Farkas & H. H. Shorey (1976), snails were exposed to a light breeze. If the air bore the odor of a food plant, the snails moved upwind.

2.3.4 Heat

Like light, heat is a form of energy. In studying behavior, we are usually concerned with temperature, that is, the ratio of the amount of heat in a system to the heat capacity of the system. Temperature itself has no directional effect on an animal's movements, but it determines the amount and direction of transfer of heat between the animal and its surroundings. The animals with which we are now concerned are poikilothermic: their internal temperature (unlike that of mammals or birds) usually follows quite closely that of the temperature outside. Below a certain temperature, all muscular contraction ceases, but the animal may survive in a state of stupor. Sheep blowflies, *Lucilia cuprina,* studied by A. J. Nicholson, are all inactive at 5°C or below; but, as the temperature rises, increasing numbers of flies begin to move; and the rate of movement also increases (figure 2-18). Hence, within a certain range of temperatures, the effect on behavior of increasing the amount of heat available is partly through an effect on metabolism: metabolic rates rise, and speed of movement rises correspondingly. Such an effect is independent of the direction of movements.

But, as figure 2-18 shows, the relationship between temperature and activity may not be as sim-

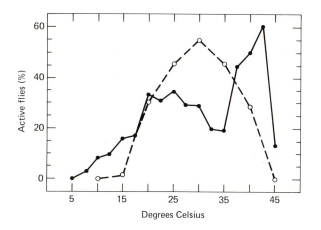

FIGURE 2-18 Sheep blowflies, *Lucilia cuprina,* are most likely to be active (crawling) at temperatures between 25° and 40°C. The continuous line represents the proportion of flies moving at different temperatures while the temperature was raised about 7°C/h. The broken line represents the proportion active when the flies had been in a constant temperature for 12 h before they were observed. (After A. J. Nicholson, 1934)

ple as one would expect: one is not justified in assuming that the activity (rate of movement) of a poikilotherm will vary with temperature in the same way as a chemical action in a test tube. Another example is provided by slugs, *Agriolimax reticulatus,* studied by B. H. Dainton. At temperatures between 4 and 20°C, for movement to begin, the temperature must fall slightly. The result is that, as a rule, the slugs begin to move in late afternoon. A rise in temperature inhibits movement, and so they become inactive in the morning. It is easy to surmise the survival value of this conduct, but the mechanism remains unknown.

Another complication arises when we observe animals that adjust their behavior so that they are heated by the sun. The desert locust is an example. These insects are torpid below 17°C. In the morning, when the temperature rises, the hoppers assemble on surfaces facing east, where they bask in

the sun, with their bodies at right angles to its direction, until the temperature reaches about 28°C. While basking, they may lie almost on their sides, in a position that exposes the maximum surface. These postures are adopted, but not so readily, even when the eyes are painted over. Evidently, basking is oriented in part by radiation from the sun acting on unknown receptors. The same applies to a change of attitude that occurs above 40°C: the insects turn to a position that presents only the head to direct sunlight.

The postures of locusts in the sun do not involve directed locomotion; they are therefore neither taxes nor kineses. But one would expect that many species would have a preferred (or eccritic) temperature. Figure 2-19 gives an example from a parasitic nematode, *Terranova decipiens,* taken by

FIGURE 2-19 Preferred (eccritic) temperature of a parasitic nematode, *Terranova decipiens.* In a temperature gradient, most settle at about 35°C. This is the deep body temperature of one of their hosts. (After K. Ronald, 1960)

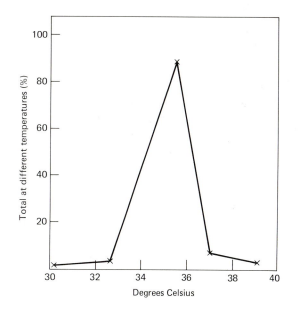

K. Ronald from the muscles of codfish, *Gadus callarias.* The high temperature selected by these larvae is evidently related to the next stage in their life history: they do best if ingested by a harp seal, *Phoca groenlandica,* of which the deep body temperature (35°C) is lower than that of other seals (Phocidae). Parasitic worms are not prominent features of the ethological literature. This example reminds us that even they often depend on distinctive kinds of behavior for their survival.

The same, of course, applies to free-living nematodes. A soil-living species, *Caenorhabditis elegans,* may be cultured in the laboratory at temperatures from 16 to 25°C. E. M. Hedgecock & R. L. Russell have studied these worms in a thermal gradient: those reared at 16°C moved to the part of the gradient at that temperature and remained there; those reared at 25°C similarly preferred that temperature. Hence the eccritic temperature of these animals depends on the temperature at which they were reared. Moreover, not all individuals, reared in given conditions, behave in the same way. Among the very large numbers of worms studied, a few were mutants that did not respond to the temperature gradient. This work, then, illustrates two sources of individual variation, environmental and genetical.

It is difficult to give an unequivocal demonstration of a thermotaxis. The best examples are from ectoparasites on homeothermic animals. *Rhodnius prolixus,* a large hemipteran that sucks the blood of human beings, has been studied by V. B. Wigglesworth & J. D. Gillet (1934a,b). It can go straight to a source of heat, such as a test tube containing warm water, from a distance of about 35 mm. Blinding makes no difference; but, if the antennae are removed, the response does not occur. Before it begins to move, *Rhodnius* waves its antennae (which are long) laterally, and perhaps

in this way detects the temperature gradient. But its walking toward a source of heat is in a straight line. If one antenna is removed, the animal does not circle, and so does not give evidence of tropotaxis. It is believed that these bugs are klinotactic, like the fly larvae described in 2.2.2.1 above, but that movements of the antennae substitute for the swinging of the whole body of the larvae.

The sheep tick, *Ixodes reduvius,* studied by A. D. Lees, uses its forelegs in the same way as *Rhodnius* uses its antennae. These animals move toward a warm object only when they have not fed: when gorged with blood, they are negatively thermotactic.

2.3.5 Chemistry

Some animals find their way to food by moving upwind when stimulated by an appropriate odor (2.3.3). But, if an animal finds food by its odor, one might expect its movements to be directed by odor gradients. The animal would then move toward regions of higher concentrations. Animals, indeed, often seem to be behaving in just this way, that is, chemotactically. But to achieve this they must be able to distinguish, from moment to moment, very small differences in the concentration of odorous substances. In fact, however, apparent chemotaxis is often an anemotaxis (2.3.3). Such a response can bring the animal to the source of the odor, but the orientation itself is determined by the air movement.

Nonetheless there are examples of genuine chemotaxes. The best demonstrations are in still air or water. Experiments on *Planaria lugubris,* a pond-living flatworm (figure 2-20), are described in detail by Fraenkel & Gunn. If, when a planarian is keeping still, in a glass dish, fragments of snails or liver are put in the water, the animal soon begins to move about. At first, the path taken is ir-

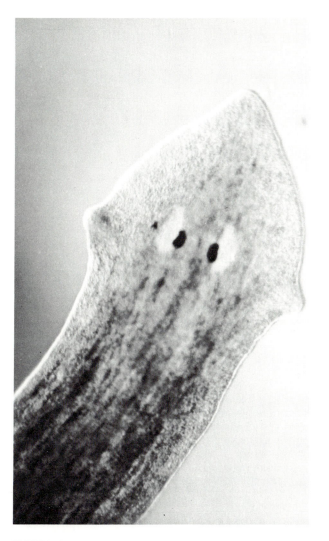

FIGURE 2-20 A turbellarian, *Dugesia tigrina,* with paired receptors at the head. (P. S. Tice)

gests that the animal first displays a chemokinesis, next a chemoklinotaxis, and lastly a chemotropotaxis. If so, it is obviously an ideal, textbook animal.

Another group of worms, the ubiquitous Nematoda, also depend on responses to chemical stimuli (reviewed by N. A. Croll; W. L. Nicholas). *Caenorhabditis elegans,* already mentioned (2.3.4), has been the subject of elegant experiments by S. Ward. These worms live in soil and eat bacteria. A number of substances attract them, including ions such as sodium and chloride, several amino acids, and cyclic adenosine monophosphate (cAMP). Ward used chemical gradients: the substance to be tested was put in a culture medium in the center of a dish, and the nematodes at the edge; the percentage of worms that had arrived at the center after a few minutes was recorded. This method gives an index of attractiveness for each substance.

Ward also followed the movements of the worms. Paired chemoreceptors in the head are evidently responsible for the orientation: the worms undulate as they move; and this, it is believed, allows them to compare the concentration of the substance in the gradient on the two sides. The orientation is therefore held to be a chemoklinotaxis. Convincing evidence was obtained by using a number of mutant forms. One mutant has a bent head, and has an abnormal orientation because it always moves so that the head is toward the source of stimulation; hence the body moves in the wrong direction. Other mutants, too, with other head defects, fail to move normally.

Chemical signals also play a part in the social interactions of nematodes. C. D. Green describes how males of the genus *Heterodera* are attracted to females. The movements of these plant parasites (which are of great economic importance) can be

regular, but it brings the animal nearer to the food; next, the direction of movement is toward the food, but the animal raises its front end and swings it from side to side occasionally; lastly, movement is direct and without swinging. This sequence sug-

studied in an agar gel. If a female has been present in the gel, and recently removed, males are attracted to the site, evidently by a substance (a pheromone) secreted by her. At a distance, the male's response is probably a klinokinesis: a decrease in concentration of the pheromone induces a change of direction (but an increase in concentration has no such effect). Later, when close to the source, the male's response is a klinotaxis. The pheromone is believed to act in a similar way in soil and on the surface of parasitized roots.

Sometimes an animal is directed by its own secretions (2.1.2). M. J. Wells & K. L. Buckley describe observations on *Physa acuta,* a Mediterranean snail common in the tropical tanks of aquarists. Snails were kept in flasks, each with a Y-tube of which the upper arms ended in the air (figure 2-21). In these conditions a snail visits the surface every 20 to 30 min. When it does so, it regularly selects the same arm of the Y. Rotating the apparatus has no effect. Hence the snail is not guided by light or some other agency outside the flask. If, however, the Y is very thoroughly scrubbed between visits, and left exceptionally clean, the snail no longer reliably selects the same arm as before. Evidently *Physa* lays a trail as it slithers, and follows the trail once it is laid. Exchange of Y-tubes between flasks showed that a snail will also follow the trail of another. Moreover, the trails are, astonishingly, directional. This may be shown in a T-maze (figure 2-22). The animal is put in the stem of a T. A trail has already been laid in the cross piece. The animal then usually turns in the direction in which the trail has been laid.

Movements impelled or directed by chemical stimuli are of vast importance in social interactions (13.2.3). M. K. Rust and others have analysed the responses of male American cockroaches, *Periplaneta americana,* to the sex pheromone se-

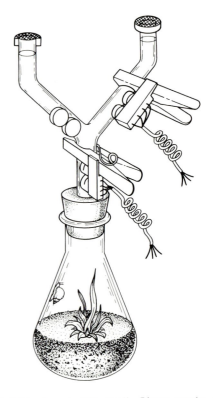

FIGURE 2-21 An aquatic snail, *Physa acuta,* scraping food from the inside of a flask. At intervals of about 20 min, it ascends one arm of the Y-tube, and regularly selects the same arm. Experiments show that the snail follows a trail it has previously laid. Pairs of photocells record movements in the arms. (After M. J. Wells & K. L. Buckley, 1975)

creted by females. Exposure to the pheromone provokes increased movement by males and orientation toward the source. The very long antennae carry chemoreceptors; and the immediate response to the pheromone includes a deflection of the antennae outward, and then sweeping movements. Males in natural conditions often lose an antenna. If a male has an antenna experimentally removed, and is then exposed to the pheromone, it makes circling movements toward the intact side, in the manner described above (2.2.2.2) for phototropo-tactic species. But after two days the head movements alter and the circling ceases: the cockroach once again directs its movements to the source of the stimulus. As so often, there is a fail-safe mechanism.

Cockroaches also provide an example of an *aggregation pheromone,* that is, a chemical signal which tends to bring conspecifics together. That of *P. americana* has been studied by W. J. Bell and others. The substance is secreted with the feces, and is detected (again) by receptors on the antennae. If the antennae are crossed, and fixed in that position, the cockroaches, on stimulation by the odor of conspecific feces, go in the opposite direction to the normal. Hence, when these insects have both antennae in the normal state, they are believed to respond to the pheromone by a chemo-tropotaxis.

Cockroaches move, as a rule, on foot. The most remarkable of responses to chemical stimuli are by flying insects. The subject of aerial odor trails has been reviewed by S. R. Farkas & H. H. Shorey (1974). The problems of how an insect reaches the source of an odor are the same whether the goal is food or a mate. They are partly discussed under the heading of chemotaxes in 2.3.5. An aerial trail may arise from diffusion (which is slow), but it is more usually a product of wind. (There are also trails in water carried by currents.) In a wind, there is an elongated trail, of which the diameter increases with distance from the source; there is also a gradient in concentration from the axis of the trail to the periphery.

Often, as we know, the direction of movement is determined, not by any gradient in concentration, but by the movement of the wind itself: we then have an anemotaxis. This requires a visual response to the substratum. In still air, an insect stimulated by an attractant substance flies at random. Even when the flight is directed, there is often a lateral zigzag. (Some ants zigzag when following a trail on foot. A chemotropotaxis is then a probable mechanism: the ant, *Lasius fuliginosus,* turns when it detects a lower concentration in an odor trail.) As Farkas and Shorey remark, there remains much doubt about how insects are guided to their goals by odors. All that is certainly known

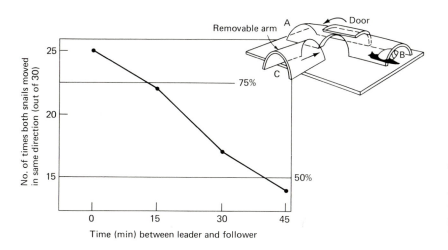

FIGURE 2-22 T-maze used for studying trail-following by *Physa acuta* (see previous figure). The graph summarizes the experimental findings. In each of 120 experiments, a snail moved through the maze from A to B or from B to A. The removable arm was then added and the door opened. A second snail was now placed at C; and, on coming to the point where it could turn left or right, it usually followed the direction of the first snail, unless more than 15 min had elapsed after the first snail laid its trail. (After M. J. Wells & K. L. Buckley, 1975)

is that they are very successful in reaching them and that they do display directed movements.

2.3.6 Interactions

At the beginning of the chapter, I give examples of movements, observed in natural conditions, influenced by more than one physical feature. Here follow three examples analyzed in more detail in the laboratory.

2.3.6.1 Snails of the Spray Zone:

The first concerns marine snails that survive in vast numbers on the inhospitable rocks of the spray zone several meters above the high-water mark (figure 2-23). Figure 2-24 illustrates experiments on *Littorina neritoides,* an unobtrusive European species, in a geometrically simple situation. (We have seen, in 2.3.1.2, that members of this genus sometimes direct their movements by the polarization of the light falling on them from above.) The snail is usually geonegative: on a vertical or sloping surface it tends to move up. On the other hand, if it is out of water (its usual position in nature), it is photonegative. It can, however, be photopositive: it moves toward light when it is in water *and* upside down. Hence, if the animal begins in water, it moves toward dark rocks and up the rock surface. While under water, if it crawls into a crevice, as in the figure, it goes on crawling and gets out again. But, once out of water, it remains in a crevice. In such a position, it is to some extent protected from drying up; and it feeds on the microscopic plants on the rock surface. In severe conditions of drought the snail withdraws into its shell and closes the operculum. It may then fall into the water, or merely remain immobile—if necessary—for months.

The notable features of this case history are the changes in responsiveness evoked by different conditions, the interaction of two physical agencies (gravitation and light), and the effectiveness of a series of simple orientations in getting the snails into a specific habitat.

FIGURE 2-23 Marine snails that occupy the spray zone above high water. The smooth species is *Littorina unifasciata;* the other, *Noddilittorina pyramidalis.* They are in a depression in rock on the coast of New South Wales. (I. A. Fox)

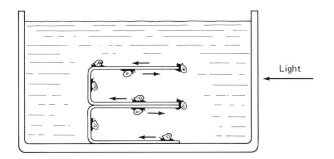

FIGURE 2-24 Orientations of a snail, *Littorina neritoides,* that lives in the spray zone. In the situation shown, it first responds photonegatively; but on a vertical wall it is geonegative; and when upside down, it is photopositive. As a result, it is found in crevices in rock above high-water mark. See previous figure. (After G. S. Fraenkel & D. L. Gunn, 1961)

2.3.6.2 Bloodsuckers:

The second example is provided by the mosquito, *Aedes aegypti,* already mentioned in 2.2.1.3. Experiments on the orientations of this important insect have been described by R. H. Wright and by P. N. Daykin and others. One disconcerting feature of its conduct is an element of unpredictability. Suppose that a number of female mosquitoes are in a cage in constant conditions at a temperature of about 25°C. Most of the time, the mosquitoes remain still on the walls; but occasionally one takes off, flies around, and settles elsewhere. Wright describes how his colleague, Daykin (a physicist), timed these unpredictable flights. It took about 1 h for half of the mosquitoes to move. This observation may be expressed by saying that the half-life of the stationary condition of mosquitoes is 1 h. The analogy is with radioactive decay, and suggests that the flights of undisturbed mosquitoes are truly random. Daykin obtained confirmation by waiting until half the mosquitoes in a population had moved, and then separating that "active" group from the rest. He then compared the half-lives of the two groups. They were the same. Hence there was no evidence that some mosquitoes in such a population were active, and others not.

Perhaps, then, there is some random feature in the functioning of the insect nervous system. Any experimenter who has faced the variation and unpredictability of animal behavior in general is likely to suspect that such effects are widespread. In this case, however, it is possible to give an orderly account of the flights. Mosquitoes in natural conditions are activated by the combined effects of carbon dioxide, water, and heat, all of which are provided by the presence of a human being (figure 2-25). When they are so stimulated, they fly upwind, and use surrounding objects and the ground pattern as visual clues to wind direction. Movement upwind takes the insects into the zone where the heat from the host produces convection currents. If an insect goes off course, that is, out of the current, it displays a momentary increase in the rate at

FIGURE 2-25 Tsetse fly, *Aëdes aegypti,* in the act of "biting". (S. A. Smith)

which it changes direction. Such an increase in turning rate is an example of a klinokinesis (2.2.4).

We now return to experiments in which the stimulating factors are studied in isolation. The half-life of the resting state of a mosquito is reduced by carbon dioxide, from about 1 h to perhaps 5 min. But the action of carbon dioxide gradually wears off (an example of habituation). Insect repellants, such as dimethylphthalate, have a similar effect: they initially provoke extra activity, but habituation follows. If insects have habituated to dimethylphthalate, they are also unresponsive to carbon dioxide; hence, if the air in a building contains a low concentration of the repellant, the activity normally induced by carbon dioxide is suppressed. The insects then fail to become active in the presence of their human hosts.

Repellants evidently act by reducing the input from peripheral sense organs. (Perhaps they should be called tranquilizers.) Some sensilla respond to changes in humidity. Discharge rates from such receptors increase when the relative humidity of the air passing over them is raised, but repellants prevent this response. Therefore, in the presence of a repellant, the changes of direction made by an insect take it away from its target instead of keeping it in the right direction.

Aedes, then, illustrates the combined effects of responses to heat, to chemical stimuli (carbon dioxide and water), and to mechanical stimuli (air movements); and, finally, there is a random element in its behavior.

2.3.6.3 Locusts

When it was morning, the east wind brought the locusts. . . . They covered the face of the whole earth, so that the land was darkened; and they did eat every herb of the land, and all the fruit of the trees: and there remained not any green thing in the trees, or in the herbs of the field, through all the land of Egypt.

This celebrated passage, translated from the writings of an early Iron Age civilisation, does not describe a myth. For thousands of years locusts have descended unpredictably, and left starvation behind them (figure 2-26). The sizes of their swarms are almost beyond belief: one swarm of African migratory locusts, *Locusta migratoria migratorioides,* carefully measured when in flight, was over 90 km long and nearly 5 km wide.

The locusts belong to the Acrididae, the family of grasshoppers (reviewed by B. P. Uvarov). Most species are solitary: they live in grassland, in a population scattered over a large area. A baffling feature of locusts was that they were seen only during outbreaks, and nothing was known of how the swarms originated. But in 1921 Uvarov published the first indication that locusts exist in two forms. When they are not swarming, they have a different appearance and live as ordinary, solitary grasshoppers.

The change in behavior depends primarily on the population density and on the resulting social interactions. The effects of weather are probably especially important in producing the huge numbers that form dense populations. Solitary locusts live in rather dry regions, and breed only when there is a certain minimum rainfall. Occasionally, exceptional rains greatly increase the food available. The survival rate of the locusts rises, and an unusually dense population develops. Frequent encounters with other locusts make locusts more gregarious. When immature insects of the solitary form are crowded together, they begin to move as a group of hoppers, at first on foot; later they develop the color pattern of the crowded form (figure 2-27). (One species, *Zonoceros elegans,* never migrates in flying swarms, but marches in dense crowds in the hopper state.) In laboratory experiments on the desert locust, *Schistocerca gregaria,* P. E. Ellis has found contact stimuli to be espe-

FIGURE 2-26 Part of a swarm of desert locusts, *Schistocerca gregaria,* in Ethiopia. The swarm caused much damage to the staple crops (maize and millet), and was over 1000 km² in area. (C. Ashall, Centre for Overseas Pest Research, London)

cially important in the marching of hoppers. She describes a number of possible interactions between immature forms. At one extreme, two insects meet and immediately run away from each other. At the other, they touch antennae repeatedly, and remain together. The second type of response arises gradually as a result of repeated encounters, and leads to the formation of groups. "Locusts [she writes] are not [hatched] with an ability to group with one another, but have to learn to do so."

S. D. Gillett (1973, 1975) has described in de-

tail how early social experience determines adult interactions. She tested the insects in a circular arena. The solitary type tended to move to the edge of the arena; the gregarious insects moved toward each other. The type of behavior, solitary or aggregating, depended on the density in which the insects were reared: early crowding leads to aggregation later. One of the factors is an airborne pheromone produced by the gregarious adults.

Structural changes come after the changes in behavior. They include not only an alteration in appearance but also an increased storage of food re-

FIGURE 2-27 The desert locust, *Schistocerca gregaria,* in its strongly pigmented, gregarious form. (S. Dalton)

serves. The crowded, fatted up locusts eventually, after transformation to winged adults, take off and fly in swarms. The resulting emigration may take them thousands of kilometers down wind from their original habitat. One swarm was followed, in 1951–1952, from the Somali peninsula to a region in Jordan and the west of Iraq—a distance of more than 3000 km. The swarms are kept together because locusts in flight retain their gregarious tendency: insects at the edges turn in to the swarm if they drift away. Hence the orientations of locusts in their swarming phase depend in part on stimuli from other locusts.

Knowledge of the movements of locusts is of great economic importance. In the early 1930s swarms from a single outbreak area near the middle Niger did enormous damage in vast areas of Africa. During the 1940s similar outbreaks threatened, but by then there was a control organization with its headquarters in London. At that time only hoppers could be controlled, by poisoned bait; but the first systematic experiments were being done on the control of the adults by spraying insecticide from aircraft. And in 1955, for the first time in history, Africa survived a period of locust attack without serious loss.

2.4 BIRD MIGRATION

The mass movements of locusts are called emigrations, for locusts never go back. In contrast, some species, especially of birds, make spectacular two-way journeys. In this book, I reserve the word migration for the movements of whole populations from one region to another, and their subsequent return. The word then covers movements of salmon down rivers and back again, and much else; but this section is almost entirely devoted to birds (reviewed by J. Dorst; D. R. Griffin (1965); G. V. T. Matthews; R. T. Orr).

Not all mass movements of birds are migrations. Like many other animals, notably the locusts just described, some occasionally break out in *irruptions.* The budgerigar, *Melopsittacus undulatus,* a member of the parrot family well-known to bird fanciers, lives in large flocks in rather inhospitable, arid regions of central Australia. The climate is erratic, and the weather sometimes allows a great increase in numbers. Drought and food scarcity return, usually quite soon, and the birds may then invade areas on the coast and elsewhere (figure 2-28).

2.4.1 The Facts of Migration

The function (or survival value) of migration seems usually to be related to avoiding the hazards of winter and to rearing young in favorable condi-

FIGURE 2-28 An irruption. The budgerigar, *Melopsittacus undulatus,* occasionally breaks out into massive swarms that emigrate from their usual habitat. (Courtesy Vincent Serventy)

tions. The latter may include not only food and warmth but also light. An American house wren, *Troglodytes aedon,* may feed its young 1000 times in a day. For this it needs plenty of light.

The Pacific golden plover, *Pluvialis dominica,* nests in Alaska and Siberia but avoids the northern winter by flying, without benefit of landmarks, to Southeast Asia and to many remote Pacific islands. Some Arctic terns, *Sterna macrura,* nest in the Canadian Arctic, fly south across the Atlantic, down the west coast of Africa, and settle for the winter on the ice of the Antarctic. A. M. Gwynn reports on three, banded in Arctic Russia or Swe-

den, that were recovered in Australia. One bird must have flown at least 14,000 km. These terns and many other species perform feats of navigation that became possible for men only after the invention of astronomy and mathematics.

The speed of flight, over great distances, is impressive. By the use of radar or of aircraft, 72 km/h has been recorded for ducks, *Anas,* swifts, *Apus apus,* and even humming birds of the family Trochilidae. Migrants start with a considerable reserve of fat, but must stop to rest and eat. Nonetheless, a semipalmated sandpiper, *Calidris pusilla,* weighing only about 15 g, has flown 3800 km from

Massachusetts to Venezuela in 26 days. A lesser yellowlegs, *Tringa flavipes,* of about 100 g, has reached Martinique from Massachusetts—about 2500 km—in six days. As Griffin has remarked, bird migrations are "limited not by the capabilities of the birds, but by the size of the planet".

The achievements of at least one reptile match those of the birds (A. L. Koch and others). The green turtle, *Chelonia mydas,* has feeding grounds on the coast of Brazil. There the females spend much of their time, though the males never come ashore. Every two or three years the females swim to Ascension Island to breed. This speck of land is about 2240 km away in the south Atlantic, and only 8 km wide (figure 2-29). Mating takes place off the breeding ground. Each female then goes ashore and lays about 100 eggs, each 5 cm in diameter. (A large turtle may weigh 2200 kg.) As soon as they hatch, the young turtles head for the sea, even if it is not visible. Experiments have indicated that the quality of the light over the sea is an essential clue. But despite much research, we still do not know how turtles contrive to reach Ascension without navigating instruments.

Sometimes, the route of a long migration is clearly related to the shape of the land. The bar-tailed godwit, *Limosa lapponica,* breeds in west Alaska but winters in New Zealand. It migrates southwest along the Pacific coast of Asia, and then south and southeast across the Malay Archipelago and along the Australian Coast. Similarly, the white stork, *Ciconia ciconia,* nests in a large area of central and south Europe (figure 2-30), but winters in southern Africa. These birds travel by day and are never out of sight of land. Their migrations have been intensively studied, sometimes with the aid of African arrows found in healthy, nesting birds: the structure of the arrows has made possible close identification of the places where the birds were shot at. Storks undertake sea crossings only when the further shore is in sight; hence at the Mediterranean their flight routes narrow to the Gut at one end and the Bosphorus and Gulf of Suez at the other.

There are two distinct stork populations in Europe. One nests west of the Rhine and includes a Spanish group; the other occupies a large area of eastern Europe. Those in the west migrate via Gibraltar; the others go east of the Mediterranean. Young storks of the eastern group have been reared in captivity, and released in a region of western Europe; at the time of release all the native storks of that region had already flown off. The young

FIGURE 2-29 The green turtle, *Chelonia mydas,* feeds along a great length of the Brazilian coast, but breeds on the tiny Ascension Island. The map shows the results of tagging turtles on the island, and identifying them after their return to the mainland. Triangles show where tagged turtles were found. (After A. L. Koch and others, 1969)

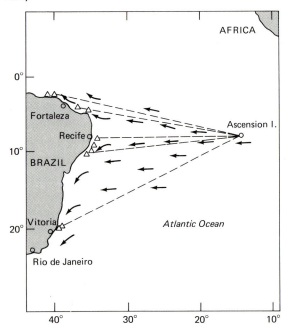

FIGURE 2-30 A white stork, *Ciconia ciconia,* and its nest, in a European city. These birds spend the winter in southern Africa. (A. Bernhaut, Photo Researchers)

storks therefore had no older birds to follow. They flew southeast, that is, in the direction appropriate to their place of origin. It is therefore suspected that the two populations are genetically distinct, and that the difference in their migratory routes is genetically determined.

2.4.2 Physiology and the Internal Clock

Captive birds of a migratory species display, at the time of migration, a change in behavior called *Zugunruhe* ("journey unrest"). In late winter, before breeding, the restlessness is accompanied by enlargement of the gonads (reviewed by P. Berthold). In late summer, before the flight to winter quarters, the gonads regress. At both seasons much fat is deposited in and under the skin. The usual proportion of fat is less than 10% of a bird's body weight. In the week or two before migration, it may rise to 50%.

The changes before flying off are precisely related to season. The external agency is the alteration in day length. Donald Farner has given a detailed analysis of these processes in the white-crowned sparrow, *Zonotrichia leucophrys* (see D. S. Farner & R. A. Lewis). This small bird breeds in the north of the North American continent, but for the winter it flies around 4000 km to the south of the United States or Mexico.

Birds were kept in captivity with a daily cycle of 8 h of light and 16 h of darkness (8L:16D). The regime was then changed to 16L:8D. The result was an increase in the secretion of gonadotropic hormones and prolactin by the anterior pituitary and a consequent enlargement of the gonads. More food was eaten, and much fat was deposited.

To respond to the change in day length, the bird must possess an internal clock (2.1.3); more precisely, there must be an internal process, based on a 24-h (circadian) rhythm influenced by light. The action of light is probably directly through the tissues of the skull on the brain. The circadian rhythm of sleep and activity undoubtedly depends on light, but it is unaffected if the eyes are covered by opaque goggles. And on a 16L:8D regime the gonads of a blinded bird enlarge as usual.

Now consider the changes, described above, that take place before breeding, during the period of lengthening days. Suppose that, during each 24-h period, a central nervous control system becomes, for a few hours, sensitive to light; and suppose that, in winter, the photosensitive period occurs during the hours of darkness: there will then be no effect. But when the days have sufficiently lengthened, the photosensitive period will occur during daylight and so be activated.

If so, it should be possible to activate the control system by subjecting birds to an abnormal cycle of light and dark. Accordingly, male white-crowned sparrows, in winter, were subjected to a regime of 8L:28D. Hence they received no more light than in winter (indeed, less), but the light periods were out of phase. As a result, the sparrows were occasionally in daylight at a time when they would, in an ordinary winter, be in darkness. In these conditions their testes enlarged. This finding confirms the hypothesis. Evidently, under the abnormal regime, the period of light sometimes coincided with the photosensitive period.

It is necessary to assume some corresponding process before the autumn migration, at the time of shortening days. On this we know something from studies of a congener, the white-throated sparrow, *Z. albicollis*. There is a circadian rhythm in the rate of secretion of the two hormones, prolactin (produced by the anterior pituitary) and corticosterone (produced by the adrenals). In spring, the two are out of phase: the interval between their respective maxima is 12 h. But this interval gradually diminishes, until by autumn it is only 4 h. A. H. Meier kept these birds in unchanging dim light and injected them with prolactin and corticosterone. The interval between injections was varied. In this way he induced the behavior and internal changes characteristic of spring, summer, or autumn, according to the interval between injections.

2.4.3 Problems of Navigation

The abilities of birds to keep on course, or to navigate, over vast distances present similar problems whether they are concerned with feats of migration or with those of homing. Homing, as we know, is return to a nest or other center, and does not entail migration. Usually, homing by birds depends at least in part on landmarks. But now we are concerned with behavior that cannot be explained in this way. A distinguished example was provided by albatrosses, *Diomedea exulans* (figure 2-31),

FIGURE 2-31 Albatross, *Diomedea exulans,* courting on Macquarie Island. These birds have an enormous range and capacity to home. (I. A. Fox)

which were interfering with the United States armed forces on Midway Island. The birds were humanely removed, and some were released thousands of miles away. They returned. One flew over 5000 km across the Pacific, at an average of about 510 km/d. A shearwater, *Puffinus puffinus,* was sent by an ornithologist, G. V. T. Matthews, from the Welsh island of Skokholm to Boston in the United States. It reached Skokholm again 12 days after its release, before the letter warning Matthews to expect it.

For experimental analysis we turn to the European starling, *Sturnus vulgaris,* whose mass aerobatics are familiar in the evening sky of many cities during autumn. Starlings do not migrate over vast distances. Some, including those in Britain, are sedentary. But many from northern Germany winter in Britain, while some Scandinavian starlings,

like wealthy people of an earlier period, visit the south of France. Starlings were introduced into North America in 1890 and have spread widely. There, again, they perform modest migrations, along the Atlantic coast north to south and back, or along the Mississippi valley.

A. C. Perdeck banded more than 11,000 starlings during their autumn migration from the Netherlands to France. The birds were then taken to Switzerland and released. Young birds, without previous experience of migration, flew off to the southwest, in the direction that would have been appropriate had they been released in the Netherlands. But adults, which had already migrated at least once, flew northwest to their usual winter quarters (figure 2-32). The young birds, then, displayed a feature essential for any migratory species, that is, the ability to fly in a fixed direction at the

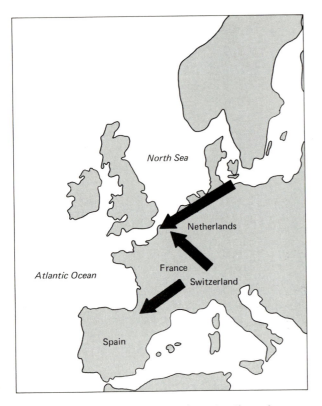

FIGURE 2-32 Experiments on the migration of young starlings, *Sturnus vulgaris*. The top arrow represents the normal autumn movement of birds that breed in the Netherlands and winter in France. Inexperienced birds were moved, before migration, to Switzerland: they flew on the correct compass course into Spain (lowest arrow). Experienced birds, similarly treated, flew to their proper winter quarters (middle arrow). (After A. C. Perdeck, 1958)

they disperse apparently at random: certainly, there is no preferred compass course. But if the sun is visible, the birds fly in a specific direction. (Similar observations have been made on other species, of which an unexpected example is a reptile, the box turtle, *Terrapene carolina*. The range of turtle migrations is modest, but their movements have been followed over 9 km.)

In a circular cage, designed for experiment, a starling can be observed trying to fly off in the normal direction. If the apparent position of the sun is now altered by mirrors, the bird makes a corresponding change in the direction of the attempted flight (G. Kramer). The same ability is displayed if birds are trained to fly in one direction by giving them food in that direction always at a given time of day. If they are then tested at a different hour, they fly, roughly, in the correct direction, just as a man in the northern hemisphere, wishing to travel east, faces the sun in the morning but keeps it on his right at noon.

Sun-compass orientation has been demonstrated in experiments on other species, such as the meadow lark, *Sturnella magna,* and the red-backed shrike, or butcher-bird, *Lanius collurio*. The sun, then, certainly enables some birds to fly on a particular compass course. But formidable problems arise when we come to sun *navigation*. To account for some of the achievements of migrating or homing birds, we must postulate abilities analogous to those of mariners on long voyages out of sight of land.

Our ancestors gradually learnt, over many generations, how to determine their position on the earth's surface by observation of the sun. The sun's apparent movement makes an arc of which the maximum height above the horizon (at noon) depends on the season and on the latitude. If a man or a bird in the northern hemisphere moves some distance north of home, say, during the night, the

season of migration. But the adults also displayed an ability acquired in a previous season: they had learnt to find their way to their winter quarters from (presumably) any direction.

Now consider what happens when these birds are held captive and released, at the time of migration, in chosen conditions. If the sky is overcast,

altitude of the sun at noon on the next day will be lower than before to an extent proportional to the distance traveled. A move to the south has an opposite effect. Displacement to east or west results in a change in the time at which the sun is at its highest point (hence "jet lag"). Human navigators traditionally made use of these facts with the aid of instruments: they required a sextant with which to take the "noon sights" and an accurate (external) chronometer.

We have seen that many animals possess internal chronometers. To account for bird navigation, G. V. T. Matthews has proposed a sun-arc hypothesis. The proposal requires that a bird compares the form of the sun's arc with that which would be observed at home (figure 2-33). It has inspired ingenious experiments and much controversy but not yet general agreement. Matthews

FIGURE 2-33 The sun-arc hypothesis of bird navigation. A diagram to show changes in the sun arc resulting from a move to south and west at noon. B shows the highest point of the arc in the new position, C the highest point at home. The altitude of B is greater by ϕ. The inclination of the arc (λ) is also greater. In addition, the sun (A) has not moved so far round its arc (by θ) as it would have done at home. (After G. V. T. Matthews, 1968)

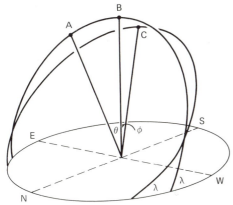

kept homing pigeons, *Columba livia,* without a view of the sun for about a week at the time of the autumnal equinox. The birds were then released a little south of their lofts. They flew south, away from home, as predicted by the hypothesis. Unfortunately, other experimenters have failed to confirm this observation. There has also been debate on whether birds could make observations of the accuracy required. The arguments associated with this and allied hypotheses have been summarized by S. T. Emlen (1975) and by W. T. Keeton.

Even if birds can navigate by the sun, those that navigate at night must have other means of orientation. G. V. T. Matthews followed the movements of mallards, *Anas platyrhynchos,* after dark by fastening lamps to their legs. They were expected to fly roughly northwest; and they did so on clear, moonless nights but not under cloud. An experimental shift of the internal clock did not affect this ability. The question whether birds can navigate (as men can) by the stars has also been investigated in planetaria, in which the artificial sky can be adjusted to show the star pattern of any season. It is said that lesser whitethroats, *Sylvia communis,* were very bewildered when, during spring, they found themselves beneath a summer or a winter sky. As usual, the findings from these experiments (which were on small numbers of birds) have aroused much argument. In 2.3.2 we saw that honey bees use the earth's magnetic field during comb building. A recent finding by W. & R. Wiltschko (1975, 1976) suggests that navigation by birds at night depends primarily on response to the earth's magnetic field, and only secondarily to the stars.

When magnets are fastened to homing pigeons, the birds take longer to get home; but the effect is evident mainly or solely in cloudy conditions. In Wiltschko's experiments warblers were kept in special cages that allowed registration of their movements. Under a clear sky and with the normal, local magnetic field of the earth, the birds tended to prefer a direction corresponding to the expected migratory movement. The birds were then subjected to an artificial magnetic field, which in effect turned the magnetic north through 120°. Again on clear nights, three species of this genus preferred the direction corresponding to the artificial field. Like bees (2.3.2), then, pigeons possess an unexpected sensory ability. And, like bees, they have now been shown to possess microscopic magnets. These structures are between the brain and the skull (C. Walcott and others).

The warblers nest in Europe and winter in Africa. It is suggested that star navigation, in so far as it occurs, represents an ability acquired during initial migration under the influence of the earth's magnetic field.

There is evidence of such combined effects of the magnetic compass and star navigation from findings on the European robin, *Erithacus rubecula.* These birds were exposed to a magnetic field while under an artificial sky with 16 simulated stars. They oriented, as expected, according to the magnetic field. The next night, they were put under the artificial sky, but in a magnetic field too weak to have any effect. They then oriented by the artificial star pattern. Evidently, only one night's exposure was needed for the birds to adapt their behavior to the pattern visible overhead.

The migrations of indigo buntings, *Passerina cyanea,* studied especially by S. T. Emlen (1967, 1970), are also guided by the stars. These birds have been kept in containers with a central ink pad surrounded by a circular blotter that shows footprints. Birds have been kept indoors, with a light-dark cycle shifted by 6 h from the correct one: their day may then begin at 1200 hrs or at 2400 hrs. When this is done with birds that fly by the sun, their direction is correspondingly altered; but the star-guided buntings are unaffected. These birds have been tested under various incomplete star patterns: they prove to be able to direct their movements by only parts of the night sky in the northern hemisphere.

The ability of indigo buntings to fly by the stars is species-typical, but depends for its development on early experience. Birds raised in captivity with no night sky (and no planetarium simulation) fail to direct their movements correctly; but exposure to a suitable planetarium sky allows them to do so. Indigo buntings, then, early in life, learn how to use the night sky during migration.

To sum up, despite much ingenious experiment (only sketched here), both the migration and the homing of birds present many mysteries. Birds of many species can undoubtedly fly over vast distances, and can end their journey in a small, precisely defined region, sometimes even in the nest they formerly occupied. The choice of their main direction and route is often independent of any special previous experience: they do not find their way around the planet by exploring and then storing topographical information so acquired. In this respect the orientations of birds resemble the taxes of invertebrates. Birds may, however, acquire further relevant information during individual development. Final homing on a nest certainly depends on the use of landmarks. Moreover, some other kinds of orientation, for instance by the stars, may depend on experience.

The cues used in orientation probably include the outline of the continents, the direction of the sun, the patterns of the stars, the earth's magnetic field, and other agencies I have not mentioned. Both the timing of migration and also navigation depend on internal chronometers.

2.5 SUMMING UP

In this chapter we begin with movements, observed in nature, that put animals in favorable conditions. Such orientations, especially of lowly invertebrates, can sometimes be analyzed experimentally as if the animals were equipped to respond mechanically to single features of the environment. In the simplest cases, posture, rate of locomotion, or direction of movement can be explained solely by such features as the relative humidity or the direction of light. An animal then behaves like a guided missile with one kind of sensor and one system for correcting departures from a predetermined course.

Simple orientations can be classified by sensory modality. But they are named according to a different system. First are stationary orientations, based on gravity receptors or on the response to light: responses to light include the dorsal light reaction. Second, kineses are not directional, but are alterations of rate of movement or direction, with a quantitative relationship to an external feature such as humidity or temperature. Third, taxes are movements in a straight line; they often but not always depend on balancing input between paired receptors. Lastly, there are transverse orientations, in which movement is at a fixed angle to a source of stimulation such as the sun.

Usually, even animals such as marine larvae, with a minimum of neural equipment, have several sense organs and also some capacity to alter their responses as circumstances change. One kind of alteration is cyclic: movements may reflect an internal circadian rhythm.

More complex animals learn their way about a structured environment. They may then use stored topographical information in returning to a nest; or they may be guided by odor trails. The last case is an example of a social effect.

The homing and migrations of birds are the most difficult of species-typical movements to explain. Among the probable means by which direction is maintained are (1) the use of landmarks, (2) sun navigation, (3) star navigation, and (4) orientation by the earth's magnetic field.

Other aspects of movement in the living space concern the relationships between predators and prey. These appear in the next chapter; and in chapter 8 we consider the exploratory component of behavior.

3

PREDATION
AND PROTECTION

So may the outward shows be least themselves:
The world is still deceived with ornament . . .
The seeming truth which cunning times put on
To entrap the wisest.

Shakespeare

3.1 TYPES OF INTERACTION BETWEEN SPECIES

Many animal species are predatory: they eat other animals, usually smaller than themselves. And many, except those of the larger species, are subject to predation: even predators themselves are often prey to others. In this chapter, we turn therefore to movements resulting from the interaction of members of different species.

Interspecific relationships may be distinguished from intraspecific or social interactions. The difference is evident both in mutually beneficial associations and in those that cause illness, injury, or death. Beneficial associations include *symbiosis,* in which members of two species are associated with mutual advantage: for example, bees both feed from and pollinate flowering plants. (Symbiosis sometimes has a wider meaning; see review by M. P. Starr.) Such interactions may be contrasted with social conduct, such as the behavior we see

when members of the same species come together to mate, to rear young, or for protection. But the two kinds of phenomena have in common that they are beneficial to all the actors. In contrast, in parasitism and predation the individual that harbors the parasite or is eaten by the predator is not benefited. There is a superficial analogy here with what happens in intolerant social interactions. But, as we see later (chapter 10), even when such interactions do lead to injury, they fall in a category quite distinct from that of predator–prey relationships. For reviews of the latter, the books by E. Curio and M. Edmunds should be consulted.

3.2 THE VARIETY OF PREDATORS

Predation may be defined as the capture and consumption for food of one animal by another. In this section I try to give a notion of the diversity of predatory behavior.

3.2.1 Protozoa

All the protozoans might be thought of as natural prey, but there are in fact many predatory species. Among them are holotrichous ciliates such as *Di-*

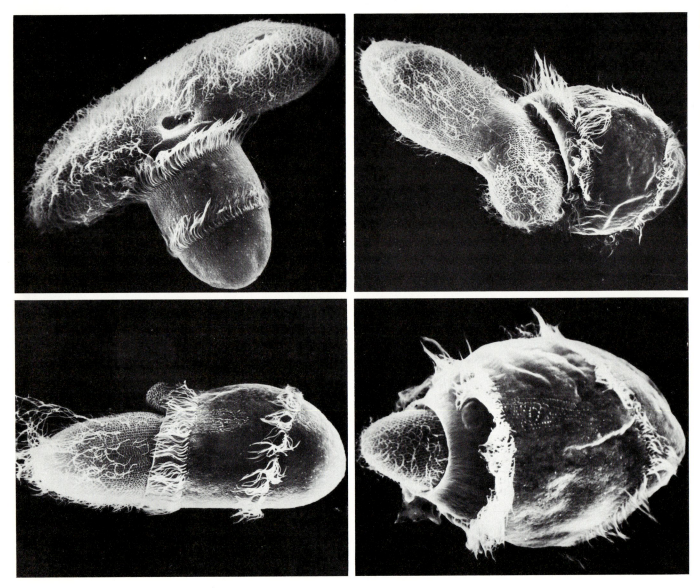

FIGURE 3-1   Stages in the ingestion of *Paramecium* by the predatory protozoan, *Didinium nasutum.* (Courtesy H. Wessenberg & G. Antipa)

dinium. H. Wessenberg & G. Antipa describe how *D. nasutum* ingests *Paramecium* (figure 3-1). Two kinds of organelle are discharged from the surface: short pexicysts adhere to the surface of the prey, and longer toxicysts penetrate the *Paramecium,* which is then drawn into the predator's "mouth" (cytostome).

G. W. Salt has described experiments on *Woodruffia metabolica,* which too feeds on *Paramecium.* Two or three *Woodruffia* were kept in about 100 μl of water together with about 200 *Paramecium.* *Woodruffia* usually glides over surfaces, but can swim. It does not, for unknown reasons, attack every *Paramecium* it meets, but it quite rapidly consumes five of its prey and then divides. If the experimenter allows the supply of *Paramecium* to run short, the predators encyst. In an intermediate situation, that is, a sparse population of *Paramecium,* 10 *Paramecium* have to be ingested before division takes place.

Woodruffia moves about more when the population of prey is sparse. Although this is a very simple, artificial situation, it presents many unanswered questions. For example, it is not known whether the extra activity when prey is scarce causes the need for extra food, which in turn leads to dividing. Similar situations and questions are presented even by some flagellate protozoans. As an instance, *Peranema* eats its plant-like relative *Euglena* (figure 3-2).

3.2.2 Headless Hunters

Protozoans manage to find and devour their prey without nervous systems. The coelenterates do so with only a nerve net. *Hydra* (figure 3-3) ingests small crustaceans, such as *Daphnia.* Movement of the tentacles is stimulated by substances, produced by prey animals, of which glutathione is probably

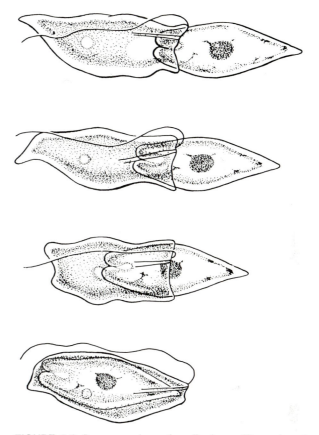

FIGURE 3-2 *Peranema* ingesting *Euglena.* (Reproduced from H. Curtis: *The Marvellous Animals,* 1968, Fig. 1.6, drawings by Shirley Baty, by permission of Doubleday & Company, Inc.)

the most important. The prey is enmeshed in the tentacles; nematocysts are discharged into its body; and the victim is finally engulfed.

The coelenterates are radially symmetrical and headless. So are the echinoderms. Starfish, of the genera, *Asterias* and *Echinaster,* are (like people) predators on bivalve mollusks, such as the mussel, *Mytilus edulis.* On disturbance, the shell of this bivalve is firmly closed by the powerful adductor muscle. The starfish fastens itself by many tube feet to both valves of the shell, and exerts a steady

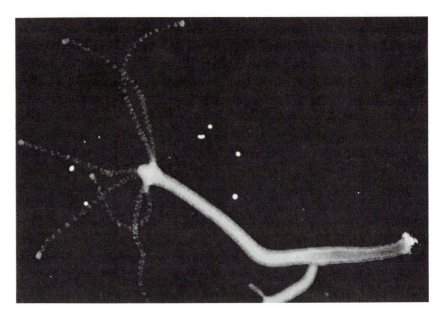

FIGURE 3-3 *Hydra,* a predator with only a nerve net. (American Museum of Natural History)

pull which eventually overcomes all resistance. J. C. Castilla has studied *A. rubens* in a simple laboratory situation, and has shown that, like *Hydra,* the starfish is stimulated to predatory activity by substances released into the water by the mussels. It responds by a movement that is perhaps a chemotaxis (2.3.5).

3.2.3 Carnivorous Snails

The Gastropoda are typically plant eaters, but some are carnivorous. Among the flesh eaters are the whelks, oyster drills (figure 3-4), and mud snails; these and their relatives are notorious as pests that eat fish caught in nets, lobsters trapped in lobster pots, and oysters and mussels cultivated for the table.

M. Copeland has described feeding by *Alectrion* (*Nassa*) *obsoleta* and a whelk, *Busycon canaliculatum,* both of North American waters. There is a

well-developed siphon, into which water is drawn and passed over the osphradium (an olfactory organ). During movement the siphon swings from side to side. The snails can evidently detect food substances in very great dilution. A fragment of oyster wrapped in cheese cloth stimulates a snail to activity; and the direction of movement is quickly adjusted to that of the odor source. Extract of fish is also effective. Copeland writes: "A snail can be led about an aquarium by squirting dilute food extract over the end of the siphon when it is pointed in [a given] direction."

3.2.4 Striking Precision

Other predators snatch, spear, or crush their prey. The mantis shrimps, or stomatopods, a group of vigorous crustacean predators, provide examples (Hugh Dingle, 1969, 1972). Most use the forelimb as a rather complex spear (figure 3-5);

R. L. Caldwell & H. Dingle describe the strike made with this organ, the dactyl, as one of the fastest of animal movements. Its velocity is more than 100 m/s; and the movement is complete in 8 ms or less. A few stomatopod species smash the shells of mollusks. These too strike with great speed, and with a force said to be nearly that of a bullet of small caliber. *Hemisquilla ensigera*, which may be about 250 mm long, broke an aquarium wall made of two layers of safety glass. These alarming animals are said to stalk their prey, which includes crabs, by sight. Crabs, hermit crabs inhabiting snail shells, snails themselves, and bivalves are all consumed. Each stomatopod has a lair, a cavity in rock, to which it drags its food and in which most of the demolition is carried out. Sto-

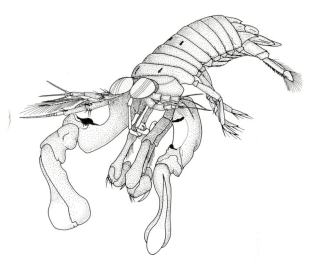

FIGURE 3-5 A mantis shrimp, *Gonodactylus bredini,* a predatory crustacean that strikes its prey at high speed. (Courtesy H. Dingle & R. L. Caldwell, 1969)

FIGURE 3-4 A predatory gastropod, the whelk, *Buccinum undatum.* On its shell is *Alcyonium digitatum.* (H. Knudsen, Marine Biological Laboratory, Elsinore)

matopods show considerable individuality in the details of their feeding behavior. Moreover, if they are given unfamiliar food, they are at first inefficient at dealing with it, but improve with practice.

Stomatopods, both spearers and smashers, are examples of animals that can strike at prey with extreme precision. There are many others. Among them are the insects of the family Mantidae. These animals wait in a characteristic posture. When a moving object, such as another insect, comes near, it is followed by movements of the head. The strike consists of very rapid extension and flexion of the forelegs, and is followed by tibiofemoral flexion so that the prey is grasped. The prey is then brought to the mouth and eaten.

Susan Rilling and colleagues have described what evokes this sequence. Mantids of the genus *Heirodula* were fasted, fixed to a cardboard disc, and then presented with dummy prey made of paper. The insects took 75 ms or less to strike at the dummies (or at real prey); and 85% of the strikes were successful. (Figure 3-6 illustrates some of the dummies.) Striking occurred most often when the object was in reach of the forelegs, and when its appendages moved rapidly and jerkily. Size and shape were of small importance; and there was no evidence of an effect of color or odor.

Here, then, is an example of what has sometimes been called a releasing stimulus, or *releaser* (17.2.5)—a pattern of stimulation (in this case visible) that evokes a stereotyped response. The "fixed" or highly predictable character of the response was examined by the same authors. Mantids of one group were fed normally throughout life on live flies; those of a second group were hand fed; and those of a third were fed on meal-worms, which have a low value as "releasing" stimuli. All three groups, when tested later, were equally efficient at striking. Hence the strike develops in full without practice. The experiments showed, however, that (as with the mantis shrimps) both catching and eating improve with experience.

Lastly there are the squids—active cephalopod mollusks that hunt largely by sight. The eyes of squids resemble those of vertebrates (figures 3-7, 3-8). The cuttlefish, *Sepia officinalis,* lives in shallow waters, where it captures quickly moving prey, such as prawns (Crustacea, Decapoda) and fish. The prey is detected with one eye, the eye moves correspondingly, and the body is then aligned on the prey. The cuttlefish is cryptically colored, but at this stage its color changes. It swims toward its prey until it reaches attacking distance, when it

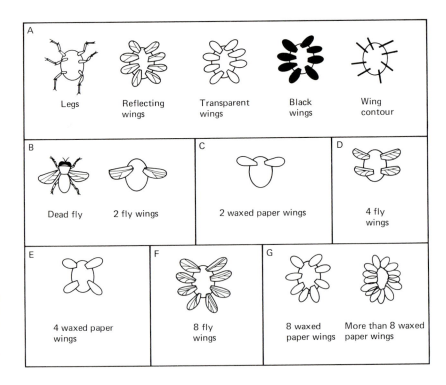

FIGURE 3-6 Models used to analyze the patterns of visual stimulation that evoke striking by a praying mantis, *Mantis religiosa.* Those of group A were least likely to evoke a response, those of group G, most likely. (After S. Rilling & others, 1959)

FIGURE 3-7 A molluskan predator, the squid, *Sepietta oweniana.* One of the highly developed eyes is shown. (H. Knudsen, Marine Biological Laboratory, Elsinore)

FIGURE 3-8 Section through the eye of a squid, *Sepia,* to show the resemblance in structure to the eye of a vertebrate. (After C. L. Prosser, 1973)

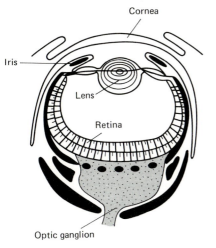

pauses for about 3 s. If the prey moves, the cuttlefish moves also. The strike itself consists of a slight forward movement of the whole animal, and a shooting out of the tentacles, which reach their target in less than 15 ms. The prey is then embraced by the arms, bitten, and injected with a poison (J. B. Messenger, 1977).

This behavior, illustrated in figure 3-9, is once again an example of an action with machine-like features. But, as might be expected with a large-brained animal, it is also capable of modification. For example, if a prawn is repeatedly offered in a glass tube, the animal learns *not* to strike at it. An even more instructive finding, on the ontogeny of the behavior, has been described by M. J. Wells (1958). Young *Sepia,* when they have just begun to feed, attack only prawns of the genus *Mysis.* Later they generalize their predatory response to a variety of species. Hence *Sepia* has a very specific and predictable kind of response, which is nevertheless to some extent adaptable to circumstances even in the adult phase; and it has a complex development that depends partly on individual experience.

Among the vertebrates, many amphibians use their tongues rather as mantids use their forelegs (reviewed by J.-P. Ewert). Figure 3-10 illustrates experiments by G. Roth on the salamander, *Hydromantes italicus.* This species is (with others) described by an appropriately tongue-twisting adjective—bolitoglossine. It leads a double life: in winter and summer it occupies limestone caves, often in total darkness; but in spring and autumn it emerges and lives under rocks or leaves. Whereas a mantid's strike is guided exclusively by sight, *Hydromantes* also responds to odor.

In the light the strike is most readily evoked by an object of area 4 mm², at a distance of about 40 mm, moving jerkily at 5 to 25 mm/s. But a

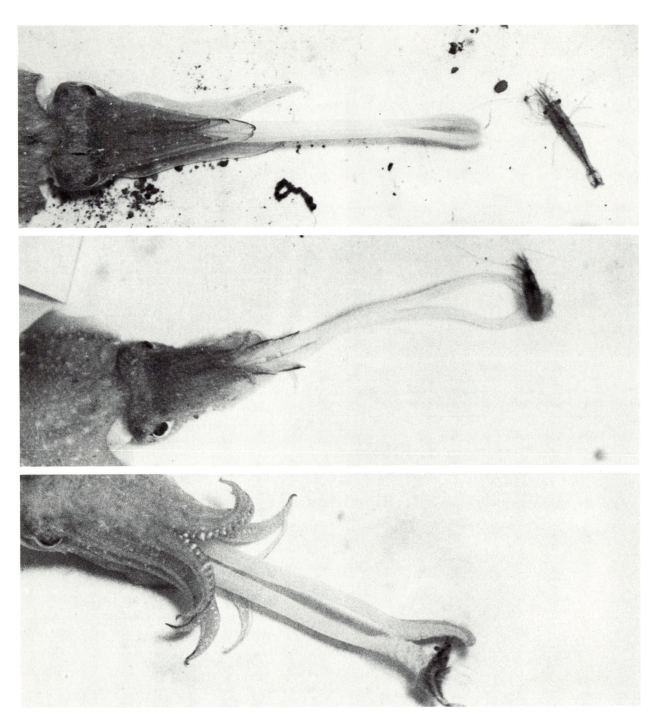

FIGURE 3-9 The rapid strike of a squid, *Sepia,* attacking its crustacean prey.
(Courtesy J. B. Messenger)

FIGURE 3-10 The rapid strike of an amphibian predator, the salamander, *Hydromantes italicus,* catching a fly with its tongue. (Courtesy G. Roth)

stationary object may be attacked, especially if it contrasts with its background and has a distinctive odor. Most surprising is the ability to make an accurate attack in darkness, on the basis of odor alone. Dead, crushed flies evoke a high response rate (shown by the movements of the prey recorded on an oscilloscope).

Whether hearing is also used by these salamanders seems not to be known; but the versatility in the use of two sensory modalities is typical of vertebrates, and is in contrast to what we find among the insects.

Despite this versatility, the use of the tongue by predatory amphibians usually depends on vision. A paper by J. Y. Lettvin and others, entitled "What the frog's eye tells the frog's brain", is based on ex-

periments in which the eye of a frog is stimulated by simple shapes, and recordings made of the impulses in single fibers of the optic tract. The authors used a hemisphere of about 36 cm diameter, painted grey on the inside, placed so that it was concentric to a frog's eye. Magnets on the outside moved black objects inside. Several types of receptor cell were identified. One, of obvious importance to an animal that catches rapidly moving prey, is referred to as a "bug detector": it responds to a small moving object, especially if the movement is jerky. This type does not respond to a change in the total amount of light falling on it, but others respond to dimming. There are also separate receptors for moving edges, whether the object is light on a dark background or dark on light. Each of the types of receptor mentioned is represented in a different layer of the optic tectum of the midbrain.

3.2.5 Sensory Specialization

When the motor equipment of predators is studied, as we saw in 1.1.4, it is not always obvious what senses are operating. The sharks (Squaliformes) provide examples. A. J. Kalmijn describes experiments on a small but notorious species, the dogfish, *Scyliorhinus canicula*—a scavenger as well as predator. Portions of dead fish were put in a chamber buried under sand, and a current of water was passed through the chamber. The fish made attacking movements at the outlet. Evidently, they were using their olfactory sense. In other experiments, a live fish was put in the buried chamber, and the fish then directed their attention to the sand immediately above the buried chamber, not to the water outlet. But no such attacks were made when the live fish had its chamber covered with an insulating material. But, when an electrode was put under the sand, and a 1-Hz sine wave current at 4 μA amplitude was passed, the fish attacked the electrode as if it were live bait, despite the presence of a tempting morsel of dead fish nearby. The fish were responsive to electrical properties of their prey. (Compare the account of electric fish in 2.3.2.)

Unlike the sharks, some fish hunt by sight. E. J. Denton describes a fish, *Pachystomias,* which lives in the deep sea where daylight hardly penetrates, and has photophores, or light-emitting organs. Large photophores near the eyes are covered with filters that transmit only orange and red light. Most fish of the deep seas are insensitive to light of these wavelengths. *Pachystomias* emits flashes of such light at intervals. As Denton remarks, such a fish resembles a night sniper with an infrared snooperscope: it can see its prey without itself being seen.

Some animals detect their prey with their ears. Owls are night flying predators. The barn owl, *Tyto alba,* studied by R. S. Payne and by M. Konishi, can strike accurately and seize a small mammal in total darkness. The owl is guided by the sounds made by its prey as it moves. The error of its aim is less than 1° in both the vertical and the horizontal planes.

More remarkable are the bats (Chiroptera), whose sonar is mentioned in 1.1.4. Insectivorous bats not only avoid obstacles by echo sounding, but also detect the presence of insects such as moths. D. R. Griffin (1958) has described how, as bats of certain species fly around a familiar region, they make cries at about the rate of 10 a second; each lasts about 10 ms; the frequencies covered are about 60 down to 30 kHz. (The highest frequency detectable by man is about 16 kHz, but depends greatly on age.) When such a bat encounters obstacles, instead of producing a series of squeaks it increases the rate of its cries to over 100 a second; each cry then lasts only about 1 ms. This buzz is also produced when a bat closes on its prey. The victim is seized in the teeth, or sometimes first with the tip of the wing.

An extraordinary finding, described by D. C. Dunning, concerns Arctiid moths that make regular, short clicking noises of high pitch when in flight. These clicks make bats alter course and so miss their prey.

3.2.6 Complex Behavior Patterns

Prey catching by a crustacean's or insect's appendage, or by an amphibian's tongue, lends itself to a mechanistic interpretation. In the late 20th century we are accustomed to machines that home on targets and make subtle discriminations. Similarly, the special features of predation by fish or even by bats can be conveniently analyzed, at least up to a point, in the language of physics. But the hunting of the most familiar animals, the birds and mammals, can usually not be described in this way.

C. H. Fry has described how the bee eaters (Meropidae) cope with insects equipped with stings. The prey is caught in flight and carried to a perch. The head of the insect is hammered, and the abdomen battered so that the venom is squeezed out of the sting gland. After a few more blows to the head, the insect is swallowed head first. This sequence, though fairly uniform and predictable

for each species, looks extremely purposeful and intelligent. The same applies to the flycatchers, *Muscicapa striata,* observed by N. B. Davies (1977). These birds distinguish wasps, *Vespula,* and bumblebees, *Bombus,* and remove their stings before eating them. Such behavior belongs in the category of what used to be called complex instinctive behavior (chapter 17).

An additional type of complexity appears in communal hunting. African wild dogs, *Lycaon pictus,* (figure 3-11) have been observed by R. D. Estes & J. Goddard and by W. Kühme. A pack in the Serengeti plain of East Africa, described by Kühme, consisted of 6 adult males, 2 adult females, and 15 pups in two litters. In February

FIGURE 3-11 African wild dogs, *Lycaon pictus:* two females (right) approach a male. These predators hunt in packs, and bring back meat to their young and to females that have stayed behind. (Courtesy G. W. & L. H. Frame)

1964 the hunting range was over 30 km but, when the numbers of prey later declined, it was three or four times that area. Hunting was around sunrise or sunset, was usually directed toward a gazelle, *Gazella,* and was always successful. A lone dog could overtake its prey, but often several pursued one gazelle and so wore it down more easily. When the prey was killed, all the dogs in the hunt assembled at it, tore open the belly, and bolted large masses of meat. They then returned to the lair, where the whole pack was fed. These animals have no status system: a male leader determines the direction of movement but is not dominant in any (other) sense (10.1).

3.2.7 The Use of Tools

In their cooperative behavior, hunting dogs resemble man. But human hunting is always aided by tools or other equipment. We now turn to examples of such external aids, used by other species. Among invertebrates the most familiar predators include the spiders (Araneida). I defer an account of their web building (figure 3-12) to 17.2.4.4. A good example of their diversity is an Australian species, *Dinopis subrufus,* studied by D. Clyne and by N. L. Roberts. These spiders live in shrubs, and hunt after sunset. A web can be constructed in about 30 min. It is then held in the manner shown in figure 3-13; when an insect comes within range, the web is dropped or thrown upon it, and so the web acts like a butterfly net.

Some predatory animals use tools. G. C. Millikan & R. I. Bowman observed six captive woodpecker finches, *Cactospiza pallida,* from the Galápagos Islands. These birds feed on insects concealed in crevices, for instance in bark. They disturb their prey by probing with a stick or a cactus spine held in the beak. In experiments, toothpicks made

FIGURE 3-12 Web of the garden spider, *Araneus diadematus.* (John Clegg)

FIGURE 3-13 A spider, *Dinopis subrufus,* with its net which it casts upon its prey. (Courtesy A. D. Blest)

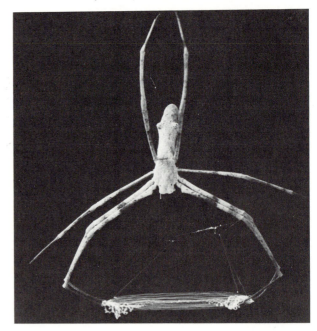

convenient substitutes. A stick may be modified: if it is too long, it may be shortened; or if it is forked, one prong may be removed. The sight of prey in a crevice, out of reach of the beak, provokes this behavior, but twigs are sometimes picked up in the absence of such a stimulus. In captivity, these finches were more inclined to use tools after a fast than when they were sated. The measure was the number of toothpicks removed from a supply provided by the experimenters.

The manipulative ability shown with sticks does not entail a general dexterity. Some true finches, for example, of the genera *Fringilla, Chloris,* and *Serinus,* studied by M. A. Vince (1958), can get a fragment of food by pulling on a string attached to it. But the woodpecker finches show no unusual abilities of this kind.

Among mammals (Primates excepted), the most celebrated tool user is the sea otter, *Enhydra lutris.* E. M. Fisher has described how an otter takes a piece of rock and a mollusk, lies on its back with the rock on its belly, and bashes open the mollusk by hammering on the rock (figure 3-14). K. R. L. Hall & G. B. Schaller also saw crabs and sea urchins treated in this way; and they describe play pounding by young otters.

Apes generally eat plants, but chimpanzees, *Pan troglodytes,* are versatile in their food habits: they may eat animals ranging from small mammals to insects. The most numerous insects in the tropics, ants and termites, are probably an important component in chimpanzee diet. W. C. McGrew has described how chimpanzees feed on driver ants, *Dorylus nigricans.* The insects have underground nests, which the apes open with their hands. A stick is dipped into the nest (figure 3-15); ants then walk on it, and are licked or chewed off. The sticks chosen are straight and of appropriate strength, without branches. Leaves are pulled off. Hence chimpanzees not only use tools, but—in the removal of leaves—go some way toward making them.

In this section we have covered a range of complex behavior patterns, from the least adaptable (represented by spiders) to the most nearly human (represented by chimpanzees). Some examples resemble the orientations described in chapter 2, for they are extremely uniform and predictable throughout each species. Others illustrate behavioral adaptability (intelligence, or the capacity to adapt behavior to circumstances). We return to these general topics in later chapters.

FIGURE 3-14 Sea otter, *Enhydra lutris,* uses a rock to hammer open a mollusk shell. (Reproduced from C. Singer et al., eds. *A History of Technology,* v. I, 1954, drawing by M. Wilson based on E. Fisher, by permission of Oxford University Press, Oxford)

FIGURE 3-15 Chimpanzees, *Pan troglodytes,* catching ants for food by dipping sticks into a hole. (Courtesy J. D. Bygott)

3.3 PREDATORY SEARCHING

3.3.1 The Concept of Searching

Despite the diversity of predators and their prey, some features of predation are quite general. Most predators search for prey: they range about their living area until contact is made with a source of food. The movements sometimes seem to be random, but we assume that, as a result of natural selection, they make an efficient pattern. If we knew the distribution of the various species of prey in space and time, and their nutritional value, we could perhaps calculate the optimum strategy for a given predator. Such a strategy would produce the maximum intake for a given expenditure of energy. But the necessary information is never completely available. Moreover, calculation should allow both for variation in the behavior of both predator and prey, and also for the demands on the predator of competing activities, such as avoiding other predators and mating.

We can therefore make only very simplified models or predictions from an armchair, even with the aid of a computer. To know just what a predator does, it is necessary to make detailed observations of many individuals.

3.3.2 Some Hunters

3.3.2.1 The Three-spined Stickleback:
J. J. Beukema has described prey catching by the three-spined stickleback, *Gasterosteus aculeatus.* This unobtrusive but much-studied fish, common in European freshwaters, eats small worms, crustaceans, and insect larvae. It lives in a structured environment, in which water weed is important. Figure 3-16 illustrates a "maze" in which sticklebacks were observed; it also shows hypothetical tracks, two random, one orderly. In some experiments, a single worm, *Tubifex,* was put in a compartment of the maze and a fish released into the maze. The fish had been without food for a period. When the worm was eaten, another was put in an-

other compartment, until 40 min had elapsed. Most fish ate about 5% of their body weight, after which they stopped eating.

The chance that a worm will be eaten in these conditions depends on how long the fish has been without food, that is, on "hunger" (4.5.4). We are concerned now with the chance that the predator will *encounter* a worm. What Beukema calls the "encounter efficiency" was independent of the duration of fasting. As figure 3-16 suggests, maximum efficiency in covering all the compartments of the maze requires an absence of turns by the fish. Beukema calculated the strategy that would give a fish the best chance of finding a worm in these artificial conditions. Although none of his fish swam at random, none adopted the ideal pat-

FIGURE 3-16 "Maze" for sticklebacks, *Gasterosteus aculeatus.* On the left, two hypothetical random tracks are shown; on the right, a track without turns. These alternative strategies, and the actual behavior of the fish, are discussed in the text. (After J. J. Beukema, 1968)

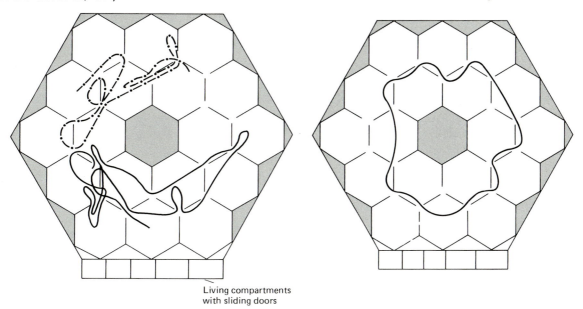

Living compartments with sliding doors

FIGURE 3.17 Carrion crow, *Corvus corone*, with one kind of food, an egg. (Courtesy H. Croze)

tern of movement: all tended to turn when, for the best result, they should not have done so. But, with repeated experience of the conditions, they improved: that is, they turned less. Hence they adapted their behavior, to some extent, to the experimental situation.

The failure of sticklebacks to search Beukema's maze in an optimum manner is perhaps not surprising. The conditions in pond or stream, to which sticklebacks are (presumably) adapted, are very different. For example, most prey animals are probably grouped, not spaced out at equal distances. Such bunching would affect the optimum strategy for a stickleback in nature: in particular, frequent turns would often be profitable.

Accordingly, G. Thomas made observations on the effect of capturing a prey animal on the subsequent movements of a stickleback. If the prey is eaten, there is an increase in the number of turns compared with the rate of turning when no prey is encountered. This phenomenon, *area-restricted searching*, like many findings based on elaborate

research, conforms with common sense. It is *as if* the animal, having found a food object, concluded that here was a promising place in which to search for more. Given that prey animals tend to group, such a response would pay off.

Sticklebacks sometimes capture an object and then spit it out. Thomas also observed movements after such rejection. They, too, corresponded to common sense: the animal swam away from the area in which the rejected prey was encountered. Thomas calls this *area-avoided searching*.

3.3.2.2 The Carrion Crow:

Some birds display similar behavior. The question of hunting strategy has been examined by H. Croze in experiments with the carrion crow, *Corvus corone,* living on a sandy shore in the north of England. These birds are both predators and scavengers (figure 3-17). Croze put portions of meat under mussel shells, *Mytilus edulis* (figure 3-18). Crows are wide-ranging exploratory birds and quickly found the meat. After this, the shells of both mussels and cockles, *Cardium edule* (figure 3-18), were put out, but with no meat under either type. The crows turned over most of the mussel shells, few of the cockles.

Crows were next trained to find meat under mussel shells painted a reddish color and partly concealed by being put on shingle. They quickly learnt to disregard shells painted a slightly different color. Once crows have found food in an area, they hunt around in it, and they also return to it persistently during later periods of foraging. Given a new kind of shell with food under it, they find the food more quickly if it is in such a familiar area. Hence these birds give two, contradictory impressions: they seem to be very alert to possible new sources of food, yet rather unadaptable in their foraging once a good source has been found. Perhaps they have to be deprived of food for some

FIGURE 3-18 Tracks of carrion crow near bivalve shells, photographed during experiments on food finding. The crows quickly found new food put out within their range: meat under mussel shells (above). Cockle shells, which provided no reward, were investigated but were soon abandoned (below). (Courtesy H. Croze)

time before they explore for new sources; but on this, nothing seems to be known.

3.3.2.3 Thrushes, Tits, and Chickadees:
J. N. M. Smith (1974a,b) has recorded the movements of thrushes and blackbirds (*Turdus*), in an English garden, when the birds had captured an earthworm; he also sometimes supplied cryptically colored artificial prey, made of flour, fat, and water. When the birds were feeding on earthworms, they tended to zigzag across the area of search: they made small, alternating turns and so avoided searching the same ground twice. But whenever a bird caught a worm, the pattern altered, and there was some evidence of area-restricted searching. Correspondingly, when the artificial prey was offered in higher density than usual, the changes of direction were larger, and there was less alternation.

J. N. M. Smith & Richard Dawkins also studied great tits, *Parus major,* in an aviary with four separate areas, each of which could be searched by the birds. The prey consisted of larvae (mealworms) of the flour beetle, *Tenebrio molitor,* and were offered in pots covered with foil caps; the birds readily learned to tear off the caps. The highest density of prey was 16, spread among 256 pots, the lowest, 1 in 256. The birds quickly learnt to concentrate on the area with the highest density, but they did not discriminate between different lower densities. After a series of trials, the areas with highest and lowest densities were interchanged. The birds nonetheless persisted, over many trials, in preferentially searching the area of formerly high density.

Hence, like the crows studied by Croze, these great tits displayed a repetitive kind of behavior or perseveration. Such conduct has been examined by J. R. Krebs and others (1974) during observations of the black-capped chickadee, *Parus atricapillus.*

They asked: when does a chickadee decide to leave a patch in which there is a group of prey? They used artificial trees hung with "pine cones" made of wood blocks with holes in them. A bird might be expected to adjust the time it spends on a patch (a tree) by its experience of the numbers of prey on such a patch: after a certain time (or when a given number of prey have been captured), it would no longer pay off to remain there. Its decision on when to leave the patch would then be based on information recently acquired. But the chickadees did not behave in this way: they gave up foraging in a patch at a constant time from their last capture in the patch. This finding confirms the impression of some degree of rigidity in foraging behavior.

3.3.2.4 Small Mammals:
Similar questions arise (but have not been fully answered) when we look at the behavior of some mammals. C. S. Holling has described experiments on deer mice, *Peromyscus,* shrews, *Sorex,* and others feeding on cocoons of the European pine sawfly, *Neodiprion sertifer.* The larvae of this insect, after feeding on pine needles, fall from the trees in June, and pupate in the pine dust on the ground. Small mammals dig into the dust and eat the cocoons. In experiments, healthy cocoons were buried 20 mm below the surface of sand in enclosures. The mammals studied by Holling, evidently guided by olfactory stimuli, dug accurately for the cocoons. (Many novel odors were found to evoke digging.) During trials spread over three or four days, the rate of capture increased—an effect of practice. The most interesting finding is illustrated in figure 3-19. A simple assumption is that rate of capture would increase in proportion to prey density. In fact, as the figure shows, at low densities captures are fewer than expected.

Holling suggests that these findings represent

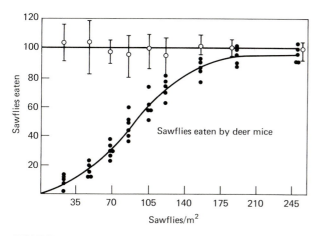

FIGURE 3-19 Deer mice, *Peromyscus,* were given a choice between sawfly cocoons and fragments of dog biscuit. The total amount of food eaten was fairly constant (upper line); but the number of sawfly cocoons detected and consumed varied with their density. The vertical bars on the points in the upper curve represent standard errors of the means. Each filled circle represents a single observation. The proportion of sawflies in the food is not a linear function of their density. (After C. S. Holling, 1966)

adaptation to a particular situation by predators that feed on a variety of prey (not only sawfly larvae). If there are only a few larvae, it pays to stop searching for them and to look for another kind of food.

3.3.3 Exploration and the Search Image

The descriptions in the preceding section omit much that is important in predatory conduct: they could indeed be misleading, by giving an impression of unadaptability. The tendency to persist in searching a locality, even when no prey remain, looks ineffective. But in fact most predators range widely, even in regions in which they have not found prey.

J. R. Bider and others give an example of exploratory behavior by a predator in natural condi-

tions. Raccoons, *Procyon lotor* (Carnivora), are usually active at night. They eat frogs and fish, small mammals, and a variety of plants. Those observed fed principally before midnight. When sated, they moved around in areas in which less food had previously been found. If a new source of food was found in these areas, on subsequent nights it was visited earlier. Such findings, though in accord with expectation, are important because we know so little of what nocturnal animals do in nature.

We now turn to the hypothesis of the *search image.* Luuk Tinbergen studied birds and their insect food for a period of eight years. In a plantation of pine trees, *Pinus sylvestris,* the main predator was (once again) the great tit, *Parus major.* The birds were observed supplying caterpillars to their young: when a bird touched down at a nest box it was automatically photographed; and the species of caterpillar could then usually be determined. Like Holling's small mammals, the birds tended to disregard species of edible insects when they were at low densities. Tinbergen also recorded what happened when a prey species suddenly became numerous: there was always a delay before the birds turned their attention to the new source of food.

Tinbergen's hypothesis of the search image states that a bird (or other predator) needs to experience the stimulus of a particular prey species at a certain threshold frequency if it is to respond to the presence of that species. But an alternative explanation for Tinbergen's findings is implied in the work described above on sticklebacks and the various species of predatory birds. If a predator tends to concentrate its search in particular patches, in which prey density is high, the result will be just what Tinbergen observed. There is then no need to assume that the predator has to store special information about the visual properties of prey species.

T. Royama studied great tits in England and Japan. He used both direct observation and the record from an automatic camera. His findings resembled Tinbergen's, but with some qualifications. First, there was the confusing observation that the parents' diet differed from that of the young. Second, some common and palatable prey were taken less than expected, and some rare species were taken with unexpected frequency. Lastly, some prey species began to be taken less *before* their numbers declined. An interesting question is whether these birds ever vary the prey eaten as if they were sampling them or selecting for novelty (8.1.3.3). Royama's hypothesis is that birds sample, if not the prey, at least all the accessible habitats; and then develop the habit of going for particular prey species in particular habitats. In this way hunting efficiency is held to be maximized.

Nonetheless, the search image hypothesis remains attractive. How can it be tested rigorously? In experiments with domestic chicks, *Gallus bankiva,* Marian Dawkins (1971a,b) offered not living prey but colored grains of rice. The birds' early history was controlled, so that their previously formed habits did not interfere with the results. In one experiment they were fed for three weeks on green or orange grains on a white background. They were then tested for ability to pick up grains on either a contrasting or a matching background. As expected, at first it took them much longer to find the matching grains. But their performance improved, until eventually they were equally quick at picking up either kind of grain.

Evidently, at first the birds responded to color, but later they developed the habit of responding to other visible features of the grains, such as shape. In later experiments chicks were trained either on conspicuous grains, that is, grains on a contrasting background, or on cryptic grains on a matching background. They were then offered a choice between conspicuous or cryptic grains (figure 3-20). The birds that had been trained on cryptic grains initially ignored the conspicuous grains standing out against their background, and picked up a cryptic grain.

Anybody interested in the design and interpretation of behavioral experiments is recommended to study the full account of this work. Dawkins concludes by justly criticizing the term search (or searching) image, because it has been used in various senses. But her findings do lead to a conclusion that supports the original concept. Her birds developed an increasing ability to detect inconspicuous grains; and this change was evidently due to a process in the central nervous system of the kind that in ourselves we call *recognition.*

3.4 CRYPSIS

Many animals are difficult to see because they match their background. Such crypsis may depend on coloration or shading; but sometimes it is due to a resemblance, of bizarre exactness, to a particular background feature (reviewed by H. B. Cott, 1940). Some critics have found it impossible to believe in natural selection for concealing coloring. Others have taken crypsis uncritically for granted. The question that can be answered is whether certain appearances (or disappearances) do in fact protect animals from predators today.

3.4.1 Countershading

A rabbit, *Oryctolagus cuniculus,* a trout, *Salmo trutta,* the caterpillar of an eyed hawkmoth, *Smerinthus ocellatus,* and a squid of the genus *Abraliopsis* have an important visible property in common: all display countershading (figures 13-4 and

FIGURE 3-20 Diagram to illustrate an experiment in which birds were offered concealed or conspicuous rice grains. Birds that had been trained on cryptic grains (right) at first ignored conspicuous grains standing out against their background (left). (Reproduced from M. Dawkins, *Animal Behavior,* 1971, p. 575-82, by permission of Bailliere Tindall, London, and M. Dawkins)

13-21). In natural conditions, in daytime, there is usually light from above. The ventral part of an animal's body is then shadowed. But many animals are paler below than above; hence there is compensation for the ventral shadow. Animals whose usual position is upside down have reversed countershading. This is a simple example of the way in which appearance and behavior are related.

L. De Ruiter studied the predatory behavior of jays, *Garrulus glandarius,* which had been reared in captivity; the birds had had no experience in finding the caterpillars on which they were tested. Caterpillars were killed and fastened to twigs either in their normal position or upside down. Eight spe-

cies were used. As predicted, more of the inverted larvae were eaten than those in the normal position. In experiments with some hundreds of caterpillars, the ratio of inverted to normal eaten was about three to two—more than enough for countershading to have survival value. (If all prey species were completely protected, there would be no predators.)

Other experiments studied the ability of birds to distinguish apparently flat from rounded models. Two jays, named respectively Samson and Delilah, could, with careful training, readily make the distinction.

Ruiter also studied the behavior of captive jays toward lepidopteran larvae of two genera, *En-*

nomos and *Biston*. These caterpillars accurately resemble twigs, and in natural conditions in daylight adopt a posture that makes them astonishingly difficult to distinguish from the real thing (figure 3-21). The birds were accustomed to feed in their aviary, but again had experienced no caterpillars. When first exposed to the larvae, they usually failed to find them. The delay in one series of experiments ranged from 7 to 40 min. This contrasted sharply with findings on the behavior of the jays faced with grasshoppers (Acrididae) for the first time. Even when they were hidden, each bird found one within 10 s.

During the delay before finding the first caterpillar, the birds, which had been without food for at least 12 h, moved around as if expecting food. The birds, however, had previously experienced twigs, and evidently at first did not distinguish between twigs and caterpillars. Sometimes a caterpillar was first detected because the bird trod on it. When live caterpillars were used, movement by a caterpillar commonly at once attracted a bird's attention. Once a caterpillar had been eaten, some birds pecked at both caterpillars and sticks. The behavior suggested the existence of perceptual learning or a search image. If, in further experiments, a bird were offered sticks and no caterpillars, it soon gave up its habit of pecking at sticklike objects.

Some animals that match their background do so only by their color. A. P. di Cesnola took advantage of the color polymorphism of *Mantis religiosa:*

FIGURE 3-21 Cryptic larva of peppered moth, *Biston betularia.* (S. C. Bisserôt)

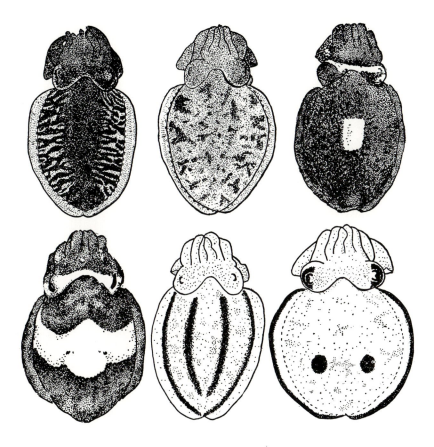

FIGURE 3-22 The cuttlefish, *Sepia officinalis,* has chromatophores in its skin, which allow rapid changes of color and pattern. On a background of sand or pebbles, mottled patterns seem to provide concealment. Other patterns startle prey, or have social functions. A single individual may have any of the appearances shown. (Reproduced from A. C. Hardy, *The Open Sea,* 1956, drawing after W. Holmes, by permission of Collins Publishers, London)

some are green, others brown. He fastened some of each color both on a green background and on a brown. All the matching mantids survived, but none of those on a contrasting background. H. B. Cott (1940) summarizes later work in which this very striking finding was confirmed; but he also describes yet a further experiment, in which not only green and brown mantids were used but also yellow; on this occasion crows, *Corvus,* quickly ate nearly all the mantids regardless of color or background. Once again, we may guess that the birds had learnt to recognize the insects in a variety of situations. Such a series of studies shows how it is possible for apparently inconsistent findings to arise

from carefully designed experiments. Predators do not always behave with mechanical regularity.

Nor do their prey. There are many examples (reviewed by M. Edmunds) both of change of color or pattern to match the background and of selection of background to match an animal's appearance. Flatfish such as flounders, *Pleuronectes,* slowly change the pattern of pigmentation in the skin until they match the sand or gravel most beautifully. William Holmes has described how the cuttlefish, *Sepia officinalis,* has a disruptive, zebra-like pattern when swimming; but on a background of sand it has a matching, mottled pattern; and on pebbles there is yet another pattern (figure 3-22).

These animals can change color in two-thirds of a second—almost as quickly as a human being can blush or pale: the chromatophores are under neural control, and their pigment spreads or contracts within its cellular processes with astonishing speed. Presumably this system helps to protect cuttlefish from the dolphins, *Tursiops,* and other cetaceans that prey on them.

Some squids have light-producing organs, or photophores. The cephalopod, *Abraliopsis,* lives mainly at a depth of about 600 m during the day, but at less than 100 m during the night. It possesses a large number of ventral photophores (figure 3-23), which produce light only when there is illumination from above (R. E. Young; R. E. Young & C. F. E. Roper). In experiments, when the light was switched off, the photophores were switched off too. Evidently, this is a kind of countershading. When the light from the photophores matches that from above, the squids become invisible, or barely visible, from below: the authors call these squids ghosts. Other oceanic species have photophores; and the same authors describe crustaceans and fish from deep waters, in which change in light production is related to illumination.

Selection of background and adaptation of posture to its special features are probably much commoner than change of color. The work of T. D. Sargent (1968, 1969) provides examples. He gave moths of two species a choice between black and white backgrounds. A dark-colored moth, *Catocala antinympha,* was more likely to settle on the black surface; a pale moth, *Campaea perlata,* turned up more frequently on the white surface. These unsurprising findings lead to the general question: how is the choice between backgrounds made by the animal? Can such behavior be interpreted in terms, say, of taxes? A related question is whether the behavior is typical of the whole species and independent of any special previous experience.

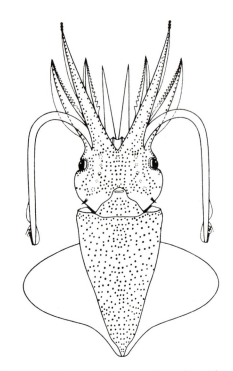

FIGURE 3-23 Drawing of the ventral view of a squid, *Abraliopsis,* to show the distribution of photophores. When these organs are producing light, the animal becomes ghost-like and is hardly visible from below. This is evidently a special form of countershading. (Reproduced by permission from R. E. Young and C. F. E. Roper, *Science,* v. 191, pp. 1046-48, Fig. 1, 12 March 1976. Copyright 1976 by the Amer. Assc. for the Advancement of Science)

Sargent submitted some of his insects to a number of treatments, none of which affected the choice of background. In some, the scales around the eyes of dark moths were painted white and those of pale moths, black. There was still no alteration in behavior. Hence selection of background evidently does not depend on matching. Similarly, another moth, *Cosimbia pendulinaria,* usually light colored, can be made dark by exposing the larvae to low temperatures. But both forms prefer to settle on a light background.

Sometimes, selection of an appropriate background depends on a response not to color or shade, but to some accompanying feature. A yellow moth, *Schinia florida,* habitually settles on the flowers of the evening primrose, *Oenothera biennis,* which, too, are yellow. But the moth will settle on a flower hidden by a muslin bag; it does so even if simultaneously offered visible yellow flowers of other species. In this case, the response is evidently to the odor of the flower.

Sargent also observed the behavior of a moth, *Melanolopha canadaria,* which resembles bark. This insect was put in a cylinder that offered a choice between horizontal and vertical black and white stripes made by stretching black tape on a white surface. Most of the moths settled in the appropriate position, that is, with the long axis of the body at right angles to the stripes (figure 3-24).

FIGURE 3-24 Experiment to show how two species of moth, each cryptically colored, align themselves on a striped background in a position that aids crypsis. (After T. D. Sargent, 1969)

Melanolophia canadaria

Tape strips	Alignment of moths			
	Correct		Incorrect	
Vertical		13		4
Horizontal		10		1

Catocala ultronia

Tape strips	Alignment of moths			
	Correct		Incorrect	
Vertical		14		1
Horizontal		0		3

This corresponds to the position adopted in nature, namely, the long axis at right angles to the axis of the tree or branch. Sargent then repeated the experiment with the stripes covered with clear cellulose acetate. In the absence of any tactile cue, the moths' resting positions had no regular relationship with the stripes. The figure also illustrates a similar finding from another species.

These, then, are examples of species-typical responses to backgrounds that aid crypsis. There is no reason to think that they depend on any form of learning by practice. To this extent, they resemble the taxes described in the previous chapter. Sometimes, they are said to be *innate;* but I defer a discussion of this difficult concept to chapter 17.

3.4.2. Genetical Variation and Natural Selection

In the present century nearly all biologists have assumed that the structural, chemical, and behavioral phenomena of crypsis are a product of evolution by natural selection. The examples of the protective value of crypsis, given above, are not, however, in themselves adequate evidence for this assumption. Evolution is a process of change. The evidence that countershading is protective comes from animals already countershaded: selective mortality from predation must tend to keep the animals of successive generations as they now are, by eliminating those that depart from the typical. Such *stabilizing selection* is widespread.

Part of the answer to such an argument is that stabilizing selection usually requires a constant environment. If conditions change, selection "pressures" change also. Just this has happened in large regions of Europe during the period of rapid growth of industry. The pollution of the air by the smoke from factory chimneys has made a vast (unintentional) ecological experiment. Many cryptic species of Lepidoptera, and even some Hemiptera and spiders, have been affected; but only one species has been studied in great detail, the peppered moth, *Biston betularia* (reviewed by H. B. D. Kettlewell).

The usual resting place for the adult moth is the trunk of a tree covered with lichen, where its light, speckled coloration makes it barely visible. In the middle of the 19th century, in England and else-where, a dark, almost black form of this species was known as a great rarity (figure 3-25). By the beginning of this century, in certain industrial regions, 95% of this species were of the melanic form. In the southwest of England, however, at least 90% were still of the typical form. In the areas in which the melanics predominated, the lichens that had formerly covered the tree trunks

FIGURE 3-25 The peppered moth, *Biston betularia*. On the left, three color forms, or morphs, on bark covered with lichen. On right, three specimens on bare bark. (Courtesy D. R. Lees & E. R. Creed)

FIGURE 3-26 Black and white surface on which moths, *Biston betularia,* were allowed to settle: the moths tended to settle on the surface that they matched. (Courtesy H. B. D. Kettlewell)

had been killed by substances in the polluted air. In these conditions, the melanic form was cryptic, but the peppered form conspicuous.

Breeding experiments showed the difference of the melanic condition from the normal to be due to a single gene substitution, and melanism to be dominant. There was therefore clear evidence of a genetically determined difference in fitness (in the Darwinian sense), related to a particular feature of the environment. But there was still the question whether the behavior of predators corresponded to this assumption. Experiments by Kettlewell fully confirmed, partly by direct observation, differential mortality of the two forms, due to predation by birds. Kettlewell also studied the behavior of the moths. He provided a surface, resembling the bole

of a tree, marked in black and white stripes (figure 3-26). The moths tended to settle on the surface that they matched.

R. C. Steward has experimented more recently on a moth, *Allophyes oxyacanthae,* which, too, has typical and melanic forms: all typicals tended to settle on a matching background, but only some melanics did so. There is evidence of genetically determined differences in behavior among the black forms. Perhaps there is a transient polymorphism, and the "matching melanics" are replacing the others.

Some further developments have been described by J. A. Bishop and others. The melanic forms today are darker than those captured in the 19th century (and carefully preserved). The latter retain small white patches. Probably, there has been selection not only for the gene for melanism but also for modifier genes that have made the dark coloring more effective. A second new development has been the introduction of smokeless zones in some regions of England. In an area near Liverpool, in the period 1961 to 1974, there was an increase in peppered (nonmelanic) forms from 5.2 to 10.5%. The change accompanied the reappearance of lichens on the trees with the lessening of pollution.

A third finding introduces an unexpected complexity. D. R. Lees & E. R. Creed have made a further study of the distribution of color types in England. In some areas they find a high incidence of melanic forms where these are at a disadvantage: that is, where the dark forms are more preyed upon than the light. They conclude that the melanic genotype confers some, as yet unidentified, "physiological" advantage, which can sometimes more than compensate for a high incidence of predation. If so, this is a case of pleiotropic or multiple effects of a gene (discussed further in chapter 16). Such findings warn us to take nothing for granted.

Nonetheless, we have in "industrial melanism" a rare example, not only of the value of crypsis, but of genetical variation that allows populations to become rapidly adapted to a change in their environment.

FIGURE 3-27 Three examples of animals subject to predation, yet extremely conspicuous: a lepidopteran, *Bunaea alcinoe;* a coleopteran, *Anthia sexguttata;* and the marble tree frog, *Hyperolius marmoratus.* (Reproduced from H. B. Cott, *Looking at Animals: A Zoologist in Africa,* pp. 163 and 183, by permission of Collins Publishers, London)

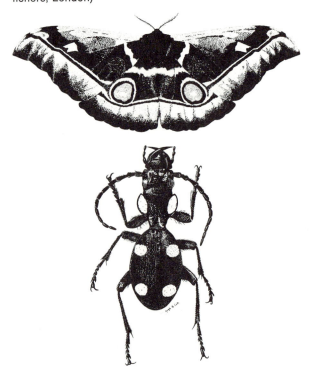

FIGURE 3-28 Wasp, *Vespula:* an example of a conspicuous species also equipped with a sting. (F. W. Long)

3.5 APOSEMATISM

Some animals are preyed upon, yet have colors and structure that make them blatantly conspicuous (figure 3-27). Such features may be a means of social communication; but for certain species they have a protective function. (They may have both functions.) Conspicuousness can protect against predation when it is accompanied by some aversive property, such as a repellent taste, poisonous tissues, or a sting. Animals so equipped are said to be aposematic. The members of the wasp family (Vespidae), for instance, combine a sting with a body garishly striped in black and yellow (figure 3-28). The concept of aposematism, therefore, implies three statements about the behavior of predators. (1) Animals of some species, on being attacked, somehow cause the predator to withdraw. (2) The predator, as a result of such an experience, later refrains from attacking other members of those species. (3) The predator identifies the prey by its conspicuous features. Aposematic effects can therefore be confidently identified only by experiment.

3.5.1 The Habit of Avoidance

W. Windecker observed the behavior of young birds of many species toward larvae of the cinnabar moth, *Callimorpha jacobaeae,* which is striped yellow and black (compare figure 3-29). Inexperienced birds readily try to eat them; but when seized the caterpillars are quickly rejected, and the bill is vigorously wiped. If the caterpillars were offered after their "hairs" had been shaved off, the birds ate them. Hence the hairs are the distasteful feature. The hairs, however, were not the feature that the birds responded to when they avoided the larvae. After he had trained birds in this way, Windecker offered them other insects, such as wasps of the genus, *Vespula* (figure 3-28). All were rejected, although the birds had not encoun-

FIGURE 3-29 Caterpillars of the monarch butterfly, *Danaus plexippus* —another example of potential prey animals that are nevertheless highly visible: like wasps, they are striped yellow and black. (American Museum of Natural History)

tered them before. Other insects, not colored in this way, were accepted. Hence the birds refuse anything that looks like the distasteful caterpillars.

Similar findings have been described by J. V. Z. Brower (1958a,b,c). The predator was the Florida scrub jay, *Cyanocitta coerulescens*. The monarch butterfly, *Danaus plexippus,* is distasteful: when attacked by a bird, it is usually rejected. After such an experience a bird is much less likely to attack a monarch when one is offered again. Moreover, a bird so trained rejects a butterfly that resembles a monarch (a "mimic"), such as the viceroy, *Limenitis archippus.* The habit of refusing such butterflies is retained (remembered) by some birds for more than two weeks. Similarly, birds readily learn to avoid the swallowtail, *Battus philenor,* which is distasteful. And if they have done so, they avoid three species of *Papilio* which mimic the swallowtail.

The capacity of birds to *generalize* (6.2.2) has also been studied by G. Mostler, in a study of the behavior of young birds toward wasps. These insects have both a deterrent sting and distasteful tissues. Birds soon learn to avoid them. A number of species of hover flies (Syrphidae) quite closely resemble wasps (figure 3-30), although they belong to a different insect order. But once the birds have learnt to avoid wasps (or bees), they also avoid the flies that resemble the distasteful insects.

Nearly all examples of aposematic patterns are

of insects, but aposematism is not confined to them. Figures 3-31 and 3-32 show a moray eel, *Gymnothorax meleagris,* which has a conspicuous pattern of light spots on a dark background and is noxious to predators (J. E. McCosker). It lives in shallow Pacific waters and the Indian Ocean, where it occupies rock crevices but is easily seen because its head usually protrudes. A much less common fish, *Calloplesiops altivelis,* similarly colored, lives in the same places; and when disturbed it takes cover in rock or coral, where it expands its fins. The dorsal fin has a conspicuous eye-like marking; hence the rear end of this fish resembles the front of the eel. McCosker has tested *C. altivelis* on other fish and has tasted it himself. It is evidently not noxious, but derives protection from being a mimic of *G. meleagris.*

3.5.2 Mimicry

We are concerned here primarily with the feeding behavior of predators, especially their capacity to develop new habits (of avoidance) as a result of experience. But a digression is now due on the subject of mimicry. The preceding paragraphs describe the capacity of predators to generalize from one species to another. In one example, hover flies—which are evidently highly palatable—are shown to be protected by their resemblance to wasps or bees.

Such a protective resemblance is called *Batesian mimicry,* after the naturalist, H. W. Bates (1825–1892). It is supposed that the mimics have evolved a progressively closer resemblance to aposematic species, and so have acquired an increasing degree of protection from predators. The mimics have

FIGURE 3-30 Hover fly, *Eristalis:* a mimic of wasps. Compare figure 3-28. (F. W. Lane)

then been able to acquire protection by conspicuousness, without any equipment of sting or repellent substances. Such a hypothesis raises many questions. For example, if the mimicry is to be effective, the aposematic model should presumably be more numerous, or more accessible to predators, than the mimic. The ecological evidence (reviewed by E. B. Ford, and by C. W. Rettenmeyer) on the whole conforms with what is expected.

J. G. Sternburg and others have provided experimental evidence. They painted some day-flying moths yellow to make them look like the tiger swallowtail, *Papilio glaucus,* which is edible; other moths were painted black to resemble a poisonous swallowtail. Large numbers of moths were released; and thereafter, on each day for a week, as many as possible were caught again. As predicted, a higher proportion of black moths were recaptured. And injuries to the wings showed that most attacks on moths were by birds, and that the yellow-painted moths were attacked more.

A behavioral question is whether a very incomplete resemblance confers an advantage. If not, it is difficult to imagine how existing resemblances could have evolved.

Several workers have therefore experimented with artificial prey: in this way predators can be tested with mimics of varying degrees of resemblance. G. M. Morrell & J. R. G. Turner put dummy insects made of pastry, on colored cards, and spread

FIGURE 3-31 Apparent Batesian mimicry. The top photograph shows an uncommon fish, *Calloplesiops altivelis,* in its normal position in a rock crevice; the eye can be seen, and also an eye-like marking on the dorsal fin. The middle photograph shows the fish when disturbed: this is the rear view, with a conspicuous eye spot. It now resembles the predatory eel, *Gymnothorax meleagris,* shown below. (D. Powell, Steinhart Aquarium, San Francisco)

FIGURE 3-32 Close-up of head of moray eel (above) and of posterior of *Calloplesiops* (below). Compare previous figure. (T. McHugh, Steinhart Aquarium, San Francisco)

them on a garden lawn. Visiting birds, mostly starlings, *Sturnus vulgaris,* were first accustomed to eating pastry from green cards (controls). Next they were offered more controls but also an equal number of baits on red cards; the latter had been soaked in a solution of quinine hydrochloride, and represented aposematic prey, or models. The birds soon came to avoid the models, but they continued

to eat the controls. The birds were then offered not only controls and models, but also edible mimics of the models. In each of a series of experiments, there were twice as many models as mimics. One kind of mimic was identical with the model; others differed in color or by the addition of a black bar. The perfect mimics were hardly ever eaten. The partial mimics were also protected, but less well: similarity of color proved to be especially important.

H. A. Ford made pastry into artificial caterpillars, and predators (birds that visit suburban gardens in Britain) were trained to avoid red prey made aversive with quinine. Blue prey were palatable. Partial mimics were made either bicolored, with contrasting colors at each end, or varying shades of purple. Incomplete mimicry again partly protected the prey from the birds; and the more nearly the shade of purple resembled the red of the model, the greater the protection.

The experiments described in this section are usually discussed under the heading of the evolution of mimicry. If mimicry has evolved by natural selection, it can hardly have done so—it is presumed—except by gradual improvement from a slight resemblance to a close one. The experiments fit the presumption: incomplete resemblances are shown to be capable of reducing predation. The actual observations, however, are not of an evolutionary process: they concern the ability of birds to develop new habits.

3.6 DEIMATIC EFFECTS

The preceding section describes interactions in which predators develop the habit of avoiding prey. Approach is *punished* by sting, poison, or taste. A possible alternative for a prey species would be an action or feature that induces withdrawal regardless of the previous experience of the predator. There are many apparent examples. If one corners a wild rat, *Rattus,* it jumps up and down and screams. I find this very disconcerting, and evidently other predators do so too. Paul Leyhausen has described how cats flinch from a screaming rat. Some insects, when disturbed, suddenly reveal a striking pattern. Hence in zoological writings there are references to startle displays, and to *deimatic* (or "dymantic") behavior—from a Greek word meaning frighten.

As usual, many apparent examples have been reported, but few experimental studies. Here I describe some successful experiments by A. D. Blest (1957). Most of Blest's predators were birds of the three genera, *Fringilla, Parus,* and *Emberiza.* The main component of the presumed deimatic display was the presence of patterns resembling eyes on the wings of many lepidopterans (figure 3-33).

Six yellow buntings, *E. citrinella,* were offered, on a number of occasions, the opportunity to feed on butterflies of the species, *Nymphalis io,* which have two pairs of eyespots. When disturbed, the insect lowers its wings, and the eyespots are revealed. This sequence of movements may be repeated many times. The butterfly also tilts its body so that its dorsum is toward the source of the disturbance. A bird, faced with such a display, may hop or fly away. Blest removed the eyespots of butterflies, and presented birds with them and with equal numbers of normal butterflies. Four times as many escape responses were made to the normal insects as to those without eyespots. The response of the birds was not, however, constant. Most escape responses were made on the first encounter with a butterfly. The birds rapidly lost the apparent "fear" engendered by the insects' display: that is, they habituated to the stimulus. There was also individual variation among the whole group of birds studied.

FIGURE 3-33 Io moth, *Automeris io,* (Lepidoptera) with eye spots. (E. Slonneger)

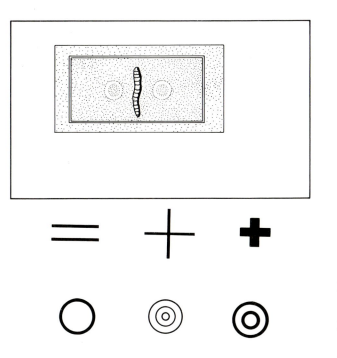

FIGURE 3-34 Method of experiment to show the deterrent effect on birds of an eye-like pattern. When a trained bird approached the worm on the platform (above), a pattern was illuminated on each side of the worm. The more the patterns resembled a pair of eyes, the less likely was the bird to take the food. Compare figure 3-33. (After A. D. Blest, 1957)

Blest also carried out experiments with the device shown in figure 3-34. The bait or prey was a mealworm. The birds were first accustomed to feeding on the platform illustrated. In the experiments, when a bird landed on the platform, a pattern was lit up on each side of the worm. The principal finding was that the more eye-like the pattern, the more likely it was to make a bird withdraw without eating the worm.

Experiments by M. Scaife on domestic chicks, *Gallus bankiva,* have examined just what features of eye-spots have the most deterrent effect. He compared circular with rectangular patterns; some were single, others paired; and some seemed to look at (track) the chick, others to look away. Paired, circular, and tracking "eyes" were the most effective.

3.7 HUNTERS AND HUNTED: SUMMING UP

The animals that eat other animals range from the Protozoa to the Primates. Their ways of hunting are correspondingly diverse: some wait for their prey, others pursue them; some depend on the simultaneous use of several senses, others on highly developed single senses; and some use special organs, others special external structures, such as webs.

Active hunters seem to employ species-typical strategies of search; these probably maximize success in their natural environment. Such strategies are to some extent adaptable to varying conditions: predators, especially vertebrates, alter their hunting patterns with experience.

Prey species similarly vary in their means of avoiding being eaten. Many run (or swim or fly) away; others withdraw into shelter. Apart from these responses, there are three main types of anti-predator device. Crypsis, or concealing pattern and coloration, is accompanied by behavior such as adopting a suitable posture or selecting an appropriate background. Aposematism, or warning coloration, depends on an animal having aversive properties, such as a repellent taste or a sting.

Predators then learn to avoid species that are both aversive and conspicuous. Some animals resemble toxic or repellent species, but are themselves palatable; they are then said to be mimics. All such conspicuous species tend to behave in such a way that their gaudy patterns are readily seen.

Lastly, there are deimatic species, that deter predators by startling them. An eye-like pattern is especially effective. The action of deimatic patterns does not depend on the formation of a habit by a predator.

Cryptic and other coloration is usually typical of whole species; but it can change quickly over generations, in response to a new environmental demand. Such changes provide good examples of the action of natural selection.

4

HOMEOSTASIS
AND BEHAVIOR

Our stability is but balance, and conduct lies
in masterful administration of the unforeseen.
Bridges
The Testament of Beauty

4.1 THE CONCEPT OF HOMEOSTASIS

A feature of many-celled animals is the regulation
of their internal states. Body fluids, such as blood
plasma, often vary little in their tonicity and in the
proportions of their main chemical constituents.
Constancy of the internal milieu, or *homeostasis,*
depends on internal regulatory systems, and makes
a large component of physiology. But regulation
also depends on behavior. The previous two chapters have given many examples: a directed movement may bring an animal into conditions of (for
instance) favorable humidity; predatory searching
enables an animal to find food. In this chapter we
are concerned with experimental studies of behavior closely linked to supplying urgent bodily
needs.

Regulation depends on internal "mechanisms"
that can sometimes usefully be described in the
language of the physical sciences. Especially rele-

vant is the notion of *feedback* (reviewed by D. J.
McFarland 1971; W. T. Powers). In chapter 2 we
had examples of postures and movements controlled by external variables, such as light and
temperature. In the present chapter we are concerned with internal variables that regulate behavior.

The direction of an animal's movement may be
determined by the direction of a target at a given
moment; and the movement may be performed
without any correction for error. An analog is the
flight of a bullet: an old-fashioned missile, once
fired, continues on its path regardless of what the
target does. The same applies to certain very rapid
movements by animals, such as the strike of a
cuttlefish, *Sepia,* at its prey (3.2.4; figure 3-9).
The speed is so great, that the strike is usually effective though not corrected. Such an arrangement
is called an open-loop system (figure 4-1).

For homeostasis, closed-loop systems are all-
important (figure 4-1). The familiar examples are
from equipment in which variables, such as temperature, are controlled automatically. A departure
from a reference value acts back on the input to
the system, so that the value is restored to the level

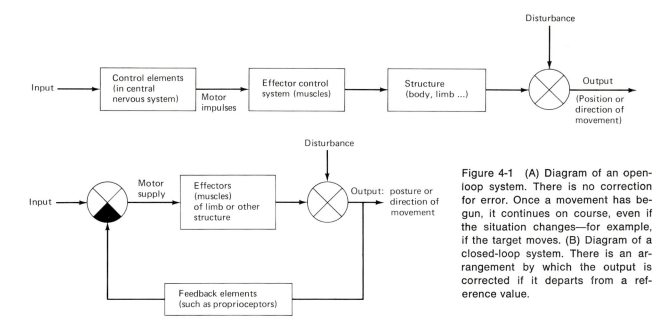

Figure 4-1 (A) Diagram of an open-loop system. There is no correction for error. Once a movement has begun, it continues on course, even if the situation changes—for example, if the target moves. (B) Diagram of a closed-loop system. There is an arrangement by which the output is corrected if it departs from a reference value.

set for it. An electric heater switches on when a sensor goes below a given temperature, and off when it goes above. In such a case we have *negative feedback:* the effect of the output of the system tends to reduce variation of input.

A closed-loop system can have a *positive feedback:* the output of the system then tends to increase further output. If not stopped, such a system produces a runaway effect which can be self-destructive: a system that went on heating itself up would eventually melt or explode.

The notion of closed-looped systems can be applied at many levels, not only to physiology. At the level of populations (chapter 10), for example, increase in numbers sometimes reflects a positive feedback: the more breeding individuals there are, the higher the rate of increase. But, of course, that statement applies only up to a point: eventually, the increase stops; and if the factor or factors that stop it are themselves regulated by the population

density, then we have an example of negative feedback.

The concepts introduced above can be greatly elaborated, as McFarland shows. Later in this chapter we see that physiological and behavioral systems usually seem to depend on many interacting negative (and sometimes positive) feedbacks; and we are only at the beginning of an analysis in these terms.

4.2 BREATHING

An animal's most urgent need is usually to take in oxygen (and, as a corollary, to lose carbon dioxide). But the cycle of the movements of breathing is usually too quickly over to be included in accounts of behavior. Exceptions are found among animals, such as some amphibians, that breathe air but spend much time under water. Helen Spurway & J. B. S. Haldane studied a newt, *Triturus cris-*

tatus. In an aquarium a newt often spends much of the time resting on the bottom. At intervals it rises to the surface, takes a lungful of air, releases an air bubble (this is called "guffing"), and swims or sinks down again. While the newt is under water the level of carbon dioxide in the blood rises (though much is released through the skin); the breathing center of the brain is therefore probably increasingly stimulated, but the newt continues to hold its breath until it surfaces. Spurway & Haldane suggest that submersion inhibits breathing; but the physiology of the inhibition is not known.

The relationship of breathing movements with the need for oxygen is shown when the air over the aquarium is replaced by pure nitrogen or pure oxygen. The intervals in minutes between ascents of a number of newts in such conditions have been recorded. A female gave the following mean intervals (with their standard errors) before, during, and after a period when the air was replaced by nitrogen:

air:	46.7 ± 1.1
nitrogen:	4.1 ± 0.4
air:	23.8 ± 5.1

It is not known why the intervals on return to air were shorter than before exposure to nitrogen, but the experimenters remark that such "changes of mood" are often observed. There is also much individual diversity. One factor not assessed was the absorption of oxygen through the skin; this could have varied (W. G. Whitford & V. H. Hutchison, 1963, 1965). Another newt, exposed to pure oxygen, gave the following means of intervals between ascents:

air:	6.9 ± 0.5
oxygen:	23.7 ± 4.6
air:	10.7 ± 1.1

What happens when a newt is simultaneously stimulated to breath and to perform another activity, such

as courtship? T. R. Halliday & H. P. A. Sweatman describe experiments on this question, in a paper entitled, "To breathe or not to breathe; the newt's problem". During courtship (17.2.4.2), the male approaches the female and performs a display, or sequence of stereotyped movements. A receptive female responds by movements mainly of approach and withdrawal. The culmination is the transfer of a spermatophore, containing spermatozoa. Whether transfer is achieved depends both on the response of the female and on the state (libido) of the male. The latter is measured by a detailed analysis of the male's movements.

Halliday & Sweatman held females in a harness (figure 4-2), and so were able to control their behavior. If a female made the appropriate movements, the male's breathing was delayed; such delay was most marked when male libido was high. If a female was removed during courtship, the male at once rose to the surface to breathe. Breathing was never observed during transfer of the spermatophore, but usually occurred immediately after transfer was completed.

Breathing is therefore described as inhibited during courtship: disinhibition occurs when courtship

FIGURE 4-2 Drawing of a female newt, *Triturus cristatus,* harnessed so that her movements can be controlled by an experimenter. (After T. R. Halliday, 1975b)

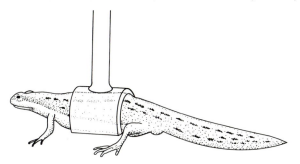

is completed or when the female is removed. The male newt might have either courted or breathed. Causal factors were operating for both activities. The dominant activity was courting. If a male had broken off courting, and swum to the surface to breathe, that would have represented competition of breathing with courtship. The causal factors for breathing would presumably then have reached such a level that they cancelled those for courtship. (This statement could lead to testable hypotheses about the physiological changes involved.) When, in contrast, courtship ends and breathing follows, disinhibition is said to occur: the significant change is then in the causal factors for courtship.

4.3 THERMOREGULATION

Like the demand for oxygen, the need to remain within a narrow temperature range is a general feature of animal life. In 2.3.4 there are examples of invertebrates that become torpid when chilled, and of direct movements related to variation in the temperature of the surroundings. We are now concerned with behavioral thermoregulation—behavior that ensures maintenance of a specific internal temperature.

4.3.1 Poikilothermic Vertebrates

Reptiles, especially lizards and snakes, can move about only within a certain range of temperatures; and for maximum activity body temperature needs to be held steady at a figure that varies with the species. The metabolic rate of reptiles is lower than that of birds or mammals; and, without feathers or fur, their insulation is poor. Behavioral thermoregulation is therefore especially important (P. J. Regal 1966, 1967). Figure 4-3 shows a

FIGURE 4-3 Skinks, *Egernia cunninghami*, immobile in a winter grouping. (Courtesy R. E. Barwick)

group of skinks immobile in a typical winter assembly.

The blue-tongued lizard, *Tiliqua scincoides,* studied by K. Myhre & H. T. Hammel, has, when active, a brain and colon temperature of about 29°C; and it can regulate its temperature by moving from one place to another. In the inactive phase it settles in a cool place, where it loses heat. Similarly, the garter snake, *Thamnophis siralis,* becomes inactive at an ambient temperature below 17°C and settles in a shady place. In environmental temperatures of 18 to 30°C it is active, and tends to keep a body temperature of 29 to 30°C. Its Q_{10} for metabolic rates is then low. That is, for a given rise in temperature, there is a relatively small increase in metabolic rate. When cooled, the snake not only takes shelter but also develops a high Q_{10} and hence a lowered metabolic rate; feeding stops. In this case, described in detail by M. Aleksiuk, we see how behavior and physiology operate together. These examples also show that, although reptiles regulate their body temperature, they do not keep it at a single reference value: there may be two such set points.

The thermotaxes described in 2.3.4 are, as far as is known, developed without practice and cannot be altered by training; but this does not apply to the thermal responses of vertebrates. Fish can develop quite novel habits which keep them at an eccritic temperature. P. N. Rozin & J. Mayer trained goldfish, *Carassius auratus,* to keep themselves cool. The water in their aquarium was heated much above the optimum level; but, if a fish pushed a disc, cold water was released. The fish learned to do this often enough to keep the water and themselves at a normal temperature for their species.

Similarly, F. D. Kemp trained desert iguanas, *Dipsosaurus dorsalis,* to push a disc attached to a microswitch. (See B. H. Brattstrom, for other ex-

amples.) The animals were kept in a terrarium heated by infrared lamps. Pressing the disc turned off the heat and switched on a fan. The iguanas learned to do this when their body temperatures were at the abnormally high level of about 45°C. In more natural conditions, this reptile keeps its body temperature at about 41°C by selecting a suitable spot wherever there is an appropriate temperature gradient. P. J. Regal (1967) similarly describes the thermoregulatory behavior of lizards (*Klanberina* and other genera), given a laboratory environment in which there is a thermal gradient. At night, low temperatures are usually selected; and these help to make the lizards inactive. But not all have a circadian rhythm of eccritic temperatures: lizards of the genus *Sceleporus* burrow into cool sand only about once a week.

We may suppose that the ability of some fish and reptiles to develop such new habits has survival value in natural conditions. Most of the invertebrates described in chapter 2 respond positively or negatively to heat or cold, humidity or dryness, and so on; but they do not develop new habits of movement as a result of finding favorable conditions in one place rather than another. Such an ability to adapt behavior to circumstances is especially prominent among the mammals; and we now turn to them.

4.3.2 Homeotherms

Most mammals, most of the time, have a deep body temperature of about 37°C, with daily fluctuations of less than a degree. Such homeothermy depends primarily on thermal insulation and on reflex and metabolic responses to changes in external conditions. An increase in the rate at which heat is lost from the body is countered by raising of the hair—if any (piloerection), peripheral vasoconstriction, and by increased heat production through shivering and other means. Local cooling of the hypothalamus can induce such responses. A rise in temperature is met by peripheral vasodilation, sweating or panting, and salivation, and perhaps by lowered heat production. Both sets of changes are reinforced by behavior.

4.3.2.1 The Response to Cold:

For a resting adult mammal of a given species there is a *zone of thermal neutrality* at which metabolic heat production is at a minimum. For a small mammal, such as the house mouse, *Mus musculus,* the zone is narrow and around 34°C; for a naked human being in still air it is about 26 to 29°C (H. Swan). The *critical temperature* is the lowest at which metabolism is not raised. Even small mammals can adapt themselves to a much lower environmental temperature than the critical, and still maintain a steady growth rate (reviewed by S. A. Barnett & L. E. Mount). The most obvious behavioral change is an increase in food consumption (figure 4-4). Such increase occurs after a brief delay, during which the animal is exceptionally inactive.

Given the opportunity, a mammal avoids the necessity for a much raised rate of heat production: it selects an environmental temperature that puts little demand on metabolism. R. H. Stinson & K. C. Fisher put deer mice, *Peromyscus maniculatus,* in an aluminium tube in which there was a temperature gradient from 6 to 50°C. The mice settled in the region between 20 and 30°C: that is, they selected a point a little below the critical temperature. It is uncertain why the eccritic temperature is not within the zone of thermal neutrality. Moreover, the details of the behavior seem not to have been analysed. Does the mouse learn by trial and error just where the eccritic temperature is? As D. M. Ogilvie & R. H. Stinson have shown, both mice and rats, even when very young, have some capacity to wriggle from a cold place to a warm one: perhaps the movement is random until warmth inhibits it. This is an example of how apparently simple behavior, such as moving to a more comfortable place, raises difficult and often unanswered questions.

Another means by which mammals economize on heat loss is huddling. Figure 4-5 gives the food consumption of laboratory mice at three environmental temperatures; some mice were alone, some in pairs, and some in groups of five. At the low temperatures the sparing effect of huddling on food consumption is very marked. Even quite large mammals benefit: the oxygen consumption of piglets can be reduced by 30% by huddling (L. E. Mount).

Many mammals, especially small ones, reduce heat loss by making a shelter—a burrow or a nest. Figure 4-6 illustrates the constancy of temperature of burrows, contrasted with the fluctuation outside.

FIGURE 4-4 Effect of transferring young laboratory mice from a warm environment (21°C) to cold (−3°C): food consumption rises, but only after a delay. Weight alters correspondingly.

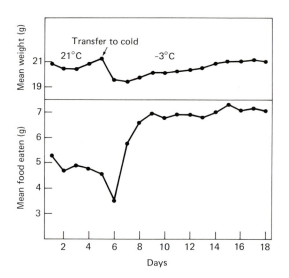

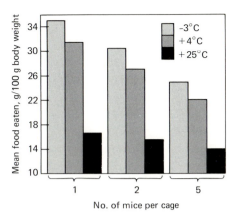

FIGURE 4-5   Effect of ambient temperature and of huddling on the food consumption of laboratory mice. At low temperatures the presence of other mice reduces heat loss and consequently the amount of food needed. (After W. Prychodko, 1958)

In experiments, laboratory rats have been given strips of paper: the weight of paper used for making a nest increased as the ambient temperature was lowered. Cold resistance is impaired by removal of the thyroid gland. Thyroidectomized laboratory rats make better nests, at a given temperature, than intact controls.

Such observations describe changes in the performance of activities that are within the normal repertoire of the species. Mammals can also learn completely new habits, in response to thermal needs, similar to those described above for fish and reptiles. Rats have been kept in cages in which pressing a lever switches on a source of heat for a few seconds (figure 4-7). At a low temperature, a rat spends most of its first few hours crouching in a corner and shivering; the lever may be occasionally pressed. Then there is a sudden change: the heat is

FIGURE 4-6   The thermoregulatory effect of burrowing. Temperatures in three burrows of the deer mouse, *Peromyscus maniculatus,* are compared with those above ground. (After J. S. Hayward, 1965)

FIGURE 4-7   Apparatus (Skinner box) in which the animal is rewarded for pressing the panel by the switching on of a source of heat. Rats adjust their response rate to need. (After B. Weiss, 1957)

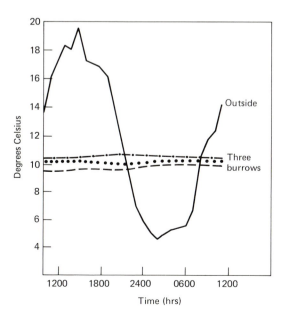

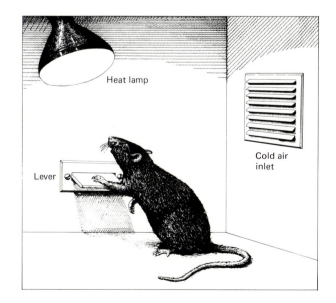

switched on regularly, at intervals determined by the amount of heat given and the surrounding temperature. Such behavior is adjusted to internal state: rats short of pantothenic acid have a low tolerance for cold, and they press the lever correspondingly more often. Pigs, too, as B. A. Baldwin & D. L. Ingram have shown, can develop a similar habit.

4.3.2.2 *The Response to Heat:*

Shelter, as illustrated in figure 4-6 above, can protect animals from heating as well as cooling. Mammals also have means of increasing heat loss in a hot environment. F. R. Hainsworth & E. M. Striker have made a detailed study of laboratory rats, and W. W. Roberts and others of several rodent species. None has sweat glands. One response to an ambient temperature of, say, 40°C is to lie in a splayed out position that evidently allows maximum heat loss from the surface. Another is copious salivation: the saliva is spread by licking the body, and so is an alternative to sweat. Dogs and others similarly use panting and evaporation of dilute saliva from the tongue as a means of cooling the body.

Once again, novel habits can be learnt to achieve cooling. A. N. Epstein & R. Milestone put rats in a cage with a bar which, if pressed, released a fine shower of water. At an ambient temperature of 40°C the rats took many showers. In these conditions rats can keep a normal body temperature even when their salivary glands have been removed and they are therefore unable to lose heat by the normal means.

4.4 DRINKING

In any cell, and in an animal's body fluids, the proportion of dissolved substances is usually regulated within a narrow range: this is *osmoregulation* (reviewed by Bengt Andersson; J. T. Fitzsimons; G. J. Mogenson).

The body of a mammal contains about 70% of water by weight. Intracellular water is about 50%, and contains, as its principal cation, potassium; the main extracellular cation is sodium. Isotonicity between the cytoplasm of the cells and their surroundings is maintained by the movement of water. The hypothalamus probably contains osmoreceptors: if there is too little water or too much sodium ion, there is increased secretion of an antidiuretic hormone by the pituitary, which leads to retention of water and lowered output of urine; at the same time, if water is available, the animal drinks.

Osmoregulation, considered in these terms, might be thought of as based on a negative feedback; but, since drinking occurs only at intervals, the feedback must act after a delay. The findings of some experiments fit this picture. L. I. O'Kelly and others put rats in a cage in which they could get water by pressing a lever (6.1.2). The rats were deprived of water for a day, after which some of them also had various amounts of water or sodium chloride solution injected directly into the stomach. They were then given access to the lever for 3 h. Some had to press the lever 5 times to get a sip of water, others 10 or 20 times. The rate at which the lever was pressed corresponded precisely with the need for water.

But in other circumstances the findings on water consumption are less simple. The complexities involve both the onset of drinking and stopping. The preceding account implies that the animal waits to drink until there is a deficit. This is not the case. If rats are given a continuous infusion of water by a tube into the stomach, they still drink quite a lot of water. Such rats have developed a habit of drinking early in life, and persist with it even in the absence of need. In general, laboratory mammals (and perhaps mammals in natural conditions too), given unlimited water, drink more than is needed to compensate for loss. Evidently, the signals that reach the brain as a result of a water deficit (in subjective terms, thirst) occur only in an emergency. Drinking usually anticipates need, and so is an example of feed-forward.

There are similar findings on what makes a mammal stop drinking: signals from the mouth, pharynx, and stomach may make it stop before it has made up a deficit. This is shown if an animal is allowed to drink, but the water is drained away by a fistula in the esophagus or stomach: after drinking for some seconds or minutes, the animal stops although the water has not been absorbed. Again, this behavior may be a result of habit formation in early life. Such findings show a simple explanation of drinking in terms of negative feedback to be untenable. In this and other features, bodily "mechanisms" are far more elaborate than anything an engineer would design.

4.5 FEEDING

The greatest volume of work on behavior and homeostasis concerns feeding. Some animals seem to feed continuously: sedentary filter feeders, such as barnacles (Cirripedia) and tube worms (Polychaeta), are examples; little is known of how their intake is regulated. More usually, feeding is discontinuous: it is divided into meals; and the frequency and duration of meals are related to the maintenance of a steady body weight or a steady rate of growth. We are now concerned with the analysis of such relationships. In the previous chapter I describe experiments on predatory feeding; but such experiments usually deal with hunting methods, not with hunting in relation to need. Very few species,

predatory or not, have been studied in detail. Hence most of this section is devoted to only three: a fly, a rat, and the human species.

4.5.1 The Black Blowfly

4.5.1.1 The Fly Observed: An outstanding study has been made of the black blowfly, *Phormia regina,* by V. G. Dethier and his associates. Blowflies are found near decaying matter, in which females lay their eggs; and they sometimes feed on rotting fruit. Each fly weighs about 25 mg; its brain weighs about 0.84 mg, and probably contains fewer than 100,000 cells. The male completes its growth, in all respects, before the end of the pupal stage: as adult or imago it can live for its full span of about five weeks on water and sugar (and oxygen). It emerges from the puparium with its adipose tissue (fat body) full of fat. Most of this reserve is used up in the four or so days after emergence; and, provided the fly has plenty to eat, the fat is replaced by stores of glycogen in the fat body, flight muscles, and elsewhere.

A fly is, of course, poikilothermic. At night, low temperature and absence of light induce torpor. Dethier describes how a fly begins its day with an empty gut and its blood sugar (trehalose) at the minimum concentration of 1.22 g/l. Movement begins when the surrounding temperature reaches about 21°C: for about 30 min the fly thoroughly cleans its body surface with an elaborate, stereotyped system of movements. With a further rise in temperature, it takes off and flies around, at first apparently at random: that is, the direction of flight changes frequently, and seems to be unrelated to external features such as wind or light.

During flight at 25°C the wings beat at 12,000 strokes a minute. To keep this up for 3 h without stopping requires 1.8 mg of 1 M glucose solution.

Such a meal would be quite appropriate, for the energy used in flying probably comes entirely from oxidation of carbohydrates. A first stage in getting a meal is to encounter the odor of fermenting sugar, as from rotting fruit. Flying now forms a pattern: the general direction is upwind, but on a zigzag course; here evidently is an anemotaxis (2.3.3). Directed flight depends on sense organs, mainly on the antennae, which are stimulated by odorous substances; impulses from them alter the output of the brain to the flight muscles, so that a systematic response is made to air movement. Remove the antennae, and the ability to respond to odors in this way almost disappears.

The zigzag flight continues until *Phormia* is about one meter from a surface, when it becomes direct until touchdown. Landing on a surface does not depend only on the odor of food. If flies have already been there they leave their own odor, and this too is attractive. Such social effects are better known among the social insects that leave odor trails (7.4.3). The sight of other flies on a surface (as if feeding) also makes a touchdown more probable.

A further, nonsocial factor is novelty: blowflies, and the common house fly, *Musca domestica*, both tend to fly toward strange rather than familiar surfaces (see also 8.1.3).

When a fly has settled on a surface, it begins to walk. Until it reaches a source of food, the direction of its movements is again apparently random. If a foot now touches a drop of sugar solution, the fly turns toward it, extends its proboscis, and sucks. Sucking is at first continuous for about 70 s; the proboscis is then retracted; the fly moves away, grooms, and defecates. After about 20 s, it begins to walk again, and may have another brief period of sucking. After that, there may be a third brief walk on the surface, but contact with the solution no longer evokes sucking.

4.5.1.2 The Receptors: The sense organs that enable *Phormia* to respond to chemical stimuli are of two kinds: the olfactory receptors are mainly on the antennae, and respond to airborne substances; the contact chemoreceptors are on the legs and the proboscis and correspond to the taste organs of the vertebrates.

The tarsi of the legs bear many "hairs" or sensilla. Stimulation of only one sensillum can evoke extension of the proboscis; and extension is therefore used as a test of responsiveness to different substances. A sensillum contains several receptors. The impulses in the sensory nerves from the receptors can be individually recorded. By this means four kinds of receptor have been identified, for sugars, sodium chloride and other salts, water, and pressure. The last kind is called a mechanoreceptor.

As usual, the response of a receptor alters with repeated or continuous stimulation. If a single sensillum is repeatedly stimulated with sugar solution, proboscis extension occurs at first, but the response rapidly wanes. Such a change could be either in the receptor itself or in the nervous system. The test is to stimulate another sensillum with the same solution. When this is done, the proboscis is fully extended. Hence the change comes under the heading of sensory "adaptation" or "fatigue". But repeated stimulation can also produce a central nervous effect. If the receptors on one leg are stimulated by sucrose solution, it becomes increasingly difficult to evoke proboscis extension: the concentration of sucrose has to be raised, or a longer time has to be left between successive stimuli. If the leg on the opposite side is now stimulated, the lowered responsiveness is still evident. In such a case, it is not the peripheral receptors that have changed but the central nervous system. Such a change may be called a central inhibitory state.

There can also be a central excitatory state. Let us suppose a fly has been allowed to drink its fill of plain water. It is now stimulated with a very weak sugar solution, and does not extend its proboscis. The stimulation is repeated a second or two later, and the proboscis is extended. What is more, although a water-saturated fly is not ordinarily stimulated by water, it responds to water if it is first given a brief stimulation with sugar. Each stimulation is given to a separate sensillum. The sugar receptor stops firing impulses in its sensory nerve as soon as the sugar is removed. Hence a central change must be responsible for the reaction to water.

Not all substances evoke proboscis extension. A solution of sodium chloride is not only rejected, but also raises the threshold for proboscis extension: that is, after stimulation by salt solution, it is necessary to supply a stronger positive stimulation to persuade a fly to extend its proboscis.

4.5.1.3. Starting and Stopping:

Since *Phormia* does not feed continuously, internal processes must insure that it begins a meal and also that it eventually stops. An active fly might, of course, feed whenever it is not inhibited by some consequence of feeding. Such a consequence would constitute a negative feedback. Beginning a meal would then result from the ending of an inhibition.

At the beginning of adult life, for 24 to 48 h after emergence, a fly is inactive. It then begins intermittent spells of activity (flying or walking), which become more frequent until, if no food is found, activity reaches a peak on the fourth day. A meal is followed by a period of inactivity. After an interval, movement is resumed and, as the amount of sugar in the crop (figure 4-8) declines, movement increases: the increase is not in the speed of movement (which is constant at a given temperature) but in the frequency of the spells of activity. The change in frequency is probably not due only to release of an inhibition: there is evi-

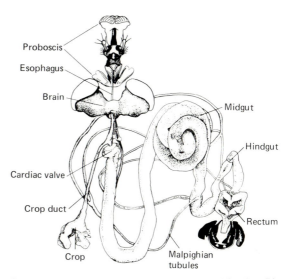

FIGURE 4-8 The alimentary canal of the blowfly, *Phormia regina*. (Reproduced from V. G. Dethier, *The Hungry Fly*, 1976, p. 68, by permission of Harvard University Press)

dently a bloodborne factor that provokes activity. The evidence comes from experiments in which two flies are linked, by a delicate operation, so that their blood systems (hemoceles) are continuous (figure 4-9). Initially, one such parabiotic fly may be active, the other inactive; in such a case the second fly becomes active. The blood factor has not been identified; nor is it known whether the correlation of increased activity with loss of sugar from the crop is significant.

More is known about what makes feeding stop. There is first a short-term effect of stimulation of the receptors, both on the tarsi and on the proboscis. A meal is liable to be interrupted by brief pauses, resulting from the sensory adaptation already mentioned. The sensory change is rapid when the solution is dilute, slower when it is concentrated. Hence the rate of sucking and the duration of a spell of continuous sucking are both proportional to the sugar concentration. (This presumably has the advantage that a fly needing food does not

FIGURE 4-9 Two flies in parabiosis, that is, with their hemoceles continuous. Such an arrangement allows study of the effects of blood composition on behavior. (Reproduced from V. G. Dethier, *The Hungry Fly,* 1976, p. 249, by permission of Harvard University Press)

spend much time filling its gut with fluid containing little nourishment.)

Temporary changes in the sense organs cannot, of course, account for the end of a meal. We are now concerned with periods of some hours during which a fly may be totally inactive. During a meal the midgut is filled first, then the crop (figure 4-10). As the contents of the midgut are digested, the crop releases more food to the midgut. Digestion results in raised blood sugar. The blood sugar is depleted by tissue metabolism. The main factor that regulates release of food from the crop is tonicity of the blood: as sugar is lost to the tissues, tonicity declines and the crop is stimulated to discharge its contents. Crop emptying can be experimentally regulated by altering blood tonicity.

An obvious hypothesis was that raised blood tonicity also made feeding stop. Experimental tests showed this to be wrong. Another possibility was that a full midgut or a full crop led to the end of eating. This, too, was shown to be wrong. Eventually, the inhibition was traced to stretch receptors in the esophagus or foregut. If the nerve that runs from these receptors to the brain is cut (figure 4-11), the fly continues to eat until it bursts. Any pressure on the receptors makes the animal stop eating. A fly will readily accept a sugar, fucose, which it cannot digest. It sucks up the solution as usual, until the foregut is filled; then it stops. No sugar reaches the blood. Hence, as Dethier remarks, the fly starves with a full gut.

Intensive study of a single species has some disadvantages. I therefore now digress to the work of E. A. Bernays & R. F. Chapman on *Locusta migratoria.* Nymphs of this species were fasted for 8 h, then allowed to eat grass until satiated. Some had the posterior pharyngeal nerves cut; these insects then ate larger meals. Once again, stretch receptors in the gut wall are evidently important. This was confirmed by filling the foregut with indigestible

FIGURE 4-10 Part of the alimentary canal of a blowfly, *Phormia regina;* the relationships with the recurrent nerve are shown. (After V. G. Dethier, 1976)

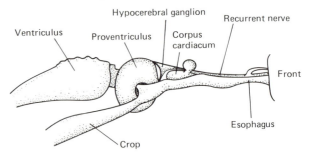

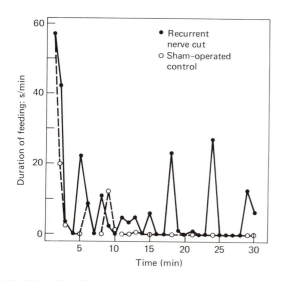

FIGURE 4-11 Effect of cutting the recurrent nerve of a blowfly, *Phormia regina:* the fly with the cut nerve continues to feed at intervals, after the control fly has stopped. (After V. G. Dethier, 1976)

agar without stimulating the mouthparts: feeding stopped. On the other hand, intake of sugars by these locusts is regulated partly through adaptation of chemoreceptors on the mouthparts.

4.5.1.4 Protein Intake: Although an adult male *Phormia* can live on a diet of carbohydrates and water, a female cannot do so: oogenesis, at least, requires an intake of amino acids. These substances, needed for the synthesis of the protein in the ova, can be offered experimentally as liver homogenate or as an extract of (mammalian) brain and heart. Chemoreceptors on the tarsi detect them as before. A male or a virgin female, if given a choice between sugar solution and proteinaceous mixtures, takes little of the latter, but a gravid female takes much (figure 4-12). Moreover, the laying of a batch of eggs is followed, in 24 h, by an increase in amino acid consumption. Correspond-

ingly, a protein-deprived female takes proteinaceous materials rather than carbohydrates. The adaptability of female feeding behavior does not, however, depend on any ability to learn the way to alternative food sources. Many attempts have been made to train *Phormia* to adopt new habits (that is, to "learn"), but they have usually been unsuccessful (but see 5.5.3). As we find in the next section, this deficiency is a major difference of flies from mammals.

4.5.2 The Rat

The species to which we now turn is *Rattus norvegicus,* which in its wild form is the common brown or Norway rat. Most of the work on the feeding of rats has been on domestic varieties: all laboratory rats are of this species and can be bred with the wild type. Rats are convenient because they are omnivorous: they will accept a great variety of foods (reviewed by S. A. Barnett 1975; D. A. Booth; N. Mrosovsky & T. L. Powley). Although they are rodents and therefore especially equipped to deal with the hard parts of plants, such as seeds, they also eat insects, mollusks, and the tissues of vertebrates; and they are occasional predators on smaller mammals, birds and even fish.

4.5.2.1 The Feeding Rhythm: A poikilotherm, such as *Phormia,* is active only when warmed up in the day time. Hence it has a circadian rhythm of activity, and therefore of feeding. A homeotherm, such as a rat, can be active in a wider range of temperatures. It can therefore feed at any time of day. Nonetheless, it has a marked circadian rhythm: free-living wild rats emerge from their burrows mostly at night; and rats of all types in captivity move about and feed mainly during the dark period. The alternation of activity and

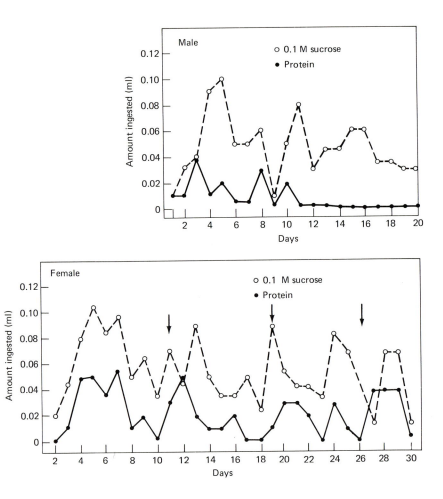

FIGURE 4-12 Above, intake of sucrose solution and a protein-containing mixture by a male blowfly, *Phormia regina*. Below, consumption by a gravid female in a similar situation; arrows show days on which eggs were laid. (After V. G. Dethier, 1976)

rest can be modified in the laboratory by changing the periods of light and dark. Experimenters are active mainly in daytime: they may therefore darken the laboratory during the day, and leave the lights on only at night: the rats then feed and perform most of their other activities during the day. Their rhythm is consequently entrained or locked to the daily cycle of illumination (2.1.3). (The laboratory norm is an unchanging sequence of 12 h of light and 12 h of dark. Natural conditions are similar only near the equator.)

Rats still maintain a rhythm even in conditions of constant light and temperature, but then do not keep quite to a 24-h cycle. The source, internal or external, of such a rhythm is much debated (reviewed by J. D. Palmer).

The feeding rhythm can easily be disrupted. If food is daily available only at a certain time, rats will feed at that time, even in bright light. Free-living wild rats adjust their behavior in the same way. (I have seen *R. norvegicus* feeding at 1500 hrs in an alley in Bombay; their food was refuse provided by the human inhabitants. A similar species, *Bandicota bengalensis,* is regularly fed in bright sunlight in a park in Calcutta.) Yet another complication is the carrying of food to the nest: wild rats hoard food in their burrows, sometimes in large amounts, but nothing is known of when they eat it.

We know, however, the usual pattern of feeding in the laboratory: this consists of a series of substantial meals during the dark period, and smaller meals in the light. A typical interval between meals is 140 min; and a rat weighing about 250 g may eat about 2.5 g at a meal; this is more than one tenth of its daily total.

4.5.2.2 Regulating Energy Balance:

Despite much individual variation in the timing and duration of meals, rats—given continuous access to a complete diet—maintain a steady rate of growth throughout life. (Other mammals stop growing after sexual maturity and maintain a constant body weight.) A rat's regulatory powers are more clearly seen if conditions are altered (reviewed by M. I. Friedman & E. M. Stricker). If ethanol, C_2H_5OH, is added to the drinking water, rats eat less food, and so compensate for the calorigenic value of the alcohol. A more drastic experiment is to administer insulin, and so to induce excessive feeding: the rats then become grossly obese. When the insulin is withdrawn, they become hypophagic: they eat little until normal body weight is restored.

Other experiments require an animal to increase intake. After a fast, the lost weight is gradually made up. Given additional nondigestible matter, such as cellulose, intake is increased correspondingly. Similarly, if transferred to a colder environment, where the demands on heat production are greater, a rat eats more (compare figure 4-4). The increase in consumption is a result of taking larger, not more frequent, meals.

These findings, and those shown in figure 4-13, are in accordance with common sense. Others,

however, are not. For example, J. Le Magnen allowed laboratory rats to feed only three times daily, for 1 h at a time. The intervals between meals were 7 h. Then one meal was omitted, so that the animals had an interval of 15 h, in each 24-h period, without food. Initially the rats increased their food intake after the 15-h gap. But, after a few days, food consumption increased during the meal *before* the gap. Hence compensation became anticipatory—another example of feedforward.

Another complicating feature is the existence of *positive* feedbacks. Figure 4-14 illustrates detailed observations of laboratory mice which had been deprived of food for 24 h. A period of feeding of about 5 min consisted of bouts of continuous eating, each lasting several seconds, broken by intervals, also of several seconds, during which no food was taken. The figure shows how the duration of successive bouts increases up to the fifth bout. Once again, "appetite comes with eating" (4.4).

As for *Phormia,* an important question is what, at the end of a meal, makes an animal stop eating. The obvious hypothesis, that pressure on the wall of the gut is responsible, turns out to be partly true: there is a limit to the amount of food that can be forced into the stomach; if rats are allowed to feed for only 2 h in each 24-h period, they readily accept a mixture of kaolin (which has no nutritive value) and water. And when they have filled their stomachs, they stop eating for a time, although no metabolic benefit results.

The larger a meal, the longer the interval before the next meal. If the stomach contents are removed shortly after a meal, the delay is correspondingly reduced. The effect of the stomach contents is partly from its bulk, but partly from its chemical properties. Even when, after a normal meal, the stomach has completely emptied, there is likely to be a further delay of at least 1 h while

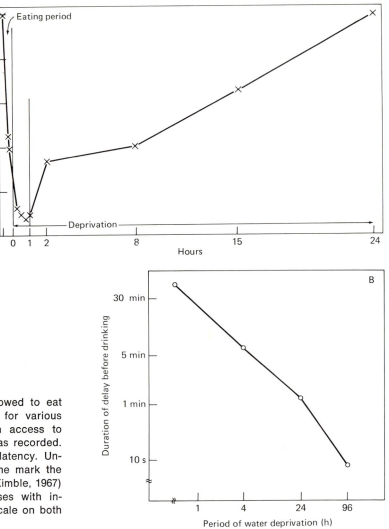

FIGURE 4-13 (A) Laboratory rats were allowed to eat their fill, and were then deprived of food for various periods. The interval between being given access to food and beginning to eat it (the latency) was recorded. The graph indicates the reciprocal of the latency. Unsurprisingly, the animals were quicker off the mark the longer they had been deprived. (After G. A. Kimble, 1967) (B) Similarly, the latency to drink decreases with increasing period of water deprivation. (The scale on both axes is logarithmic.) (After R. C. Bolles, 1962)

the products of digestion are being metabolized by the liver.

The state of the stomach, and in particular the degree of repletion, is signaled by the discharges in the branch of the vagus that innervates the stomach. If this nerve is cut, the usual pattern of meal taking is disrupted; but regulation according to need still occurs by means of smaller and more frequent meals. Rats can indeed regulate food intake even if the stomach itself is removed. There are evidently several means by which food intake is controlled—a common type of finding in physiology.

In human experience, appetite is considerably

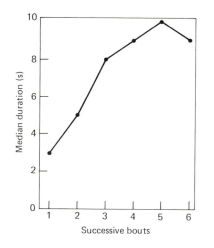

FIGURE 4-14 "Appetite comes with eating." The behavior of laboratory mice was observed for about 5 min during which bouts of eating were interrupted by intervals of nonfeeding. The duration of successive bouts initially increased—an example of positive feedback. (After P. R. Wiepkema, 1971)

affected by the taste of food and by other features of the conditions in which one eats. The same applies to the appetite of other mammals. J. W. Pack (1978a,b) has studied the body weights of rats given foods of different palatability, or required to work more or less hard to get food. If a rat were a straightforward homeostatic mechanism, maintained by negative feedbacks, it would keep the same weight by accepting the same amounts of bitter or sweet foods, and by working harder for food when the situation demands it. But, in fact, rats given food made bitter with quinine lose weight; the same applies if they are required to press a lever many times to get food. In either case they finally stabilize at a body weight lower than that maintained on a palatable diet for which they do not have to work.

The findings on the effect of quinine concern taste. We now therefore turn to the effects of the passage of food through the mouth and pharynx. A simple question is this: if food is taken without stimulating the oropharyngeal receptors, has it the same effect as food taken normally? The answer is not simple. In the short term, food injected straight into the stomach through a fistula has less satiating effect than the same amount taken by the usual route. For example, rats were trained to operate a lever which, when pushed, released a drop of milk (M. Kohn; figure 4-15). For one group, the milk was injected into the stomach; for another, the same amount of milk could be drunk in the ordinary manner. The rats were tested 5.5 min later. Those that had received milk through the mouth worked less hard for additional nourishment than those that had received it straight into the stomach. Stimulation of the mouth and pharynx has therefore some inhibitory effect on feeding.

On the other hand, as C. T. Snowdon (1969, 1970) has shown, in some conditions the absence of oropharyngeal stimulation diminishes intake. In Snowdon's experiments, rats were required to feed themselves for some days solely by injecting food into their stomachs. (It is indeed fortunate that the docile laboratory rat will function satisfactorily in a bar-pressing apparatus and with a permanent gastric fistula.) The experimental rats, like those studied more recently by J. W. Peck, "lost appetite" to such an extent that intake was only 75% of the amount taken by normal means. Consequently, these rats, instead of growing, achieved no more than a constant body weight. Behavior changed in other ways: the rats fed intragastrically did much more licking and chewing than the controls.

Although impulses from the gut are clearly important, they do not fully account for the regulation of intake. Current hypotheses emphasize the importance of the availability of substances that

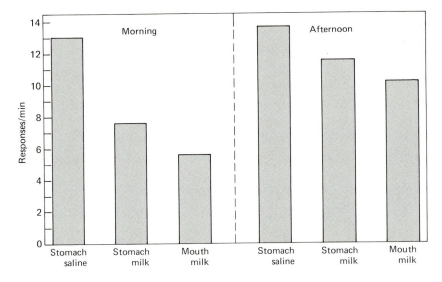

FIGURE 4-15 Satiation depends on the route by which food is taken in. Domestic rats could obtain milk or salty water by pushing a panel; some received the milk directly into the stomach, others drank it. Milk taken by the mouth was the more satiating: that is, the rats stopped pressing the panel sooner when they had milk to drink. There was also some effect of the time of day at which the experiments were done. (After M. Kohn, 1951)

can be used in energy production. The substances are sugars, fatty acids, and amino acids. We have seen that feeding is delayed for a time after the stomach has been completely emptied. A similar delay in feeding may be induced by injecting a solution of fructose or glucose into the hepatic portal vein. The liver may be the main source of peripheral information that regulates intake. Alternatively, or in addition, the fat depots in adipose tissue may play a part in controlling eating.

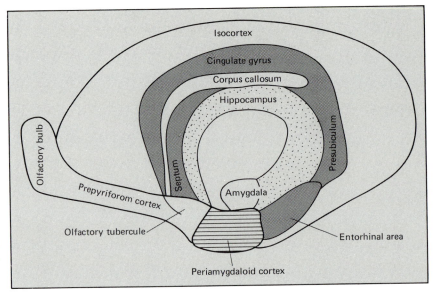

FIGURE 4-16 Diagram of sagittal section of rat brain showing the main parts of the limbic system. (From S. A. Barnett, 1975)

4.5.2.3 The Central Nervous System:

Attempts have been made to find out how the brain deals with information from the periphery. The results are of great interest in themselves; they also illustrate the limitations of the methods used in relating brain function to behavior.

It would be convenient if we could describe a particular region of the brain as "the center" for feeding. Such a notion has a long history. In the late 18th century, a serious pioneering attempt was made by F. J. Gall (1758–1828) to analyse the functions of the parts of the brain. Unfortunately, the successors to Gall allowed his ideas to degenerate into phrenology, according to which one can determine character by feeling the "bumps" on the outside of the cranium (reviewed by E. H. Ackerknecht and by R. M. Young). Later, localization of function in the (mammalian) brain was inferred from the results of carefully placed injuries. As many critics have pointed out, such experiments resemble an attempt to find out how a large and

FIGURE 4-18 Stereotaxic equipment which allows an experimenter to make very small, precisely placed injuries in the brain. (I. A. Fox)

complex computer works by destroying parts of it with a hammer.

Other methods exist, but have been less used. A sated rat can be made to eat or drink by injecting into the brain, with a micropipette, minute quantities of drugs. Several regions of the limbic system (figure 4-16) respond in this way. But most of the relevant information comes from experiments in which the hypothalamus (figure 4-17) has been injured. A delicate stereotaxic technique (figure 4-18) allows an experimenter to make very small

FIGURE 4-17 Ventral view of brain of cat, especially to show position of hypothalamus and pituitary.

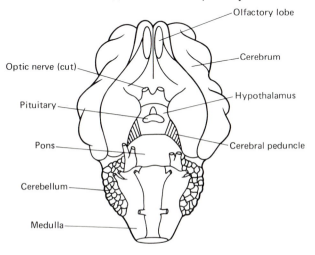

Olfactory lobe

Optic nerve (cut)

Cerebrum

Pituitary

Hypothalamus

Pons

Cerebral peduncle

Cerebellum

Medulla

injuries in precisely determined regions of the brain. When the ventromedial region of the hypothalamus is destroyed on both sides, the animal overeats until it roughly doubles its weight; it then settles down in a constant state of obesity (figure 4-19). Hence the ventromedial hypothalamus has been called a satiety center. But it is doubtful whether this name is appropriate. First, injury to certain other sites in the brain has a similar effect. Second, the metabolic effect of the hypothalamic

FIGURE 4-19 Effect of lesions in the ventromedial region of the hypothalamus: there is initial over-eating, and a doubling of body weight. The operation was on the second day of the record. (After P. Teitelbaum, 1955)

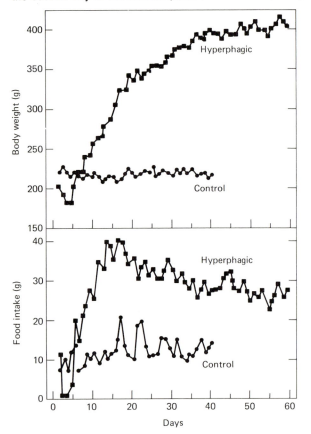

lesions seems to be an increased rate of fat deposition in adipose tissue. The overeating, or hyperphagia, is evidently a response to the excessive withdrawal of fatty acids from the circulation. If rats have already been made obese by other means, and then receive ventromedial hypothalamic lesions, they do not overeat.

An opposite effect is produced by injuries in the lateral part of the hypothalamus. The animal stops eating completely, but can be kept alive by forced feeding. Disconcertingly, rats kept alive in this way can gradually recover: eventually they feed normally and keep a steady body weight or rate of growth.

4.5.2.4 Special "Hungers" and Acquired Aversions:

An omnivorous animal such as a rat could maintain its intake of calorigenic food but yet have an inadequate diet. Unlike an adult male blowfly, it requires amino acids, vitamins, and inorganic salts, as well as carbohydrates. We know little of how wild rats achieve a balanced diet in natural conditions; but in captivity both laboratory and wild rats can do much to adjust their choice of foods to need. Such experiments have been done on wild rats by W. J. Griffiths & C. T. Harmon, and by O. Maller; and A. E. Harriman has found similar ability in experiments with wild wood rats, *Neotoma micropus*. But most have been on domestic forms of the Norway rat. An ability to balance the intake of certain inorganic salts and of some vitamins has been clearly shown. In addition, very strictly designed experiments, for example those by D. A. Booth & P. C. Simson, have brought evidence of adjustment to the need for amino acids.

For experiments on "dietary self-selection" there are two main methods. In one, the animal is presented with a cafeteria situation: a number of dishes or bottles offer solids or liquids containing components of a complete diet. The question then is whether the animal's choice results in a balanced diet. Often, it does.

In the second, an animal is given a choice between two mixtures, of which one is without an essential substance. The substance is most often a water-soluble vitamin or an inorganic salt. Usually, the animals are first put on a deficient diet: for example, the earliest major study, by L. J. Harris and others, required rats deficient in a vitamin (thiamine) to make a choice between a mixture containing thiamine and others without it. In such conditions laboratory rats soon develop the habit of eating the appropriate food. They are aided if the alternative mixtures are distinctively flavored. The flavor associated with the favorable internal effects of a vitamin comes to be preferred. A thiamine-deficient rat is aided in its development of a suitable habit by an enhanced tendency to sample all the available foods, instead of persevering with a single mixture.

When two foods are offered and one is preferred, it follows that the other is rejected. Such rejection of an unsuitable mixture is more clearly shown when a rat has taken a small quantity of a poisonous mixture. While the original work on dietary adjustment was by nutritionists working in Cambridge (England), that on the effect of poison was initiated by ecologists working in the not distant manufacturing town of Oxford. Dennis Chitty & H. N. Southern, and their colleagues, were concerned, during the Second World War, with the protection of food, some of it imported at desperate risk from overseas. Their observations were almost entirely on wild *Rattus norvegicus,* and largely on free-living populations. They were dealing with pests popularly held to be exceptionally wary and intelligent (1.1.3).

Their reputation proved to depend on two distinct behavioral features. First, the wild type of this species tends to avoid any novel object in a familiar environment (neophobia). The object avoided may be a pile of food. If so, it is eventually sampled, but at first—as a rule—in small quantities. If the food contains poison, a likely consequence is a period of illness during which feeding stops. Second, on recovery, the animal rejects the mixture which has contained the poison, but instead samples any alternative food. The first, or neophobic response is displayed without regard to any previous adverse experience. The second is an acquired aversion: it is a result of the particular experience of the ill effects of a poison, and should not be confused with the entirely distinct phenomenon of neophobia. Such an aversion is the obverse of a habit of selecting a food as a result of its favorable effects.

Wild Norway rats, then, compensate for their strong exploratory tendency or "curiosity" (8.1.4) by avoiding strange objects in familiar surroundings ("fear", new-object reaction, or neophobia). The latter, combined with the ability to develop aversions, makes rats exceedingly difficult to kill by poison baiting.

These findings have led in two directions. First, they made possible more efficient methods of poison baiting. If small amounts of plain food are put in carefully selected places in an area infested with rats, they are eventually eaten. After, say, 4 days, poison can be added to the now readily eaten mixture, and will be taken in lethal quantities. The method of *prebaiting* has been widely and successfully used.

Secondly, psychologists have analyzed the development of aversions in much greater depth (reviewed by John Garcia and others). For example, saccharin is readily taken in dilute solution by rats;

given a choice between such a solution and water, they take more of the former. Saccharin has no nutritional value: its effect on choice represents a *hedonic* effect—one determined by an action on the (chemical) senses and without previous association with reward or punishment (6.2). The sweet taste can also be used, in experiments of the type described above, to make it easy for rats to discriminate between two mixtures, one nutritionally superior. The saccharin may then be associated with either mixture.

In experiments on aversion, consumption of saccharin solution has been accompanied by an injection of lithium chloride, LiCl. A suitable dose causes illness: activity diminishes, and eating stops for a time. On recovery saccharin flavor is refused, even if it is offered some days later. These observations, on laboratory rats, conform with those, described above, on wild rats. They illustrate the lasting character of an aversion induced by poisoning.

In an ingenious further development, low doses of ionizing radiation have been used to cause illness. A single dose may be given when a rat is drinking flavored water. The result is subsequent refusal of that flavor, or at least a reluctance to accept it. A similar lasting aversion is, however, *not* induced if the radiation accompanies visual, auditory or tactile stimuli (table 4-1). Evidently rats (and no doubt other mammals also) have a special capacity to relate a taste or odor to an illness that follows after a substantial delay. The survival value of such an ability is obvious: it makes possible acquired aversions to unfavorable mixtures whose action takes place only some hours after the mixture has been ingested (reviewed by John Garcia & R. A. Koelling).

Another development of this work has been a return to economic zoology. The problem was to

TABLE 4-1 Acquired aversions. The ability of a laboratory rat to learn to avoid a taste or a sound, when one of these is coupled with an aversive external stimulus or internal state.

	Internal state (nausea)	External stimulus (shock)
Cues:		
Taste (sweet)	*acquires aversion*	*no aversion*
Sound (click)	*no aversion*	*learns to avoid*

prevent predators, such as coyotes, *Canis latrans,* and bald eagles, *Haliaëtus leucocephalus,* from attacking lambs, without killing the predators. The latter are believed to have (when not attacking lambs) a favorable ecological effect. Lamb meat containing lithium chloride has been put out for the predators to eat, and has led to long-lasting aversion. The method may prove to be widely useful.

4.5.2.5. Influence of Early Experience:
The adult behavior of a rat does not emerge suddenly, fully formed: unlike that of *Phormia,* it goes through a gradual development.

Of the various components of feeding behavior, some are easily modified by special rearing, others are not. When I tried to induce weanling wild rats to acquire a taste for flavors such as that of cod-liver oil, I was unsuccessful: as soon as they had the opportunity, they ate an alternative food with a different taste (1956). But the preferences of young rats can be modified by influences acting at an earlier age (B. G. Galef 1976). Wild nestlings received milk from mothers on different diets; their preference for the diets was tested later, and proved to be influenced by the composition of the milk they had drunk.

Galef has also described social influences on the

feeding of weanling wild rats. When young rats first venture from the nest, they tend to follow their parents or other adults. In experiments, adults were made bait-shy as a result of taking a small dose of poison. They were then given access, with their young, (1) to the mixture (without poison) of which they were shy and (2) to an alternative. The young rats followed the adults to the alternative food, and developed a habit of eating that food. Such habits persisted for longer among young wild *R. norvegicus* than among a domestic variety. The crucial behavior in this case is evidently the following of adults by the young. The adults take no special action: they do not teach; and not even imitation is involved (8.4.2).

4.5.3 Human Beings

The last case history in this chapter is that of humankind, *Homo sapiens*. Statements that human conduct resembles that of other species in important ways have become suspect (14.2.1); but such comparisons are exceedingly fruitful in physiology, and the same applies to some aspects of behavior. One is feeding (reviewed by Paul Rozin).

At first sight the differences are more prominent than the resemblances. Man is not only omnivorous: in different places or periods populations have thrived on diets ranging from the totally vegetarian to that of the Eskimo, which is largely meat. Foods, such as insect larvae, regarded as delicacies in some communities, are rejected with horror in others. Local taboos, such as those against eating horse or pork or reindeer, are widespread (reviewed by F. J. Simoons, and in a collection edited by T. K. Fitzgerald).

4.5.3.1 Energy: Cultural diversity is, however, superimposed on regularities that resemble those

we find among the mammals generally. J. V. G. A. Durnin recorded the food intake of 69 people, each for a week. There was much variation in intake from day to day, usually with no relationship to energy expenditure. Hence, if one confines oneself to daily rates, people may seem not to be balancing intake against output. But over the whole week nearly all Durnin's subjects were in energy equilibrium. In confirmation, N. Taggart weighed everything she ate during 11 weeks. And she weighed herself daily (except on Sundays). To quote Durnin and Passmore:

Her mean daily intake from Monday to Friday was 2300 kcal, on Saturdays it was 2580 and on Sundays 3050 kcal. During the weekdays she lost on average 480 g . . . Evidently she went to bed on Friday nights with an energy deficit of the order of 700 kcal: yet she did not feel hungry, and the deficit was made good only gradually during the next weekend.

Such weekly cycles of regulation are presumably imposed by the custom of resting every seventh (and, often, every sixth) day. If so, a cultural pattern derived from an ancient Middle Eastern civilization acts as a *Zeitgeber* (2.1.3). Among gatherer-hunters, or cultivators uninfluenced by the Judeo-Christian week, the findings might be different.

These findings refer to adults. An obvious question is how infants or young children regulate intake. The milk intake and growth of children in their first months has been studied by Margaret Ounsted & Gillian Sleigh. They were particularly interested in infants whose birth weights were exceptionally small or exceptionally large ("small-for-dates" and "large-for-dates"). The small babies took substantially more milk relative to their body weight than the large babies. Correspondingly, the small babies had a higher daily weight gain. Both large and small babies tended to revert to the median, that is, the typical weight for the population from which they were drawn. Breast-fed babies reverted more quickly than bottle fed; hence infants can regulate their food intake and weight gain, but especially if they are fed from the breast, for milk secretion is adjusted to demand (B. Hall).

M. Manciaux and others have also recorded the spontaneous regulation of food intake by 40 children aged from 18 months to three-and-a-half years. Their feeding is described as anarchic in the short term, but regulatory over longer periods, like that of adults.

Some studies of energy intake have been experimental. T. A. Spiegel persuaded 15 people to live for up to three weeks on a liquid diet. For the first few days the diet provided about 4200 J/ml; after that, the energy value of the mixture was halved. Six of the subjects "compensated dramatically" (but not completely) for the low energy value by increasing the frequency and size of meals. The adjustment took several days. Others would perhaps have adjusted too, had they endured the experiment for longer. Another group, studied by R. G. Campbell and others, were given nothing but a liquid diet (dispensed from an apparatus) for 121 days. The energy content of the mixture was altered without warning, and most of the victims quickly adjusted their intake accordingly; the exceptions were a few extremely obese subjects.

There is a general implication in all these findings. Human beings regulate their food intake; but their ability to do so depends on experience: patterns of feeding are habits acquired gradually. In a sense, we have to learn to be hungry (F. Bellisle; H. Bruch).

4.5.3.2 Food Selection:

Although human beings regulate their energy intake, they often fail to select food of the right quality (reviewed by A. Burgess & R. F. A. Dean; D. N. Walcher and others). A celebrated example, which has affected many millions of people, comes from the habit of eating milled rice instead of the whole grain. In populations that live on rice and little else, the result may be a high incidence of a debilitating and often fatal disease, beriberi. The example is striking because beriberi is due to deficiency of thiamin—the vitamin on which much of our knowledge of dietary self-selection by rats is based.

Nonetheless, we have some ability to select a favorable diet (without the aid of biochemists). Perhaps children, with no firmly developed habits, are better than adults. C. M. Davis (1928, 1939) offered young children (in hospital), over long periods, freedom of choice among about 20 foods presented together at each meal. Milk, meat, cereals, and fruit or vegetables were included in all meals; other items varied from meal to meal, but were offered every day. Sometimes (as also described in the work of Manciaux mentioned above) the response was disconcerting: for a few days a small child might eat nothing but one food. But these "binges" ended spontaneously. Sometimes individual meals were, in the author's words, "a dietician's nightmare—for example, a breakfast of a pint of orange juice and liver; a supper of several eggs, bananas and milk". But over longer periods a balanced diet was achieved; all children grew well and were healthy. The results might have been less satisfactory had foods made chiefly of white flour and sugar (cakes, cookies, biscuits) been offered. But with this qualification, the findings not only confirm our similarity in this regard to rats but must also be reassuring to parents.

Another similarity is in our ability to develop long-lasting aversions as a result of a single experience. For instance, a child of four developed influenza just after eating prunes and milk. The result was an aversion from this nourishing mixture that persisted for years. The example is from an inquiry, by J. L. Garb & A. J. Stunkard, in which more than 600 Americans were questioned. Over one-third reported food aversions, most of them associated with, and presumably derived from, some alimentary disorder. The aversions were most often acquired during the ages of 6 to 12 years. As a rule a taste (less often an odor) was related to illness. There was usually an interval of hours before illness developed. The aversions lasted for up to 50 years.

A last comment may be made on common salt, NaCl, an essential component of our diet. People who sweat heavily lose much salt, and develop a "salt hunger": miners in deep hot mines drink salt beer and eat exceptionally salty foods. In this case there is evidently a change in, literally, taste. A degree of saltiness in food or drink, which would normally be repellent, becomes highly palatable. Such a change, distinct from merely associating a flavor with a favorable effect, again parallels findings from experiments on rats. A grim but instructive example, described by L. Wilkins & C. P. Richter, concerns a child who, from the age of a year, had developed a habit of eating exceptional amounts of salt. His parents acquiesced in this strange behavior: they allowed him to dip his fingers in raw salt and lick it off. In his fourth year the child had to go into hospital. There he was denied his salt; and in seven days he was dead. At postmortem a severe adrenal cortical defect was found. This endocrine insufficiency, which has been fully studied in experimental animals, is fatal unless exceptional amounts of salt are taken.

4.5.4 The Concept of Hunger

In the preceding account I have hardly used the word hunger: sometimes, instead, I have referred to the time since the last meal or to some measure of internal state. Yet in ordinary speech one may remark that a dog, say, is hungry. Such a statement is usually based on the dog's behavior—barking, whining, or scratching at an empty bowl. D. O. Hebb (1949), in a celebrated book, initially defines hunger as the tendency to eat. The definition, which is not very precise, is in terms of behavior, and so corresponds to ordinary usage. But the colloquial use of hunger often implies some reference to feeling: one may say that one feels hungry; and similar feelings are often attributed to other species. We have seen that this is a hazardous procedure (chapter 1).

If we are concerned only with overt behavior, can we properly continue to use "hunger" as a descriptive term? In experiments by N. E. Miller (1955) laboratory rats were trained to press a lever for the reward of a pellet of food. (The apparatus is described in 6.1.2, figure 6-6.) The mechanism is next set to deliver a pellet not each time the bar is pressed but irregularly and unpredictably. The rate at which the animal presses the bar is then, up to a point, proportional to the time since its last meal. Similarly, quinine, which is distasteful to rats, is accepted in food after a fast (or, when the rats are "hungry"?): the longer the fast the greater the tolerated concentration of quinine. The bar-pressing rate and tolerance of quinine have been described as measures of hunger. But now consider rats made hyperphagic by hypothalamic lesions (4.5.2.3); these animals eat more, and are therefore sometimes described as more hungry, than normal rats. Yet they press a bar for food at less than the normal rate, and they are less tolerant of quinine. Hence, on these measures, they are *less* hungry than normal rats.

Such findings are disconcerting if we assume, consciously or unconsciously, that there is some single process or state, named "hunger" (or "hunger drive"), that is responsible for all the phenomena of feeding behavior. When the behavior is analyzed, we find evidence of many internal processes that influence feeding. These processes are not always positively correlated.

The reference to "hunger drive" raises a number of problems, discussed more fully in 17.1.2. But some general questions of method may be faced now. If we are asked to *explain* an action such as eating, several kinds of answer are possible. Here is an incomplete list of possible responses to the question: why is that animal eating that food?

1. The animal is hungry.
2. The animal likes that food.
3. The animal is accustomed to (has the habit of) eating at this time of day.
4. The animal has had no food for 12 h.
5. The animal's blood sugar is low.
6. The animal is imitating other members of its species.
7. The animal developed the habit of eating that food in early life.
8. Animals of this species usually feed at this time of day because they are then safer from predators.

The first two answers are colloquial and imprecise. The first seems to give no further information. It could, however, be a short way of saying that the animal has fasted (for a specified period). The second again adds nothing to the statement, "the animal is eating that food", unless it implies that the food preferences of the animal (or of conspecifics) have been tested.

The next five answers are unambiguously objective. They can give precise information from which we might predict the behavior of other animals. The reference to time of day in the third answer signifies that the animal has formed a habit of eating at a particular time; such behavior could be analyzed in the same way as other examples of habit formation (chapters 6, 7). Answers four and five refer to the animal's internal state. These statements are reductionist (19.1.3): they try to explain behavior by physiology. The reference to imitation in the sixth answer introduces the social aspect of eating: the feeding of many animals is influenced by the conduct of conspecifics (8.4). Feeding is, as the seventh answer implies, not influenced only by the animal's immediate situation: previous experience, even quite remote in time, may have an effect.

The eighth and final answer is, at first sight, a statement about the present ecological relationships of the animal's species. If so, it is empirical and objective: such relationships can be investigated (though not easily). But when we look at the answer closely, the word "because" raises some difficulties. One implication could be of genetical variation in the timing of feeding. There might then be selection favoring genotypes that tend to feed, say, at dusk and dawn. Again, such a statement might be testable by study of existing populations. But statements on species-typical features sometimes refer to the evolution of the species. Hence the eighth answer might imply (or be taken to imply) that feeding at a certain time is a product of natural selection in the remote past. It is then not testable as are the third through the seventh answers. I return to such questions in chapter 18.

4.6 SUMMING UP

The homeostatic function of behavior can be thought of in a very simple way: an animal depends for its survival on maintaining some measurable feature, such as deep body temperature or blood sugar, at a particular reference value. Departure from this value provokes behavior that restores it. Constancy then depends on a negative feedback. But the facts are not so simple. (1) There may be more than one reference value; a reptile, for example, may have alternative set points for its body temperature. (2) In all the examples studied, there are many negative feedbacks, at both the physiological and the behavioral level; these interact; often they seem to provide a failsafe mechanism. They may, however, act only after a substantial delay. (3) Sometimes there are positive feedbacks; up to a point, "appetite comes with eating". (4) There may be a feed-forward: drinking often occurs in advance of need, that is, when there is not yet any water deficit. (5) There may be competition between incompatible responses, as when a newt has the alternatives of courting or breeding. (6) Homeostasis may depend in part on social interactions.

Maintenance activities, especially among invertebrates, often consist of orientations, and similar species-typical responses, that are not adapted to individual circumstances. In contrast, much of the feeding and similar behavior of vertebrates, especially that of mammals, depends on habits formed as a result of the experience of favorable or unfavorable individual conditions. This is the topic of the next part.

III

ADAPTING TO CIRCUMSTANCES

This part deals with topics usually discussed under the heading of learning. For reasons given more fully at the end of chapter 8, I do not use the word learning as a collective noun; the main reason is that the word is used in many senses, with no agreed definition, and is therefore a source of confusion. But I do use the verb in the ordinary sense, as in the phrase, "learning the way to water": a new habit (what is learned) is the specified.

Chapter 5 begins with reflexes, and examines the ways in which they are modified as a result of individual experience. The two main concepts are habituation and the conditional reflex (commonly mistranslated as conditioned).

Habituation looks deceptively simple: as applied to man, it might be casually described as what happens when we get used to something; but, as we find, the waning of a response as a result of repeated stimulation, even when observed in invertebrates with the simplest nervous systems, presents many problems. These are analyzed both in behavioral and in physiological terms.

Habituation entails loss or attenuation of a response. In the conditional reflex something more positive occurs. A response is repeatedly evoked in association with a stimulus that previously had merely attracted the animal's attention. As a result, a modified version of the response comes to be made to the new stimulus. In the usual type of experiment the response is a simple one, and is observed in an animal harnessed so that few movements are possible. Nonetheless, many questions arise from the attempt to analyse the conditional reflex. Among the results of such analysis are findings on the functioning of the human nervous system.

In chapters 6 and 7 we turn to behavior more obviously relevant to what animals do in natural conditions. When an animal develops a habit, it often seems to do so as a result of initially random movements or at least of movements not directed by the needs of the situation. Eventually, after repeated exposure to a situation or problem, it performs an effective sequence of acts with economy of time and effort. The sequence may be movement from its home to a place where some need can be satisfied. Such trial, error, and success has been minutely studied in the laboratory, especially in relation to the effects of reward and punishment. But attempts to find laws of high generality about such behavior have so far had little success; and the physiology of habit formation remains enigmatic. On the other hand, much has recently been found out about the variety of what animals of diverse types can and cannot learn to do.

Lastly, in chapter 8, we face the most formidable achievements of the most complex animal nervous systems. Many animals can store information about the environment, and can use it later, for instance in taking a direct way from one place to another. The storage may occur during exploratory movements in the living space. Such movements are often provoked by new things in the environment, or by access to a new place. In human terms, many animals show marked curiosity.

Among the Primates, habit formation and problem solving usually occur in a social context. The development of abilities often then depends on imitation. The teaching of skills, however, is confined to human beings.

Some vertebrates, especially Primates, not only solve problems but develop an ability to solve *classes* of problems, just as human beings learn to answer novel mathematical questions on the basis of previous study. Such cognitive abilities represent one of the major unsolved problems of biology: how do nervous systems generate such elaborate behavior?

5

REFLEX BEHAVIOR

I lay me down and slumber
And every morn revive.
Whose is the night-long breathing
That keeps a man alive?
                                    A. E. Housman

Many of the movements of animals, especially of
the simpler invertebrates, clearly "reflect" the pattern of stimulation falling on their external senses.
Such movements, and similar glandular responses,
are therefore called *reflexes*. In this chapter we are
concerned mainly with changes in reflex responses;
but first something must be said about the reflexes
themselves.

5.1 REFLEXES

5.1.1 The Mammalian Spinal Cord

The most familiar examples are from the mammals.
The stretch reflexes of the limbs have been much
studied by neurophysiologists and are regularly used
clinically.

If the tendon below the kneecap is hit with the
side of the hand (or with a tendon hammer), the
muscles in front of the thigh contract: if the leg is
free, the result is a brief kicking movement. The
function of stretch reflexes is to maintain posture.
When a mammal is standing still, the limb muscles
are contracted to keep a constant length. If the animal begins to fall to one side, some of the muscles
are stretched, the stretch reflex operates, the length
of the muscle is restored, and balance is kept. Such
adjustments may take only a few milliseconds.

The structures that regulate these reflexes are in
the spinal cord. If an animal such as a cat is anesthetized, and then killed by severing the brain from
the cord, the cord can be kept in a responsive state
if the body is kept warm and the movements of
breathing are artificially maintained. Such a "spinal
preparation" can still respond to stimulation with
movement of the limbs. Stretch reflexes can be
elicited.

The relationships of sense organs, sensory (afferent) nerves, connecting neurons (interneurons)
in the cord, motor neurons, and muscles are often
shown in a simple diagram (figure 5-1). The "reflex arc" is, however, only a diagram, for it omits
many complexities. Some of the latter are parts of
classical neurophysiology.

The diagram suggests that one of each kind of

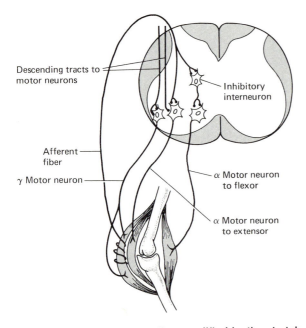

FIGURE 5-1 The "reflex arc", exemplified by the stretch reflex described in the text.

cell is connected to one of the next, in a simple chain. This is far from true. Suppose that stimulating one group of sense organs produces a partial contraction of a group of muscles, and that a separate stimulation of other sense organs produces a similar contraction. If the two stimuli are applied together, the combined effect may be greater than the sum of the two separate partial contractions. This is *summation*. But sometimes the result is less than expected: such *occlusion* is due to overlap of sensory pathways. These phenomena are, of course, not confined to the spinal cord.

A simple diagram is misleading for other reasons. When a sensory fiber enters the cord, it branches extensively, and these branches end close to many other neurons. Figure 5-2 illustrates a few of the tens of millions of neurons in the mamma-

lian nervous system. Each is in synaptic connection with hundreds of others. A synapse is the site at which two neurons are in a functional relationship; the relationship may be excitatory or inhibitory.

Moreover, communication in the nervous system is not one-way: while afferent impulses are arriving from the sense organs, there are always efferent impulses acting back on the periphery. Figure 5-3 gives an example on a small scale: the axons of certain motor neurons have collateral branches within the gray matter of the spinal cord; these run to interneurons (Renshaw cells), of which the output goes back to the motor neurons. The action of the Renshaw cells is inhibitory; hence we have here an example of a negative feedback loop (4.1). The

FIGURE 5-2 Cells in the mammalian cerebral cortex. The pyramidal cell has a long axon that extends into the spinal cord. Each of the many millions of such neurons is in synaptic connection with hundreds of others. In this type of preparation only some of the cells take up stain; and these cells stand out clearly. (After J. Z. Young, 1975)

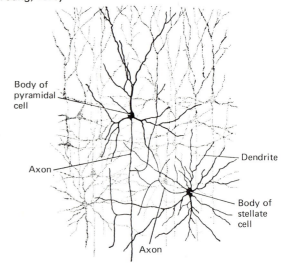

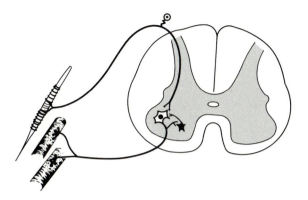

FIGURE 5-3 Another aspect of the spinal reflex arc. (Compare figure 5-1 above.) A Renshaw cell is shown with a collateral from the axon of a motor neuron making synaptic connection with the Renshaw cell body; its own axon in turn makes a synapse with the body of the motor neuron. A sensory fiber from a muscle spindle is also shown. (After T. D. M. Roberts, 1967)

loop is supposed to prevent the rate of firing of the motor neurons from exceeding the optimum value for maintaining contraction of the muscle cells.

The mechanism of the stretch reflex also provides examples of motor (efferent) innervation of sense organs. The sense organs are the muscle spindles, of which the activity is primarily determined by the extent to which the muscle is being stretched. But each spindle is itself innervated by motor fibers (gamma efferents or fusimotor fibers). Stimulation of one kind of gamma fiber increases the sensitivity of the spindle to stretching: that is, in a given state of the muscle, its firing rate increases. A second kind influences the response of the spindle to *change* in the state of the muscle.

These features of the proprioceptive system of a mammal warn us not to think of central nervous activity in terms of highly simplified diagrams. They also remind us that even simple behavior is more than just stimulus followed by response.

5.1.2 Examples from Invertebrates

5.1.2.1 Pedicellariae: Our knowledge of reflex physiology is founded on study of the mammalian spinal cord—among the most complex of all reflex systems. Many workers have now turned to invertebrates for examples of simpler arrangements. They have been helped by technical developments, such as those that allow recording from an electrode of which the tip is inside a nerve cell body.

Sometimes a stimulus evokes a response without intervention by a central nervous system. The Echinoderms, such as starfish (Asteroidea) and sea urchins (Echinoidea), have on their surfaces many small pincer-like organs, the pedicellariae (figure 5-4), which are believed to pick off intruders such as the settling larvae of sedentary animals (reviewed by M. S. Laverack). Our knowledge of these structures goes back to the work of H. S. Jennings (1868–1947) at the beginning of the century. He describes how, if one lightly touches the back of a starfish, the pedicellariae nearby bend toward the point of contact and open and close. A touch on the outside of the pincers evokes opening; a similar touch inside causes closing. All these responses are performed even in a fragment of starfish disconnected from the nerve cords that constitute the Echinoderm's central nervous system. Hence the whole reflex mechanism is a local one and can operate independently. This is perhaps the nearest approach among many-celled animals to a system corresponding to the reflex arc diagram. It corresponds to certain general peculiarities of the Echinodermata (3.2.2).

5.1.2.2 Nerve Nets: The simplest nervous systems are those of the Coelenterata. There is usually no well-defined concentration of nerve cell bodies—nothing that may be called a brain or even a gan-

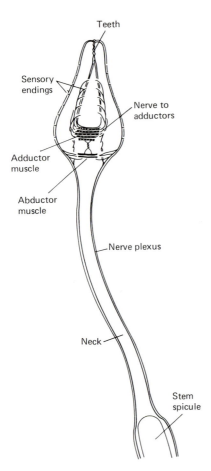

FIGURE 5-4 Diagram of a pedicellaria of a type found on sea urchins such as *Echinus*. The control of the opening and closing of the pincers is extremely simple, and is independent of any central nervous activity. (After D. Nichols, 1962)

glion. A coelenterate may have as many as 100,000 neurons in a network (figure 5-5). The neurons are fired off by sensory cells in the ectoderm (reviewed by T. H. Bullock & G. A. Horridge).

Nerve cells are usually stimulated so that they conduct in only one direction, but those of a nerve net often transmit impulses both ways. Correspond-

ingly, impulses spread in all directions from a source of stimulation. Such a system has no sustained, autonomous activity: it seems always to depend on a push-button effect of the sense organs. The Scyphozoa or jellyfish (figure 5-6) have statocysts (2.2.1.2). If all the statocysts are removed, the regular contraction of the "bell" or "umbrella"—which produces movement—ceases.

Nonetheless even the coelenterate nerve net can produce quite complex behavior. The most elaborate performance known has been described by

FIGURE 5-5 Part of the nerve net of a coelenterate, *Hydra:* an example of the simplest kind of nervous system. (After P. Semal-Van Gansen, 1952)

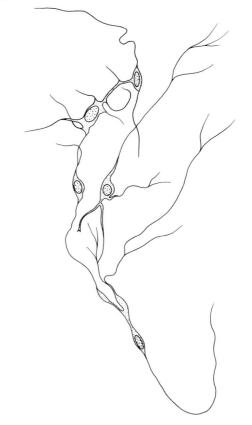

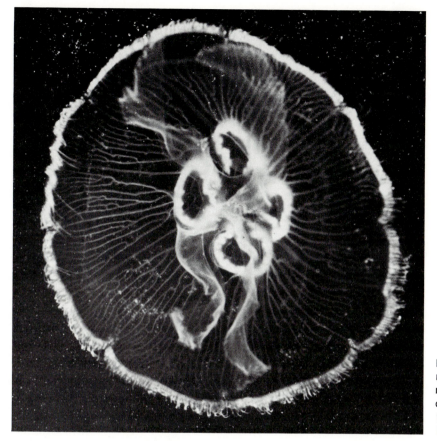

FIGURE 5-6 *Aurelia aurita,* a common scyphozoan, of which the movement (contraction of the umbrella) depends on a continual input from the statocysts. (D. P. Wilson, Marine Biological Laboratory, Plymouth)

P. N. Sund. A sea anemone, *Stomphia,* when at rest, often sits on the shell of a mollusk, *Modiolus* (compare figure 3-4); but, if substances produced by a nearby starfish reach its chemical receptors, *Stomphia* detaches itself and swims off by means of rhythmic contractions of the body. Just what makes possible such an efficient directed movement is not known. Another example is illustrated in figure 5-7.

The important features of a nerve net include: (1) the effects of facilitation at the synapses; (2) variation in the properties of neuromuscular junc-tions; (3) the existence of local concentrations of cells and of directional conduction almost as if there were a nerve; and (4) the presence of two nerve nets with different properties (T. H. Bullock & G. A. Horridge). Whether these are sufficient to account for all the observed behavior is doubtful.

5.1.2.3 Giant Neurons: A kind of reflex system, much investigated because of its accessibility, is that based on giant neurons. Many annelids have a few fibers of exceptionally large diameter which provide a continuous rapidly conducting strand

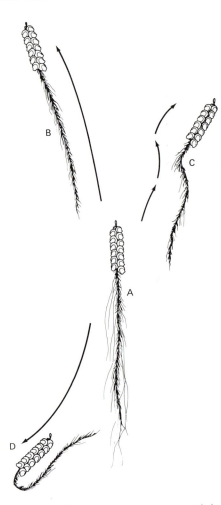

throughout the length of the nerve cord (shown in figure 5-8). These giant fibers make possible rapid withdrawal into a tube or a burrow. A squid or a cuttlefish (figure 5-9) similarly has a system of giant fibers (figure 5-10). When a squid is disturbed, it not only releases a cloud of ink (1.1.4), but also makes a very rapid movement backward. This escape response is jet propelled: water is forced out of the mantle cavity through the funnel. Hence giant neurons can produce a single, violent response as a result of stimulation from a number

FIGURE 5-8 The nervous system of a polychaete such as *Nereis*. (After R. Buchsbaum, 1976)

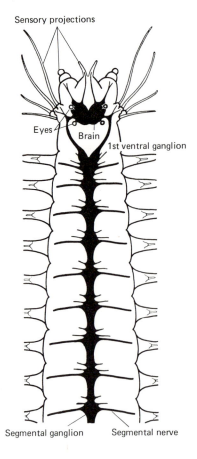

FIGURE 5-7 *Nanomia cara,* a coelenterate of the order, Siphonophora. The units of which this "colonial" animal is composed include nectophores specialized for swimming. Their contractions are often synchronized, and produce well-organized forward (B) and reverse (D) movement. A shows the animal at rest, and C illustrates zigzag swimming in which the nectophores contract asynchronously. All this is achieved without a central nervous system, but with two nerve nets. (After G. O. Mackie, 1964)

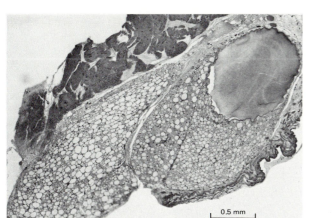

FIGURE 5-9 Giant neuron. Section of a nerve in the mantle sac of a squid, *Sepia.* Many small nerve fibers appear as empty circles. This is one giant fiber, in which impulses are conducted exceptionally quickly to the jet propulsion muscles. (Courtesy J. Z. Young)

of possible sources. Cephalopod giant neurons have an exceptionally high rate of conduction, correlated with their large diameter.

An analogous system has been described in the Crustacea Decapoda. Giant axons have been investigated in an American freshwater lobster or crayfish, *Procambarus clarkii.* These animals can move abruptly backwards by forceful flexion of the abdomen. In each abdominal segment (figure 5-11),

FIGURE 5-10 Diagram of the arrangement of giant nerve fibers of a cephalopod, the squid, *Loligo.* (After D. Burkhardt, 1967)

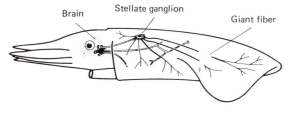

five excitatory neurons supply the flexor muscles on each side (figure 5-12). (There are also inhibitory neurons that go to the extensor muscles.) Withdrawal depends on simultaneous activation of the total of a hundred or so excitatory neurons in the abdomen. Such activation can result from stimulation of a single large interneuron (described by D. Kennedy and others and by R. S. Zucker and others).

5.1.3 Significance and Definition

The reflexes described above are examples of behavior of exceptional simplicity. The neural arrangements on which reflexes depend are correspondingly simple, and progress has been made in giving a physiological account of some of them. Nonetheless, the neurophysiology has not been easy to unravel, and many questions remain. What has been achieved gives some notion of the formidable task of analyzing more complex behavior physiologically.

The aspect of complexity with which we are now mainly concerned is the modification of reflex responses as a result of individual experience. But first I must say something about definition. The term "reflex" is not a precise one. It is usually reserved for muscular or glandular activity with the following features. The response is (1) an immediate and simple reaction to stimulation; (2) always produced by the same effector; (3) highly predictable; (4) consistently related to a particular kind of stimulation; and (5) species-typical. But the best way to find out what is meant by "reflex" is to look at examples.

5.2 HABITUATION

The term habituation is sometimes defined as the loss or waning of a response as a result of repeated

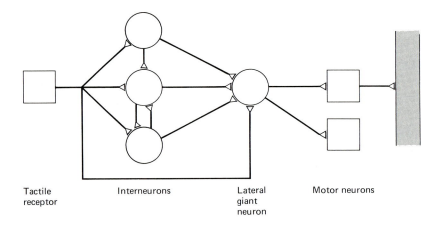

FIGURE 5-11 Flexion of the abdomen of the crayfish, *Procambarus clarkii*, depends on the operation, in each abdominal segment on each side, of the system shown diagrammatically. The system may be activated by stimulation of tactile organs; these stimulate interneurons, which connect via lateral giant neurons with motor neurons. (After R. S. Zucker and others, 1971)

stimulation. (We see later that it is more convenient to use a narrower definition: a stimulus-specific decline in a response, resulting from the effect on the central nervous system of repeated stimulation.) The phenomenon is subjectively familiar: the loud tick of a clock is eventually not noticed; the stiffness of new clothing is soon disregarded; an odor, initially strong, becomes quickly imperceptible. Habituation, as defined, occurs when a response, such as turning the head toward a clock, ceases.

The definition given in the first sentence of this section, taken literally (as a definition should be), includes effects of sensory "adaptation" or "fatigue". In the account that follows, we see that habituation is often a result of changes in the central nervous system, and is specific to a particular kind of stimulation.

5.2.1 Invertebrates

5.2.1.1 Behavioral Analysis: For the study of habituation, a convenient kind of response, widespread in the animal kingdom, is sudden with-

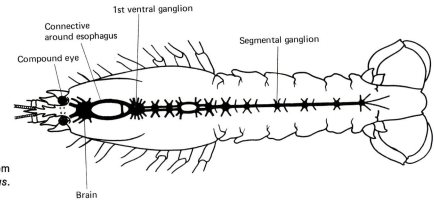

FIGURE 5-12 The nervous system of a lobster, such as *Procambarus*. (After R. Buchsbaum, 1976)

drawal from stimulation. If a stimulus that induces withdrawal is regularly repeated, it commonly comes to have less effect, until sometimes the response disappears altogether (reviewed by E. J. Wyers and others).

Animals equipped with only a nerve net can habituate in this way to a variety of stimuli. The responses of *Hydra pirardi* (Coelenterata Hydrozoa), a rather large species of its well-known genus, have been described by N. B. Rushforth. In its usual state *Hydra* has a long, slender body, and still longer, fine tentacles that sweep the water until food is touched (figure 3-3). A sudden increase in light, or a mechanical disturbance, can cause general contraction. Rushforth's animals were mechanically shaken at intervals of 15 s. At first, all contracted at each stimulus; but gradually the number responding declined to about one in five. If animals habituated in this way were stimulated with light, all contracted. Hence the decline in the response to vibration was not due to failure of the muscles ("fatigue", or the accumulation of metabolites): it was specific to a particular stimulus.

Fully habituated animals were rested for 1 h and then retested. Most now contracted again: the effect of "training" had been largely lost. But the loss was not complete: these animals habituated more quickly to a second training session than to the first; evidently some trace was retained during the interval without stimulation.

Figure 5-13 illustrates a similar finding, by R. A. Westerman, on Turbellaria ("planarians"). These flatworms (compare figure 2-20) turn away from a beam of light on their front ends. On each day of experiment, the animals were exposed to the light on 25 occasions at intervals of 30 to 60 s. On the first day animals responding to the light declined from over 30 to below 20%. On the 16th day the initial proportion was about 28%, but the final

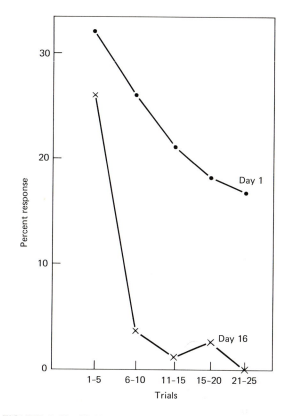

FIGURE 5-13 Habituation of the withdrawal response of *Dugesia dorotocephala*. On Day 1, over 25 trials, the lowest percentage responding to sudden illumination was about 17 (upper curve). On the 16th successive day of such experiments, the decline in the percentage responding during the series of trials was much steeper; and the final proportion responding was zero. (After R. A. Westerman, 1963)

figure was zero. There was evidently a lasting effect that expressed itself in a higher rate of habituation as a result of repeated training. In such a case two processes seem to be involved: one brings about the short-term change observed during one day; the other is responsible for the persistent effect of training; but the physiology is not known.

Habituation can take place to diverse kinds of stimulation, but not always at the same rate. Bristle worms of the genus, *Nereis,* have been subjected by S. M. Evans (1969a,b) to repeated contact, light, or vibration, all of which cause contractions. There was a rapid decline in the response to the first two; but habituation to tactile stimuli was slow. Such a finding suggests that the different sense organs respond differently. Certainly, the internal processes responsible for the change in behavior are local and not in the supraesophageal ganglia (figure 5-14): decerebrate worms habituate in much the same way as normal worms. Similarly, as S. C. Ratner & A. R. Gilpin have found, earthworms, *Lumbricus terrestris,* can habituate to an air puff when deprived of their cerebral ganglia.

An important question is whether habituation to one kind of stimulation is affected by applying another kind. We have already seen that habituation to, say, vibration leaves the response to a quite different stimulus, such as light, unaffected. We are now concerned with the effect of an "irrelevant" stimulus on the original response.

E. J. Wyers and others describe experiments on the sea hare, *Aplysia californica* (Opisthobranchiata). This splendid mollusk can reach a length of more than 30 cm. (Another species is shown in figure 5-31.) A jet of water directed onto its mantle induces withdrawal of the gills. If the stimulus is repeated regularly, the response declines. If, now, a stronger jet of water is applied, the response to the original stimulus returns. Similarly, another part of the animal's surface may, after habituation to the water jet, be gently stimulated with a soft brush; again the response to the water jet is performed. This type of interaction is called *dishabituation:* the effect of repeated stimulation of one kind is canceled by new stimulation of another kind.

A similar finding is described by K. Lukowiak & J. W. Jacklet. They stimulated the isolated siphon of *Aplysia* either with light or with touch. The with-

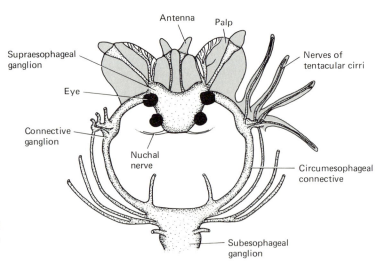

FIGURE 5-14 The anterior sense organs and front part of the nervous system of the polychaete, *Nereis.* (After P. Flint, 1965)

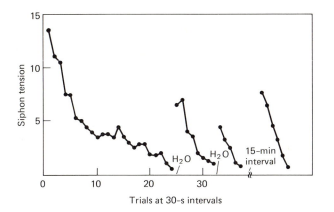

FIGURE 5-15 Habituation of the isolated siphon of *Aplysia* to light. The stimuli were applied at intervals of 30 s. On additional stimulation by drops of water, dishabituation occurs. Similarly, the response recovers after some minutes of rest. (After K. Lukowiak & J. W. Jacklet, 1972)

drawal response habituates to either stimulus. If such a preparation is habituated, say, to stimulation by light, and is then provoked by touch, the response to light is restored, or dishabituated (figure 5-15).

A last, rather different example is provided by the work of H. Mourier (already mentioned in 4.5.1.1) on the response of houseflies to unfamiliar objects. Novel surfaces, put in a cage containing these flies, are at first strongly attractive, but their effect declines. Such a decline is, of course, implied in the statement that "novel" objects are attractive. The decline in the response takes about 20 min, and is specific to the stimulus; hence it is not due to muscular fatigue or to a decline in the functioning of sense organs. If a second novel stimulus acting on the same sense organs is introduced into a cage, not only is this stimulus attractive, but the attraction of the first stimulus is restored.

5.2.1.2 Neurophysiology:

The observations on decerebrate worms show how much goes on in each segmental ganglion. There is a contrast here with the vertebrates: in them, for the neural processes of habituation, one must usually turn to the immensely complicated brain with its vast numbers of neurons. We saw (5.1.2.3) how neurophysiologists have therefore used the nervous systems of annelids and other invertebrates for the analysis of reflex action. We now turn to similar studies on the neural basis of habituation (reviewed by W. J. Davis, and by F. B. Krasne).

G. A. Horridge (1959) examined the rapid shortening, mediated by the giant neurons, of two polychaetes, *Nereis virens* and *Harmothoë imbricata*. When such withdrawal is repeatedly elicited by contact, vibration, or a visual stimulus, it habituates. The synapses at which the underlying change of function takes place are between lateral giant command neurons and the giant motor neurons; they soon become refractory on repeated stimulation, whereas the other synapses in the "reflex arc" do not.

Krasne reviews more detailed studies on the crayfish, whose reflexes are described above (5.1.2.3). The crayfish segmental system for the escape response (the tail flip) is disynaptic (figure 5-11): an input from sensory organs activates a giant command neuron, which in turn stimulates giant motor neurons. There is, however, an alternative pathway, through interneurons between the sensory neurons and the command neurons.

During a series of stimulations, the tail flip declines slightly in vigor, but the main feature of habituation in this case is a sudden loss of response. In one kind of experiment the giant command neurons have been repeatedly stimulated by direct shock. Such a procedure cuts out the sensory side of the "reflex arc"; and it does not lead to sudden habituation. Hence the loss of response must be on the afferent side of the system. Records were made with intracellular electrodes in the giant neurons. These showed that excitation in the direct (monosynaptic or alpha) route is stable with repeated stimulation; but it is not by itself sufficient to fire the giant motor neurons: excitation in the alternative path (of beta cells or interneurons) is also required; and it is here that a decline in responsiveness occurs when stimulation is repeated. Habituation, then, depends on changes in the responsiveness of a particular category of neurons.

In the intact crayfish each segmental ganglion is of course connected with all the others. Attempts have been made to discover whether the input to the ganglia from other ganglia or from the brain contribute to habituation. Some of the effects of the longitudinal pathways are certainly inhibitory. Correspondingly, if the nerve cord is cut between the thorax and abdomen, the escape response is more easily provoked than before; but there is no evidence of an effect on habituation of the tail flip when it is repeatedly stimulated. Probably, therefore, the neural basis of habituation of this response is located entirely in the abdominal ganglia.

In the previous section I give examples of habituation with both a short-term and a long-term component. The crayfish is a further instance. Habituation of the tail flip fades over a few hours, but testing several days later reveals some persisting effect of training. The neurology is not known; the answer may have to be sought outside the abdominal ganglia. A still further complexity has been described by J. S. Bryan & F. B. Krasne. Repeated tactile stimulation does *not* always induce habituation of the tail flip. The exception is when the stimulation is a result of the animal's own movements. Again, the neurology is not known.

A last example is provided by extensive studies of the sea hare (5.1.2.4). Studies of "learning" by such gastropod mollusks have been reviewed by E. R. Kandel and by A. O. D. Willows. They describe experiments on the preparation shown in figure 5-16: the head and the greater part of the nervous system are kept intact, but most of the body is removed. Drops of water applied at intervals of 10 s are used to provoke withdrawal of a gill. As already described, the response habituates. Microelectrodes were implanted in giant neurons in the ganglia. Excitatory potentials in these cells were recorded at precisely the time of withdrawal of the tentacle. As the tentacle reflex declined, so did the excitatory potential decline in amplitude. If stimulation was stopped for a few minutes, the response recovered and so did the potential. Simi-

FIGURE 5-16 Isolated head of *Aplysia* with part of the nervous system attached. This preparation is used in experiments on the neurophysiology of habituation, described in the text. (After J. Bruner & L. Tauc, 1966)

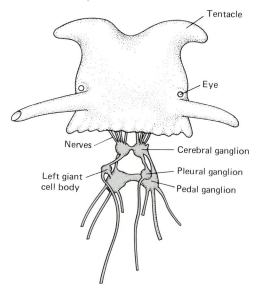

larly, dishabituation brought about by scratching the skin was accompanied by reappearance of the potentials as well as the reflex. Further measurements of the changes taking place in the ganglia showed that the giant cells remain responsive during all these changes: they are not themselves the site of the decrement in function. It is the cells that excite the giant neurons in which refractoriness develops when stimulation is regularly repeated.

5.2.2 Vertebrates

5.2.2.1 Behavioral Analysis: The vertebrates provide a diversity of examples of habituation (reviewed by R. A. Hinde, 1970).

Hinde himself has made a detailed study of the *mobbing response.* Many species of small birds form a group around a predator, such as a hawk or an owl, and fly at it while uttering alarm calls (12.2.1). Mobbing is assumed to confer some protection on the prey. Chaffinches, *Fringilla coelebs,* mob not only predatory birds, but also carnivorous mammals such as dogs and stoats, *Mustela erminea.* Hinde exposed chaffinches to such stimuli. In some experiments he used a stuffed tawny owl, *Strix aluco,* and so ensured that the stimulus was a constant one; in others he used a live little owl, *Carine noctua.* When a stuffed owl is presented continuously for 30 min, the response, recorded as the rate of calling, declines rather erratically toward zero. On repetition of the experiment next day, the response is evoked again, but less strongly.

Hinde examined the question of stimulus specificity. If the object presented on the second day differs from that used on the first, the mobbing response is usually more fully restored than when the second object is identical with the first. Hence there is some discrimination of the various objects that evoke mobbing, but habituation to one spills over into the response to another. The experiment with a live owl showed that habituation of the kind observed with models occurs also with a natural object.

Mobbing is evoked by a rather specific group of objects, namely, predators. Sometimes, strange objects and strange conditions in general induce a well-defined response. In 5.2.1.1 above the attraction of novel stimuli for houseflies is mentioned. Mammals too tend to approach unfamiliar objects and conditions (8.1.3.3). If a wild rat (or a laboratory rat), of the genus *Rattus,* is put in an unfamiliar environment it spends some time moving around sniffing. Figure 5-17 illustrates a maze in which a rodent can live and in which such conduct can be recorded. The maze has a central nest box and four arms (S. A. Barnett & P. E. Cowan). If, when a rat is put in, only three arms are open, the animal makes many visits to each during its first day. On later days, the rate of visiting is much lower (habituation). If, after three days, the fourth arm is opened, there is initially a high rate of visiting as before: although the fourth arm is structurally identical to the other three, it still evokes a "new place reaction". There is no general decline in responsiveness, but a specific loss of "interest" in the places already explored.

Lastly, there are examples from human beings. Seventy infants aged one to three days were exposed to harmless mixtures of odorous substances, such as aniseed oil and asafoetida (T. Engen & L. P. Lipsitt). The breathing rate increased; but this response declined with repeated exposure. If the infant was then exposed to only one component of the mixture, the response reappeared. Hence the decline was not solely a consequence of "sensory fatigue": the authors describe it as a novelty effect, that is, as due to a change from a familiar to an unfamiliar stimulus.

FIGURE 5-17 Artificial environment in which an animal can be kept for many days. There is a central nest box, from which four arms may lead to food, water, other incentives, or nothing. When a small mammal is put in such an environment, at first it makes many visits to the arms; but after a day or two, the visiting rate declines to a much lower level. (Philip Boucas, courtesy World Health Organization)

Similarly, A. K. Bartoshuk observed babies when a varying tone was sounded: there was an acceleration of the heart rate, but as usual the response declined when the tone was repeated. Suppose the tone rose in frequency. After habituation, a similar tone, but one changing from high to low frequency, was sounded; the response then returned. In this case a subtle change in the structure of the stimulus was enough to restore the habituated response.

One of the distinctive acts of a newborn child is turning the head (rooting), especially toward a touch on the lip or cheek. Normally the movement brings the infant to the nipple. H. F. R. Prechtl made observations on over 500 babies, many of them in the first few weeks of life. The babies were evidently being fed at intervals, of 3 or 4 h, determined by the convenience of their parents. They were usually tested shortly before a feed was due. By the age of two or three weeks the head turning evoked by a touch around the mouth is directed toward the source of the stimulus. If this response is evoked repeatedly, it declines; but the response is made if contact is now on the other side of the mouth.

Such observations on our own species parallel those on many others. They all give a "mechanical" impression. But even the newborn infant, as Prechtl shows, is much more complex than an abbreviated account indicates. Both the head turning itself and habituation to the stimuli that evoke it depend greatly on the infant's state: allowance must be made, not only for when the baby last fed, but also on whether it is sleepy and perhaps on the character of the social situation in which the baby finds itself.

5.2.2.2 Neurophysiology:
The neural basis of habituation has been investigated in both the spinal cord and the brain. Experiments at the neuronal level (reviewed by Gabriel Horn) may be compared with those on the nerve cells of invertebrate ganglia.

C. L. Prosser & W. S. Hunter studied two kinds of reflex in rats. One was a monosynaptic tendon reflex (5.1.1). A "spinal" animal was used, that is, one in which the spinal cord had been severed from the brain; responsiveness is maintained by keeping the animal warm and by artificial respiration. When the reflex was repeatedly evoked, there was no sign of habituation. In contrast, the startle response of an intact animal, involving interneurons and hence more than one synapse, habituated quite quickly. Such findings imply that the neural basis of habituation is in the interneurons.

Experiments by G. Horn & R. M. Hill have identified individual neurons, concerned with habituation, in the brain stem of rabbits, *Oryctolagus cuniculus*. The stimulus, a tone of 1000 Hz, was repeated at intervals of 1.5 s. At first the tone elicited a response by the brainstem neurons; but after 28 presentations the response had faded almost to nothing. A tone of 1500 Hz was now presented in the sequence of repeated tones: this evoked a strong response. Similar findings came from the use of tactile instead of audible stimuli. And there was some evidence that habituation was specific to the kind of stimulus: habituation of a neuron to an audible stimulus was apparently independent of response to a tactile stimulus.

Certain types of neurons in the mammalian brainstem are probably especially important in ha-

bituation to all kinds of stimuli. These cells belong to the reticular activating system (RAS). The RAS is a network of small cells extending from the anterior part of the spinal cord forward into the thalamus (figure 5-18). It receives fibers from afferent tracts as they run toward the thalamus: all the inputs from the organs of special sense contribute to it, directly or indirectly. Hence information from every sensory modality converges on it. From the RAS a vast number of fibers run to the whole of the cerebral cortex. This diffuse projection to the cortex is in contrast to the more familiar system that carries the main sensory inputs, via the thalamus, to the special sensory regions.

The RAS has been called, not very precisely, an organ of consciousness. If it is put out of action by injury or drugs (including anaesthetics), the animal is made comatose. The input from the senses by the direct routes is still reaching the cortex; but

FIGURE 5-18 Diagram of cat's brain, to show the relationships of the reticular formation (RAS). The RAS receives inputs from all the exteroceptors: those indicated are from the spinothalamic tracts. From the RAS there are diffuse projections to all parts of the cerebral cortex. These are in contrast to the specific projections of individual sense organs to particular cortical localities. (After T. E. Starzl and others, 1951)

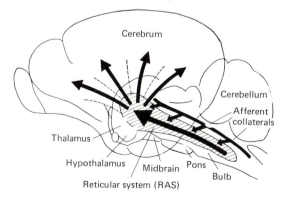

responsiveness requires the additional cortical facilitation evoked by impulses from the RAS. The output of the RAS to the cortex alters during behavioral habituation. S. Sharpless and H. H. Jasper used sounds that initially evoked the "orienting response" (OR) of a resting cat. The OR includes turning the head and pricking the ears; and it is accompanied by activity in the RAS. The latter diminishes in parallel with increasing habituation. The effect is stimulus specific. A puff of air, which acts on different sensory modalities, still evokes the response. Sharpless and Jasper also produced habituation to a simple melody. An isolated tone was then sounded from among those that formed part of the tune. This evoked the OR and caused activation of the RAS, although the complete tune did not do so. Hence loss of responsiveness by a mammal during habituation is evidently a result of changes in the mass of interneurons in the brainstem reticular system.

Nonetheless, this is far from the whole story. Hans Vale and others elicited the OR of cats by direct electrical stimulation of the cerebral cortex. Their animals were not anesthetized and were unrestrained. The OR produced in this way could not be distinguished from that resulting from stimulation through the external senses. Repeated stimulation resulted in habituation, although the method bypassed the RAS. Stimulation of the external senses, for example by switching on a light, produced the usual dishabituation. Hence in this case habituation depended, evidently, on changes in cortical synapses.

The electrical stimulation also sometimes resulted in other responses, such as movement of a forelimb and contraction of the muscles of the back and neck. These, too, habituated. From their findings Vale and his colleagues suggest a further implication: It has been suggested that habituation by a mammal always involves recognition of a particular pattern of stimulation of the external senses. But in the experiments by Vale, the external senses were not involved. Hence the underlying changes in the brain were in this case evidently due to increasing refractoriness of synapses as a result of repeated stimulation.

5.2.3 The Concept of Habituation

In 5.2 above, habituation was provisionally defined as the loss or waning of a response as a result of repeated stimulation. We now see that the phenomena covered by that definition are inconveniently diverse. Taken literally (as any definition must be), it includes two kinds of change that are better analyzed separately—and are indeed usually treated as part of physiology. The first is a decrement in behavior resulting from muscular fatigue, that is, exhaustion of the substances, such as hexoses, required for muscular contraction. The second, sensory "adaptation", is a result of continuous or repetitive stimulation, and it, too, can lead to a change in behavior. (See the account of feeding by blowflies in 4.5.1.2.)

If we omit the effects of muscular fatigue and of sensory adaptation, we are left with behavioral changes that depend on a decline in activity within the nervous system itself. But, once again, a qualification is desirable. If there were a decline in an animal's responsiveness to all stimuli (as a result of repeated stimulation), that would be a kind of change distinct from those described in the preceding pages. The examples already given are stimulus specific: that is, they leave responses to other stimulation unimpaired. Correspondingly, they are subject to dishabituation by stimulation of another sort. Hence a convenient definition of habituation is: a stimulus-specific decline in a response, resulting from the effect of repeated stimulation on the central nervous system.

The object of paying so much attention to definition is, as usual, to avoid confusion and failure to communicate. One should always view with suspicion writings that refer to "true habituation", unless it has been made quite clear what the writer means by "habituation" unqualified. Given an unambiguous definition, phenomena are perhaps found that resemble habituation but do not fall under the definition. Still more suspicion should be evoked by talk of the "essence" of habituation: such an expression usually indicates a disregard of the need for clarity. These principles apply, of course, quite generally.

We may now perhaps accept that the term habituation (as defined) refers to a fairly distinct set of phenomena. One reason for considering these phenomena together is that the function of habituation is easily surmised. If an animal repeatedly responds to some harmless stimulus, such as a shadow, by withdrawal, the time available for essential activity, such as eating, may be excessively reduced. Moreover, sudden movements that involve most of the muscles exact a heavy cost in energy expenditure. We make the assumption (though we cannot test it) that the rate at which habituation occurs is a product of natural selection, and that it represents a balance between security on the one hand and carrying out essential activities on the other.

Statements on the present survival value of behavior are, however, testable. For example, animals that have a withdrawal response could be given a stimulant. What would be the effect on a bristle worm or a bivalve mollusk of keeping it in a state of continual agitation? As far as I know, such experiments have not yet been attempted, perhaps because the results would be difficult to interpret.

5.3 SENSITIZATION

5.3.1 Increased Responsiveness

The obverse of habituation is sensitization, defined as a persistent increase in responsiveness due to repeated stimulation (reviewed by R. A. Hinde, 1970). Here are some examples.

If the dorsal skin of a frog is gently touched with a bristle, the frog responds by wiping the stimulated area with a hind limb (figure 5-19). Frogs,

FIGURE 5-19 The wiping reflex of a frog, *Rana esculenta*. (Courtesy L. Franzisket)

Rana pipiens, were stimulated in this way 100 times on each of 12 successive days (D. P. Kimble and R. S. Ray). The bristles used and the force with which they were applied were standardized. When frogs were stimulated on each occasion at exactly the same spot on the skin, there was a decline in the response over days (figure 5-20)—a typical case of rather long-term habituation.

Frogs of a second group were similarly stimulated except that the point of contact varied. This procedure resulted, not in a declining response, but in an increase (figure 5-20). Evidently, in this case, habituation requires a highly specific input. When the input is more varied, the result suggests that an opposite process of central facilitation predominates.

FIGURE 5-20   Wiping reflex of frogs, *Rana pipiens.* The lower curve illustrates habituation: it resulted from standardized and repeated stimulation at exactly the same spot on the skin. The upper curve illustrates sensitization: in this case the point of contact varied. (After D. P. Kimble & R. S. Ray, 1966)

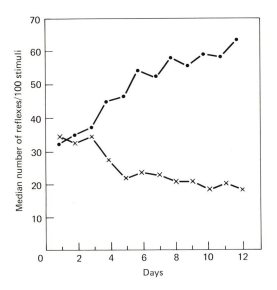

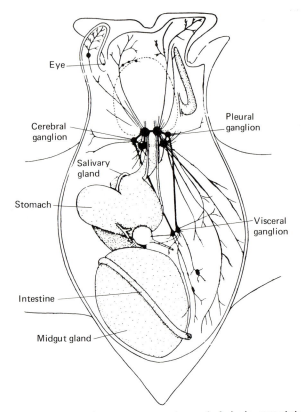

FIGURE 5-21   The nervous system of *Aplysia punctata* from above. Not all the nerves are shown on both sides. (After T. H. Bullock & G. A. Horridge, 1965)

Another instance comes from the work of Dethier on blowflies (4.5.1.2). In that case, however, not only were different sense organs (sensilla) stimulated, but two substances were used, water and sugar.

An attentive reader will have realized that dishabituation (5.2.1.1) falls in the same general category as the preceding examples: in all instances, stimulation increases responsiveness. Usually, it is possible only to *assume* that central facilitation is responsible; but there is the beginning of neuro-

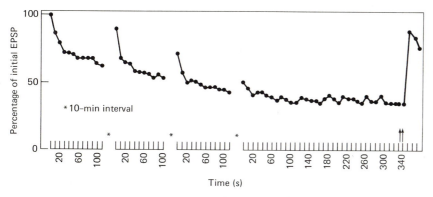

FIGURE 5-22 Findings from an experiment on *Aplysia.* Stimulation of a sensory pathway evokes an excitatory postsynaptic potential (EPSP) in motor neurons. Habituation of the EPSP, on repeated stimulation, is shown, and its partial recovery after 10 min rest. On the right the two arrows indicate more vigorous stimulation of a sensory nerve which, too, leads to recovery of the EPSP. (After J. Bruner & L. Tauc, 1966)

physiological analysis. W. J. Davis reviews findings on gill withdrawal of the sea hare, *Aplysia,* in response to stimulation of the mantle. The visceral ganglion (figure 5-21) has two large motor neurons, stimulation of which leads to withdrawal of the gill. These neurons receive inputs both from the posterior siphon (by the siphon nerve) and from an anterior gland (by the brachial nerve). Stimulation of one of these nerves results in an excitatory postsynaptic potential (EPSP) in the motor neurons. The EPSP declines with repeated stimulation; but if the nerve from the cerebral ganglia to the abdominal ganglion is stimulated electrically, the EPSP is restored (figure 5-22). Moreover, if the EPSP has not declined, this extra stimulation increases the amplitude of the EPSP to a still higher level. The effects of electrical stimulation are, in fact, a neurophysiological counterpart of sensitization.

5.3.2 Pseudoconditioning

Sensitization, then, may be regarded as the behavioral expression of increased responsiveness in the nervous system. But it is also important in other ways. S. M. Evans (1966a,b) has studied the polychaete, *Nereis diversicolor,* one of the bristle worms

that live on the seashore in tubes made in sand or mud (figure 5-23). In the laboratory, the worms enter any narrow channel, such as one made by two blocks of Perspex. Whenever a worm enters, it always swims out of the other end, even after many repetitions. Evans "trained" worms by applying a shock each time the exit of the channel was reached. The worms so treated slowed their movements, and

FIGURE 5-23 *Perinereis novaehollandiae,* a polychaete worm that closely resembles those used for experiments on sensitization or pseudoconditioning (next two figures). (I. A. Fox)

sometimes even stopped entering the channel. They had evidently learnt to avoid the shock. Such "learning" is commonly described as resulting from the association of a particular action (in this case entering a channel) and a consequence (in this case receiving a shock). But Evans also shocked some worms after they had left the passage, and others before they had the opportunity to enter it. The result was exactly the same: the worms slowed down and tended not to enter the channel (figure 5-24).

Similarly, Evans used shock to evoke the withdrawal response (mediated by the giant fiber system). On a series of occasions, he preceded the shock by a sudden decrease in illumination. The question asked was whether the animals would learn to associate the change in lighting with the unpleasant stimulus. The worms did indeed progres-

sively increase their response to light-off; but, as before, a similar increase occurred even when the shocks were applied, not at the time of the change in lighting, but between trials. When there was no shock at all, the effect of light-off gradually diminished—a typical case of habituation (figure 5-25). Evidently, the change in behavior is independent of any association in time between the unpleasant stimulus and the animal's movements in relation to the passageway. It is therefore called *pseudoconditioning*.

M. J. & J. Wells (1971) give another example from experiments on *Physa acuta*. These freshwater snails spend much time moving about; and their transparent shells allow observation even of the contracted animal. Withdrawal can be provoked by a mild electric shock. Such shocks were preceded by light-off or by mechanical disturbance—a "thump" (S_1). After a number of such trials, the S_1 in each case evoked withdrawal. It seemed that the snails had learnt to associate the S_1 with shock. But giving a series of shocks alone produced the same effect, that is, withdrawal at light-off or vibration. The change in behavior was therefore an example of sensitization.

Stimulation often produces a general change in responsiveness rather than an alteration in the response to a particular stimulus. G. A. Kimble (1961) reviews experiments in which mammals are exposed to a stimulus, such as a loud noise, which induces agitated behavior. An animal so treated may become more responsive to other stimuli, of diverse kinds, that evoke avoidance, withdrawal, or some kind of startle response. W. F. Grether describes the effects of sudden, explosive noises on rhesus monkeys, *Macaca mulatta*. Exposure to such violent stimuli leads to a response to the mild stimulus of a bell, even when the loud noise has not been paired with the bell. There is

FIGURE 5-24 Findings from experiments by S. M. Evans on *Nereis diversicolor*. The apparatus is shown diagrammatically above. If the worms were shocked in the channel, their readiness to enter it diminished. But the same result was obtained if they were shocked, not in the channel, but some seconds before or after entering it. Hence the change in behavior is not a result of associating shock with a particular situation but falls in the category of pseudoconditioning. (After G. Razran, 1971)

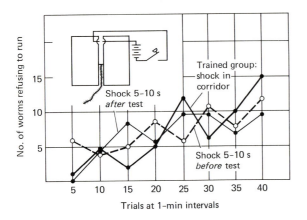

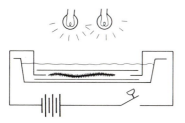

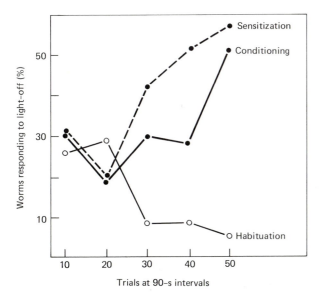

FIGURE 5-25 Findings from further experiments on *Nereis diversicolor.* (See figure 5-24.) The apparatus is shown diagrammatically above. In one kind of experiment there was a sudden dimming of the light only: the worms at first responded by contracting, but on repetition the response diminished (habituation). In other experiments the dimming was followed by a shock: this led to an increase in the proportion of worms that responded to light-off by contracting. But a similar change resulted from administering shocks between trials of the effect of dimming. Hence the effect of the shocks is an example of pseudoconditioning or sensitization. (After G. Razran, 1971)

evidently, in such a case, a nonspecific change in the central nervous system which might be called heightened arousal.

The term pseudoconditioning, then, is the name given to sensitization that can be mistaken for a specific effect of training. Confusion is most likely to occur when the effects of stimulation last for many hours. Hence some writers prefer to treat short-term sensitization and pseudoconditioning as distinct phenomena. Pseudoconditioning was initially studied by workers concerned with the ways in which animals develop new, adaptive habits. In ordinary terms, they were interested in how animals learn to find what they need and to avoid danger. Such adaptation of behavior must be related to specific stimuli, favorable or unfavorable. A general, undiscriminating excitability is a different kind of phenomenon. Hence for some types of experiment it is essential to control for sensitization. The work on polychaetes and snails, cited above, provides particularly clear examples.

Most, perhaps all, nervous systems can display both increases and decreases of response as a result of repeated stimulation (M. J. Wells, 1975). We may guess that such simple variations in function represent an early stage in the evolution of nervous tissue. What we colloquially call learning or intelligence—we suppose—grew gradually on that foundation.

5.4 THE PROBLEM OF THE PROTOZOA

Intermittently, throughout this century, the question has been asked: "Can Protozoa learn?" A suitable response to such a question might be: "Learn what?" For example, P. B. Applewhite, in an account of the behavior of protozoans and rotifers writes: "Habituation . . . can be considered to be a form of learning if fatigue, injury and local sensory adaptation can be ruled out." Such a proposition states clearly only what learning is *not*. In this section, I describe experiments on the behavioral plasticity of Protozoa (reviewed by W. C. Corning & R. VonBurg). The general question asked is whether Protozoa adapt their behavior to circumstances and, if so, in what ways.

5.4.1 Habituation?

The foundation of our knowledge of protozoan behavior is the work of H. S. Jennings (1906).

Jennings studied sessile ciliates such as *Stentor* (figure 5-26). A fine jet of water may be used to induce contraction. After about 30 s, the animal extends again; and, if the stimulation is now repeated, withdrawal may not occur. The refractory state persists for some hours. If, however, a different or stronger stimulation is applied to a refractory animal, the animal contracts; hence the failure to contract is not a result of a general inability to do so: that is, failure is not due to fatigue.

More recent experiments on *Stentor,* and on other protozoans, have been reviewed by T. C. Hamilton, and by E. M. Eisenstein and his col-

FIGURE 5-26   The sessile ciliate, *Stentor.* (P. S. Tice)

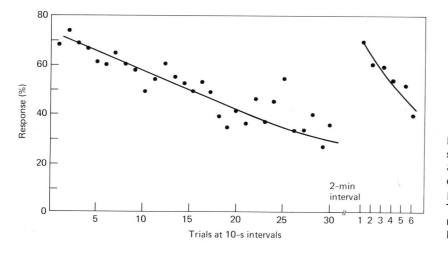

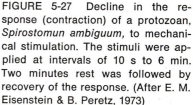

FIGURE 5-27 Decline in the response (contraction) of a protozoan, *Spirostomun ambiguum,* to mechanical stimulation. The stimuli were applied at intervals of 10 s to 6 min. Two minutes rest was followed by recovery of the response. (After E. M. Eisenstein & B. Peretz, 1973)

leagues. Mechanical stimulation of *Stentor,* repeated at intervals of 1 min, leads to disappearance of the withdrawal response after about 60 trials; but stimulation by light still induces contraction. Similarly, repeated exposure to a change of illumination results in loss of the response, but the response is still made if the animal is mechanically stimulated.

The modern workers have also used *Spirostomum,* another large ciliate protozoan that contracts when disturbed. Again, vibration usually, but not always, causes contraction. The stimulation can be applied mechanically with precise regularity. The individuals that contract four or five times during the first five stimulations thereafter tend to lose the response; but others do not contract at first, and these tend to "facilitate"—that is, to respond increasingly after further repeated stimulations. This anomaly resembles the findings, described above (figure 5-20) on the wiping response of frogs. Figure 5-27 illustrates some features of the loss of response of this protozoan.

When *Spirostomum* collides with an obstacle, it reverses its ciliary beat and swims backwards. This "avoiding reaction", originally described by Jennings, is classified as a klinokinesis (2.2.4.2). But, unlike many kineses and taxes, its performance declines on repetition. The decline, as Hamilton shows, is in the duration and distance covered during each avoiding response: the rate of swimming is unaltered. The decrement in the response is observed over only four to five trials, and is therefore much quicker than the decrement in contraction described in the preceding paragraph. Presumably the internal processes differ.

The physiology of these changes in behavior is unknown. For each response, receptor and effector are within a single cell; and the analog of conducting tissue (nerve cells) is in the same mass of cytoplasm. Unicellular animals cannot undergo habituation, as it is defined above, for the definition applies only to animals with a nervous system. Given the definition, it would be logically unacceptable to say that Protozoa habituate. Nonetheless, some species undergo changes of behavior which parallel with some exactness the habituation of Metazoa. Perhaps we should name such changes protohabituation.

5.4.2 The Question of Habit Formation

Protozoa, then, are certainly capable of an adaptive loss of responsiveness. A more difficult question is whether they can develop new, adaptive habits.

If *Paramecium* is drawn up into a capillary tube so fine that it cannot easily turn round and swim back, it eventually escapes by means of a bodily contortion. If it is repeatedly trapped in this way, its performance improves: that is, the time taken to escape declines. This observation has been repeated on several occasions. The problem is to interpret it.

In ordinary language, the animal has, as a result of experience, learnt to escape more quickly. P. B. Applewhite & F. T. Gardner repeated the experiment, but found the change in behavior to be preventable. First, the tubes were specially cleaned before use; and second the protozoans were repeatedly drawn up into a tube and expelled before the experiment. Such findings suggest two possibilities. First, the mechanical properties of the animal, especially of the cuticle, may have altered (by unknown means) during movement in the capillary tube. Second, the environment in the tube may, in the usual type of experiment, alter as the experiment proceeds. Such an environmental change could influence the behavior of the animal.

The other important example is the work of Beatrice Gelber. If a platinum wire is lowered into a culture of *Paramecium,* some attach themselves to the wire. In experiments, the protozoans were rewarded for attaching themselves in this way. *Paramecium* eats bacteria. The wire was therefore baited with *Aerobacter aerogenes.* Each culture of

Paramecium was then exposed to the wire on 40 successive occasions, but with bacteria on the wire only on every third occasion. The interval between exposures to the wire was 25 s. Controls were similarly exposed to a platinum wire, but for them there were no bacteria. Exposure to the wire with bacteria resulted in a progressive increase in the number of the protozoans on or near the wire. If such "trained" protozoans were then exposed to the wire on a number of occasions without bacteria, the number clinging to the wire decreased. Here is an analog of *extinction* (discussed in the next section of this chapter and in the next chapter). There was some recovery from extinction if a culture were tested 2 h later. Finally, the altered behavior persisted for a total of at least 10 h.

These findings, with their parallels to the habit formation of animals with central nervous systems, were rather sensational. But, as D. D. Jensen has shown, they are not easy to interpret. *Paramecium* clings more to objects in its environment, and also groups together, as the acidity of the environment increases. One possibility is of an increase in the acidity of the region around the bacteria: the latter produce carbon dioxide, and so do the protozoans themselves as they accumulate on or near the wire.

It is uncertain whether the accumulation of carbon dioxide is the full explanation of Gelber's findings. In fact, "protohabituation" excepted, the question whether Protozoa can "learn"—and, if so, in what sense—remains open.

5.5 CONDITIONAL REFLEXES

5.5.1 The Classical Experiments

5.5.1.1 Procedure: If lemon juice is placed on the tongue of a mammal, the rate of secretion of saliva is greatly increased. This is a simple reflex (5.1.3). In contrast, the sound of a doorbell (for example) does not ordinarily induce salivation. It can, however, do so, if the bell is rung, on a number of occasions, shortly before the salivary reflex is evoked. An observation of this kind led I. P. Pavlov (1849–1936) to his celebrated researches (published in English in 1928), at the beginning of the 20th century, on conditional reflexes (CRs). (The commonly used "conditioned" is not only a mistranslation, but is also often used casually where "trained" would be appropriate.) His work on behavior depended on a strictly defined and limited experimental procedure: its main feature was evocation of a reflex response by a stimulus that had not previously done so (reviewed by G. A. Kimble 1961, 1967).

Pavlov was the principal founder of our knowledge of salivation and the secretions of the stomach glands. In his experiments on digestion he used

dogs; and an experimental animal was often seen to begin to produce digestive secretions *before* it ate the food. In colloquial terms, the dog had learned to associate food in the mouth with some feature of the experimental situation. Pavlov called this "psychic" secretion, but he emphasized that it was a consequence of the activity of the brain.

In his most prominent experiments, he concentrated on measuring the rate of salivation. The experimental animal was made to stand in a harness on a table, with a fistula in the duct of one of the salivary glands. W. G. Reese & R. A. Dykman describe the long and laborious preparation of a dog for such an experiment: many months may be taken in accustoming the animal to the experimenters and situation. Moreover, once the dog is in place and harnessed, disturbance by irrelevant stimuli must be prevented. Pavlov's biographer, B. P. Babkin,

FIGURE 5-28 Dog in a sound-insulated room, behind one-way glass, harnessed for study of conditional reflexes. (Courtesy Jackson Memorial Laboratory)

describes how, in early experiments, assistants would establish a conditional reflex and invite the professor to see it; but as soon as Pavlov arrived, the dog would fail to salivate. Later, therefore, the dog was always behind a screen; and in modern laboratories the animal is usually in a sound proof room (figure 5-28).

In a typical experiment, the dog is first kept without food for some hours. When the animal is standing passively, harnessed on the table, a plate bearing powdered food is presented. The food is the *unconditional stimulus*. The dog, unsurprisingly, takes the food, chews, salivates, and swallows.

If, when the dog is installed, a buzzer is sounded, the dog performs the orienting response (OR) already described (5.2.2.2): the ears are pricked, the head is turned, the eyes move, and the pupils dilate; in addition, the heart and respiration rates change (reviewed by D. C. Raskin). The strange sound is the *conditional stimulus*. On hearing it, the animal is made ready to respond rapidly to whatever happens next. In the classical experiment, the food is offered a few seconds later and is duly eaten. This sequence is repeated on a number of occasions. To describe the findings from such experiments, the symbols and names below are often used.

Symbol	Name	Examples
S_1	conditional stimulus (CS)	sound of buzzer; light on
S_2	unconditional stimulus (UNCS)	food in mouth; sudden noise
R_1	unconditional response (UNCR)	eating; eyeblink
R_2	conditional response (CR)	salivation; eyeblink

We now turn to the consequences of such training. One is that the OR declines (habituation).

Sometimes it disappears after a few trials, but there is much individual variation. The decline in the visible OR is accompanied by a return of the heart and respiratory rates to normal.

The main consequence of training is a tendency for salivation to occur, in increasing amounts, before the food arrives. This, the *conditional reflex* or R_2, may properly be called a new response: it is not the original response (eating), but only a component of it; and its relationship in time to the arrival of food has changed: it is anticipatory. Its anticipatory quality has been brought out in Russian experiments, described by N. E. Miller (1961), which required the simultaneous presentation of two dishes. A dog is trained to salivate to a sound, by presenting it with meat on one of the dishes. It is separately trained to salivate to light-on, by giving it bread on the second dish. The fully trained dog is then presented with bread on the meat dish. Like a diner offered claret with fish, the dog displays disturbed behavior: the conditional salivation fails, and the animal looks from one dish to the other.

Another new feature of R_2 is its relationship to the intensity of S_1: if S_1 is increased or decreased, the response diminishes or disappears. There is *discrimination* of the intensity of the stimulus (figure 5-29). In contrast, the magnitude of an unconditional response is, within limits, proportional to the intensity of the stimulus.

5.5.1.2 Limitations: Pavlov's method hardly allows the animal any activity. What is recorded is a single aspect of its total behavior. From the behavioral repertoire of the experimental animal only existing reflexes can be used. As a rule, when the subject is a mammal, the response is mediated by the autonomic nervous system: it is either glandular or a movement produced by smooth or cardiac

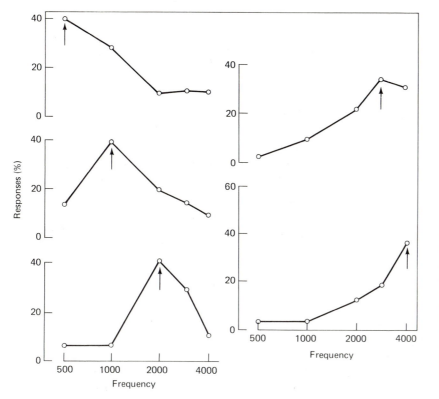

FIGURE 5-29 The conditional eyelid response of rabbits was evoked by sounding a tone before administering an electric shock. Five groups of rabbits were studied, each trained with a tone of different frequency from the others; the frequencies are shown by the arrows. The graphs give probabilities of responding to the sounding of tones of various frequencies. (After S. Siegel and others, 1968)

muscle. Correspondingly, descriptions of the experiments often disregard what the animal does, and give only the record of secretion rates or of muscular contraction.

The prolonged process of training a dog to play its part is mentioned above. K. Zener has described what dogs do during an experiment, when the conditional stimulus (S_1) is the sound of a bell. In the early stages, when the bell rings, the dog turns quickly and points toward the bell; but when the food arrives the dog at once lowers its head, takes the food, and eats with its head over the plate. When the dog has been trained, its behavior during the delay between S_1 and S_2 varies. Often, there is no evidence of attention to the bell (especially if the dog has been fasted for many hours). But some dogs look at the bell and then at the source of food, or even oscillate between the two. Other individual variation is in bodily orientation—which includes adjustment for convenient eating from the dish. Restless movements such as stamping are nearly always seen. Chewing and licking occur sometimes. Zener remarks that, except for the component of salivary secretion, the conditional behavior is not the same as the original unconditional response.

If the dog is not restrained, its conduct becomes more complex and more familiar: when S_1 occurs, the animal approaches the food dish and waits as if expecting food.

5.5.1.3 General Features of Habit Formation:
Despite its restricted scope, the conditional reflex
includes important general features of habit formation.

1. A formal account of the conditional reflex, in
terms of S_1 and S_2, disregards the need to pay attention to the total sensory input. We saw above
that a CR is likely to fail if the surrounding circumstances are altered. To achieve a reliable response, the experimental conditions must be the
same during both training and subsequent testing.
Failure of the response on presentation of an unfamiliar stimulus Pavlov called *external inhibition:*
the OR overrides the CR.

2. The second principle concerns the animal's
internal state, and is illustrated in the previous
chapter: in 4.3 I describe how animals can develop
new habits and so maintain an eccritic temperature; and in 4.5.2 I give instances of habits developed in relation to feeding. In the first example,
a particular skin temperature is a *reward;* in the
second, the reward is food (in the mouth). For
food to be a reward, the animal must have been
fasted beforehand. In 4.5.4 I mention the question
whether it is helpful to talk of "hunger" or "hunger
drive" in this context. But, whatever terminology
we use, in experiments on conditional reflexes the
animal is often in a state of deficit (not always of
food), and the reward matches the deficit.

3. The CR is lost if the conditional stimulus
(reward) is repeatedly presented, over a short period, without the unconditional stimulus or reward.
The loss was originally called "internal inhibition";
but it is now usually, though less appropriately,
named *extinction*. Such a change is to be expected
if one considers the function of the CR: it is no
use salivating if there is no food. Extinction of the
salivary response (and of many other CRs) is a
corollary of the relationship between the animal's
internal state and the reward.

Extinction is not the same as forgetting: the latter is a gradual loss with lack of practice. Suppose
a CR to be extinguished, in the manner described,
on one day. What happens if the animal is exposed
to the experimental situation (without reward)
after a night's rest? In fact, the response reappears:
in the classical kinds of experiment, S_1 evokes almost as much salivation as it did before extinction
occurred. Evidently, extinction is not a simple un-
doing of the changes in the nervous system that
underlie CR formation. The CR must be due to
one set of neural processes, and extinction to another.

4. Not all simple habits depend on reward: some
enable an animal to *avoid* stimulation. A stimulus
that makes an animal withdraw, or that it tends to
avoid, is called *aversive*. Examples are given above
(3.5.1) of birds learning to avoid toxic prey and
also similar harmless species. Here we are concerned with reflex responses observed in the laboratory.

H. S. Liddell studied a response of the skeletal
musculature, that is, one mediated by the "voluntary" nervous system. His animals were sheep,
Ovis. S_1 was the sound of a metronome set to tick
at one beat a second for 5 s; S_2 was an electric
shock delivered by electrodes on the left foreleg.
The shock made the sheep (harnessed as usual)
raise its foreleg; at the same time respiration deep-
ened and became irregular. Initially the metronome
had no obvious effect on the sheep; but, after 11
trials, the sound alone induced flexion of the leg
and the accompanying change in respiration.

5.5.1.4 Experimental Neurosis: The clearest behavioral indication of the nonmechanical character of CRs is experimental neurosis (reviewed

by P. L. Broadhurst), a disruption of behavior which, too, was first described by Pavlov. Pavlov upset the behavior of some of his dogs by presenting them with confusing stimuli. Consider, for example, a dog trained to expect food at the sound of a tone. The animal is next trained not to salivate at the sound of a different note. The experimenter now, on separate occasions, sounds tones that are closer and closer together on the musical scale, until they are difficult to distinguish. Eventually, in this sort of situation, the animal, instead of readily running to the experimental room, jumping on the table, and patiently submitting to the harness, rebels: it struggles when brought out for experiment; it howls, and displays other signs of agitation; and, even when no experiments are being done, its behavior may be seriously disturbed. The form of the disturbance is characteristic of individual animals: some become very inactive (inhibited) and cower in a corner; others become excessively active and continually agitated. These upsets can be remedied, if at all, only by patient and prolonged retraining.

5.5.2 The Human Species

5.5.2.1 Adults:
A question that has aroused much interest concerns the scope of CRs in human conduct. B. W. Feather describes findings on 37 undergraduates. The subjects were treated in much the manner of Pavlov's dogs: S_1 was a tone of 0.7 kHz sounded for 8 s; S_2 was lemon juice in the mouth. The lemon juice was squirted in after the tone had been on for 6 s. Saliva was carefully collected to give an accurate record of the rate of secretion. There was a control group to test for sensitization: they experienced both S_1 and S_2, but S_2 never occurred less than 60 s after S_1. The procedure fitted the working week: on four successive days each subject had six acquisition trials; on the

fifth day there were two further acquisition trials, and six extinction trials. In the last, the subjects received no lemon juice. A conditional response of salivation was duly established, but extinction was rapid. There was no clear relationship to swallowing; hence the findings resembled those with dogs, in that the CR represented only part of the total original response.

G. Razran (1961) has described experiments which have evidently arisen from the special interest in CRs displayed by Russian physiologists. As an example, three patients who, for clinical reasons, had tubes in their bladders, were equipped with manometers that recorded the pressure of urine. They could observe the manometer readings, and were asked to report when they felt the need to urinate. They therefore became accustomed to needing to pass urine (through the fistula constructed by the surgeon) when a certain reading was reached. After this training, the experimenter made the manometer give false readings. As a result the patients reported the urge to urinate when manometer readings were high, but the true bladder pressure was low. If the manometer showed a low reading, they even failed to report an urge when they should have done so. Hence the readings had become conditional stimuli for contraction of the bladder muscle.

Experiments on healthy volunteers have shown how vasomotor responses can be "conditioned". Each subject swallowed an inflatable gastric tube. The stomach could then be heated or cooled internally by passing in water of a suitable temperature. When the stomach was heated, the blood vessels of the arm dilated; correspondingly, cooling caused vasoconstriction. In some experiments a flashing light was switched on, and cold water then poured in. After a series of such experiences, the light alone was followed by vasoconstriction, although it normally had no such effect. It had become a conditional stimulus for the vascular response.

In the work by Feather described above, much individual variation was found. The people who took part fell into two groups, high salivators and low salivators. Only the high salivators developed CRs. On the other hand, Feather remarks that "voluntary and attitudinal variables" had little influence on performance. In other words, there was no evidence of an important effect of what the subjetcs said or thought about the experiment.

Such "irrelevant" influences do, however, exist. They may be illustrated from experiments on the eyeblink. A number of sudden stimuli, such as a loud noise, reliably elicit a brief closing of the eyes. The stimulus most used by experimenters is a puff of air directed at the face. Figure 5-30 shows how

FIGURE 5-30 The influence of the subject's attitude on the development of a conditional response. People were exposed to a conditional stimulus (light-on), followed by an unconditional stimulus for blinking the eyes (a puff of air on the face). The response curves show the effects of giving different preliminary instructions. (After M. F. Nicholls & G. A. Kimble, 1964)

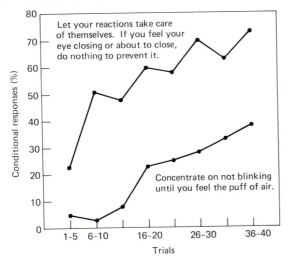

the blink can be evoked by a stimulus, the switching on of a light, which did not evoke it at first, and it illustrates how the instructions given by the experimenter can influence the outcome. Other, more detailed studies are described by G. A. Kimble (1961). Russian psychologists use the expression "second signaling system" to refer to language. Whatever terms we use, the effects of social communication clearly take us right away from the simplicities of Pavlov's original design.

5.5.3 Invertebrates

If CRs can be demonstrated in both dogs and people, one might suppose it would be easy to do the same with invertebrates. In fact, however, there are severe problems of controls in all such experiments.

The response studied is usually contraction or some other kind of withdrawal; S_1 may be mechanical (perhaps, a vibration), but often it is electric shock—a rare phenomenon in natural conditions. The primary feature of the experiments is the attempt to evoke withdrawal by a stimulus that initially does not have this effect; and the procedure, as in the classical experiments, is to present such a "neutral" stimulus (S_1) shortly before an unconditional stimulus which does.

J. V. Haralson and others have studied the withdrawal (folding of the oral disc) of a sea anemone, *Cribrina xanthogrammica* (Coelenterata Anthozoa). These animals have only a nerve net (5.1.2.2). Electric shock causes withdrawal. The authors state that light-on can be made to have the same effect, by coupling it with shock. To justify this conclusion a number of controlled experiments were needed. Perhaps, for example, repeated exposure to light-on alone would have produced the same effect (sensitization, 5.3): similarly, repeated exposure to shock could have increased the response to light, without pairing the two stimuli. A third type of control was to present shock and light at random intervals, instead of regularly paired. None of these had the same effect as pairing the stimuli. A further finding concerns the *latency,* that is, the interval between stimulus and response: the latency of the CR was nearly twice as long as that of the unconditional withdrawal. Such a finding supports a comment by N. B. Rushforth. He quotes a remark, made in 1952, to the effect that we are nearer a complete analysis of the structural units on which coelenterate behavior is based than that of any other animals; and he adds, "The behavioral simplicity of these animals has proved to be more apparent than real, for today, twenty years later, we seem further from a complete analysis than was previously expected."

The Turbellaria, or flatworms, too, have caused much debate (reviewed by W. C. Corning & S. Kelly). It has been said that they can learn simple tasks, and that the physiological changes which underlie the altered behavior are present in all parts of the body. Planarians have notable powers of regeneration. Cut one into several parts, and the result may eventually be the same number of complete, if at first smaller worms. It is said that if the original worm has been trained, the results of the training are still evident in each regenerating portion—even one from the back end.

Research on this question has attracted agreeably unconventional people to it. Some have produced a journal, *The Worm-Runners' Digest,* from which I take the following stanza:

> Causally or randomly
> Thoughts re-grow rapidly
> My anterior
> Is not superior
> Nor my posterior
> At all inferior.

It has even been said that a planarian which eats a portion of a conspecific can then display the "learning" previously acquired by its prey (for example, R. A. Westerman). The intellectual advantages of cannibalism for these (or any other) animals have not been satisfactorily established (reviewed by M. J. Wells, 1974); but planarians can at least develop CRs. P. B. Applewhite & H. J. Morowitz describe observations on *Stenostomum.* They used a very brief electric shock, which caused the animal to stop moving. In the experiments, immediately before each shock, a light was switched on for 5 s. The pairing of S_1 and S_2 was repeated every 30 s. After about 27 such pairings, the animals reliably stopped moving when the light was switched on, although the light had had no such effect before. There were controls for sensitization: one group was exposed only to the light, and another to the shock. Neither led to the appearance of a response to the light.

A parallel investigation of an earthworm, *Lumbricus terrestris,* by S. C. Ratner & K. R. Miller, had the merit of using as S_2 a stimulus (vibration) that would be important to the animal in natural conditions. It led to similar findings.

Yet a further study has been made by P. B. Applewhite & H. J. Morowitz (1966) of a crustacean, the freshwater ostracod, *Cyclocypris forbesi.* The length of this animal, 0.6 mm, leaves little room for a complex nervous system, but allows observations to be made in a cube of only 2 mm side. A light was switched on for 5 s; during the last second, as with the planarians, a 3-volt shock lasting 100 ms was given. On experiencing this (the unconditional stimulus), the animal stopped swimming and closed its shell. The procedure was repeated every 2 min. After about 13 experiences the animals closed their shells as soon as the light went on. Extinction was observed when the light was repeatedly switched on once a minute without shock. After about five such repetitions, the animal stopped responding. Controls for sensitization were the same as those for the preceding experiments.

The arthropods whose behavior has been most studied are of course the insects; and in the next chapter there is much to say about their abilities. Insects have, however, sometimes been said not to develop CRs. The work of M. C. Nelson on the blowfly, *Phormia regina,* is an exception (4.5.1). She observed several hundred flies from a stock that had been bred in the laboratory for 22 years. They were therefore domesticated flies, and must have been different genetically from the original wild population (16.1.2.4). Contact of sugar solution with the mouthparts makes a fly extend its proboscis (4.5.1.2). In Nelson's experiments these were S_2 and R_1, respectively. S_1 consisted of contact of the tarsi with water and then with salt solution. The latter, as we know, is usually an aversive stimulus. When this double stimulus was applied shortly before S_2, some of the flies began to extend the proboscis in response to S_1 alone. There was great individual variation: only about 39% of the flies were "good learners".

The variation observed by Nelson may have been genetically determined. In further experiments laboratory populations of *P. regina* were selected, over many generations, either for ability to develop a CR ("good learners" or "bright"), or—on another line—for inability ("poor learners" or "dull"). There was a rapid improvement, over generations, in the first line, and a decrement in "conditionability" in the line selected for dullness (J. Hirsch & L. A. McCauley; T. R. McGuire & J. Hirsch). Hence there must have been considerable genetical variation that influenced the observed differences of behavior in this stock of blowflies.

A last example comes from the work of G. J. Mpitsos & S. D. Collins on *Pleurobranchia californica* (figure 5-31)—another large marine mollusk.

This animal has a body weight of around 150 g, and is a voracious carnivore. G. P. Mpitsos & W. J. Davis had already been able to train these animals to perform feeding movements in response to a tactile stimulus. Controls showed the new habit not to be a result of sensitization. The later work is of especial interest because the animals were trained to respond to food, of a kind which normally evoked approach and eating, as an aversive stimulus; this was done by giving them an electric shock when they fed. Again, there were controls for sensitization. Another notable feature was the timing of the development of the new response. The effect of the treatment was at a maximum 12 h after the end of training. Such delay in the effects of training, or *consolidation,* has been more fully described in the behavior of mammals. Evidently the training induces a process that continues after training has stopped. The physiology is, however, not known.

5.5.4 The Significance of the Conditional Reflex

The expression "conditioned reflex" has passed into colloquial speech. In reference to human behavior it commonly means a habit performed without thought—mechanically. It is still possible to find people who assume that all "learning" is in some sense a matter of acquiring such responses. The concept, perhaps not clearly acknowledged, is of a mind or brain functioning like one of the familiar man-made machines.

Such a concept, though grossly misleading, is even to be found in writings in the behavioral sciences. I. Kohler, in a paper entitled "Pavlov and his dog", gives an account of a quite simple electrical system that, according to the author, can develop a conditional reflex. The secretion of saliva

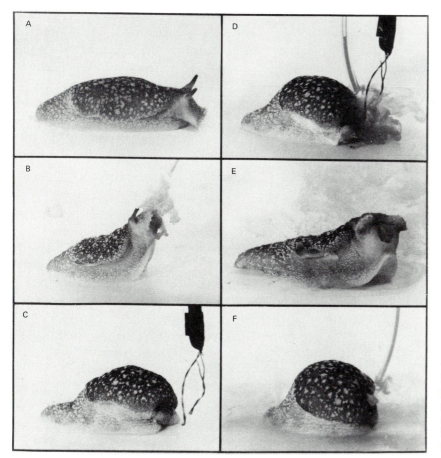

FIGURE 5-31 A carnivorous marine mollusk, *Pleurobranchia californica*, is shown in A. In B it is offered food that it readily accepts. The other illustrations in the sequence show how it is shocked on presentation of such food; eventually, as in F, it contracts when food is presented, instead of eating it. (Courtesy G. J. Mpitsos)

is represented by the shining of a light; the unconditional stimulus is the closing of a switch; the conditional stimulus is the ringing of a bell. As a result of the repeated pairing of these two events, the light eventually comes to switch on at the sound of the bell alone. The "memory store" is represented by a condenser; and, since the charge is gradually lost in the absence of practice, the system also displays "forgetting".

The author, although he grants that his "artificial dog" is more stupid than a real one, states that the eyeblink of man can be interpreted in terms of a system precisely analogous to his electrical gadget.

He also states: "actions of . . . this kind require neither mind nor soul". There are, however, more prosaic matters overlooked in this light-hearted paper. They include the orienting response and the accompanying internal arousal; the fact that R_2 differs from R_1; and many others, including the possibility of external inhibition. The construction of models (now often consisting of computer programs), as D. J. McFarland (1974) shows, can help in the design of hypotheses about behavior and its physiological substrate. But, if such models are to be useful, they must correspond more closely to what is already known about the behavior.

On the historical role of the concept of "conditioning", I have more to say in chapter 15. The significance of the CR in the repertoire of a mammal—and probably of vertebrates in general—is as a component in the more complex behavior to which we turn in the next chapter.

6

TRIAL, ERROR,
AND SUCCESS

I sometimes feel, in reviewing the evidence on the localization of the memory trace, that . . . learning just is not possible. It is difficult to conceive of a mechanism which can satisfy the conditions set for it. Nevertheless, in spite of such evidence against it, learning does sometimes occur.

K. S. Lashley

In the previous chapter we were concerned with simple responses common to all members of a species. The ability to perform reflex acts seems to develop in each individual regardless of particular experiences; it is therefore sometimes loosely said to be "built in" to the animal. As we saw, reflex responses can be diminished or enhanced, and they can come to be evoked by new stimuli. But in none of this do we find anything about the development of *novel* habits.

Earlier chapters contain many examples of such habits. Pigeons learn the landmarks around their loft (2.4.3); predators respond appropriately to new signs of food (3.3.2) or to distasteful prey (3.5.1); animals develop new habits in order to keep warm (4.3) or to avoid toxic substances (4.5.2.4). Such "learning" usually entails the gradual acquisition of a habit. The habits that animals can develop are exceedingly diverse; and the natural surroundings of an animal contain too many variables for easy analysis. Hence experimenters have devised very simple, artificial situations for the study of habit formation in the laboratory; and they have usually preferred tractable domestic animals (or human beings) as their experimental subjects. The study of conditional reflexes, described in the previous chapter, is one example. The pioneers who introduced such methods have given us a vocabulary, and a number of experimental techniques.

6.1 EXPERIMENTAL METHODS

6.1.1 Mazes and Discrimination

If an animal lives in a structured environment (not, for example, the open sea), it often needs to develop habits of movement along fixed paths; or it may regularly return to a nest or lair from sources of food in a surrounding region. To investigate such abilities one usually needs an artificial environment. For a burrowing species such as the Norway rat—the most frequently used laboratory ani-

FIGURE 6-1 Above: elevated T-maze in which a laboratory rat has just turned right after being put on the stem of the maze. Below: an enclosed Y-maze in which the goal arms offer different visual stimuli. Both are examples of mazes with a single choice point. (I. A. Fox)

mal—a branching system of passages has often seemed to present suitable problems (reviewed by N. L. Munn; M. H. Sheldon). Such *mazes* may be walled passages, raised runways, or canals filled with water. At first they were very elaborate. Later, a popular design was one with a single choice point: the shape was then that of a T or a Y (figure 6-1).

Behavior, even in (or on) a T-maze, can be quite difficult to interpret: the animal may wait for a long time in the vertical arm; it may turn around and face away from the choice point; it may go to the choice point and then vacillate; it may raise itself on its hind legs and sniff the air. A rat unaccustomed to the situation is likely to release one or two exceptionally wet fecal boluses. If the maze is raised above floor level, the animal may spend

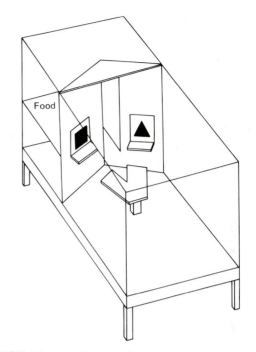

FIGURE 6-3 Jumping stand for experiments on visual discrimination. Of the two doors marked with patterns, one is unlocked and gives access to food when a rat jumps at it. If a rat chooses the wrong door, it bumps its nose and falls into a net (not shown) below. (After K. S. Lashley, 1934)

FIGURE 6-2 Plan of a complex enclosed maze. (After Y.-C. Tsang, 1934)

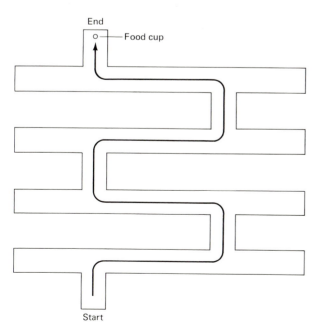

some time looking over the edge. (It may also fall off.) Usually, much of this behavior is disregarded: the experimenter records, perhaps, the time taken from start to goal, and—if a complex maze is used—the number of blind alleys entered (figure 6-2). If there is only one choice point, the record may consist simply of whether the subject turns left or right.

One of the components in the behavior of an animal in a maze is *discrimination* (5.5.1.1). When it habitually turns one way rather than another, it is discriminating the stimuli presented by the alternative routes. Figure 6-3 illustrates a situation in which an animal has only one decision to make: assuming that it does not merely remain at the starting point, it can jump either to the left-hand or to the right-hand gate. The visible stimuli presented by the gates are different. One gate falls open when the animal touches it, and allows the animal to find food. The other is fixed. This, the *Lashley jumping stand,* has—as we see later—many uses.

6.1.2 Simple Operations in Problem Boxes

For some purposes experimenters have required an animal to be caged in a box in which a single movement produces a result. Formal experiments of this kind were begun by E. L. Thorndike (1874–1949). Thorndike presented cats with the problem illustrated in figure 6-4. Some hours after its last

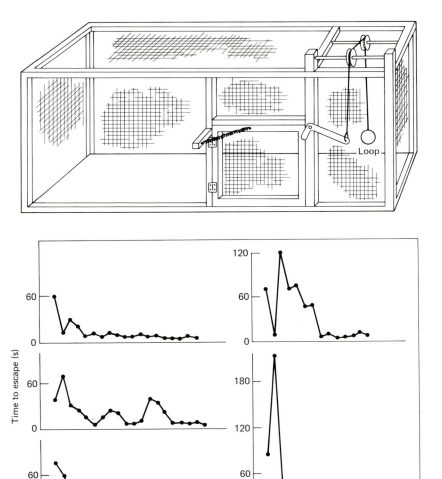

FIGURE 6-4 A problem box: an animal such as a cat can get out if it pulls the string. (After N. R. F. Maier & T. C. Schneirla, 1935)

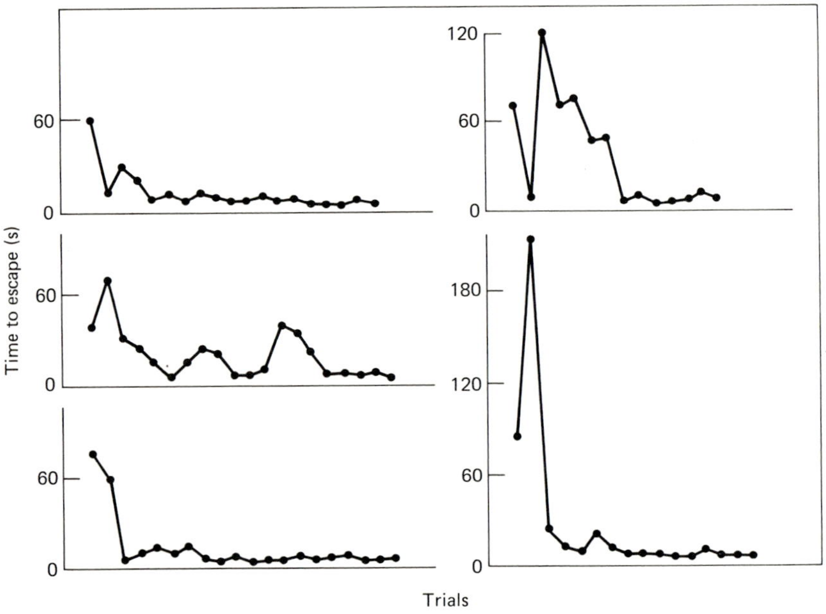

Time to escape (s)

Trials

FIGURE 6-5 A cat put in a box such as that shown in the previous figure at first takes some time to get out. After a few trials, it becomes very efficient. The graphs give five examples. (After E. L. Thorndike, 1898)

meal, the animal was put in the cage and food was put outside. To escape and to get food the cat had to pull a string. On the first occasion each animal made many ineffective movements not directed by the needs of the situation. Eventually, the string was pulled, the door opened, and the cat sprang out and ate the food. Thereafter, during a series of repetitions, the time spent in the cage declined, until the animal pulled the string with elegant economy of effort as soon as it was put inside (figure 6-5).

B. F. Skinner has been the most prominent advocate of Thorndike's method, but in an attenuated form (reviewed by R. A. Boakes & M. S. Halliday; by C. B. Ferster & B. F. Skinner; and by W. S. Verplanck). Just as Pavlov concentrated on measuring the output of saliva, so Skinner recorded the single movement of pecking by a bird, usually a pigeon (*Columba livia*). The bird is faced with a key of which the color can be varied: a number of pecks at one color, but not the other, leads to delivery of a reward, such as an edible seed. The pecks are recorded, and the food delivered, automatically: there is no need for the experimenter to pay any attention to the bird's behavior. A still better known form of the Skinner box is adapted for mammals: usually the subject is a laboratory rat, but it may be a mouse, a monkey, or some other guinea pig. The crucial movement is the depression of a lever or bar (figure 6-6). Again, this action may release a reward. The reward may consist of the switching on of heat (4.3.2.1).

The experimenter's exclusive preoccupation with a single act (bar pressing) is reflected in the term

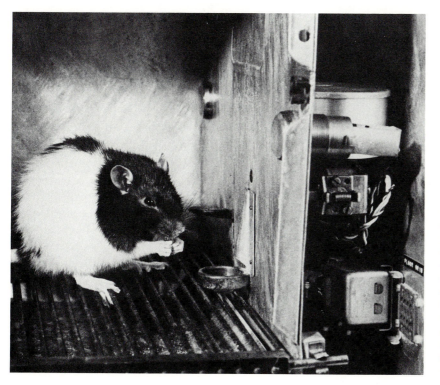

FIGURE 6-6 "Skinner box" in which a laboratory rat is shown eating after pressing the lever. The equipment may be programmed so that a pellet of food is released on each bar pressing, or only after a specified number of pressings or a specified interval. A source of light (above the rat) may be used as a cue, or as a reward in itself. The floor grid may be used to apply a shock to the feet. (Philip Boucas, courtesy World Health Organization)

operant, which is used for the one act recorded. The method accepts the operant as given: how it comes to be performed initially is not investigated. The method induces a change in the rate at which the operant is performed.

Animals develop not only positive habits, but also habits of escape or avoidance. A typical Skinner box allows the experimenter to apply an aversive stimulus—usually, a slight shock to the animal's feet (M. Sidman). An alternative system for applying shocks is the *shuttle box* (figure 6-7). Typically, the shock is signaled in advance by light-on or by a sound. To avoid the shock, the

FIGURE 6-7 Shuttle box. An animal in one compartment can be shocked through the floor grid. It can escape the shock by moving into the other half of the box. If a light is switched on before each shock, an animal can learn to avoid shock by moving in response to the light. In the photograph, the lids of the box, each with a signal light, have been turned back. See next figure. (I. A. Fox)

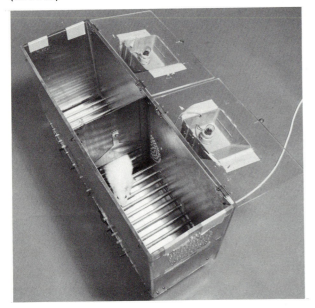

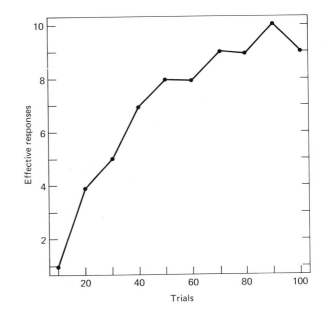

FIGURE 6-8 The gradual learning to avoid a shock in a shuttle box (previous figure) by a laboratory rat. (After O. H. Mowrer, 1960)

animal must move into another compartment of the cage within a few seconds of the signal. Small mammals can readily, if slowly, be trained to develop this habit (figure 6-8).

6.1.3 Classical and Instrumental

The formation of a conditional reflex, described in the previous chapter, is sometimes referred to as classical conditioning; and the CR has been called CR type I (reviewed by G. A. Kimble 1961). These terms are designed to distinguish Pavlov's procedure from that of Thorndike and his successors. The methods described in the preceding two subsections all study *operant* or *instrumental conditioning,* or CR type II.

What are the important differences between

them? The term instrumental implies that the act has some effect on the animal's environment, whereas the classical CR has been held not to have such an effect. But, as D. O. Hebb (1956) has pointed out, salivation does have an effect: it dissolves the food, and makes possible stimulation of the taste buds.

The most important feature of instrumental conditioning is conveyed in its alternative name, trial-and-error behavior. Thorndike used the expression, "trial, error and accidental success". An animal in, say, a problem box at first makes a great variety of movements: the problem set by the experimenter is then solved incidentally. Gradually or rapidly inappropriate conduct is given up: eventually the one procedure that leads to the goal is performed with little expenditure of energy. Pavlov's method, in contrast, makes it impossible for the animal to perform a variety of movements.

Since, in the typical Pavlovian experiment, the animal is immobile, the response studied is usually glandular or visceral; and it is mediated by the autonomic nervous system. Instrumental responses are inevitably, as a rule, movements produced by the skeletal muscles. But this distinction does not always hold. A tendon reflex, which depends on skeletal muscles, can be used in a Pavlovian experiment. More important, animals have been trained to make visceral responses for rewards (reviewed by N. E. Miller, 1969). Great difficulties had to be overcome, including the belief of Miller's graduate students that the task was impossible.

In some experiments rats were paralyzed with a drug of the curare group. (A human being under curare cannot move, but can afterward report what has happened: that is, he is conscious.) An animal in this state can be rewarded by electrical stimulation of certain regions of the brain. Light-on or a noise was the conditional stimulus. By this procedure rats were trained to accelerate or to slow their heart rate, or to increase or decrease the peristaltic movements of their intestines. In human terms, they had learnt to control "involuntary" responses. This phenomenon is now sometimes discussed under the heading of biofeedback.

6.2 THE ANALYSIS OF TRIAL AND ERROR

The procedures described above represent the main experimental designs used in investigating trial and error. I now summarize findings from the use of these traditional methods.

6.2.1 Reward

6.2.1.1 Habit and Homeostasis: In chapter 4 we saw how behavior often has a homeostatic function. More generally, it has survival value, if not for the performer then for offspring or other kin. Correspondingly, as a rule, habit formation is usually closely linked (1) to some feature of the environment that influences survival, and (2) to the internal state of the animal. The latter is often discussed under the headings of *motivation* or *drive* (17.1.2). If a rat is to learn a maze, or a monkey a manipulation, for a reward of food, the experimenter should deprive the animal of food beforehand. There is often a systematic relationship between duration of fast (food deficit) and behavior (4.5.2.2); and the same applies when other deficits are used.

A reward (or *positive reinforcer*) is defined here as a stimulus which produces a lasting increase in the strength of a response that evokes the stimulus. In running a maze, there is a starting point and a goal. At the goal there may be food, or there may be some other object or condition. If animals can readily be trained to run from start to goal, then whatever is (or occurs) at the goal constitutes a reward, by definition (reviewed by M. E. Bitterman & W. M. Schoel).

For experiments of this sort, there must be a clearly defined measure of habit strength. Pavlov used the amount of saliva secreted, that is, the *amplitude* of the response. In some kinds of problem box, the *frequency* of responding may be used: the rate at which a rat in a Skinner box (figure 6-6) presses the bar is an example. A third measure is *latency:* in experiments with mazes, the interval between the start of the experiment and the attainment of a goal may be used; alternatively, a reciprocal measure, the *speed,* may be preferred. Last is *resistance to extinction.* As we see later, these measures do not always give the same results.

We now turn to the effects of quantity of reward on habit formation; and we find—as so often—observations that conform with common sense. In many experiments (reviewed by S. A. Barnett, 1975) laboratory rats have been required either to run a passage (frivolously called an I-maze), or to press a bar, for a drink. The solution offered may be of saccharin in water (sweet), of dextrose in water (nutritious but not sweet), or of sucrose in water (both nutritious and sweet). By varying the character of the reward, one can produce variation in the amount of solution drunk. In general, one finds a corresponding variation in the speed of running or the rate of bar pressing.

The elaborate demonstration of the obvious sometimes leads to discovering what is not obvious. Examples come from the relationship of habit strength to *change* of reward. L. P. Crespi asked the question: what happens if an animal has been trained to take an action for a standard amount of reward on each run, and is then either given much more reward or much less? Suppose the action re-

quired is again traversing a runway, and suppose the animals (again, laboratory rats) have been fasted for 22 h. The rats are trained initially on either 1 unit of food or 16 units. Once trained, they are all offered, on a series of occasions, 4 units, and so in this final phase all are given the same amount of reward. Yet those that have been trained on 1 unit speed up, while those trained on 16 units slow down. They display, in fact, behavioral counterparts of elation and disappointment.

Such behavior suggests a state of expectation by the animal. As we know (5.5.1.1), Pavlov's dogs were disturbed when offered a familiar reward in unfamiliar conditions. Similarly, rats are upset when they receive an unfamiliar reward in familiar circumstances. One group of rats is trained to run a maze with a reward of wet mash. Another is rewarded instead with sunflower seed. The second group does not learn the maze as quickly as the first. But, after 10 trials, the group that has been receiving the mash is given the seeds instead. At once its performance deteriorates, and even becomes worse than that of the group rewarded throughout with sunflower seeds (figure 6-9).

A more elaborate example is provided by D. Premack (1969). He trained laboratory rats in two tasks on alternate days. The schedules of reinforcement for the two tasks were different. The amount of reward for performing the first task was then reduced, but that for the second task, on the alternate days, was unchanged. Nonetheless, the rate of responding in the second task went up. In other words, the changed situation on one day altered behavior on the next day, despite the absence of change in reward on that day. (It was as though the rats were relieved, and therefore elated, to find the second reward intact.)

Such findings warn us not to think of trial-and-error behavior as a simple, quantitative reflection

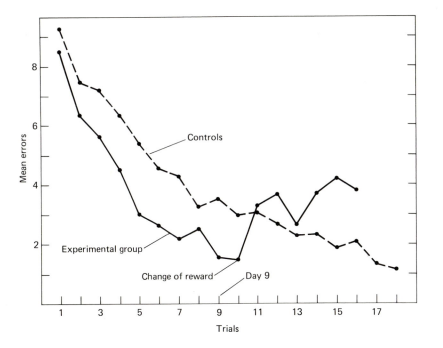

FIGURE 6-9 Change of reward. Habit formation by laboratory rats in a maze was recorded by the decline in the number of errors with time. After Day 9, the experimental group was rewarded with sunflower seeds instead of the wet mash previously given. Their error rate then rose above that of controls, which were given seeds throughout the experiment. (After M. H. Elliott, 1928)

of the reward. An animal such as a rat displays, in much of its behavior, responsiveness to the total situation and to the influence of its past experience. Similarly, as described in chapter 4, behavior is sometimes precisely homeostatic in its effect, but there are nonetheless circumstances in which simple homeostatic relationships do not hold.

6.2.1.2 Self-Stimulation of the Brain:

An extreme example of nonhomeostatic behavior is provided by animals that work to give themselves electrical stimulation of the brain (reviewed by James Olds, 1977). An electrode is implanted, and the animal—usually a monkey, a cat or a rat—can pass a brief charge through it by pressing a lever. The result depends on where in the brain the electrode is implanted (figure 6-10). In an early study, J. M. R. Delgado and others found an

aversive effect of very mild electric shocks in regions around the thalamus: the rats used in these experiments behaved as though the stimulation were painful; that is, they refrained from further bar pressing. The surprising finding was that stimulation of other, adjacent regions of the brain (shown in the figure) produce not avoidance, but repeated self-stimulation: the stimulation may be at the rate of 30 every minute. It seems that the experimenter, by suitable placing of the electrode, directly influences the system of rewarding or punishing effects in the brain. Correspondingly, an animal may learn a maze when the reward is the opportunity to perform self-stimulation of certain brain structures.

6.2.1.3 Delayed Reward:

A further quantitative relationship concerns the interval between action

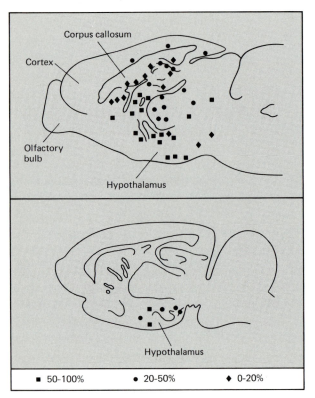

FIGURE 6-10 Rat brains in sagittal section: effects of self-stimulation. Squares show points where stimulation was highly rewarding; circles indicate moderate reward; and diamonds neutral or punishing effects. (After J. Olds, 1958)

and reward. In most experiments on trial and error, the subject is rewarded promptly as soon as the required act is performed: the delay may be only 1–2 s. The effect of longer delays has implications for the study of memory: for how long can an event be retained in the absence of reward? G. R. Grice required laboratory rats to discriminate white from black: this is a simple problem for rats, but they failed it when the reward was de-

layed for 10 s. Other examples are given by G. A. Kimble (1961).

In a maze with several choice points there must, however, be a substantial delay between responses in the first part of the maze and the ultimate reward. A possible explanation is based on the notion of *secondary reward* (reviewed by R. C. Bolles 1967). It is supposed that conditions or stimuli, initially not rewarding, come to have reward value as a result of association with a primary reward. As an example, I. J. Saltzmann asked: if rats had previously had food in a particular goal box, would they show a preference for this box, even when it was empty, over another? He trained his rats to run a straight alley for food offered in a distinctive box. When they had been trained, they were run in a maze with a single choice point: on one side was the box in which they had received food; on the other, there was either a completely strange box or one in which they had previously experienced absence of reward. The second box was distinguished from the reward box by being black instead of white, or white instead of black. In these conditions, the rats preferred the box in which food had been experienced: the color of the box had come to act as a reward. (Once again, we see that habit formation is not always straightforwardly homeostatic.)

From such experiments, we may suppose that some habits depend partly on prolonged retention based on secondary reward. There are, however, examples of retention that cannot be explained in this way. As we know (4.5.2.4), an animal can learn to avoid a toxic mixture when illness develops some hours after ingestion (an example of the delayed action of *negative* reinforcement); and a food containing, say, a needed vitamin may be preferred, although the favorable action of the food is

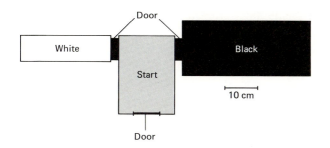

FIGURE 6-11 T-maze used for study of "delayed re-ward learning". The inside of the starting box was grey; the alternative goal boxes were of different shapes and sizes, and one was painted white, one black. If the rat made the correct choice (previously designated by the experimenter), it was put in the start box and given food after an interval that varied from 30 s to 8 min. If the in-correct choice was made, the animal was put in the start box and allowed to run again. In these conditions, the habit of choosing one box (the correct one) was readily developed, even when there was a long interval between making the choice and receiving the reward. (After B. T. Lett, 1973)

not instantaneous. B. T. Lett (1973, 1975) has also demonstrated "delayed reward learning" in a truncated T-maze (figure 6-11). She put a rat in the start box and then raised the doors into the two arms. One arm was designated as the correct arm. If the animal entered that arm, it was returned to the start box and there, after a varying interval, given its day's ration of food. If the animal made the wrong choice, it was at once returned for an-other run in the maze. Each animal therefore al-ways received one reward on each day. The crucial feature of the experiment was the interval between a run and a reward. The delays ranged from 30 s to 8 min. On conventional assumptions, a delay of 8 min should have prevented the animals from de-veloping the habit. In fact, the habit was acquired equally readily with all the delays used. Hence the effects of delays previously reported are partly a

function of the experimental procedure. A rat's (unrewarded) memory is not as bad as has been supposed.

We see later (for example, in 8.1.3.3; 8.1.4.1), that a reward need not contribute directly to ho-meostasis (or reproduction), and that information may be stored for long periods without any evi-dent effect on behavior. For a full discussion, with examples from human activities, consult D. Pre-mack (1965).

6.2.1.4 Extinction: If a CR is set up, and the animal is then exposed to the conditional stimulus but not to the unconditional (the reward), the CR declines, eventually to zero. Such extinction has also been much studied in experiments on trial and error. Figure 6-12 gives an example. Rats are fasted, and then given the opportunity to press a bar in a Skinner box for food. They duly develop the habit of pressing the bar at a high rate. The

FIGURE 6-12 Extinction: response rates in a bar-press-ing apparatus after reward has been withdrawn from trained rats. At first, the rate rises; extinction begins only after the third day. (After D. D. Wickens & R. C. Miles, 1954)

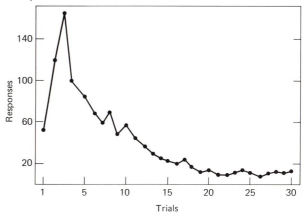

animals are now put on an extinction schedule: that is, no food is released. At first, as the figure shows, the rate of bar pressing rises; eventually, however, it declines, as expected. But now suppose that the rats are rested for 24 h. On return to the Skinner box, they resume a high rate of response. Just as with a conditional reflex, there is spontaneous recovery of the habit. The recovery is, however, not complete. The animals are evidently, in a sense, developing a new habit during extinction: they are learning not to respond. The process is different from forgetting, which is loss of a habit with time and lack of practice.

The rate at which extinction occurs may be used as a measure of habit strength. One important question is how this measure relates to others. In a Skinner box the proportion of acts rewarded can be varied; the higher the ratio of reward to acts (bar pressings), the more quickly is a high rate of responding achieved: there is a positive correlation between the incidence of reward and the readiness with which a habit is formed. A habit developed with 100% reward (food from every bar pressing) might be expected to be more resistant to extinction than one acquired slowly with, say, 30% reward (only three pellets from every 10 bar pressings). In fact, the opposite is found: habits developed with partial reward are *more* resistant to extinction.

Such findings suggest that two distinct processes in the central nervous system are responsible respectively for learning to act and for learning not to act. Correspondingly, certain substances that influence the functioning of the brain have opposite effects on habit formation and extinction: sodium bromide (NaBr) is proverbially a depressant, and it does delay habit formation; but it accelerates extinction. Correspondingly, stimulants such as caffeine and amphetamine, which can improve the rate of habit formation, delay extinction. (Unfortunately, these findings on laboratory animals provide a poor guide for the use of such drugs by human beings: their action on different individuals varies greatly, and can be adverse.)

This is one example from many of how, as investigation becomes more detailed, an apparently simple phenomenon, such as the habit of depressing a lever, is found to require plural analysis: such a habit is no longer seen as a unitary process.

The need for a plural interpretation is disappointing if one is looking for general principles or laws. One question is whether the findings on extinction match those on habituation (5.2.3). Extinction may be said to be habituation of a pattern of response acquired as a result of experience; it depends, of course, on absence of reward. It may then be hypothesized that extinction is "the same" as other kinds of habituation. If we ask what this could mean, at least two kinds of answer are possible: one, at the behavioral level, concerns the pattern of loss of the response; the other concerns central nervous function. J. W. Kling & J. G. Stevenson give an experimental example. They used the procedure, already described (5.2.2.1), of exposing chaffinches, *Fringilla coelebs,* to a stuffed owl and recording the rate at which the birds make their chink (alarm) calls. They also trained their birds to peck at a disc to get seed, and then recorded extinction of that habit. Figure 6-13 shows that the two curves differ: over a period of 6 min the rate of alarm calling rises at first, but then declines; but pecking, on withdrawal of the reward, shows a smooth decline at once. The authors remark, with restraint, that the hypothesis of a single underlying neural process for the two phenomena is premature.

FIGURE 6-13 Comparison of extinction with habituation. On the left is the record of three periods of extinction of a pecking response by 12 chaffinches, *Fringilla coelebs:* the upper curve records the first test, and the bottom curve the third. On the right, curves of habituation of an alarm call (the "chink" call) on exposure of nine birds to a stuffed owl: the upper two curves refer to the first and second habituation tests given just after the birds were brought into the laboratory; the lower two curves refer to eight birds kept in the laboratory for six weeks before two successive tests. (After J. W. Kling & J. G. Stevenson, 1970)

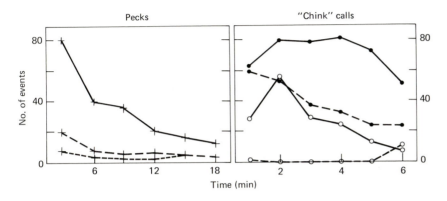

Pecks   "Chink" calls

6.2.2 Generalizing

When, in laboratory experiments, an animal is trained to respond, say, to something visible, we usually speak as if its responses were always to exactly the same stimulus. But in fact the pattern falling on the retina, even from a single object such as a cube, is not constant. Hence animals respond to populations of stimuli: each population has a mean value for each of the measurable attributes of its members, and variation—which may be considerable—about the mean. Such variation is very obvious in natural conditions: an animal may learn to respond to a class of objects, say, all the members of a particular species, which themselves vary greatly in appearance.

A formal, quantitative example of generalization, is provided by a laboratory rat trained to respond to a tone of 1000 Hz; this is done by sounding the tone and then applying a slight shock to the animal's feet. When the animal is trained, a tone of 900 Hz is presented, and the animal moves, but less vigorously than before. At 500 Hz there is hardly any response. A similar effect is observed if the pitch is raised.

Such a simple example, however, understates the importance of generalizing. Generalization sometimes involves what in human conduct we should call concept formation or abstraction. Figure 6-14

FIGURE 6-14 Patterns used to test the ability to generalize. (After D. O. Hebb, 1958)

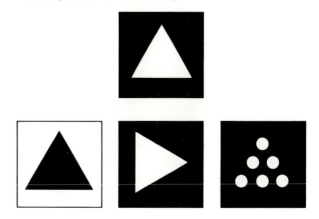

shows how generalization of shapes, that is, response to certain relationships shared by a number of patterns, may be tested. It is easy to train a rat to respond to a white triangle on a black background. (Figure 6-3 shows suitable equipment.) The alternative might be a white circle. The question now is whether animals so trained will respond to triangles in general; and this is tested by offering a black triangle on a white ground, a white triangle at a different angle from the first one, and a triangle made up of a group of dots. In fact, a rat fails all these tests; a chimpanzee, *Pan troglodytes,* fails the last one; but a child of two years succeeds with all three.

6.2.3 Discriminating

In experiments in which a rat responds to a tone, it not only generalizes to tones of lower and higher frequency, but it may also discriminate frequencies very different from the original 1000 Hz: the latter evoke little or no response. The classical CR allows analogous observations (figure 5-29). Further analysis has been based mainly on the use of a Lashley jumping stand (figure 6-3) or some similar arrangement.

In the simplest situation an animal is rewarded for approaching one stimulus but nothing much happens if it approaches the other. ("Nothing much" may include bumping its nose against a locked gate, or falling into a net; hence there may be an element of punishment for making the wrong response.) An important question is whether an animal can readily change habits so developed. Such an ability is tested by discrimination reversal. The animal, trained to approach a triangle and not a square, is suddenly faced with the opposite situation: approach to the square is rewarded, but not to the

triangle. A rat soon acquires the new habit. Moreover, further reversals are learned more quickly still: the animal eventually adopts the optimum strategy of win-stay, lose-shift; hence every time the experimenter switches the reward, the animal, after its first failure to achieve reward, turns to the alternative stimulus. R. J. Schusterman (1963) has demonstrated the use of this strategy also by adult chimpanzees, *Pan troglodytes,* and children aged from three years.

A further development is the overtraining reversal effect (ORE). Suppose an animal is trained to make a discrimination; and then the training continues, long beyond the point at which it would usually be regarded as complete. The question is whether such overtraining makes a reversal easier or more difficult. A habit might be supposed to become progressively more fixed as a result of its being repeatedly evoked. But, in fact, overtraining makes reversal easier. The explanation is uncertain. Perhaps the overtrained animals attend more to the relevant stimuli, and are less distracted by other features of the environment.

In another kind of problem, reward is associated with each of two stimuli, but with different frequencies. Approaching a square may be rewarded on 70% of occasions, and approaching a triangle only on 30%. On any given trial it is impossible to predict which is the correct choice. The optimum strategy is then to choose always the stimulus more often rewarded. And rats, like men, do just that: they maximize.

6.2.4 Punishment

There are, of course, circumstances in which the optimum strategy, in contrast, is to minimize. Some stimuli and conditions are aversive, that is they tend to cause withdrawal (reviewed by M. E. Bitterman & W. M. Schoel; and by R. M. Church). In the laboratory the stimulus may be a shock, a blast of air, a loud noise, a bright light, immersion in water, or other assaults on the senses. An animal may learn to *escape* such conditions: for example, it may run from one side of a shuttle box to another more comfortable side; in a Skinner box it may learn to press a bar and so switch off a stimulus. But, in a shuttle box, if the shock is signaled in advance, the animal later learns to *avoid* the shock by moving to the other side before the shock comes on. Similarly, in a Skinner box, an animal may learn to prevent an aversive stimulus by pressing the bar.

If an act leads to an aversive stimulus, the act is said to be punished. Punishment is conveniently defined as a response-contingent aversive stimulus; and removal of such a stimulus is called *negative reinforcement*. An example of punishment, as defined, is eating a food that causes illness (4.5.2.4). A single such experience by a rat can lead to a lasting aversion. The same applies to man (4.5.3.2). In the laboratory small mammals regularly encounter another experience similar to one that occurs in natural conditions: handling by an experimenter resembles being seized by a predator, and is sometimes aversive for domestic rats as well as wild ones; but few experimental studies of handling have been published (reviewed by S. A. Barnett, 1975). The taming of an animal often involves habituation to handling, or to other aversive conditions, such as the mere presence of a human being; but again little systematic work has been done on taming.

Most experimental findings in this field come from the use of shock, which has the advantage of being exactly reproducible, and easily varied in intensity. A single severe shock can cause long-lasting avoidance of the conditions in which it occurred. The effect resembles that of eating something toxic. But the most important effect of severe shocks is a general disruption of effective behavior.

In contrast, experiments that use mild stimulation sometimes lead to unexpected findings. K. F. Muenzinger trained rats in a visual discrimination under three conditions: one was food for the correct response and mild shock for the wrong response; a second was food reward alone; and the third was food *accompanied* by mild shock. As might be expected, the habit was most quickly developed in the first condition. But, when shock accompanied the reward, performance was better than when the only incentive was food. Hence a stimulus that is usually aversive can, when offered with a reward, enhance the effect of the reward. In general, in certain circumstances an aversive stimulus facilitates the performance of a punished act. Perhaps such a stimulus can make it easier for an animal to discriminate between two situations. Other explanations are possible, but none has been established.

A last feature of experiments in which punishment is used concerns the association of conditional reflexes with the formation of habits by trial and error. J. H. Banks and others put rhesus monkeys, *Macaca mulatta*, in separate cages in which they could be given a mild but disagreeable shock. Each shock was preceded by a visual stimulus. The shock could be prevented if the monkey pressed a bar when the visual stimulus was applied. At intervals, the monkeys were also subjected to another visual stimulus, which did not signal the onset of shock. While the monkeys were learning to press the bar, there was always an increase in their heart rate when the stimulus that signaled the shock was switched on. The other stimulus had no effect on the heart rate. Some monkeys failed to develop the habit of pressing the bar; and they did not develop the discriminated cardiac response. The heart rate of a mammal is regulated by the autonomic nervous system. Changes in the rate, such as those observed in monkeys, must be expected whenever a new habit is developed.

The last example illustrates, once again, how much is going on internally when a mammal acquires even a simple habit. An interesting question is whether it is easier to analyze habit formation by animals with simpler nervous systems. We now turn to them.

7

TRIAL AND ERROR
IN THE ANIMAL KINGDOM

World is suddener than we fancy it.
World is crazier and more of it than we think,
Incorrigibly plural.

MacNeice

7.1 TURBELLARIA

In many experiments on habit formation by invertebrates, the reward or unconditional stimulus is food that has to be approached on the application of another stimulus. The procedure is often different only in detail from a classical maze experiment.

The question whether flatworms (Turbellaria) can learn a route to food has caused much debate (reviewed by W. C. Corning & S. Kelly). Evidently they can. Figure 7-1 illustrates the method of a successful experiment by P. H. Wells (1967). The upper diagram shows food (meat) on the end of a wire and the worms moving about mainly on the bottom of the tank; this represents the situation before training has been attempted. The other diagrams show stages in the training of the worms: at first the food is at the surface, hence easily accessible; later it is lowered by stages, until it is 32 mm below the surface. When the food is presented in this manner to trained animals, they

quickly move up the side of the tank, along the surface and down the wire. They also do this when the wire is completely clean, provided that meat juice is added to the water; hence the worms are not merely responding chemotactically to the food. Flatworms may also be trained to move in this way in response to light-on. How this sort of ability is used by flatworms in natural conditions is not known.

7.2 ECHINODERMATA

Our knowledge of echinoderm behavior is small. Attempts of various kinds to train these animals in new habits have met with mixed success (reviewed by A. O. D. Willows & W. C. Corning). D. E. Landenberger provides an exception. The pacific starfish, *Pisaster giganteus,* is a versatile predator that feeds especially on mussels, *Mytilus.* The individuals studied were living beneath a pier in California, supported on pilings on which mussels were growing in large numbers. Most of the predation by the starfish was on mussels that fell off. The distribution of the starfish coincided closely with the area beneath the pier where this food was

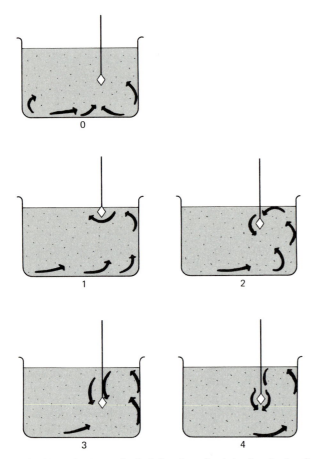

FIGURE 7-1 A method, fully described in the text, of training flatworms to find meat. (After W. C. Corning & S. Kelly, 1973)

available. Landenberger writes: "This distribution can be explained if we suppose that the starfish recognise the limits of the pier and confine their movements to within these limits. This requires learning, and the simplest kind of learning that would suffice is . . . association of certain clues . . . with presence of food."

Accordingly, eight of these animals were kept in tanks, in near darkness, without food for two

weeks. In these conditions the starfish stay on the walls of the tanks, near the water surface. They descend only to get food. The conditional stimulus was light-on. Control experiments showed that light had various effects on the animals: sometimes movement in the horizontal plane occurred; but light did not make them go to the bottom. The response to light was therefore analogous to the orientation reflex of a mammal (5.2.2.2).

Training consisted of light-on and putting a damaged mussel at the bottom of the tank. This was done on eight occasions on alternate days. On 10 further occasions the light was switched on without the simultaneous presentation of food. The animals nevertheless responded by moving to the bottom of the tank. When they had done this, they were given their reward of mussel. In the final stage, the light was switched on but no food was offered until 12 h later; this represents an *extinction schedule*. The animals soon stopped responding, that is, extinction occurred.

This example from the echinoderms resembles that from the planarians; but it has the unusual feature of being related to the ecology of the animals observed.

7.3 OLIGOCHAETA

An early experiment on invertebrate habit formation was that of R. M. Yerkes, published in 1912, on an earthworm, *Eisenia* (*Allolobophora*) *foetida*. An animal was put in a maze with a single choice point (compare figure 6-1). One arm led to a dark, humid chamber; the other, which was lined with sandpaper to give it a distinctive texture, led either to a source of electric shock or to a strong salt solution. The animal was set moving by shining a bright light on its hind end. After 20 to 100 trials the worm usually turned regularly right or left, that is, in the direction in which it had previously found humid darkness.

Today Yerkes's paper would be (rightly) rejected by most scientific journals, because he used only one worm. Yet at the time this was an important pioneering observation.

One problem in such work is the reluctance of the worms to move from the starting point: often they have to be prodded. Hence it is important for the experimenter not to guide the worms in the way he thinks they should go. Another question, studied especially by J. H. Reynierse, concerns the temperature at which worms are kept: it is usual to keep the worms in a refrigerator, and to warm them up for testing at room temperature. This procedure substantially reduces the ability of worms to develop new habits. Yet a third problem arises from the circadian rhythm of the activity of earthworms. These animals are most active (that is, most likely to be moving about) during the first hours of the dark period; and this is the best time to train them. There is some doubt whether worms can learn new habits at all in the morning. But not all species have the same abilities, and this is yet a further hazard for the experimenter.

Despite these difficulties, Yerkes's findings have been confirmed on several species (reviewed by J. A. Dyal). As an example, L. C. Aranda and others repeated Yerkes's experiments on 19 specimens of *Lumbricus terrestris*. After more than 200 trials, spread over about seven weeks, the worms regularly succeeded in avoiding shock and achieving refuge in a burrow. Yerkes had also cut off the first four and a half segments of his worm after training, but found that the effect of the training persisted. Aranda and his colleagues confirm this. They seem also to have confirmed that the habit is lost when the front end regenerates. The interpretation of this finding is obscure, and raises the un-

answered question of the function of the cerebral ganglia of earthworms.

Although, on this evidence, earthworms are slow learners, they seem to have quite good memories. L.-G. Datta also studied *L. terrestris* in a T-maze similar to that designed by Yerkes. Her worms were, when necessary, driven from the stem of the T by bright light, heat, or shock. Treated in this way, they retained their habits well for at least five days.

Another question concerning memory arises if we consider the effects of varying the *intertrial interval* (ITI). In most of Datta's experiments the ITI was 5 min. In some it was only 1 min. In either case habit formation was observed. But when the ITI was 25 min, no habit formation developed. Whatever trace is left by a single experience in the maze evidently fades in that time.

It would be interesting if a similarly thorough investigation of habit formation by worms could be carried out without the aid of electric shock.

7.4 INSECTA

7.4.1 Cockroaches: Reward and Punishment

Among the insects, the cockroaches (Dictyoptera, Blattidae) have been popular subjects for behavioral experiments. The species used are large and easily bred in captivity. They are active but tractable. We might expect the movements of such animals to be taxes (2.2.2) and therefore unadaptable; and we saw in 2.3.4 that their responses to a temperature gradient are indeed fixed. Certain species are, however, apparently very adaptable in the general sense: they are highly successful in man-made environments throughout the world. The finest population of *Blatta orientalis* I have encountered was in the Great Eastern Hotel in Calcutta; but this species and *Periplaneta americana* also do very well in cooler climates, especially in warm buildings, such as bakeries, which supply plenty of food.

Cockroaches live in buildings in the same conditions as rats or mice. If they are run in a maze in bright light, and the reward is a dark refuge, their performance improves with practice (reviewed by T. M. Alloway). They will also cope with a dark maze if the reward is a cup smelling of cockroach.

Odor is not, however, the main source of cues in acquiring the maze-running habit, at least for *Blattella germanica:* cleaning a brightly illuminated maze does not interfere with this behavior. Nor is vision essential: cockroaches with their eyes painted over perform quite normally. But the eyes evidently play some part: if the direction of the light is changed during training, performance is impaired. The antennae are probably essential—or, at least, one antenna; and they must be mobile. A. Hullo ran *Blattella germanica* in a maze with five choice points. If the antennae were fastened back lightly with glue, the insects could not cope with this task. These findings conform with the ecology of cockroaches: the insects typically live in dark corners, and are in continuous contact with surfaces.

7.4.2 Cockroaches: Adapting to Amputation

The importance of the antennae for normal movement suggests that both must be present for survival. Yet in natural populations it is quite common to see cockroaches, apparently thriving, which have lost an antenna. Cockroaches can evidently adapt to having only one (2.3.5). Equally remarkable is their ability, described by J. V. Luco, to compensate for amputation of legs. *Blatta orien-*

talis, like other cockroaches, regularly cleans its body surface. When an antenna is cleaned it is held by the opposite foreleg. If an adult has both forelegs removed, the antenna is held by a middle leg; at first the insect cannot stand on the three that remain, but after four or five days it becomes able ("learns") to use them as a tripod.

Young cockroaches have the same ability, but their legs regenerate. When this has happened, the normal method of cleaning antennae is restored. If, now, the front legs are again removed, the insect at once returns to its adapted pattern.

Such findings show how individual adaptability may be found where it might not be expected. Cleaning antennae is an example of a species-typical, "fixed" action pattern (17.2.4.1) of a kind that used to be called instinctive or innate. Yet the apparently fixed sequence of movements can be to some extent altered to meet a new situation.

7.4.3 Ants: Maze Learning

In 2.2.3 we saw something of the ability of ants (Formicidae) to find their way about: foragers of various species can go out, get food, and make use of the sun to return direct to the nest. Evidently they need some practice before they can allow for the sun's apparent movement; but such transverse orientations are not equivalent to maze learning. Behavior in a maze is, however, relevant to what they do in nature (figure 7-2).

Figure 7-3 illustrates a maze with many turnings and six choice points (T. C. Schneirla, 1953). The last alley leads to the ants' nest; hence returning home is the reward. Eight ants of the species, *Formica incerta,* acquired the habit of running the maze, almost without error, after 28 trials. Eight laboratory rats were trained in a maze of identical pattern with food as the reward. As the figure

FIGURE 7-2 Site of the nest (N) of a harvester ant, *Pogonomyrmex rugosus,* with two tracks (T) leading from it. Such tracks are marked with pheromones. (Turid Hölldobler)

shows, their performance resembled that of the ants, but they acquired the habit more quickly.

Schneirla's comparison suggests only a quantitative difference between ants and rats; but other differences are more fundamental. Suppose workers of the genus *Formica* learn a complex maze, and are then required to run it in the reverse direction: their performance is as if they were experiencing the maze for the first time (B. A. Weiss & T. C.

Schneirla). In contrast, rats in such a situation—as we see later (8.1.4.1)—would benefit from their previous experience.

Ants of the species, *Formica rufa,* do however, acquire visual discriminations with a facility similar to that of an octopus, a rat, or a macaque. D. M. Vowles ran ants in a T-maze, again with return to the nest as the reward. He painted patterns of vertical, horizontal, or oblique stripes on the maze walls; and the ants used these visible stimuli in developing the maze habit.

The family of ants is large, and few species have been studied. Fortunately, L. O. Stratton & W. P. Coleman have experimented on the fire ant, *Solenopsis saevissima,* a predatory species far removed taxonomically from *Formica.* When these insects return home alone, after finding food, they too are guided by the sun (2.2.3). During the walk back they leave an odor trail, which can be followed outward by other ants. Stratton & Coleman used a maze of the design in figure 7-4. Ants walked into the maze from their nest and found their way to an incentive such as a recently killed fly larva. The importance of odor trails was confirmed. The maze, in one set of experiments, was washed on alternate days. Ants reached the goal more quickly when the maze was left unwashed. If the maze was moved, so that the visual cues outside were altered, this too impaired running speed. The most important question was whether the ants would learn their way entirely without odor cues. In a separate experiment, therefore, the maze was washed daily after each trial. Figure 7-5 shows the progressive improvement that nevertheless took place over days. The curve represents the time from the entry of the first ant into the maze until the first three ants had reached the goal.

Such findings complement those on the orientations of ants given in 2.2.3. Evidently, ants can ac-

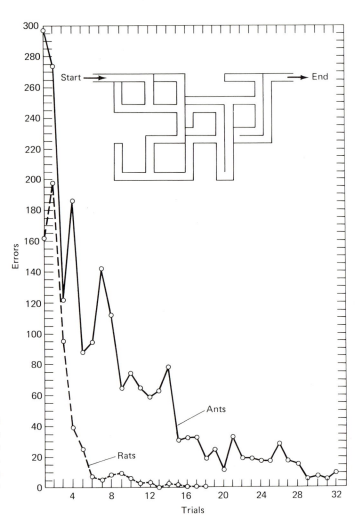

FIGURE 7-3 Design of a maze in which habit formation by ants, *Formica incerta,* was studied and compared with the maze-learning abilities of laboratory rats. The findings are summarized in the graphs. (After T. C. Schneirla, 1953)

quire new habits of movement about their living space in response to the positions of food and their nest. As one would expect from their foraging behavior, they do not depend merely on "forced movements", but can adapt their conduct to their individual circumstances.

7.4.4 Bees: Discrimination and Memory

Honey bees, *Apis mellifera,* like ants, can learn their way through a maze (reviewed by E. O. Wilson, 1971). K. Weiss used one with a number of choice points. Correct turns were signaled by col-

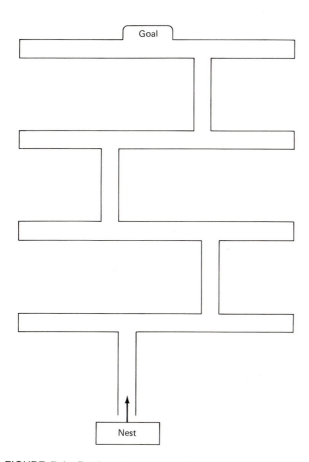

FIGURE 7-4 Design of maze used to study habit formation of the fire ant, *Solenopsis saevissima:* the ants
found their way to food in a maze of which the starting
point was just outside their nest. (After L. O. Stratton &
W. P. Coleman, 1973)

sucrose) at the far end. Bees were trained to leave
the hive and to feed at this source in response
either to light-on, or to smoke blown through the
hive. In some experiments, to reach the food the
bees had to pass one of two differently colored

FIGURE 7-5 Fire ants were run in the type of maze
shown in figure 7-4, and in conditions that prevented
their following an odor trail left by other ants. Nonetheless, the time taken to run the maze diminished to a
minimum during 10 days—a typical "learning curve".
(After L. O. Stratton & W. P. Coleman, 1973)

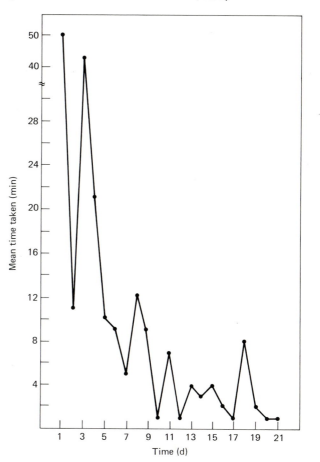

ored markers. Habits were retained for at least six
days.

In other experiments (figure 7-6), bees were
kept in a hive that allowed direct observation of
their behavior. The insects could leave the hive
from an opening outside the building; they could
also enter a runway with a source of food (2 M

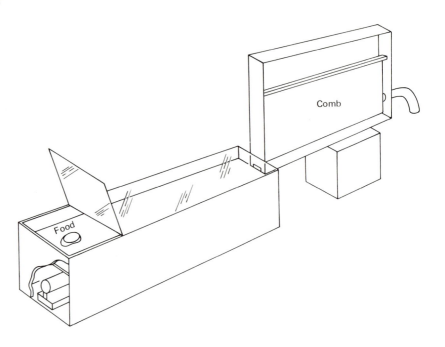

FIGURE 7-6 Apparatus in which hive bees, *Apis mellifera,* were trained to enter the runway (on left) to feed, in response to light-on or to smoke blown through the hive. The bees could also forage in the open air by leaving through the entrance on the right. (After A. M. Wenner & D. L. Johnson, 1966)

doors. They quickly learned to go to the color associated with food.

R. Menzel and his colleagues have made use of such abilities in studies on the memory of bees. Most of their observations have been on free-flying workers fed on a table about 40 m from their hive. The table has three discs of ground glass. Each disc can be illuminated with different colors. During training, the center disc is lit, and bees are rewarded for visiting it: when they touch down, they are allowed to take their fill of 2 M sucrose solution. Each bee studied is marked so that it can be individually identified. A bee that has been trained with food on, say, a yellow background returns to the table for another helping. It is then tested: the light under the center disc is switched off, and the two other discs are illuminated, one with yellow, the other with blue. Previous tests have shown no preference for one of

these colors over the other: untrained bees, given a choice between them, are equally likely to choose either. Figure 7-7 gives a typical "learning curve" from such experiments: there is a substantial effect of even one reward; and after five rewards the bees give 90% correct responses. There is, of course, a close similarity in this behavior to normal foraging from flowers.

Menzel and his colleagues, in ingenious experiments, have analyzed some of the factors in the development of such habits. Their findings refer to various stages in the storage of information.

1. There are first some questions about the action of different levels of reward. Evidently the *amount* of sugar solution sucked up does not, in itself, influence the strength of the habit formed; but there is a strong effect of the *duration* of sucking. If bees are allowed to suck for only 2 s on a

single visit, they give a high proportion of correct responses during the first 4 min after the reward, but later performance deteriorates. On the other hand, if sucking is allowed for 15 to 30 s, there is an *improvement* after 4 min, despite the absence of further training. I return to the phenomenon of delayed improvement below.

2. Next there is the question of long-term retention, or memory in the usual sense. Bees were rewarded three times on one of two colors; tested after an interval of two weeks they still remembered: their score was then about 80% correct choices.

3. Another important phenomenon is *registration,* the stage at which the input through the senses first has an effect on the nervous system. This effect is independent of reward. For training to have any effect, the stimulus (the color) must

have a certain time relationship with touchdown: the color must be visible for at least 2 s before the insect lands on the disc. If the color is on only after touchdown, there is no effect of training. Evidently there is a brief period of information storage before reward. For this the term "sensory memory" is used.

4. Lastly, observations have been made on changes that take place during the period immediately after registration. "Learning curves" usually have, as the horizontal axis, a measure such as the number of trials or of reinforcements, as in figures 6-8 and 6-9. An alternative is to study change in performance with time after a single reward. Bees may be allowed only one training visit, during which they suck for 10 s. If they are tested not more than 1 min later, they score 80% correct responses. But after that their performance declines: at 2 min it is only about 65%. It might be expected that it would soon fall to 50%, that is, the chance value, indicating complete loss of the habit. In fact, as figure 7-8 shows, during the next 10 min performance improves again: bees retested 3 min after reward still score below 70%, but at 12 min they are back to 80%. (These figures are each based on many hundreds of observations.) Evidently, after reward, at least two processes in the nervous system influence performance. One undergoes an early decline, but the other, slower process has the opposite tendency.

The improvement, or consolidation, that takes place without practice is not confined to bees. An example, from experiments on mice, is given in figure 7-9. Moreover, consolidation in bees can be experimentally prevented by treatments originally applied to mammals: one is electroconvulsive shock; a second is a brief period of narcosis by immersion in 100% carbon dioxide. A third treat-

FIGURE 7-7 Given a choice between two colors, bees quickly learn to respond to the one associated with a reward of sugar solution. The vertical bars represent standard errors of the means. (After R. Menzel and others, 1974)

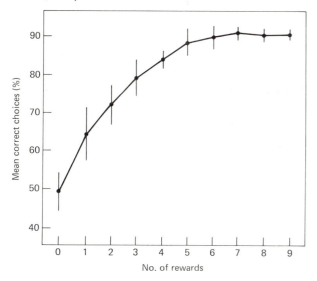

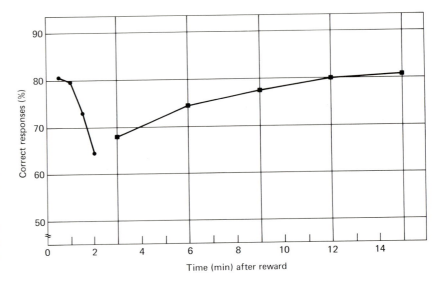

FIGURE 7-8 Effect of the interval between experiencing a reward and the time of testing on the performance of bees. The task was to select the correct one of two colors. The bees had received one reward: this consisted of 10 s feeding from a sugar solution. The immediate effect was a correct response rate of about 80%; but if the bees were tested 2 min after receiving the reward, only about 65% of responses were correct (as if the bees had "forgotten"). But, tested after yet a further interval of 12 or more minutes, bees again scored 80% correct. (After R. Menzel and others, 1974)

ment effective for bees is cooling to 4°C. All allow complete recovery and normal subsequent behavior. The treatments have been applied at various intervals after the training visit. If shock is applied within 30 s of training, the bees, on subsequent testing, show no effect of the training: there is total retrograde amnesia; and there is a marked interference with memory (or information storage) up to at least 3 min from training. By 7 min there is no effect. These figures define the period during which consolidation takes place.

7.5 CEPHALOPODA

7.5.1 Octopus and Adaptability

The last invertebrates to be discussed are those with the largest brains, the cephalopods, of which a common Mediterranean species, *Octopus vulgaris,* has been most studied. This work, initiated by J. Z. Young, has been reviewed also by G. D. Sanders and by M. J. Wells (1978).

Octopus, like squids (figures 3-7, 3-9), have large eyes similar to those of vertebrates; there are eight arms, each with a double row of suckers, bearing a vast number of receptors of touch and chemical stimuli; and there are paired statocysts that resemble in function those of vertebrates. In natural conditions octopus live in rock crevices or similar shelter, and move out to feed on a variety of prey. An octopus can be kept in the laboratory in a tank with a lair at one end; in these conditions many experiments have been done in which the animal is required to attack or to avoid prey. While the animal is in its shelter, a crab may be dangled on a black thread at the other end of the tank (figure 7-10). Within 10 s the octopus will have attacked the crab. These are voracious animals: an octopus of about 500 g will readily eat more than 10 g of food in 24 h. If it is rewarded with small helpings on each occasion, an experimenter can give it 40 training trials a day.

A main objective of the work on these animals has been to analyze their ability to discriminate visual stimuli, and to relate such abilities to brain

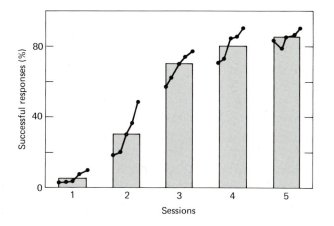

FIGURE 7-9 Acquisition of an avoidance response. On each of five days, mice had a session of 100 trials in a shuttle box. Mean success for each run of 20 trials within sessions is shown by the points connected by lines; mean success for whole sessions, by rectangles. There is evidence of improvement (a) within sessions, (b) from day to day, and (c) between sessions 1 & 2 and 2 & 3 (consolidation). (After F. Bovet-Nitti, 1968)

function. The magnitude of this task is reflected in the size of the brain of an octopus, with its estimated 168 million neurons. A bee's brain has fewer than one million.

Another index of the scope of such work is the range of adaptability found in the conduct of octopus. Sanders describes the behavior of a number of blind octopus that were kept in aquaria in the Zoological Station at Naples. Their food was crabs. The arrival of food was preceded by removal of the lid of the aquarium. As soon as the lid was taken off, the octopus swam to the water surface at the front of the aquarium, turned on their backs and spread out their arms and interbrachial web. If a crab was now dropped at the front of the aquarium it was easily caught. Sanders therefore tried dropping crabs out of reach of the spread arms, so that they fell to the bottom of the aquarium. A blind octopus would then swim to the bot-

FIGURE 7-10 Octopus attacking crab. (Courtesy J. Z. Young)

tom at one end, spread its arms from one side to the other and "move along the length of the tank collecting the crabs like a snow-plow". Obviously octopus are extremely adaptable, "intelligent" animals.

7.5.2 Visual Discriminations

In early experiments on habit formation by these animals, carried out by B. B. Boycott & J. Z. Young, both reward and punishment were used. Octopus were trained to attack crabs presented alone, but *not* to attack when a white square was shown with the crab: this restraint was imposed by applying, with a probe, a mild electric shock whenever a crab accompanied by a square was attacked (figure 7-11). It was similarly possible to train octopus to attack crabs only when a white square was present.

This procedure allowed experiments on the visual discrimination of shapes. An octopus can readily distinguish a vertical rectangle from a horizontal; but it cannot distinguish similar rectangles, one pointing up to the left and the other to the right. In such experiments it is necessary to allow for certain preferences that seem to develop independently of experience. The shapes are most effective if in continual slight movement. If rectangles are being moved up and down, octopus prefer (that is, tend to approach) the vertical rather than the horizontal; but if the rectangles are moved horizontally, the opposite preference is shown. N. S. Sutherland concluded from discrimination experiments that octopus distinguish shapes especially by the differences in their horizontal and vertical extensions.

If an octopus is so dependent on accurate assessment of vertical and horizontal extensions, then there must be some means by which the orientation of the retinae is kept constant. In fact, the statocysts of an octopus enable it to maintain a constant relationship to gravity. If the statocysts are removed, the ability to distinguish vertical from horizontal fails: in some experiments, such unbalanced octopus were tested when their retinae were at right angles to the normal position; they then responded to vertical rectangles as if they were horizontal.

As might be expected, further study showed the original hypothesis to be too simple. Figure 7-12 gives an example of two patterns, readily distinguished by octopus, which do not differ in their vertical and horizontal extensions. It is now believed that the brain of an octopus has more than one system for the analysis of the visual input. In this it resembles the brain of a mammal. Certain discriminatory abilities, too, are remarkably similar to those of mammals. Suppose an animal is trained to approach (attack) pattern A and to avoid pat-

FIGURE 7-11   Result of training an octopus to discriminate between a crab alone and a crab shown with a white square; after the first two days, an attack made when the square was present was punished with a slight electric shock. (After B. B. Boycott & J. Z. Young, 1955)

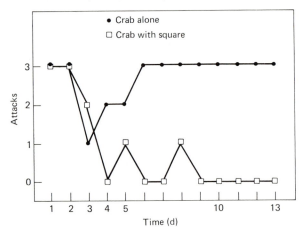

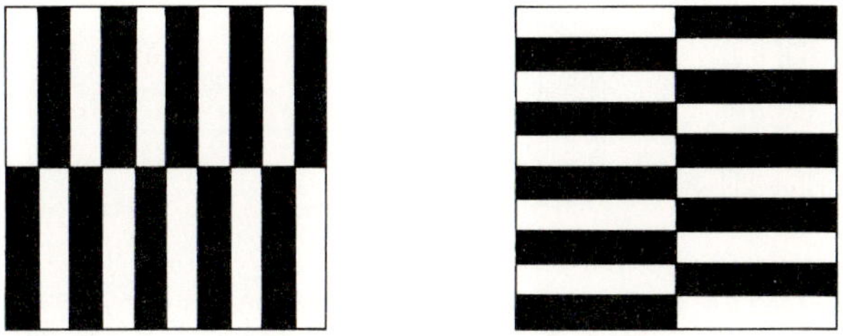

FIGURE 7-12 Two patterns that can be easily discriminated by octopus, although they do not differ in their
vertical and horizontal extensions. (After N. S. Sutherland and others, 1963)

tern B, and then required to do the opposite. As
with a mammal, performance improves with successive reversals (6.2.3). Another example is the
overtraining reversal effect (ORE), also described
above (6.2.3). For octopus, as for mammals, overtraining makes reversal easier. Evidently, these
mollusks have independently evolved neural arrangements that might otherwise have been supposed to be confined to the vertebrates.

7.5.3 Tactile Discriminations

Octopus are highly manipulatory, and their capacity for making tactile discriminations is well
developed. M. J. Wells (1962) describes how an
octopus emerges from its lair from time to time to
explore its surroundings, and to poke its tentacles
into any place to which they can penetrate.

Anything that projects is pulled at, and anything movable within arm's length of the home is gathered into
the heap of debris among which the animal lives. Apparatus left in the tank is examined, and generally
broken up (the expectation of life of a floating thermometer, for example, is about twenty minutes).

Wells has shown how octopus can distinguish
natural shapes, such as the shells of bivalve mollusks; these, however, even after cleaning, could
differ in taste. (We have seen that the arms of an
octopus have many chemoreceptors, as well as
touch receptors.) Wells therefore used artificial
shapes (figures 7-13 and 7-14). He first blinded
his animals. An octopus so treated usually settles
with its arms spread out. If the back of an arm is
touched with an object, the arm turns and grasps
the object with the suckers. The object may then
be passed to the mouth. Training in tactile discrimination consisted of rewarding an octopus for
this action with one object, and punishing it if it
did the same thing with the other. The reward was
a piece of fish; the punishment, as before, was a
slight shock. These discriminations required about
the same number of trials as visual discriminations.
The crucial factor in making such discriminations
seems to be the proportion of grooved to flat
surface.

It might be supposed necessary, in experiments
on objects with different textures, to control for
differences in weight. But in fact octopus are unable to distinguish objects, such as cylinders, which
differ only in weight (figure 7-15). This may seem
an extraordinary anomaly. They pick up a great
variety of objects; and to do so must adjust the
contractions of muscles in the arms according to
the weight of the object. Evidently, this is a local
action; and there is no corresponding central nervous process to enable them to distinguish objects
by their weight.

7.5.4 Memory and the Brain

The central questions in the work on cephalopods
have been on how the brain stores and retrieves
information. These are also the questions asked in
the more recent work on bees (7.4.4). Some of the
findings on retention are the same for both groups.

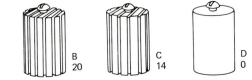

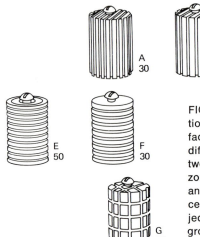

FIGURE 7-13 Objects used to test tactile discrimination by octopus. The proportion of grooved to flat surface diminishes from left to right. The top four objects differ in the number of vertical grooves they bear; the two objects in the center differ in the number of horizontal grooves; and the bottom object has both vertical and horizontal grooves. The numbers represent the percentage of surface of each object that is grooved. Objects A, F, and G, each with about the same amount of grooved surface, are hardly distinguished by octopus. (After M. J. & J. Wells, 1957)

J. B. Messenger (1973) describes experiments, not on octopus but on cuttlefish, *Sepia officinalis* (figure 3-9). These, as we know, are predatory animals with highly developed eyes and tactile sense. They readily attack prawns offered in an aquarium. Messenger trained them not to do so when the prey were presented behind glass: the animals had to learn not to batter their heads against the glass wall. Training was for 20 min. The question asked was how well the effect of training was expressed at different periods thereafter. For the first 15 min after training, performance was high; it then declined. But by 60 min it had recovered. Evidently, just as with bees, "memory" depends on at least two processes with different temporal properties. Sanders describes similar findings from observations on octopus.

Much work has been done on the effects of brain injuries on the ability to register or to retain information. The "higher centers" of the octopus brain are, appropriately, those at the top (figure 7-16): above the structures that receive inputs from the sense organs, there is a group of lobes whose working has been examined largely through the effects of injury.

Both octopus and cuttlefish have a vertical lobe, at the top of the brain, which displays no electrical activity when the external senses are stimulated. If this lobe is extensively injured, the animal's behav-

FIGURE 7-14 Diagram of part of the arm of an octopus in contact with a grooved object. (After M. J. & J. Wells, 1957)

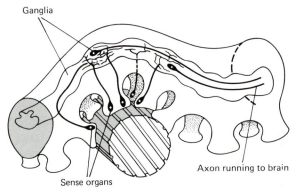

Ganglia

Sense organs

Axon running to brain

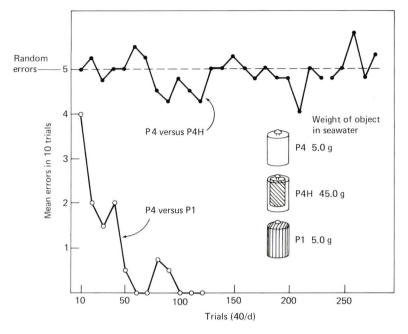

FIGURE 7-15   Results of trying to train octopus to discriminate objects that differ only in weight, and objects of the same size that differ in texture. When they were required to distinguish P4 from the much heavier P4H (which had the same tactile properties), the number of errors was that to be expected from a choice made at random (upper curve). The lower curve shows successful training to discriminate P4 (which was smooth) from P1 (which was of the same weight but grooved). (After M. J. Wells, 1962)

ior, in the uneventful conditions of an aquarium, is not visibly changed. But a cuttlefish cannot hunt effectively without its vertical lobe: for, if the prey goes out of sight behind an obstacle, the pursuer is baffled. A normal cuttlefish deals with such a situation without difficulty. In colloquial terms, destruction of the vertical lobe of a cuttlefish seems to reduce its "intelligence"; or perhaps it impairs "drive"—the readiness to take trouble. On present knowledge these expressions cannot be given any precise meaning, when they are applied to cuttlefish.

Octopus in an aquarium attack crabs with great reliability. If about 90% of the vertical lobes are destroyed, the animal, though still superficially normal, no longer attacks crabs reliably; it also takes longer over the attacks it does make. Once again, this suggests that the vertical lobe is con-

FIGURE 7-16   Sagittal section of part of the brain of an octopus. (Reproduced from J. Z. Young, *A Model of the Brain,* 1964, by permission of Oxford University Press, Oxford)

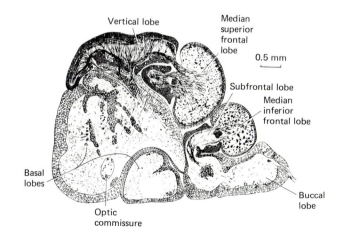

cerned with "hunger drive" or some aspect of motivation; but, as J. Z. Young has remarked, this adds little to our picture of how the vertical lobe functions.

Injury to the vertical lobe also alters the effects of training. Suppose an octopus has been trained (as described above) not to attack a crab when a white square is shown. If the vertical lobe is removed from an animal so trained, the effect of the training is lost: attacks are not prevented by the presence of the white square, or even by further shocks. It is still possible partly to train these animals again, but the effects of such training do not last long. There is a quantitative relationship between the amount of injury to the vertical lobe and the number of errors (inappropriate attacks) made by the animal (figure 7-17).

This remarkable finding parallels earlier observations on the effects of injuring the cerebral cortex of a rat. The most celebrated of such studies are those of K. S. Lashley (1890–1958). (See reviews by Lashley, 1950, and by R. L. Isaacsohn.) The implication of such experiments is that the representation or "engram" in the brain, resulting from training, is not localized, but is diffusely present in a large mass of neural tissue.

When an octopus learns—however imperfectly— a visual discrimination without its vertical lobes, the information is presumably stored in the optic lobes. It is evidently separate from that of tactile discriminations: tactile habits are formed normally by octopus from which both optic lobes have been removed. An astonishing amount of brain tissue can be lost with little effect. On the other hand, if there is damage to the inferior frontal, subfrontal, or buccal lobes, there is a marked decrement in performance. In particular, if the subfrontal lobe is removed, an acquired tactile discrimination fails completely. Indeed, an animal so damaged fails to

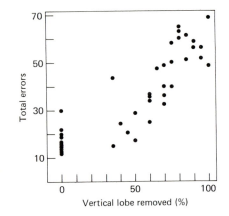

FIGURE 7-17 Relationship between performance in a visual discrimination by octopus and the percentage of the vertical lobe of the brain removed. The animals were rewarded if they attacked on presentation of a white horizontal rectangle, punished if they attacked a vertical rectangle. Their discriminatory ability was reduced only if more than 50% of the vertical lobe was removed. (After J. Z. Young, 1958)

respond to further training in such discrimination.

The independence of the "memory stores" for visual and tactile discriminations is remarkable. A feature shared in common by the two sets of structures is the presence of very large numbers of small neurons, linked not by massive tracts but by comparatively short dendrites. Both insects and vertebrates have similar brain tissue; and in both groups it is involved in information storage.

The brain of an octopus, like that of a mammal, is bilaterally symmetrical, and the two sides are linked by many fibers. If these tracts are cut, an octopus survives with two half-brains. One side of the animal may now be trained in a tactile discrimination by allowing only the arms on that side to touch the objects. When this is done, only that side develops the discrimination; the other side can, however, be trained either in the same discrimination or another. (Octopus, conveniently, are neither right-handed nor left-handed.) M. J. Wells (1968) has remarked on the convenience of this bilaterality.

Since there is no left or right-handedness in octopuses . . . the performance of one side of the animal can be used as a control for the effect of a brain lesion on the performance of the other. Doing experiments in this way eliminates many of the variables that otherwise make it difficult to interpret the results of . . . experiments. An animal that is hungry, or sick, may perform badly and one normally has no means of determining the precise extent to which the poor performance of animals with brain lesions is due to this sort of factor. With split preparations, it is fair to assume that the two sides of the same animal are equally cheerful or miserable and that they were equally experienced and equally intelligent at the start of the experiment.

One finding concerning the relationship of the two sides of the brain is highly relevant to the question of information storage. Suppose one side of a blind octopus is trained in a tactile discrimination, it may be asked whether the other side of the intact brain stores relevant information simultaneously. In fact, it does not. It takes about 1 h for the other side to catch up with the trained side. The long-term store can, then, hardly be a change merely in electrical relationships. Probably, the initial registration and storage are in the form of patterned sets of impulses passing among the neurons; but the repetition of these patterned discharges leads to structural changes, presumably at the synapses, in the hour that follows the relevant experience.

7.6 FISH

7.6.1 Varieties of Adaptability

Of the more than 20,000 species of fish, few have been studied ethologically. Often, experiments are on the domestic goldfish, *Carassius auratus.* Substantial differences of behavior must be expected between pelagic fish, which live in the nearly homogeneous environment of the open sea, and those that live among rocks or plants, or in pools on the shore.

Ethologically the most celebrated species is the three-spined stickleback, *Gasterosteus aculeatus.* Male sticklebacks build nests (9.2.1), and in doing so often remove objects, such as stones, from the nest site. Bernadette Muckensturm studied this behavior experimentally, but did not use a conventional method: instead she gives an impression of the natural animal. She stuck miniature wood posts in the sand around a nest, and the male pulled them out and took them away. She also put a piece of nylon over a nest, and weighed it down with small stones; the fish removed the stones, and then the nylon. The observations were made on a number of males, and there was much individual variation. The presence of obstacles led not only to their removal but also to much extra activity, including momentary attacks on plants growing in the aquarium. Unfortunately, nothing seems to be known of the way in which this type of behavior develops.

A clear example of adapting behavior to experience comes from work, by R. Hoogland and others, on two predatory species, the perch, *Perca fluviatilis,* and the pike, *Esox lucius,* toward two sticklebacks, the three-spined and the ten-spined, *Pygosteus pungitius.* All species are well distributed in European freshwaters. Sticklebacks (figure 7-18) are quickly snapped up by perch or pike (figure 7-19); but their spines, which are raised when the fish is disturbed, make the predators reject them.

Such rejection involves "coughing"—a reflex response. But a pike or perch that has begun to eat

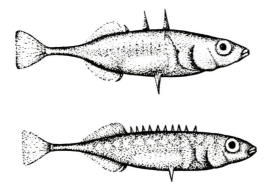

FIGURE 7-18 Above, three-spined stickleback, *Gastero-steus aculeatus;* below, the ten-spined, *Pygosteus pungi-tius.* The spines of both protect them from predation. (See figure 7-19.) (Reproduced by permission from R. Hoogland et al., *Behaviour* 10, 1957)

a stickleback, and has (with difficulty) spat it out, usually refuses another stickleback on sight: an aversion has been developed for this kind of prey. Experiments have been done with sticklebacks deprived of their spines; as expected, the spines provide the main aversive stimulus: spineless sticklebacks are usually not spat out but are ingested.

A third example of adaptability in natural conditions concerns the behavior of fish, especially salmon, *Salmo,* which live in the sea but migrate up rivers to spawn (reviewed by A. D. Hasler; and by H. Gleitman & P. Rozin). The behavior includes their astonishing movement against a formidable rush of water and even the leaping of obstacles that one would think would be unsurmountable. Eggs are laid upstream, and the young fish spend their early life in freshwater. They then move back into the sea where they travel over vast distances: The North American Chinook salmon, *Oncorhyncus tschawytscha,* may range up to 4000 km from home and the Atlantic salmon, *Salmo salar,* 2500 km. When they are sexually mature, they return to the river or stream of origin. How do they achieve

this? Each river evidently differs subtly from all others in its chemical properties. It seems that the fish can discriminate these differences, and that early experience determines their choice of spawning ground. There is an analogy here to the imprinting by which some young birds and mammals become responsive to members of their own species (12.3).

Elaborate experiments have been needed to justify these conclusions. Eggs are moved from the stream in which they have been laid to another;

FIGURE 7-19 Pike, *Esox lucius,* with a three-spined stickleback in various positions in its mouth. A pike rejects such spiny objects; and, once it has experienced a stickleback's spines, it rejects such prey on sight. (Reproduced by permission from R. Hoogland et al., *Behaviour* 10, 1957)

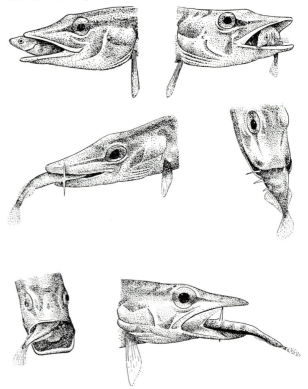

and the young fish are marked, by clipping their fins, before their migration to the sea. Then traps are set in both streams annually for some years. All findings from such work support the hypothesis that salmon "remember" the chemical properties of the stream in which they were hatched. Moreover, adult salmon in spawning condition have had their olfactory sacs infused with the waters of various sources, and the resulting electrical activity in the olfactory bulbs was recorded: the activity was most marked when the sacs were stimulated by home waters. Clearly salmon have long memories.

7.6.2 Mazes

We now turn to conventional experiments in the laboratory. W. H. Thorpe (1963) has reviewed early studies of route-learning by fish. Some have differed from the usual maze-learning experiments: the reward (food) was visible behind glass, and the fish had to make a detour to get it. In other experiments the food was not visible at the starting point. Wrasse, *Ctenolabris rupestris,* a European freshwater species, have been presented with food behind a glass plate or in a pot. After some experiences of this kind, the fish rather suddenly acquired the habit of going round the obstacle or into the pot.

Several species of the tropical freshwater Cichlidae have been required to cope with a glass plate; but in this case they had to get over it. Since the top was only just below the surface, they had either to turn on their sides to swim past, or else to jump. Some did the one or the other; but there was much variation between individuals of the same species and between different species. Some fish succeeded even when the glass was frosted and the reward was out of sight.

Another tropical species, the Siamese fighting fish, *Betta splendens,* lives in turbid waters; but it has long been bred in captivity for the gorgeous coloring of the males' fins and for readiness to make vigorous attacks on other males (S. R. Goldstein). It is therefore, like the white rat, a domestic animal (M. J. A. Simpson). These fish can learn to make a detour through a hole in an obstacle. Initially the movements are apparently at random. If the food is visible when the hole is passed, the fish swim straight toward it. If it is not visible, there is further apparently random movement until the food is found. Once this has been achieved the fish are economical in their movements on later trials, and often take the shortest route to the goal. The fish can learn new routes if the arrangement of obstacles and food is altered. In some experiments the fish were required to make a vertical detour. When the obstacle was gradually moved so that its top was at the surface, they jumped over like a flying fish.

These and other experiments show not only topographical learning by fish, but also their ability to adapt the kinds of movement they make to achieve a goal.

Fish can learn not only to approach but also to avoid. W. H. Riege & A. Cherkin give an example from experiments with goldfish. These useful animals tend to swim against a current. In the experiments they swam into a calm water well; arrival in the well acted as a reward. It was found possible to induce avoidance of the well by giving the fish a shock on entry. Only one such experience was needed. The retention of this habit was observed at various intervals after the shock. (Compare the experiments on bees after a single reward, 7.4.4.) The index of retention was the *latency* of reentry: that is, the experimenters recorded the interval between being again exposed to the situation and entry into the well. If the fish were tried again immediately after the shock, there was marked avoidance; but after that there was at first a decline, and then a rise to another peak at about 60 min. Once again we find evidence of two kinds of storage in the nervous system, one brief and one more prolonged.

An electric shock is, of course, at first sight a very unnatural aversive stimulus. A question I have not seen discussed is how often fish encounter it in natural conditions. There are animals, notably electric eels, *Electrophorus,* and rays, *Torpedo,* which produce shocks of a force sufficient to stun their prey. Probably, however, this does not justify us in saying that the electric shocks of experimenters simulate a natural event.

7.6.3 Discriminations

It is easy to guess at the function of maze-learning ability for freshwater, shore-living or benthic fish in natural conditions. The problem box is a different matter. Nonetheless, Haralson & Bitterman have succeeded in designing a Skinner box (compare figure 6-6) suitable for fish. Their subject was a cichlid, *Tilapia macrocephala,* an African mouthbrooder. The specific name indicates a large (swollen?) head, but this may not be relevant. Instead of pressing a bar like a rat, the fish had to thump its head against an object. Reward for doing so was provided by the automatic release of a small worm into the water. Discrimination could be studied by providing two targets, differently colored, of which only one was a source of reward. Similar experiments have been carried out with goldfish. M. E. Bitterman (1975) and M. H. Sheldon have reviewed the resulting findings.

1. Suppose one target is colored red, the other green, and that only hitting red is rewarded. When the fish have developed the habit of nearly always

hitting the red, the arrangement is reversed: reward now comes from hitting the green. The reversal is learnt by a fish or rat equally well. (The rat, of course, would be tested either in a conventional Skinner box or in a T-maze or on a jumping stand, such as that of figure 6-3. And the discrimination would not be based on color.) There follows a series of further reversals. As we know, rats improve in these conditions (6.2.3); but fish (those that have been tested) do not: fish can learn a single reversal, but they do not *learn to reverse* in general (figure 7-20).

2. A rather similar finding comes from the study of extinction. If a fish, trained in a discrimination, repeatedly hits the previously rewarding target with no result, it loses the habit of hitting that target. Suppose, then, the fish is subjected repeatedly to further positive training and further extinction; on each occasion it has to relearn the extinction as before: there is no improvement such as a rat shows in analogous situations.

3. A further example of failure of transfer of training is provided by the *dimensional transfer effect.* Again I take an example involving color and therefore suitable for a fish but not for a rat. The experiment requires that the stimuli to be discriminated differ in two respects ("dimensions"). For example, they could be straight lines that differ both in color and in orientation: they could be red or green, horizontal or vertical. Now suppose that approach to red is rewarded regardless of orientation. Color may then be said to be the "relevant dimension". The trained animals are next tested with another set of stimuli that differ in the same respects, say, yellow versus blue, and opposite slopes. For some animals color is again relevant, for others it is now the angle that has to be attended to. Monkeys, *Macaca,* and even rats improve on this second test if the relevant dimension

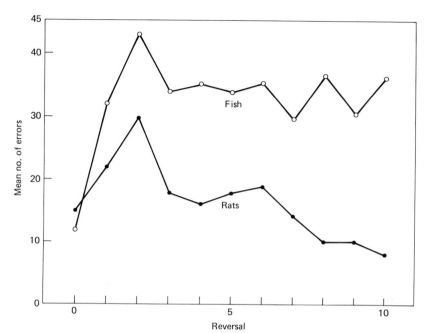

FIGURE 7-20 Results of giving fish and rats successive discrimination reversals. The animals are first trained to discriminate two visible stimuli. Once trained, they are required to learn to avoid the previously positive stimulus and to approach the one formerly negative. Their error rate then rises; and it rises still further after a second reversal. The error rate of fish then remains high; but that of rats declines. Hence fish, unlike rats, do not learn to reverse. (After M. E. Bitterman, 1968)

is the same as in the first. "Intradimensional transfer is better than extradimensional transfer." But fish show no such effect.

4. Now let us look at some features of reward. Goldfish have been trained to strike a target for worms as described above; and in this case the latency was recorded: that is, the time between the moment when the target becomes available and the occurrence of the response. Some fish were rewarded on each strike with 4 worms, others with 40 worms. Those that received the larger reward were quicker to strike. When they had been fully trained, some of those receiving the larger reward were shifted to receiving only four worms. Unlike rats, they displayed no signs of disappointment, but continued to strike with the same promptness as before. The main work with rats on the depression effect of a reduced reward was done in a runway,

not a discrimination apparatus. Fish have been tested similarly also in a swimway (and so have turtles, *Chrysemis picta*), with the same finding of no depression.

5. Lastly, experiments on *probability matching* may be mentioned. In a discrimination apparatus, it is possible to reward approach to one stimulus on 70% of trials and approach to the other stimulus on 30%. The sequence is randomized. Hence on each trial the betting ratio is 7 : 3 on the first stimulus. In such a situation, the most profitable strategy is always to approach the first stimulus; and this is what a rat (or a monkey, or a human being) does. But a fish does not: on the contrary, it shows probability matching: the "better" stimulus is approached on only 70% of trials, at random. When faced with visual problems, the painted turtle also behaves in this respect like a fish.

7.7 BIRDS

Birds are, like mammals, homeothermic; but they have evolved from a reptilian ancestry separate from that of the mammals since the Triassic. Their brains, larger relative to their bodies than those of reptiles, are structurally different from the mammalian type: there are large cerebral hemispheres; but the dorsal pallium (highly developed in mammals) is little more than a membrane, while the ventrolateral regions form a great mass of tissue.

The intellect of birds is popularly not highly regarded: the expression "bird-brained" is hardly complimentary. Nonetheless, as we know, in their food getting some birds are quite adaptable. If their searching movements reveal the presence of hidden food, they adapt the search accordingly (3.3). They also quickly learn to avoid noxious species and retain the habit of avoidance for long periods (3.5). Thier discriminatory abilities are of a high order. Homing requires an acquired knowledge of topography, and the navigation of experienced migrants may depend on storage of information about star patterns or other features (2.4.3). Some even more remarkable achievements of the bird's brain are discussed in the next chapter. Here I give some examples of experiments on trial-and-error behavior.

Many experiments have been done on domestic pigeons, *Columba livia,* in Skinner boxes, which can be operated by pecking (6.1.2). The findings from such work (reviewed by M. E. Bitterman & W. M. Schoel; C. B. Ferster & B. F. Skinner) resemble those on rats tested in similar equipment (chapter 6). The similarity is not surprising: the experimental design obliges the subject to perform a single, narrowly defined act—pressing a bar or pecking a key; no other activity is (as a rule) recorded; and no other has any significant effect on the animal's surroundings.

A Skinner box therefore gives little opportunity for different species to reveal their special qualities (7.8). Yet pigeons trained to peck for a reward do not behave like automata. A much-discussed example is *autoshaping* (reviewed by B. R. Moore). Suppose a fasted pigeon is put in a Skinner box. The equipment is programmed so that, at intervals, the response key is lit up and a food reward is delivered after a brief delay. This happens regardless of what the bird does: there is no need for the bird to peck the key. In those conditions the pigeon nonetheless pecks the illuminated key: that is, it performs a stereotyped, species-typical act although doing so has no evident outcome. The interpretation of this conduct is debatable; but it does illustrate once again that the relationship between activity and reward is not simple (6.2.1).

In earlier work with problem boxes (reviewed by W. H. Thorpe, 1963), the tasks allowed rather more variation of response. Birds were fed in a food cage inside their living cage. Later the food cage was shut; but it could be opened from outside by pulling or pressing on a string that was stretched tight between two supports. Birds of several species learned to open the cage, some by pulling the string with beak or claw, others by pressing the string with their heads. In further experiments, some birds learned to solve the problem by alighting on the string. This was typical trial-and-error behavior: solving the problem for the first time required many inappropriate movements, but after a number of successes the solution was rapid and economical. House sparrows, *Passer domesticus,* displayed great persistence and coped with the problems very well. They also alternated between uninhibited approach ("boldness") and avoidance or withdrawal ("fear"). There is a resemblance here to the wild rats (4.5.2), which are also very successful in human communities.

A comment on method may also be made. These

experiments, carried out in the first decade of this century, used only simple equipment: there were no elaborate electronic devices for recording the subjects' movements or for imposing a calculated "schedule of reinforcement"; but the findings are much more relevant to the animal's life in natural conditions than many of those based on the use of modern electronics.

Some species of birds run about and feed on the ground; but even for them a laboratory maze seems an inappropriate environment. Nonetheless, E. Diebschlag found little difficulty in training pigeons to waddle mazes: in some respects the birds did as well as, or better than, laboratory rats. But they did not display as much adaptability: once they had thoroughly learned one maze, they did not readily alter their movements to cope with a changed problem.

An interesting question, apparently as yet unanswered, is whether other species would do better than pigeons. The birds commonly regarded as most "intelligent" are the crows (Corvidae). L. W. Kruschinski and others presented members of this family with an unusually difficult problem. They were allowed to see two boxes through a screen; One box contained food, the other not. The two boxes were moved in opposite directions. To get the food, each bird then had to go round the screen in the appropriate direction. Members of the crow family did well in this test, but two domesticated types, pigeons and fowls, did not.

In some other tests, however, pigeons and domestic fowl have done quite well. Fish, as we know, do not improve with practice when given a series of discrimination reversals (7.6.3); but pigeons do (M. E. Bitterman, 1975). Domestic fowl have been shown by R. J. Plotnik & R. B. Tallarico to be able to develop a learning set. Four white Plymouth Rock roosters were given a series of 50 discriminations. The stimuli were three-dimensional objects.

A progressive improvement in performance on second trials was observed. Evidently some species of birds have evolved a brain that makes possible adaptive behavior of a complexity similar at least to that of rodents.

7.8 ACHIEVEMENTS AND CONSTRAINTS

7.8.1 Comparative Studies

Most people, even zoologists, speaking informally, will agree that a man is more intelligent than a macaque, and a macaque than a mouse; but to express this notion precisely is not easy; and still greater difficulties arise if we wish to compare, say, a squid with a cichlid. At first it might seem that differences in the ability to solve problems could fit an evolutionary sequence from lower to higher; but here, too, we meet great difficulties. Among them is that what is rewarding for one species is not necessarily so for another (J. A. Hogan & T. J. Roper).

An obvious procedure is to set members of each species one or more problems, and to use conventional measures of performance in assessing them. Such measures include (1) the time taken to attain a specified level of performance; (2) the numbers of errors before success; (3) the proportion of successes during a series of trials after training. Unfortunately, this method does not work. Figure 7-21 gives "learning curves" for laboratory rats and two species of monkey; the task was to learn the simplest possible maze—one with a single choice point—for a food reward. Of the three species, the rats did best. Similarly, in experiments by Ø. Skard, laboratory rats were compared with human beings. Fourteen rats were required to learn a maze with 14 choice points for a food reward; and 20 blindfolded students were "run" in a maze of identical geometry: they used a stylus and ran it along a

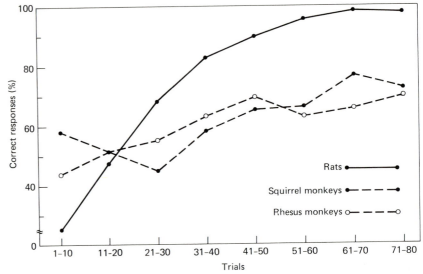

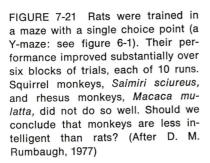

FIGURE 7-21 Rats were trained in a maze with a single choice point (a Y-maze: see figure 6-1). Their performance improved substantially over six blocks of trials, each of 10 runs. Squirrel monkeys, *Saimiri sciureus,* and rhesus monkeys, *Macaca mulatta,* did not do so well. Should we conclude that monkeys are less intelligent than rats? (After D. M. Rumbaugh, 1977)

groove in the maze walls. The reward for the students was getting out of the maze. In these conditions the rats learned the task about as quickly as the students. In an earlier study by V. C. Hicks & H. A. Carr, rats improved in speed of running a maze to a much higher degree than human beings, but in other respects had a rather similar "learning" score. As the authors remark, the facts are not explicable in terms of intelligence.

Another type of example comes from experiments on discriminations. As we know, some kinds of discrimination can be rapidly acquired. Bees learn to go to one color rather than another in only a few trials, and indeed they develop the habit to some extent in only one (7.4.4). Similarly, avoiding an intensely aversive stimulus is often learned in one trial. There is little scope for comparative assessment here.

There are also examples of great variation between species, or between other taxonomic groups, which do not match any simple phylogenetic

scheme. Within the great subphylum of the Insecta, the bees (Apidae) and the houseflies (Muscidae) may be regarded as pinnacles of evolutionary achievement. The former have notable ability in the learning of topographies and discriminations; the flies, by contrast, usually behave like extremely efficient automata: habit formation by dipterans can be demonstrated only with difficulty (4.5.1).

Not all comparative studies lead to confusion. The work of M. E. Bitterman (7.6), in which fish are compared with other vertebrates, has given a clear picture of certain differences between vertebrate taxa. The method is to take a clearly defined type of problem, appropriate for any vertebrates (and for many invertebrates), and to observe the response to it. One finding concerns reversal learning: fish evidently do not improve their ability to reverse when they have practice at reversing, but mammals do. There is also, as we saw, a difference between the taxa in dealing with probabilities. Such observations allow precise statements on differences, sometimes qualitative, between types. They refer to particular, clearly specifiable abilities. In such comparisons, there is, however, no place for statements about "intelligence" in general.

A critical reader may now have noticed a gap in the argument. A habit is usually developed either to remedy a deficit or to escape or to avoid some external stimulus. How can this aspect be made uniform for very different species? Fasting, say, a snake for 12 h after a meal would have little effect, for most snakes take their meals at longer intervals; but most mammals and birds feed much more frequently. The remedy is to test each species in a range of conditions: different durations of fast or intensities of shock may be tried; for the principal experiments the most effective level of deprivation

FIGURE 7-22 "Intelligence test" for rats. Above: an enclosure with movable barriers. The other diagrams show different arrangements of the barriers, each of which presents a detour problem. (After D. O. Hebb & K. Williams, 1946)

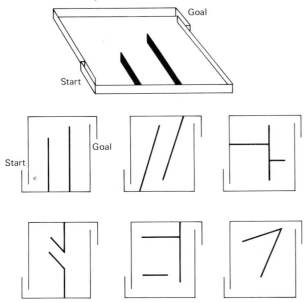

or stimulation is used. In this way each species is given the fullest opportunity to show what it can do.

A second example of successful comparison concerns variation within a species. D. O. Hebb & K. Williams were interested in differences in behavior between two types of domestic rat. They began by training them to find food in one of four containers in a spacious arena, but no difference between the two groups emerged. They were therefore led to design an "intelligence test" for rats of the type shown in figure 7-22. A series of tests is set, each in the same apparatus. Each item requires the rat to follow a particular route to the goal; and this route is varied. Each rat must be accustomed to the apparatus, to being handled, and to eating food at the goal. The whole procedure is highly standardized. When all these precautions are taken, the method proves to be reliable: that is, retests give scores closely similar to those of initial tests.

P. J. Livesey (1966, 1967) has also compared three domesticated mammalian species by this system. Rats, rabbits, and cats were run on raised pathways. Rats and rabbits were about equal, but did not do as well as cats.

The ability of a wasp to remember where it has dug holes, of a bee to learn visual discriminations, and of an ant or a rat to learn mazes all exemplify a biological axiom: each species has its ecological niche, and all its characteristics may be expected to be related to that mode of life. The same can often be said of what an animal cannot do. An extreme case is that of a sedentary bivalve mollusk, which has hardly any behavior at all: its capacity for developing new habits is almost zero.

Such limitations are sometimes due to sensory deficiencies. Primates excepted, mammals are not equipped to distinguish colors, and so cannot learn discriminations based on them: a gray rag can be as effective to a bull as a red rag. A human being cannot detect sounds of pitch above, say, 20 kHz (without instruments), but a dog or a bat can. Other examples are given in 1.1.4.

Some sensory limitations are central and do not reflect the properties of the sense organs. As we know (7.5.3), an octopus can adjust the movements of its limbs to compensate for the weights of objects picked up; but it cannot be trained, as a mammal can, to discriminate objects by weight. J. M. Warren (1973) reviews comparisons between the domestic cat, *Felis ocreatus,* and the rhesus macaque, *Macaca mulatta.* Cats can easily be trained, on presentation of a signal, to approach a box for a reward of food. Suppose the box is indicated both by the sound of a buzzer and by a flashing light; the alternative box is silent and unlighted. Cats so trained have been tested in three conditions: (1) the correct box is indicated by light alone; (2) the box is indicated by the buzzer; and (3) the correct box is indicated by one of the two signals while the other signal is shown on the alternative box. The buzzer alone was then almost as effective as if buzzer and light had still been combined. The light alone was less effective. And when the cats had to choose between light and buzzer, they always chose the latter. In contrast, rhesus monkeys, although they have excellent hearing (tested by other means), learned to approach a reward signaled by a sound only with difficulty.

One way of describing such findings is to say that cats pay more attention to sound than do macaques. Cats hunt at night, largely by ear. In contrast, monkeys feed off plants during the day. Hence the behavioral differences observed experimentally correspond to the ecological differences between the two species. There may, however, be another factor: according to some observations, the sounds used are aversive to monkeys.

Rhesus monkeys may also be compared with dolphins, *Tursiops truncatus,* in their capacity to make sounds at need. Two dolphins, a male and a female, were trained by J. Bastian to cooperate in solving a problem. The solution required that the female (out of sight of the male) should utter a particular sound; the male had to respond by approaching the source of reward. The training succeeded, although the experimenter was unable to identify the precise sounds involved. In contrast, as S. Yamaguchi & R. E. Myers have shown, it is difficult to train a macaque to make a sound for food reward. Monkeys that failed this test quickly learned to press a bar when a red light was switched on and not to do so when it was off. They also learned to make a particular arbitrary movement, with the head up, when the light was on.

In this case, we are dealing with a species, the dolphin, which (in common with other Cetacea) has an elaborate system of communication by sounds. There is no reason to think dolphins more "intelligent" than monkeys; but they are evidently better at controlling their voices and at responding to auditory cues. In contrast, visible signals dominate in the social interactions of macaques. Macaques can learn to communicate the whereabouts of food to other macaques. W. A. Mason & J. H. Hollis arranged that one monkey could see a reward, but only the partner (who could not see it) could get to it. To achieve this, the partner had to select the correct one out of four possible responses. Communication was by gesture. Once again, however, we must not take statements on modes of life as explanations of the experimental findings. There seem to be relationships between the abilities of the two species and their respective niches in natural conditions, but we do not know under what selection pressures the differences evolved.

7.8.2 Species-typical Preparedness

In some recent ethological writings special attention has been paid to "constraints on learning" (R. A. Hinde & J. Stevenson-Hinde). It may seem strange to emphasize deficiencies rather than abilities. There is, however, a reason that is both historical and practical (reviewed by K. H. Brookshire). "Learning" has traditionally been the field of psychologists, not zoologists. Psychologists are primarily interested in man, but have ventured into the animal kingdom, at least as far as the albino rat. They have, reasonably enough, sought general laws of behavior. Accordingly, they have often disregarded the facts of biological diversity. In the preceding section are examples of the kinds of interspecific differences they have ignored.

M. E. P. Seligman has published a general discussion. He uses the terms "preparedness" and "contrapreparedness". The existence of species-typical abilities and limitations does not, however, justify the expression (also used by some writers) "inherited predispositions to learn": as we see further in chapter 16, it is misleading to refer to *characteristics* as inherited: the significant property of these predispositions is that they are difficult to alter during the development of the individual.

S. J. Shettleworth has made a systematic study of the conduct of hamsters, *Mesocricetus auratus,* when fasted (hungry). The question she asks is whether her animals can be trained to perform any of their stereotyped actions by rewarding them with food. It proves to be easy to train them to dig, to scrape at a surface, or to rear up on their hind legs; but other prominent action patterns, such as face washing and scent marking, can hardly be evoked by such training (figure 7-23). Shettleworth comments that in natural conditions face washing and

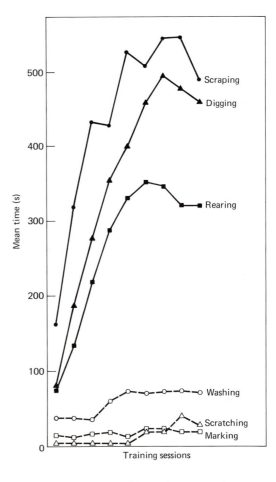

FIGURE 7-23 Hamsters, *Mesocricetus auratus,* were rewarded with food when they performed one of six acts: if the act rewarded was scraping, digging, or rearing up, the extent to which it was performed increased with the training; but there was no such effect of rewarding washing the face, scratching, or scent marking. (After S. J. Shettleworth, 1975)

scent marking, unlike the other activities, are not associated with food getting.

As another example, I refer again to the work of J. Garcia and others on the learned aversions of rats (4.5.2.4). The aversive effect of a toxic food lasts for some hours, even when the rat has not been exposed to the food during that period. Most work on habit formation by rats had used situations (described in 6.1) in which a rat's retention span has to be measured in seconds or at most minutes. Garcia, then, showed rats to have abilities superior to those previously assumed. But, as we know, he also displayed their limitations. A delayed illness can be related to a taste or an odor, but not to a sound or to a visible stimulus.

These findings fit the evident needs of an omnivorous animal with poor eyesight. They may be compared with observations on birds. Bobwhite quail, *Colinus virginianus,* studied by H. C. Wilcoxon and others, resemble rats in several respects: they can develop an aversion to a flavored solution when drinking the solution is followed by illness. The aversion can arise from a single experience, and the onset of illness may be as long as 30 min after drinking. But, unlike rats, quail can develop an aversion to a colored but flavorless mixture. Similarly, G. M. Martin and others have induced young chickens, *Gallus,* to develop aversions specific to the color red by giving them novel red food followed by a dose of poison.

The preceding findings concern maintenance activities. The same principles can be applied to so-cial interactions. P. Sevenster (1968) has studied courtship and attack by the three-spined stickleback, *Gasterosteus aculeatus.* In some experiments males in the breeding state, in their territory, were trained to swim through a ring. One effective reward was the opportunity to court a female for 10 s. Another, equally effective, was the sight of a second male behind a glass barrier, again for 10 s. The response to the male was threat or attack (9.2.1). Sevenster also trained sticklebacks, again in their territory, to bite the tip of a rod. For this purpose, the sight of another male was again an effective reward: the sticklebacks displayed at the rival male behind glass, then swam to bite the rod and back again to display at the rival. But in this case a female was not an effective reward. When a female was offered, there were very long intervals between bites; and during the intervals the male behaved toward the rod rather as if it were a female to be courted, not something to be bitten.

Such findings, unfortunately, do not provide us with "laws of learning": on the contrary, they emphasize variety. But we have by no means exhausted the variety of abilities, even among the few species that have been well studied. In particular, nothing has yet been said about the ability to improvise. We turn to this in the next chapter.

8

EXPLORING, IMPROVISING, AND IMITATING

Animals manifestly enjoy excitement, and
suffer from ennui, . . . and many exhibit *Curiosity*.
                         Darwin
                      The Descent of Man

The previous two chapters are concerned principally with gradual changes in behavior related to reward or punishment. Animals can learn their way to food, nest sites, and other necessities; and they can learn to avoid adverse features of the environment, such as predators. Such behavior, adapted to the special circumstances of each individual, requires storage of information in the nervous system. The storage can occur, however, without reinforcement: the phenomena of delayed reinforcement (6.2.1.3) provide examples. In the present chapter a major theme is the use of information stored on a number of occasions without reinforcement, then combined later. Many animals evidently acquire information as they move about, and can use it later in taking the shortest route to a goal such as a nest. If that route has never been taken before, the behavior falls quite outside the category of trial and error: there has been no previous error or even trial.

Such abilities are subjectively familiar. A human being who knows an area of countryside or of a city can often go by the shortest route between two points without ever having done so before. One speaks of having a map in one's head.

The storage of topographical information allows, then, sudden solution of a new problem. In general, acquaintance with a class of problems may make possible the instant solution of a novel problem from that class. For us, mathematics provides many obvious instances. We see later that, although few (if any) animals can count, other species too can learn to solve general kinds of problems.

One kind involves a social interaction. If an animal, D, performs an unusual set of movements, can another, O, of the same species, at once make similar movements? That is, can O *imitate* D? We see below that imitation, which is such a prominent feature of human conduct, is also important for a number of mammalian species.

8.1 ACTIVITY AND EXPLORATION

8.1.1 Observations in the Field

8.1.1.1 Insects: As we know, many species have a settling place, nest, hide, or lair; this they leave at intervals, usually provoked by the need for food or a mate. Once satisfied (or exhausted) they have to return. Sometimes they leave traces on the outward journey; and these guide them on the way back (2.3.5).

Among animals that do not depend on such traces are the hunting wasps of the family Sphegidae. W. H. Thorpe (1950) has watched *Ammophila pubescens* on an area of gravelly heath in England. The females lay their eggs in holes and stock the holes with caterpillars. The caterpillars are first stung, then dragged along the ground sometimes over distances of nearly 100 m. Thorpe interrupted the return of a wasp by catching it, putting it in a box, and carrying it some distance before releasing it (figure 8-1). The wasp made a rapid and accurate return journey from the new position. Another, similarly treated, briefly circled before setting off in the correct direction.

Such observations suggest the presence, in the small brain of the wasp, of a representation of its living area. The wasps are said to be very "exploratory": that is, they often fly about apparently aimlessly. The assumption is that in doing so they learn their way around; but no experiments were done by Thorpe to test this.

A more detailed study has been made of sand wasps, *A. campestris,* in the Netherlands. G. P. Baerends (1941) spent five summers recording the behavior of more than 100 of these insects while they made their nests, laid their eggs, and stocked their nests with food. He marked the wasps with paint for individual recognition; and the nests, visible to human beings only with difficulty, were identified by wires pointing to them. Sometimes he made an artificial nest of plaster of Paris, to replace an authentic one, since an ordinary nest is liable to disintegrate on inspection.

When an egg hatches out and the larva begins to eat, it has to be supplied with more caterpillars, according to need. The female visits each of her holes daily. What is found during these visits determines whether she will return with more food.

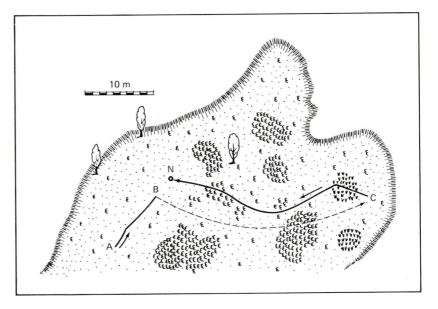

FIGURE 8-1 Sketch map to illustrate the experiment on a wasp, *Ammophila pubescens,* described in the text. The wasp was observed dragging prey along the line AB. At B it was picked up and put in a box, in which it was taken to C. Its remarkably direct flight path from C to its nest (N) is shown. The observations were made in a depression in heathland in which there were patches of ericaceous plants and small trees (indicated by the symbol Ɛ). (After W. H. Thorpe, 1950)

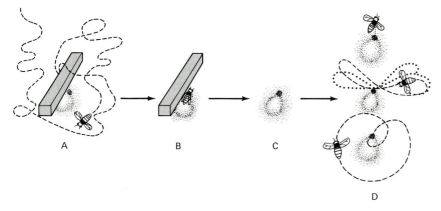

FIGURE 8-2 Diagram to illustrate experiments on a wasp, *Bembix rostrata.* (A) A strange object has been put by a hole previously dug by the wasp: the wasp performs an orientation flight and (B) enters the nest. (C) The object is now removed. (D) On emerging, the wasp closes the entrance, and then usually performs an orientation flight of one of the kinds shown. (After J. J. A. van Iersel & J. van den Assem, 1965)

Sometimes, she returns after a delay as long as 15 h; she has evidently remembered the exact place of the hole and what is in it. Moreover, a female can keep several holes stocked in this way at one time. Hence, when a wasp makes a visit of inspection to one of her holes, the information she acquires is retained and—if necessary—acted upon after an astonishingly long period.

The homing of these insects depends on the use of landmarks. Wasps of another genus of this family, *Philanthus,* have been studied by N. Tinbergen & W. Kruyt, and by G. van Beusekom. The prey in this case are honey bees which, too, are paralyzed and brought to a burrow for the larvae to feed on. In many experiments, patterns of landmarks around the burrow were set up and then altered. An important observation was on the effect of a drastic change in the arrangement of such objects while the insect was in its hole. On emerging, the insect flew around for a short period. Such an "orientation flight" needed to last only 9 s: the animal could then home accurately on the hole with its new landmarks. The information stored in this way evidently persisted, sometimes, for several days.

J. J. A. van Iersel & J. van den Assem have made a still more detailed study, also in the Netherlands, of *Bembix rostrata.* This wasp preys upon flies but, like the others, digs nests with barely visible entrances. The wasp homes on her nest with speed and accuracy. If, however, the immediate surroundings of a nest are extensively disturbed, the result is "searching" behavior. Experiments, in which objects were put near a nest, and later moved, illustrate the precise memory of these insects for the relationships of structures to the nest entrance (figure 8-2). Such information storage always requires an orientation flight. This wasp does not, however, use only nearby landmarks, but also distant ones; and if nearby objects are repeatedly moved, it directs its flight to the nest by others that remain unaltered (J. J. A. van Iersel).

The honey bee, *Apis mellifera,* is another insect that stores information in this way. In 7.4.4 I describe findings by Menzel on the memory of bees. His experiments depended on the tendency of bees to range widely in their flights, and so to be exposed to new sources of food. The function of this behavior in natural conditions is obvious: plants may newly come into flower, and exploratory behavior is essential for bees to make use of such additional resources.

Probably, bees similarly store information dur-

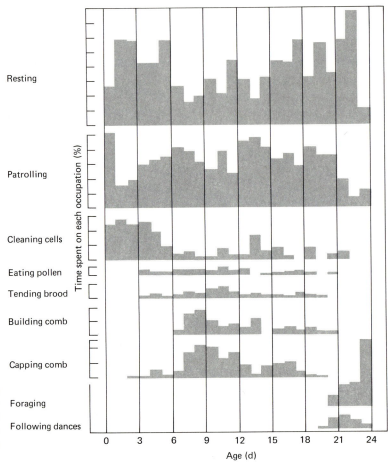

Resting

Patrolling

Cleaning cells

Eating pollen

Tending brood

Building comb

Capping comb

Foraging

Following dances

Time spent on each occupation (%)

Age (d)

FIGURE 8-3 Record of the time spent in various activities by a honey bee, *Apis mellifera,* observed throughout her life. Time spent patrolling the hive is especially notable. The record of some minor activities is omitted. (After M. Lindauer, 1961)

ing movements in the hive. M. Lindauer (1961) marked bees and recorded their activities continuously over long periods. These proverbially busy insects proved to be remarkably "idle". One, observed regularly for 20 days from emergence, worked for only 50 h out of the 139 h during which she was watched. For about another 50 h she moved slowly around, occasionally inspecting a cell or making contact with another worker (figure 8-3). The apparently random wandering is believed to enable a worker to respond to the needs of the hive as they arise (13.3.2).

8.1.1.2 Vertebrates: Searching by predators (3.3.1) is usually related directly to feeding: it has an immediate homeostatic function (4.5). Other movements allow storage of information that can be used later. From observations in natural conditions we can infer that such movements occur, although there is hardly any experimental evidence.

Among fish we should expect to find examples from those that make nests (such as sticklebacks, *Gasterosteus*), or from those that regularly return to a home. Among the latter is the shore-dwelling goby, *Bathygobius soporator* (figure 8-4), studied

FIGURE 8-4   A shore-dwelling goby, *Bathygobius soporator*. (Courtesy L. R. Aronson)

by L. R. Aronson (1951, 1971). Individual gobies can be identified as occupying the same rock pool day after day, at low water. But at low tide they also move from one pool to another by jumping. The jumps cannot be guided by sight of the next pool: one pool is quite invisible from a neighboring one. (Aronson also gives evidence against orienta-

tion by the sun.) He moved fish to unfamiliar pools and tried to induce them to jump out by prodding them. Such treatment quickly induces a jump when a fish is in a familiar pool, but never when in a strange pool. A fish removed from a familiar pool for 40 days and then put back could still jump accurately into neighboring pools. The most prob-

FIGURE 8-5   Artificial pools in which the movements of gobies (see figure 8-4) were studied. (Courtesy L. R. Aronson)

able explanation is that these fish swim around at high water, and acquire information about the rocks and pools in their area while doing so. In experiments with artificial pools (figure 8-5), the fish were found to direct their movements correctly only after swimming over the pools. G. C. Williams (1957) has described similar behavior by the wooly sculpin, *Clinocottus analis,* a "sluggish" species of the rocky shores in California.

There is surprisingly little exact information on the exploratory behavior of birds. Incidental observations have been made, such as those on crows described in 3.3.2; and W. H. Thorpe (1963) mentions possible examples, rather unexpectedly, from birds that have no nests of their own. Many cuckoos (Cuculiformes) are nest parasites: their eggs are laid in the nests of other species and the young are fed by the hosts. During the breeding season a female cuckoo may occupy a perch for many hours while birds of other species build their nests around her. The positions of these nests (often well concealed) are evidently remembered, and visited for egg-laying when the cuckoo is ready.

When we come to the mammals, we find a similar lack of precise information. An exception is provided by the work of J. R. Bider and others on the raccoon, *Procyon lotor.* This nocturnal mammal feeds as a rule before midnight. When it is sated, it moves around more widely; and if further sources of food are then found, on subsequent nights it visits them at an earlier hour.

Probably, most mammals are intensely exploratory: they either move around a large area when sated with food and other necessities; or, if they are large and live in the open, they scan the region around them by looking. The exploratory activity of wild rats has already been mentioned in the context of feeding behavior (4.5.2.4). But the exploratory behavior of even the much-studied *Rattus*

norvegicus is known principally from experiments in the laboratory. We now turn to them.

8.1.2 The Analysis of Activity

Observations in the field suggest that many animals (1) move about their living area when sated with necessities, (2) store information in doing so, and (3) make use of the information much later. These statements may be regarded as hypotheses. They have been tested rigorously in the laboratory, almost entirely on a few species of mammals (reviewed by S. A. Barnett, 1975; F. W. Finger; C. G. Gross; L. W. Reiter & R. C. Macphail). The first hypothesis implies that animals are sometimes active when not impelled by the demands of homeostasis or reproduction. An initial step is therefore to examine the ways in which activity is measured, that is, how "activity" is defined.

1. Figure 8-6 presents observations on two species of harvest mice. These animals have a marked circadian activity rhythm, if we define activity as *the time spent outside the nest.* Figure 5-17 illustrates an artificial environment that allows accurate recording of the same measure in the laboratory.

2. The time spent out of the nest tells us nothing about distance run. The traditional means of recording running is a wheel or treadmill (figure 8-7): this provides a record of *wheel activity.* Unfortunately, a wheel provokes running by an animal such as a rat or a mouse. Indeed, laboratory rats with restricted daily access to food may be so distracted by the wheel that they starve themselves (A. Routtenberg & A. W. Kuznesof). J. L. Kavanau has recorded another striking effect of running wheels. Deer mice, *Peromyscus,* were observed in artificial environments with many branching pas-

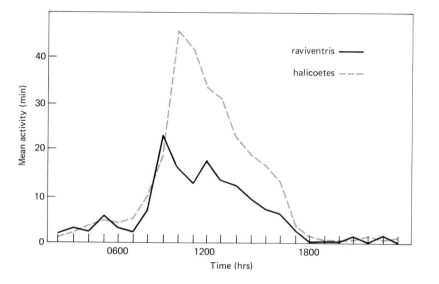

FIGURE 8-6 "Activity" as time spent outside the nest. Two species of harvest mice, *Reithrodontomys,* have a marked circadian rhythm. (After G. F. Fisler, 1965)

FIGURE 8-7 Wheel or treadmill, with rat. The revolutions of the wheel are automatically recorded. (I. A. Fox)

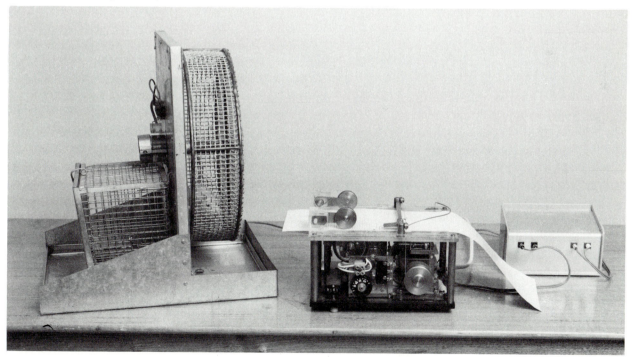

sages and other amenities, as well as wheels; and the structure of the wheels was varied: in some, the mice had not only to run but also to jump hurdles. They ran more in the more complicated wheels. Hence wheel activity measures an animal's special response to a wheel—usually in conditions in which it has as much food and water as it needs.

3. Sometimes it is desired to measure movement in the cramped conditions of an ordinary cage. The cage may then be mounted so that it is tilted by the animal's movements; and each roll or pitch is recorded mechanically or electrically. Such stabilimeter cages do not give the same results as a treadmill. We may therefore speak of *cage activity*.

4. Another much-used situation is the *open field* (reviewed by J. Archer, and by R. N. Walsh & R. A. Cummins). The subject, probably a laboratory rat or mouse, is picked out of its cage and put on a flat, featureless surface—usually with a wall to prevent the animal from jumping or falling off (figure 8-8). Its movements are recorded for a few minutes. The findings from such experiments vary with the species studied. Laboratory rats respond differently from laboratory mice; and R. C. Wilson and others have described diverse, species-typical responses of 12 species of mouse-like rodents. Neither the physiology nor the behavioral significance of open-field activity is fully understood.

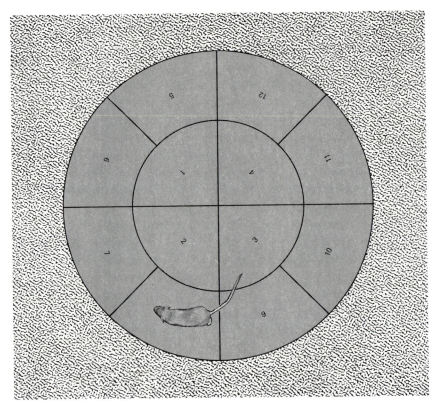

FIGURE 8-8 An "open field" with mouse. All marked sections are of the same area. In a typical experiment, the number of sections entered in, say, three minutes is recorded. Edge activity and center activity may be distinguished. (I. A. Fox)

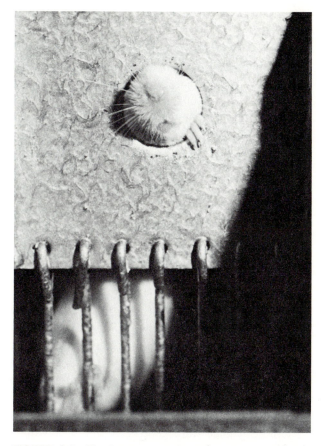

FIGURE 8-9 The frequency with which a small mammal pokes its nose into holes or crevices may be used as an index of exploratory activity. (Philip Boucas, courtesy World Health Organization)

5. A small mammal, during its wanderings, pokes its nose into holes and crevices (figure 8-9). Hence a board with holes in it may be included in the environment in which movements are to be studied. The number of occasions on which an animal responds to these holes by "head dipping" may then be recorded, and used as an index (S. E. File & A. G. Wardill, 1975a,b).

6. One accompaniment of the movements of most animals is the contraction of muscles. As S. D. Morrison has shown, it is possible to record the total activity, in this sense, of freely moving laboratory rats. A sensitive micromanometer is arranged to respond to a rat's movements in a small chamber: even respiratory movements may be detected by this means. At the same time, oxygen consumption (or loss of carbon dioxide) is measured. About 25% of total energy expenditure is then found to result from the animal's movements. Fasting the animal induces no change of activity in this sense; but there is an increase in the movements not related to feeding. Such experiments on energy expenditure show how something quite properly called total activity can be precisely measured. But in behavioral analysis we are usually interested in quantitative statements about particular kinds of behavior.

This list of methods illustrates the dangers of using vague expressions in describing behavior. It is not appropriate to say that fasting an animal increases its activity: it is necessary to state exactly what has been recorded. Nor is it appropriate to speak of general activity, unless one states just what observations have been made.

8.1.3 What Impels Movement?

8.1.3.1 Exploring Some Examples: One of the expressions to be used with caution is exploration. We may say casually that an animal is exploring when it is moving about (and if the animal is a mammal, probably sniffing as well, as in figure 8-10), and if the animal's movements have no evident relationship to need. Such a definition is too vague to be acceptable. In this section, instead of giving a more precise definition, we ask what makes an animal move about. Here are four examples of

FIGURE 8-10 A wild rat, *Rattus norvegicus,* rears up and sniffs during its movements about a strange environment. Rearing may be used as an index of exploration. (I. A. Fox)

the kinds of phenomena with which we are concerned.

1. Roger Darchen has studied the movements of a cockroach, *Blattella germanica.* These creatures hug corners (thigmotaxis) and shun light (2.2.2). Give them access to a vertical column and they climb it. This suggests negative geotaxis. But wait for a short time and they come down; then up again; and so on. With repetition, the rate of marching up and down declines. The same happens if a horizontal platform is provided. If a cockroach,

accustomed to one object, is offered another, the new one is explored. Novelty is evidently crucial. Similarly, if one of these insects is put in an empty Y-maze, it tends on successive runs to alternate between turning right and turning left: evidently the less familiar path is more attractive.

2. H. Kleerekoper and others describe the movements of goldfish, *Carassius auratus,* in a large tank. Each fish swims around in one part of the tank and then moves to another part. The movements are not random, but suggest that the fish go through a systematic process of familiarizing themselves with their new environment.

3. David Chiszar and others describe the movements of the garter snake, *Thamnophis radix.* Snakes had previously been described as lacking in "curiosity". These reptiles (and snakes of other species), put in an open field without food or the odors of other snakes, crawl around flicking their tongues. Rates of movement and tongue flicking are higher among fasted than among sated snakes; but the snakes also move and flick their tongues more when the open field is not familiar.

4. A final example is illustrated in figure 8-11. Laboratory mice were kept in an environment, of the kind illustrated in figure 5-17, during late pregnancy and early lactation. Activity, in the sense of both movement outside the nest and time spent outside, was (as expected) at a minimum around the time of parturition. Yet a part of the environment that never contained any incentive was regularly visited by every mouse on every day of the experiment. Hence all parts of a region around the nest are regularly inspected even when doing so is apparently fruitless.

To analyze such findings we need experiments in which animals' movements are altered by a single factor. In this way two kinds of hypothesis may be tested: (1) that internal deficits provoke activity in some sense; (2) that activity may reflect a tendency to vary the input through the external senses; in that case movements may be called novelty seeking or neophilic.

Both hypotheses are to some extent correct. Concerning the first, if an animal is deprived of food or

FIGURE 8-11 Movements of 20 laboratory mice in an artificial environment (figure 5-17), during late pregnancy and lactation. The number of visits made to all parts of the environment outside the nest, and the time spent outside the nest (A) were both at a minimum around parturition (Day 0). Nonetheless, an arm of the maze that was left empty was regularly visited by all mice on all days (B). (After S. A. Barnett & I. M. McEwan, 1973)

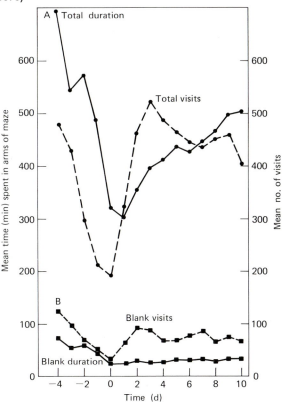

water, or is excessively cold or warm, it must be expected to move about more: in natural conditions such movement would improve its chances of returning to its optimum state (though this statement tells us nothing of the means by which the changed behavior is brought about). Even the apparently futile wheel running of a caged rat increases when the animal is fasted. Similarly, a female laboratory rat runs more in a wheel when she is in estrus and therefore receptive to a male, than at other times. Such movements, related to deficits, have been called appetitive behavior (17.1.2.1). The evidence bearing on the second hypothesis is described below.

8.1.3.2 Exploring: Laboratory Rats:

The notion of an appetitive component in behavior, provoked by an internal condition, is allied to that of behavior as a means by which the body is maintained in a steady state (chapter 4). Correspondingly, the preliminary to a consummatory act such as eating may be wide-ranging movements without any obvious orientation; or, at the other extreme, the movements may be along a well-marked track from a home to a source of food. The searching or appetitive phase of a behavioral sequence is therefore one in which the adaptability of behavior is especially marked. Animals develop new habits of movement as a result of what they find when they move about their range.

There is therefore no sharp distinction between searching impelled by a deficit and the movements that we call exploratory. Nonetheless, the latter seem to be independent of special incentives or needs; and they often occur after satiation, not before. The regular patrolling by parturient mice described above (figure 8-11) was not provoked by any evident incentive. In the same kind of situation, wild (and domestic) rats, *Rattus norvegicus,* make brief visits to all parts of an artificial environment after a meal. Such wanderings are not random but ordered: they tend to put the animal in unfamiliar, or at least less recently visited, parts of its range. Such conduct has been analyzed in great detail in the laboratory (reviewed by R. A. Butler; S. A. Barnett & P. E. Cowan, 1976).

The simplest case is that of an animal put in one of the three arms of a Y-maze, that is, a maze with a single choice point (figure 6-1). It walks to the choice point and turns, say, left; it is then picked up and replaced, walks to the choice point, and turns right. Laboratory rats in these conditions display alternation on at least 8 out of 10 trials. Such alternation is the simplest case of exploratory behavior: it is displayed when the alternative routes are each bare of any incentive; and in one pair of trials it maximizes an animal's range of movements.

The detailed analysis of spontaneous alternation has thrown light on the nature of exploration in general. One question is whether the animal is responding to external stimuli (stimulus alternation); the other possibility is that it is alternating the response, that is, the pattern of movements, regardless of external stimulation (response alternation). E. L. Walker and others used plus-shaped mazes

(figure 8-12) that could be rotated so that any of the four arms could point toward any feature of the laboratory. The arms of the maze were painted black or white, and any arm could be blocked, so that the cross could be converted into a T. The effects of three factors could then be distinguished: (1) the response, that is, turning left or right; (2) the visual stimulus provided by the differently painted arms of the maze; (3) the visual stimulus provided by the background outside the maze. On any given occasion, the maze could be arranged so that the animal had the choice between alternating either its response or the input from some aspect of its surroundings. In these conditions, the rat always varied the visual stimulus: there was no tendency to vary the response, that is, to alternate between turning right and turning left. The effects of the color of the maze walls and of the laboratory background were about equal. Many other experiments (reviewed by S. A. Barnett, 1975) have confirmed that spontaneous alternation consists of avoidance of external stimulation recently received, in favor of less familiar stimulation.

In some experiments it has been possible to provide novel stimulation from the internal senses. A maze has been used in which the entries to the goal

FIGURE 8-12 Test for stimulus alternation versus response alternation. On the left, arrows show direction of movement on successive trials, when the response is alternated; on the right, place or stimulus alternation is shown. (After E. L. Walker and others, 1955)

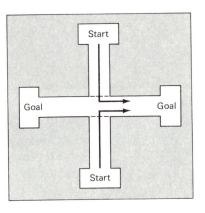 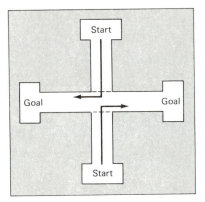

arms were complicated: each involved twists of the animal's body and changes of direction; and the contortions required were quite different in the two arms. The tendency to alternate the response (the movements) was then nearly as great as that to vary the input through the external senses.

Alternation is not a peculiarity of domestic rats. The polecat, *Putorius putorius* (Carnivora), has been studied in Y-mazes by R. N. Hughes and by A. M. Eastment & Hughes. The responses of these animals, like those of rats, are consistently neophilic. Polecats tend to approach an arm that is visibly more complex than the alternative. An appetitive effect is also observed: the animals move more quickly if fasted than if sated.

In all such experiments, it is desirable to allow for the possibility that, during a previous run, the animal itself has altered one of the runways. As we see later (13.2.3.4), small mammals, as they move about, deposit odorous substances that influence their own later behavior as well as that of conspecifics.

8.1.3.3 Novelty Rewarding:

In the experiments just described, the animals discriminate between the less and the more familiar, and tend to approach (select) the former. Many other experiments have shown that novel stimulation can operate as a reward: that is, animals will form a habit that enables them to vary the input through their external senses. One goal arm of a Y-maze may have a spacious goal box at the end, while the other leads merely to a featureless blind alley. The former is then entered more frequently, just as it would be if the animal had been fasted and offered food in that arm.

Such findings are not confined to behavior in mazes. In a Skinner box (figure 6-6) in the usual type of experiment, an animal has to press a bar

for a reward such as food. Provided the animal needs food, it will develop the habit of pressing the bar at a high rate. If pressing the bar has no effect, no such habit develops. But the expression "no effect" requires critical examination. Suppose pressing the bar produces a sharp click. Laboratory rats or mice press the bar at quite a high rate to produce this effect only. Similarly, they press a bar for light-on *or* for light-off (figure 8-13). Indeed, they will work for an increase or decrease of illumination in conditions in which there is always some light (reviewed by D. E. Berlyne, 1969).

There are analogous observations on Primates. Macaques, *Macaca mulatta,* have been kept alone for many hours in a featureless cage from which it was possible to get a view of the outside world only by pressing a lever. When the monkey did this, it opened a peep hole. Sometimes only an empty room was revealed; at others, the monkey could see palatable food, a toy train trundling round its circular track, or another monkey. All proved to be attractive, and the subjects spent much time exerting themselves to open the window and gaze out. There was, however, some discrimination: the sight of another monkey evoked the strongest response, next the train, then the food, and finally the empty room. Monkeys took many hours to get tired of this passive viewing.

Auditory exploration also occurs. To show this the box was partly insulated against sound, but its furniture included a loud speaker and two levers. Pressing one lever had no effect, but the other switched on the speaker and released the sounds of a nearby monkey colony. Again, monkeys showed no signs of quickly becoming bored with this entertainment. But in further experiments they did, once again, indicate preferences: a monkey calling to its mate was preferred, for instance, to a dog barking.

It may be asked whether it is appropriate to dis-

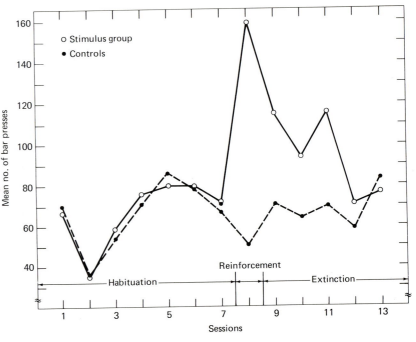

FIGURE 8-13 Reinforcing effect of light-on. Laboratory mice were put in a Skinner box (figure 6-6) in which, during the first seven sessions, pressing the bar had no effect. During the eighth session, it switched on a light, and the rate of bar pressing rose steeply. A control group was run with no light, and their rate of bar pressing did not rise. During the last part of the experiment there was again no light for the experimental group, and the response underwent extinction. (After G. B. Kish, 1955)

cuss such findings under the heading of exploration. We usually think of exploring as movement about a large region; but an animal such as a monkey, a bird, or even an octopus, all of which have good eyesight, can explore an area visually while keeping still. Such scanning insures variation in what is seen. Similarly, some animals can work for the sounds they hear.

Variation may also result from investigating and handling objects (R. A. Butler). Monkeys are readily trained to perform manipulations (figure 8-14). They are indeed likely to manipulate all accessible objects: they move them, break them, throw them, and so on without any obvious benefit. To solve the puzzle illustrated in figure 8-15, it was necessary to raise a pin, unlatch a hook, and swing back a hasp. Macaques readily learned to do this and repeated it again and again, although they achieved nothing further by doing so. They also solved more complex puzzles of a similar kind. Monkeys easily learn to distinguish objects that can be moved from others that are fixed. A board was offered, with differently colored screw eyes all apparently fastened down; in fact, those of one color could be pulled out. The monkeys quickly discovered those that could be detached and inspected. In fact, they learned to distinguish objects by color, simply for the reward of handling them.

Many mammals, then, work for stimulus change. But this statement disregards the possibility of working for a preferred level or kind of stimulation. If, for instance, an animal persistently turns a light off, it could be working either for a change of stimulation or for darkness. Will the animal also work to turn the light on? As we know, laboratory rodents will do both. Hence they are held to be

FIGURE 8-14 Chimpanzee, *Pan tro-glodytes,* performs an elaborate manipulation. In this case, the reward was a bunch of grapes; but it is doubtful whether the grapes were necessary. (See figure 8-15.) (Fox Photos Ltd)

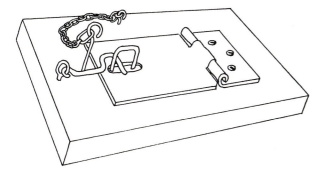

FIGURE 8-15 To solve the puzzle, three operations have to be performed in the correct order. Monkeys work at this and solve it without any additional incentives. (After H. F. Harlow and others, 1956)

working primarily for stimulus change, and not for a preferred, or eccritic, illumination.

N. K. Humphrey & G. R. Keeble have studied the same kind of question in experiments on macaques. They used a bar-pressing apparatus to demonstrate that these monkeys *prefer* certain colors and levels of brightness: they work for these colors and levels in preference to others. In their terminology, this behavior reflects the factor of pleasure. But monkeys also work to see something complex in preference to something simple—for example, a movie rather than a plain field of light. Such behavior is described by these authors as reflecting interest. The determining factor is believed to be the information content of the stimulus.

Clearly, a given stimulus may be to some extent both interesting and pleasurable (to continue with the same terminology). When an unchanging stimulus is presented to a monkey, interest rapidly fades (habituation); but pleasure remains constant.

8.1.4 The Effects of Exploration

8.1.4.1 Storing Information: The findings on what impels exploration, described above, are a notable example of detailed analysis, at the behavioral level, of an important kind of behavior. An obvious question is: what is the survival value of such conduct? Novelty seeking is not to be expected if it does not lead to some useful consequence. An animal's general movements about its living space increase its chance of encountering something useful. We are now concerned with a much less obvious effect, usually called latent or exploratory learning.

The classical experiments were done by H. C. Blodgett. Laboratory rats or mice put in an empty maze usually move around. The same thing happens if they are put in a maze, with food at a goal

point, just after they have eaten. In neither case do they develop the habit of running from the starting point to the goal. But if later, after a fast, they are given a series of runs with food at the goal, they learn the way more quickly than controls without previous experience of the maze (figure 8-16).

These and later similar observations led to much

FIGURE 8-16 Experiment on exploratory (latent) learning. Above: plan of maze. Below: error scores of three groups of rats. Group 1 were trained when fasted in the usual way, with food in the goal box on each run. Rats of the other groups were not at first rewarded; but, at X, reward was introduced: this led to a sharp reduction in errors, attributable to previous storage of information. (After H. C. Blodgett, 1929)

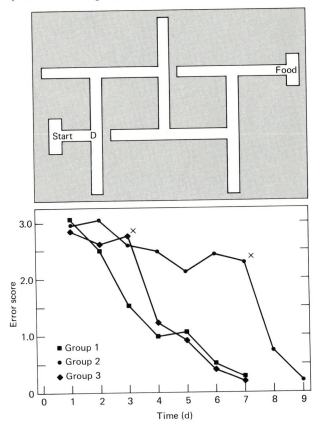

debate. For a long time it had been supposed that "learning" could occur only as a result of reinforcement (6.2). We now see that movements may also be accompanied by storage of information that can be used later. This is sometimes called *perceptual learning* (compare 12.3.5). From later behavior, when an animal quickly adapts itself to a new situation, we infer that storage has occurred. Such a rapid change in behavior is not shown by animals that have had no previous experience of the area.

To sum up, exploration and the accompanying exploratory learning have three important features: (1) wide-ranging movements increase the likelihood of the animal encountering something useful; (2) information storage is shown to occur sometimes "by contiguity"; (3) the stored information allows an animal to improvise a new response, or sequence of movements, when it is advantageous to do so.

8.1.4.2 Deutero-learning:

At the beginning of this chapter I mention the ability to solve *classes* of problems; and in chapters 6 and 7 there are examples of generalized abilities such as the ability to reverse a discrimination. Colloquially, we say general problem-solving capacity is a measure of intelligence. We are now concerned with the development of intelligence in this sense (reviewed by B. Meyers). Gregory Bateson has called the acquisition of such ability *deutero-learning*. The ability is then distinguished from acquiring a specific habit or from solving a particular, single problem. Here the term is defined as the development, during previous diverse experience, of an ability to solve problems.

We may begin with an informal experiment by D. O. Hebb (1949). He took some young laboratory rats home and, with the strong approval of his children, allowed them to wander about the house. When they were adult, he compared them with similar rats that had been reared in the usual confinement of small cages. The two kinds of rat, free living and confined, were given "intelligence tests" of the type described in 7.8.1. The free animals proved to be much superior.

This domestic experiment clearly had imperfections. The animals were few; and there were many differences between the conditions of the two groups of rats: the environment of the experimental rats must have differed in complex ways from that of the controls. But Hebb's colleagues confirmed the original findings. Both maze learning and acquiring discriminations are superior when laboratory rats have received complex early experience. Rats that have been allowed, in early life, to move about a large enclosure containing a variety of objects, later learn a maze more quickly than those confined to small cages. Similarly, rats were accustomed from infancy to seeing a variety of patterns fixed to the walls of their cages like pictures or murals: they were then quicker at visual discriminations when tested as adults.

W. R. Thompson & W. Heron have made similar observations on dogs. Some of their animals had their movements restricted, early in life, by confinement to a small cage. (They showed no signs of distress.) These dogs were later compared with a control group which had been allowed to run freely: and they proved to be much inferior in their ability to solve simple problems, such as learning to go to the correct place to get food. They lacked the ability to discriminate relevant and irrelevant aspects of the environment; and they failed to adapt their behavior quickly to changes in the experimental situation. They are described as easily distracted by minor disturbances. Domestic cats, too, have been reared, some in restricted environments and others in complex conditions. They have been tested, like Hebb's rats, in Hebb–Williams mazes (figure 7-22). Those that had experienced the more stimulating early environment, in which they could make many exploratory movements, scored higher.

Rearing in an "impoverished" environment, then, impairs problem-solving ability. There are other conditions with similar effects. Among them is hypothyroidism. Deficient secretion of the human thyroid hormone in early life results in cretinism—a severe form of mental deficiency. A similar thyroid deficiency can be induced by administering thiouracil. If this drug is given to female laboratory rats for some days before and after parturition, their young display a number of behavioral defects. The method has been used also on dogs and macaques. J. W. Davenport begins an account of such experiments by asking the question: can mental deficiency be alleviated by environmental stimulation? Rats whose mothers had been treated with thiouracil were tested as adults in a form of Hebb–Williams maze. Those that had been reared in ordinary small cages performed much worse than controls whose mothers had not been drugged. But some rats were reared in a "superenriched" environment, that is, a spacious arena containing diverse objects and opportunities for exercise. The deficit in maze learning of the hypothyroid rats was then greatly reduced; and maze retention, too, was hardly inferior to that of controls reared also in the stimulating environments. Davenport writes of "improved learning capacities of . . . a general nature".

Observations on the early behavior of Primates have usually been made in contexts different from those on rats, cats, or dogs. H. F. Harlow and his colleagues (1950, 1956) were interested in what they call the "manipulatory motivation" or "ex-ploratory-investigatory drive" of infant rhesus monkeys. Healthy young monkeys spend much time moving about, handling all accessible objects and especially strange ones. Such conduct is pursued with as much persistence as are eating or drinking. The solution of a manipulatory problem (compare figures 8-14 and 8-15) is quickly learned without any additional incentive to do so: indeed, offering a reward of food may disrupt performance of the manipulation.

As we see later, Primates nearly always develop new habits in a social context. Correspondingly, the development of primate abilities has recently been studied in relation to early social experience (reviewed by G. P. Sackett & G. C. Ruppenthal). In its early explorations, an infant monkey uses its mother as a base and ventures on increasingly distant expeditions. If it is reared in a laboratory without a mother and in social isolation, normal exploration does not occur. Reluctance to enter a strange arena persists for years. Figure 8-17 shows a double cage that allows observation of responses both to a strange environment and also to visual complexity.

Monkeys that had different conditions of rearing were observed in this cage at ages from three-and-a-half to five years. The delay or latency before moving from the starting cage to the test cage was a measure of the tendency to enter a novel environment. Those with the lowest latency were monkeys that had been reared in natural conditions. Monkeys that had been in the laboratory all their lives, but had been brought up with their mothers and young of their own age, also had a low latency. Various kinds of social deprivation in early life increased the latency. Animals that had been isolated for 9 to 12 months during their first year were the most reluctant to enter the test cage. (There was also a difference between the sexes:

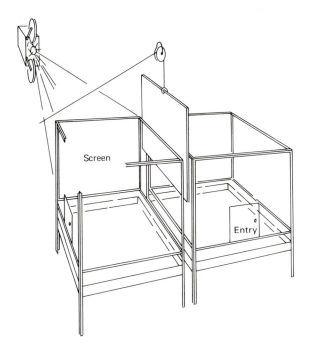

FIGURE 8-17 Cage for studying the responses of monkeys to novelty. The delay before moving from the right-hand to the other compartment measured readiness to enter a strange environment. In the left-hand compartment a screen allowed projection of a pattern. The time taken by monkeys to explore such patterns (figure 8-18) was recorded. (After G. P. Sackett & G. C. Ruppenthal, 1973)

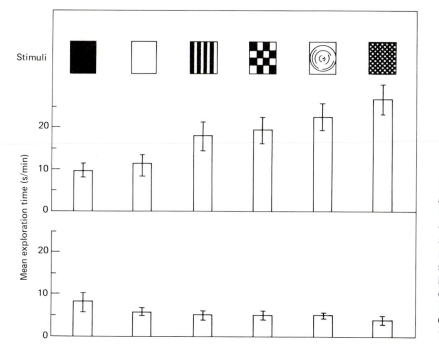

FIGURE 8-18 Patterns used in the apparatus shown in the previous figure to test the exploratory responses of monkeys. Upper histogram shows a high rate of response by monkeys reared in the wild; lower histogram shows a low response rate by monkeys that had been socially isolated during their fourth trimester. Vertical bars represent standard errors. (After G. P. Sackett & G. C. Ruppenthal, 1973)

the females of all deprived groups explored more than the males.)

Figure 8-18 illustrates further experiments. One of the patterns shown was projected on to the wall of the test cage. Each monkey was briefly exposed to the pattern, and the time it spent investigating the pattern was recorded. The monkeys that had been reared in the most complex environments spent the most time in exploring the pattern, especially those that were most complicated. Monkeys that had been isolated for 9 to 12 months in infancy did little investigating and showed no clear preference for any patterns.

An important question is whether such deficiencies in exploratory behavior are correlated with impaired problem-solving abilities. The answer is not simple. A general consequence of early social deprivation is delay in adapting to the experimental situation. When monkeys are, for example, to be faced with a problem in the Wisconsin general test apparatus (figure 8-19), they must first be "shaped", like Pavlov's dogs described in 5.5.1.1: they are taught to reach through the bars for food.

Normally reared monkeys (controls) may require two weeks of such training; but those reared in isolation may take many months. Nonetheless, once the shaping is achieved, the deprived monkeys may do as well as the controls. Hence from these experiments, in the words of Sackett & Ruppenthal, "intellectual impairment does not seem to be produced by even the most extreme forms of early social or environmental deprivation."

Such findings show once again how difficult it is to investigate intelligence. If we say that by intelligence we mean problem-solving abilities, we find that it depends on a number of factors. One is responsiveness: if an animal is too distractable, or too inert, to respond regularly to the stimuli chosen by the experimenter, it may be rated as of low intelligence. Yet we may ask whether there is some quality, independent of responsiveness, that may be suitably named intelligence. The only satisfactory way of settling such a question is by experiments in which the factors, hypothesized as influencing the behavior, are separately measured. This seems not yet to have been done.

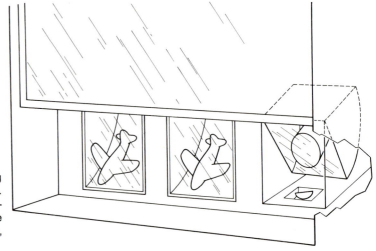

FIGURE 8-19 Apparatus for testing ability to solve the "oddity problem". If the animal pushes back the correct panel, food is revealed in the well below. (After D. M. Rumbaugh, 1970)

8.1.5 Human Applications

Human beings are insatiably restless and inquisitive, unless quelled by repressive upbringing or debility. D. O. Hebb (1955) has commented on the additional tendency for people to demand stimulation, even at risk of severe discomfort, evident in some kinds of sports and games. The need or demand for stimulation, and the ill effects of withdrawing it, are known from experiments on volunteers in the laboratory (reviewed by D. E. Berlyne 1960; D. P. Schultz; and J. A. Vernon). Some of the early experiments were inspired by the effects of solitary confinement in prisons. Since then, the problems of space flight have become prominent.

Some subjects have been required to endure prolonged, monotonous, repetitive stimulation; others have been put in conditions in which all external stimulation was at a minimum. Young men, well paid to lie on a couch, in a warm room, with hands and eyes covered, find such so-called sensory deprivation exceedingly disagreeable and even intolerable after a few hours. Some of those who endure the conditions longest develop hallucinations, and their perception and coherent thinking are impaired. And some, after release, display prolonged disorder: they become interested in the occult, telepathy, and other such notions although they were indifferent to them before the experiment. Given the opportunity, during the experiment, the subjects will work to switch on a pattern of lights in the ceiling. More remarkable, they will listen, repeatedly, to a recording of a boring lecture, rather than suffer in silence.

These observations contradict a psychoanalytic assumption sometimes called the Nirvana principle. S. Freud (1955) wrote: "The mental apparatus endeavours to keep the quantity of excitation present in it as low as possible or at least to keep it constant." This assertion, which is almost the op-posite of the truth, is an example of a conclusion based on the imagination unchecked by empirical study.

Critical analysis of these findings raises a number of questions. (1) In the experiments described above the subjects are inactive. If they are allowed to take exercise, the effects of isolation and monotony are greatly reduced or even annulled. (2) Previous knowledge concerning the experimenters' hypotheses can influence the results: ill effects may be generated by expectations. (3) The subjects are nearly always young and working—usually as students—in a university. Members of other groups might respond differently.

There is, indeed, still much to be learned about the demand for varying stimulation and—still more important—its effects. Diverse experience is likely to have its most significant effects early in life. Can we then confirm the Shakespearian assertion that "homekeeping youths have ever homely wits"?

Partly as a result of findings on experimental animals, hypotheses have been made, or questions asked, about the upbringing of children. Children are restlessly inquisitive. To what extent should this curiosity be encouraged, and with what useful outcome? What are the effects of discouraging it?

D. G. Beswick has discussed the possibility of training children of school age to exercise curiosity. By applying a number of standard tests he has given evidence of a positive correlation of curiosity with intellectual attitudes, and a smaller correlation with achievement at school. (He also states that curiosity is negatively correlated with noisiness.) His investigation emphasizes the great individual variation to be expected in even a small group of human beings.

Beswick's study concerns the desire to acquire knowledge. Evidence is also beginning to appear of effects of stimulation in the years before schooling, and even in infancy (the first year); but at these ages the responses are rather to general stimulation, to contrast, or to discrepancies. Visual exploration by infants and reaching with the arms can both be increased by handling the infants; giving them extra things to look at provokes more visual exploration, but reduces the movements of the limbs (reviewed by K. Connolly; B. L. White and others). J. Kagan & S. R. Tulkin have studied the responses of infants to change and contrast. At the age of a few days a moving or intermittent light holds an infant's attention especially well; so does a black figure on a white ground. Later, at about two months, attention begins to be attracted more by moderate discrepancies from what is expected (that is, from what has been experienced before).

Later still, the child's mobility allows more elaborate experiments. H. S. Ross presented children aged 12 months with either novel or familiar toys. To induce "familiarity", the child was allowed to play with the toys for 5 min before observations began. Familiar and unfamiliar toys were then offered, in the presence of the child's mother, in either a familiar or an unfamiliar room. The two rooms were adjoining. The unfamiliar toys were played with most, though the others were not ignored. When an unfamiliar room was made accessible it was quickly entered. As well, in some experiments, the toys offered a choice between simple and complex; the latter were preferred. The opportunity to respond to stimulation varies greatly with the environment provided by the parents. From about eight months there are differences (in North America) between social classes in the responsiveness of infants to change; and Kagan & Tulkin suggest that such differences influence cognitive development. In other words, the more stimulating the early environment, the brighter the child (and perhaps the adult) later on.

This statement represents only a hypothesis. Kagan (1976) has more recently emphasized the possibilities of compensating for early lack of stimulation. Correspondingly, there is beginning to be evidence that stimulation is especially important for older children that have suffered severe deprivation early in life. M. Winick and others (1975, 1978) have been led, as nutritionists, to a hypothesis about human development which they state in these words: "Malnutrition and environmental deprivation act synergistically to isolate the infant from the . . . inputs necessary for normal development." This proposal, based on findings from experiments on laboratory animals (8.1.4.2), led to the suggestion that children underfed in early life might derive special benefit from extra stimulation. These authors tested this notion by examining Korean children who had been adopted into American homes at around the age of 18 months. The findings fitted the hypothesis; and, if confirmed, they have obvious implications for future action.

To sum up, hypotheses on the effects of stimulation in early human development, based on studies of animals, have already been fruitful; but they have not yet revealed any simple correlations between conditions of upbringing and later ability. "Stimulation" is itself a vague term. The needs and the responsiveness of children change rapidly with age, and also vary among individuals. Much more work needs to be done.

8.2 LEARNING SET

8.2.1 Discriminating

We know that many animals can learn to approach or to avoid an object or place (chapter 7). Such a habit usually results from repeated exposure to a single situation: it depends on trial, error, and success. In this section we are not concerned with the acquisition of individual habits, but with the ability to solve classes of problems, or *learning set* (reviewed by A. J. Riopelle & C. W. Hill; D. M.

Rumbaugh, 1970; J. M. Warren, 1973, 1974). This is one of the phenomena that—in human activities—we regard as an aspect of intelligence. In studies of trial-and-error behavior, "random" movements are emphasized. Here we deal with solving problems suddenly with little or no error.

Learning set has been principally studied in experiments with Primates. Rats, however, improve their ability to make discrimination reversals with practice (6.2.3, 7.6.3). Such improvement is a minor example of a learning set.

There is now evidence that laboratory rats can develop a learning set of a more complex kind. B. M. Slotnick & H. M. Katz designed equipment that allowed them to present olfactory discriminations to rats. In experiments on visual discriminations the alternative stimuli are usually presented together. In the experiments with odors the alternatives were presented separately. The odors were floral perfumes; and each problem required a response to one and not the other. When a key was pressed during exposure to the correct odor, water was released and the rat could drink. The rats were trained in a series of such discriminations. Each problem involved presenting a different pair of odors.

As with discrimination reversals, the optimum strategy is win-stay, lose-shift. The question asked in an experiment of this kind is whether an animal will reach such a strategy or at least approach it. In fact, in one series of experiments, rats came near to this criterion after only 4 of the 16 problems had been presented.

Among the mammals, domesticated types that weigh about 25 g (mice) or even 250 g (rats) are convenient. At the other extreme, there is the Indian elephant, *Elephas maximus*—also domesticated, but very expensive. Nonetheless, Bernhardt Rensch describes formal experiments with an elephant aged five years in a zoo in Germany (see also B. Rensch & R. Altevogt). The elephant was presented with two boxes, of which one contained a piece of bread. The lids were marked with different patterns. The first pair of stimuli were a black circle and a black cross. To get the food, the elephant had to lift the lid marked with the cross. Over 300 trials were required before the elephant had acquired the habit of opening only the right box. A series of further discriminations was then presented; and the elephant improved greatly in the speed with which she learnt the successive tasks. She reached a satisfactory standard with the fourth pair of stimuli after only 10 trials. She was also able to retain 20 discriminations simultaneously.

This one elephant, then, illustrates typical learning set for visual discrimination. Other mammals that can form discrimination learning sets include domestic cats, raccoons, *Procyon lotor,* and several species of monkeys. H. F. Harlow (1949) gave rhesus macaques 344 pairs of stimuli in a situation resembling that shown in figure 8-19. At first, the monkeys made many mistakes. The crucial question was how well they did at the end of their long period of training. The maximum success would be to get each discrimination right on the second trial: that is, if on the first presentation the choice made was incorrect, then the animal should turn to the alternative on the second trial; but if the first choice was correct, then on the second trial the same one should be chosen. In fact, the score during the last 56 problems was 97% correct.

Human beings excepted, the chimpanzees, *Pan troglodytes,* studied by R. J. Schusterman (1964), seem to have done best. They were trained on a single pair of stimuli, and then given two other reversal tasks. To these they transferred almost without error. Chimpanzees are also proficient in a different kind of discrimination. R. C. Gonzalez and others presented these apes with three boxes of different sizes. The requirement was to pull in the box of intermediate size. The reward was food. When trained, the apes were presented with another three boxes; and now the box of intermediate size was the same absolute size as the largest or the smallest box used in the first stage of the experiment. In this situation, it was the intermediate box that, once again, tended to be selected. The authors use the expression "relational process" to describe this performance: the animals were generalizing the relationship of "intermediacy" from one situation to the other.

Learning to select an object on the basis of a general relationship, such as intermediacy, is an example of learning set. Other tests have been devised for the study of similar abilities, especially of Primates. One is the *oddity problem* (figure 8-19). This requires two pairs of objects, for example, two triangular and two circular blocks of wood. On each trial, the animal is presented with only three of the objects; reward depends on choosing the odd one. The test then is of the ability to learn a general relationship, that is, oddity, and not merely to discriminate between objects of different shapes. Laboratory rats were at first thought incapable of this feat; but J. Wodinsky & M. E. Bitterman used animals that had been extensively "shaped" by previous experience. The procedure resembled that illustrated in figure 6-3, but the animal had to choose one of three doors, not two. Rats that had received training in this situation were presented either with two black doors and one white, or with two white doors and one black; and they were required to choose the odd one. They succeeded. Macaques, if patiently trained, can certainly solve this problem; and chimpanzees solve it more easily than macaques.

The obverse of solving the oddity problem is *matching*. The animal is required to select from among several objects the one that corresponds to the one presented by the experimenter. Again, macaques and chimpanzees cope with this demand, but only after 1000 trials or more.

These findings, then, demonstrate the ability to respond to relationships that we represent by terms such as "different from", "resembling", and so on. All involve discriminations. As we have seen, discriminating and generalizing are complementary (6.2.2; 6.2.3). Human beings not only distinguish between subtly different phenomena, but also group sense data into large categories such as "insects" or "flowers". To what extent can other species generalize in this way? Little is known about this; but E. Lehr has described relevant experiments on a female rhesus monkey and a male capuchin monkey, *Cebus apella*. The monkeys were given two kinds of training. In the first, they were required to select pictures of insects instead of withered leaves, bits of twig, or fruit. In a trial they were offered one pair of pictures, each with the same area and of the same color. In the second training sequence, they were required to select pictures of flowers instead of comparable pictures of other objects. After training, they were tested on a number of insect species contrasted with a great variety of alternatives. They duly preferred the insects. Similarly, after training with flowers, they preferred flowers. They also identified simple flower-like patterns as flowers. The selections made were not a result of any initial preference, for the preferences were only gradually learned.

It is difficult to interpret these findings. Perhaps the two monkeys were generalizing visible patterns—as we know, an essential feature of all responses to classes of visible objects (6.2.2). One way of describing what the monkeys achieved is to say that they formed the concepts of insect or flower. An objection to such a statement is its vagueness: it adds nothing to what we already know. In human conduct, concept formation is usually inseparable from the use of language. I return to the linguistic abilities of apes below (8.3).

8.2.2 Counting

Another achievement usually linked to language is *number sense*—or the ability to count (reviewed by W. H. Thorpe, 1963). The most notable studies, rather surprisingly, have been of birds. One source of our interest in the number sense of birds is the fixed clutch size of many species: a female lays, say, three eggs, and then stops. If an experimenter removes one or more eggs, she lays again: hence a particular egg number is an example of a reference value or *Sollwert* (2.2.1). A constant clutch size is, however, not evidence of a number sense: the bird, for instance, may be responding to the contact of the eggs with the brood spots on her ventral surface.

Number sense includes the ability to respond to the *n*th of a series of objects or events, regardless of what the objects or events are. Human beings easily learn to recognize groups of quite different objects as being similar, when their only resemblance is in the number of items they contain. To test for this ability in other species, it is necessary to control for other cues. The elephant studied by Rensch (8.2.1) was taught to discriminate objects marked with different numbers of black circles; but she did not have to count to do this: she could merely be responding to a larger or a smaller amount of black on the white background.

There is, however, evidence of authentic number sense from carefully designed experiments on jackdaws, *Corvus frugilegus*, ravens, *C. corax*, and gray parrots, *Psittacus erithacus*. In these experiments, the observer was out of sight of the birds and so could not give them accidental clues (compare 1.1.3). Sometimes behavior was recorded by an automatic cine-camera. One procedure involved matching: the bird was presented with a key card marked with a number of spots (from two to six). The task was to open a box marked with the same number of spots. The spots varied in size and were arranged in various patterns. The positions of the boxes and other features of the arrangement were also varied irregularly. Eventually a raven and a parrot learnt to open one of five boxes, in accordance with the number (again from two to six) of objects lying on the ground.

Another type of problem is to perform an act *n* times only, and to give no clue when *n* has been reached except the number of acts. For example, birds were trained to take only *n* seeds from a large heap. In a variant of this problem, a bird was faced with a row of boxes, some of which contained one or more seeds. The task was to open the boxes and take the seeds, if any, until *n* seeds had been taken; and then to stop. Jackdaws were successfully trained to do this. To quote W. H. Thorpe (slightly shortened):

A Jackdaw, given the task to raise lids until five baits had been secured (which in this case were distributed in the first five boxes in the order 1, 2, 1, -,1) went to its cage after opening only the first three lids and consequently eating only four baits. The experimenter was about to record an incorrect solution when the Jackdaw returned to the boxes. It bowed its head once before the first box it had emptied, made two bows in front of the second box, one before the third, opened the fourth lid (no bait) and the fifth and took out the last (fifth) bait. It then went home.

Such observations suggest that in this case a crucial feature was the number of times on which a specific movement (picking up the seed) was performed. But this notion does not account for the matching achievements reported from the other experiments. It does, however, fit the observations of C.-S. Chen on laboratory rats. Chen required his animals to run around a circular passage a specified number of times from two to seven. The size of the circle was sometimes varied, so that time spent or distance traveled could not be used as a clue; and in some experiments the runway was made elliptical, to change the proprioceptive input that resulted from running. Several rats were successfully trained in this way. Chen describes the behavior at the entrance to the passage in which the reward was given. While circling, "the animal would usually come to a stop at the entrance, swinging its head toward the stem or standing still for a moment, before starting the next turn".

It is hardly surprising that few well-designed experiments on "counting" have been done. They are laborious and difficult to interpret, even when successful. Thorpe, on the basis of a full review, suggests that two "pre-linguistic faculties", which he calls "simultaneous and successive unnamed number sense" have been demonstrated by some species of bird. (And we may now add that "successive number sense" is also evidently possessed by laboratory rats.) But these abilities of birds are "still not true counting in the fully human sense". The two obvious features in which human counting differs are, of course, (1) that speech is used, and (2) that human number sense has a much higher generality and a much wider application, even in its simplest form, than anything demonstrated in other species.

8.2.3 Manipulating

We now return to the Primates. The tests of "intelligence" outlined in 8.2.1 include nothing that involves the use of tools or improvising equipment to attain an end. Yet the monkeys and apes (An-

thropoidea) are dexterous animals and are liable to handle anything they can reach (reviewed by J. M. Warren, 1976).

The manipulations of chimpanzees in natural conditions have been described in detail by Jane van Lawick-Goodall (1970) and by W. C. Mc-Grew. Chimpanzees eat ants and termites in large numbers. To get them out of their nests, a chimpanzee pokes a stick into an entrance of an ant hill and then draws it out; the insects clinging to the stick are licked off (figure 8-20). Chimpanzees select sticks for their straightness, and may remove leaves and branches to make them more serviceable. Sometimes they crush leaves and use them as a sponge to scoop up water that cannot be reached with the lips; or they use crushed leaves as a brush to clean the fur. Lawick-Goodall describes the waving and even the throwing of sticks as part of threatening displays toward other chimpanzees. A chimpanzee sometimes seems to aim a stick at an opponent before throwing it, but accuracy is low: in a series of 44 observations, the apparent target was hit only five times.

Other observations on the use of sticks to reach objects have been made on chimpanzees in captivity. The most celebrated study is that of W. Köhler (1887–1967), during a period of forced isolation in the First World War. Köhler (1925) had few human companions, but there were several chimpanzees. The apes were given problems, such as fitting sticks together, so that a banana outside the cage, or hanging from a string, could be reached. As we know, these animals carry out manipulations without reward (8.1.3.3). Probably the banana was not important as food, but only as part of the problem.

The last statement is supported by an anecdote, described by D. M. Rumbaugh (1970). The Canadian psychologist, D. O. Hebb, persuaded a female

FIGURE 8-20 Above: chimpanzee, *Pan troglodytes,* catches ants by poking stick into hole. Below: it licks the ants off. (Courtesy J. D. Bygott)

chimpanzee to solve a series of problems for the reward of slices of banana. She did not eat the slices, but arranged them in a row. Hebb then ran out of bananas, but offered another problem with no reward in the box. The female now put a slice *in* the box on each occasion when she solved a problem. Hebb ended up with 30 slices of banana.

Köhler's most interesting observations were on what his apes did when faced with difficult problems. Chimpanzees proved to be able to fit two sticks together, to pull in a banana otherwise out of reach. Another achievement just within chimpanzee ability is to pile up two or more boxes and climb to the top—again to reach an object. Similar observations have been described by B. B. Beck. Gibbons, *Hylobates,* were required to get fragments of food by pulling strings. The gibbons soon learned not only to pull a string straight into the cage but also to alter the angle of the pull so as to bring the reward within reach.

Köhler's problems often baffled his apes; but sometimes, after apparent withdrawal from the situation, one of his subjects returned and solved it at once. It was as if the solution had been silently worked out by reflection. Köhler emphasized such evidence of reasoning, and he has been criticized for disregarding the extent to which apes solve problems by trial and error (reviewed by W. A. Mason, 1976). H. G. Birch investigated this question experimentally. His six chimpanzees had been reared in captivity and were four to five years of age. All had had experience of string-pulling problems, but none had solved problems by the use of sticks. They had, however, lived in an enclosure in which they had the opportunity to handle twigs; and one (J) had developed the habit of manipulating twigs. Birch presented the problem of pulling food into a cage with a hoe, that is, a stick with a crosspiece at the end. J solved the problem

quickly and economically in 12 s; and one of the others solved it at its first presentation. All the animals were then released into an enclosure, where they were allowed to handle sticks. Later they were again tested with the hoe; and all solved the problem within 20 s.

A sudden adaptive reorganization of performance is sometimes called "insight behavior" (for example, by W. H. Thorpe, 1963). Such expressions emphasize the internal processes that go on in the absence of overt activity, and that culminate in a successful action. Evidently, like human beings, apes solve manipulatory (and other) problems by a combination of trial and error and other processes. The latter still lack detailed analysis.

8.2.4 Cognition, Comparisons, and Complexities

The phrase, in the previous paragraph, "internal processes that lead to successful action", could also be applied to the phenomena of exploratory (latent) learning (8.1). The "insight behavior" of chimpanzees solving problems and the maze running of rats making use of information stored during general wanderings have important features in common. They can by no means be interpreted in stimulus-response terms: the animal is not responding simply to the immediate situation. The behavior evidently depends on the combined representations in the brain both of separate previous experiences and of current inputs. (By "experiences" I mean patterns of input through the sense organs.) Such internal interactions are often referred to as *cognitive* processes. The conduct of an animal solving a problem on the basis of several previous experiences resembles that of a human being who acts effectively after "thinking it out".

When problem solving by monkeys is studied,

the experimental situations allow a much simplified account of the behavior. (The same applies to other kinds of experiments.) We are told, say, the mean number of errors made by so many rhesus macaques in precisely specified conditions. Such procedures are essential if one wishes to produce repeatable findings, but they often obscure much of interest. A. J. Riopelle & C. W. Hill have a relevant passage in a review of experiments on learning sets. They remark on the individual biases and "erroneous or irrelevant response tendencies" that each monkey displays when faced with a problem. For example, a particular monkey may persistently prefer left to right; it may have a strong tendency to explore alternative stimuli even when response to the first stimulus chosen is rewarded; and each individual is liable to have a number of preferences and aversions. In solving each problem, these interfering tendencies gradually disappear; but, Riopelle remarks, they reappear when the next problem is presented. They presumably represent the effects of the special circumstances encountered by the individual monkey, perhaps early in life; but we know little about the ontogeny of such traits.

At any time, an animal may be invisibly recording information that it can use (or misuse) later. A difficult question concerns the extent to which such recording actually occurs. At every moment a mammal (for example) is exposed to sounds that can induce discharges in the auditory nerve, odors that affect the olfactory nerve, and so on through all the sensory modalities, both external and internal. Habituation (5.2) as we know, insures that some inputs are without effect, but there are other means of *stimulus-filtering*.

In 7.8 I give examples of species-typical abilities and limitations. The same principles apply to the kinds of information an animal can store. The work of Slotnick & Katz (8.2.1) suggests that laboratory rats acquire an olfactory discrimination set much more readily than one based on vision. We may guess at the relationship of this ability with the needs of a nocturnal animal, for which odors are more important than sights.

In future, with more knowledge, it will perhaps be possible to give a comparative account of the abilities of species in relation to their respective ecological niches. Such an account is unlikely to be based on a simple linear measure of "intelligence": it will probably be based on the analysis of many particular abilities, possessed to different degrees by different species.

8.3 APES AND LANGUAGE

When an experimenter makes animals learn something, the task is usually determined by the interests of the experimenter. The behavior required may then be analogous to that of a circus animal riding a bicycle—a performance not closely related to the ecological niche of any species. An extreme case is that of attempts to teach chimpanzees to communicate by using a human language (reviewed by R. S. Fouts & R. L. Rigby; P. Marler, 1974; D. Premack 1976; and in a volume edited by D. M. Rumbaugh, 1977).

The sounds made by apes, like those of other animals, reflect the signaler's state (chapter 13): they may tend to cause a fellow ape to approach or to withdraw; they may inhibit another's action; or they may be warnings of danger. But, warnings apart, they are not referential: in natural conditions even a chimpanzee does not, as far as we know, name a series of objects with arbitrary sounds. A further contrast with human behavior is seen very early in life: the babbling of human infancy is a precursor of speech; apes hardly babble at all.

Apes are extremely imitative (8.4.2.3); but even those reared in human families have never imitated speech. W. N. & L. A. Kellogg reared a female chimpanzee, Gua, with their own child. A child, from before two years, steadily learns to speak, partly by a complex kind of imitation. Gua never did so. A celebrated and strenuous attempt was made by K. J. & C. Hayes to *teach* another young female chimpanzee, Viki, to speak. Viki, too, was reared like a child. She achieved only some semblance of "mama", "papa", "cup", and "up", uttered on appropriate occasions. These are described as unvoiced whispers. Yet both Gua and Viki seemed in other respects very intelligent; and they *responded* appropriately to simple spoken English.

It is now realized that the plan of trying to teach an ape to *speak* is wrongly conceived. Apes are not structurally equipped to make the subtle variety of noises required (P. H. Lieberman and others). The same applies to some human beings: they are dumb owing to a neurophysiological defect, but they are not necessarily deficient in other ways. B. T. & R. A. Gardner accordingly had the brilliant notion of teaching a chimpanzee, Washoe, to use the gestural system, Ameslan (American sign language for the deaf). Washoe, given a diverse and stimulating environment and plenty of human companionship, after about four years learned 132 signs either by imitation or by molding; the latter consists of moving the limbs into the proper position. When the Gardners conversed in Ameslan in Washoe's presence, she picked up some signs by observation.

Early reports of these remarkable findings were criticized on the ground that nothing equivalent to human language had been learned. Here is a comment by Ian Robinson.

It is *not* naming, but idiocy, to say "dog" every time one sees a dog; and nobody reports that Washoe has anything to say . . . about dogs but "dog". (If she were to begin "thinking about" dogs when no dog was present, . . . and if she began making the dog sign with a thoughtful expression on her face, the experiment would be thought to have failed.)

As far as I know, no chimpanzee has begun to make a sign "with a thoughtful expression on her face"; but some further developments suggest that chimpanzees have a rudimentary capacity to learn a human language. This capacity has been revealed both by the Gardners' method and by other means. Premack taught another female, Sarah, born in the wild and about six years old at the beginning of his experiments, to use colored, plastic shapes for words. The shapes could be put on a magnetized board, and so a spatial array was possible. Rewarded with fruit, Sarah learned 130 words by this method. Yet a third method, used by Rumbaugh, entailed a computer-controlled training situation. Lana, about two and a half years of age, was taught to use white geometric figures as words: to produce a "word", she had to press the appropriate key on a keyboard; an illuminated figure then appeared (figure 8-21).

Of these, the Gardners' is the method most appropriate to the normal conduct of a chimpanzee; it also allows the subject to be independent of the experimenter. But each of the chimpanzees mentioned above (and others, too) have proved to be able not only to use single words but to form short sentences; moreover, they have made novel sentences from single words previously learned. They also respond correctly to questions such as, "What [is] that?" or "where [is the] banana?".

Among the words learned by Washoe and other chimpanzees, there were nouns such as "flower" and "dog", adjectives such as "red" and "white",

FIGURE 8-21 The chimpanzee, Lana in the computer-controlled situation described in the text. (Courtesy D. N. Rumbaugh)

verbs such as "go" and "help", and adverbs such as "up" and "down". Examples of sentences include "you me go-out hurry"; "give-me sweet drink". The correct destinations of movements may be indicated by expressions such as "go-in" and "go-out". As a result, compound sentences have been achieved, such as "Sara put banana [in] pail [and] apple [in] dish". One chimpanzee, Lucy, when taught Ameslan, invented combinations of words, such as "drink fruit" for a water melon; after tasting a strong radish, Lucy called it "cry hurt food".

Lana, at her keyboard, achieved sentences such as "Lana want drink milk eat bread". Premack's Sarah learned to use words such as "same" and "different", which indicate general relationships; she also learned the use of "if . . . then". And she was able to describe something not present. For example, she was first required to describe an actual apple—its color, shape, and whether it had a stalk. She was then asked to describe the blue triangle that was the symbol for apple. Sarah once again described an apple, not the triangle.

Many aspects of the procedures required for the

work with chimpanzees are fascinating to read in the original. As a rule, learning was based on reward, but one apparently intelligent male refused to respond to such training. Eventually, the experimenter threatened him. At once he began to make the required sign over and over again. (Analogies with human situations, though almost irresistible, should of course be resisted.) But usually the relationships between experimenter and chimpanzee seem to be good. Indeed, when Lana was being trained, there were difficulties when she was required to face the keyboard in the absence of the experimenter. An indication that she had made an incorrect response led to fits of screaming. These diminished when the experimenter stayed in the room. On the intellectual side, an interesting difficulty arose when Sarah was required to present a specific shape before receiving a particular fruit; she often presented the wrong shape. Investigations showed that she was asking for a preferred fruit and disregarding the one on offer.

As Eugene Linden has described, findings on the linguistic abilities of apes have led to controversy and even to resentment. (See the passage from Robinson quoted above.) The ground for resentment is not obvious. We accept that our species has evolved from early apes. If so, a period when our ancestors had only rudimentary linguistic ability is likely (15.2.1.1). Perhaps chimpanzees represent such a stage. According to workers such as the Gardners, their level of communication resembles that of a child of more than two years; but a child, unlike a chimpanzee, does not have to be painstakingly taught to speak. There are, however, experimental grounds for doubt. H. S. Terrace and others trained an infant chimpanzee, named Neam Chimpsky, to communicate by gestures. Many words were learned; but these experimenters hold that the ability of their chimpanzee to communi-

cate in this way reflected imitation of his teachers, not any true linguistic ability. Perhaps some of the differences in the findings of different experimenters reflect individual variation among chimpanzees. The experiments and the debate will no doubt continue for a long time.

Further work will no doubt reveal much more of the abilities of chimpanzees and probably of gorillas too (F. G. Patterson). A question open to study is how the abilities experimentally revealed are related to what happens in nature. There are now captive groups communicating among themselves by Ameslan. Does such communication already occur in African forests? As far as I know, the only relevant findings concern other captive groups, which have been shown to communicate among themselves by unidentified signs (11.2.4.2). There is perhaps much to be learned by combining what we know of the social interactions of chimpanzees with the observations described in the preceding paragraphs.

8.4 SOCIAL INFLUENCES

8.4.1 Local Enhancement

8.4.1.1 Birds: In most experiments on "learning" the subject is isolated from all other animals (except, sometimes, the experimenter); but in natural conditions habits are often formed during social interactions. In human affairs imitation provides obvious examples. It is often asked whether imitation occurs in the conduct of other species. To answer rigorously we have to decide on just what behavior, if any, we call imitation. There are social effects on habit formation which do not involve imitation in any sense, but are nevertheless important. To emphasize this, M. P. Crawford introduced the expression *social facilitation,* defined as "any increment of activity resulting from the presence of another member of the same species". Such a general definition covers all social effects, whether they involve imitation or not. In this section we examine instances of apparent imitation which do not qualify as imitative behavior.

First, I take the celebrated mystery of the missing milk. In the 1940s, in the south of England, householders began with increasing frequency to find that the bottles of milk delivered to their doors had their tops taken off and some of the contents removed. Some indignant victims therefore awaited the thieves from a concealed place. The culprits proved to be blue tits, *Parus caeruleus,* which had developed the habit of drinking the cream from the nonhomogenized milk (R. A. Hinde & J. Fisher). Later, the habit spread to the mainland of Europe. Moreover, other species joined in.

How should we interpret these events? On the obvious anthropomorphic assumption one bird, accidentally or through some flash of insight, took to stripping the caps off bottles; this conduct proved rewarding, and so other birds imitated the innovator. It might even be supposed that the innovator indicated by some signal that the result of cap stripping was beneficial.

We now turn to actual observations. E. R. A. Turner has described in detail the social feeding of two other species, the chaffinch, *Fringilla coelebs,* and the house sparrow, *Passer domesticus.* Flocks of such small birds are a familiar sight in winter. A group of birds feeding attracts other birds of the same species. Such interactions are important in inducing a change to unfamiliar foods. Juvenile birds tend to be more neophilic than adults, and perhaps lead the way. J. R. Krebs and others discuss the effects of flocking in general and describe experiments on the great tit, *Parus major.* The diet of this species in winter resembles that of the blue tit, with which the great tit often forms mixed flocks. The experiments were carried out in aviaries in which there were artificial trees. Birds were studied searching for food alone or in flocks of four. Those in flocks tended to find food more quickly. When one member of a flock had found food, others soon went also to the source.

The implication of such findings for the blue tits and the cream is then an anticlimax. Part of the usual feeding behavior of these birds is stripping bark off branches of trees and eating the insects below. Such a stripping movement is also appropriate for the cap of a milk bottle. A bird drinking the cream would be likely to attract others. We are therefore evidently dealing with *local enhancement,* or an increment of response to an environmental feature resulting from the response of a conspecific to it. In addition, a bird that has found food in a milk bottle is likely to develop the habit of visiting other milk bottles.

The ability to adapt behavior to circumstances, partly by social means, may be quite widespread among birds (and, no doubt, among mammals also). M. Pettersson describes the spread of a new habit among greenfinches, *Chloris chloris.* A shrub, *Daphne mezereum,* cultivated by gardeners, has a scarlet, plum-like fruit. The stones of the ripe fruit are hard and cannot be opened by these birds; but those of unripe fruits can be cracked, and the seed can then be eaten. Pettersson describes the spread of a habit by greenfinches of stripping unripe fruits off the bushes. The culprits are usually a mated pair with young in the nest.

A more detailed study has been made by M. Norton-Griffiths (1967, 1969) of oyster catchers, *Haematopus ostralegus.* These birds open the shells of mussels, *Mytilus edulis,* which make much of their diet on British shores: some carry the mussel to firm sand, on which they bang the ventral surface; others swiftly insert their beaks in the slightly open shell while it is under water. No bird is known to use both methods; and young birds follow their parents to the mussel beds where, evidently, they learn the parental technique of feeding. This case, and those of the blue tits and greenfinches, seem to be examples of tradition—the transmission of habits by social means from one generation to the next. Tradition is a central feature of human societies, but is otherwise rather unusual. Generally, the behavior of an animal species is adapted to new conditions as a result of genetical change in populations—a slow process. Social transmission can be more rapid, and so can enhance the ability of a species to adapt itself to a changed environment.

Such transmission is aided by flocking. As we know (3.3.2) the clumping of food items is important for predators. Given the existence of local enhancement, flocking appears to be advantageous when food is clumped. J. R. Krebs and his colleagues (1972) write:

Some tropical-forest mixed-species flocks are formed around one or two "leader species" which, as a result of their movements through the canopy, flush insects which are eaten by other members of the flock . . . Similarly, . . . Anis *Crotophoga ani* and Cattle Egrets *Ardeola ibis* feed more efficiently when following herds of cattle, which flush insects eaten by the birds . . .

We now look more closely at these social interactions. P. H. Klopfer trained greenfinches, *Chloris chloris,* to feed on sunflower seeds at a point marked by one pattern and to avoid another pattern. Avoidance was induced by offering moist aspirin inside a hollowed-out seed. The question asked concerned social effects on the rate at which the discrimination was acquired. If an untrained conspecific were present, the rate was lower than when the bird was alone while it solved the problem.

Moreover, incorrect responses by an untrained partner sometimes led birds to fail to make a discrimination which had previously been learned. The presence of a trained partner did not interfere with the acquisition of the habit. Here, then, we have evidence of a social effect, but not of imitation in any sense.

John Alcock (1969) describes experiments on the fork-tailed flycatcher, *Muscivora tyrannus,* the white-throated sparrow, *Zonotrichia albicollis,* and the black-capped chickadee, *Parus atricapillus.* He asks whether these birds could learn to uncover hidden food merely by observing the behavior of a bird that had been trained to do so. He used a food tray with three depressions, in one of which was a mealworm concealed by a flat wood lid. Experimental birds were allowed to observe a trained (demonstrator) bird remove the lid and eat the worm. Control observers watched an untrained bird moving about in similar conditions. Observer birds always seemed to pay a great deal of attention to the demonstrators. After this experience, they were tested alone with a worm concealed in the food tray. Both experimental and control birds moved around in an exploratory way; but the experimental birds approached and manipulated the tray much more than the controls. The principal effect of the demonstrator's behavior on the observer seems to have been in enhancing the observer's exploratory activities. Hence the chance of uncovering the concealed prey was increased; but none of the birds learned by observation alone where the mealworm was to be found. Once again, local enhancement is seen to be important. But imitation, in the sense of copying the exact movements of the demonstrator, did not occur.

8.4.1.2 Mammals: A special case of local enhancement is provided by the conduct of some young mammals in following their parents or other conspecifics. Young rats may follow older rats to a food source (4.5.2.5). They are consequently guided to food and are likely to eat the same food as their elders. But the choice of food is then evidently an indirect result of following.

An interesting question is how the following response develops. Is it a result of experiencing food (milk) in association with the mother? The ontogeny of the response seems, however, not to have been studied. But we do know that adult domestic rats can be trained to follow another rat. N. E. Miller & J. Dollard ran rats on a raised T-maze (figure 6-1). A rat already trained to turn to one side was put on the short arm; behind it was another rat. In some experiments the second rat was rewarded with food for following the first; in others, it was rewarded for not following. Both kinds of training were successful. Clearly, in each case the leading rat was a cue for the second rat; but when the second rat followed the first we need not assume anything that we would ordinarily call imitation.

8.4.2 Imitation and Tradition

8.4.2.1 Defining Imitation: In the previous section I avoid defining "imitation"; but the critical reader will have noticed, in one passage, an approach to an implied definition. The everyday concept of definition is difficult to analyze rigorously (reviewed by J. M. Davis, and by B. G. Galef). The difficulty may be expressed in formal terms. Consider the situation (described in the previous section) in which animal D has learned to go to a particular place where there is food. Animal O is now put where it can either follow D or take an alternative path. After a few such experiences, O regularly follows D, and so receives food also.

Would we call this imitation? The obvious answer is that if a lifeless object had been substituted for D, the result would have been the same: no question of imitation would then have arisen.

What, then, would we accept as imitation? The most quoted definition is that of W. H. Thorpe (1963). The full passage, with the original emphasis, follows:

By true imitation is meant the copying of a novel or otherwise improbable act or utterance, or some act for which there is clearly no instinctive tendency. Defined in these terms, we see that true visual imitation becomes something which apparently involves self-consciousness and something of intent to profit by another's experience; and it becomes doubtful whether (except possibly in cats) we can find any certain examples of such behavior anywhere in the animal kingdom below the Primates.

The first part of the first sentence is a good *description* of the conduct usually called imitation in ordinary speech (if we assume that the word "true" is put in merely to remind us of the contrast with phenomena such as those described in the previous section). The rest of the passage involves us in questions to which we return in 8.4.2.5.

8.4.2.2 Predatory Mammals: In 1930 Z. Y. Kuo published a paper on the development of the hunting behavior of domestic cats. Some of the kittens he studied saw their mothers kill either rats or mice; others did not. Most of the first group became killers themselves, but only about half of those that had not been set this example.

Such observations raise the question whether kittens copy their mothers (or other adults) and, if so, in what sense. H. E. Adler describes experiments in which cats were required to get food by pulling it into their cage. The main part of the experiment resembled that carried out by John Alcock on birds (8.4.1.1). One cat (the observer) is allowed to see another (the demonstrator) perform the food-getting action. In some experiments the observer sees the demonstrator go through the process of learning the task. Unlike Alcock's birds, cats evidently do *learn by observation* to perform a specific motor act: observer cats, presented with a problem they have seen another cat solve, become proficient at solving it more quickly than do controls. Kuo's kittens too, may have learned by observation, though we cannot be certain of this.

The domestic dog is capable of similar achievements. L. L. & H. E. Adler describe experiments on miniature dachshund puppies. In this case the demonstrator and the observer were both juvenile. By the age of 38 days a puppy was shown to be capable of learning by observation when a demonstrator puppy pulled a food cart into its cage by tugging a ribbon. Sometimes, like cats, the pupil performed the appropriate act at the first opportunity. Also like cats, the pupil did not perform with full efficiency until the observer had had some practice.

The only other mammals, Primates excepted, which are believed to be imitative on the basis of clear evidence, are dolphins, *Tursiops,* studied by C. K. Tayler & G. S. Saayman. Bottle-nosed dolphins, *T. aduncus,* were kept in a vast tank with Cape fur seals, *Arctocephalus pusillus,* and repeated the patterns of movement of the seals—even those of sexual interactions. A diver entered the tank to scrape algae from an observation window; one dolphin then copied the diver's movements and made sounds resembling those of the air valve on his equipment. Another dolphin used a scraper, succeeded in removing algae with it, and ate the algae.

8.4.2.3 Primates:
To *ape* another's actions is traditionally associated with the Primates. As with

carnivores, the precise scope of such behavior can be revealed only by quite elaborate experiments. W. A. Myers studied a pair of stumptails, *Macaca speciosa,* and another pair of rhesus macaques. As controls he had one stumptail, one rhesus, and—oddly—one baboon. Of each pair of monkeys, one was an observer and the other a demonstrator. The demonstrator was required to learn a complex task in the equivalent of a Skinner box (figure 6-6). The observer watched from an adjoining compartment for up to 210 h. The observers were then tested on the tasks they had seen performed, and they made the appropriate pattern of responses much sooner than the controls. The total sequence included not only learning, according to a complex pattern, to press a bar for a reward but also to stop pressing the bar when no reward was offered. An important feature of these observations was that the precise movements of the demonstrators were repeated by the observers.

In an earlier study by C. L. Darby & A. J. Riopelle, on four rhesus macaques, the observer monkeys were required to achieve an end, but precise repetition of movements was not involved. The problems were of a type already described: there were 500 discriminations in each of which two objects were presented with food beneath one. Each observer saw another monkey presented with such a discrimination; it was then required to perform the same discrimination itself. On 50% of all such occasions, the observer monkey saw the demonstrator make the correct choice; on the remainder, it saw the observer monkey make an incorrect choice. Clearly, in a sequence of such trials, the "intelligent" thing to do is to choose the same object as the demonstrator if doing so was rewarded, and the alternative object if the demonstrator had not been rewarded. The question was whether the observers would in fact acquire such a habit. During the first block of 50 such discriminations, the observers scored only at chance level on the first trial, that is, 50% correct. By the end of the long sequence of discriminations they were scoring about 75% correct. In such an experiment, there is an element of delayed response and also of matching. The experimenters remark that the performance satisfies the requirement for a test of reasoning.

The evidence so far gives us some notion of the scope of social interactions in the habit formation of Carnivora and Primates; but it tells us little about its significance in natural conditions. Experiments on forest baboons, *Mandrillus sphinx,* by Pierre Jouventin and others, though also carried out in captivity, have some bearing on what happens in the wild. The experimenters used slices of banana colored with tasteless dyes. Some bananas were made unpalatable with quinine. In one experiment, a young female, Intacte, watched the behavior of adults offered three yellow, palatable bananas, and three green and unpalatable. Intacte could not herself reach the bananas. Training continued until each adult, offered the six bananas, ate all three yellow and no green bananas. Intacte was then given a tray with sixteen yellow and four green slices. Green was already known to be an attractive color to her, for she readily ate green leaves. Yet she ate all the yellow slices and none of the green. A day later, the discrimination was still intact. Other experiments on similar lines, but with different colors, gave similar results. Here, evidently, is a means by which the behavior of older animals can protect young conspecifics from distasteful or harmful foods or other objects.

8.4.2.4 Tradition:
As we know, one general effect of "social learning" is that it offers the possibility of rapid adaptability to strange or fluctuating conditions. If an adult or group of adults adapt themselves to, say, a novel source of food, it may be advantageous for their young to copy their el-

ders, instead of repeating a slower process of learning the new pattern independently. Such copying could be the basis of a tradition. Information, in the technical sense, is usually passed from one generation to the next through the genome. In human affairs there is the prominent alternative means of tradition, usually verbal: we "inherit" knowledge through the media of speech, written words, and so on. But if young animals copy older animals, a tradition need not be verbal.

The clearest evidence of nonhuman traditions in natural environments is in the feeding behavior of Primates. Indirect evidence comes from observations of differences in the habits of different troops or larger populations. A. Kortlandt has described feeding by groups of chimpanzees. In west Africa, maize, sugar cane, avocados, and other plants are eaten by these apes. The same species are present in the Congo, but there they were much more recently introduced; and in the Congo, evidently, chimpanzees do not eat these crops.

Similarly, F. E. Poirier describes changes in food habits of langurs, *Presbytis johnii,* in southern India. A tree introduced from Australia, *Eucalyptus globulus,* has for economic reasons been planted in regions occupied by the monkeys. Adults are described as now eating the petioles from these trees, but the young are beginning to eat the whole leaves, despite their exceptionally aromatic properties. In the Nilgiri Hills, some troops are raiding fields in which potatoes and cauliflowers are grown. Certain troops have developed the habit of pulling up entire plants.

Such observations do not reveal the precise character or role, if any, of social learning in these new developments. But, in a celebrated series of observations on the Japanese macaque, *M. fuscata,* social transmission of food habits has been recorded in remarkable detail by K. Imanishi (1957, 1960), by M. Kawai, and by S. Kawamura. Again, early observations were of differences in the conduct of neighboring troops. Some dug out the roots of plants, while others did not. Some raided rice fields but others, with equal access, disregarded rice as a source of food.

The most important observations have resulted from adding to the foods available. The sequence of events reflects different responses by different age groups. In one region caramels were offered, and were quickly accepted by monkeys aged three and younger. When this new habit had become general among them, some of the mothers evidently acquired the habit from the juveniles. These females passed it on to their own infants. It took 18 months for just over 50% of the troop to become caramel eaters.

Of all introductions, the most important was that of sweet potatoes on Koshima Island. The sweet potatoes were put on the beach. When the monkeys visited the beach they took the sweet potatoes, and—after a year—adopted an extraordinary new habit.

A two-year-old female (named Imo) took to dipping her potatoes in water and so washing off the sand. Monkeys of about Imo's age began to follow suit, and after five years about 80% of the monkeys aged two to seven years were washing their potatoes. Older monkeys, for the most part, did not learn the new trick; but some females were evidently less conservative than the males. After 10 years, about 90% of the troop of all ages washed their potatoes, excepting infants and adults aged more than 12 years. As with the caramels, there was a tendency for mothers to learn from juveniles and for infants then to learn from their mothers. Later, Imo—who has been called a "monkey genius"—made another invention. The Japanese zoologists also offered wheat to the monkeys, again by scattering it on the beach. The grains had to be separated from the sand. At the age of four years, Imo took to scooping up mixtures of sand and wheat grains, carrying the mixture to the sea, and throwing it in. The sand sank, but the grains floated and were gathered in and eaten. Once again, this innovation began a tradition; and, once again, the adult males failed to accept it.

As a last example, described by A. Tsumori, experimenters buried peanuts while watched by a troop of macaques. A few, four to six years of age, quickly dug them up again; and—as before—the habit spread from them to most of the other members of the troop.

Much more remains to be learned about the traditions of monkey troops. For example, S. Green has given additional information on what happens when food is put out for Japanese macaques. One immediate consequence is a great deal of noise from the monkeys. Green gives evidence that the noises made are specific to particular places. He also suggests the existence of cultural transmission of patterns of sounds, and hence the existence of local dialects.

Potato washing and digging up nuts are manipulatory. Another important kind of manipulation is the use of tools. Chimpanzees use sticks when they are feeding on ants or termites (8.2.3). J. van Lawick-Goodall (1970) has described how young chimpanzees watch adults using tools; when an adult drops a tool, the young ape may pick it up and use it in the same manner. Sometimes a chimpanzee uses leaves to wipe its bottom. A young chimpanzee has been observed to copy this act with some exactness, although its bottom at the time was clean.

W. C. McGrew and others have evidence of social interactions in the use of ladders and sticks by chimpanzees climbing out of an enclosure. These apes were in captivity, and displayed considerable ingenuity in learning how to climb over a barrier. When they had "escaped", they ate items of food and played with objects; they then returned without prompting from their captors. Much of this behavior evidently depended on innovatory acts by one individual which were then copied by the others.

8.4.2.5 Human Imitation:

In discussing apparent imitation by other species, a general problem is what to include. In contrast, when we come to social learning by human beings, the problem is what to omit. A small child copies the movements made by parents and others, including most notably the movements of speech (reviewed by J. Ryan). A youth apprenticed to a skilled tradesman copies the master's methods. The clothing style of a prominent person is adopted by admirers. The moral principles stated by a philosopher are repeated by his followers.

Most systematic studies of human imitation have been on children. Usually they have examined how imitation contributes to social development (reviewed by A. Bandura and by W. W. Hartup & B. Coates). In experiments on other species (8.4.2.2) the observer is usually rewarded for copying the demonstrator. Similarly, imitation by children may, as we all know, be strengthened by reward; but the reward may be merely verbal: "Good!". As an example from a simple society, I take the account by M. J. Konner of gatherer-hunters in the Kalahari Desert. The infants, by the end of their first year, already copy adult activities, such as pounding with a mortar and pestle, digging, singing, and even dancing; and adults spend much time encouraging such conduct. Year-old children may also be encouraged to catch and bite large insects.

Such findings tell us something of the social factors that influence imitation. More important is the scope of the effects of imitation. B. J. Zimmerman & T. L. Rosenthal show how a great variety of generalized skills and concepts can be "taught" simply by encouraging imitation. Such behavior is, of course, quite distinct from the copying of a pattern of movements.

8.4.2.6 Social Play:

One of the characteristic features of young mammals is behavior which resembles that of adults but is not carried to completion. Young mammals seem to run (and climb) when there is nothing special to run from or to; they go through movements that seem apotreptic but do not lead to any lasting withdrawal by another; they manipulate objects and materials, without eating them, making a nest, or doing anything else that (to a human observer) seems useful. Such behavior, which is also sometimes performed by adults, is often discussed under the heading of play. The heterogeneous character of this grouping is brought out in a volume edited by J. S. Bruner and others: some of the descriptions are of novelty responses that seem to contribute to deutero-learning (8.1.4.2); others are instances of problem solving (reviewed also by A. Weisler & R. B. McCall).

In this section we are concerned with "social play", that is, with social interactions that have some or all of the following features (reviewed by M. Bekoff, 1976; R. M. Fagen): (1) they are not due to any evident internal need and are not induced by the external stimuli that normally provoke them; (2) they lead to no outcome apart from that entailed in the movements themselves; (3) they are quickly and frequently repeated; (4) the roles of the performers are rapidly reversed; (5) the motor patterns resemble those of adults, but are incomplete, exaggerated, distorted,

or in the wrong sequence; (6) the movements require more expenditure of energy than seems
necessary.

Most motor patterns can be classified by the
ends they serve—their functions, such as feeding,
reproduction, and so on. The patterns called "play"
cannot: the activities seem to be performed as ends
in themselves; obstacles may even be sought or
created so that they can be surmounted. Hence
"play" must be defined structurally, that is, in
terms of movement patterns. Moreover, it is a
"cluster concept": that is, play is identified as activities that have *some* of the features listed in the
previous paragraph, but not necessarily all. The
concept of play is therefore unsatisfactorily vague.

Nonetheless, it is often easy to get agreement on
what should be called play. As an example, F. F.
Darling describes conduct by calves of the red deer,
Cervus elaphus, which seems to parallel a familiar
game played by children. A calf stands on a hill-
ock, and is then displaced by another that runs up
and pushes it off. The interactions include "mock
fights", but these are momentary; and the whole
sequence lasts only a few minutes. The hillocks are
regularly used for this purpose. Other games described by Darling include chases in which first one
and then another calf pursues a companion.

It is sometimes stated that the Primates are the
most playful of mammals. Such an assertion is
usually unsupported by quantitative evidence; but
J. van Lawick-Goodall (1968) gives quantitative
evidence of the familiar fact that young animals
play much more than do adults. The form taken
by play included chases, grabbing of twigs or other
objects held by another, wrestling, and tickling. A
young chimpanzee invites social play with two distinctive signals. One is a special kind of walk: the
back is hunched up, the head is pulled down and
back, and the steps are short. This pattern is ob-

served in no other context. The other signal is the
"play-face": the mouth is opened so that the teeth
are exposed; but the expression is quite distinct
from the open-mouth threat.

The usual assumption is that the various activities called play provide useful practice, and so
make an animal more efficient when it comes to
perform social and other acts in earnest. So stated,
the practice theory, though obvious, evokes at least
two comments. First, many kinds of behavior are
called play, and their functions may be correspondingly diverse, even if all provide some sort of practice. Second, does experimental evidence exist or,
if not, can appropriate experiments be devised?

There is much evidence of short-term favorable
effects of practice on the functioning of the nervous
system; and, as we see in chapter 17, normal early
development of central nervous function requires
diversity of experience. Hence we may suppose
that some kinds of play contribute to the development of the nervous system. Such effects do not,
however, necessarily entail social interactions.

For other (fragmentary) evidence on function,
we turn again to the Primates. The play of Primates
is often imitative (compare 8.4.2.3). P. H. Schiller
describes an example from young, captive chimpanzees. For a year, from the age of two years, he
kept two animals without access to sticks. Normally, both in captivity and in the wild, young
chimpanzees, once they have reached the age of two
years, frequently manipulate, break, and even throw
sticks (J. van Lawick-Goodall 1968). (Older chimpanzees also behave in this way.) Schiller's deprived animals were much less skilful in using
sticks to get food than were others reared more
normally. Schiller also made observations on the
use of two sticks joined together to reach for an
object (compare 8.2.3). He states that chimpanzees less than five years old never join sticks to-

gether; and that only those that have previously joined sticks in play can do it to achieve a reward. Unfortunately, although Schiller observed large numbers of chimpanzees, he gives no details of his findings nor quantitative analysis.

There is little formal evidence on the role of play for our own species. J. L. Dansky & I. W. Silverman describe a study of 90 children around five years of age. Their main concern was with the effects of the opportunity to play with objects; but there was a social component: one group of children had the opportunity to imitate an adult. The objects included a screwdriver, paper clips, matchboxes, and others. One group of children were allowed to play with the objects; a second group was asked to imitate an experimenter turning screws with the screwdriver and performing other acts; and a third (control) group saw nothing of the objects, but were given crayons and sketches to color. Immediately after the sessions of play, imitation or coloring, each child was shown an experimental object and asked to suggest the variety of things it could be used for. Hence the question asked in the experiment was whether play had an influence in imaginative or creative use of objects.

The responses of the children were classified as standard or nonstandard. Standard responses were those that mentioned a use for which the object had been designed. As figure 8-22 shows, there was no effect of imitation on nonstandard responses, but a vast effect of play. The authors comment as follows.

The protocols of the play subjects provided numerous examples of . . . free combinatorial and associative activity. . . . Children stated that they could "wrap (a paper towel) around a bunch of paper clips and throw it", use an empty matchbox to "put sand in it for a little house for ants", and use paper clips to "make a chain out of them and tie up dogs with it".

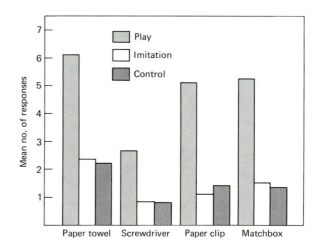

FIGURE 8-22 Children were allowed to play with objects or to observe an adult manipulating the objects; a control group had neither experience. The test, given immediately afterward, was to show a child one of the objects and to ask for suggestions on what it could be used for. There was a marked effect of playing with the objects. (After J. L. Dansky & I. W. Silverman, 1973)

One child suggested that he could use a matchbox to make either "a little T.V." (or) "a big swimming pool". Another claimed that "If you turn it (a screwdriver) like this, it will be a merry-go-round."

The observations by Dansky and Silverman, then, have some bearing on a possible general effect of play. A study by K. Sylva and others examines effects on the development of a specific ability, and is derived from the experiments in which chimpanzees are required to join sticks to make a tool (figure 8-23). The question was whether the opportunity to play with sticks and clamps would later help children to solve a problem involving their use. Again, some children merely had the opportunity to play, others to imitate a demonstrator. It might be supposed that, as a preparation for dealing with the problem, a demonstration of a manipulative procedure would be

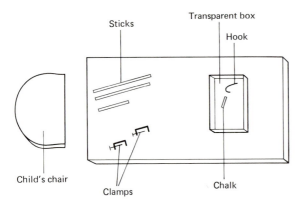

FIGURE 8-23 Arrangement of materials used to test the effects of playing with objects on subsequent use of the objects for solving problems. The transparent box could be opened by pulling on the hook. The colored chalk it contained could then be pulled into reach. To do this, the sticks had to be made into a single tool by clamping them together. (After K. Sylva and others, 1976)

more helpful than undirected play. But, in fact, children that played with the objects did just as well as those that received a demonstration; and both groups did much better than controls with no relevant previous experience.

Such experiments are of great interest; but they inevitably leave unanswered questions on the long-term effects of the opportunity to play. In general, play is one of the most important and most enigmatic of familiar activities. When more work has been done, this vague category will no doubt be analyzable into a number of distinct phenomena, and we shall know much more about how to promote the full social and intellectual development of children.

The role of imitation (and, as we shall see, of teaching) for human beings is so vast that it separates the human species rather sharply from all others (15.1; 15.2).

8.4.2.7 Theoretical Questions:

The preceding sections describe the range of phenomena usually discussed under the heading of imitation. If we return to Thorpe's definition (quoted in 8.4.2.1), we can now see more clearly why the definition emphazizes the novelty of the act performed. Suppose one animal is attracted to a place by another; and further suppose that it then performs a probable act as eating: that is an example of local enhancement (8.4.1.1). We distinguish such conduct from the copying of a complex habit, when the latter must first be acquired slowly by a demonstrator animal.

Thorpe adds, in effect, that we call a copied act "imitation" if it is one for which "there is clearly no instinctive tendency". Many of those who cite his definition omit this phrase: behavior that used to be called "instinctive" (chapter 17) is species typical and highly predictable. Hence it is far from "improbable"; the additional phrase therefore seems redundant. The phrase does, however, emphasize that an action we call imitative is usually one that has to be acquired by practice.

In his own comment on the definition (also quoted), Thorpe suggests that imitation, as he defines it, "apparently involves self-consciousness". A human being imitating another can state in words something of the internal processes—the thoughts—that underlie the imitative act; and we may say that that person is conscious of what he is doing. In describing animal behavior it is more convenient to state exactly what we observe (and what we know or hypothesize—if anything—about the accompanying internal changes). What we do know is that such copying requires the retrieval of various sorts of information previously acquired on a number of separate occasions. *In that sense* it involves, if not self-consciousness, at least cognition.

To sum up, there is a useful objective distinction

between local enhancement, on the one hand, and imitation on the other. We speak of imitation when O observes D and, as a result, develops some habit that O would not otherwise have achieved or would have achieved more slowly. The end may or may not be attained by a precise repetition of the movements performed by D.

8.4.3 Encouragement and Teaching

Nearly all accounts of "social learning" treat the conduct of the model or demonstrator as something given and independent of what the observer does. Many experimental arrangements insure that the demonstrator cannot be influenced by the observer. Yet in natural conditions social effects are usually *interactions* between two or more individuals.

If a model is interacting with an imitator, the model can behave in a way to make it easier (or more difficult) for the imitation to occur. Examples come from the carnivores. The large cats (Felidae) have been described as encouraging their young to hunt: for example, an adult may pull down a prey animal and leave it for the cubs to kill. Rudolph Schenkel (1966) has observed lions, *Panthera leo,* behaving in this way. R. F. Ewer (1963) describes how meerkats, *Suricata,* learn to eat insects. When, on leaving the nest, the young begin to eat solids, the mother catches insects and, instead of eating them, holds them in her teeth. The young then take them from her. Discouragement can also evidently occur. Young chimpanzees, like children, are adventurous feeders. A mother or older sibling may take an unfamiliar food from an infant or juvenile, and so restrict its food habits (J. van Lawick-Goodall 1973). This conforms with the observations on mandrills described in 8.4.2.3.

In the development of human behavior, imitation plays a large part, but it is aided by teaching;

and teaching is more than encouragement. (Sometimes it involves a great deal of discouragement, but that is another story.) If a parent takes children to the seashore and leaves them to play, they may learn to swim without further adult intervention; but we would not call that teaching: we might classify it as encouragement. On the other hand, in many (though by no means all) of the activities we call teaching one individual persists in and adapts behavior until another, the pupil, achieves a certain standard of performance (reviewed by S. A. Barnett, 1977).

To what extent do other species behave in this way? The answer, on present knowledge, is that they do so only in a special category of interactions—those that induce separation of individuals, or withdrawal of one from another. There are three main kinds of such behavior, all described further in later chapters.

1. The most familiar situation, in which one mammal persistently drives another off, is weaning. H. L. Rheingold gives a number of examples. Among domestic animals, it is a common sight to see a bitch batting her independent puppies away. A macaque, *Macaca,* or a langur, *Presbytis,* drives off her year-old offspring—sometimes with cries from the victim. It may be objected that these acts are not teaching; but they do fall in the category of conduct that induces a particular response (avoidance or withdrawal), and they are persisted in until that end is attained. The alert reader will have noticed that, if we do call this teaching, it is teaching by punishment (6.2.4). The deterrent behavior constitutes something that the young animal tends to avoid; and the punished act is approach.

2. Another category is behavior observed in the maintenance of a status system (or dominance hierarchy, 11.3). Again, proximity is punished. One

member of a group approaches or is approached by another. One gives a standard signal, and the other moves away. Among Primates, the signal may be blinking the eyes or slapping the ground. Habit formation results from such encounters: a subordinate learns to keep away from a dominant animal.

3. A similar type of relationship is seen in the maintenance of territory (10.4). Status refers to conduct within a group, while territorial interactions are between groups or, sometimes, between isolated individuals. Again, what is learned is avoidance.

There is no evidence that punishment is ever used by animals in the teaching of *skills*. Such a statement is purely descriptive. This needs emphasis because, in another context, the statement might be used as a basis for moral exhortation. On the one hand, the reader might be urged to look to the animals, who never use punishment to teach their young skills. But from another bias, one might exclaim that because human beings are so adaptable, pain can help them to develop useful habits.

With the exception of dispersive interactions, teaching—in the sense of conduct adapted to a pupil's performance—seems to be confined to mankind (S. A. Barnett, 1977). It appears to be universal in human communities, but it has not been systematically studied. Accounts of gatherer-hunter and simple agricultural communities include only scattered references to the teaching of children, usually during comment on socialization. In simple communities, children are encouraged to take part in adult activities from an early age; and imitation of adults is prominent and welcomed. The adults of some groups deny that they teach their children at all. But, probably, in all such communities, older children teach younger ones, as an accompaniment of looking after them.

We have seen how difficult is the analysis of complex habit formation and problem solving, even when the subject is isolated. When the social dimension is added, we reach the most intricate—and the most important—of the processes studied under the heading of learning. In all human groups, but in no other species, such processes depend on verbal communication. I say more about that in chapter 15.

8.5 THE CONCEPT OF LEARNING

After four long chapters on conditioning, habit formation, problem solving, imitation, and related phenomena—defined with various degrees of precision—a reader may be tempted to ask: "What is learning?" I now try to explain why this temptation should be resisted.

A committee of ethologists once deliberated on the definition of ethological terms, and for "learning" proposed "internal change causing adaptive change in behavior as a result of experience" (W. H. Thorpe, 1951). This definition is interesting partly because it is reductionist (19.1.3): the word "learning" is applied to *internal* processes, presumably mainly in the brain. J. A. Dyal & W. C. Corning have given a convenient survey of other definitions. They consider it inappropriate to define "learning" in terms of mechanism, if only because so little is known about the physiology of the behavior discussed under this heading.

A leading worker on the physiology of behavior, N. E. Miller (1967), has proposed the following formula:

Learning is a relatively permanent tendency for a stimulus to elicit a response that is based on previous association between the stimulus and the response . . . or the response and a reward, that can be established between any one of a considerable number of arbitrarily selected *S–R* combinations, and that can be reversed by specific retraining.

This passage is notable for omitting much that is commonly labeled as learning, for example, habituation and also the storage of information that sometimes takes place in the absence of behavioral change. Moreover, the expression "relatively permanent" is vague.

E. M. Eisenstein and his colleagues have an interesting passage in a discussion of what I have called "protohabituation" (5.4.1). They write:

One question to consider is whether the response decrement to repetitive mechanical stimulation "really" is learning. This is not a question to be answered by an arbitrary assertion or definition. It is an empirical question. It requires knowing the molecular substrate of the decrement and how this substrate is similar or dissimilar to that underlying such generally accepted forms of learning as Pavlovian conditioning and instrumental learning. . . .

Behavioral characteristics not yet demonstrated and which most workers would like to see before they would agree that the above phenomenon is related to learning seen in organisms with a nervous system are: (1) stimulus discrimination, i.e., is the response decrement specific to the stimulus used to produce it, and not a general decrement to all stimuli to which the animal is capable of responding? (2) Can dishabituation be shown?

In this passage there is an attempt to interpret "learning" in both behavioral and physiological terms. It does not, however, lead to any position or definition that would be generally accepted by workers in this field.

The position I adopt in this book is that colloquial terms with many lexical definitions, such as learning, are useful only as labels for general, ill-defined categories of phenomena. If we see a book on behavior with the word "learning" in the title, we know that it is probably about some kinds of change in response to repeated stimuli or situations, and that the changes described are likely to appear adaptive (that is, promoting survival). To find out more, we have to look at the table of contents. On this view it is inappropriate to ask what is the essence or the definition of learning. We need to examine the various kinds of change, to classify them in an orderly way, and to attempt explanations of how they come about. For this purpose there are two main kinds of explanation: (1) we may observe behavior in relation (a) to the animal's immediate situation and (b) to its previous experience; (2) we may attempt a physiological analysis (reductionism).

The preceding chapters have described the principal methods used in the attempt to establish "laws of learning", that is, explanations based on phenomena such as the effects of reward or punishment. There is much less on physiological analysis, because not much is known about the physiology of "learning". Indeed, at present, there are no unifying theories at all. Earlier in this century some people thought it would be possible to bring all "learning" into a single scheme. The study of conditional reflexes, or of bar pressing in Skinner boxes, seemed to provide unifying concepts. The baffling complexities of exploratory learning and other cognitive processes were glossed over. Today, in contrast, we are in a phase of diversification of methods, of kinds of behavior, and of species. Perhaps there is also a corresponding need for new ideas.

IV

SOCIAL CONDUCT

Social interactions are mentioned in several previous chapters, especially chapter 8. We now turn to systematic study of social ethology, that is, to relationships between members of the same species.

Chapter 9, on reproductive activities, illustrates the variety of the means by which fertility is insured and young are reared. As usual, most of the words we use to describe the behavior were first applied to human beings. And so the mating systems of animals include promiscuity, polygamy, and monogamy, as well as other less familiar strategies. Experiments on a few species have told us much about the physiology of their reproductive behavior.

In chapter 10, the principal themes are territorial behavior and the structure of status systems ("dominance hierarchies") within groups. Related topics include crowding, social stress, and "aggression"; all these have given rise to controversy, and still do so. There are no universally accepted definitions for any of the key terms. The lack of agreement arises partly from the variety we find in the animal kingdom, partly from the diverse interests of different workers.

The Primates have a chapter of their own, because of their special interest and the vast mass of description of their societies now available.

Most of the patterns of social behavior of animals are species-typical. They often seem to be exceedingly rigid and unadaptable. But in fact there is always some variation. Sometimes individual recognition, for example, by members of mated pairs or by parents of young or young of parents, is possible. Variation may be studied by experiments on the ontogeny of social patterns. Ontogenetic studies, such as those on bird song, on imprinting, and on the social development of monkeys, illustrate fundamental principles of behavioral biology.

The last chapter of this part, on communication in general, gives an account of social signals, and of the special problems of method that we meet in studying them.

9

COURTSHIP
AND PARENTHOOD

For the reproduction of the race, there are two instincts needed, the sexual and the parental, and the way these are organised is to say the least curious.

Darwin (1901)

Much of the complex, bizarre, and fascinating behavior in the animal kingdom arises from the problems of insuring that eggs are fertilized; and the most agreeable behavior to watch is often that of parents and young together. Courtship, mating, and parenthood are the principal occasions of animal cooperation. They also provide many of the best examples of complex, species-typical social activities—conduct that used to be called instinctive or innate. This chapter gives examples. The question of general rules concerning the reproductive behavior of animals is deferred to chapter 18. A review of animal courtship has been published by Margaret Bastock (1967).

9.1 ARTHROPODS

9.1.1 Courting Couples

Some arthropods have an elaborate courtship but do not look after their young. A common European butterfly, the silver-washed fritillary, *Argynnis*

paphia, has been closely studied (D. Magnus). These pretty creatures occupy clearings and the edges of woods, where adults may be seen in July and August. Much of their behavior may be interpreted as orientations (chapter 2) to narrowly defined features of their habitat. Moving models have been used to evoke these responses (figure 9-1).

Females are seen in flight mainly during the morning; males become active later and feed principally in the afternoon. Hence mating depends on brief encounters around lunchtime. When a male is feeding it flies on a fairly straight course, and tends to approach yellow, green, or blue objects. But a mating flight has a distinctive zigzag pattern; and a male, when flying in this manner, is attracted by orange-yellow objects. This is the predominant color of a female. For an orange-yellow object to be maximally attractive, it should be fluttering, preferably at a high rate. Its shape is unimportant; but if it is larger than a female—even four times the size—it is very attractive indeed.

In natural conditions, nubile females, and only they, have a hovering, fluttering flight. The males go for these fluttering virgins, and then begin to flutter themselves. The female flies away, again in

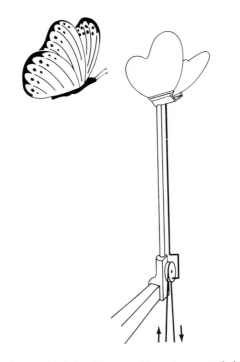

FIGURE 9-1 Model with movable wings used in experiments on the courtship of the silverwashed fritillary, *Argynnis paphia*. (After D. Magnus, 1958)

be called a *social signal;* and a group of such signals occurring together is sometimes called a *display*.

Another insect courtship, described by M. Bastock & A. Manning, is more one-sided: in the mating of fruit flies of the species, *Drosophila melanogaster* (also known as the vinegar fly), the male does most of the work. Insects of this genus, famous for their contribution to genetics, feed on the yeasts that multiply in decaying fruit. The females lay their eggs near such food.

Courtship begins when a male taps another insect with its forelegs. Like the blowfly (4.5.1.2) a fruit fly has chemoreceptors on the tarsi. The "taste" of other insects helps the male to discriminate between females of its own species and other males or members of other species. The discrimination is, however, not very precise. But, if a mistake is made, the fly that is wrongly approached rapidly kicks the erring male off: females are more discriminating than males.

a distinctive manner, on a straight line, whereafter an aerial pas de deux is performed, during which secretions from the male are wafted to the female. The female then settles on a convenient plant, but continues to flutter, and probably releases odors also. The male approaches closely, "bows" (figure 9-2), clasps the female with his wings, releases more odor, and vibrates his antennae and middle legs against the female's hind wings. Coitus takes place with the two insects alongside each other, and their abdomens bent toward each other.

These butterflies evidently respond in a highly specific way to sights, odors, and contacts. A stimulus, or set of stimuli, from one individual sets off a response by the other, which in turn acts as a stimulus. Each visible pattern, odor, or contact may

FIGURE 9-2 Male fritillary on right bows to female during courtship. (Reproduced from M. Bastock, *Courtship: A Zoological Study,* 1967, drawing after D. Magnus, 1958, by permission of Heinemann Educational Books, London)

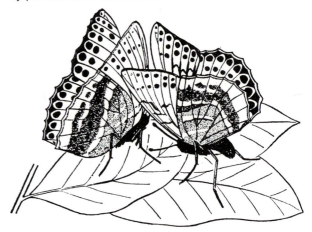

When a suitable female is identified, the male goes through the sequence of acts illustrated in figure 9-3. In the phase of orientation, the male faces the female and may circle around her. Next, one wing is vibrated. A third component accompanies orientation and vibration: the male licks the female's genitalia from behind. After licking, mounting occurs, but is often at first unsuccessful. The whole process, including several attempts at mounting and ultimate coitus, may take 3 min. It may be readily studied under a low-power binocular microscope, with the flies in small glass vessels.

Mating by *D. melanogaster* evidently does not depend on visual stimuli, for it occurs normally in darkness. Vibration of the wings stimulates the female: wingless males may take 20 min before the female accepts them. The current of air produced by the wing vibration acts on receptors on the female's antennae. A female without antennae responds in the same way to a male with wings and to one without: both have to court her for about 20 min before coitus.

The courtship of other species of *Drosophila* has also been observed in some detail. Within this one genus there is much variation. *D. subobscura* seems to depend on visual stimuli, for it mates only in the light. Others evidently depend more on tactile stimuli—not only licking, but also leg rubbing. And when we turn to flies of different families, there is still more variation. One extreme is that of the housefly, *Musca:* the male lands on the female's back without warning.

It might be expected that such unceremonious behavior would be especially found among insects

FIGURE 9-3 Courtship of the vinegar fly, *Drosophila melanogaster.* The male approaches the female (A), vibrates his wings (B), and licks the female's genitalia (C). D and E show mounting and coitus. (Reproduced from B. Burnet & K. Connolly, in J. H. F. van Abeelen, ed., *The Genetics of Behavior,* 1974, Chap. 9, by permission of Elsevier/North Holland Biomedical Press)

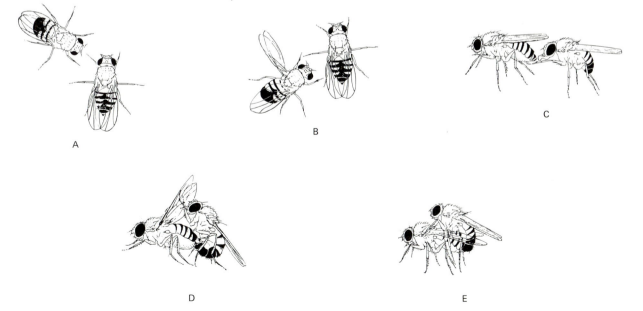

A

B

C

D

E

that live crowded together, and therefore require no special means of bringing the sexes into contact. But this is not always the case. L. M. Roth and others (1952, 1956) have studied a cockroach, *Nauphoeta cinerea,* an Asian species with a worldwide distribution in association with man. Sexually mature males move around their warm, damp, dark environment, and touch antennae with any other cockroach they meet. The antennae of virgin females secrete a substance that excites the male to further antennal stimulation. After this, the male poses in a standard position, sometimes for as long as a minute, with raised wings and lowered abdomen. This posture allows the female to nibble at the secretions of glands on the back of the abdomen. In this way she ingests a substance (seducin) that both attracts her and also makes her keep still. The male is thus enabled to grasp the female with his claspers, which are at the rear end; insemination takes place with the pair in a straight line, facing away from each other.

The sedative properties of seducin are an example of an inhibitory effect of a courtship signal. Inhibition is especially evident in the mating of spiders (Araneida) (reviewed by W. S. Bristowe). Most spiders are rather indiscriminate predators, and discharge poison from their fangs or chelicerae. The females are larger than the males. Correspondingly, a male usually approaches a female rather gradually, with a number of preliminary signals.

A male of a web-building species begins his reproductive activities alone. Soon after reaching full size, after the last moult, he constructs a miniature web on which he deposits a drop of seminal fluid—a functional masturbation. This is now picked up by the swollen tips of the palps, that is, the first pair of leg-like appendages. The next step is to approach the female in a species-characteristic manner. Males of the orb-web family (Argiopidae) commonly court at night. When they reach a female's web, they drum on it with a rhythm typical of their species. The effect is quite unlike that of the struggles of a prey organism trapped in the web. If the female moves, the male runs off; but he soon returns and resumes drumming. If she remains still, he eventually approaches, and strokes her with his appendages. Finally, she turns on her back, and the male inserts his spermatophore and

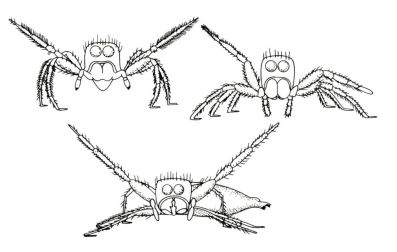

FIGURE 9-4 Female's-eye view of courting male salticid spiders. The appendages are moved in a regular and characteristic fashion, as if the animals were semaphoring. Upper left, *Corythalia chalcea.* Right, *Mago dentichelis.* Below, *Ashtabula furcillata.* (After A. Portmann, 1961)

discharges seminal fluid. The last movement apart, the female has only to remain still: such immobility is evidently induced, as a rule, by the male's signals.

Many spiders have large and elaborate eyes and hunt by sight; courtship then involves elaborate visible signals, such as those illustrated in figure 9-4. Jocelyn Crane (1949) has described the displays of spiders of the family Salticidae. The male's slow approach is accompanied by movements that show off striking patterns of colors typical of the species; often, there are systematic semaphore-like movements of the limbs. These animals are well equipped with chemoreceptors, and odors are probably important as well as visible stimuli; but little is known about them. Something is, however, known of audible signals. J. S. Rovner describes drumming by *Lycosa rabida*. During courtship the male vibrates his palps on the ground in bursts of up to two seconds. A receptive female responds by waving her legs. Courtship can be carried out in the dark; but in daylight these spiders can mate without the aid of sounds. Hence the sequence of acts during mating is not invariable.

Another example of versatility is described by R. R. Jackson. A male jumping spider, *Phidippus johnsoni* (figure 9-5), courts a female outside her nest with a typical series of movements: he walks toward her and then away; he also walks sideways, to the left and then to the right; and he waves his forelegs in a typical fashion. The performance consists of an elaborate visible display. But in an encounter in the nest the male vibrates the silk of which the nest is made, and this type of courtship is independent of vision.

Some of the forms of spider courtship are astonishingly elaborate. A male *Pisaura mirabilis* catches a fly, webs it up, and, on finding a female, adopts a peculiar posture with the fly held in front. The fe-

FIGURE 9-5   Above, male jumping spider, *Phidippus johnsoni,* courts a female by facing her with raised forelegs. Below, another form of courtship, in which the male stands on the female's nest and tugs at the silk. (Courtesy R. R. Jackson)

male, if ready to mate, begins to eat the fly; the male moves into position below, and inserts a palp. Coitus may last an hour, during which the male occasionally refreshes himself, too, from the fly. A male *Xysticus cristatus* begins his courtship by seizing one of the female's legs; he then ties her to the ground with "silk" threads and, having made all safe, embarks on coitus. After an hour or more he leaves, and the female struggles free.

Nonetheless, as O. Drees has shown, experiments are practicable. Figure 9-6 illustrates the use of models to determine what an object should look like to evoke courtship by a male salticid. The size of the "body" was one factor; others were the thickness of the legs, their number and their angularity. When in use, all the models were in

FIGURE 9-6   Models used to induce courtship by male salticid spiders. The models were in motion during the experiments. The size of the model and the position, number, size, and angle of the legs were all factors that influenced the probability of a response. (M. Bastock after O. Drees, 1967)

	No. of tests	Responses (%)
	88	58
	80	85
	82	49
	69	36
	72	36
	44	23
	54	52
	36	17

motion. The right-hand part of the figure shows that the models often evoked attack, rather than courtship, especially if the male had been kept without food for some time. These models, of course, do not represent the total situation during the mating of these spiders: in particular, they had no odor. But the experiments illustrate how one aspect of a display, in this case the visible aspect, can be analyzed.

9.1.2 The Eusocial Insects

The most notable examples of family life among invertebrates are those of the *eusocial* insects (reviewed by O. W. Richards; E. O. Wilson 1971). Eusocial species have the following features: (1) conspecifics act together to care for the young; (2) some individuals, of low fertility or sterile, feed and otherwise support one or more fertile individuals; (3) at least two generations coexist, so that fertile individuals are at some stage aided by their offspring. Two orders, the Isoptera and the Hymenoptera, include highly organized societies with these characteristics. Some species of Hymenoptera, among the wasps and bees, have some of the eusocial features but not all. They are regarded as representing earlier stages of the evolution of sociality; and from them it is inferred that the initial selective advantage of a complex social organization was in the protection and feeding of the young.

9.1.2.1 Termites: The Isoptera, or termites, have no metamorphosis from a larva into a different adult form. In many species the young contribute to the activities of a colony; but in some (of the family, Termitidae) the immature forms depend on the adult workers. All species of termites produce large numbers of infertile individuals of both sexes. All live in large groups—some even of millions of individuals. Many are architects on a vast scale: their nests may then be made of an astonishingly hard mixture of clay and saliva; when these are to be destroyed, on ground destined for planting, they must be blown up. The common name of "white ants" for termites is related to the habit of these insects of shunning the light: the insects are burrowers and lack brown pigment.

As a rule, a new colony is founded by a newly mated pair. Clouds of winged nubile females and fertile males appear for a brief time. These sexual forms meet in the air or on the ground, and shed their wings; the two insects touch each other with their antennae and mouth appendages; there follows a nuptial promenade, which ends with the selection of a nest site. A tunnel is dug jointly, and coitus takes place in it. The first young are, necessarily, reared by the "royal" pair; later workers feed the young with predigested foods.

This food has a special property. Termites can use wood as food (J. A. Breznak). Many species owe this ability to the presence in the gut of a protozoan, *Trichonympha,* which can digest cellulose and other, usually indigestible, carbohydrates. If the protozoans are killed by exposing termites to high oxygen pressure, the insects starve. Infection with *Trichonympha,* from one generation to the next, depends on the presence of the protozoan in the predigested food fed to the young. Other species (the majority) are aided by bacteria.

9.1.2.2 Ants:

When we turn to the Hymenoptera, we find that all the ants (Formicidae) are eusocial. All, like termites, protect the eggs and young, usually in nests. There are remarkable parallels to the termite kind of organization, although the two groups must have evolved their social systems independently.

From their behavior the ants may be grouped as hunters, food gatherers, farmers, or stockbreeders, though some species practice more than one of these activities. Among the hunters are the army ants (Dorylinae). These carry out raids in vast numbers, and can kill pigs in their sties or hens in their cages (T. C. Schneirla, 1956, 1971). A large species, *Eciton burchelli,* of Central and South America, has been closely observed. A phase of active, *nomadic* movement alternates regularly with one in which a temporary nest or bivouac is made—the *statary* phase. This cycle is related to a cycle of egg laying by the queen—which is the only fertile female. Every five or six weeks, in a few days during a statary period, she lays 100,000 eggs or more. These are tended by workers. The period during which the colony is active begins when the eggs have hatched, and continues while the larvae are growing. The workers carry the larvae on the march, and feed them with the proceeds of the many raids now made. A period of quiescence begins when the larvae pupate; and it ends just before they emerge.

Among the harvesting ants of the genus, *Pogonomyrmex,* we find a caste misleadingly called soldiers: with their vast heads and powerful mandibles, they crush seeds and so benefit the whole colony. Such food gatherers live principally on the seeds of grasses. There are, however, many other sources of food. Among the oddest are the excreta of aphids and other Hemiptera. These liquid excreta are sugary, and it is sometimes possible for an ant to induce an aphid to produce a drop of the fluid by poking it. There are food gatherers, the honeypot ants, of the genera, *Camponotus, Myrmecocystus,* and others, of which some of the workers (repletes) specialize as repositories of stored food: they are fed with a vast excess of the sugary liquids obtained from other insects; they then swell enormously and hang from the ceilings of underground cavities in the nests. They resemble the blowflies that overfeed after the recurrent nerve has been cut (4.5.1.3). When suitably stimulated, a replete surrenders some of the stored food to an ordinary worker; hence it acts as a reserve against times of scarcity. These species live in arid regions.

The existence of food stores suggests that an ant colony possesses means of regulating the intake and supply of food, in relation to need and to food availability outside. Exchange of food among colony members, or *trophallaxis,* seems to provide a means of control. This long held hypothesis has been confirmed for *Myrmica rubra* by M. V. Brian & A. Abbott. The rate at which food is collected is regulated by the demand from the larvae: little food is gathered in the absence of larvae that will accept it from the workers.

The harvesting ants, like the honeypot species, also store food, but in the more ordinary form of grain, again in underground chambers. If the seeds become damp, the ants bring them out to dry when the sun shines. Germination may be prevented because the ants bite off and eat the part of the seed which produces a shoot. It has been said that these ants plant some of the seeds outside their nests, and harvest the resulting growth next year. In fact, any seed that has germinated is taken from the nest and, if covered, may grow.

The leaf-cutting ants are systematically "agricultural": they carry plant fragments into their nests, and fungi grow on them. Fungus growers include *Cyphomyrmex* and *Atta* (Myrmecinae). The fungi are evidently different for each species of leaf cutter, and they are found only in association with the ants. Growth of the fungus depends partly on manure provided by the feces of the workers, which are mixed with the fragments. The network of fungal threads produces knob-shaped growths on which the ants browse. Some of the workers keep the fungus gardens in order: for instance, they have to be weeded, that is, kept free of molds. The larger grubs lie in the fungus gardens, and feed themselves on the fungi.

How are fungus gardens started in a new colony? When a virgin female flies out to mate, she has with her a small pellet containing fungal spores. The pellet is deposited on the floor of the underground cavity she makes after mating. The fungus grows there, and is manured with the female's excreta. From time to time, the female takes a fragment of fungus and holds it against her anus, from which she deposits a fluid on it. Hence cultivation of these fungi is a product of a most complicated system of stereotyped activities.

Finally, there are the stockbreeders. Their mode of life (trophobiosis) has perhaps developed from the food gathering of species that ingest the excreta of aphids and others. A number of species (for example, of the common genera, *Lasius* and *Formica*) keep aphids or other Hemiptera in their nests. These inquilines have been called ant cows. Some ants take in the eggs of aphids in the autumn and put them out again in the spring, on plants on which they can develop.

The words we use to describe these marvelous creatures represent an orgy of anthropomorphism. They would be misleading if they made people think that, say, the fungus gardens of ants were, like our farms, a product of a few thousand years of tradition, and were managed by methods learned anew in each generation. A similar absurdity would be to condemn, on moral grounds, the "child labor" observed among the species of termites in which the early instars contribute to the work of the colony. Fortunately, such confusions rarely appear, at least in modern writings.

9.1.2.3 Wasps and Bees:

The ant family (Formicidae) is classified in the same group of families as the social wasps (Vespoidea), together with several families of species that are not euso-cial. The latter tell us something of the stages by which complex social organizations could have evolved. The hunting wasps and sand wasps pro-vide food in the form of paralyzed or dead cater-pillars for their young (8.1.1.1). But once this mass provisioning is accomplished, the young are left to fend for themselves; hence no colony de-velops.

Among the simple wasp societies are those of the genus, *Polistes*. These insects represent a sub-stantial advance on any of the solitary wasps. The "queen" closely resembles the workers except in behavior: she stays in the nest and does most or all of the egg laying; and she receives an extra ration of the food brought in. If this one fertile female is removed, the workers soon take to lay-ing eggs themselves; but, since the eggs have not been inseminated, all the eggs are parthenogenetic; hence, as a result of the rather odd mode of sex determination in this group (18.2.3.3), all produce males. Evidently, the presence of a queen inhibits egg laying by the workers.

At least one species of wasp, *Polistes gallicus,* founds colonies with several fertilized females. Later, in some varieties, one female becomes the single monarch: she "attacks" the other females with open jaws and much loud buzzing. Eventually, the ovaries of her rivals degenerate. The end result is said to be a dominance system, with the single queen at the top. Dominance is mainly a matter of prior access to food and sites for oviposition. Per-haps the survival value of confining egg laying to one female lies in releasing other individuals for nest building, care of young, and food gathering.

The commonest social wasps of Europe and North America, notably those of the genus *Vespula* (see figure 3-28), are socially among the most ad-vanced. The queens are much larger than the work-ers, and are fertilized during the brief period, at the end of the summer, when males are produced. Survival during winter depends on the inseminated queens. In spring they select a site and begin a nest. This is made from "paper" produced by mix-ing fibers of wood, scraped from dead trees or fences, and saliva. The cells in which the young develop are covered by dome-shaped envelopes, of which there are several. This provides as good heat insulation as could be made with such material.

Adult wasps can ingest only liquid food; but they prey on other insects to provide the larvae with a nutritious, proteinous paste, made by chew-ing with the mandibles.

By the end of a good summer a successful nest contains several thousand wasps. The rapid growth of the young is no doubt aided by the nest tem-perature, which is kept at 26 to 36°C. When a nest overheats, the workers collect at the entrance, hold on, and fan vigorously. Some species bring in water as an additional means of cooling. Similarly, the construction of cells, supports, and envelopes is a communal task, regulated in ways that have not been discovered. The result is an elegant, highly functional piece of architecture (figure 9-7).

9.1.2.4 The Honey Bee:
According to J. P. Spradbery, by 1973 about 100,000 scientific pub-lications had appeared on the social Hymenoptera and the termites. From these a substantial library could be made of works on *Apis mellifera* alone. Moreover, new and fascinating information (7.4.4) appears almost every month. The subject has been reviewed by J. B. Free, Karl von Frisch (1967), Martin Lindauer (1961), and E. O. Wilson (1971). (I defer the story of communication by honey bees to 13.3.2.)

Most of the members of a bee colony are sterile females—the workers. A newly emerged adult worker, within a few hours, becomes a house bee: she cleans cells, builds or repairs combs with secre-

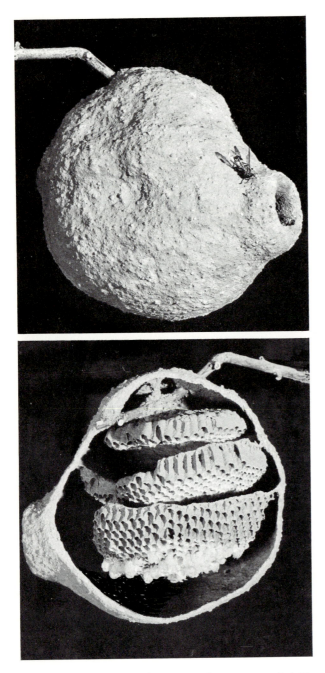

FIGURE 9-7 Above, the nest of a wasp, *Polybia emaciata;* below the nest open to show the combs. (Max Renner)

tions of her wax glands, and feeds larvae with secretions from her hypopharyngeal glands; she also receives and stores nectar and pollen brought in by older bees. During summer the queen has a group of bees, usually young, around her: they lick her and touch her with their antennae. Some young bees become, for a time, guard bees: they investigate incomers with their antennae; strangers are recognized by their odor and are driven away; when food is scarce, intruders are so ruthlessly attacked that they may die. This sequence of duties is not fixed: a worker in her first three weeks or so of adult life can turn to any activity in the hive.

House bees spend much time moving about, evidently exploring (8.1.1.1, figure 8-3); this behavior includes investigation of cells and larvae: a house bee makes a full examination of a larva before feeding it. An experimenter may divide a colony so that one part contains only older bees, which have become foragers; they have ceased to look after larvae, and their hypopharyngeal glands have atrophied. Yet some resume nursing, and the glands enlarge again. Similarly, by supplying large numbers of larvae, bees can be made to continue nursing until more than seven weeks from emergence—long after they would ordinarily have turned to foraging.

The exchange of food, or trophallaxis, is believed to be an important means of integrating behavior in a colony (figure 9-8), as it is among ants. A forager, returning with a load of nectar, does not store it in a cell, but passes it to house bees. They in turn may transfer it to yet other bees; hence only some is stored, or none in times of scarcity. The spread of food through a colony has been shown by experiments in which a few foragers from an experimental hive were allowed to take a syrup containing traces of radioactive phosphorus; the phosphorus could be traced, and was found soon to be widely dispersed among colony members.

FIGURE 9-8 Trophallaxis: worker bees exchange food. (J. B. Free)

During food transfer, other substances of social importance may be passed on by contact. The presence of a queen influences the behavior of all the many hundreds of workers of a large colony (1.1.1). The influence depends on substances that also prevent the ovaries of the workers from developing, and inhibit the building of large cells in which other queens could grow.

9.1.2.5 Caste and Division of Labor:

The eusocial insects are distinguished by the existence of females specialized for producing eggs: there may be only one such queen in a colony of many thousands of individuals. This is one aspect of the differentiation of function among types, or castes, of which the structure, longevity, and behavior differ. Every colony of eusocial insects has, in addition to one or more fertile females and some fertile males (not necessarily at all times), large numbers of workers; of the latter there may be only one type, or there may be several (reviewed by M. V. Brian, 1965, 1979; E. O. Wilson, 1971). Division of labor, or polyethism, commonly depends on the existence of castes; but, as in the honey bee, workers may have a series of roles according to age.

When modern studies of eusocial insects began, the contrasted structures of the various castes within each of many species (figure 9-9) suggested genetical differences; but it is now clear that, apart from the differentiation of the sexes, caste depends on upbringing.

Among the Isoptera the castes of *Kalotermes flavicollis* have been closely studied by Martin Lüscher (1964, 1969). These termites tunnel in dry wood, and their colonies consist of no more than a few hundred individuals. There is frequent exchange of fluids among colony members. Workers are of both sexes. The classical experiment on caste differentiation in this species, described by E. O. Wilson (1971), illustrates the way in which developmental lability allows a colony to adapt its structure to circumstances. A dozen or so individuals can produce a complete colony. If the initial group has no reproductives, some individuals develop gonads and so develop into kings or queens. A complete colony includes workers with large

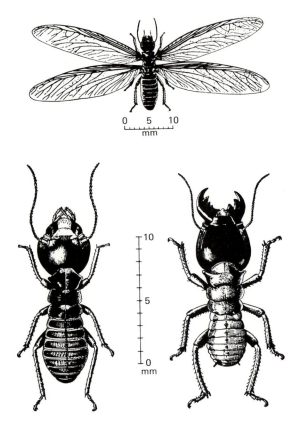

FIGURE 9-9 Three castes of a termite, *Hodotermes mossambicus:* above, a winged reproductive; left, a worker; right, a soldier. (Reproduced from W. V. Harris, *Termites, Their Recognition and Control,* 1961, Fig. 1, by permission of the Longman Group Limited, Essex)

heads ("soldiers"): if these are at first missing, some individuals develop into them. The implication is that a newly hatched larva can develop into any form or caste (allowing for the limitations of its sex). If so, the environment in which the larva develops must determine how it differentiates. Experiments by Lüscher have revealed a number of environmental effects on workers which retain the capacity to undergo further development after what would normally be their last molt. If there are no fertile individuals (reproductives) present, such workers can become fertile. They are normally pre-

vented from doing so by pheromones, produced by the reproductives, that are passed among the members of the colony during the constant allogrooming, and the regurgitation and consumption of secretions. There is also evidence of a pheromone, again produced by reproductives, which stimulates workers to develop into soldiers.

Similar complexities are found among the ants. Some, of the genus, *Myrmica,* have been minutely studied by M. V. Brian (1965, 1977). Each colony has many thousands of individuals and a number of queens. Most colony members are workers, that is, sterile females. (Male ants have only a reproductive function.) The brood produced in summer spends the winter as larvae. Many female larvae are capable, in spring, of developing into queens. Whether they do so is related to their growth rate: those that become queens are heavier, at all except the earliest stages, than those that become workers: the latter do not go beyond about 4.5 g; queens weigh about 8.0 g, have wings, three ocelli, sperm sacs, and large, functioning ovaries. Hence a worker is a female of which some structures fail to develop during metamorphosis. The structures of the adult (imago) are present in the larva only as rudiments, the imaginal discs. Of these discs, those that give rise to the legs, mouth parts, and central nervous system are ventral, and they develop in both queen and worker; but in the workers a dorsal group of discs, from which the wings, gonads, and ocelli arise, fail to grow.

Whether queens or workers are produced depends on a number of factors. The presence of queen pheromones inhibits the development of more queens by altering the behavior of the nurse workers: the latter, if offered both large and small larvae when a queen is present, feed the small larvae more than they would in the absence of a queen, and the large larvae, less. Hence their behavior reduces the number of larvae that become queens. Another factor is temperature: the chances of a larva developing into a queen are increased by some degree of exposure to cold, such as occurs in winter. The optimum temperature for larvae, measured by survival, is 22°C. If larvae are exposed to 24°C, the proportion of larvae developing into workers greatly increases. Yet a further factor is the age of the queen: the eggs of young queens are more likely to develop into workers than are those of old queens. The total picture is one of an intricate system of checks and balances, which determines the structure of a colony as it changes with seasonal and other environmental fluctuations.

9.2 FISH

9.2.1 The Three-spined Stickleback

The courtship and reproduction of only a few vertebrates are known in detail. Among them is a rather unobtrusive freshwater fish, the three-spined stickleback, *Gasterosteus aculeatus,* studied by J. J. ter Pelkwijk & N. Tinbergen. The fish are common in the ponds and streams of Britain and western Europe. Except in the breeding season, they live in schools. In winter they are rather inactive, but in spring the males move more widely, until each finds a place with a sandy bottom and water weed growing in it. The male now builds a tunnel-like nest in the sand, with pieces of weed. If another male approaches, a characteristic posture may be adopted with the head pointing down. An intruder may also be attacked with darting movements as if the defender were biting. In this way the males space themselves out in territories (10.4). The change from schooling to territorial behavior and nest building depends on a rise in the temperature of the water, such as normally occurs in spring.

A territory does not extend to the surface of the water. But, when the nest is nearly complete, the male spends much time swimming in a characteristic way near the surface above the nest. The females, too, swim in this neutral zone. If a female approaches a male she may be "attacked", but this does not drive her away as it would a male. If the female is receptive, she adopts a characteristic attitude, with the head pointing up, which deters further attack by the male. The male, in this early stage of courtship, may swim up from below and stab the female with his erect dorsal spines. This evidently has a favorable effect on the female's response.

The male next swims in a rapid zigzag toward the nest. The female follows and, after some delay, enters the nest; and the male now places his head against her tail and quivers. The quivering, which may be imitated by an experimenter with a glass rod, provokes the female to release her eggs. The male then releases sperm. He now chases the female away, and advertises for another by again swimming near the surface. The males are polygynous, and can evidently cope with the eggs and young of up to five females. There is some progressive change in successive courtships: in particular, the attacking movements of the male diminish, as if he had become accustomed to a new, nonattacking attitude toward females.

The young of this species are elaborately cared for: the male remains near the nest while the eggs develop; he continues to drive away intruders, and maintains a current of water over them by a swimming movement called fanning. Fanning insures that the eggs develop in oxygenated water; and, as P. Sevenster (1961) has shown, its intensity varies to some extent with the amount of carbon dioxide present.

The territorial and sexual responses of a male stickleback depend largely on the visible features of other sticklebacks. A male at this time has a shiny blue back, a dark red belly, and eyes of brilliant blue. He will attack a crude model which has been painted red on the underside to resemble—in this respect—a male in the breeding season. An accurate model of a male, without the red coloring, evokes little response (figure 9-10). A female in the breeding state also has a characteristic appearance: she too develops a silvery sheen; and the mass of large ripe eggs gives her a swollen belly.

FIGURE 9-10 The accurate model of a stickleback, without a colored abdomen, evokes little response from a territorial male; but the others, with red bellies, tend to provoke a vigorous apotreptic response. (Reproduced from N. Tinbergen, *The Study of Instinct,* 1951, Fig. 20, by permission of Oxford University Press, New York)

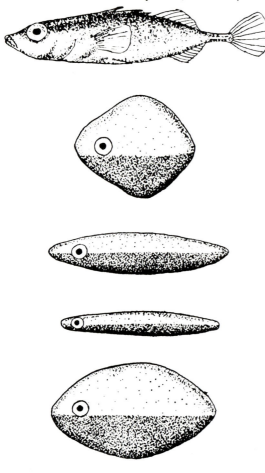

Correspondingly, the courtship display of a male can be evoked by a simple model, provided it has a ventral swelling.

These findings give an impression of a machine-like fixity of response to narrowly defined stimuli. Such an impression is enhanced by a chance observation: Tinbergen (1953) daily noticed territorial postures by the sticklebacks in his laboratory, induced by the distant passage of a mail van painted the same red as a rival's belly. But in fact responses to models habituate more quickly than those to the real thing (Sevenster 1961). Hence experimenters who wish to evoke persistent displaying often use a live stickleback in the appropriate state, but inaccessible in a glass tube (R. J. Wootton, 1972b).

All the observations so far described were made in the laboratory. An important question is whether they correspond to what happens in natural conditions. Wootton (1972a) made prolonged observations of these fish in the River Wear in the north of England. More than 40 nests were studied, spaced at distances of 50 to 250 cm. The males usually spent only 20 to 30 s out of 20 min on territorial displays; but such displays were important, for a male that succeeded in reaching another's nest was likely to damage it and to carry eggs back to its own nest. In courtship, zigzag swimming and pricking with the spines were observed. Males also fanned developing eggs in the manner observed in captivity. Hence the accounts of captive sticklebacks evidently conform with what happens in their natural habitat.

9.2.2 Cichlids

Other fish observed in great detail belong to the family, Cichlidae. The jewel fish, *Hemichromis bimaculatus,* is found in tropical freshwater and in many aquaria (figure 9-11). Like the stickleback, it is territorial during the breeding season but oth-

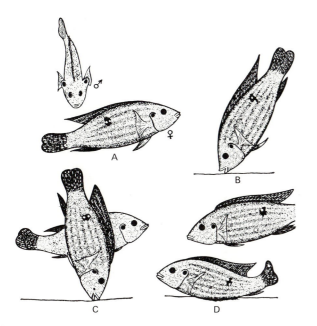

FIGURE 9-11 Courtship by the jewel fish, *Hemichromis bimaculatus.* The initial response of the male to the female is apotreptic (A); later the courtship displays include quivering (B), nipping (C) and skimming (D). (Reproduced from M. Bastock, *Courtship: A Zoological Study,* 1967, drawing after Baerends and Baerends van Roon, 1967, by permission of Heinemann Educational Books, London)

erwise lives in schools. G. P. Baerends & J. M. Baerends-van Roon describe how, before mating, females hold territories of their own. Another notable feature is that these fish pair for a whole breeding season.

At the beginning of the season both males and females have territories, and the females are nearly as brightly colored as the males. The significance of female territories is obscure, for rather suddenly the females give up territorial behavior and enter the territories of males. The females are attracted by the bright red markings of the males: they can distinguish them even from those of other females. Such discriminations are most precise among fish that have already mated at least once: evidently they depend in part on experience.

A male in his territory displays to intruders or even attacks them: he may butt them or, if the attack is from the front, each may grip the jaw of the other (figure 9-12). Such interactions occur not only between males, but at first also between males and females. But gradually both become more tolerant and turn to indicating sites for depositing the eggs. Movements are made toward a stone or other object, and a display follows in which the head is jerked from side to side or the whole body quivers. Later still the stone is cleaned: plants or other matter are removed in the mouth. This behavior, called nipping, occurs even if the surface is already clean. Lastly, the fish skim over the stone so that the abdomen touches it; and eventually the female lays eggs during one of these movements and the male follows and releases his sperm.

Several such groups of eggs are laid. The female remains near them and drives conspecifics away—sometimes even her own male. When the young

FIGURE 9-12 Male jewel fish (see previous figure) in an apotreptic encounter. (Reproduced from M. Bastock, *Courtship: A Zoological Study,* 1967, drawing after Baerends and Baerends van Roon, 1967, by permission of Heinemann Educational Books, London)

hatch, they are carried to small pits in the sandy bottom; and the male and female then share the task of guarding the young and patrolling the territory.

There is much variation in the reproductive behavior of cichlids. The same authors have described the conduct of *Tilapia natalensis*. The male, like that of the three-spined stickleback, is polygynous; and he prepares a pit for eggs before any female arrives. But in this case the female goes off with the eggs in her mouth, where the young are carried until they are quite well grown. Throughout this time the female goes without food: the whole set of responses connected with feeding is temporarily in abeyance. Hence there is no cannibalism of the young. Still other mouthbrooding species continue to feed, and parents of both sexes retrieve straying young by picking them up in the mouth and returning them to a nursery—a pit dug in the substratum. Evidently, there is something about the young of these species that inhibits eating.

The young themselves are not passive. G. P. Baerends (1957) describes experiments on another mouthbrooder, *T. mosambica*. When the young fish are disturbed by movement in the water or by a large object, they swim vigorously. When a model is used to replace the female, the young tend to swim toward its underside; they also approach dark patches; and, if there are holes in the model, they enter them. In natural conditions these responses usually bring them into the female's mouth.

Variety in this family is further illustrated by the unusual family pattern of a New World cichlid, *Aequidens paraguayensis,* studied by A. M. Timms & M. H. A. Keenleyside. The adhesive eggs are laid on dead leaves, where they are fanned and guarded for about 32 h by both parents. When the young hatch, both parents continue to look after them by mouthbrooding. Such diversity, in a single, though

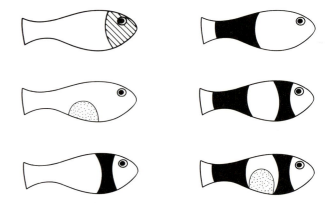

FIGURE 9-13 Diagrams of models of female *Pelmatochromis subocellatus:* only those with two vertical bands evoke courtship by males; a red patch on the flank (indicated by stippling) directs the male's movements. (After N. Monfort-Braham & J. C. Ruwet, 1967)

widespread, group, shows how difficult it is to relate species-typical social patterns to ecological niche (18.3.2). Why should this species be, most exceptionally, "biparental"?

As a last example of this fascinating family, we turn to *Pelmatochromis subocellatus,* a tropical form studied by N. Monfort-Braham & J.-C. Ruwet. Here the female is the gaudy sex: the background color is yellow; the neck and the tail region have black collars; and ventrally there is a large patch of dark red. In courtship, a female approaches a male; he responds by swimming toward her and touching the red patch. Models (figure 9-13) have been used to test the response of the male to the various visible features of the female. Only models with two vertical bands attract a male; and even to these the male's response is wrongly directed unless the red patch is also present. An interesting question, apparently still unanswered, is whether the narrow channeling of the male's response to such a specific visible pattern depends on exposure, in early life, to adult females.

9.2.3 The Siamese Fighting Fish

The final case of fishy conduct concerns the Siamese fighting fish, *Betta splendens,* also found in tropical freshwater—an adaptable animal (7.6.2) that has been domesticated for uncounted generations. The male makes a nest of mucus-coated bubbles at the water surface; the eggs develop protected by the bubbles and guarded by the male. Defense by a male of one of the domesticated varieties includes a magnificent visible display (figure 9-14) with gorgeously colored raised fins and prominent expanded gill covers (described by M. J. A. Simpson).

C. M. Robertson & P. F. Sale have analyzed "sexual discrimination" among these fish. Their experimental arrangement (figure 9-15) allowed them to present a series of stimuli to males protected by a transparent partition. The stimuli included live male and female *Betta splendens,* and a series of models (figure 9-16). The models, fashioned from balsa wood and (for the fins) stiff plastic, evoked patterns of response very similar to those made to live fish.

The males responded in one of two ways. All the male models, and the one female model that resembled a threatening male, were treated "agonistically": that is, the male alternated between facing the stimulus with raised opercula, and turning broadside on with extended fins. Included in this *apotreptic behavior* was a rapid tail beat and frequent biting. When responding to a female, or to a model of a female, the male usually remained near his nest, with head pointing up at about 45° to the vertical; sometimes bubbles were added to the nest, and sometimes the male also displayed by tail-beating and by raising the opercula.

A feature of the work by Robertson and Sale is

FIGURE 9-14 Male Siamese fighting fish, *Betta splendens,* in an apotreptic display directed toward the conspecific on the left. The two fish are separated by a glass partition. (Courtesy S. R. Goldstein)

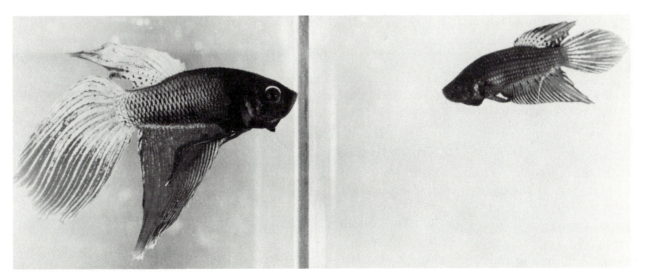

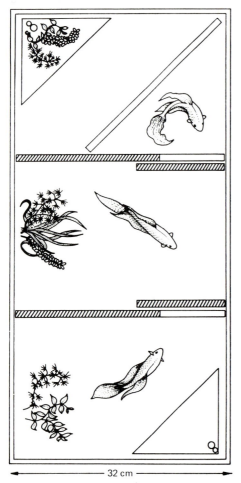

FIGURE 9-15 Experiments on Siamese fighting fish (see previous figure): the fish are in tanks with movable opaque and transparent partitions. (Reproduced by permission from C. M. Robertson and P. F. Sale, *Behaviour* 54 (1975), p. 4)

the analysis of the roles of several visible features by the use of models in which the features are variously combined. Discrimination between the sexes depends mainly on three characteristics. Long fins, raised opercula, and an unpatterned body indicate a male. For a model to be treated as a male, it must have one of the first two. Short fins and patterned

body indicate a female. Sometimes, during conflict between two males, one of the males folds his fins and changes color to resemble a female. This is called a "submissive" response. The other male now tends to behave as if his opponent were female. Hence, by his new posture, the submissive individual protects himself from damage.

9.3 BIRDS

Diversity in reproductive behavior is illustrated more clearly by the birds than by any other group. The class Aves is quite small (about 8500 species) and structurally it is a uniform group. But behaviorally it is full of surprises.

FIGURE 9-16 Models used to test the responses of Siamese fighting fish (see figures 9-14 and 9-15) to visible stimuli. The two at the top are life-like; the others are stylized, and represent various features of the natural fish. (Reproduced by permission from C. M. Robertson and P. F. Sale, *Behaviour,* 54 (1975), p. 5)

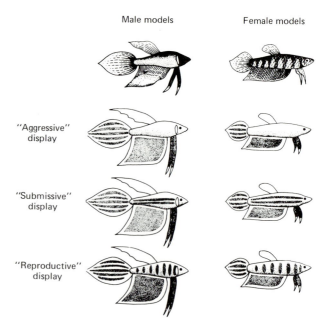

9.3.1 The Yellowhammer

We begin with a common bird of European hedge-rows and farm land, the yellowhammer, *Emberiza citrinella,* studied in great detail by R. J. Andrew (1957). In winter both sexes feed and roost in flocks. In February the males disperse to territories, where they sing loudly from prominent positions. They are visited by the drab females, which are evidently attracted by both the color and the song of the male. The next stage is not what one would expect: the female visitors make attacking motions toward the males, and drive them off. The female has nothing that can be called an "appeasement" posture: that is, she gives no signal that prevents attack by the male, but the male at this stage often makes no attack; on the contrary, he allows himself to be supplanted. (His response to another male is, of course different.) Soon a female increasingly visits one male; he is now allowed to return, and the pair settle down to feeding and perching together; they also begin to collect material for a nest.

During this engagement period the male makes mock attacks on the female: and when the female flies away she is vigorously pursued. These "sexual chases" evidently end when the male is tired out. They occur in many other species, and may be needed for the maturation of the female's ovaries. Early in May both partners turn to nest building: the male only collects material, while the female builds the nest on the ground under cover. Eventually, the female attracts the male to the nest. There (and elsewhere) he gives a distinctive call and displays with his body horizontal, bill lowered, and wings extended and vibrating. He also performs more elaborate displays. One consists of very brief runs with fluffed body feathers, flexed legs, drooping tail feathers, and quivering wings trailing

on the ground. (This resembles a distraction flight, by which a predator is drawn away from a nest.) In the other principal display, the male runs toward the female instead of away from her; his body, wings, and tail feathers are raised. If the female now solicits, by adopting a specific horizontal posture and uttering a special call, he mounts her.

We have here a detailed example of social signals, and responses to them, by both members of a mating pair. Reproduction evidently depends, in this species as in others, on the performance of a series of typical activities, each evoking a similarly predictable response by the partner. The predictability is, of course, not complete: there is individual variation; but this brief account is valid for the whole species in its ordinary habitat.

9.3.2 Thermometer Birds

The female yellowhammer is responsible for incubation of the eggs, but the young in the nest are fed by both parents. In our second example, the pattern of relationships is completely different. The mallee fowl, *Leipoa ocellata,* also known as the thermometer bird, belongs to the Megapodiidae, a family of large-footed birds, related to the domestic fowl, which live mainly in Australia and Niugini. The mallee fowl lives in open bushland in arid and semiarid regions of southern Australia, where there are great fluctuations of temperature, both seasonal and within each day. It has been studied in great detail by H. J. Frith.

The female lays up to 33 large eggs in a season; but a single nest usually contains 12 eggs. The season lasts about 10 months, beginning in April or May. The eggs are laid, at intervals of around four days, in a nest made in and above a pit about 1 m deep (figure 9-17). The pit is filled with plant fragments which are also piled up above ground level.

FIGURE 9-17 (A) Mallee fowl, *Leipoa ocellata,* on a mound in which eggs have been laid. (B) Male and female during egg laying. (Courtesy H. J. Frith)

Sand is put on top of the heap and smoothed down. Most of this work is done by the male.

The compressed plant matter soon begins to ferment, and its temperature rises. By August it has reached 34°C, and the female now lays her first egg. The nest is an incubator, and its temperature is accurately maintained, to within about 1°C, throughout the period of incubation. Before the female lays, the male digs a brood chamber in the compost. He then puts his head in, takes some of the compost in his mouth, and spits it out again. Evidently his mouth contains temperature-sensitive receptors. The female then checks the temperature too. If the temperature is not right, the male has to find another position in the compost. When the female has laid her egg, the male closes the pit. When she is ready to lay again, he reopens it.

The incubation period for the whole clutch lasts six to seven months. During all this time the temperature of the nest is taken daily, except in very hot weather when the mound is opened less frequently. In spring, if the nest heats up, ventilation shafts are made and later closed when the temperature has fallen. In summer, sand may be added to the top of the heap as an additional protection from the sun. In the morning, in both spring and summer, when the temperature of the surroundings is lowest, the sand may be spread out to cool and then replaced. In the fall, cooling is prevented by removing most of the sand in late morning. What remains is warmed by the sun.

Frith and his colleagues, during years of work, accustomed the birds to their presence, and so were able to put recording instruments close to the eggs. They even put in a heater, and raised the nest temperature: the birds then opened the nest, and so cooled it, more often. But when a nest was artificially warmed in autumn, the birds left it untouched instead of taking their usual actions to heat it up.

Such elaborate and prolonged care of the eggs suggests that the mallee fowl are—in human terms—devoted parents. Yet, when the chicks hatch, they are left to dig their way out; and this takes up to 15 h. (Big feet are now essential.) Once they are out the chicks take only an hour before they can run, and 24 h before they fly. They have no contact with their parents at all.

9.3.3 Green Herons

The yellowhammer and mallee fowl represent contrasted species in which a territory is held by a pair in isolation. The green heron, *Butoroides virescens,* a North American species described by A. J. Meyerriecks, breeds like other herons in colonies near water (figure 9-18). The nests are grouped in tall trees. A male advertises himself by posturing with up-pointed bill on a treetop, and by uttering a call represented as "skow". (Attempts at written versions of bird calls rarely mean much except to those who have actually heard them.) A female perches outside the male's small territory and calls "skeow". There are duets of skow-skeow. The female attempts entry into the nest territory, the male "attacks" her, she persists, and finally the male accepts her. There is now an engagement period, during which both birds perform complex aerial displays near the nest. These show off their gorgeous coloring, of chestnut neck, dark green plumes, and orange-red legs. The dark yellow eyes also contribute to the total picture; but we do not know what features are important for a heron. The same features are prominent in a nest display by the male: he stands with head and neck up and plumes displayed, sways from side to side, and utters a soft "aroo-aroo". He also points his bill down, snaps it sharply, and bobs and bows; these movements re-

FIGURE 9-18 Displays of the male green heron, *Buto-roides virescens:* top, flapping flight at the nest site; middle, "threat"; below, stretch, which is epitreptic, not a "threat". (After A. J. Meyerriecks)

semble those of nest building, and have perhaps evolved from them.

All this might be interpreted as a frenzied exhortation to the female to come to nest. In fact, this consummation is delayed, for when the female does venture to the nest she is "attacked". Eventually she enters, and now the male's conduct changes: threat and aerial and snap displays cease: they are replaced by coitus and nest building.

9.3.4 The Jungle Fowl

The green heron is social in the sense that it nests in large groups; but there is no special social structure within the group. The common domestic fowl, and its wild forebears (thought to be the Burmese red jungle fowl, *Gallus gallus*), form social groups in which there are relationships of dominance and subordination (10.1). The conduct of the wild type has been described by J. P. Kruijt, and that of the domestic fowl by D. G. M. Wood-Gush. They differ only in detail.

In natural conditions jungle fowl move about on the ground, usually in dry open country with low plant cover. Groups are of both sexes. The female may indicate readiness to mate by crouching in front of a male; but mating is usually initiated by the cock. The cock performs a variety of displays, of which one is shown in figure 9-19. Any tendency to peck the female now disappears; and she is allowed to pull at the cock's feathers and to peck him. Paradoxically, his displays are similar to those performed during threatening encounters toward inferiors. Evidently these performances stimulate a female: the more a cock displays, the more he is likely to induce a female to crouch before him.

This ground-living species has the special interest of being kept in its domesticated forms in most countries. Its mating and other social conduct can therefore easily be observed almost anywhere.

9.3.5 Penguins, Jays, and Jacanas

Most people probably take it for granted that young birds are exclusively cared for by their parents; and monogamy and pairing at least for a season are the rule among birds. Such relationships seem "natural" and familiar to us, partly because of our own customs. But they are not universal.

Sometimes an exceptional type of behavior is obviously related to the special conditions in which a species lives. The emperor penguin, *Aptenodytes forsteri,* studied by Y. Le Maho, lives in conditions that, one might think, preclude survival (figure 9-20A). The temperature of the Antarctic habitat often falls to −35°C. There are blizzards of 125 km/h in which a man without shelter dies quickly. These birds weigh up to 40 kg and stand 1 m high. They have a notable capacity for standing still: this no doubt conserves energy, and also reduces loss of heat from the surface; in a blizzard they huddle together and so protect both themselves and their chicks.

To breed they may travel as much as 120 km from the sea to the rookery, where the female fasts for 40 to 50 days, loses 25% of her body weight,

and lays an egg. The female now returns to the sea, and the egg is incubated by the male on the upper surface of his feet, where it is covered by a flap of ventral skin. The male fasts for 115 days and loses 40% of his body weight. The chick hatches about midwinter, and the female returns and helps to care for it by regurgitating sea food and keeping it warm (figure 9-20B). There is a high mortality, up to 90%, among the chicks; but an unprotected chick is pushed on to the parent's feet or to the feet of any adult. Such intensely communal behavior is no doubt crucial for success in the ferocious climate of an Antarctic winter.

It is, however, not always possible to guess plausibly at the selective advantage of an unexpected type of behavior. As an example, J. L. Brown (1970, 1972) has described communal feeding of young by the Mexican jay, *Aphelocoma ultramarina,* in southeastern Arizona. These birds usu-

FIGURE 9-19 Male domestic fowl, *Gallus gallus,* waltzing to a female. (Reproduced from D. G. Wood-Gush, *The Behavior of Domestic Fowl,* 1971, p. 19, by permission of Heinemann Educational Books, London)

FIGURE 9-20 Emperor penguins, *Aptenodytes forsteri* (above) huddled together; (below) attend to their young. (Y. Le Maho)

ally live in flocks numbering 8 to 20; but a flock may include only two breeding pairs. Brown put color bands on all the members of one flock; and he also banded many members of four flocks that together formed a population of about 68 birds. His detailed records showed parents as often responsible for only about one-third of the feeding of their young in the nest, and rarely more than one-half. Other members of the flock coped with the rest. Birds that are not parents, but nevertheless behave parentally, are called helpers. They also take part in feeding of the young after they have left the nest. The behavior of helpers is sometimes said to be altruistic but, as we see later (15.3.3; 18.2.3), this is a misnomer.

In human societies, polygamy is quite common but polyandry is rare. The same applies among the species of birds (reviewed by D. A. Jenni), but the American jacana, *Jacana spinosa,* is an exception. D. A. Jenni & G. Collier, who observed these birds for four years in Costa Rica, define polyandry as the simultaneous mating of a female with more than one male. (As they point out, in the field it is difficult to distinguish such a relationship from promiscuity.) The American jacana is a shore-living bird that nests in swamps and marshes. The males build nests, incubate the eggs, and rear the young. The sexes are identical in plumage, but the females are much larger than the males. Breeding takes place all year round. Each male has a territory of about 0.15 ha, but females have larger territories which include up to four male territories. While each male defends his own territory, the female that he shares with others defends only those portions of her territory not defended by males. Defense by the males ιis by "loud, strident calls" and by flying up toward the intruder with a whirring of wings. The females have a territorial display in which they stand opposite a neighbor and flick

their heads rapidly from side to side. The population studied by Jenni & Collier was always polyandrous: over the whole period of observation there were 15 females and 34 males. One "superterritorial" female laid at least three clutches of four eggs each. This female had four males in her territory. During these observations a territory-holding female died; and her territory was then divided up by two previously unmated females.

The authors of this study remark that polygamy allows the presence of fewer adults in a territory than does monogamy. Nonetheless, among birds such systems are rare. I return to these and similar questions in 18.4.

9.3.6 Feeding Nestlings: Behavioral Analysis

Although some birds, such as the mallee fowl, completely neglect their young, most feed them and protect them from predation. The young of many species spend their first days helpless in a nest; on the arrival of a parent they gape to receive food (figure 9-21). A number of experiments have investigated the exact nature of the stimuli that induce this familiar response.

N. Tinbergen & D. J. Kuenen describe the "begging" of nestling blackbirds, *Turdus merula.* If a parent alights by the nest and shakes it, gaping may occur at once. An experimenter can imitate the effect merely by shaking the nest; but the response of the nestlings will not occur if the experimenter's presence has made the parents give their alarm call.

The most important stimulus for gaping is, however, the appearance of a parent at the nest. At first, gaping is always upward; but soon it is directed toward the beak of the parent. The evidence for these statements comes from the use of models.

FIGURE 9-21 Young black red-starts, *Phoenicuros ochruros*, gape at the approach of a parent. (Courtesy E. Weitnauer)

For an object to induce gaping, it must move, and its diameter must be above 3 mm. When a model has a projection on it (resembling a head or a beak), gaping is toward the projection. Some models in these experiments had two "heads"; gaping was then directed to a projection that had a certain proportion to the size of the body.

Similar but still more detailed experiments have been described by Tinbergen & A. C. Perdeck on feeding by the chicks of the herring gull, *Larus argentatus* (compare figure 9-22). The adult has a white head, yellow iris, yellow beak, and a red spot on each side of the beak. The bill is the important feature: varying the shape or color of the model's head has no effect on the chicks, but there must be a pointed bill-like structure with some red on it. A completely red bill is especially effective. These statements are based on many hundreds of observations of chicks taken from the nest a few hours after hatching—probably before they had been fed by their parents. Figure 9-23 illustrates some of the findings.

D. A. Quine & J. M. Cullen applied the same method to another species, the Arctic tern, *Sterna macrura*. The birds they studied had been incubated; hence they had had no experience of adult terns at all. The chicks of this species, too, proved to have color preferences—for red, blue, and silver. They are fed with small fish; and attaching a fish-like object (a rectangular piece of metal foil) increased the response to a flat model of a tern's head.

The response of a herring gull chick to an adult beak is pecking; and this makes the parent regurgitate a morsel of food which the chick swallows. Similarly, pecking by a tern chick makes the parent release a fish. The original descriptions of such behavior by young birds give an impression of a predetermined, highly stereotyped response to a pattern of stimulation (or "sign stimulus"). This

FIGURE 9-22 Female lesser black-backed gull, *Larus fuscus,* with chick. (Photo by N. Tinbergen from *Signals for Survival* by N. Tinbergen and H. Falkus, © Oxford University Press, 1970)

impression is reinforced by the work of Quine & Cullen on terns, for these authors studied incubated birds. They were therefore able to observe the responses of recently hatched chicks with no experience of a parent, or anything resembling a parent. Once again, we are dealing with behavior that, partly because of its apparent fixity, is of the kind formerly called instinctive or innate. The behavior is, however, not as fixed as it seems. Further work has shown the filial conduct of gull chicks to be less

stable in development than has been thought. (For a further account of species-typical movements, see 17.2.4.)

9.3.7 Physiological Analysis

9.3.7.1 Ringdoves: In 2.4.2 we saw how annual endocrine changes are related to bird migration. Similar changes occur, as a preliminary to breeding, even in nonmigratory birds. They have been studied in great detail in the ringdove, *Streptopelia risoria,* by D. S. Lehrman (1919–1975) and his colleagues (Lehrman 1955, 1964). M.-F. Cheng has described experiments in which lengthening the daily light period to which ringdoves were exposed led to an increased secretion of gonadotropic hor-

FIGURE 9-23 Models of the heads of herring gulls, *Larus argentatus,* used to test the responses of newly hatched chicks. The color of the mandible patch was varied in the top four figures. The rectangles indicate the relative frequencies of response by the chicks. (After N. Tinbergen, 1951)

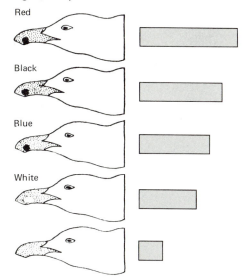

mones by the pituitary. But the increased secretion of pituitary and gonadal hormones which precedes egg laying is not merely a response to the longer days of spring. Usually, birds lay eggs only if a male is present. Mating, egg laying, and care of young by ringdoves are all influenced by both social and other features of the environment (figure 9-24).

Ringdoves, like others of their family, breed well in captivity. If an adult male and female are put together in a cage with some hay and a nest bowl, they go through a regular sequence of courtship, nest building, incubating the eggs, and feeding the young (squabs).

A solitary female in these conditions, even if provided with a well-made nest, rarely lays eggs; and, given a nest with eggs in it, she does not brood. When a male is present, there is an initial period of up to three days during which the male spends much time strutting around, bowing, and cooing. Both partners also indicate the nest site by crouching over it and giving a special cooing sound. The next phase is of nest building, which lasts for about a week. The male gathers material, and the female assembles it. Coitus takes place during this period.

After 7 to 11 days with the male, the female lays two eggs, and then incubates them for 18 h daily; the male sits on them for the remaining 6 h.

FIGURE 9-24   Ringdoves, *Streptopelia risoria,* courting at nest bowl. (R. Silver)

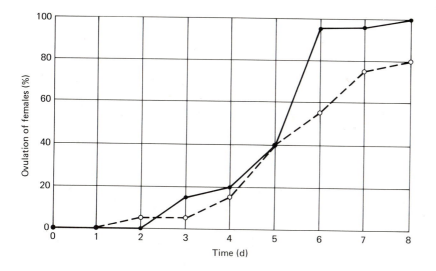

FIGURE 9-25 Ovulation by a ring-dove (figure 9-24) is influenced by the presence both of a mate and of nesting material. The percentage of females ovulating after a number of days with both mate and nesting material (continuous curve) or with a mate only (broken curve). (After D. S. Lehrman and others, 1961)

A female does not incubate, as a rule, unless she has previously gone through the period of shared nest making.

During incubation, the crop of each bird enlarges greatly; this organ, an expansion of the alimentary canal below the mouth, is the source of the "pigeon's milk" with which the squabs are fed. Hatching occurs after 14 days of incubation, and for 10 to 12 days the squabs remain in the nest, fed by both parents. Even when they have left the nest, they are still fed both with seeds and with regurgitated liquid. They induce such feeding by "begging" from the parents. When the squabs are three weeks old, the reproductive cycle of the parent can begin again.

It is commonly assumed that the prolonged courtship of birds stimulates the internal processes that culminate in ovulation, brooding, and caring for the young. The work on the ringdove is exceptional in giving detailed evidence (figure 9-25). A simple experiment is to put a female with a castrated male. Such a male does not bow or coo. In the absence of this stimulation by eye and ear, a female usually fails to lay eggs. Another index of her state is the growth of the oviduct. In the normal situation this organ grows during courtship, and reaches a maximum after six days. Growth depends on the rate of secretion of gonadotropic hormone by the pituitary. R. J. Barfield has shown development of the female reproductive tract to be precisely correlated with the duration of exposure to courtship by a male. Readiness to sit on the eggs is influenced in the same way.

Courting by a male provides the most important stimuli for the female's reproductive cycle, but others have some influence. If there is no nest material, the probability of normal behavior by the female is decreased. This is an example of an effect of the "physical" environment. The general social environment also has an effect: D. Lott and others describe experiments in which some birds were kept in auditory isolation. In this case the measure used was the development of the ovary. The birds that could hear other ringdoves had heavier ovaries.

The implication of such findings is that external

stimulation acts on the brain and, via the hypothalamus, causes an increase in gonadotropin secretion by the pituitary (compare figure 9-27). The pituitary hormones in turn act on the ovaries, and increase the rate of output of ovarian hormones. Confirmatory evidence has come from experiments in which hormones were injected. Some of the most notable findings have been on the interactions of hormonal effects with those of past experience. Some birds, already with experience of eggs and squabs, were injected with the ovarian hormone, progesterone. Each was then offered a nest containing two eggs. Half of them were sitting on the eggs within 22 min, and all within three hours. In contrast, inexperienced females, similarly treated, often do not sit at all; and it is 24 h before half of them are beginning to incubate the eggs.

Enlargement of the crop also depends on the secretion of a hormone—in this case, prolactin—by the pituitary. The crop wall thickens, and the epithelium sloughs off to form the cheesy mass regurgitated for the squabs. Prolactin also changes behavior: injection can induce feeding of squabs by doves that would otherwise ignore them; if there is no secretion from the crop, birds so treated may feed the squabs with regurgitated seeds. Again, injecting prolactin makes experienced birds feed squabs aged six days, but it does not have this effect on the inexperienced. (Newly hatched young are more stimulating: they are fed even by inexperienced females.)

The route by which prolactin changes behavior has been examined. The hormone could act directly on the brain, and so increase readiness to respond to the young by feeding them. Or it could act through its peripheral effect: the engorged crop could stimulate the brain through its afferent nerves. In fact, both seem to occur. When the crop of birds is treated with local anesthetic, their feeding behavior is impaired. Hence there is evidence of a peripheral effect from the crop. But prolactin also has an effect on the pituitary, presumably via the hypothalamus: it reduces the output of gonadotropic hormones. The hormones of the ovaries or testes are no longer secreted in the amounts needed for sexual behavior; hence courtship and coitus, which would interfere with feeding the young, do not occur.

These and many other experiments illustrate both the interactions of external stimuli with internal (endocrine) states and also the multiple actions of hormones. But there are still aspects of the breeding of ringdoves which we know only at the behavioral level. There is no physiological account of the effects of previous experience. Another feature concerns pairing. Ringdoves, in natural conditions, are—like most birds—monogamous: that is, male and female remain together at least for a breeding season. Another way of saying this, commonly used, is that there is a "pair bond". R. L. Morris & C. J. Erickson have tested the strength of this "bond" experimentally. They paired ringdoves in the laboratory and allowed them to complete two reproductive cycles. The doves were then isolated for periods of up to seven months. Groups, each members of three such pairs, were introduced into test cages. They again paired, and always in their original pairings. A similar tendency to reinstate an original pairing was shown even when females could only see males behind a glass partition. Since the initial pairings were determined arbitrarily by the experimenter, and not as a result of choice by the birds, the persistent association must have been due to the formation of a habit during courtship and reproduction.

9.3.7.2 Canaries: The interaction of external and internal events, on which reproduction (and other achievements) depend, has also been revealed, in exceptional detail, by R. A. Hinde (reviewed 1970) and others. In experiments on female canaries, *Canaria serina,* the external conditions, especially nests and nest material, and internal (endocrine) states have been varied.

The female begins to come into the breeding state as the days lengthen (compare 2.4.2), but a similar change can be induced by injecting gonadotropic hormones. The resulting behavior includes courtship and mating, and also nest building. If a male is present, the process is more rapid than if he is not. His activities augment the endocrine changes already begun, such as growth of the ovaries and a rise in the secretion of ovarian hormones.

As the time of incubation approaches, a ventral brood patch is formed: feathers are lost; there is a local increase in vascularity; skin sensitivity is enhanced; and edema develops. The first three changes depend on endocrine action, but the edema is influenced by external stimuli.

These experiments illustrate, not only multiple interactions, but also the importance of negative feedback. As we know (4.1), a process often brings about a change which inhibits that process: feeding brings about changes which inhibit further feeding, and so on. A canary building a nest is at first stimulated to build by the nest site; and construction of the nest is stimulated by the previous actions of gathering and carrying nest material (positive feedback). But the bird does not go on building indefinitely: eventually the nest inhibits further building. Similarly, there is a limit to the number of eggs laid: the presence of eggs inhibits further laying.

9.4 MAMMALS

9.4.1 Reproductive Cycles

All the activities of mammals connected with reproduction depend on hormones. The special con-tribution made to our knowledge by study of mammalian reproductive behavior is physiological. It begins with the connection, known to stockbreeders for several thousand years, of the testes and ovaries with the behavior of cattle and horses. Remove the testes of a bull calf, and the adult bullock that results never displays much interest in cows. A gelding, or castrated horse, has similarly altered behavior. It has also been known for more than 2000 years that removing the ovaries of a sow abolishes her sexual behavior.

9.4.1.1 The Male: When removal of the testes has ended sexual behavior, sexual activity can be restored by injecting testosterone. This substance is one of the group of oils, the steroids, to which the hormones of the gonads and the adrenal cortex belong. Testosterone itself is an androgen—one of the substances that promote masculine behavior. Its rate of secretion rises steeply at puberty, that is, when a mammal becomes sexually mature.

Many large mammals, such as the deer (Cervidae), are sexually active only during a breeding season or rut. Courtship, coitus, and displays directed against other males (described below) are confined to this season and depend on a raised level of androgens in the blood (reviewed by B. L. Hart).

Androgens alter behavior mainly by a direct action on the brain; but they also have peripheral effects. We saw in 9.3.7.1 how prolactin acts on the crop of ringdoves. Similarly, androgens are required for the normal development of epidermal papillae on the penis both of rats and of cats. The papillae are associated with nerve endings, and are evidently sense organs. Since, however, a rat or a cat will still mount a female when the penis has been desensitized, the peripheral effect of androgen is evidently not essential for sexual behavior.

We infer from behavior that androgens act directly on the brain; but something is also known of probable sites of action. The anterior hypothalamus and the adjacent basal part of the forebrain, in front of the optic chiasma (figures 5-18, and 6-10) seem to have a special role in sexual behavior. If male rats are stimulated electrically in this region, they become sexually much more active: for example, they attempt coitus with inappropriate objects. If radioactively labeled testosterone is injected, it is possible, by autoradiography, to identify tissues in which it is taken up; and a particularly high uptake is observed in this region of the brain. It is also possible to implant small amounts of testosterone in this region. A castrated and sexually inactive male so treated becomes sexually responsive.

An account in these terms might give the impression of male sexual behavior as a unified pattern of activities somehow driven from the anterior hypothalamus. This would be misleading for at least three reasons.

First, other parts of the brain influence sexual behavior. F. A. Beach (1940) removed various amounts of cerebral cortex from male rats. Loss of small amounts had little effect; but large injuries reduced the proportion of rats still able to copulate. These findings have been qualified by further study: K. Larsson (1962, 1964) prevented sexual behavior entirely by making small injuries in particular regions of the rat cortex.

Second, not all the components of sexual behavior respond to androgens in the same way. R. E. Whalen and others gave different amounts of androgen to male rats and observed the decreasing lack of discrimination (already mentioned) in the objects mounted; the males also displayed a corresponding decrease in latency: that is, they became quicker off the mark. Rats have several intromissions before ejaculation is achieved. The increasing doses of androgen had no effect on this measure of

performance. Hence the timing of ejaculation was uninfluenced by treatment that had a marked effect on other features of sexual activity.

Such findings have theoretical implications (further discussed in chapter 17). They indicate that it is inappropriate to think of a unitary "sex drive" (reviewed by R. A. Hinde, 1970). Sexual behavior consists of a number of components; and these are not all regulated by the same physiological processes.

Third, the effect of castration (and of other treatments) depends partly on experience: a castrated tom cat with sexual experience continues to be sexually active; but an inexperienced male often does not.

9.4.1.2 The Female: Many male mammals are continuously sexually active, but females of all species (except one) have a marked cycle of behavioral changes. (The exception is the human species: there is no period in the monthly cycle during which a woman's libido is totally absent. There may, however, be cyclical changes of mood; these vary greatly among individuals.) There may be only one or two periods of receptivity in a year; or a female may be receptive at frequent intervals (polyestrous). When not in estrus ("in heat"), a female repels a male's advances; when she is in estrus, she invites them. Behavioral estrus occurs at the time of ovulation: thus a female allows insemination only when it is likely to be effective.

The cyclical alterations of behavior, like those in the functioning of the reproductive organs, depend on hormones secreted by the ovaries and the pituitary (figure 9-26). Estrogen, produced by the ovaries, evidently activates processes in the brain which make a female responsive to a male. A number of substances are known with this effect. One, stilbestrol, has been implanted by G. W. Harris and others in the hypothalamus of spayed cats.

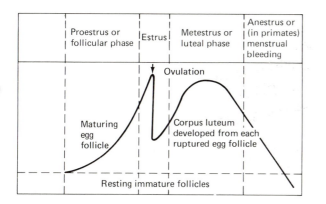

Proestrus or follicular phase	Estrus	Metestrus or luteal phase	Anestrus or (in primates) menstrual bleeding

FIGURE 9-26 Diagram of the estrous cycle. (After M. Bastock, 1967)

Such females, deprived of both ovaries, are sexually unresponsive. The implant restores normal sexual behavior, although none of the cyclical changes in structure of the reproductive tract occurs. Experiment had also shown that the sexual behavior of female cats does not depend on stimulation from the genital organs. Hence in this case all the behavior associated with mating depends on central nervous activity primed by a hormone.

In the intact female, the control of the secretion of estrogen is complex and itself depends primarily on the brain (figure 9-27). The immediate provocation to the ovary to secrete it comes from the follicle-stimulating hormone (FSH) of the anterior pituitary; but the pituitary is itself controlled by the hypothalamus. These statements do not apply only to cats. As R. D. Lisk (1962) has shown, spayed rats implanted with estradiol similarly become again sexually receptive (figures 9-28, and 9-29); and so do similarly treated rabbits.

9.4.1.3 Ontogeny:
Steroid hormones influence, not only adult behavior, but also development: if a young mammal is spayed or castrated, the typical structural and behavioral changes of puberty do not occur; mammary glands do not develop in the female, nor do the characteristic bodily proportions of an adult male appear. In the human species a boy's voice does not change in the absence of the testes: this fact has been used in the past to insure that cathedral choirs have plenty of good altos. The female parts even of the operas by Handel (1685–1759) were written for *castrati*.

Early castration, then, prevents normal sexual development; but it does not follow that sexual behavior will develop automatically if the proper

FIGURE 9-27 Diagram showing the relationship between the hypothalamus, which produces neurosecretions, and the pituitary of a mammal. The neurosecretions stimulate the synthesis and release of hormones, which in turn regulate the production of hormones by other organs, including those of the ovary. ACTH = adrenal corticotrophic hormone; TSH = thyroid-stimulating hormone; GH = growth hormone; LH = luteinizing hormone; FSH = follicle-stimulating hormone; ADH = antidiuretic hormone. (After R. M. Rose, 1969)

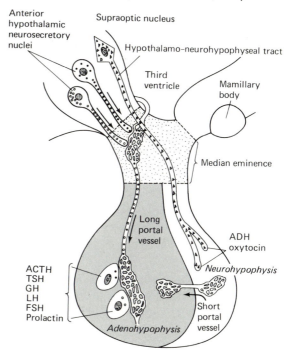

FIGURE 9-28 Coitus of rats, *Rattus norvegicus:* a receptive female adopts a posture (lordosis) which allows intromission. (Drawing by Gabriel Donald, from a photograph; from S. A. Barnett, 1975)

hormones are present: external factors also have an influence. E. S. V. Valenstein and others reared cavies (guinea pigs), *Cavia,* in isolation. When exposed to the opposite sex, adult animals were sexually aroused but were unable to organize their responses effectively. To some extent, sexual conduct depends on learning by practice to perform sequences of acts. The same applies to the domestic dog and cat (reviewed by W. C. Young, 1961) and

to Primates (12.4.1), including our own species. This is yet another example of how the development of species-typical ("instinctive" or "innate") responses may depend on experience.

As we know, some of the effects of castration have been familiar for millennia. A recent finding concerns the action of hormones either before birth or shortly afterward. Hormonal treatment during an early *sensitive period* (12.3.2) can permanently

FIGURE 9-29 Effect of a hormone on the brain. Sagittal section of rat diencephalon. Triangles indicate sites where implanted estradiol (an estrogenic substance) restores the postural response (previous figure) to sexual stimulation. Circles show where estradiol causes growth of the reproductive organs. (After C. H. Sawyer, 1962)

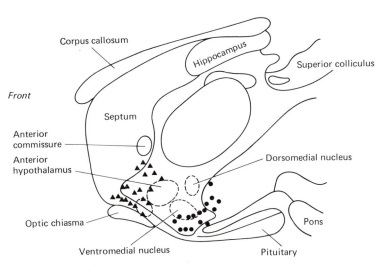

change the development of the reproductive tract and sexual responses. Prenatal action is exemplified by the cavy. W. C. Young (1969) reviews experiments in which pregnant females were given testosterone: the genitalia of the female young then were of the male form and there was a corresponding tendency toward male behavior later.

The corresponding sensitive period of rats is after birth (reviewed by G. W. Harris). Normal male behavior develops only if testosterone is present in the blood during the first few postnatal days. In its absence (by castration) the adult, though chromosomally male, behaves like a female: there is even an analog of the estrus cycle. If females are given testosterone at the age of four days, they later behave like males.

9.4.2 A Diversity of Creatures

9.4.2.1 Courtship and Coitus:
The mammals are the only large group of animals of which all species feed their young from maternal secretions. Fertilization is always internal, and is usually preceded by some sort of courtship. The mother and young of every species display complex, complementary systems of responses to each other, which insure that the young are fed and protected. The most detailed descriptions and analyses we have of their reproductive behavior are those of domestic forms, such as the laboratory rat (figure 9-30) and mouse and the domestic cat. I have reviewed work on rats elsewhere (1975). Many of the descriptions of wild mammals have been summarized by R. F. Ewer (1968).

A lengthy courtship is not always needed. P. Paulian describes the mating of a seal, *Arctocephalus gazella*. The male and female have already been together for some days. Before coitus, they circle round each other, and each grooms the

FIGURE 9-30 Female wild rat, *Rattus norvegicus,* with young. Licking the young is an important feature of maternal behavior. (Philip Boucas, courtesy World Health Organization)

other's head and neck. The female extends her body, the male utters a cry and a snort, and mounts. The whole process may take 4 min. The African elephant, *Loxodonta africans,* as described by I. O. Buss & N. S. Smith, is even more abrupt: the male walks up to the female and rests his tusks on her back: she then either remains still and allows mounting, or she moves away. At the other extreme, a female is often followed for many hours before the male can mount her. And after that, coitus may be prolonged. Marsupials are particularly notable for the duration of coitus: the small shrew-like *Antechinus* (figure 9-31) may copulate for 12 h. The best-known cases of prolonged coitus among eutherians are those of the dogs (Canidae): when the penis is inserted it is held by a vaginal contraction, while the partners stand back to back for many minutes. This is the lock.

Mammalian social signals are diverse, but odors are nearly always of prime importance: dramatic visible displays are unusual; except those of whales (13.2.2), the sounds made are less elaborate (and, to our ears, less musical); but cutaneous stimulation is often important.

The role of odors is indicated by scent marking, and by sniffing, which is often a prominent feature of courtship. The pheromones, or chemical social signals, in the urine of a bitch "in heat" attract dogs from a whole neighborhood. Typically, a female becomes attractive in this way before she is fully receptive. Hence she has a good chance of already having the company of a male when she comes into full estrus.

When a male mounts a female, he provides a stimulus by pressing on her flanks or back. Pressing on the back of a sow is a test of whether she is in estrus. If she is, she remains still in the posture which allows a male to mount. Similarly, a female rat in estrus responds to pressure on her flanks by adopting the position, called lordosis, shown in figure 9-28.

Among the cloven-hoofed mammals (Artiodactyla), tactile stimuli again seem to be important (F. R. Walther, 1977). The kudu, *Tragelaphus strepsiceros,* goes through a gradual process that includes mutual sniffing, urination by the female, *Flehmen* (wrinkling of the nostrils) by the male, and pursuit. At a critical moment, the male presses with his neck on the female's back. This stimulus is evidently necessary for the female to allow

FIGURE 9-31 A pair of *Antechinus stuartii.* The coitus of these shrew-like marsupials may last for up to twelve hours. The mating season of the members of this genus lasts about a fortnight in late winter or early spring. All the adult males then die. (I. A. Fox)

mounting. Thomson's gazelle, *Gazella thomsoni,* has a similar but more striking courtship, which includes rapid chases and drumming on the ground. At the end of a quite prolonged interaction, the male taps the female's hind leg with his forefoot. If the female now keeps still, he mounts.

It is sometimes easy to imagine how a social interaction has evolved, but such speculation may lead one into difficulties. Ewer discusses the difference between the prolonged, continuous coitus of marsupials and the often brief but repeated copulations of eutherian mammals. As she remarks, the question usually asked is why the coitus of, say, *Antechinus* should last for hours; and she comments that perhaps instead one should assume a single copulation to be primitive; the mating pattern of many eutherian mammals should then be seen as reducing the danger of predation during coitus.

Unfortunately, this argument brings us no nearer an explanation of the prolonged coitus either of marsupials or of the Canidae. It might be argued that its significance is enjoyment; but this proposition does not go well with the axiom that virtually all evolution is a product of natural selection. In the Darwinian context life is real and earnest, and pleasure must not be expected unless it has survival value. To sum up, there is an immense variety of coital practices (and positions) among the mammals; and we have no satisfactory explanation for them.

9.4.2.2. Maternal Care:

Infant mammals are reared in one of four ways. (1) The marsupials carry their young for some time in a fold of skin or a pouch. Eutherian mammals (especially Primates) sometimes carry their young too; but as a rule the young are either *altricial* or *precocial.* (2) Altricial young are initially almost helpless, often without hair and blind, and are usually kept in a nest. Typically they are members of a large litter (figure 9-30). Most small mammals are of this type. (3) Precocial young, of which the most familiar are those of the hoofed mammals, are mobile within a few minutes or hours of birth. Hence, if they belong to a herd on the move, they can keep up with it. (4) Some young are *cached*—some species, both of Artiodactyla and Carnivora, leave their young in concealment (but not in a nest) for long periods.

Detailed knowledge, based on experiments, is principally of domestic mammals, especially the cat and the laboratory rat and mouse (reviewed by D. S. Lehrman, 1961; in a symposium edited by H. L. Rheingold; and by M. P. M. Richards). During pregnancy, a female's behavior changes. She moves about less (figure 8-11), and her nest building alters. In 4.3.2.1 I mention the thermoregulatory function of nests. A pregnant female builds a substantial brood nest even in temperatures in which she would otherwise build a small one. If a female hamster, *Mesocricetus auratus,* is given straw, she makes a sleeping nest that weighs about 14 g; but during pregnancy, in the same environment, she gradually increases it to about 30 g. If the nest is damaged or removed, she restores it. If she is not allowed to build a nest, her behavior is disrupted, and many of her young are likely to die even if they are in a favorable temperature.

The change in behavior during pregnancy probably depends on hormones. During pregnancy progesterone is secreted in increasing amounts by the corpora lutea of the ovaries. Two injections, each of 5 mg progesterone, into a virgin hamster induce building of a brood nest. Evidently progesterone acts not only on the developing embryo but also on the brain, and so alters behavior. Estrogen may play some part in conjunction with progesterone:

R. D. Lisk (1971) describes experiments on laboratory mice in which spayed females were induced to build brood nests by a combination of small amounts of estrogen followed by progesterone a week later. Even some males, treated in the same way, built "maternal" nests.

There are also important external effects on nest building. If a litter of mice dies or is removed just after birth, the mother reverts to building only a small nest; but if one pup remains, a brood nest is retained. Even virgin female mice sometimes behave maternally when presented with a litter (figure 9-32). Such a female builds a brood nest. Hence, once a litter is present, the building of a maternal nest does not depend on the endocrine changes of pregnancy or lactation.

At parturition the female often uses her mouth (or, if a Primate, her hands) to help the young to emerge. She licks the amniotic fluid and the young, and may eat the placenta. Placentophagy has been described among bats, artiodactyls, rodents, carnivores, and Primates. Many species that practice it are otherwise exclusively plant eating. It is an anomaly that females just after parturition should become flesh eaters.

The young are, of course, as a rule not eaten. But they are nearly always energetically licked. A rat licks her infant as it emerges. The newborn has its membrane neatly stripped off, and it is then further licked especially in the genital region. The process seems analogous to a human infant's first bath; but in fact, at least for some rodents, it has

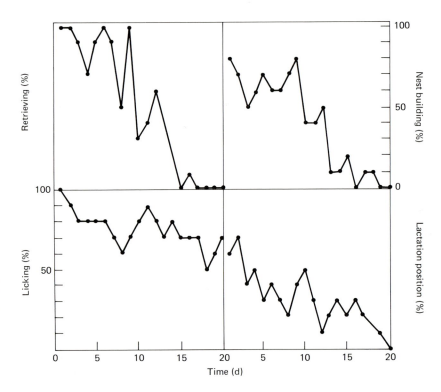

FIGURE 9-32 Responses of virgin female laboratory mice to young of different ages. The vertical axes represent the percentages of females responding in the way indicated; the longitudinal axes represent the ages of the young. (After E. Noirot, 1964)

an additional significance. This emerged when J. A. Reyniers & R. F. Ervin tried to rear rats from birth artificially. Like human babies, the infant rats accepted milk from a "bottle"; but, unlike babies, they did not develop the reflexes of elimination: urine and feces were retained, and death resulted. But when maternal licking was simulated by stroking the perineal region, the reflexes developed normally. Here is an unexpected example of the dependence of development on environmental influences.

When the young of the familiar rodents (or monkeys) have begun to suck, the female initially remains with them much of the time. In these species we find, in effect, "demand feeding"; but mothers of other species visit their young only at long intervals. A monotreme, the spiny anteater, *Tachyglossus,* observed by M. Griffiths, fed her single infant at intervals of one-and-a-half to two days. European rabbits, *Oryctolagus cuniculus,* keep their young in a nest in a burrow, and feed them at intervals of 24 h. R. D. Martin (1966) describes what is probably the extreme case. The female tree shrew, *Tupaia belangeri,* visits her young in their nest only once every 48 h. Martin did "test weighing": a typical increase in weight of the newborn at its first feed is from 9 to 15 g. These animals stay in the nest initially, but are precocial; at birth their eyes are open, they have fur, and they can regulate their body temperature. They can also groom themselves.

There is a relationship of feeding practices with the composition of milk. When feeding occurs only at long intervals, the milk contains high concentrations of protein and fat; at the other extreme, the demand feeders have a dilute kind of milk (D. M. Ben Shaul). These differences cut across the orders of the Mammalia: within the Artiodactyla, for example, the milk of species that cache their young is more concentrated than that of species whose young follow the mother from birth.

Milk secretion requires the presence in the blood of hormones from the anterior pituitary, of which prolactin is the best known. If the action of the hypothalamus on the pituitary is prevented by cutting the pituitary stalk, the milk flow is reduced. The presence of young is of course essential for milk secretion: if the young are removed from a lactating female, the mammary glands regress. Such regression is sometimes localized: soon after birth kittens develop the habit of each sucking from a preferred teat; the milk supply to unused teats then dries up. Similarly, infant rats in small litters usually suckle only from the anterior nipples, and the posterior glands regress. Correspondingly, lactation can be prolonged by repeatedly giving a female young nestlings instead of older ones. The effects of sucking by an infant are not only local, on a particular teat and gland, but also systemic: prolactin secretion by the pituitary of a rat or a rabbit is increased by the action of the young on the sensory nerve endings in mammary glands.

During lactation, many females, when necessary, carry their young in their mouth to a nest or a place of concealment (figure 9-33). Such "retrieving" may be important if young are liable to stray from the nest; in addition, if a female suddenly leaves her young, they may be dragged out of the nest while still on the teat, and unable to get back. F. A. Beach & J. Jaynes (1956a,b) observed lactating female laboratory rats in a standard situation, which required that they retrieve young to their nest. Some of the young presented an abnormal set of stimuli: for example, some had been smeared with an odorous substance. By this means, females were shown to be influenced by visible properties (especially size), chemical and tactile features, and temperature. Yet a further source of

FIGURE 9-33 Female laboratory mouse retrieves her young. (Philip Boucas, courtesy World Health Organization)

stimulation is the squeaking of young, including their production of sounds of a frequency above the range we can detect—ultrasounds (R. W. Bell; E. Noirot; E. E. Okon). If infant rats or mice are slightly chilled, as when they are exposed outside the nest, their squeaking changes, and evokes attention from the female.

Such findings have a general implication for the social interactions of mammals. When a mammal responds to a conspecific, several sensory modalities are likely to be involved. One consequence is a "fail-safe" effect: if one kind of input is absent, others may allow an effective response.

9.4.2.3 The Infant Responds: From its earliest minutes after birth, a mammal displays responses that help it to establish contact with a nipple. A newborn kangaroo (Macropodidae), though in many respects still embryonic, makes it way to the pouch without any help from the mother. The red kangaroo, *Megaleia rufa,* described by G. B. Sharman & J. H. Calaby, takes about 3 min to complete the journey. The forelimbs are well developed and clawed. The movements are evidently guided by odor.

The newborn "helpless" young of altricial mammals move their heads from side to side once they are free from the membranes; when the female adopts a nursing posture, this "rooting" enables them to find a nipple. Again, the olfactory sense is important. J. K. Kovach & A. Kling removed the olfactory bulbs of kittens and so prevented them from responding to the mother's nipple. Most infant mammals also have a "milk tread" or something similar: altricial young massage the area around the nipple with their forelimbs; precocial young butt at the udder.

9.4.3 Human Lactation

For each species of mammal we can describe a single pattern of courtship, coitus, and care of young. Individual variation is on only a small scale. The human species has reproductive organs and reflexes like those of other mammals, but no such uniformity of behavior. Study of the vast variety of marital relationships and infant care makes a substantial part of social anthropology. Nonetheless, two aspects of the interactions between human mothers and their infants can usefully be studied ethologically—the stereotyped behavior patterns of infancy (chapter 14) and lactation (reviewed by N. Blurton Jones, 1972). Despite the diversity of infant feeding practices, it is legitimate to ask whether the human species is physiologically adapted to carrying of the young and continuous feeding, or to caching the young and intermittent feeding. Among people with a simple technology, it is common for mothers to carry their infants much of the time and to feed them on demand. In some technically advanced communities, infants are fed at arbitrary intervals such as four hours.

Primates usually carry their young and feed them at any time. Since we are Primates, it might be argued that we should do the same. But this argument is not valid. As we have seen, a single mammalian order can include species adapted to a great variety of modes of life. A female chimpanzee carries her infant about with her, but it does not follow that a woman should do so too.

The only clearly relevant facts concern the composition of milk (D. M. Ben Shaul). As we know, mammals that feed their young at intervals have a more concentrated milk than those that feed them continuously or frequently. Human milk resembles that of apes in being dilute; moreover, although the fat content rises during each single feed (F. E. Hytten), it remains dilute throughout lactation. Hence in this respect our species seems to be adapted for carrying and for demand feeding, not for caching and feeding at intervals.

Supporting evidence comes from the study of crying. It may seem naive to ask why a baby cries: the answer, one might think, has been known for millennia; but this is one of many seemingly absurd questions that, if studied in a scientific context, lead to useful findings. In practice, what we ask is what action will stop crying. If a healthy, warm infant is crying, merely picking it up may silence it. S. M. Bell and M. D. S. Ainsworth describe a detailed study of 26 American infants during their first year. In its early months an infant cries most often when it is not with or near its mother. By the end of the year, crying is more usual when the mother is nearby: the child has learnt to direct its "signal" toward a person. In either case, picking it up is the appropriate response.

Hence crying is often a demand for contact. But of course it may reflect hunger. Judy Bernal & M. P. M. Richards made a study of English babies, some of whom were breast fed, others bottle fed. The mixtures given to bottle-fed babies are more concentrated than is human milk. Correspondingly, bottle-fed babies often last 4 h between feeds without crying, but breast-fed babies do not. In communities in which bottle feeding is customary, it is sometimes assumed that 4 h is the proper interval between feeds. Hence women who are impressed by the many advantages of breast feeding may be misled about the timing of feeds. According to Bernal and Richards, they may even become disheartened and give up breast feeding, when what they should do is feed their infant more frequently.

Observations of this kind illustrate four important principles. The first concerns what we can learn about human beings from the conduct of other species. The answer is that we can learn nothing certain: we can derive only ideas or hypotheses; these can sometimes be tested by the direct study of human beings.

The second principle is that the variety of ways in which mothers feed their young is an example of our lack of stable, species-typical behavior. Here is a passage from a review on human milk by D. B. & E. F. P. Jelliffe.

In most urbanized countries, to advocate breast feeding is regarded as unrealistic, unnecessary, and faddist, out of touch with scientific trends and technical development. That this is not the case becomes evident as new . . . advantages of human milk continue to be brought to light by modern research.

This comment brings out very strikingly our ability to survive unaided by fixed behavior patterns: we are born helpless and equipped with only a few simple responses (chapter 14); yet women have no standard repertoire of maternal responses such as we see in other species. They have to learn what to do, usually from their own mothers or neighbors—or, in technically advanced communities, from people with special knowledge. Indeed, as the quotation shows, whole communities may reject what members of other groups regard as natural.

The third principle is a corollary of the second. We may feel that certain customs are natural, others unnatural; but there is often no objective basis for our presumptions. There are people who regard breast feeding as, if not unnatural, at least improper. Such attitudes are culturally influenced.

Lastly, any debate on what is held to be natural, desirable, healthy, normal, or decent raises questions of ethics. In the 1970s, in some communities, anyone who seems to be advocating more exacting tasks for mothers is liable to be criticized as a supporter of the continued subjection of women. Correspondingly, in a matriarchal society an argument for breast feeding would, no doubt, be treated as an additional support for female privilege. But, whatever one's concern for liberation, two other principles are equally important. One is that, if the welfare of infants or young children demands a particular kind of action, that action should be taken. The other is that relevant facts, even if unwelcome, should be stated.

9.5 SUMMING UP

Courtship, coitus, and parental and filial behavior may be analyzed in terms of signals and responses to them (see also chapter 13). Some signals, especially of invertebrates, evoke orientations of the kinds described in chapter 2. Even among vertebrates there are examples of narrowly defined signals that evoke stereotyped responses. Hence the reproductive behavior of a species often comprises a set of patterns common to all members of that species of a given sex and age.

There is, however, some versatility. Certain species, even among the spiders, have alternative patterns of courtship, adapted to different environmental conditions. Among the mammals, relationships between the sexes, and between parents and young, are influenced by all the external senses; and, if one sensory modality is out of action, behavior may be hardly changed.

Among different species there is great variety (see also 18.4). Courtship may be long and elaborate, or it may be almost nonexistent. At one extreme it may be followed by prolonged association of the partners while they rear their young; at the other, it may end with the female eating the male. Care of young may be by the female only, the male, or by both sexes.

Sometimes, conspecifics other than the parents take part. The eusocial insects have such helpers on a vast scale. The study of these insect "societies" has revealed analogs of agriculture, stockbreeding, and other human activities; but these differ from those of human beings in being species-typical, whereas human patterns depend on tradition and can change rapidly from generation to generation (chapter 15). The behavior of a colony of eusocial insects can, however, be adapted to fluctuating demands of the environment, such as changes in weather and food supply. Each colony is to some extent homeostatic, in a manner analogous to that of a single animal.

Helpers also occur among birds and mammals.

Much is known of the physiology of the reproductive behavior of a few species of vertebrates.

The timing of courtship, insemination, and the production of eggs or young may be related to seasonal changes in external factors such as light. It always depends on endocrine feedback and feedforward (4.1). The endocrine and other changes on which female fertility depends may be influenced both by the behavior of the male and by features of the inanimate environment, such as the presence of nest material.

Care of young involves an interaction between parent and offspring in which signals from the young play an important part. Studies of such interactions have led to fruitful hypotheses about our own species.

For many species reproduction, and social relationships both within and between groups (especially territorial conduct), are closely related. We turn to this subject in the next chapter.

10

GROUPING
AND DISPERSION

Many of the most important terms in biology are commonly used without adequate definition . . . A great number of the words used in biological books are nothing more than ink marks without a clear meaning, [hence] much biological controversy is apt to be . . . fruitless. . . . Neither is it of any avail to accumulate measurements unless you have clear concepts relating to what you are measuring.

J. H. Woodger

10.1 TERMINOLOGY

When Tennyson wrote of "Nature, red in tooth and claw", he reflected a popular notion of animal life. Yet all organisms depend on other organisms. More obviously, collaboration within a species is common, if only for mating. The previous chapter gives examples. We are now concerned with other relationships within groups, and also with interactions between groups. Many animals live in families, shoals, flocks, or herds. These groupings are not due merely to a preference for a particular habitat: the attraction lies in the other individuals, and is often strong enough to maintain large, stable groups of healthy individuals of both sexes and all ages. Yet the very species that present marvels of social

cooperation also ruthlessly reject some individuals of their own kind. The honey bee has in the past been for moralists a model of communal conduct; yet it drives away intruders from another colony; and in winter, even a colony's own males (drones) are killed and thrown out. But dog does not eat dog, and it is not usual for an animal to kill another of its own kind, or even to inflict serious injury on it.

The social interactions of animals are, as we know, usually described, even by ethologists, in human terms, such as aggression, submission, threat, and so on. Such terms cannot be entirely avoided; but, for reasons which I hope will become clear, we need for some purposes expressions without emotional associations. In addition, the neutral terms chosen should not imply any unjustified presumptions about an animal's internal state. Accordingly, many of the social interactions of animals may be objectively classified into those of approach and those of withdrawal (T. C. Schneirla, 1966). The accounts of courtship in the previous chapter give a number of examples. The word *treptics* may conveniently be used for all such social interactions: *epitreptic behavior,* then tends to cause approach by a conspecific, and *apotreptic behavior,* withdrawal. The prefix epi- is familiar in biology from words such as epizoite and epiphyte, for an animal or plant that lives attached to another.

An alternative to "apotreptic signal" would be "threat"; but in the dictionary a threat is not a signal that tends to cause withdrawal by a conspecific: it is a statement of an *intention* to punish or hurt; it refers to the state of the actor, not to an effect of the action. I have often used threat as a technical term; but, owing to its quite different colloquial meaning, it is inevitably misleading. Moreover, the term is not used consistently in ethology. Valerius Geist, for example, distinguishes threats from displays. In his usage, a threat is a signal with one or

more of the following properties: it may be a movement similar to that of the actual attack—one which indicates "incipient attack with a specific weapon" (figure 10-1); or it may be an action that makes the performer look big ("looming") and so induces withdrawal; or it may be a "severe distortion of body form". Such a usage attempts, in effect, a description of some apotreptic signals; but it is not precise, and is therefore difficult to use consistently.

A much used word, introduced by J. P. Scott & E. Fredericson, is *agonistic.* They recommend its use for a group of activities, which they call attack, escape, threat, defense, and appeasement. A short, but not very precise definition for agonistic might be "conduct associated with threat [apotreptic be-

FIGURE 10-1 Encounter between two Uganda kob, *Adenota kob.* How should such incidents be classified ethologically? In different writings they are named "aggressive" or "agonistic"; they may also be called rituals or "ritualized" displays (18.5.4). (Courtesy O. R. Floody)

FIGURE 10-2 Apotreptic displays by hoofed mammals. The male oryx, *Oryx gazella,* presents his flank to an opponent and adopts a characteristic head posture; the opponent (on the left) withdraws. A Grant's gazelle, *Gazella granti,* thrashes at plants with his horns. A wildebeest, *Connochaetes taurinus,* goes on his knees. But an ibex, *Capra ibex,* rears up on his hind legs. Similarly a guanaco, *Lama guanacoe,* rears up and jumps at an opponent. But a topi, *Damaliscus lunatus,* merely stands erect and turns his head to one side in a territorial encounter. (Reproduced from F. R. Walther in T. A. Sebeok, ed., *How Animals Communicate,* 1977, by permission of Indiana Univ. Press)

havior] and the responses to it". Whatever the definition, the acts called agonistic differ from one species to another. It is therefore always necessary, in a serious study, to specify with great exactness just what postures and movements are referred to. It is usually also desirable to illustrate a verbal account with photographs or drawings (figure 10-2).

In addition to approach and withdrawal, an animal's signals may have two other kinds of social effect: they may *inhibit* an activity of another; and they may act as *warnings,* for example of a predator (18.6).

Social interactions are observed in four main contexts: (1) mating; (2) parental activities; (3) other conduct between members of a group; (4) relationships between groups (or, sometimes, between isolated individuals). The first two are discussed in the previous chapter. *The social interactions in all these contexts are usually in some sense cooperative:* that is, the conduct of each animal tends to increase the chances of survival of conspecifics. A special case is that of filial behavior: the conduct of young animals toward their parents (and, sometimes, toward others) may contribute only to their own survival.

Some interactions within or between groups are not cooperative, but *disruptive* (T. H. Clutton Brock & P. H. Harvey, 1976): that is, they tend to *reduce* the chance of survival of a conspecific.

Within a group there is often a *status system* (also known as a peck order or a dominance hierarchy). In such a system certain individuals are *dominant* to others; the latter are *subordinate.* By dominant I mean having prior access to food, a place, a mate, or other requirement; this includes "victory in a fight"—which often means that one animal turns away from an opponent. When the word dominant (or subordinate) is used, it is always necessary to say just what it signifies for the species described. The cooperative character of status relationships is seen when, for example, an animal, while feeding, is approached by another and moves away leaving the newcomer in possession.

A dominant animal is not necessarily the *leader* of the group: the latter is the animal that goes ahead of the rest or otherwise determines the direction of march. Nor is priority in access to, say, place necessarily correlated with access to a mate.

Groups, pairs, or individuals sometimes occupy a region to the exclusion of conspecifics. This is one definition of *territorial behavior.* More usually, a territory is defined as a region defended against conspecifics. In this book, on the grounds of convenience, I use the first definition. I also distinguish the ability of an animal to drive a conspecific from its territory (intergroup) from dominance (intragroup). The two types of interaction are usually distinct. Territorial behavior, like status conduct, is cooperative. Often, as we see later, animals behave as if there were a negotiated boundary between them. A territory is not necessarily the same as an animal's *home range:* the latter is the whole region regularly visited.

Two additional comments are needed. First, exclusion does not signify that all conspecifics are driven away: for example, sometimes males are excluded but females admitted. Second, entry by members of other species, too, may be prevented; but this, *by definition,* is not territorial conduct.

10.2 GROUPS

The social groupings that have been most studied are those of the eusocial insects (9.1.2) and the Primates (chapter 11). In 9.1.2.3 I describe dominance among wasps. We now come to examples of dominance and subordinacy among vertebrates.

10.2.1 The Domestic Fowl

The concept of the peck order was originated by T. Schjelderup-Ebbe, from studies of the domestic fowl and other birds. The sexual relationships of the fowl are described in 9.3.4. Group structure has been studied mainly among the domestic varieties (reviewed by D. G. M. Wood-Gush). In a simple case of, say, six birds, A pecks all the others, B pecks all except A, and so on to F, which is pecked by all the others. This is an example of a *peck-right* system: an inferior never pecks a superior. In groups of more than about 10 domestic fowl, the straight-line order breaks down, and there are sometimes triangular or more complex pecking relationships.

Such complications may be a consequence of domestication and crowding. N. E. & E. C. Collias (1967) describe groups of jungle fowl observed in India in natural conditions. A typical group consists of a cock and several hens, with subordinate cocks in company but at a distance.

Dominance among these birds is, then, defined by pecking relationships. If an artificial flock of domestic birds is set up, such relationships soon develop: and, once status has been settled, it may be reinforced merely by a movement toward another as if a peck were intended. When such a flock includes both sexes, males and females have separate peck orders; and males are always dominant to females. If the flock is left undisturbed, relationships remain stable for months; the birds also eat more, grow better, and produce more eggs than others among whom social relationships are less stable. If a bird from a stable flock is removed, and returned even after two weeks, its social behavior is unchanged: it remembers its place in the order.

Dominance (defined by pecking) is accompanied by priority of access to food, nests, and roosting places. It might also be supposed that dominance would be correlated with sexual prowess or success. Among males in natural conditions, this may be the case. But among domestic fowl detailed observation does not always reveal any correlation between the mating frequency of the cocks and their position in the peck order. A similar anomaly is observed among hens: those high in the peck or-

der are likely to be courted less than those lower down. (No parallel should be drawn with the situation in human communities.)

10.2.2 Whiptail Wallabies

The marsupials, though put in the same class as the eutherian mammals, have had the whole of the Tertiary in which to evolve their own forms of social conduct. With some exceptions, the extant species are rather quiet animals. The whiptail wallaby, *Macropus parryi,* has been studied by J. H. Kaufmann (1974) in natural conditions in New South Wales. These small kangaroos feed mainly on grass and, while doing so, they move around in groups of up to 50 or more (figure 10-3). The groups or "mobs" described by Kaufmann occasionally met, mingled, and fed together. When one watches kangaroos (Macropididae) casually, they give an impression of living in groups with no special social structure. The males of this species, however, maintain a straight-line status system.

Interactions are quite frequent. Often, one wallaby merely made another move away by approaching and sniffing or touching the nose. More lively interactions are called fights: one male stands upright in front of another, and perhaps also touches the other with his forepaws. The other then stands up too, both rise to their full height, and paw each other (figure 10-4). Occasionally wrestling follows, and rarely kicking. No harm results. Such clashes usually end when one male turns away or withdraws: that male was then recorded as subordinate. Kaufmann describes the fights as stylized, harmless, and almost gentlemanly.

Dominance, defined by the outcome of clashes, is correlated with access to females in estrus. Such females are often followed by several males, but only the male of the highest rank achieved coitus.

FIGURE 10-3 A group of whiptail wallabies, *Macropus parryi,* feeding. (Courtesy
J. H. Kaufmann)

There is no evidence that dominance has any other effect.

10.2.3 Cattle

We now turn to a species that, like *Gallus gallus,* is known mainly as a long-domesticated form. M. W. Schein & M. H. Fohrman studied a herd of dairy cattle at an experimental station in Louisiana. The conditions were not those of wild cattle, for the animals were segregated by age and reproductive state. They had also had their horns removed. Such findings are nonetheless useful in several ways.

First, the conduct of domestic varieties can often illustrate phenomena observed among wild types, and is usually much easier to record. Second, knowledge of the conduct of farm animals, even if different from that of the wild type, may be of practical importance. Third, such studies remind us that students of ethology can often learn a lot by observing the animals most readily available.

The work of Schein & Fohrman is notable for its detailed account of actual behavior: instead of saying merely that some cows behaved aggressively, they describe the actual movements of their animals. A cow is said to be subordinate to another when it ends an encounter by turning or running away. The encounters typically include a slow approach by one cow to another, with head lowered, and occasional pawing of the ground. The cow so approached may turn away with her head up; or she may face the first cow with head lowered. Butting then follows.

Some thousands of such encounters were recorded; and the authors concluded that there was a straight-line status system like that observed in small groups of domestic fowl. Both weight and age contributed to status. When, however, strange cows were introduced to a herd, their eventual status was lower than would have been predicted from these features.

FIGURE 10-4 "Gentlemanly" apotreptic behavior by two male whiptail wallabies (see figure 10-3). (Courtesy J. H. Kaufmann)

Not all status systems among cows are straight-line orders: when a group of four was set up, the result was a circular dominance system influenced by relationships previously established. The importance of previous experience has been shown more fully by M.-F. Bouissou, who also studied groups of four heifers. These animals were observed on their first encounter with strange conspecifics, and also during later encounters with strangers. Experience increased the amount of social interaction, but reduced the amount of butting, though not the amount of preliminary gestures ("threats"). Experienced animals established dominance relationships within a few minutes, and these relationships were more stable than those set up among inexperienced heifers. Hence in these experiments the animals were seen not only to learn to respond in specific ways to particular companions: they also learned how to form relationships quickly.

A final comment on cattle concerns leadership. As R. Kilgour & T. H. Scott have shown, in a herd of cows there is no necessary correlation between dominance and going ahead of the rest. Dominance is defined by the results of encounters in which one animal displaces another, or by the result of clashes in which butting occurs. Dominant cows tend to occupy the middle of the herd when it is on the move; cows of middle rank are usually ahead of the rest. These authors found "rearship" to be even more evident than leadership. Social relationships in a herd are perhaps most evident when it is moving to a new place.

10.2.4 Rhinoceros

We now return to wild-type animals in their normal environment. R. Schenkel & L. Schenkel-Hulliger (1969a) have observed the black rhinoceros, *Diceros bicornis,* in a national park in Kenya.

These formidable mammals make conspicuous tracks leading to wallows and watering places. There is no evidence of a well-defined group structure or of status. The animals might therefore be expected to space themselves out in territories. It has sometimes been stated that mammals of certain species mark their territories with odorous secretions or with dung or urine containing pheromones. Black rhinoceros leave much of their dung at special sites ("lavatories"), often at a bush or tree. Usually, each site is used by many individuals. Defecation is preceded by sniffing, and is followed by scraping, which spreads the dung. This certainly suggests scent marking. Moreover, urination is of two forms: a large volume of urine is released in a continuous stream directed mainly downward; but a male sometimes directs a shower of fine drops horizontally onto a bush (figure 10-5).

Nonetheless, all tracks, wallows, and watering places are used by many individuals. There is no clear evidence of territory. The only stable association observed is that of a female with her young; this lasts for two to three years.

Males sometimes display intolerant behavior among themselves: they may face each other, and then move off in different directions; sometimes,

FIGURE 10-5 A white rhinoceros, *Ceratotherium simum,* directs a shower of urine backwards on to a bush. (Courtesy R. N. Owen-Smith)

FIGURE 10-6 Two male white rhinoceros (see also figure 10-5) face each other before going their different ways. (Courtesy R. N. Owen-Smith)

evidently, they prod each other, and scars resulting from such encounters may be seen; screaming, scraping the ground, and circling occasionally occur when two males meet; and the authors observed one chase. Considering the equipment possessed by these animals, such encounters are remarkably harmless.

The Javan rhinoceros, *Rhinoceros sondaicus,* observed by the same authors (1969b), is also a rather solitary animal (again, apart from mother and young), but it may be found in groups of two

to four. This species not only leaves scent marks but also makes a loud whistling noise that perhaps helps to keep such groups together.

An account by R. N. Owen-Smith of white rhinoceros, *Ceratotherium simum* (figure 10-6), studied in Zululand, seems at first to differ sharply from those of the other species. They are described as having territories with sharply defined boundaries regularly patrolled and scent marked. This author uses the term territory to name an occupied and marked area. The males that behave in the way stated do not drive other males away; and visitors are regularly allowed to pass through a "territory" to reach water. Evidently, the mammals of this family form only the loosest of associations (apart from mothers with their young), and do not display, even to careful observers, the definitive features of either status or territorial relationships.

10.3 SPECIAL CASES OF COOPERATION

We have seen that status relationships are cooperative, as when an animal, while feeding, is approached by another and moves away leaving the newcomer in possession. But for some species cooperation goes much further. The eusocial insects represent one extreme (9.1.2). The birds (9.3.5) include species in which care of the young depends on more than collaboration by the parents: additional helpers make a substantial contribution. Among the mammals there are some further instances, though there has been little detailed study. Strangely enough, the Primates (ourselves excepted) do not provide good examples.

10.3.1 Dolphins and Elephants

Dolphins (Delphinidae) have recently attracted attention because of entertaining but nonsensical writings about their supposed intelligence (7.8.1). Fortunately, authentic descriptions of their conduct also exist (reviewed by W. E. Evans & J. Bastian). These superb swimmers move over vast oceanic distances in groups or schools. A small school may consist of, say, six adult females with their young; another may be of a similar number of young males. Sometimes, a single male accompanied by a female is seen. The larger schools, however, may number hundreds of individuals; they presumably include both sexes and all ages.

As we know (7.8.1), the Cetacea have well-developed systems of communication by sound. Dolphins of the genus, *Tursiops,* have also been known for millennia for a special kind of cooperation: as described by J. B. Siebenaler & D. K. Caldwell, they sometimes "school" or group together when disturbed; and, if one has been injured, it is held up (so that it can breathe) or otherwise protected by the others. Similar conduct by *Delphinus delphis* has been observed in the Mediterranean; and it is from there that we have the well-based legends of human beings supported or carried in the water by dolphins.

Cooperation by females in the care of young has also been observed among captive bottle-nosed dolphins, *Tursiops truncatus* (M. C. Tavolga & F. S. Essapian). Care includes retrieving the young dolphin if it moves away from its mother. When, however, the mother is feeding, she may leave her offspring with another female (an "aunt"). If a strange dolphin approaches, the newcomer may be driven off by slapping the water; or the young may be removed.

We have more detailed descriptions of the social conduct of the African elephant, *Loxodonta africana,* notably those by J. F. Eisenberg and others, by R. M. Laws & I. S. C. Parker, and by W. & B. M. Leuthold. Females and young live in family groups of about 15 females with their offspring. There is usually an oldest and largest female who goes ahead on the march and evidently determines the direction of movement; but, during retreat from danger, she takes the rear position. When age enfeebles her, she is replaced by a younger female. Family groups sometimes come together to form a larger assembly, called a kinship group, believed to consist of closely related individuals. Individual recognition does not seem to have been studied in detail; but elephants that have been parted for a time greet each other in a formal way: the tip of

FIGURE 10-7 A newborn African elephant, *Loxodonta africana,* is attended by several females. (Courtesy Walter Leuthold)

the trunk is placed in the mouth of the other, in the manner of a calf taking food from its mother.

Cooperation is notable in at least four ways. First, after the birth of a calf, the newborn is given intensive care not only by the mother but by her companions (figure 10-7). Second, any female in milk allows any calf to feed from her (figure 10-8). Young cows not in milk control the movements of calves by preventing them from going too far ahead, and by waking them if they doze off during the march. Third, there is a remarkable parallel with dophins in conduct toward an injured companion: a member of the group that falls over is often raised by the efforts of the others. This is important: an elephant lying down in the sun is liable to overheat; moreover, it may suffocate. Lastly, when a group is threatened, it forms something like the military square, with the young protected by the females, all of whom face outwards.

When the bulls reach the age of about 13 years, they are driven away. Adult males live either in bands less organized than those of females, or as solitary individuals. They form a status system based on the outcome of harmless clashes. These encounters are most vigorous when a female in estrus is present.

FIGURE 10-8 An African elephant calf (see figure 10-7) can feed from any lactating female. (Courtesy Walter Leuthold)

10.3.2 Carnivores

We now return to the Canidae (3.2.6). The wolf, *Canis lupus,* the ancestor of our domestic dogs, is an example of an energetic predator with a largely peaceful and cooperative home life. Wolves are proverbially a threat to people, but in fact have been nearly wiped out by human action. These magnificent animals have been studied by M. W. Fox, by L. D. Mech and by R. Schenkel (1947). Like the hunting dogs of Africa (figure 10-9), they cooperate both in bringing down their prey and in feeding the pack—especially the young. The prey include large mammals such as moose, *Alces alces,* and caribou, *Rangifer arcticus,* but also small ones

the size of mice. Packs are evidently family groups: they begin with a mated pair and their litter. Later, two straight-line status systems develop, one for each sex, initially headed by the founding parents. Status is determined in encounters that begin when puppies go through the motions of fighting. Clashes between adults are usually formal and soon end. The superior stands with stiff legs, raised and quivering tail, raised hair and bared fangs; he growls. The other may, in the extreme, crouch with flattened tail and ears; he is silent (figure 10-10). Such postures are familiar from our domestic dogs. Snapping of the teeth, or mock biting, is frequent; true biting is rare, but serious injury can occur, especially among males during the breeding season.

FIGURE 10-9 A group of hunting dogs, *Lycaon pictus.* (Courtesy L. H. & G. W. Frame)

Like other mammals, wolves have a formal "greeting ceremony", in which a subordinate grips and licks the mouth of a dominant. As with elephants, there is a resemblance to the conduct of a young animal begging food.

A curious myth, derived from a popular work by

FIGURE 10-10 Postures of male wolves, *Canis lupus.* On the left, dominant, on the right, subordinate. (Reproduced from A. Portmann, *Animals as Social Beings,* 1961, by permission of Hutchinson Publishing Ltd)

K. Z. Lorenz (1952), has been widely propagated and accepted. A subordinate animal has been said to present its neck (the part most vulnerable to biting) submissively to a dominant animal. This extreme example of anthropomorphism implies that a wolf can regard a posture as a symbol of surrender—an abstract notion of which only human beings are capable. The story, however, is in any case based on incorrect observation. Of two male wolves, the one that presents his flank or neck is the dominant animal; the other, being a subordinate, makes no attack (R. Schenkel, 1967).

Wolves range widely, but packs usually keep to their own area. There is elaborate cooperation in hunting large mammals. These are not easy prey: deer and even mountain sheep can run faster than wolves; a moose can defend itself without running, and can indeed kill a wolf. In natural conditions, most pursuits are unsuccessful. Success may result from remarkable collaboration by pack members:

some drive the prey toward others lying concealed. (The ability to herd hoofed mammals is, of course, reflected in the marvelous skill of sheep dogs and their management of flocks of sheep.) When prey is cornered, it may be torn down by many wolves attacking it together. The successful hunters do not then monopolize the food: wolves, like hunting dogs, bolt meat and regurgitate it for their young. Excess food is cached. A female may draw upon such a store, and regurgitate it for her young.

Lastly, in this section, we come to a predator that has provided even more proverbial lore than the wolf. The lion, *Panthera leo,* a member of the cat family (Felidae), has been observed in accurate detail by B. C. R. Bertram, by G. B. Schaller (1972), and by R. Schenkel (1966). The "king of beasts" proves to be largely a scavenger, to be the zoological equivalent of an extreme male chauvinist, and to practice infanticide.

Unlike the other cats, the lion does not walk by itself but forms groups. A pride commonly consists of around 15 lionesses and young. The group structure is therefore primarily "matriarchal"—like that of elephants. The young are kept out of sight—in a "creche"; a female feeds mainly her own infant, but any other is allowed to suck; a cub may complete a meal with milk from as many as five lactating lionesses. Cooperation in hunting has some resemblance to that of hunting dogs and wolves. The lionesses spread out in a fan and stalk their prey—which may be a formidable opponent, such as the gnu, or blue wildebeest, *Connochaetes taurinus,* a giraffe, *Girafa girafa,* or a buffalo, *Syncerus caffer.* At a critical moment, each closes in on the prey in a sudden rush.

Young males usually leave the pride in which they were born, but may eventually join another. The powerful adult males associated with a pride are peripheral to the main group and are led by the females. When a kill has been made, they dis-place the females (who have done the hunting) and the cubs. They then make a good meal before allowing the others access to the food.

There is a status system for each sex, maintained in noisy clashes which, though frightening to a human observer, are usually harmless. Males have, however, been known to be killed in fights with conspecifics. Moreover, if a pride of females or a territory, lacking males, is occupied by intruders from neighboring areas, the resident cubs may be killed and eaten. Such behavior presumably increases the chances of survival of the offspring of the invading males, at the expense of the descendants of the males they are replacing.

10.4 TERRITORY

10.4.1 Case Histories

We now turn to interactions between separate groups or individuals. These, usually described in terms of conflict or antagonism, may—as we know—also be treated as cooperative. Such a statement has, however, no moral significance (1.1.2; 15.3.3). In a natural and stable environment, territorial conduct, though diverse, entails an orderly and often peaceful spacing out of a population in conditions that allow many individuals to rear young.

10.4.1.1 Invertebrates: Bristle worms, such as *Nereis* (5.3.2), lurk in rock crevices or, in the laboratory, in glass tubing (R. B. Clark). A worm with no tube moves around until it finds one; but if the tube is already occupied, the incomer may leave at once—an example of withdrawal from an occupied region. But sometimes there is a clash, in which each grasps the other with its proboscis; sometimes the resident is driven out, perhaps because the incomer fits the tube better (see photo on opposite page).

Among the arthropods are the shore-living fiddler crabs, *Uca* (Jocelyn Crane, 1941, 1975). At low water these animals emerge from burrows, and the males advertise themselves by incessant waving of a vast claw, by displaying colored markings, and by making noises (figure 10-11). These signals evidently drive off other males but attract females. Each species has its own code of waving, honking, or rapping (M. Salmon, 1965, 1971); and sensitivity to sound varies correspondingly among species.

Peter Weygoldt (1974, 1977) has closely observed similarly formal "fighting" among the whip spiders, *Charinus brasilianus,* and other species (figure 10-12). Two of the legs of these arachnids are long and fine (antenniform), and are used to make contact with conspecifics during both mating and also apotreptic encounters. In meetings between two males (and sometimes two females), each initially taps the other with its whip-like appendages; then the agonists separate to the full length of one antenniform leg and tap or strike each other. "Suddenly", writes Weygoldt, "they stop and . . . each steps forward. A short but vehement pushing-and-pulling struggle follows, after which the animals separate." After such a clash, a

Bristle worms, Nephthys, in a clash. (Lennart Nilsson)

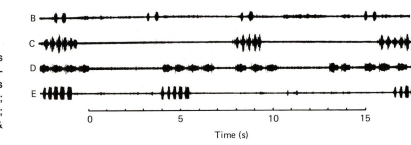

FIGURE 10-11 Species-typical sounds of male fiddler crabs. The oscillograms show the distinctive patterns of *Uca pugnax* (A); *U. virens* (B); *U. longisignalis* (C); *U. mordax* (D); *U. rapax* (E). (From M. Salmon & S. P. Atsaides, 1968)

gesture by the antenniform leg of one animal may drive off the other. Such interactions are believed to be sometimes territorial.

Among the insects some of the dragonflies

FIGURE 10-12 Two stages in an encounter between whip spiders, *Charinus brasilianus*. (Courtesy Peter Weygoldt)

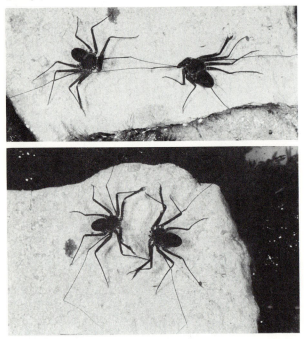

(Odonata) are territorial. Male and female *Aeschna cyanea* (figure 10-13) visit ponds to mate, where the females also lay eggs. A male in his mating area pursues other males with a buzzing noise. In a study by H. Kaiser, the rate at which males arrived at a breeding area varied from about 3 to 24 an hour. Yet the density of males present remained about constant. The higher the arrival rate, the lower the duration of stay. This is a notable example, from a natural environment, of a relationship between intolerant behavior and density.

10.4.1.2 Fish: The descriptions of mating by sticklebacks and jewel fish, in 9.2.1 and 9.2.2, include their territorial conduct. These are examples of species whose mating and defense of a region are inextricably related. C. R. Robins and colleagues describe a more consistently territorial fish, the pike blenny, *Chaenopsis ocellata,* an inhabitant of shallow marine waters. In natural conditions the males probably live in the empty burrows of bristleworms. Unlike stickleback males, they are territorial at all times. If an animal approaches a male to within 25 cm, the male raises his head and dorsal fin. If the animal is a conspecific male, there is next a marked darkening of part of the dorsal fin and head, the pectoral fins are spread, the mouth gapes, the branchiostegal membranes are spread, and the respiratory rate goes up (figure 10-14). The interloper now usually withdraws. Here, in fact, is a splendid example of species-typical apotreptic behavior. Less often, there is a clash in which the mouths are in contact and there is the appearance of a struggle. The clashes do not result in injury. Females are not threatened. The perhaps unusual pattern of permanent territories held by individuals may be related to the use of worm tubes as permanent refuges.

Another example of permanent territories has been described by T. A. Clarke. The garibaldi, *Hypsypops rubicunda* (Pomacentridae), lives on rocky bottoms just below low water mark. It feeds on algae growing on the rocks. Adults of both sexes each defend a region that includes a rock crevice used as a shelter and also a grazing area.

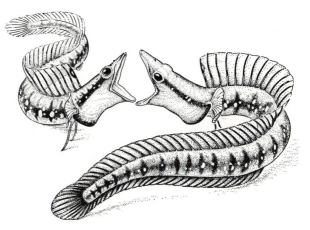

FIGURE 10-14 A territorial encounter between two male pike blennies, *Chaenopsis ocellata*. (Reproduced from E. O. Wilson, *Sociobiology: The New Synthesis*, 1975, p. 25, by permission of Harvard University Press)

The territories of some males include a nest—a patch of red algae, to which the female is admitted for spawning. The female is then expelled, and the eggs are guarded by the male. Males rarely leave their territories, but females tend to roam. Territories are contiguous. The fish are colored a brilliant orange, and so must be easily visible to each other. Wanderers without a territory are chased away by means of a rapid swimming movement accompanied by tooth snapping. The size of territories, and hence the population density, is evidently determined by the food supply: the denser the growth of algae, the smaller the territories, down to a certain minimum.

Spacing out induced by apotreptic behavior may occur even among species that live in unstructured environments. Fish such as the cod, *Gadus callarias*, live in shoals in open waters. Yet V. M. Brawn has observed apotreptic conduct among cod caught in the North Sea and kept in aquaria. Their display included fast swimming toward another fish, lowering of the floor of the buccal cavity, arching of the

FIGURE 10-13 *Aeschna cyanea,* a dragonfly of which the apotreptic conduct has been closely studied: males at their breeding sites drive away other males by means of buzzing flights. (Spang Larsen)

back, and adjustment of the pelvic fins at a prominent angle. Sometimes the displaying fish turns to give a side view to its opponent and also makes a grunting noise. The response of the other fish is often to raise all its dorsal fins and then to swim away.

There are two seasons of apotreptic conduct in the year. One, during September through November, is when cod are difficult to catch in the North Sea, probably because the fish spread out widely over their feeding grounds. Around midwinter the fish evidently shoal closely; but during the spawning season of February and March apotreptic behavior occurs again. At this time some of the fish kept in aquaria established territories. Unfortunately, we do not know what happens in natural conditions.

The observations of blennies, the garibaldi, and cod were made on undomesticated species. They contrast with the many studies of the Siamese fighting fish, *Betta splendens,* of which the mating is described in 9.2.3. When put together in a small tank, domesticated males come into prolonged conflict: they have been bred to fight. Nonetheless, such males, given plenty of space, can behave differently. S. R. Goldstein recorded three kinds of behavior. The first is the striking display described in 9.2.3 (figure 9-14); the second consists of clashes in which injurious biting occurs; and the third is the mouthlock in which each fish grips the mouth of the other. The fish were observed both in typical small aquaria and in a large L-shaped tank. The mean time spent in displaying was much the same in both conditions; but the incidence of injurious clashes and mouthlocks was much higher in the small tanks. In the large tank, after brief clashes, the fish formed, in Goldstein's expression, a stable community. These animals are commonly said to be strongly territorial, but stability in these experiments did not depend on the setting up of territories: a territory, in the sense of a clearly marked, exclusively occupied region, was observed only when a male made a bubble nest. An unanswered question is: what happens to wild *Betta splendens* in natural conditions? If the waters in which they live are turbid, perhaps the fish display some intolerance of strangers without setting up territories, except in relation to nests. If so, the reputation of this species as a ferocious, territorial fighter is based on the study of atypical, domesticated forms in abnormal conditions.

10.4.1.3 Reptiles: We now return to a natural environment—that of *Crocodilus niloticus.* Although it can weigh as much as 1000 kg, the Nile crocodile is still widespread, and is a highly efficient predator with an elaborate social life (M. L. Modha; A. C. Pooley). The males hold territories. On an island in Lake Rudolph they occupy regions of shore varying in length from 60 to 230 m and extending about 50 m into the water. Territories are regularly patrolled and are evidently stable: there are few transgressions across boundaries. Any conspecific that does intrude is chased away: apotreptic conduct includes roaring and snapping of the jaws; the last, performed in water, produces a formidable crash. Few actual clashes are observed.

Territorial behavior is linked with breeding. Courtship, which includes a splash display by the male, induces a female to dig a nest near the water, in a shady spot in the male's territory. During the three months of incubation the female rarely leaves the nest. Meanwhile the male continues to defend the area around it. When the young are ready to hatch they make noises which induce the female to open the nest. The female now takes the eggs or young in her mouth (which is equipped with a ventral buccal pouch), and carries them to water. At the water's edge a nursery is established where the young are guarded by both partners for at least six weeks. In several respects the territorial pattern of this reptile resembles that of many birds. Perhaps the survival value of monogamy, and of clearly defined defended regions, is the same for birds and for crocodiles.

Like birds, reptiles have diverse social relationships. I give three examples from the lizards (Lacertilia). A large, rock-dwelling iguanid, the chuckwalla, *Sauromalus obesus,* is an inhabitant of North American deserts, and is polygamous (K. H. Berry). Large, vigorous males, accompanied by several adult females, defend regions against intruding males. These territory holders are called "tyrants". Success as a tyrant depends on possession of an intact tail: if the tail is lost, for example, through predation, the ability to hold a territory is lost too (at least, until the tail regenerates). Nonetheless, the main apotreptic signals recorded are movements of the head. Each individual has its own distinctive pattern of headbobs, performed during the first 3 or 4 s of a display: this is called the "signature". A display may lead to the withdrawal of a smaller male; if it does not, the intruder is charged and then chased. The breeding season (June) is the only period in which territorial or indeed any apotreptic behavior occurs. During that season, about 10% of encounters between males involve actual clashes and not merely threat and withdrawal.

Sometimes, females are territorial. J. A. Stamps describes a lizard, *Anolis aeneus,* in the Lesser Antilles, of which individuals can be distinguished by their markings. Experiments were done in which lizards that had first been accustomed to handling were tethered in regions occupied by others. This species lives in a variety of habitats and has at least two kinds of social organization; but there is no precise correlation between habitat and social system. In some places the females are territorial, but in others they live in groups in which there are relationships of dominance and subordinacy. Different kinds of headbobbing are performed in the two types of social situation.

Another lizard, a gecko, *Gehyra variegata* (figure 10-15), is of special interest because H. R.

FIGURE 10-15 The gecko, *Gehyra variegata.* (I. A. Fox)

Bustard studied it in an artificial environment. During the day this lizard lives under the bark of trees. There are two or three females to a tree, and only one male: others are kept away by apotreptic behavior. An artificial tree stump can be made of linoleum. Altering the amount of food has no effect on the number on each tree stump: even a fast of six weeks has no effect; evidently, population density depends on the shelter available.

10.4.1.4 Robins: Our understanding of territorial behavior has until recently been based almost wholly on observations by bird watchers, above all by the Englishman, Eliot Howard (1875–1940). The territorial conduct of birds is usually closely related to breeding (Howard, 1920). Moreover, like sticklebacks (9.2.1) and some other fish, birds in the initial stages of courtship seem often to combine apotreptic and epitreptic displays, as if they were oscillating between courtship and defense.

The European robin, *Erithacus rubecula,* has been intimately observed by another English ornithologist, David Lack (1910–1973). This bird holds territories in autumn and early winter, as well as the breeding season; both sexes have a conspicuous breeding color, the red breast; and the female as well as the male may sing. But territorial activity is mainly in spring and summer, and is principally performed by males (Lack, 1943).

A male settling in a new region begins with quiet song from near the ground; if he is unopposed, he gradually works up to full song from conspicuous perches. He sings only in his own territory. This resembles a prison willingly entered: he cannot readily be driven from it for, if pestered to its boundary, he suddenly flies back over the head of his pursuer. If a strange male approaches, the song of an established male becomes louder. Often, the intruder withdraws at once—another example of apotreptic conduct without any clash. Even birds confined in an aviary and unable to get at incomers directly can drive them away in this harmless fashion. If song fails, apotreptic conduct may next take the form of postures that expose the red breast; or there may be a combination of song and pursuit. Sometimes the resident is then driven away. Just what determines which agonist wins cannot be told by watching the encounter. Clashes are rare. When they occur, the birds use both legs and beaks, feathers fly, and both may fall to the ground while grappling; but even then, severe damage is exceptional.

Evidently, both sounds and sights act as signals for this species. Lack studied the importance of the red breast experimentally. He used a shop-soiled, stuffed robin, bought for one shilling. This object, set up in a robin's territory, evoked both postural threats and actual attacks. It did so, indeed, even after it had been beheaded by an exceptionally energetic hen. But models, however realistic, lacking a red breast, were neither threatened nor attacked. In these experiments, as in ordinary encounters, great individual variation was revealed, both in the intensity of the behavior and in its style. Nothing is known of the sources of this variation. It makes quantitative study of this, as of other species, very difficult.

10.4.1.5 Red Grouse: The red grouse, *Lagopus lagopus,* though closely related to the domestic fowl, is adapted to cold climates. Its territorial interactions on Scottish moorland have been studied in detail (reviewed by A. Watson; and by Watson & R. Moss). They and their colleagues were able accurately to estimate populations with the aid of trained dogs. Breeding depends on acquiring a territory; every year about half the population fail to do so, and are driven away from the moors where territories are held. The unsuccessful birds spend much of their time in scrub where food is scarce; many die. The immediate cause of death is then predation or perhaps sometimes shortage of food; but the primary cause is social.

Territories are established in autumn, and the successful birds usually survive the winter. Most are held by pairs; but some males, whose displays are evidently exceptionally vigorous ("aggressive"), have larger territories than the others and mate with two females. All suitable moorland is occupied by territory holders; and the size of the breeding population varies with the sizes of the territories. If territory holders are shot in autumn, others replace them, and do well. An important question is therefore what determines territorial size. This feature, which changes from year to year, is related to the supply of food. It might be expected that territorial behavior in autumn would be adjusted to the food supply, but this is not observed. Territorial size is probably related to the nutritional state of the birds' parents. Certainly, if parents are short of food, the fertility of their young is lower than usual, and the population declines. Hence there is a delayed effect of food supply both on the population and—probably—on territorial behavior. High fertility is correlated with *low* mean size of territory. This situation accompanies an abundant food supply of good quality, namely, green heather tips, *Calluna vulgaris*. These statements are based not only on correlations recorded in undisturbed populations, but also on experiments: the quality of the heather, on which the birds feed, has been improved by adding fertilizer. The result was, as predicted, a decrease in the mean size of territories and an increase in the mean number of young reared.

Other experiments have been done on apotreptic behavior. Displays include a song in flight which incorporates the typical cackling call, often given in response to a neighbor. Territorial interactions among these ground-living birds also include walking along a boundary in company with the neighboring territory holder. Clashes sometimes occur. Implanting males with androgenic hormone improves their chances of establishing a territory; correspondingly, their survival rate goes up and so does their chance of breeding. These easily measured consequences are accompanied by a high level of apotreptic conduct.

The extensive studies of this attractive bird give us an unusually comprehensive picture of ecological, behavioral, and physiological interactions.

10.4.1.6 Australian Magpie: The territories of another conspicuous and highly audible bird, the Australian magpie, *Gymnorhina tibicen* (figure 10-16), have been described by R. Carrick (1963, 1972). He writes: "Its aggressive carol, energetic defence of the territorial boundary and readiness to attack intruders, including ornithologists, . . . assist field study." In eight years more than 3000 birds were banded; 650 were individually identified by color banding. Successful breeding depends on occupying a territory of around 4 ha of open woodland. A territory may be occupied by a pair, but the group is usually larger, up to 10, but with not more than three adults of each sex.

Many birds occupy less favorable areas, including open pasture. Some assemble in large flocks. They may breed, but nearly all fail to rear their young. Members of this peripheral population move in when a prime territory is left unoccupied. A notable observation concerns differential susceptibility to infectious disease. During a cold and wet winter, a bacterium, *Pasteurella pseudotuberculosis,* killed many flock birds. The infection is

FIGURE 10-16 An Australian "magpie", *Gymnorhina tibicen*, in its territory. From such a perch it utters its characteristic fluting call. (I. A. Fox)

spread by contact, and no banded territorial birds, living close by, were killed by it. Here is an unusual example of evidence that territorial spacing can prevent disease.

10.4.1.7 Squirrels:

The squirrels (Sciuridae) are solitary mammals. Both male and female red squirrels, *Tamiascurus hudsonicus*, hold territories, of area 0.4 to 0.8 ha, in North American conifer forests. In summer only about one-third of the total population hold such territories. But in deciduous woodland, where the food supply is poor, others hold temporary territories; and this floating population can provide incomers to prime territories when these are vacated. In the breeding season each female is in estrus for one day, during which she accepts several males. After this, she returns to a solitary existence (C. C. Smith; G. A. Kemp & L. B. Keith).

Female ground squirrels, *Spermophilus richardsonii* (also North American), hold territories from year to year, except during hibernation. Males are kept out except during mating, and their territories are smaller than those of females. Territorial defense is by typical postures with the body arched, the tail fluffed, and a flank presentation. When holders of neighboring territories are repeatedly encountered, such interactions decline, as if the squirrels recognized each other (R. I. Yeaton; G. L. Michener).

The round-tailed ground squirrel, *S. tereticaudus,* is more sociable: at first, after hibernation, burrows may be shared. Later, intolerant behavior is the rule, except for coitus and for interactions between mother and offspring and among sibs. In July and August even juveniles become territorial. Closely related females often set up territories in the area occupied by their mother. C. Dunford regards these "kin clusters" as rudimentary social groups.

The females of another member of this family, the yellow-bellied marmot, *Marmota flaviventris,* do live in groups, each with one male (K. B. Armitage). The male regularly patrols his region with raised and waving tail; but actual clashes are rare. If a male is removed or dies, he is quickly replaced, often by a male previously without a territory.

Squirrels, then, provide examples of (1) territories held by single individuals of both sexes; (2) females holding the larger and more permanent territories; (3) both promiscuity and polygamy; and (4) the existence of a "floating" population living in conditions that prevent breeding. Researches on a few species of this one family illustrate the diversity of social patterns to be found even in a small group.

10.4.1.8 Prairie Dogs and Rabbits: We now turn to examples of group territories. J. A. King (1955) has published a detailed study of prairie dogs, *Cynomys ludovicianus,* in natural conditions; and W. J. Smith and others have observed them in seminatural conditions in the Philadelphia zoo. These noisy rodents form vast colonies of up to at least a thousand individuals; the area they occupy may be as much as 30 ha. Within each colony, or "town", there are groups (coteries) each of which has a territory. The coteries consist of one or two adult males, with several females and their young. Members of the same coterie greet each other with characteristic gestures, especially mouth contact and mutual grooming. The encounters of strangers from different coteries are different: in particular, the tails are raised and the anal glands are thus exposed. After this apotreptic display, the two animals separate. Territorial defense is aided by a noise, called a bark, which is distinct from the loud barking used as an alarm call in response to disturbance from larger animals.

In the breeding season coterie territories break down, but nest territories are uncompromisingly maintained by the females. When the young emerge, the adults treat them with forbearance: the young have a low mortality rate, suck from any available female, and are gently groomed by any male they encounter. These idyllic conditions do not persist: coterie territories are gradually restored; the young learn from intolerant treatment by members of other coteries where the boundaries lie; and there is a high death rate among yearling males.

Another much-studied burrowing species, the European rabbit, *Oryctolagus cuniculus,* also assembles in large colonies. R. Mykytowicz & P. J. Fullagar review the social ethology of this popular pest, and especially the effects of social interactions on reproduction. A colony is divided into small breeding groups, each with a territory. All members of the group defend the territory; and boundaries are usually respected by members of neighboring groups. For each group, the warren is the center of activities, and most movement is near it. There is a status system for each sex: dominance is defined primarily in terms of access to place. In an unstable situation, individual status is determined by vigorous apotreptic encounters; later, when the group has settled down, there may still be chasing, with occasional more energetic interactions especially at a time of breeding. Despite all this, rabbits are highly gregarious: given a large area for colonies, they often crowd into only a few warrens and leave plenty of empty space.

For both sexes status has a marked influence on reproductive success. In particular, dominant females have larger and healthier young than have those lower in the order.

The fertility of rabbits is usually less than the maximum. Mykytowicz & Fullagar attribute this to social interactions. When populations of low density have been observed in enclosures, there has been a very high rate of increase. At their first breeding season, such populations may increase to 10 times the original number; but in the next season the corresponding factor may be only three or four. When dispersal is possible, its rate, as one would expect, increases with density. One factor in dispersal is the hostility of senior males to young adult males. Whether such findings are sufficient to account for the regulation of rabbit numbers is uncertain (10.4.3.1).

10.4.1.9 The Vicuña and the Topi: Group territories are also held by the vicuña, *Vicugna vicugna* (Camelidae), described by C. B. Koford. It is remarkable that so much is known about this animal, for it lives at high altitudes in the treeless wastes of the central Andes called the puna. A territory is held by a single adult male with a "harem" typically of four adult females and some juveniles. An average area for a territory (based on observations in a Peruvian game reserve) is 17 ha. There may be no evident territorial boundary, but a demarcation line may be identified by a human observer from the conduct of the vicuñas: two males face each other and display at a distance of only 3 m; if a male steps across the line between them, he is driven back.

In each territory there are piles of dung. All members of the group regularly visit the piles and add feces and urine. It has been suggested that some mammals use such marks, made of special secretions or of excreta, as threats; the expression "territorial marking" has been used to suggest that an occupier's pheromones have an apotreptic effect on intruders. There is, however, no evidence that scent marks operate in this way, for this species. (What little good evidence exists for apotreptic odors is mentioned in 13.2.3.4.) Territories are unhesitatingly entered by wandering vicuñas when the occupiers are absent. The dung heaps may be mnemonic devices to remind the occupiers themselves of their boundaries. Authentic threats by males are said to include a posture with extended legs and with head and tail held high. There is also a loud screech or whistling cry—a distinctive signal that lasts about 4 s and seems to be an alarm call as well as an apotreptic signal.

A new territory is set up when a male moves into an unoccupied region. After a few days he begins to threaten males in adjoining regions, and so evidently establishes his boundaries. He then rounds up unattached females, especially year-old virgins that have been driven away by their parents and older, widowed females. Males, too, are driven out by their fathers. There are always groups of such nonterritorial males, similar in size to the territory-holding family; and sometimes a male from such a group takes over a territory when the resident male dies or becomes enfeebled.

The topi, *Damaliscus korrigum* (figure 10-17), has a social structure rather similar to that of the vicuña. N. Monfort-Braham has observed this an-

FIGURE 10-17 Two topi, *Damaliscus korrigum,* in a clash. (Courtesy N. Monfort)

FIGURE 10-18 Pair of elephant seals, *Mirounga leonina,* hauled out for breeding on Macquarie Island in the Antarctic. (I. A. Fox, courtesy Australian National Antarctic Research Expeditions)

telope in Rwanda. Large territories with rather isolated groups, each of a male with his harem, are, however, confined to wooded regions. The species occurs also in savanna, where the population is more dense, perhaps because there is more food. There the males set up small territories in breeding arenas. Hence, in these conditions, social interactions are much more numerous. (It would be interesting to know something of the physiological consequences.) This versatility of social structure is clearly related to habitat.

10.4.1.10 Sea Lions and Elephant Seals: Steller's sea lion, *Eumetopias jubata,* is an Arctic species that T. C. Poulter calls the "most portly" pinniped. In the breeding season, the bulls arrive

at a rookery before the females. There each establishes a territory on which much time is spent swaying and crooning; if a male intrudes, the occupier growls and snorts. Intruders are sometimes severely gashed during fights, but such clashes are rare; and, when they occur, a gashed male usually retreats to a bachelor herd before he suffers serious injury. When the females arrive, they are herded into harems numbering up to 25. They are attracted by noises described as rapid, low-level rattling grunts, accompanied by a nodding of the head. The females themselves moo rather in the manner of dairy cows.

Each female stays with her newborn young for several days, before beginning to make trips out to sea—presumably to feed. On her return, she makes calls, and her pup answers, gallops toward her, and sucks. If another pup tries to suck, it is attacked, and may be thrown some distance. Once again, we have an example of polygamy, combined with territorial behavior (though the territories are very small), and individual recognition of the young.

B. J. Le Boef has described the rather similar conduct of northern elephant seals, *Mirounga angustirostris,* on Guadalupe, an island off Lower California, and has given detailed evidence on the effect of social status on reproductive success. Adult males, which are three times the weight of females (compare figure 10-18), haul out on remote islands in December and form a stable status system: dominance, in the sense of supplanting, depends on gestures and growls that are followed by withdrawal of the opponent; less often there is an attack and a bite; least often, there is a fight. Pregnant females arrive later than the males, and assemble in harems to which only dominant males have access. Birth takes place six days after landing, and lactation lasts for 28 days. During the last four days of lactation the female is in estrus, and accepts coitus several times.

All females copulate, but fewer than one third of the males do so. The opportunity to copulate, and its frequency, are related directly to social status. Moreover, the same individuals are often dominant for three consecutive breeding seasons. As a result, many males fail to reproduce, but those that do so are likely to have many offspring. We see later, however, that dominance (in the sense of having priority of place) is not necessarily related to reproductive success (chapter 11).

10.4.2 The Concept of Territory

10.4.2.1 Definitions: It is often said that "territory" (in ethology) is a difficult word to define.

This apparently illogical statement means in practice that it is impossible to devise a definition to cover all ethological uses of the term. The word is often used loosely. Sometimes different definitions reflect the different interests of the writers.

Some writers are concerned with the means by which territories are maintained. Others, especially ecologists, investigate the effects of territory. The former are likely to prefer a definition in terms of defense, that is, positive action by the animals concerned. Those interested in ecological effects perhaps lean toward a wider definition. But a definition that covers all exclusively occupied areas (10.1) can conveniently be used by anybody. If we observe groups or individuals of one species, each occupying an area separate from that of others, it is convenient to call such an area a territory, even if nobody has seen the animals taking defensive action. (Perhaps preoccupation with defense is a concealed anthropomorphism: the boundaries of a territory are possibly thought of as frontiers.)

Mountain lions, *Felis concolor,* have individual and apparently undefended territories. In winter in Idaho, the females each occupy regions of up to 50 km², and males still larger areas. But, during observations lasting four years, M. G. Hornocker saw no evidence of defense. The lions make claw marks especially on trails and on high ridges, and they urinate and defecate on them. But the lions often cross the territories of others. As another example, the quokka, *Setonix brachyurus,* a marsupial, has a home range of around 4 ha, part of which at least is exclusively occupied; but there is no evidence of defense (W. N. Holsworth).

Given the wide definition, there are four kinds of factor that might confine an animal to its territory. The first, which we may ignore, is the existence of structural barriers to movement. The second is the attraction of place, exemplified above by the European robin (10.4.1.4). Third, there may be specific apotreptic behavior that keeps animals apart. Of this we have had a number of examples. Lastly, animals may withdraw on detecting the presence of a conspecific, regardless of what the latter is doing. The last two, both social effects, are not mutually exclusive.

M. Bekoff (1977a) has discussed the dispersal of mammals in the absence of apotreptic conduct. It is often taken for granted that some members of a family group are driven away as they approach sexual maturity—usually by the elders. But, as Bekoff shows, mammals may disperse without evident apotreptic conduct.

Coyotes, *Canis latrans,* though of the same genus as wolves, are much less social: they do not usually form packs. Young wolves spend much time in social play, and the family is likely to remain together. Coyotes early perform vigorous apotreptic behavior that leads to the formation of a status system and later to separation by the end of the first year. It might be supposed that the more threatening individuals would drive out others. But, on the contrary, the least tolerant individuals are often the ones that disperse. The mammals among which this relationship has been observed include the prairie dogs (described in 10.4.1.8) and the house mouse, *Mus musculus.* The extent to which exploratory behavior (8.1) plays a part seems not to have been studied.

Dispersal into separate territories, then, need not, and often does not, depend on apotreptic signals. A feature of recent studies is the emphasis on individual variation. The signals that make an animal either withdraw from or approach a conspecific are stereotyped and typical of each species; but there are individual differences both in the intensity of social conduct and in the readiness to part from companions.

FIGURE 10-19   The short-tailed field mouse, *Microtus agrestis.* (John Markham)

An important question is whether variation within a species reflects *genetical* differences between individuals (chapter 16). The study of population genetics in relation to behavior is a rather new venture. A notable attempt in this field has been made by C. J. Krebs and others (1973) in a study of dispersal among two species of voles of the genus, *Microtus* (figure 10-19). These mouse-sized rodents are territorial animals: they are not colonial, like prairie dogs, but solitary; and members of both sexes occupy defended areas of grassland. They are celebrated for the instability of their numbers (reviewed by C. S. Elton; D. Chitty 1960, 1967, 1977). At intervals of about four years, their density reaches a peak; there follows an abrupt decline, or crash, often to levels at which, in the area affected, voles are difficult to find. During the peaks, they tend to disperse.

Krebs and his colleagues studied populations of voles confined in large areas of grassland. Populations with no opening for emigration reached exceptional densities; they then ate so much food that some voles showed signs of starvation. In natural conditions such signs are not found. Members of other populations were allowed to emigrate, and were compared genetically with the stay-at-homes. The comparison was of the presence or absence of genes detectable by differences in the blood proteins (serum polymorphisms). The two types were genetically different. The meaning of this difference has still to be discovered; but the hypothesis is that the genetical differences also influence behavior. Perhaps there is genetically determined variation in the tendency to emigrate, and in the forms or intensity of apotreptic behavior (figure 10-20). Here is an example of a new and probably important method of study in which ethology, ecology, and

genetics are combined (see also C. J. Krebs, 1978).

To sum up, territory as defined here refers to exclusively occupied regions maintained by various means. Sometimes mutual avoidance seems to occur; sometimes individuals leave a region without evident provocation; most often, the members of a species, whether they are solitary or gregarious, are spaced out by species-typical signals: when a signaler is in a region it has already occupied for some time, its signals usually lead to the withdrawal of an intruder without a clash.

10.4.2.2 Classifying Territories:
The examples given in this and the preceding chapter show that there are many kinds of territory. Despite all this variety, we can see three main types:

1. The first is a region in which most or all of an animal's activities are carried out. Occupation may be confined to a breeding season. Examples are the territories of sticklebacks, crocodiles, robins (and many other birds), and vicuñas.

2. The second is a region, smaller than the animal's total area of movement (home range), in which courtship and mating occur. Dragonflies provide an example. The *lek* (18.4.4) is a special case. This is a region in which males group together, each in his own small territory, and display to visiting females. R. H. Schuster describes the breeding of the lechwe antelope, *Kobus leche,* of Zambia. In the rutting season, groups of 50 to 100 males occupy circular areas of about 0.5 km in diameter. When females are present there are liable to be 10 to 20 closely grouped around one or two of the males. The females are evidently attracted by a male display in which the head is high, the feet are prancing, the tail is vibrating, and the head shaking. In the absence of a female, this performance is directed toward another male. Between males

FIGURE 10-20 A scheme to illustrate how density-related factors might account for the fluctuations in numbers of small rodents, such as those of the genus, *Microtus. See also 10.5.1.1.* (After C. J. Krebs and others, 1973)

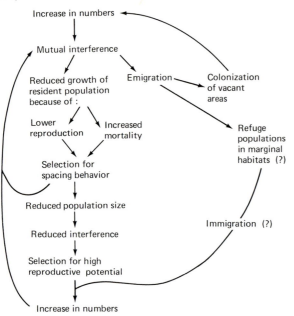

FIGURE 10-21 Gulls, Laridae, usually nest crowded together. Black-billed gulls, *Larus bulleri,* of New Zealand, on their nest. (Courtesy C. G. Beer)

there are also swinging of the head, pawing of the ground, tearing of the grass, and clashing of the horns; but Schuster observed little or no actual fighting.

3. Lastly, a female with young may drive conspecifics from her nest. Hence we have a nest territory. Gulls (Laridae) nest crowded together (figure 10-21), but vigorously prevent intrusion into their own small area (figure 10-22). Other sea birds nest in colonies also (figure 10-23). Among small mammals, small nest territories may be held within larger, group territories (W. H. Burt).

Since territories are often held only in the breeding season, they may be permanent or temporary. As an additional complication, groups of some species, especially of large mammals, hold an area while on the move. Y. Espmark describes how the rutting territory of reindeer, *Rangifer tarandus,* moves with the "harem": no fixed boundaries can be identified, but other groups of individuals remain (or are kept) at a distance, wherever the harem happens to be.

10.4.2.3 Territorial Songs: Although, for some species, there may be no evidence of territorial defense, territories are usually held as a result of signals. The illustrations in the preceding pages give examples of visible displays. The other important category is sounds. Of all audible displays, those of birds have been best recorded; and here I illustrate some additional features of territorial display from bird song.

J. B. Falls gives a thorough account of the singing of male white-throated sparrows, *Zonotrichia albicollis.* Singing occurs especially at the boundaries of a territory, in response to other males. Repeated encounters with neighboring males are accompanied by a decline in singing; but the arrival of a strange male at once evokes more vigorous

FIGURE 10-22 Above, two lesser black-backed gulls, *Larus fuscus,* in a territorial clash. Violent interactions are, however, rare. Below, a display by the gull on the right drives off an intruder. (Photos by N. Tinbergen (above) and L. C. Shaffer (below) from *Signals for Survival* by N. Tinbergen and H. Falkus, © Oxford University Press, 1970)

FIGURE 10-23 Colony of cormorants, *Phalacocorax albiventer,* on Macquarie Island. The nest territories, like those of gulls (figures 10-21 and 10-22), are small. (I. A. Fox, courtesy Australian National Antarctic Research Expeditions)

song. Evidently, the birds discriminate between the songs sung by conspecifics in their own locality and those of others from elsewhere: that is, there are song dialects (12.2.2).

Falls emphasizes the economy of effort displayed by these birds, which not only rely almost entirely on singing to maintain their territories but also sing vigorously only until stable relationships with neighbors have been established. Not all birds are so restrained. Some sing with extraordinary persistence. Among the many possibilities, the tropical barbets (Capitonidae) rank high. Hugh Whistler describes the call of the green barbet, *Thereiceryx zeylanicus,* as loud and monotonous; it starts, he says, with a "harsh sort of laugh" and continues with a call which he represented as *tur-r-r kutur-*

kotur-kotur. This remarkable noise can be heard in all seasons, but especially during breeding early in the year; it is then so persistent that it is surprising the birds have time to eat, let alone breed.

Another example is the crimson-breasted barbet, *Xantholaema haemacephala.* This bird, though common in India, is well camouflaged and not easy to see; but its "song" is inescapable: it consists of a relentlessly repeated *tok-tok-tok* resembling the noise of a distant hammer beating out metal. Hence follows its alternative name of coppersmith. In the absence of rather elaborate experiment, the significance of such apparently excessive advertisement can only be guessed at. I return to such questions in 18.6.

Another variant on territorial songs is described by R. H. & M. S. Wiley. They studied the group territories of stripe-backed wrens, *Campylorhynchus nuchalis,* observed in the Venezuelan savanna. Each group includes around seven birds and occupies a well-marked territory; vocal "duels" occur at the boundaries. The encounters are not between two antagonists, but between pairs or groups: the main apotreptic behavior consists of duets or choruses. The duet of a neighboring pair is distinguished from that of a stranger. By playing recordings of duets, the authors evoked a stronger response by residents to a strange song than to the song of a neighboring pair. In addition, if a neighbor's duet were played on the wrong side of a territorial boundary, that too evoked an especially vigorous answer.

10.4.2.4 The Confusion with Status:

Many of the species described in this and the preceding chapter hold group territories; and in each group there is a status system. Relationships of dominance and subordinacy in a group are then entirely distinct from territorial interactions. The former do not depend on where the actors are; and, among adults, status—once acquired—usually persists until annulled by death or weakness. In contrast, in a territorial situation A can drive B away when A is on his territory; but B, on *his* territory, can expel A.

In some writings, however, a territory holder is described as dominant to an intruder. Such a statement implies a definition of dominance wider than that I stipulate in 10.1. Those who prefer the wider definition may argue that the narrower one used here has at least one disadvantage: there are certain inconvenient species of which the conduct does not seem to allow a clear distinction between status within a group and territorial relationships.

I take first two examples of confusion that has seemingly arisen from study of captive groups. M. G. Ridpath (1972a,b) has described the social life of the Tasmanian native hen, *Tribonyx mortierii* (figure 10-24). In natural conditions these birds live spaced out in territories, each occupied by a pair or by a group of two males with one female. The territories are permanent. Both sexes take part in the rearing of young. The young drift away from their parents when they are aged about one year, and only a few succeed in setting up territories for themselves. Clashes in relation to territory are energetic but rarely injurious. Within the small groups of two or three, conflict is hardly seen. So far, we have an account of a species which has well-defined territorial behavior, and of which the only marked peculiarity is polyandry. No status relationships were observed in natural conditions. A status system ("hierarchy") did, however, develop in one place where additional food was put down. Ridpath points out that the apotreptic conduct of this species tends to increase with population density; and he attributes the development of relationships of dominance and subordinacy to exceptional crowding at an artificial feeding point.

FIGURE 10-24 Apotreptic conduct of a Tasmanian native hen, *Tribonyx mortierii.* The bird is described as "yelling". (Courtesy M. G. Ridpath)

He also reviews work on other birds which suggests the same conclusion.

It is hardly surprising that the social conduct of animals should be distorted by confinement in manmade environments (11.2.5.2). It is also easy for an observer to misinterpret social interactions, especially those of captive groups.

A second example is from my work (1975) on wild rats, *Rattus norvegicus.* In some experiments, artificial groups of adults have been assembled in large cages. If such groups consist only of males, conflict is rare or absent; and if status exists, the signs are so unobtrusive that I failed to observe them. Peaceful conditions depend on the rats all being put into the new environment at the same time. If they are put in at intervals, conflict follows. Evidently, a rat in a new environment, during its initial exploration, quickly comes to behave in a territorial manner: an adult male intruder is then liable to be threatened.

Nonetheless, in the account of my experiments, I used terms such as "alpha", for "dominant" animals, as if I were dealing with a status system. But the males I called alphas, instead of establishing a stable set of group relationships, were persistently and vigorously intolerant of all other adult males. Probably, the apotreptic conduct of this species is usually territorial, perhaps always. Rarely, in my experiments, a male adapted itself to the presence of another (usually larger) male, kept out of its way, and was therefore given the status of beta. Yet, when it did occur, the peaceful coexistence of alpha and betas represented an authentic status system. But the role of betas in natural conditions is not known.

Sometimes similar difficulties are met in studies of natural populations. A. D. Brian watched great tits, *Parus major,* in winter on a farm in the west of Scotland. She caught and color ringed all those that came to eat scraps put out for them. Seven males formed a straight-line status system, apart from a triangle among three. A female was associated with each male, and the females too formed a similar system. Status in this case was, in effect, defined by priority at the food: sometimes, if a bird were feeding, and another arrived, the second waited nearby or was chased away; in other encounters, a bird feeding flew away on the arrival of another. Only mated pairs fed together.

The complication arose when these relationships were related to the distance of the owners' territories from the feeding point. A clear rule emerged: "the farther away a bird's territory, the lower its status." The three birds that formed a triangle had roughly equidistant territories. Hence these birds were not living together as a group, but were holders of adjoining territories brought together by the existence of a source of food. Their relationships of "dominance" reflected their territorial status.

As the author points out, her conclusions should have been checked by observation of the same birds at other feeding points, at different distances from the various territories. Her work is nonetheless of interest, especially because a study of this kind can be attempted with patience but very little equipment. J. L. Brown (1964) has made a more extensive and critically analyzed study of Steller's jays, *Cyanocitta stelleri,* in a park in California. These birds form pairs that set up permanent residence in territories centered on their nests. Brown observed interactions at a number of feeding stations, at which supplanting relationships like those of the great tits were observed (figure 10-25). As Brown points out, it is not always easy to be certain that A has supplanted B: B might just be about to fly off when A arrives, and so give a misleading impression of having been supplanted. Nonetheless, Brown was able to establish clear relationships between distance from the nest and "dominance"; but these relationships applied only to males: the status of females was less clear. Brown writes:

> The concept of "territory" is inadequate to express accurately the dominance relationships between individual Steller Jays in respect to the topography of the areas where they lived. . . . the dominance relationships of an individual Steller Jay may be conceived as a series of concentric zones of diminishing dominance rank from the center of the nesting area outwards.

Such species, then, do not fit a conventional classi-

FIGURE 10-25 Above, Steller's jay, *Cyanocitta stelleri.* (V. R. Johnston, courtesy J. L. Brown) Below, three stages in an encounter between two male Steller's jays. The birds also made loud calls and clapped their bills. (Reproduced from J. L. Brown, *The Integration of Agonistic Behavior in the Steller's Jay* (Univ. Calif. Pub. Zool. 60 (4) 1964, p. 294) by permission of the University of California Press)

fication of social interactions, in which relationships within a group are sharply distinct from those between groups. (In this case the group is a mated pair.) But no confusion need arise, provided that the observations made are clearly described, and terms such as dominance are unambiguously defined. (For further discussion of status systems, see 11.3.)

10.4.3 Territory and Populations

The widespread occurrence of territorial behavior among vertebrates, and even among many invertebrates, makes its importance evident, but it does not tell us what it does for the animals. Its *effect* is to space out individuals or, more usually, pairs and their young or larger groups. Regions favorable to a species seem in this way to be prevented from acquiring a population above a certain density. Hence territorial behavior has attracted much attention from ecologists interested in the regulation of animal numbers (reviewed by N. B. Davies, 1978).

This has been a controversial subject. Some of the controversy has centered on the concept of density-related factors that regulate the growth of populations. In a simple case, if a population begins, in a favorable environment, with a small number of individuals, the rate of growth is slow at first, then becomes rapid, and finally slows until a maximum is reached (figure 10-26). Such slowing of increase and eventual maintenance of a maximum density must be due to the operation of an adverse effect on population growth that increases in proportion to density. Regulation of density is then based on a negative feedback (4.1). Animal populations are often fairly stable. The few that are not, such as those of locusts (2.3.6.3), obtrude themselves and may give a misleading impression of ecological chaos.

The following are the categories of density-related factors that might influence the growth of animal populations and keep them in a steady state.

1. the attacks of predators
2. the supply of food
3. the incidence of infectious disease

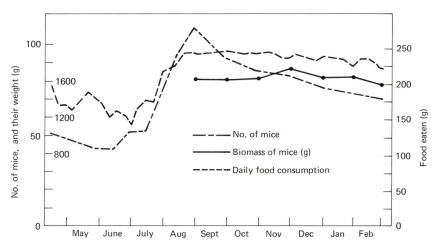

FIGURE 10-26 Growth of a population of house mice, *Mus musculus.* The number of mice in an isolated colony grew to a peak and then gradually declined; the total weight or biomass of the mice reached a plateau; and, correspondingly, so did the rate of food consumption. (After R. L. Strecker & J. T. Emlen, 1953)

4. the availability of shelter, especially nesting places

5. apotreptic behavior

It is convenient to discuss some of these categories separately; but, as we see below, in natural conditions they are likely to act in combination.

10.4.3.1 Predation:

When predator-prey interactions are studied closely, the numbers of the predatory species sometimes seem to be regulated by those of the prey, rather than the reverse (reviewed by M. P. Hassell).

As an example, a population of 17 to about 30 pairs of tawny owls, *Strix aluco,* was observed in an English wood from 1947 through 1959 (H. N. Southern). Its food consisted mainly of wood mice, *Apodemus sylvaticus,* and bank voles, *Clethrionomys glareolus.* The birds, even their nestlings, were easy to count because they were noisy. The numbers of rodents were estimated by an elaborate system of trapping. Southern calculated an index of "losses" in the owl population based on failure to breed or to achieve the maximum clutch size. This index was calculated for each year, and was plotted against the estimated density of the rodents in June of the same year. With three exceptions, the points fell on a straight line, indicating a steep fall in losses with rising rodent density (figure 10-27). The three exceptions were in years in which the rodent population was unusually large: in those years, evidently, the owl population was limited by other, unidentified factors.

It does not, of course, follow that all predator-prey relationships are of this type. Southern's work examines the effects of prey population on the predator. More often the question has been whether the numbers of prey are in any sense controlled by predation. M. Andersson & S. Erlinge discuss the effects of different kinds of predator: some special-

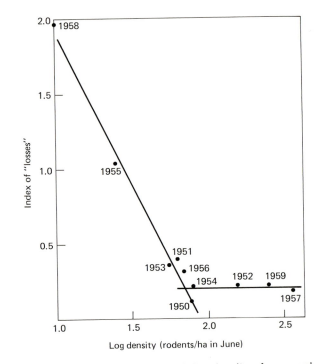

FIGURE 10-27 Relationship of the density of prey animals (rodents) to an index of "losses" of a population of owls, *Strix aluco,* in a wood. The figures for seven of the ten years shown give a linear regression. In the three exceptional years (1952, 1954, 1959), the rodent population was unusually large. Except in those years, the owl population was evidently regulated by the number of prey animals. (After H. N. Southern, 1970)

ize on one or a few species, others are "generalists"; some are permanent residents (like the owls studied by Southern), others are nomadic. These authors are especially concerned with populations of rodents, such as voles, *Microtus,* which fluctuate widely with a fairly regular cycle of about four years (10.4.2.1). They suggest that generalists, if there are plenty of alternative species to prey upon, can stabilize the numbers of rodents; but resident specialists may be responsible for cyclic changes in numbers.

A vole, *M. montanus,* in California is preyed

upon extensively by the ermine or weasel, *Mustela erminea* (B. M. Fitzgerald). These carnivores not only eat the voles but occupy their burrows and nests: they are specialists in vole hunting. It might be supposed that ermine would eat a high proportion of the total vole population when the population is at its highest, but almost the opposite is found: predation is most intense when the voles are rather scarce; and at that time, during winter, all the losses of voles from the populations studied are attributable to predation. When the voles are at minimum density, the ermine either die or emigrate. This evidently allows the voles to recover their numbers; whereupon the predators increase again. In this case, predation seems to regulate the numbers of prey at some stages in their population cycle; but there is also an effect of the prey population on the numbers of predators. Figure 10-28 gives another example.

Rodents of this and similar genera are pests of farm lands and forests. It has long been suggested that the habit of farmers of killing predators, such as foxes, weasels, hawks, owls, and snakes, has ill effects by allowing an increase in rodent numbers. It is extremely difficult to get satisfactory evidence on such a hypothesis, without experimenting on a vast scale. There is, however, some evidence of predation as a limiting factor from studies of the European rabbit, *Oryctolagus cuniculus*. This familiar lagomorph (already mentioned in 10.4.1.8) depends wholly, or almost wholly, on man; it has been introduced (as a source of food) into regions remote from Europe. In Australia it quickly became a national calamity. In that continent its numbers have been, at least temporarily, restricted by myxomatosis; but this disease was deliberately spread by man, and tells us little about the natural regulation of numbers.

J. A. Gibb describes a 10-year study of rabbits on a sheep pasture in New Zealand. The area, which was enclosed, was at first of 8.5 ha but was later reduced. During periods of maximum abundance, it allowed dispersion of the rabbits from their main occupied areas. The main predators were cats, *Felis catus,* and ferrets, *Mustela putorius.* There was also a raptor, *Circus approximans* (a harrier). The enclosure allowed ground predators in only for the first five years (1958–1963). There was a population peak in 1959–1960, and a larger one in 1965–1966. Young born late in each season of peak numbers were undersized, and had an exceptionally high mortality. At these times there was overgrazing (a phenomenon also observed outside enclosures).

Some of Gibb's findings suggest that social interactions regulated numbers. During the first five

FIGURE 10-28 Relationship of the size of a rabbit population to the number of predators. During 1958 and 1959 rabbit numbers increased, and the number of predators counted increased correspondingly. When, in 1960, the rabbit population began to decline, the predators continued at first to increase; but there was a steep decline after the rabbit population had "crashed". (After J. A. Gibb, 1977)

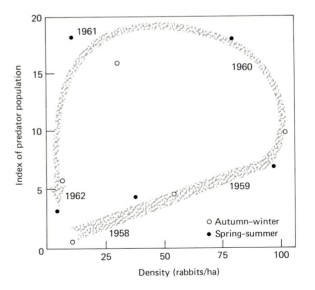

years of the study, the higher the population density, the shorter was the breeding season: hence the rate of increase was lowest when the population was at maximum. As density increased, territories became smaller, and burrows for each rabbit became fewer; and at high densities surplus rabbits occupied the less favorable ground. Social interactions are, indeed, held to have led to differences in fertility among individuals: some females, of high status, reproduced successfully, while others did not; and there may have been similar effects among the males. The chances of survival of adults are also held to have been affected by their social position. Nonetheless, social interactions seem not to have prevented overeating the food supplies; nor did they prevent predation. The numbers of predators on the area increased as the density of rabbits rose; moreover, at high densities there was more feeding in the open, and the rabbits then disregarded predators instead of avoiding them. Hence, when numbers were high, there was a high mortality from predation. This, combined with the shortage of food (which led to more exposure), is regarded as the principal controlling factor.

A comparison is made with hares, *Lepus europaeus,* whose food supply is more predictable than that of rabbits. There is a fixed breeding season; and hares never reach high densities, as rabbits do. Hares are solitary, and their normal state of dispersion evidently depends on social interactions, which may for them be the most important regulator of density.

To sum up, predation seems sometimes to contribute to the regulation of mammalian populations; but it may do so as a result of an interaction with other factors, especially the supply of food.

10.4.3.2 Shelter:

The availability of shelter, too, seems to influence some populations. The pike blennies mentioned earlier evidently depend on a special kind of shelter, the burrows left by sedentary worms (10.4.1.2). Occasionally, we have experimental evidence of shelter as a limiting factor, as from the observations on geckos described in 10.4.1.3. The population of pied flycatchers, *Muscicapa hypoleuca,* nesting in a Finnish wood, was estimated by L. von Haartman. Nest boxes were then supplied. The number of nesting pairs at once increased, and the population became stable at a higher level. The birds were directly observed to be using the boxes; and so the extra shelter was evidently responsible for the change in density.

10.4.3.3 Food and Social Interactions:

Simple relationships between shelter and the numbers of a species are, however, probably rare. At first sight, food seems the most likely of possible limiting factors. One question is then whether the sizes of territories or home ranges are related to food needs. Figures of food consumption are hard to come by, but food needs are a function of body weight (B. K. McNab); and so the relationship of body weight to occupied area has been examined. T. W. Schoener finds the sizes of the feeding territory of birds to be positively correlated with body weight. Of course, other factors are involved. Predators have territories larger than those of plant eaters of similar weight; and the home ranges of raptors are positively correlated with the density of the prey. Similarly, the dense flocks of herbivorous birds feeding during winter are held to be related to the patchy distribution of their food (compare 3.3).

A similar review has been made by K. Milton & M. L. May of the home ranges of Primates. Again there is a strong positive correlation between the area covered and body weight; and again there are other factors that make the relationship less than simple. For example, leaf-eating species have smaller home ranges in relation to body weight than have fruit eaters or omnivores.

Nonetheless, it sometimes seems impossible to attribute the density reached by a species, in a favorable environment, to predation or disease, shortage of shelter, or even shortage of food. We therefore turn to social interactions. A certain level of crowding could act by driving some individuals away from favorable ground, or by reducing fertility, or even by increasing injurious violence. The argument can be applied, not only to species that are intolerant at all times, but also to those that are territorial only in the breeding season. (Intolerance within the species may then allow each pair to rear healthy young; but such a statement concerns the survival value of the behavior, not its effect on density.)

This theoretical argument may seem to lead to the proposition that food is excluded as a means of regulating numbers. But, although supposed density-related factors sometimes seem to act alone, in many natural populations they probably interact. Indeed, there is evidence that, for some species, (1) food supplies, (2) the distribution of shelter, and (3) apotreptic behavior combine to influence numbers in a given area.

Some examples have already been given. In 10.4.1.2 I mention a fish, the garibaldi, whose territories vary in size with the amount of edible plant food available; similarly, the sizes of the territories of red grouse, described in 10.4.1.5, are negatively correlated with food supply. Other instances are scattered around the animal kingdom. A formidably large Californian limpet, *Lottia gigantia,* has been studied by J. Stimson (1970, 1973). These mollusks live on rocks between tide marks, and feed by scraping the algae from the rock surface. Each limpet has a region defended against conspecific intruders. (The region is also kept free of sessile animals, such as barnacles, which could interfere with the growth of the crop of algae.) Territorial areas are positively correlated with the size

of the occupying limpet, but are also related to the thickness of the growth of the algae. The supply of this food is greatest in spring. When, in spring, some territories were partly denuded of algae, the territories were enlarged. In other experiments, large individuals were removed from their territories; smaller limpets then moved in and set up their own territories. Hence in this case, evidently, territorial behavior and food supply combine to determine population density.

C. A. Simon describes analogous observations on the iguanid lizard, *Sceleporus jarrovi,* in southeast Arizona. All adults and most juveniles defend a rock-strewn region against conspecifics of the same size and sex. Defense is by means of head-bobbing, a lateral display, tail slashing, and occasional biting. The size of the territory is positively correlated with body size, and is negatively correlated with the food supply. Supplying extra food leads to a reduction in territory size.

C. L. Gass and others give another example. The rufous hummingbird, *Selasphorus rufus,* feeds on the nectar provided by flowers. These minute birds were studied in northwest California, in mountain meadows at about 2300 m, where their main sources of food were only two plant species. The birds rarely fed outside their territories. Gass and his colleagues estimated the yield of nectar to a unit area in different meadows in which there was a total of nearly 200 territories (figure 10-29): there was a remarkable relationship between the sizes of the territories and the estimated output of nectar in the area. Food was therefore a crucial density-related factor, but it operated through territorial interactions.

10.4.3.4 Interactions: Further Experiments: Many of the experiments on interacting density-related factors have been on rodents. They fall into four categories.

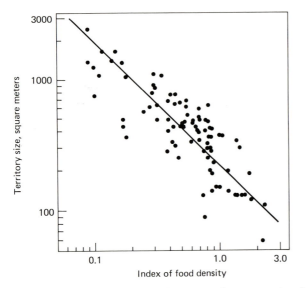

FIGURE 10-29 Relationship between the amount of food and the sizes of the territories of the rufous hummingbird, *Selasphorus rufus.* These birds feed from flowers; and the more flowers there were in a unit area, the smaller were the territories. Both axes are on a logarithmic scale. (After C. L. Gass and others, 1976)

1. One desirable type of experiment, in principle, is to induce members of a territorial species to abandon their apotreptic behavior. An approach to this is provided by observations on laboratory rats, which are very tolerant of conspecifics. J. B. Calhoun (1961) allowed such rats to breed unchecked in a structured environment. Their population density probably reached a much higher figure than it does in the burrows of wild rats even in the most favorable conditions (though this is not certain). Eventually, fertility declined, and infant mortality rose, although there was no shortage of food.

Calhoun did not study wild-type *Rattus norvegicus* in identical conditions. Colonies of wild rats have, however, been compared with domestic rats (S. A. Barnett and others, 1979). Among the wild rats many males died. From an early stage, in each colony, only one male moved about freely. Females moved about with little interference. In contrast, laboratory rats of both sexes (and two strains) moved about readily; hardly any died. Hence their population density was eventually higher than that of the wild rats. Nonetheless, such experiments do not provide a satisfactory test of the effects of territorial conduct. Wild rats differ genetically from domestic rats in many respects; and the conditions of experiments on rats in captivity, even in large cages or enclosures, differ greatly from those of any natural population.

Some writers have tried to draw conclusions on human populations from Calhoun's study of white rats. The inappropriateness of such comparisons is made still more obvious when we see that the domestic rats do not tell us even what to expect from the wild type of their own species.

2. Another lesson of this example is the difficulty of getting experimental evidence on the effects of territorial behavior. An alternative method is to allow an artificial population of animals of the wild type to grow in captivity, and to make observations on the factors that seem to limit its growth.

C. R. Terman has studied captive prairie deer mice, *Peromyscus maniculatus.* In natural conditions these rodents do not form densely packed colonies, as some rats do, but are solitary like voles, *Microtus.* Some of Terman's populations were set up in seminatural conditions in large enclosures; others were in small cages. He provided nest boxes in the enclosures. The mice settled in particular boxes, and homed on them after being removed by the experimenter. They also tended to avoid boxes already occupied. Terman emphasizes mutual avoidance as a means of spacing out individuals. In other experiments laboratory populations of his mice were allowed to grow in confined conditions with plenty of food, water, and shelter. Growth stopped before any of these resources were exhausted. Some of his populations were started with four males and four females. The population size at which growth stopped ranged from 6 to 47. When breeding continued after the maxima had been reached, numbers did not rise because there was a high death rate among the young. Females in the groups became pregnant less often than others that were kept each alone in a cage with one male: that is, living in a group reduced fertility much below its maximum. While females in isolated pairs nearly always produced healthy young, about 80% of the grouped females were barren. Terman attributes the low fertility and high mortality to behavioral interactions. Such interactions (perhaps territorial) are, no doubt, exacerbated by the impossibility of dispersion by young adults.

3. The preceding findings are consistent with limitation of density by apotreptic conduct; but others point to food as a crucial factor. Human action often leads to unintended experiments, in which animals are given access to vast concentrations of food in a small space. A garbage dump is such an experiment. P. A. Courtney & M. B. Fenton, who describe these municipal amenities as "at present unavoidable", studied one in a rural environment in Ontario. A deer mouse, *Peromyscus leucopus,* and the Eastern chipmunk, *Tamias striatus,* were in substantially higher densities on the dump than in another favorable environment nearby. Both are scavengers. Other small mammals, more discriminating in their choice of diet, were less common on the dump than on a control area with a normal amount of food.

Another example comes from the rice godowns of Calcutta, in which J. J. Spillett studied vast populations of the Indian mole rat, *Bandicota bengalensis.* The population density was estimated as 78 rats to each 100 m² of floor space. This murid also lives throughout India in the banks that border paddy fields. There it is spaced out in a network of burrows and is apparently solitary. Evidently, a high concentration of food, together with the shelter offered by dilapidated buildings, annuls the dispersive influence of intolerant conduct.

On the evidence of the preceding paragraphs, the population density of some species can be substantially increased by providing an exceptional abundance of food. Presumably, there must also be plenty of shelter. What does this signify for the role of territorial or other social interactions in regulating density? Consider two environments, which we may call respectively normal and abundant. The second is exemplified by a garbage dump or a godown. In the normal environment, density—measured by number or mass of a species in a unit area or volume—is much lower than in the abundant environment. There is no evidence of starvation or infectious disease in the normal environment; and we are led by this, and by more direct evidence, to suspect that apotreptic behavior prevents density from rising above a certain level. If so, how does supplying abundant food alter density? The answer can be only that the amount of food available influences the intensity of social interactions: the more food there is, the less the conflict. Hence food supplies and social behavior interact or combine to determine the density of certain populations. There could also be an interaction with the character and distribution of shelter.

Such findings suggest the following conclusions: (a) food and social conduct can both influence population density; (b) the effects of both these agencies vary with the season; (c) the effects of food and social conduct may interact; and (d) a full account of density regulation for a single species requires detailed study in each of the major types of environment in which that species is found.

4. An important kind of experiment is that in which a natural population is substantially reduced, and then observed during its recovery. Numbers may be restored from (a) breeding, or (b) immigration. The latter can be either from an excess of young individuals produced by neighboring populations *or* from nonterritorial adults flowing in to occupy vacated territories. Here we are concerned with the last. We have already had three examples (the red grouse, the Australian magpie, and the vicuña) of populations that include "floaters" from among which losses of territory holders are made good. Such replacement has also been observed after experimental reduction of numbers. J. R. Krebs (1971, 1977a) describes observations of the great tit, *Parus major,* in England. This much-studied bird nests in mixed woodland (where breeding success is high) and in hedgerows (where it is low). Mean territory size varies greatly from year to year, perhaps—like that of red grouse—in response to a varying food supply. By adding to the food in a wood in winter, Krebs was able to raise the breeding population. He also studied the distances between nests, and showed that nest sites were not distributed at random: it followed that local density limitation was due to social (territorial) interactions. In spring, Krebs removed pairs from their territories in mixed woodland. They were quickly replaced, mainly by birds, aged one year, from hedgerow territories. The latter were not refilled. Territory is therefore believed to limit the breeding population in an optimum habitat. The principal apotreptic behavior that achieves this is song.

Such culling experiments have also been done on small mammals. C. J. Krebs (1966) studied *Microtus californicus:* when natural populations of this vole were reduced by trapping, there was rapid replacement by immigrants. Evidently, some form of intolerance prevents entry by newcomers once a population has reached a certain density. Similarly, M. C. Healey, in yet another study of deer mice, set up artificial colonies in fenced areas of natural woodland. Young males were released into these plots, but soon died. But, when released into areas from which all other deer mice had been removed, they often settled down and grew well. Social interactions provide the only plausible explanation of such findings.

10.5 CROWDING AND SOCIAL STRESS

10.5.1 Birth and Death

In this chapter so far, and in chapter 9, we have been concerned with social interactions that differ in kind, according to the age, sex, status, or territorial position of the actors. A much-debated question is the extent to which it is useful to examine such interactions in terms of population density alone. On the simplest assumption, animals may be treated as if they were molecules in a gas: the incidence or intensity of encounters is then proportional to the density—the number present in a unit area or volume. In special cases the degree of crowding is certainly both measurable and significant. The behavior of locusts is crucially influenced by their density and the consequent frequency of encounters (2.3.6.3.). But most of the work and theorizing has been on populations of mammals, especially rodents and Primates.

10.5.1.1 Fertility: The fertility of rodents and probably of some other mammals seems to be negatively correlated with population density. If a population of, say, deer mice is experimentally reduced, it is quickly replaced by an influx from neighboring areas (10.4.3.4). What happens if there is no source of rapid replacement? R. L. Snyder studied populations of the woodchuck, *Marmota monax,* in a region with abundant food. When he removed a large fraction of a population, the rates of pregnancy and of survival among the young rose, and there was a rapid return to the original density. D. E. Davis made a similar study of wild rats, *Rattus norvegicus,* living in residential areas in Baltimore. By trapping he removed about half the population of a substantial area. The pregnancy rate rose by 60%. Hence again numbers increased rapidly from their low level.

Such observations do not tell us how crowding acts. Here are some possibilities.

1. Delayed maturity
2. Reduced ovulation or spermatogenesis
3. Diminished implantation of embryos
4. A higher death rate in utero
5. A higher death rate among the young

All these have been observed in very crowded artificial colonies of house mice, *Mus musculus,* and other species (reviewed by S. A. Barnett, 1964; J. A. King, 1973). Their scope in natural populations is not known; but there is increasing indirect evidence of social effects acting early in the reproductive cycle. As an example, there is the "Bruce effect", or pregnancy block, first described by H. M. Bruce (1961, 1967). If a female laboratory mouse is inseminated, and the stud male is replaced by a strange male (preferably of a different strain) early in pregnancy, implantation usually fails (figure 10-30). Such pregnancy block can be brought about merely by the odor of a strange male. The pheromone responsible is present in the urine.

Pregnancy block also occurs among rodents of the genera, *Peromyscus, Microtus,* and *Clethrio-*

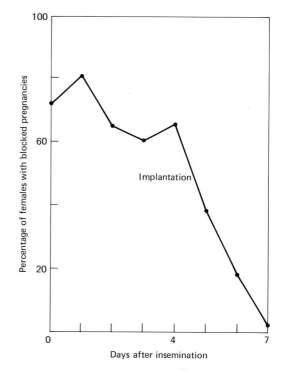

FIGURE 10-30 Pregnancy block or the "Bruce effect": exposure of a female laboratory mouse, *Mus musculus,* to a strange male blocks pregnancy. (After H. M. Bruce, 1961)

nomys. F. F. Mallory & F. V. Clulow review these observations, and describe a detailed study of the meadow vole, *M. pennsylvanicus.* The ovaries after pregnancy block can be identified histologically (figure 10-31); and Mallory and Clulow report such ovaries from a wild population. Presumably, the more dense the population, the more likely is a female to meet a strange male just after insemination. Hence we evidently have here a physiologically economical means by which fertility is regulated by population density.

Pregnancy block seems to be confined to certain rodent genera. Among other mammals, there may

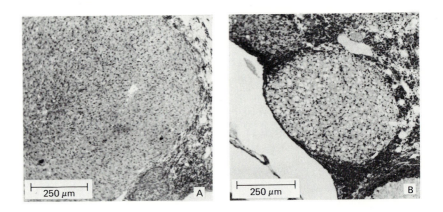

FIGURE 10-31 Photomicrographs of corporea lutea of the meadow vole, *Microtus pennsylvanicus:* (A) normal, four days after coitus; (B) four days after coitus, and two days after pregnancy block, with many abnormal (pycnotic) nuclei. (Courtesy F. F. Mallory)

be analogous density-related effects, also acting early in the reproductive cycle. In 10.4.3.4 above I mention the work of C. R. Terman on deer mice. His artificial colonies stopped growing before the resources of their environment were exhausted. A similar finding is described by L. Goldman & H. H. Swanson in a study of confined colonies of golden hamsters, *Mesocricetus auratus.* The experimental populations were each begun with two males and two females. Breeding was allowed for some months. No population increased to more than eight individuals. The main limiting factor was a high infant mortality due to cannibalism (not by the mother): pregnant and parturient females crowded in with the other hamsters, even when there were alternative nesting sites, and their young were eaten.

H. H. Swanson & M. R. Lockley describe similar experiments on Mongolian gerbils, *Meriones unguiculatus,* and review the whole field. Groups of these charming pests were kept in cages, or in enclosures of much greater area. Each was begun with a single mated pair. None of the colonies grew to more than 20 members in either condition: hence available space was not a factor in regulating numbers (figure 10-32). Regulation depended

on (1) infertility of the young females, (2) cessation of breeding by the founding female, and (3) deaths of litters. An important finding was of delay in the sexual maturation of the young owing to the presence of breeding adults. In some further experiments litter mates were left in enclosures without their parents: sexual maturation of these, too, was delayed; there was conflict until a status system arose in which there was only one breeding female. In such a system there was one male distinguished by the presence of a large ventral scent gland: this male rubs his ventral surface on objects in his living space (see also 13.2.3.4).

The last observation suggests that delayed sexual maturity could result from the presence of pheromones, just as pregnancy block is induced by odors. G. O. Batzli and others give further evidence. If litter mates of microtine rodents are kept in the same cage, or even in conditions in which they have the same air supply, their growth and rates of sexual maturation are diminished. If such "suppressed" voles are put with strangers of the opposite sex, growth and maturation accelerate. As the search for such effects widens, more evidence will probably accrue on the behavioral regulation of breeding rates and hence of population density.

10.5.1.2 Pathology of Adults: Exceptionally high population densities are usually assumed not only to reduce fertility but also to have ill effects on adults. The expression "social stress" is a general term for adverse effects of social interactions. When such effects exist, they may not be due to crowding; but it is often assumed that they become more severe with a rise in density. (Experiments that seem to support this notion are described above, 10.4.3.)

The injuries are not, as a rule, wounds due to violent clashes. As we know, careful descriptions of apotreptic behavior often include the statement that serious injury is rarely or never seen. Such behavior can, however, be indirectly harmful by expelling conspecifics from a favorable environment; but here we are concerned with more immediate effects. An extreme example, observed in laboratory encounters, is sudden collapse and death, *without wounding* (figure 10-33): sudden or gradual collapse under attack occurs among several species of wild rats, *Rattus* (S. A. Barnett, 1975). This is not an effect of population density itself: wild rats, at least of some species, can live peacefully when severely crowded. It results from the encounter of strangers; and of course such encounters are (other things equal) more likely in high densities.

Similar observations have been made of tree shrews, *Tupaia belangeri* (D. von Holst; figure

FIGURE 10-32 Colonies of Mongolian gerbils, *Meriones unguiculatus:* on left, in a cage; on right, in a larger enclosure. Space was not found to regulate numbers. (Courtesy H. H. Swanson)

FIGURE 10-33 Male adult wild rats, *Rattus norvegicus,* in a clash. An intruder under attack may collapse and die in the absence of wounds. Here the attacker, but not the defender, has raised hair and ears. (W. E. Hocking)

10-34). These live in peaceful family groups in the forests of southeast Asia. They are active during the day. Adults attack strange conspecifics of the same sex. Males were trapped and kept alone for three months. Encounters were then staged between a male in his cage and an intruding male. The resident attacked the newcomer, but the newcomer did not fight back. The victim of such attack, if exposed for long, died; but there was no obvious cause of death. A syndrome of changes occurs in attacked animals. There is loss of weight and low liver glycogen but normal blood sugar; there are pathological changes in the kidneys, of a kind associated also with severe infection; and the adrenal glands are greatly enlarged. A similar syndrome had already been observed in wild rats (reviewed by S. A. Barnett, 1975).

Before wild rats and tree shrews had been closely studied experimentally, there had been re-

FIGURE 10-34 The tree shrew, *Tupaia belangeri.* On left, in a relaxed state; on right, in an apotreptic encounter, with raised hairs on the tail. (Courtesy D. von Holst)

ports of sudden, unexplained death among small mammals in natural conditions. The word "shock" was used in the early descriptions; but such an expression explains nothing. The most prominent physiological hypothesis concerning social stress centered on changes observed in the adrenal glands (figure 10-35). The adrenals respond to a number of injurious conditions by increased secretion of steroid hormones from the cortex, and—if the condition persists—by cortical enlargement. Such changes are observed on exposure to severe cold, infectious illness, poisoning, burns, and even forced exercise. These are sometimes called "stressors"; and the adrenal response is regarded as a means by which the body resists their effects. The bodily response is often named "stress".

Attack by a conspecific can produce an apparently identical adrenal response (figure 10-36). Yet there is no evidence that this response helps the attacked animal: extra adrenal secretion and enlargement of the gland have been proposed as indices of the severity of the "stress" (reviewed by J. J. Christian and others), but they are not held to reflect an adaptive response by the animal. This anomaly has still to be resolved.

An unanswered question concerns the scope of such changes in natural populations. The review by Christian and his colleagues gives examples of crowded rodent populations, some in the laboratory and some in the field, in which adrenal enlargement appears to be correlated with density and so with the intensity of social interactions, but there are many contradictory findings (reviewed by C. J. Krebs & J. H. Myers). Wild house mice, *Mus musculus,* have been studied on an island by W. Z. Lidicker; they were initially at a high density, but declined to extinction without any sign of extra adrenal activity. The European rabbit, *Oryctolagus cuniculus,* the rice rat, *Oryzomys palustris,* and the white-footed mouse, *Peromyscus*

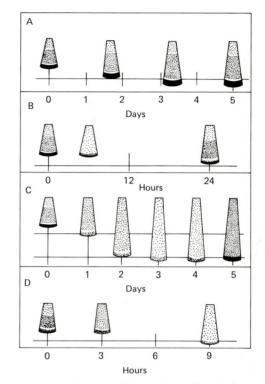

FIGURE 10-35 Diagrams illustrating adrenal responses to adverse conditions. Each section shows a portion of the adrenal cortex, with its three zones (the outer glomerulosa, the fasciculata, and the inner reticularis). The appearance is that seen after treatment with a fat soluble stain to show cholesterol. (A) Hypertrophy due to gradual environmental change. (B) Depletion and recovery after a sudden, brief exposure to adverse conditions. (C) The effect of more severe conditions. (D) Failure to recover. (After G. & M. A. Sayers, 1948)

leucopus, have all provided examples of failure to conform with the hypothesis (reviewed by S. A. Barnett, 1975). A vole, *Microtus pennsylvanicus,* which has a cycle of numbers with a peak every three or four years, has been studied by L. P. To & R. H. Tamarin: high population densities were not accompanied by changes in adrenal weights.

Much of the published work in this field is con-

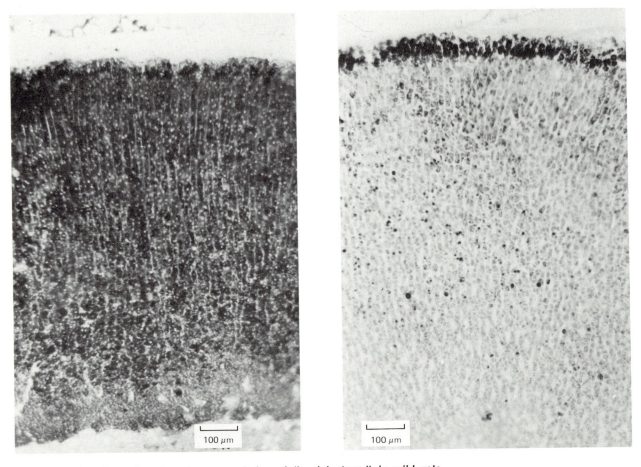

FIGURE 10-36 The adrenal cortex as an index of "social stress" in wild rats. (See figure 10-35.) On left, part of a section of the gland of a control male. The heavy staining (with Sudan black) indicates the presence of much cholesterol, a hormone precursor. The medulla (below), and the nuclei of the cortical cells, are unstained. On right, similarly treated gland of a male that had died, though unwounded, after being under attack for 14 h. The adrenals, removed at once, had lost most of the cholesterol in the zonae fasciculata and reticularis. (From S. A. Barnett, 1958b)

cerned exclusively with the ill effects of social interactions. Yet many of the species studied tolerate high population densities. Moreover, some tend to associate closely together even when there is space to spread out (figure 10-37). The question then arises whether we should also study "social sedation"—that is, the *favorable* physiological effects of contact with conspecifics.

So far little on these lines has been attempted with wild-type mammals, but B. Anderson and others have made a relevant observation on pigtail monkeys, *Macaca nemestrina,* in captivity. Each group had a number of adult females (from 6 to 15); most included several young; and all except one had one adult male. Each group was observed both in a single room of about 7 m² floor space and in a pair of rooms providing double that. Apotreptic acts such as hitting another monkey, pushing, biting, barking, and the open-mouth grimace were recorded for sample periods. Contrary to the experimenters' expectations, such acts were fewer in the more crowded condition. These authors review other findings on the effects of crowding, including some on children, which conform with theirs. Although nearly everything remains to be learned in this area, enough is known to warn us against facile presumptions.

The phenomena of social stress among mammals are summarized in table 10-1. Despite many obscurities, they illustrate important problems of method. (1) Social stress is a clear example of a behavioral phenomenon that demands physiological analysis. Debility and death may result from social interactions in the absence of any obvious pathological changes. A satisfactory explanation depends on knowing the underlying physiology.

TABLE 10-1 Apotreptic conduct: some causes and effects

	Threatener	**Threatened**
Causes	Internal states (hormonal and other) External stimuli (such as approach by a stranger)	Approach Exploration
Effects	Shorter latency of threat Raised intensity of threat Enlarged adrenals?	Flight; "submission" Enlarged adrenals Renal & gastric pathology Death

FIGURE 10-37 Wild rats, *Rattus norvegicus,* tend to crowd together, especially when sleeping, even if there is space to spread out. (S. A. Barnett)

This is true even though the phenomena would, in a human context, usually be classified as "psychological" rather than "physical". (2) It is obviously important to know what happens to animals in their natural surroundings; but what we learn from work in the field often consists only of correlations: for example, adrenal weights may rise in spring, when apotreptic behavior is also at a maximum. Unfortunately, sexual behavior and breeding also occur at this time; and there are changes of weather. Correlations may be important in suggesting hypotheses, but they do not demonstrate causal relationships. (3) Hence there is need for rigorously controlled laboratory experiments, in which—as far as possible—single factors are altered while all else is kept constant. When such experiments produce clear results, there is, however, still the problem of relating them to what happens in nature. In general, progress is most likely when field and laboratory observations go hand in hand. (4) Lastly, we always look for laws of high generality: we should like to be able to say something decisive about social stress which is applicable at least to all mammals. But we are always faced with variation between species; this may account for some of the inconsistencies in the findings on adrenal weights at different population densities.

10.5.2 Human Applications?

Research on social stress has attracted interest for its possible relevance to human problems. Here, too, there are important questions of method. Some writers seem to assume that if voles or even laboratory rats develop ills as a result of crowding, then people must be expected to do so too. I need not dwell on such absurdities. The important question is: what rational use have findings on animal populations for students of human society? In this as in other fields, the answer is that they can suggest testable hypotheses (14.2.1). And a number of workers in the social sciences have used them in just this way (reviewed by J. L. Freedman, 1975, 1978).

There have been formal experimental tests of the effects of crowding. When young American adults have been assembled for short periods in groups of different sizes and in rooms of different dimensions, no evidence of any effect on competitive or punishing behavior has emerged.

Most hypotheses about human crowding have, however, been concerned with supposed effects of continuous experience of crowding as a result of living in cities. Among the notions proposed is that of "urban malaise". Such an expression does not tell one what should be measured. Since the subjects of investigation are human, it is of course possible to ask them how they feel. When this is done in an elaborate way, by means of questionaries designed to assess attitudes, no evidence of an urban malaise is found. Similarly, a careful study of the effects of crowding in Chicago on "physical" health revealed no effects of density (R. M. Factor & I. Waldron).

Crowding has sometimes been supposed to promote crime, especially crimes of violence. One of the problems is that of measuring crowding. Freedman and his colleagues used two measures—the mean number of persons in a given residential area, and the mean number of persons to a room in all households in the area. A second problem arises when the degree of crowding is found, on a simple calculation, to be positively correlated with, say, the incidence of robbery. Such a finding does not demonstrate a causal relationship. The next step is to examine correlations with other measures, such as income. When this is done, crime rates are found to be correlated with poverty and similar factors, but not with population density itself, as measured in either of the ways described.

In New York City a very detailed analysis was made of the incidence of juvenile delinquency. It was possible to compare large numbers of neighborhoods, each with the same density but varying in other respects such as income and national or cultural origin ("ethnicity"). Crowding proved to be either unrelated to delinquency or *negatively* correlated with it.

If population density in itself is not a significant factor, perhaps there are important differences in the quality of urban life. How is this to be measured objectively? J. Passmore has proposed an index of suspicion, based on the percentage of houses or cars left unlocked, on the types of locks on doors, and on the ownership of fire arms. This suggestion at least illustrates the problems of measurement faced by social scientists.

A possible test of the quality of urban life is the incidence of mental illness. A. Robertson gives a critical review. There is first the question of identifying mental illness: definitions vary; and in practice, to estimate the incidence of such illness in a community, it may be necessary to count only those who seek psychiatric treatment: such people may not make a representative sample of all those who would, on other grounds, be regarded as mentally sick. Another kind of difficulty arises from the high incidence of schizophrenia in the poorest areas of large cities. It might be supposed that conditions in such areas induce this severe form of insanity; but probably people who develop this condition tend to drift into such areas.

Robertson, having uttered these warnings, discusses a hypothesis: that certain features of the urban environment have ill effects. The features are the size of the population, its density, and its heterogeneity. These are held to lead to fewer helpful personal relationships; in addition, work and home life are separated; and there are few clear standards of conduct, that is, of moral principles or conventional manners. In such conditions, it is hypothesized, breakdowns should be exceptionally frequent.

At the other extreme we have rural communities in which everybody has a role and plenty of support from neighbors, and in which there is a generally accepted set of religious and moral principles. Among such communities, the Hutterites, an isolated and highly organized Christian community in northwestern United States and Canada, provide an example. They, and other such communities, have an incidence of psychiatric disorder similar to that of urban populations. Indeed, the incidence of psychosis (or madness) among them is higher than it is in a Baltimore slum. Cohesive rural communities are, however, more tolerant of mental illness; and the recovery rate among them is higher than in urban communities. Robertson suggests that all populations have a similar proportion of people "predisposed" to mental breakdown, but severe social disorganization can increase the proportion of people with mental illness. He considers analogies with other species to be useless for enquiries of this sort.

Even the physiological changes of "social stress" are difficult to measure; and they are still more difficult to interpret (reviewed by Ciba Foundation; L. Levi; V. Reynolds, 1976; G. Serban). For an example I turn from crowding to a form of "stress" that might be held to be much more severe—that of war. The work of P. G. Bourne begins with the notion that the adrenal hormones provide a measure of something called stress. His specific questions were on the relationship between adrenal cortical secretion and experience in war. One hypothesis was that exposure to severe danger, such as flying combat missions, would be accompanied by a rise in the output of adrenal cortical hormones. In fact, this was not found. Moreover, the mean level of output of these hormones, whether the subjects were in combat or not, was lower than that predicted. The men are described as having adapted themselves to their situation by developing attitudes of fatalism, and by using mascots or other superstitious devices. Hence this research, as is usual in studies of human behavior, had to allow for phenomena that have no counterpart in other species. Once again, researchers on animals had suggested useful hypotheses; but simple extrapolations from animals to man proved to be inappropriate.

Lastly, there is the possibility of favorable or welcome effects of crowding. Anthropologists have described how people of some groups, with the simplest of technologies, crowd themselves together when they could easily spread themselves out. An extreme case is that of the San people of the Kalahari desert, described by P. Draper. These gatherer-hunters, in the whole of their inhospitable environment, have a population density of about one person in 26 km². But in their camps they huddle so closely together that each has only about 17 m² of personal space (or about half the minimum recommended in the United States). Each group is separated from neighboring groups by distances of 24 km or more.

The liking of people for crowds when they wish to relax is familiar. There may be scope for research on the stressful effects of visiting holiday resorts; but some workers have instead emphasized the adverse effects of a solitary existence. As usual, there are great problems in deciding on what to measure. S. D. Webb & J. Collette made a survey of the use of tranquilizing drugs in urban New Zealand. The use of the drugs was treated as an index of stress. They conclude that crowding is

negatively correlated with stress in this sense. A survey of murder and assault in cities of the United States, made by J. D. McCarthy and his colleagues, has led to the conclusion that isolation is a more serious problem than overcrowding in modern cities.

In general, social scientists who based their hypotheses on the alleged ill effects of crowding in animal communities have not had their predictions confirmed. This does not invalidate their procedure. Their findings give evidence on the factors that influence illness and crime, at least in the large and important communities that they studied. To achieve these results, they have been obliged to design elaborate methods of enquiry and of quantitative analysis.

10.6 "AGGRESSION"

10.6.1 A Case of Confusion

Much of the conduct described in this and the preceding chapter is conventionally called aggressive. Unfortunately, "aggression" has been used to name so many activities (table 10-2), that it has almost come to cover all social responses (and some that are not social). The statement that a word is ambiguous, or has many meanings, may be dismissed as merely a matter of semantics. Sometimes this is justified. If two bird watchers use the name "robin" for quite different birds, confusion may be quickly resolved by pointing out that one is *Erithacus rubecula* (the European robin) while the other is *Turdus migratorius* (the American robin). But the present case is not so simple. The diverse meanings of aggression have led some writers to say that there are many *kinds of aggression*. If I say that there are many kinds of insect, I refer to a clearly defined category of organisms, of which there are indeed many species. Or, to take a more abstract

TABLE 10-2 Some meanings of "aggression"

NONHUMAN

Signals that lead to withdrawal by conspecific:
    territorial (including those of female with young)
    maintenance of status
    female weaning young
Male controlling a female's movements
Injuring or killing conspecific
[Predation]

HUMAN

Individual	Group
Murder	Rioting
Assault	Revolution
Assault without battery	War
(verbal abuse . . .)	
Dominating behavior	
Assertiveness	
[Hunting other species]	[Hunting other species]

example, I may say there are several kinds of mating system; I am then referring to a distinct class of social interactions. But there is no well-defined category of relationships to match all the usages of "aggression": consequently, the use of the word may imply that two kinds of behavior are similar, in either their causation or their function, when they are, in fact, quite different.

Some writers urge (and other writers take for granted) that "aggression" should be confined to acts done with the *intention to hurt*. It is, however, often difficult or impossible to say what an animal *intends*. We sometimes know that an animal will persist in an activity until another goes away; but what we then observe are the effects of the activity and of the response to it, not its causes inside the actor. Moreover, much of the activity often called aggressive consists of harmless displays that tend to cause withdrawal. For instance, U. Nagel & H. Kummer tabulate studies of "agonistic" interactions among cercopithecoids (baboons, langurs,

macaques): they find few examples of wounding, and write: "aggression in animals is primarily a way of competition, not of destruction." And they add: "aggressive episodes rarely inflict damage . . . under natural conditions."

Here are two definitions which show further how confusing serious research writings are on this subject. Roger Ulrich and others write: "For purposes of laboratory and naturalistic observation . . . , aggression may be defined as behavior associated with the presentation of aversive stimulation to another organism." This form of words is vague and could be interpreted as covering rather diverse activities, from predation to an apotreptic display. The writers say that injury is not a necessary feature of the behavior defined. The second definition, proposed by O. J. Andy & H. Stephan, is even more vague: "Aggressive behavior may be defined as a sensorimotor response integrated as an emotional drive to attack." These authors seem to be attempting a definition in terms of physiology, but they do not specify any distinct kind of behavioral or physiological events. These examples are far from covering the whole range of meanings. Marc Bekoff (1977b) remarks that some writers even use the term "aggressive" as a synonym for "dominant".

Among more particular confusions, two are especially obvious: one concerns attack, the other, defense.

1. Predation is often called aggression. I therefore summarize the four major differences between predation and apotreptic conduct.

First, in predation two species are involved, the predator and the prey (3.1). In contrast, most of the other conduct called aggressive comes under apotreptic conduct: it is within species. Admittedly, cannibalism may be regarded as both social and predatory; but, although some human beings are—on tenuous evidence—said to be cannibals (W. Arens), it is rare for animals to kill and eat their own kind.

Second, the main effect of predation on the prey is death. In contrast, it is quite unusual for social interactions to be fatal.

Third, the function of predation is to supply the predator with food. Rather obviously, it has no direct survival value for the prey. In contrast, as we know, apotreptic behavior may be regarded as cooperative.

Fourth, there are species of which the movements of both predation and apotrepsis have been recorded in detail. One is the domestic cat. B. Kaada, in a review, contrasts the stalking attack (a predatory act) with what he calls the defense reaction. In the former the animal creeps forward slowly, and then jumps on to the prey and bites, usually the neck; the pupils are normal, and the hair is not raised. The defense reaction occurs during an apotreptic encounter: the head is retracted, the ears are flattened, the pupils are dilated and the hair is raised. (Figure 10-38 gives an example from another species.) The animal growls or hisses and may strike with the forelimbs without making contact with the opponent. Kaada also reviews the different neurophysiological features of the two behavior patterns. The apotreptic sequence can be induced by electrical stimulation of the posterior region of the hypothalamus. Such stimulation does not provoke attack of the predatory kind. Similarly, the endocrine basis of the two patterns is different (reviewed by K. E. Moyer): the apotreptic behavior of a mammal usually depends on the presence of male hormone in the blood; it can be reduced by castration, which cuts off the supply of the hormone, or raised by giving testosterone. But testosterone does not enhance predatory behavior.

FIGURE 10-38 Appearance of a tiger, *Felis pardus,* during an apotreptic encounter. (Zoological Society of London)

2. When we talk of aggression colloquially, we usually refer to an unprovoked or lawless attack or threat. But in animal conduct apotreptic interactions are rarely either unprovoked or lawless: they are performed in specific situations, such as the approach of an intruder on the actor's territory.

In human affairs an unwelcome intrusion may be regarded as a case of aggression—or, at least, of transgression; but in some writings on animals it is the behavior of the resident, or defender, that is casually called aggressive. There are two main kinds of defense; one is against conspecifics, and is usually related to territory or status; the other is against predators. They may be quite distinct, as they are for the domestic cat (described above). O. A. E. Rasa (1969) describes an example in her study of a fish, *Pomacentrus jenkinsi*. This omnivorous inhabitant of Hawaiian reefs maintains permanent feeding territories, in each of which is a hole or crevice. It has spines on its opercula. Apotreptic conduct includes tail beating, a lateral display, biting, and also two less common features: the eyes darken from their usual pale yellow, and each fish scrapes its spines on the head of the other while swimming backward. But when other species approach, they are darted at but rarely bitten, and the eyes remain yellow.

For all these reasons, the words "aggression" or "aggressive" are not used in this book, except in reference to the writings of others. Unambiguous accounts of social behavior, and of its causes and its effects, need to state clearly just what activities are being discussed, and to avoid words with many meanings.

10.6.2 A Nonmoral Question

In the preceding section I refer to the harmless character of many apotreptic displays. This book contains a number of descriptions of intolerant social behavior, taken from the work of meticulous observers, most of whom remark that serious injury is rarely, if ever, inflicted on conspecifics. There are, of course, exceptions. Among the insects the best known is the killing of drones by worker bees at the beginning of winter; the function of this slaughter is presumably to avoid wasting resources, during a time of scarcity, on these *bouches inutiles*. I mention above the case of infanticide by lions (10.3.2). Infanticide has also been described among Primates (W. Angst & D. Thommen). The langurs, *Presbytis entellus,* of north India, (figure 10-39) live in troops each with a status system. Sometimes, the most dominant male dies or is displaced by an intruding male. Y. Sugiyama has described how the intruder, on becoming dominant himself, may kill all the infants in his adopted troop.

The attempt to give a balanced account of such phenomena encounters at least two difficulties. One, discussed in the next chapter, is the effect on the social behavior, especially of Primates, of human interference: crowding in captivity, or exceptional population density in man-made environments, can produce social disruption. The other difficulty is the confusion with human morality or depravity. In the modern period, but before the second half of this century, much emphasis was put on competition among the members of groups or populations. I. S. Bernstein & T. P. Gordon have reviewed the literature in which apparently hostile interactions were thought to represent competition for space, food, or females. Such conduct, we know, occurs in human communities. Serious injury was sometimes assumed to be a common outcome of such strife. In contrast, N. Tinbergen (1951), in the founding work on modern ethology, describes "fighting" among animals as usually consisting of "threatening or bluff"; and he expresses

FIGURE 10-39 Group of female langurs, *Presbytis entellus,* with young. Despite the normally peaceful social existence of these animals, systematic infanticide sometimes occurs. (S. B. Hrdy, Anthro-Photo)

astonishment that "real fighting" is seldom observed.

Some writers seem to disagree. E. O. Wilson (1975) states that "murder" and "cannibalism" are commonplace among the vertebrates. He gives the example of the lions, and another from hyenas, *Crocuta crocuta.* He also refers to accounts of captive groups, and to instances of infanticide by gulls (Laridae). His book describes the social lives of a large number of vertebrate species, most of which contradict his thesis of murder and cannibalism.

Authentic knowledge in this field illustrates cer-

tain general biological principles. One is the diversity of species and their behavior. A second is the theory of natural selection, which gives us a rational, though hypothetical, explanation of that diversity in terms of events in the remote past (chapter 18). Infanticide by langurs or lions may be accounted for, in principle, in exactly the same way as apparently self-sacrificing behavior (miscalled "altruism"), such as we seem to observe when a parent risks its life in defense of its young. The crucial questions concern the survival value of genotypes (chapter 18). Given the existence of genetical variation in behavior, what pattern of co-operation or conflict will most favor survival? Moral principles are irrelevant to such questions. Zoological analogs of murder or cannibalism sometimes evidently improve the chances of survival of the "murderer's" descendants. This conclusion has no bearing on what we advocate or oppose in human communities.

10.6.3 A Question of "Drive"

10.6.3.1 Animals: Another matter of debate is the concept of an aggressive drive. In chapter 4 I give examples of behavior performed with increasing readiness or intensity as a deficit develops. The readiness with which an animal eats or drinks alters progressively with deprivation, and so we may speak of a build-up of hunger or thirst. It is easy to see how survival depends on such fluctuations.

The same does not apply to apotreptic behavior. One would expect a priori that a territorial display or an assertion of dominance would occur only when a rival appears. If there were an "aggressive drive" that had to be satisfied, a male deprived of other males as objects of deterrent display might turn on his consort or young and drive them out. But the important question is, of course, what is revealed by actual observation or experiment.

There are first the changes in conduct that occur at sexual maturity and at the time of breeding. Territorial activities are usually confined to adults. In some species they also fluctuate regularly: they may occur only in the breeding season. Accordingly, some people say that there is an "aggressive drive" only at certain times; but to say this is only to repeat that apotreptic behavior occurs at those times: no information is added by talking about a "drive". This is not only a matter of logic: it is also relevant to empirical findings. R. M. Rose and

others discuss the role of androgenic hormones in the "aggressive" behavior of Primates. Plasma testosterone rises, sometimes from zero, at puberty; and it goes up still further during the breeding season. If a male Primate loses status (as a result of defeat in an encounter with another male), his testosterone level declines. Behavioral interactions then determine androgen level, not the other way round. (But, as these authors show, this does not apply to rodents.) The internal springs of behavior must be analyzed in terms of features that can be measured, not of unanalyzable drives. The results are then sometimes unexpected.

Our primary question is, however, not whether there is *fluctuation* in a particular activity, but whether it is—to repeat—*evoked more readily with deprivation*. As a corollary, we may ask whether animals ever search for opponents in the same sense as they search for prey. There have been a number of statements on this subject not based on evidence. That of K. Z. Lorenz (1966) is often quoted. He puts forward a cathartic theory, according to which expressing "aggression" discharges tension and thereby gives relief to the performer. The anthropomorphic character of this notion is obvious: it is a case of projecting human feelings onto other species. (Such ideas are discussed in another context in chapter 15.) The question now is whether relevant experimental evidence exists.

In fact, there are few good examples, partly because the design of experiments presents difficulties. There are at least two important questions of method.

1. It is necessary to control for habituation (5.2). Suppose an animal encounters and threatens an opponent, and suppose the rate of the threatening (say, in each minute) falls off as the

exposure is prolonged. After a period of rest, the threatener is exposed again; its rate of threatening is found to be now partly or wholly restored; and the degree to which it is restored is proportional to the duration of the rest period. Such a change comes under the heading of habituation: it is not a case of deprivation leading to enhanced responsiveness. H. V. S. & S. C. Peeke give examples, from the three-spined stickleback among others. They suggest that habituation "is the major process involved in the reduction of aggressive behavior between neighboring territorial conspecifics."

2. The other problem of method arises from experiments, mainly on laboratory mice or rats, in which adults (usually males) are kept in complete social isolation for some weeks. They are then exposed to conspecifics, which they attack. Does this represent a "build up of drive"? These species, in natural conditions, live in groups. Isolation is a gross departure from their normal state; it induces a number of changes, including skin lesions, enlarged adrenal glands, lowered resistance to poisoning and others (reviewed by S. A. Barnett, 1975). These findings are of interest in themselves; but it is clearly unsafe to draw conclusions about the normal behavior of the wild type from the conduct of domesticated animals in a diseased state.

Among the animals that have been supposed to display a "buildup of aggressive drive" are fish, especially of the family Cichlidae. W. Heiligenberg has reviewed his own work and that of others. In some experiments, isolation has again been used. Male *Pelmatochromis kribensis* have been kept alone for many weeks. The hypothesis tested was that they would then attack conspecifics with exceptional vigor. In fact, they hardly attacked at all. But in this case too the use of isolation could be criticized. In experiments on *Haplochromis burtoni,* Heiligenberg used a different procedure. His fish were not totally isolated, but were each kept for many weeks with 10 young cichlids of another species. These small fish evoke attack just as conspecifics do; and the intensity with which they are attacked corresponds closely to the intensity of attacks on conspecific rivals. The apotreptic behavior consists of a rapid lunge, which may end in biting; but the bite is usually avoided. Model fish were presented to the experimental animals on a series of occasions. This species has a black bar (figure 10-40) which points down and forward from the eye. One model had the bar in its normal position, another had it at right angles to the normal, that is, pointing down and back. Repeated presentations of the "correct" model led, as the figure shows, to a progressive *increase* in the attack rate, whereas the inaccurate model had no such effect. Other activities, such as cleaning the body surface and courting, were unchanged by exposure to either model. Hence, once again, experimental findings were the opposite of those predicted by the drive hypothesis.

A further example from the cichlids comes from the work of T. E. Deiker & D. R. Hoffeld on *Cichlasoma nigrofasciatum.* The territorial conduct of these fish includes (1) a full frontal display with erect opercula, (2) a flank presentation, head-to-tail, accompanied by lateral thrusts with the caudal fin, and (3) mouth fighting with locked jaws. The question asked was whether preventing the first type of conduct by surgically fastening the opercula would cause a "buildup of drive" and hence an increase in mouth fighting. In fact, sewing up the opercula led to delayed or diminished attack. Once again, the hypothesis was not confirmed.

As a last example in this section, I return to wild rats, *Rattus norvegicus.* When my colleagues

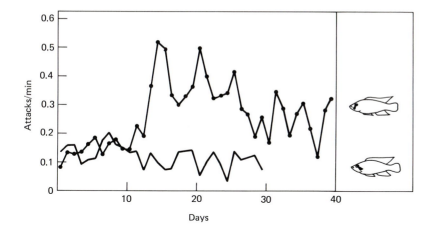

FIGURE 10-40 Increase in the attack rate of *Haplochromis burtoni* on repeated presentation of a model with the eye bar in its natural position (upper graph). There was no such increase when the model had an eye bar at the wrong angle (lower graph). Increase of the tendency to threaten or attack with experience of doing so is often found. It contradicts the notion of a "buildup" of "attack drive" which has to be "discharged". (After W. Heiligenberg and U. Kramer, 1972)

and I wish to ensure that a male will regularly attack an intruder, we expose the male to repeated intrusions by strange males. This procedure often leads to an increase in the time spent on threat and attack. It does not result in a decline. There is immense individual variation, but it has been possible to provide quantitative evidence of the change (S. A. Barnett and others, 1968). Such a change resembles the development of a habit, and is the opposite of that predicted by the drive hypothesis.

10.6.3.2 Human Beings:
Despite the findings from animal studies, the notion that, in human relationships, tension can be discharged by aggression has often been taken for granted. J. E. Hokanson remarks that a hydraulic notion of something pressing to be discharged pervades the social sciences "to a rather amazing degree". Such a concept of catharsis, partly as a result of the influence of psychoanalysis, has come to be a commonplace among laymen. It has, however, rarely been tested; but Hokanson's work provides an exception (Hokanson, 1970; Hokanson and others, 1968).

In some of his experiments the experimenter gives "aversive stimulation" (shock) to the subjects; in others, the experimenter harrasses and insults his victims. The accompanying changes in blood pressure and heart rate are recorded. Sometimes the findings correspond to the catharsis hypothesis. When a shock is administered, the result is usually a rapid vasoconstriction, with a maximum at 5 s after the shock. If the subject makes a counterresponse against the experimenter, there is a correspondingly rapid recovery. This counterresponse Hokanson calls "aggressive"; others might call it defensive. But not all Hokanson's subjects responded in an aggressive-defensive way: some made a friendly response; and this, too, was accompanied by a rapid recovery of blood pressure and heart rate. Such friendly responses were usual among women, but not men. Nonetheless, women could be trained to be "aggressive" by rewarding them with avoidance of shock when they made a violent retort.

In other experiments, it proved to be possible to train people to give themselves shock: in other words, they were trained to be masochistic. Important findings concern the effects of the details of the social situation. Sometimes the subjects (who were, of course, students) believed the person who was insulting them to be a member of the university faculty; a violent verbal retort did not then produce the expected decline in blood pressure. Hokanson's conclusion is this: "Only when aggression is learned as . . . instrumental behavior towards a . . . target . . . does it acquire tension-reducing concomitants." Both friendly and self-punishing conduct can produce a relief of "tension": in fact, as might be expected, the response depends on attitudes and habits individually acquired in a social setting, and the human situation involves many complexities not found in other species.

We return to this theme in chapters 14 and 15. The next chapter gives findings on the social interactions of Primates, and ends with a summing up on social ethology.

PRIMATE GROUPS

I confess freely to you, I could
never look long upon a monkey,
without very mortifying reflections.
William Congreve

11.1 THE PECULIARITIES OF PRIMATES

Until the second half of the 20th century, the Primates had hardly been studied scientifically in natural conditions. Splendid travelers' tales existed in abundance (1.2), often illustrated by imaginative drawings; but these tell us more about the travelers than about the animals. Now, in a quarter of a century, the study of the Primates, like that of the eusocial insects, has become a subject with its own special features and problems, and its own journals.

Primates differ from other mammals in the importance of vision in guiding their movements. Most Primates are also highly dexterous and have exceptionally large brains. These features are evidently related to the origin of the order as a tree-living group. But the Primates have radiated out in various directions, and not all are now arboreal. In addition, most Primates live, throughout their lives, in well-defined social groups. Social relationships are maintained by elaborate systems of visible and audible signals. Moreover, they have special capacities for social learning (8.3; 8.4.2).

Early scientific observations of Primate conduct were of captive animals in quite atypical conditions, or of monkeys at liberty but in man-made environments. The most celebrated captives were the baboons, *Papio hamadryas*, described by Solly Zuckerman in 1932. These animals, forced into an arbitrary group in a compound in the London Zoo, behaved with great violence to each other. Some people assumed that these were natural relationships, although they included incessant sexual activity, fighting for females, and much injurious conflict.

This genus in its natural habitat presents a quite different picture (figure 11-1). T. E. Rowell (1967) has made a quantitative comparison of a *P. anubis* group held in captivity with one living in freedom in a forested region of Uganda. Interactions were of the same kinds in both groups, but were about four times as frequent among the captive animals; those of approach and withdrawal were especially intense. The captives formed a straight-line rank order, but in the free group there was no clear evidence of status.

FIGURE 11-1 Yellow baboons, *Papio cynocephalus*. In natural conditions the interactions of these sociable animals are quiet and, in human terms, friendly. In this muzzle–muzzle contact, one may be getting information about food from another; but the gesture may be purely social and not related to feeding. (Courtesy S. A. Altmann)

Fortunately, there are now detailed descriptions of the conduct of several species in their usual environments.

11.2 SOME CASE HISTORIES

11.2.1 Titi Monkeys and Gibbons

We begin with two species, widely separated taxonomically, of which the groups consist each of a monogamous pair with their young. *Callicebus mo-*

loch, the dusky titi, a South American monkey, has been studied in thick forest in Colombia (W. A. Mason, 1971). It is a small Primate, weighing 600 g or less; and it lives in conveniently dense populations in which each group occupies a territory of around 50 m in diameter. The members of a group live and move close together. When still, they keep literally in touch, notably by each of a pair twining its tail round that of the other. Contact is also maintained during territorial interactions: two or more groups regularly meet the occupants of adjoining territories at a boundary between them, usually in the early morning. The adult male and female of each group sit in contact, a few meters from the other pair. There is an exchange of complex noises accompanied by visible displays. Contact may be broken for brief chases. Mason observed no injurious clashes.

The formation of pairs has been observed in captivity in large enclosures. The first approaches are gradual and tentative; but, once an association between a male and a female has been established, it is evidently permanent. The young titi, like other Primates, is at first very dependent, and is carried during most of the day by the male. Such paternal behavior, as T. H. Clutton-Brock & P. H. Harvey

(1976) point out, occurs also among marmosets, *Callithrix jaccus,* siamangs, *Symphalangus syndactylus,* and others, all of which are monogamous. The family life of marmosets, in particular, has been closely studied by J. C. Ingram. Not only do both parents care for the young, but older siblings may carry infants (figure 11-2), as do human children.

A further example of the "nuclear family" is provided by the gibbons (Hylobatidae), which belong among the great apes, and include the siamangs. The forest-living white-handed gibbon, *Hylobates lar,* of Southeast Asia, is highly arboreal (figure 11-3). The sexes are similar, and both males and females may weigh as much as 8 kg. Their conduct has been described by C. R. Car-

FIGURE 11-2 Marmosets, *Callithrix jaccus:* an immature male carries two younger siblings. (Courtesy Jennifer Ingram)

FIGURE 11-3 White-handed gibbon, *Hylobates lar:* female with young. (New York Zoological Society)

penter (1964) and by J. O. Ellefson. Each group, consisting of a male and female and not more than four young, occupies a territory of 100 ha or more.

Again, these are very vocal animals. Almost every day begins with loud calls from the female. The "song" lasts for about 20 s, and is repeated relentlessly for about 15 min. It consists of a series of rising hoots, and can be heard over several kilometers. These calls are evidently not deterrent, but bring the members of neighboring families together. Moreover, adult males may move several hundred meters to watch two groups interacting.

This effect of loud calls is worth emphasizing, for it is in contrast with what is observed among the howler monkeys, *Alouatta,* of Central and South America, also described by Carpenter (1965). These monkeys, too, are large: the males often weigh more than 5 kg, and they are structurally adapted for making tremendous hooting noises, audible for many kilometers, which evidently keep neighboring groups apart.

To return to the gibbons, the males as well as the females help to look after the young. Stimulation is provided by grooming and other manipulation, and by play during which the young ape makes mock attacks on the parents. The juvenile gibbon also has an alarm call that brings rapid help from the male. At puberty the young leave their parents and presumably soon pair off.

11.2.2 Baboons and Langurs

The most-studied Primates live in assemblies larger than those of titi monkeys or gibbons. Such groups may include only one adult male and several adult females; or there may be several males.

11.2.2.1 Papio: Baboons provide examples of both. These monkeys are prominent in the plains of eastern and southern Africa, where they are much more easily watched than are forest-living species (figure 11-4). There is now extensive knowledge both of *Papio hamadryas,* of eastern Africa, and *P. anubis,* in the south. (The two types can interbreed but are usually classified in separate species.) H. Kummer (1971) has reviewed work on the hamadryas. The social unit consists of a male, several females, and young. The male is much the largest, and has a prominent grey mane that makes him look larger still. He also has conspicuous fang-like upper canines. The male "herds" the females. If a female strays, she may be brought back by a gesture; but the male may rush out and slap or bite a female that has drifted away. (This is one of the many items that have been put under the heading of "aggressive" conduct. It could also be called "proprietorial", or even "protective". But such expressions often hinder an objective analysis.) The female members of the unit may come into conflict over access to the male, especially when two females each try to groom the male at the same time. The male then evidently decides between them.

Hamadryas baboons are unusual in having three levels of social grouping. The one-male units are grouped in bands during foraging for food. These groupings are less stable than the units. The members, however, defend food sources from the intrusions of other bands. Lastly, the bands themselves assemble in still larger troops for sleeping. A favored roosting spot is a rocky cliff (figure 11-5); and if there are few such places, the troop that assembles there may be of several hundred individuals.

A troop includes separate groups of bachelor males—those that have not succeeded in collecting any females. Twenty percent of a population may consist of such celibate males. It might be thought that such a situation would lead to conflict; and certainly, if a female is released into a troop, she is quickly taken over by a male. Nonetheless, actual

FIGURE 11-4 A large troop of baboons, *Papio,* on the march. (H. Kummer, Zoologisches Institut, Zurich)

fighting, as distinct from displays with open mouth and gestures of the hands, is unusual. There are relationships of dominance and subordinacy within troops, defined in terms of access to food; but these are harmless.

The means by which the one-male units are preserved has been studied by Kummer and others. They describe interactions between members of "triads", each consisting of a male and female pair and a second male belonging to the same troop. The presence of the second male is accompanied by an increase in the intensity of the interactions of the pair. It might be thought that the larger, stronger, or more dominant male would be able to annex the female, regardless of her previous affilia-tion, but this is not observed. If a female is seen by another male to be paired, the second male refrains from making an approach. Evidently, the sight of a female interacting with a male has an inhibitory effect on a rival.

Not all baboons live in one-male units. The chacma and olive baboons (which may be classified together as *P. anubis*) assemble in multimale troops sometimes of more than 100 individuals (I. DeVore). These monkeys, too, forage over large areas of grassland. The troop is the only social unit. A male may be accompanied by a female in estrus, indicated by the swelling of the "sexual skin" around the genitalia (compare figure 13-24), but such consort pairs are only temporary. Young

FIGURE 11-5 Baboons, *Papio,* roosting on a cliff. (H. Kummer, Zoologisches Institut, Zurich)

FIGURE 11-6 Male baboon, *Papio anubis,* carries an infant on the march. (H. Kummer, Zoologisches Institut, Zurich)

infants are normally carried and even touched only by the mother; but on a long march a male may carry one and thus relieve the smaller female of a burden (figure 11-6).

If a troop is observed on the move, a casual look might detect no marching order (figure 11-4), but some observers report a regular pattern. The first scientific (but nonquantitative) accounts, which are still often cited, describe a central group of females with young, around which are the largest males; an outer zone includes juveniles, young adults, and other large males. A number of later observers have failed to see this pattern. R. S. O. Harding reviews recent work, and gives the results of 1032 h of studying olive baboons in Kenya. He compares the chances of observing particular categories of individual in the lead or in the rear with their "ex-

pected" chance based on the proportion each class makes of the total number. For example, in a troop of about 50 baboons, with 4 adult males, in 76 observations, the "expected" number of occasions on which an adult male should be in the lead is about six. But in fact, Harding saw adult males in the lead on 38 occasions. The leading group as a rule consisted of adult males, adult females, and subadult males; juveniles and infants were in the middle; and another group of adult females formed the rear section.

These findings, and others like them (cited by Harding), have general implications. The pattern originally described (by I. DeVore & S. L. Washburn) was never supported by detailed, let alone quantitative, evidence. Yet it was at first generally accepted. It now seems that, if the pattern occurs at all, it is unusual. As Harding also shows, there is much variation in group relationships. Further, DeVore and Washburn build a substantial argument on what they believed to be an invariable group structure. This structure is held to be one of several means by which baboons are protected from predators. Others include large canines and the "aggressive" tendency and size of the males, aided by the mane, which makes them look larger still. There is, however, no firm evidence that these features are primarily related to defense against predators: their importance may be social. This example illustrates the need for specific, quantitative evidence to support statements on behavior patterns; it also shows how easy it is to make plausible but inadequately supported statements on the survival value of species-typical features.

We do not know what selection processes have acted on baboons in the past; but defense by the males against predation certainly occurs. The approach of a predator, such as a leopard, *Felis pardus,* is signaled by barking. The troop sheers off, but the largest males may threaten the predator and, if they are attacked, they prove formidable opponents. When a troop approaches water, even after a long dry march, it is said that the members do not drink until the leading males have had the opportunity to detect the presence of predators.

The social differences between hamadryas and anubis are undoubtedly in part genetically determined. U. Nagel has studied the conduct of hybrids between them, in a natural environment, and found it to be either on the whole intermediate or an amalgam of the parental features. But baboons are also ontogenetically labile in important aspects of their social interactions: they are usually not predatory, but S. C. Strum has described a group of anubis in Kenya in which a tradition developed of preying on other mammals and of sharing the pro-

ceeds. In 1970–1971 predation was almost confined to the adult males, and these also ate most of the meat. In 1973 there was sharing with females and young, among whom the killing habit had also spread. Such a change in feeding habits resembles those observed among Japanese macaques (8.4.2.4).

Another kind of lability is still more important. Experiments by H. Kummer (1971) have thrown a novel light on the differences between the two species. Hamadryas males control the movements of the females attached to them, and prevent their association with other males. Anubis males do not behave in this way: the females are promiscuous, and interact much more also with other females. The obvious assumption is of genetical determination of these differences. Kummer put females of both species in hamadryas troops. All adapted themselves to the hamadryas way of life, and accepted attachment to a hamadryas male. Similarly, females of both species, put in anubis troops, all adopted the anubis mode. Hence the different genotypes of the females had in this case no observed effect on behavior: conduct was adapted to the alternative environments provided by the males of the two types. This example illustrates the fundamental principle (discussed fully in chapter 16) that the phenotype is a result of the interaction between genotype and environment: we must never assume that apparently fixed differences are genetically determined.

In *Papio* we have, then, a versatile primate genus adapted to living on the ground in open country. One species (or subspecies), the hamadryas, flourishes in the semidesert of Ethiopia; its primary social group is the one-male unit. Others form much larger permanent groups, with many adult males, and live in more fertile country. Some observers believe organization in small groups to be an adaptation for life in the arid type of habitat.

11.2.2.2 Presbytis: The hanuman langur, *Presbytis entellus,* is another monkey that occupies a variety of habitats and displays diversity in its social groupings. The langurs are tree-living, but the hanuman moves about on the ground more than the others. It has been closely observed by Phyllis Jay in the north of India, by Y. Sugiyama in the south, and by K. Yoshiba in several environments.

The single-male groups are the most often observed units in the south and resemble those of the hamadryas. They occur inland, often in rather arid conditions. The usual social unit in the north is a group with several males of different ages. The most dominant male is, as a rule, both the largest and the oldest. The reference to dominance can, however, be misleading. If one observes these monkeys, even in rather crowded conditions in a town or village, intolerant conduct is rarely seen. Phyllis Jay watched them for long periods in more open country, and describes them as "peaceful and relaxed"; much of the time each individual moves about within the group with no indication of status.

Status relationships among females are indeed always indistinct; but the males of multimale groups have a status system. Dominance is defined by displacement: one male approaches another, and the second male merely withdraws. Or one stares or slaps the ground, and again the other moves off. There are other such threats. (Remember that "threat" in this book is a signal that tends to cause withdrawal by a conspecific.) They include crouching and then suddenly standing up, biting air and turning the head, lunging, grunting, and barking. Actual clashes, which are rare, include slapping, biting, and wrestling.

The relationships of females to young (figure 11-7) are a prominent feature of langur social life. Soon after an infant is born, all the females of the group, even the juveniles, surround the mother and

FIGURE 11-7   The hanuman langur, *Presbytis entellus:* female with young. (S. A. Barnett)

try to touch or lick the infant. The infant can soon hold on even while the mother is running or jumping. In the first few hours after the birth, the female licks, grooms, and strokes the infant. Soon the other females are allowed to handle it.

There is much individual variation, among adult females, in the manner in which they manage infants; and a few are evidently quite clumsy and inept. It would be interesting to know how these differences develop. Are they influenced by early experience? (See 12.4.1.) A notable difference from baboons is that male langurs pay no attention to infants.

11.2.3 Gorillas and Chimpanzees

11.2.3.1 Gorilla berengei: We now turn to the two species nearest to man. The gorilla, *Gorilla berengei,* the largest extant Primate, may weigh more than 180 kg and sometimes reaches a height of almost 2 m. It has been closely studied by G. B. Schaller (1963) in a natural habitat. Like the langurs of northern India, it lives in social units that include several males.

Schaller lived for 18 months in mountainous wilds in Uganda and Congo, and spent long periods recording the behavior of these creatures, often at close quarters. With their shining blue-black hair and gleaming faces (figure 11-8), they are formidable creatures to meet on a jungle path. They spend 80 to 90% of their time on the ground, and their climbing, though assured, is far from attaining the brilliance of that of gibbons. They spend their days eating plants—especially those with a bitter taste. Vast amounts of this rather bulky food have to be eaten, and siestas are taken after each heavy meal. Gorillas sleep also at night.

They are not distinguished for manipulative skill in the wild. They make simple nests of branches and twigs, but do not—as far as is known—employ tools. Novel objects casually encountered in their natural habitat are ignored: they are not handled as if from "curiosity", as they would be by a chimpanzee. Perhaps the gorillas are too busy eating. They do, however, stare (disconcertingly) at a human being.

The social relationships of a gorilla group in-

FIGURE 11-8 Female mountain gorilla, *Gorilla berengei,* aged about seven years. (Courtesy Michael Gorgas)

clude a status system: in a typical group of about 20 individuals, dominance is the prerogative of the oldest (and largest) male, clearly recognizable by grey hair—on his back, not his head. Such males are called "silver-backs". There is a straight-line status system among the adult males of a troop. Females are dominant to all juveniles, but there is evidently no stable order among females. Dominance consists of possession of right of way on a narrow path, or of displacing another individual from a resting place. Females sometimes clash: they bark, scream, grapple, and bite; but, if a male then advances towards them, grunting, they stop. The dominant male does not maintain his status by violence. On the contrary, his behavior is gentle. Females lean on him, and young gambol around and on him. Nor is there evidence of sexual conflict. Coitus, as far as is known, is infrequent. It occurs in public, and all males have access to all females. There is a quite prolonged, precoital play initiated by the female.

Individuals are as recognizable as human beings, and temperament varies accordingly. Some are placid, others exictable. Some males spend much of their time alone, with occasional visits to the group.

The young gorillas are imitative, lively, and playful. Follow-the-leader and sliding down slopes are popular games. In the evening, when the troop is preparing for bed, games are stopped when a female merely glances at the young. Infants are very dependent, and are carried by the mother. They sleep with the mother for their first three years. Weaning from the breast, however, is at about eight months. The rate of development may be thought of as about twice that of man. By the age of two-and-a-half a young gorilla can keep up with the troop without assistance. Yet the attachment to the mother goes on for longer, up to four years or more.

Each troop has a restricted home range. Schaller's observations did not indicate any territorial behavior, but this may have been because all the gorillas he observed closely belonged to the same group, divided into subgroups. These subgroups (if that is what they were) met, mingled, and parted without disturbance. Or perhaps gorillas are territorial, but maintain their territories without visible or audible displays.

They have a notable system of signals, some of them highly deterrent to man at least. The sight of a strange gorilla (or a man) may evoke a terrifying roar, made more impressive still by beating of the chest with cupped hands and by the gigantic male rising to his full height. This sudden uproar startles even the gorillas of the performer's own troop. Another signal is head shaking. This is a nonbelligerent attitude. If you or I suddenly met a gorilla, we should be well advised to shake our heads from side to side and avoid looking the gorilla in the eye. This is what Schaller did: and his survival reflects the effectiveness of this conduct. He describes one head-shaking duet, with a young (but large) male, that lasted for 10 min. A further signal consists of crouching down with the limbs tucked under the body. This is performed by young during rough games, and also by females during a clash. Once an individual adopts this position, there is no further attack. There is, however, no complete account of the signals of gorillas, and still less is there knowledge of just what some of their signals do. Gorillas, like us, have complex muscles of expression: they frown, bite their lips, and make other grimaces. (They also yawn and stretch.) No doubt other gorillas are specifically influenced by these movements, but we do not know in what ways.

There are other enigmas. Among them is a stereotyped sequence of acts, of considerable violence, performed only by silver-back males. According to Schaller this terrifying performance is rarely given in its complete form. The male first sits with pursed lips and gives a series of soft, clear hoots at an increasing rate. If, at this stage, he is interrupted, he looks round as if annoyed, before continuing. The hooting may be interrupted while the male takes a leaf from a plant and puts it between his lips. At about this stage, females and young withdraw. The male next rises and rips branches or leaves off a nearby plant and throws them in the air. Now comes the alarming part: chest beating begins, with cupped hands, at the rather high rate of about 10 beats in each second. This lasts for a second or two at a time, and in the intervals the male may slap his belly, his thigh, a tree or another gorilla. He may also kick a leg high in the air. Now he begins to run, at first sideways on his hind legs, then forward on all four limbs, hitting at anything in his path quite indiscriminately. The climax is a thump on the ground with the palm of the hand. Even more remarkable than the performance of this apparently socially useless, and even dangerous, sequence, is the fact that young gorillas display components of it from the age of about four months. Females may put on similar performances, but do not hoot. Without more information it is fruitless to speculate on the significance of this behavior.

11.2.3.2 Pan troglodytes:

The other great ape, of which we have intimate descriptions, is the chimpanzee, *Pan troglodytes*. Absorbing accounts of the behavior of this creature in its normal habitat have been given by Adriaan Kortlandt and by Jane van Lawick-Goodall (1968). Chimpanzees were already known, from observations in zoos, to be enterprising and "intelligent" animals. The differences from gorillas, which they display in captivity, are even more notable in the wild. Kortlandt studied a group of 48 chimpanzees from a platform, high up in a tree, overlooking a hill in the Congo. Like gorillas, they proved to be highly terrestrial: their movements even beat paths through the forest. Kortlandt regularly observed their morning approach to a clearing: at first they were cautious; the males arrived in advance of the rest, and were heralded by faces peering from cover. In the absence of danger, the males turned to a lively dis-

play of screaming, chasing, and smacking tree trunks with their hands. This conduct is often associated with the discovery of food, and attracts other chimpanzees. The females were always silent and "shy". Like gorillas, chimpanzees perform sexual acts—normal coitus and homosexual behavior—in public, and there are no regular pairs. Jane van Lawick-Goodall saw one female accept seven males in succession, without any conflict.

Something was already known of maternal behavior, partly from observations of captive chimpanzees. Unlike the gorilla, the young chimpanzee clings to its mother as soon as it is born (figure 11-9). But it soon becomes active, and is encouraged to be so by its mother in its early weeks: she stretches its limbs by holding the infant up as if to oblige it to walk. Unlike some human mothers, she encourages climbing. The infant may learn to stand by pulling itself up on its mother. Later, it may be carried to a place where it can practice climbing. R. M. Yerkes & M. I. Tomilin describe how a juvenile chimpanzee, given such an opportunity, climbs at once (rather as a baby spontaneously crawls up stairs), then cries when at the top and is quickly rescued. Climbing down, which is more difficult, develops later. A female may encourage her young to walk by dragging it with one hand, or by crouching in front of it and calling.

Some parental restraint is also exercised, even by cuffing. In general, however, chimpanzees, at least in the wild, treat their young with tolerance and restraint: they are permitted to pester their elders; and even the older juveniles, when they play their boisterous games, avoid hurting their weaker juniors and help them out of difficulty. Kortlandt describes the young as pampered. They are sometimes fed by adults other than their parents. They ask for food by holding out a hand.

Status among chimpanzees is most evident among

FIGURE 11-9 Female chimpanzee, *Pan troglodytes*, with young. (Zoological Society of London)

males: one approaches another, and the other withdraws. Most adult males are, in this sense, dominant to most females; but among females there is a separate rank order.

Social relationships in a chimpanzee troop give, in fact, an impression of being loosely organized and casual; but this may be partly because the kinds of interaction most readily recorded by a human observer are not the most important for chimpanzees. Among these apes, perhaps as among go-

rillas also, there is much silent communication by look or gesture. The role of such signals can be determined only by experiments. E. W. Menzel studied eight chimpanzees aged about four to six years. They had been born in the wild, and were now kept in a large paddock. For the experiments, they were first put in a cage at the side of the paddock. Food was hidden, and one chimpanzee was shown its whereabouts. When, later, the others were released, they followed or even preceded the first chimpanzee; and they took a direct line to the goal. Control experiments were done in which no food was shown to the first chimpanzee. The others, when released, then moved at random about the paddock.

Sometimes there was not only hidden food, but also other food in plain view. Nonetheless, the chimpanzees went to the hidden food. The most important cue seems to have been the direction of movement of the leader and the nature of the leader's gait. Rarely, there was a wave of the head or a backward glance if the others lagged behind. In further experiments there were two lots of hidden food, one much larger than the other, and two leaders indicating different goals. The chimpanzees then mostly went to the larger quantity.

The same type of experiment was done with aversive objects, such as a model of a snake. (Chimpanzees shun not only snakes but also snake-like objects.) The behavior of the group on release was then quite different: approach was tentative, and accompanied by throwing of sticks. Again, the main indication seems to have been the leader's gait, which was hesitant. There was never evidence of specific signs, such as those of the gestural language taught to chimpanzees by experimenters (8.3).

Later observations by E. W. Menzel and S. Halperin confirmed that chimpanzees can respond to the rate at which a chimpanzee moves toward a concealed object. These authors do not exclude the use also of gestures as sources of information, for much may depend on whether the apes are (as in these experiments) known to each other; indeed, they emphasize "the ability to get across the same general message by any number of alternative means". They also show that the "purposive" movements of the leader occurred only if the others were present.

Not all signals are received at a distance: contact is also important. In greeting, chimpanzees, like people, throw their arms round each other. Mutual grooming takes up much time: two adults may spend two hours going over each other's fur. More violent forms of communication, notably screaming, are employed in emergencies, or as threats. Just as silver-back male gorillas are dominant, so old chimpanzees are too. Indeed, Kortlandt describes an elderly and enfeebled male who seemed to dominate his group despite his weakness.

Apes of all species are plant eaters; but chimpanzees are now known not only to eat insects (3.2.7), lizards, and young birds, but also occasionally to hunt other mammals, including baboons and pigs. G. Teleki has described predation by groups of chimpanzees. In the first stage a male freezes and stares at the prey, with its hair partly raised all over the body. Other males are attracted, and may join the first male in rushing the prey or in pursuing it. Sometimes, the prey is first stalked. Chimpanzees are usually noisy animals; but when hunting they become quiet. The meat is always shared with others. Sometimes a chimpanzee in possession of meat is approached by another holding out its hand; a portion may then be handed over.

Such findings have led to speculation on the origin of hunting in the evolution of apes and man. It is often assumed that, during the ascent of man, hunting began among the Australopithecinae who are held to be our ancestors of about two million years ago, and who began to make stone tools. If so, chimpanzees must have developed the hunting habit independently—which is perfectly possible. Alternatively, a common ancestor of chimpanzees and man, say, 30 million years ago, was perhaps a (part-time) predator. It is imaginable that further fossil findings will have some bearing on these questions, but the alternative hypotheses cannot be rigorously tested: speculation in this field, though enjoyable, is not a reliable basis for the analysis of human conduct (14.1.1).

To man, chimpanzees are, though not uniformly harmless, evidently even less dangerous than gorillas. On an encounter with a man, a chimpanzee usually stares, scratches, and wanders off. Jane van Lawick-Goodall (1968) has been able to live so intimately among chimpanzees, that eventually she was allowed to groom one—as if she were herself a subordinate member of the company.

11.2.4 Variation and Ecology

We already know something of the capacities of Primates for imitation, and of the traditions that can arise in quite small groups (8.4.2). Where tradition exists, a population can adapt itself to new conditions behaviorally, and retain the altered behavior over generations, in the absence of genetical change (see also 11.2.2.1). Correspondingly, some of the most-studied primate species thrive in a variety of habitats; and this versatility seems to depend in part on variations in social structure. The Indian langur, described above, is an instance. But the extent to which tradition contributes to the variation is, as yet, rarely known; often, no doubt, differences are genetically determined.

11.2.4.1 Examples of Heterogeneity: It is, however, possible to give further examples (reviewed by W. A. Mason, 1976). The black spider monkey, *Ateles paniscus,* has been observed at a variety of altitudes in the tropical forests of Central America. At about 275 m its social groups include, on average, four adult males; at 889 m there is only a single adult male in each unit. Such a finding suggests adaptation to a less favorable habitat by the formation of smaller units. It recalls the difference, already mentioned (11.2.2.1), between anubis and hamadryas baboons. Unfortunately, not all species fit this notion. J. S. Gartlan (1973) describes observations on a versatile African species, the vervet, *Cercopithecus aethiops* (figure 11-10), which ranges from the semiarid Sahel savanna, through to secondary forest bordering on lowland rain forest; the mean annual rainfall of these extreme zones is 38 and 269 mm, respectively. In the arid region the social units often include over 20 individuals but, in the forest, fewer than 10: as rainfall rises, group size declines.

This is an example of the difficulties in attempting to relate group composition in any precise way to habitat. The difficulty may arise partly from the many ways in which species vary. The number of individuals, or of males, in a social unit, though a convenient index for classifying social groups, is not necessarily correlated with other features of social organization. Gartlan takes as examples the hamadryas, on the one hand, and the closely related gelada, *Theropithecus gelada,* on the other. The latter, another much-studied African species, like the hamadryas lives in single-male units. But in other respects the two species differ substantially.

A fully adult hamadryas male, on encountering an unattached female, solicits her and, if successful, adds her to his group. And, as we know, if a female of his group strays, he brings her back. Young hamadryas males at puberty have to withdraw to a celibate existence, or "kidnap" young females in the teeth of threats from a larger male.

FIGURE 11-10 Vervet, *Cercopithecus aethiops:* a "threatening" expression. (Courtesy J. S. Gartlan)

In contrast, the subadult male gelada is at first a member of an all-male group; later he becomes associated with the young females of a harem. Eventually, he leaves, evidently to set up a new unit with several adult females. The females, it seems, are never coerced, as are hamadryas females, but themselves determine which harem they will join.

On the basis of examples of this kind, Gartlan reaches this conclusion.

Neither phylogenetic affinity (such as membership of the same genus) nor ecological similarity (such as inhabiting the same forest) is necessarily of value in predicting . . . features of social structure such as group size, adult sex ratio, or the types and frequencies of social interaction.

11.2.4.2 The Rhesus Monkey: One kind of variation in behavior, within a single species, is clearly related to habitat, and is exemplified by the rhesus monkey, *Macaca mulatta.* This, the most studied of all Primates (except *Homo*), lives in large numbers in the cities and villages and on the roadsides of India. In these conditions it depends on man for food, and often there are large numbers in a small space (figure 11-11). Temples are a favorite spot for such crowds; but the grounds of your hotel may harbor a troop; and an ethologist holding classes in animal behavior in an Indian university may be able to illustrate primate social signals simply by going out into the courtyard and looking at the macaques.

In these man-made environments, C. H. Southwick (review, 1969) and his colleagues have made a massive study of macaques' social interactions. Another source of information has been a population, originally set up in 1938 on a West Indian island, Cayo Santiago. This population was (and is) artificially fed, and has reached a higher density than would have been possible in conditions of complete independence of man. Detailed accounts have been given by S. A. Altmann, by J. H. Kaufmann (1967), and by D. S. Sade.

FIGURE 11-11 Rhesus monkeys, *Macaca mulatta:* part of a group living among buildings in Jodhpur, India. Such groups depend on man for food. (S. A. Barnett)

To interpret correctly the findings from such colonies, it is essential to allow for the effects of artificial feeding. This requires experiments. Southwick and others (1976) watched four groups of rhesus monkeys in rural habitats and four urban; all were fed by the people of the locality. Such feeding, in both types of habitat, consistently led to an increase in apotreptic conduct, especially when the food items were large, or when the food was not widely scattered. R. W. Wrangham has described similar findings in a study of the effect of giving bananas to chimpanzees and baboons. His observations were made at the famous Gombe Stream Research Centre, where Jane van Lawick-Goodall has made her studies of chimpanzees.

If, however, we had to rely on observations of groups completely independent of man, we should know little about the rhesus monkey. Southwick (1969) has described the difficulties of observing troops of rhesus that are neither accustomed to nor dependent on man. D. G. Lindburg similarly tried to watch these animals in what is probably a natural habitat in a forested region of the Himalayan foothills. The dense vegetation and the shyness of the forest groups created insuperable difficulties for a thorough study; for many of his observations, he was obliged to fall back on monkeys associated with a forest research institute.

The temple groups described by Southwick and his colleagues each included a number of adult males, a slightly larger number of adult females, and young of various ages. In contrast, the groups observed by Lindburg had a substantial majority of females. J. H. Kaufman (1967) describes large groups on Cayo Santiago. Each contained several males four years of age and of similar status. But a more usual finding is of a linear system among adult males.

A linear system emerges if records are kept of

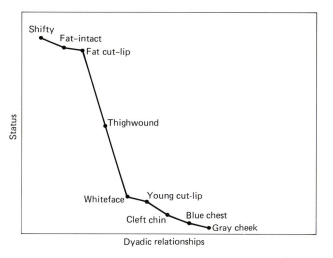

FIGURE 11-12 The status system of a group of rhesus monkeys (see figure 11-11). The name given to each monkey is shown. The most dominant was called "Shifty". Status was assessed by observing the outcome of interactions, each between two individuals (dyadic). (After C. H. Southwick, 1965)

the interactions between pairs of individuals. In a series of encounters between any two adult males, one of the two always (or nearly always) displaces the other and is said to be dominant. Such relationships are, however, by no means the whole story: they are often modified by "coalitions" or "cliques", each of two or three males. Figure 11-12 represents diagrammatically the linear order of the nine adult males of a temple group. It is based on an analysis of 119 encounters; and in only three of these did an animal displace another to which it was usually subordinate. But sometimes the tidy linear order was upset by apotreptic encounters in which more than two males were involved. As an example, the two "fat" males (the second and third in the "hierarchy") often moved, fed, and rested together. When they were associated, they dominated Shifty, the top male.

Apotreptic interactions in which one group member supplants another are diverse in form: in the principal form of threat, a tense, crouched posture is adopted; the animal stares (figure 11-13) with raised eyebrows, flattened ears, and open mouth; and it makes a repeated noise like a grunt or cough. Sometimes there are bobbing movements of the head. There may also be a lunge toward an opponent or a chase; and occasionally there is a clash in which each animal wrestles and hits or bites the other. The animal displaced most often merely withdraws. But sometimes there is a movement, described as cowering, together with a high-pitched scream; this is called a "submissive" response.

Southwick gives the following percentages, from a record of 4173 apotreptic interactions observed among roadside groups in the north of India:

threats	59.5
chases	36.4
attacks	3.7
fights	0.4

Such groups depend on man, but they are not in the most crowded conditions possible. Southwick gives figures of attack frequency and of the incidence of wounding for a number of habitats. The highest are for captive groups, especially in the first days after the group is assembled. The lowest are for forest dwellers. Groups associated with a farm or a temple are intermediate (table 11-1).

In the study of this (and other) species of Primates, there has been a great concentration of interest in apotreptic behavior; this can mislead a reader on what goes on in natural conditions. I have watched the very similar bonnet macaque, *M. radiata*, in patches of jungle near farmlands in the south of India. (A proper study of this species has been described by P. E. Simonds.) While foraging, they move slowly about, in a rather dispersed group, making very quiet grunting noises. The scene is agreeable but unexciting. Social interactions are muted. The picture is quite different from that of a troop moving about the buildings of a city, or even in spacious public gardens (where there are many people); but even in these conditions clashes are rare and brief.

The same kind of contrast is observed when one

FIGURE 11-13 Bonnet monkey, *Macaca radiata,* stops eating to present a "threatening" face to an intruder. (S. A. Barnett)

TABLE 11-1   Effect of environment on apotreptic inter-actions in groups of *Macaca mulatta* (after C. H. South-wick, 1969)

Habitat	a No. in group	b Attacks/10 h	$\frac{b}{a}$
Forest	32	0.7	0.02
University farm	12	1.1	0.09
Temple	42	4.0	0.09
Captivity	17	20.9	1.23

The number of hours of observation ranged from 30 to 110.

turns to interactions between groups. Southwick describes how three groups of rhesus monkeys, each occupying the grounds of a temple, come into noisy conflict. Sometimes there are injurious clashes. (But even these groups often merely avoid each other.) D. G. Lindburg, in his study of groups at a forest research institute, describes 41 encounters between troops; in 15, one troop merely moved off as another approached. This was at an artificial food source. More lively interactions were marked by head bobbing, staring, tree shaking, and chasing; but Lindburg observed hardly any fighting, and no injuries.

These valuable and meticulous studies of a versatile species have an unavoidable and general limitation: at best, they can only point to correlations between behavior and habitat. Only experiment can provide convincing evidence of causal relationships. I have mentioned experiments, in which the artificial feeding of rhesus, baboons, and chimpanzees increased conflict. Southwick (1966) made a detailed study of an artificial, balanced colony in Calcutta. There were four adult males and four adult females; the remainder were subadults. When the colony had settled down, apotreptic behavior was recorded in relation to a number of factors. At first, plenty of food was given, at sev-eral points in the enclosure. Later, the amount of food offered was reduced, first by 25%, later by 50%. The first reduction had little or no effect. More severe reduction led to less apotreptic and other social behavior, but (as might be expected) more exploratory activity. Food shortage had been expected to result in conflict, but this was not observed. On the other hand, when food was supplied at only one point, apotreptic interactions increased.

Two other experimental changes also increased apotreptic conduct. One was a reduction in the space available. (This is in contrast to the findings on *M. nemestrina,* described in 10.5.1.2.) The other was the introduction of newcomers to the colony. Southwick and others (1974) have further de-scribed the apotreptic response to strangers. They call this "xenophobia". They observed three rural groups in northern India and one in Calcutta. Three were large (62 to 71 individuals), but one of the rural groups numbered only 22. Twenty-three monkeys, each distinctively marked, were separately released into these groups. Except for three infants, each stranger was quickly threatened and often violently treated; most fled. This work raises the interesting question whether an apo-treptic response to strange conspecifics can be dis-tinguished from territorial conduct. Is strangeness by itself a source of conflict? At present this ques-tion cannot be answered.

Earlier work on this species had emphasized the way in which strangers rapidly form a group with a status system, and how strange individuals can be absorbed into a group after only a brief period of conflict. I. S. Bernstein (1964) cites observa-tions on the effect of putting a group of these mon-keys, strangers to each other, into an enclosure: there are at first frequent conflicts, but in all dyadic interactions one individual is consistently a sub-ordinate (in the sense of withdrawing from the other). There is, in fact, immediate establishment of status.

Bernstein describes a group, initially of four adults, to which eight more adults were added in succession. Each addition led to conflict, which was severe if the newcomer resisted. But such resistance always faded within 20 min; and all the newcomers were incorporated in the group.

11.3 STATUS

11.3.1 Patterns of Social Order

Dominance is defined in 10.1; and examples of status systems are given in 10.2; but the concept of status has still to be discussed. General questions about status systems ("dominance hierarchies") are conveniently dealt with by referring to primate groups (reviewed by J. M. Deag, J. S. Gartlan, 1968, R. A. Hinde, 1974, T. E. Rowell, 1974).

We must first dispose of a simple, anthropomorphic notion that might be called the Tarzan principle: that animal groups include a dominant or alpha individual combining superior strength and intelligence with all the features listed below.

Priority of access to: place, food, and mates	Leads group on march
More groomed by others	Defends group
	Controls members' interactions

In a human community, the items in the left-hand column would be regarded as rights, and those on the right, as duties.

The implied assumption is that, *however status is defined,* the same rank order emerges. Suppose we observe a particular male to have priority of place: others give way when he moves along a path or comes to a convenient resting place, or even when he merely approaches another group mem-

ber. The question is then, is that male dominant also by other criteria, such as access to food or to females? More generally, various features are used as criteria of rank: to what extent are they positively correlated?

11.3.1.1 The Question of Correlations: Priority of access is not necessarily correlated with being a leader, in the sense of an individual that determines where the group goes (10.1). Certainly, "leader" should never be used as an equivalent of "individual of the highest rank"; there are, however, examples of correlations between other criteria of rank. T. T. Struhsaker describes the social structure of vervet monkeys, *Cercopithecus aethiops.* The groups had from 7 to 53 members, with a mean of 24. If the status of a male vervet is defined in terms of its ability to displace other males, a linear order emerges, but with some complications due to coalitions. Given knowledge of the order so defined, an observer can predict with some confidence the outcome of an encounter over food: the dominant has priority.

There are also other correlations. These monkeys have a display in which the perineal region, which is red, and the scrotum, which is blue, are exposed to another monkey while the performer moves with a distinctive gait and tail raised. The display is a prerogative of the more dominant individual. Allogrooming, correspondingly, is performed by the subordinate monkey of a dyad. Hence certain males not only have priority over place and food, but also get their backs scratched more. In addition, Struhsaker recorded more copulations by high-ranking males than by those of lower status. Such observations have, however, been questioned, on the ground that when subordinates copulate they do so unobtrusively.

Struhsaker's findings are of special importance,

because they were made on a population unaffected by people. Other examples (given in the reviews cited) exist, but are from groups influenced in some way by human action. As we know, crowding resulting from captivity or from artificial feeding can enhance apotreptic conduct, and can make status relationships more prominent than in natural conditions.

Correlations such as those observed among vervets are far from universal: there are species in which rank determined by one criterion, such as priority of place, does not signify, say, superior reproductive success. Unfortunately, most of the evidence again comes from captive groups.

T. E. Rowell (1966) describes the social interactions of 11 *Papio anubis* kept in a large outdoor cage. These animals could be arranged in a straight-line status system, just by watching them. But, when detailed, quantitative records were analyzed, to quote the author, "no single behavior pattern could be used as a rank criterion." The "apparent rank" mainly reflected encounters in which one of a pair of animals withdrew from the other. But some encounters were not apotreptic; presenting or nosing the genitals seemed at first to be correlated with "apparent rank", but this did not apply to interactions between females.

In a simpler case H. Kummer (1957) assessed the rank of each of a group of captive males on the basis of apotreptic encounters, and made a separate rank order in terms of mating success. The two orders did not correspond.

Other work has shown that the monkeys of this genus are not exceptional. I. S. Bernstein (1970) describes findings from six species of the genera *Macaca* (two species), *Theropithecus, Cercopithecus, Cynopithecus,* and *Cercocebus.* He recorded apotreptic relationships, mounting not related to coitus, and allogrooming. In apotreptic interactions,

the question was, as usual, which of two individuals withdrew. In mounting, the animal mounted is recorded as subordinate. But in allogrooming, as we know, the animal groomed is regarded as dominant. Bernstein was able to suggest some regularities. For example, females received more grooming than did males, but they also did more. In these genera, high status, determined by results of apotreptic interactions, is usually a prerogative of adult males. And rank orders determined on this basis are stable. In contrast, grooming relationships are less stable; and, more important, there was no evidence of correlation between the three criteria of status.

11.3.1.2 Social Interactions and Hygiene:

The previous paragraph gives an example, one among many, of treating allogrooming strictly as a social interaction (figure 11-14). The reader of this and other passages might assume that the grooming of one mammal by another is always held to have an exclusively social function: or, in other words, that such conduct has survival value only as a means of regulating interactions within a group. But the notion of a social significance for allogrooming is rather new: in the past such behavior has been supposed to have a hygienic function. There is experimental evidence for this outside the Primates. For example, D. Fraser & M. S. Waddell show how mice, *Mus musculus,* depend on grooming by their companions for removal of ectoparasitic mites (Acarina) from the head and shoulders, which are inaccessible to self-grooming.

W. J. Freeland has discussed the connection of social interactions among Primates with preventing parasitism and disease; and J. J. McKenna describes detailed observations, made during more than 1500 h, of grooming by langurs, *Presbytis entellus.* One question, unfortunately unanswer-

FIGURE 11-14 Allogrooming by rhesus macaques, *Macaca mulatta.* (Courtesy
J. H. Kaufmann)

able, is whether allogrooming originated, in evolution, as a means of controlling pathogens, and only later came to be a social signal. Such a notion conforms with the evidence of selection for resistance to disease as a major component of evolutionary change (J. B. S. Haldane, 1949).

Freeland points to several features of social organization which perhaps reduce the chances of infection. (1) The first is associating and mating only with members of a single group. (The increase in respiratory infections that occurs when members of previously separate human groups meet is well known.) (2) Territorial behavior may similarly be supposed to reduce the incidence of epidemic infections (10.4.1.6). (3) A more speculative notion

concerns the effects of xenophobic behavior: if a newcomer is at first treated harshly, the result may be to reveal an existing diseased state by making it worse. (In 10.5.1.2 I describe some of the pathological effects of social intolerance among rats and tree shrews; these could be interpreted in the same way.) (4) Lastly, Primates that live in small troops allow their infants to be handled by others, but those that live in large troops do not. This difference, too, could be related to reducing the dangers of infection during a particularly susceptible period.

These ingenious proposals need to be tested by experiment, or at least by observations of actual behavior and of the incidence of disease. McKenna's findings on grooming by langurs suggest that, among these monkeys, allogrooming has a dual role. (1) Adult males receive most grooming; adult females do most grooming of others. Infants are groomed more than are adult females. One of the functions of grooming another is held, on the basis of close study, to be converting a "tense situation into a peaceful one". All this fits the notion of allogrooming as a social signal. (2) On the other hand, langurs are likely to groom the less accessible regions of a companion's body. Moreover, solitary males in the wet season are liable to infestations with leaches (Hirudinea) on inaccessible parts of their bodies. Hence there is at least some evidence of an hygienic role for allogrooming.

Once again, we see how difficult it is to form conclusions on functions. Plausible guesses are often easy to make. They are also sometimes difficult to eradicate from conventional belief, even when evidence has been brought against them. We now have detailed descriptions of the social structures of a number of species; but convincing evidence on the precise functions of individual acts, or of total social patterns, rarely exists.

11.3.1.3 Subordinacy: We now return to questions of status. We must expect to find, in any group of Primates, several kinds of relationship, each of which has to be studied independently. The precise form of these relationships cannot be predicted in advance, but must be determined by close, unbiased observation of each species. We then find that the simple concept of dominance has to be discarded. T. E. Rowell (1974) has criticized preoccupation with dominant behavior at the expense of its obverse (subordinacy). She describes the assumption of subordinate status among baboons by "provocative cringing": this conduct, together with running away and an expression called "fear-grinning", are said to provoke threat. Low-ranking animals are described as beginning to cringe as one of higher rank approaches, even if the dominant individual is moving toward a quite different goal. The dominant sometimes responds to such a gesture with an apotreptic approach. The behavior in some ways resembles "play", in which responses by others are continually provoked (8.4.2.6). It may be asked whether, in some interactions, an animal is seeking social stimulation. (Searching for other kinds of stimulation is described in 8.1.3.3.)

11.3.2 "Control" Animals

I now discuss the special roles of certain individuals in determining the conduct of others. First there is *leadership*. We know that among deer (10.1) and baboons (11.2.2.1) the direction of movement depends on a leader; but the leader may not be dominant by other criteria. Similarly, when a troop of howler monkeys, *Allouatta,* is on the move, males may enter alternative paths, and—if a suitable path is found—utter a distinctive noise; the others then follow (C. R. Carpenter, 1964).

Second, there is protection. Male baboons and macaques put themselves between their group and an external source of danger, such as a predator.

Third, the male macaques that act protectively also interfere when members of the group come into conflict. M. Oswald & J. Erwin describe observations on six groups of pigtail monkeys, *Macaca nemestrina.* They recorded "contact aggression" (grabbing, pushing, hitting, and biting); "non-contact aggression" (including chase, open-mouth threat, and bark); and "submission" (including a grimace, a screech, and crouching). All these acts are called agonistic. Each group had one adult male, eight adult females, and one or two infants. If the male was removed for 20 min, all the agonistic acts were performed more frequently by the females. If a female was removed, there was no effect.

These authors therefore refer to the male as a *control animal*—a term earlier used by I. S. Bernstein (1966) in an account of a group of capuchin monkeys, *Cebus albifrons*. These monkeys may have no clearly defined status system, but a single animal may have a distinctive dual role: he (1) threatens others outside the group and is resorted to when group members are disturbed, (2) intervenes when conflict arises within the group. A control animal may also be dominant by one of the conventional criteria; but the concept of control is distinct from that of status. The main effect of control is evidently to *inhibit* conduct that, among people, would be called antisocial.

11.3.3 The Status of Status

Despite all the difficulties, the concepts of dominance and subordinacy, and of rank order, are still often used, both for Primates and for social interactions of other animals. The new knowledge, however, makes us more critical, and more careful to say, in each account, just what behavior is referred to by these terms. Moreover, there are several kinds of social relationship apart from those of rank. Given this caution, we may still ask what type of status system exists in a particular species.

Usually, among Primates, males are dominant to females (on any of the usual criteria), but there are many exceptions (reviewed by T. E. Rowell, 1974). A troop of ring-tailed lemurs, *Lemur catta*,

FIGURE 11-15 Ring-tailed lemurs, *Lemur catta,* a species of which the females are dominant over males: that is, they have priority in access to food or place. (Zoological Society of London)

(figure 11-15) has been studied by Alison Jolly. This is one of the forest-living Madagascan family, Lemuridae, of which the social groups include more males than females. Apotreptic interactions are lively: there are visible threats and also clashes, in which the animals may slash at each other with their canines. Moreover, these prosimians employ pheromones prominently: adults of both sexes mark branches with secretions of glands associated with the genitalia. The males also have glands on their chests and their arms. During apotreptic encounters the tail is rubbed on these glands and then waved about so that the odor reaches the opponent. Such events are called "stink fights".

Males have a rank order, defined by priority of place and maintained largely by postural signals. Females among themselves have a less well-defined status system. The important feature, however, is that females have priority over males for food; they also displace males by the use of visible threats. Jolly describes how sometimes a female bounces up to the alpha male, snatches an item of food from him and gives him a cuff on the ear. Moreover, this species is yet another in which dominance, defined by access to place, is not correlated with mating success.

Although female lemurs are, in a clearly defined sense, dominant over males, they are not arrayed in a rank order with males. And females display less, or less vigorous, apotreptic conduct than males. The obvious general conclusion is that the social structure of a lemur group does not fit any simple concept of status relationships.

The same applies to the squirrel monkeys, *Saimiri sciureus* (figure 11-16), studied by J. D. Baldwin, (1968, 1971) in a park in Florida. There were four adult males in a troop of more than 100 monkeys. The troop moved about as a unit, but—except

FIGURE 11-16 Squirrel monkeys, *Saimiri sciureus*. (San Diego Zoo)

in the breeding season—the adult males formed a peripheral group; and if they approached the adult females, who formed the core of the troop, they were driven off. Hence, if we define dominance in terms of supplanting, the females were dominant over males. Even the young monkeys associated with the females threatened the males. There was no evidence of a rank order among either males or females except in the breeding season, when the males formed one (defined in terms of threat, clash, and withdrawal). But the order was unstable, and—once again—unrelated to mating success.

Recent findings on the social interactions of Primates and other animals have a clear implication for the concept of rank or status: they deflate its importance. The social relationships of members of a group are of several kinds. They include sexual, parental, and filial interactions (among which are those of "aunts" and "uncles"), combined action in finding food or in hunting prey, and leadership, control, and other "responsibilities" (11.3.1); in addition there are the various apotreptic interactions (many entirely peaceful) that are often used as criteria of status. There is much variation between species in each of these categories; and sometimes there is variation within a species. Where a single species varies, the differences between populations often seem to reflect not genetical differences but ontogenetic responses to diverse environment demands.

11.4 OCCUPIED REGIONS

11.4.1 Description

In descriptions of the movement of Primates, three terms are often used: home range, territory, and core area (reviewed by B. C. Bates and by R. L. Holloway).

The home range is the region in which an animal lives during its adult life, or during some shorter, specified period. This definition excludes regions in which an adolescent animal has roamed before settling down. It also allows for seasonal movement and other shifts perhaps determined by the availability of food. For example, D. J. Chivers recorded the regions regularly visited by neighboring groups of mantled howlers, *Allouatta palliata*. In any period of a few days the regions were quite distinct; but during a period of three months they shifted. There was much overlapping of the home ranges of adjacent troops; but, although the population was increasing, the troops did not mingle: they howled energetically at dawn, and this display seemed to keep the groups apart. Here, evidently, is an example of the dispersion of groups maintained without territorial conduct. Another example of overlap of home ranges is provided by baboons, *P. anubis,* of which the troops meet and mingle at water holes but otherwise keep apart (reviewed by K. R. L. Hall & I. DeVore, 1965).

Territory in this book means a region occupied by an individual or a group to the exclusion of conspecifics. Usually, intruders are driven from a territory by displays. Within a territory there may be a *core area* (J. H. Kaufmann 1962), in which the group is most often found, and in which there may be roosting places or some other important amenity.

A map showing areas of occupation by groups gives, however, only incomplete information about the animals' movements. Primates, especially the majority that live in trees, occupy not an area but a volume: there is a vertical dimension. Some species live in the tree tops, others lower down. More important, movements within an occupied area are often by pathways, between which the animals may rarely venture. (For the importance of pathways for rhinoceros, see 10.2.4.)

Even without these qualifications, there is much variation. The titi monkeys and gibbons described in 11.2.1 have well-marked territories. J. O. Ellefson gives details of four adjacent territories of lar gibbons, *Hylobates lar*. There were narrow undefended regions between them. Hence the home range of each group was only slightly larger than its territory.

The baboons in Kenya, described by Hall & DeVore, have large home ranges that greatly overlap, but core areas that are mostly separate. Unlike titis, howlers, and gibbons, they have no elaborate territorial displays: evidently the troops keep apart without special signals. Hence the core area of this species is a territory as defined in this book.

A third case is represented by the mountain gorilla. G. B. Schaller (1963) describes 10 groups with greatly overlapping home ranges and small regions that seemed to be exclusively occupied. He saw no evidence of territorial conduct. If males of two groups met, they sometimes mingled, sometimes separated as if deliberately avoiding contact, and sometimes threatened. In general, ground-living Primates seem rarely to have marked apotreptic territorial conduct (C. C. Wilson). The same applies to arboreal species that eat fruit, of which the supply varies with the season and is erratically distributed in space. But those that eat leaves and buds, of which the supply is more constant, are territorial: such genera include *Alouatta* (11.2.1) and *Presbytis* (11.2.2).

A correlation between type of food and territorial conduct, if it exists, suggests once again that social interactions can prevent populations from overeating their food supplies (10.4.3), but that among Primates they do so only when the food supplies are of a certain type. A. M. Coelho and others studied a howler monkey, *Allouatta villosa,* and a spider monkey, *Ateles geoffroyi,* in a Guatamalan tropical forest. The habitat produces plant food which, measured by its calorigenic value, could support much denser populations than those present. But Coelho and his colleagues point not to social interactions but to disease and malnutrition (not undernutrition) as possible limiting factors. These could interact with the social structure.

11.4.2 Apotreptic Conduct

In the past it has sometimes been assumed (1) that territories are always defended by violence; and (2) that interactions between neighboring groups are always hostile. As the preceding passages show, neither of these statements is correct. (1) Territorial displays are typically harmless, though noisy. (2) Moreover, boundary displays sometimes look more like greeting ceremonies than warnings. This applies to the dawn hootings of gibbons and to the morning encounters of titi monkeys (11.2.1). They resemble the dawn chorus of birds, which is an outbreak of audible territorial displays evoked by sunrise.

Displays, as we know from observations of birds, often *indicate the presence* of a resident (chapter 10), and we may assume that they cause intruders to withdraw. Occasionally, there is experimental evidence that the displays actually have this effect.

Since Primates depend greatly on sight, and also on sounds, their social signals are easier to study than are those of other mammals, among which odors are more important. Figure 11-17 illustrates visible displays performed during encounters. The wide open mouth and the grin are common apotreptic signals among Primates. So are slapping the ground and shaking the branch of a tree. Since such performances seem often to cause withdrawal by opponents, they are, by definition, threats. They are commonly accompanied by a stiff bodily posture and raised hair, eyebrows, and ears.

Visible threats nearly always go also with noises (reviewed by Peter Marler, 1965). The harsh noises that in man become speech are typical of primate calls. Noises made during the encounters of neighboring groups are often evidently threats but, as we know, they may on the contrary attract neighbors—as they do among gibbons (11.2.1). Casual human observers (such as the originators of the travelers' tales of earlier times) inevitably believed such seemingly violent, noisy displays to be a kind of war or riot; but this, as so often, was an unjustified anthropomorphism. If a human analogy

FIGURE 11-17 Apotreptic expressions common to many primate species: the grimace with bared teeth (left), and the "open-mouth threat" (right). Top, *Macaca mulatta;* middle, *M. radiata;* bottom, *Presbytis entellus.* (Reproduced from P. Marler in I. DeVore, ed., *Primate Behavior: Field Studies of Monkeys and Apes*, 1965, Fig. 16-6, by permission of Holt, Rinehart & Winston, New York)

is needed, it is that of bluffing opponents to withdraw without a clash (compare the Beau Geste hypothesis, 18.6). But, of course, the concept of deliberate (conscious) bluff should not be applied to species other than *Homo sapiens*.

11.5 SOCIAL ETHOLOGY SO FAR

Most of our present knowledge of social ethology is a result of the rapid expansion of behavioral science during the period since 1950. Both the species studied and the ideas of the researchers have been (and are) diverse. Attempts have been made to state general rules; and they have led to fruitful debate, but not to general agreement. Much of the controversy has arisen from proposals about the evolution of social behavior, and the role of natural selection (chapters 15, 18).

Other developments since 1950 have made the study of animal societies easier in three important ways: (1) methods of observation, experiment, and quantitative analysis have been much improved; (2) patterns of social structure have been revealed, which provide models or hypotheses on which further work can be based; (3) a beginning has been made on the vast task of relating types of social organization to ecological niche, and this too is a source of hypotheses.

Parental care of eggs or young is widespread among arthropods, cephalopods, and vertebrates. The family, consisting of a female with her offspring, is one form of primary social group, from which others seem to have evolved. In larger groups there is often a status system (peck order or dominance hierarchy). In its simplest form one adult has priority over all the rest in access to place, food, and a mate, and in determining the direction of march; and others follow in a linear order. But detailed, quantitative observation of a number of mammalian, especially primate, species has shown such systems to be rare. Leadership is often distinct from dominance defined in terms of priority of other kinds; females and males may form separate systems; dominance, defined by the ability to supplant another (that is, by access to place), may not be correlated with the chance of successful mating; cliques or subgroups may act as units that confer equal status (in terms of access to place) on their members; but such cliques may be only temporary. At first, too, superior status was assumed to be a prerogative of males; but now many exceptions are known. The original concept of a status system, even modified in minor ways, is therefore too simple to match the facts: instead, members of a group (especially of Primates) are described as having roles of various kinds, both in respect of "rights" (such as access to a mate) and "duties" (such as controlling movement or regulating apotreptic conduct).

Relationships within a group are usually distinct from territorial interactions between groups. In this book, therefore, I write of status and roles only within groups: terms such as dominance are not used for interactions between holders of separate territories. A territory is conveniently defined as a region occupied to the exclusion of conspecifics. The definition is then in terms of social relationships, not of attachment to a place (though this exists also). The definition does not refer to defense; but most closely studied territories (so defined) are in fact defended. Among birds and mammals, interactions between neighboring conspecifics are sometimes vigorous at first, but are later muted: individual birds may then be distinguished by their neighbors through distinctive song or appearance, and mammals perhaps by odor.

A population may include a large proportion of individuals without territories: these then can provide replacements for territory holders that die.

In a given region, the number of possible territories is finite; hence the existence of territorial behavior entails a limit on population density. But the density of the populations that have been studied perhaps often depends on the combined effects of social interactions and the available food and shelter.

Social signals (further described in chapter 13) that mediate behavior within groups may evoke approach by another (epitreptic) or withdrawal (apotreptic); or they may cause a conspecific to stop an activity (inhibitory).

Much attention has been given to apotreptic conduct (often called aggressive) both in and between groups. The apotreptic or intolerant interactions of many species have now been studied; nearly all species have a repertoire of characteristic signals that induce withdrawal of conspecifics without causing direct injury. In natural conditions serious injury is usually rare. (In captivity it may be common.) There are, however, well-defined instances of the systematic killing of conspecifics: examples are the autumn slaughter of males by bees, and infanticide by lions and macaques. These illustrate the amoral character of the social interactions of animals.

The account of social relationships, given in this and the preceding chapter, is restricted to the conduct of adults, and therefore disregards an important dimension, that of individual development. And so in the next chapter we turn to the ontogeny of social behavior.

12

THE ONTOGENY
OF SOCIAL CONDUCT

Train up a child in the way he should go;
and when he is old, he will not depart from it.

Proverbs 22:6

12.1 THE IMPORTANCE OF ONTOGENY

Simple accounts of species-typical social conduct
sometimes imply that these features of behavior
develop with a kind of inevitability. If we listen,
like Shelley, to that blithe spirit, the lark, we are
likely to think of its song as something given in the
very nature of a skylark. But to do this ignores the
fact that behavior develops. Young American larks,
of the genus *Sturnella,* have been reared by W. E.
Lanyon (1957, 1960) in an unusual environment,
and so made to sing quite unusual songs.

This is one example of the importance of examining the way in which apparently fixed patterns
of conduct develop in the individual. In the present
chapter we see how experiments on young animals
can reveal unexpected sources of variation in the
development of species-typical patterns.

There are not only different degrees of lability,
but different kinds. As we know, certain grasshoppers (Acrididae)—the locusts—can live either as
ordinary, solitary insects or in swarms, in which
their behavior and even their appearance are quite
different (2.3.6.3). The difference is not genetically determined, but depends on the occurrence of
special conditions in outbreak areas. In this case,
there are two main kinds of species-typical behavior, displayed by each species: locusts either swarm
or are solitary, and the environment determines
which type of behavior develops. Moreover, the
process of becoming a swarming locust depends
partly on the visual stimulus presented by other locusts. Hence the behavior is labile in development
and is affected by social experience. Other notable
examples are provided by the eusocial insects
(figure 12-1).

The next sections concentrate on three celebrated
groups of examples from the vertebrates: the ontogeny of bird song; the effect of "imprinting" in
the social development of birds; and the influence
of early social experience on the social development of monkeys. Each illustrates the phenomenon
(already mentioned in 9.4.1.3) of the *sensitive
period* in development (also called a "critical period"): at certain stages, usually soon after hatching or birth, an animal may be especially suscep-

tible to environmental action that influences its development. The researches also have important theoretical implications (chapter 17).

12.2 THE AUDIBLE SIGNALS OF BIRDS

12.2.1 Some Properties of Bird Song

Many species of birds make two distinct kinds of sound: one is a call note, which is likely to be brief and (to our ears) a mere noise; the other, the song, is a complex sequence, to us a melody, which can sometimes be represented in musical notation. Scientific investigation of song has led to some of the most elegant experimental studies in modern ethology (reviewed by R. A. Hinde, 1969; D. E. Kroodsma, 1978b; P. Marler & P. Mundinger, 1971; W. H. Thorpe, 1961). These studies have depended on the use of modern electronic equipment. In particular, the sonograph prints out a representation (sonogram or sound spectrogram) of a recorded sound (figure 12-2). This allows the experimenter to measure a number of features, including pitch and the temporal relationships of the components of a song.

Call notes may indicate the presence of food; but their most studied role is that of alarm. Fig-

FIGURE 12-1 Queen cells of the honey bee, *Apis mellifera.* (F. Ruttner)

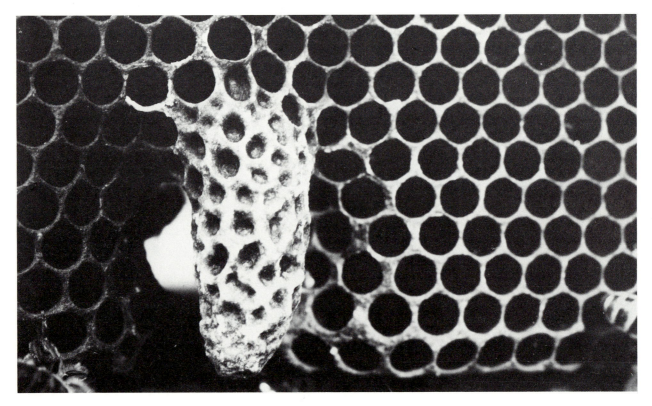

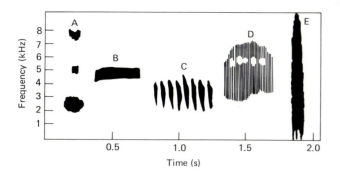

FIGURE 12-2   Spectrograms of sounds made by birds: (A) pure note, with harmonics; (B) whistle; (C) trill; (D) buzz; (E) squawk. (From W. H. Thorpe, 1961)

FIGURE 12-3   Sound spectrograms of similar calls made by birds while mobbing owls: (A) blackbird, *Turdus merula;* (B) mistle thrush, *Turdus viscivorus;* (C) Robin, *Erithacus rubecula;* (D) garden warbler, *Sylvia borin;* (E) wren, *Troglodytes troglodytes;* (F) stonechat, *Saxicola torquata;* (G) chaffinch, *Fringilla coelebs.* (From W. H. Thorpe, 1961)

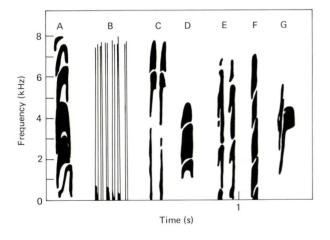

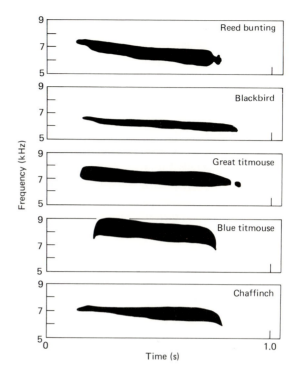

FIGURE 12-4   Sound spectrograms of calls given with a hawk overhead. (From P. Marler, 1959)

ure 12-3 illustrates the rather similar calls given by seven European species, in response to the presence of a predator, such as a hawk or a carnivore, observed in a tree or on the ground. Each includes many frequencies, and is therefore harsh: we call such repeated noises a chatter. They are easily located, and may bring a group of small birds of different species together. Such a group may then mob the predator (5.2.2.1).

A different kind of alarm call is illustrated in figure 12-4. Again, five species are shown to have very similar calls, uttered when the predator is in flight; the calling bird also flies or runs to cover, and other birds do the same. Once in cover, they continue with the same call. These calls, which are of an entirely different structure from those shown in the preceding illustration, are exceedingly difficult to locate; hence they do not guide a predator to the source.

The similarity of the alarm calls of different sympatric species is in notable contrast to the differences between the songs even of closely related species. The song is often heard only during the breeding season, and is related to mating or to the holding of a territory. Figure 12-5 gives the famous example of three European warblers. The chiffchaff, *Phylloscopus collybita,* has a rather simple song, based on two notes, but with variations of detail; the willow warbler, *P. trochilus,* is very similar in appearance, but has a quite distinct song, lasting about 2 s, and regularly repeated; the wood warbler, *P. sibilatrix,* rather differently colored, also has a distinctive song, sibilant and hurried. These

FIGURE 12-5 Sound spectrograms of songs of three closely related, sympatric warblers: (A) the willow warbler, *Phylloscopus trochilus;* (B) the chiffchaff, *P. collybita;* (C) the wood warbler, *P. sibilatrix.* The vertical axis represents 0 to 8 kHz; each time interval on the horizontal axis represents 0.5 s. (From P. Marler, 1957)

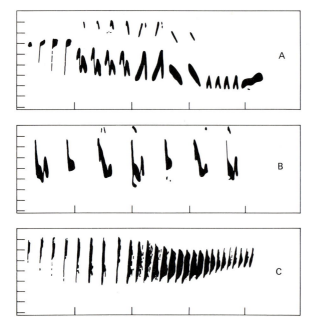

sharply differentiated songs were the first features that allowed ornithologists to distinguish the three species.

Song patterns are, in fact, usually as typical as distinctive shapes or colors or visible displays. They might therefore be expected to be quite invariable, regardless of conditions of rearing. If so, they could be described as *stable in development* (R. A. Hinde, 1959). Sometimes, they are. The species of doves (Turturidae) each have their distinctive cooing song; and in cross-fostering experiments the birds produce their species-typical coo, and not that of the foster parents (B. I. Lade & W. H. Thorpe). Similarly, song sparrows, *Melospiza melodia,* have been experimentally fostered by J. A. Mulligan on to canaries, *Serina canaria,* which have a completely different song. The fostered birds heard only canary songs during their development, but still produced songs typical of their species.

A natural experiment is provided by certain nest parasites, such as the European cuckoo, *Cuculus canorus.* These birds are always reared by foster parents of other species, but always develop their instantly identifiable song.

Nonetheless, the songs of some species are ontogenetically labile. For example, the stability of the song of *Melospiza,* mentioned above, is not complete. D. E. Kroodsma (1977a) reared song sparrows in complete auditory isolation. The birds still sang, although they heard no songs of any kind during development; but the sounds they made differed from the normal both in duration and in form. The experimental method is to rear a bird, from hatching or soon after, alone in a sound-insulated room. One reared in this way is sometimes called a *Kaspar Hauser* animal. The allusion is to the story of a boy, aged about seventeen, who was found near Nuremberg in 1828. He had evidently been reared in complete isolation (R. F. Tredgold & K. Soddy).

12.2.2 Some Songs

12.2.2.1 The Chaffinch: Many experiments have been carried out on the chaffinch, *Fringilla coelebs.* This common European bird develops its complete song during its first 12 or 13 months. The song is a major part of territorial conduct.

A chaffinch hatches in spring; and, if it is reared in a soundproof room until its second June or July, it can never sing normally. The song of a bird reared in isolation is of about the right length, and has the right number of notes, but the melody is not recognizable as that of a chaffinch (figure 12-6). Even the "chink" call note of such birds is abnormal. Chaffinches of the same age have been reared also in small groups, isolated from older birds. Each member of such a group sings a private song identical with that of the others and quite different from the usual one. Deafening during a bird's first summer also prevents development of the natural song. The critical time for song learning is the first autumn. Deafening later has little effect.

Evidently, during its first year, a chaffinch requires exposure to older chaffinches if it is to sing the normal song when adult. The song depends on imitation (8.4.2). But most chaffinches in natural conditions grow up among birds of many species. They must therefore show some discrimination in what they imitate. Attempts have been made to induce male chaffinches to sing various abnormal tunes, including the songs of other species, by rearing them in isolation and repeatedly playing a record to them during their first months. Usually, such attempts are unsuccessful.

A chaffinch readily imitates a recorded chaffinch

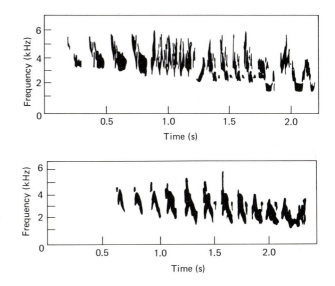

FIGURE 12-6   Above, sound spectrogram of the full song of a chaffinch, *Fringilla coelebs.* Below, sound spectrogram of a chaffinch reared in isolation from sounds of other birds. (From W. H. Thorpe, 1961)

song. Moreover, as J. G. Stevenson has shown, for a young male chaffinch to hear conspecific song is rewarding. Her birds were tested in a soundproof chamber with four perches. If a bird settled on one, it switched on a recording either of chaffinch song or of structureless ("white") noise. There was no evidence that the noise was rewarding; but there was a marked tendency to prefer the perch that switched on song. These findings, based on critically designed experiments, suggest that in natural conditions young male chaffinches tend to put themselves where they can hear adult males singing.

The sensitive period for the development of chaffinch song ends at about the age of 10 months; but this can be altered experimentally. If a male chaffinch is castrated, its singing stops, owing to the absence of androgenic hormone secreted by the testis. If a castrated bird is given testosterone at the age of two years, it begins to sing for the first time; and it then learns either the normal song or an abnormal one according to the conditions in which it is kept.

Here, then, we have species-typical and highly standardized conduct; yet its development can be substantially altered by experiment. There is also some geographical variation: although the song of all chaffinches (reared in a natural environment) is recognizable as that of the species, *Fringilla coelebs,* quite small, partly isolated populations each have their own, minor variant, or dialect.

12.2.2.2 The White-Crowned Sparrow:

An American species, *Zonotrichia leucophrys,* the white-crowned sparrow, has been studied in great detail, with similar results. Like the chaffinch, this bird has song dialects; and careful experiment has shown the differences between the dialects not to be genetically determined, but to depend on imitation during an early sensitive period between about 7 and 50 days of age: for the development of a normal song, the young bird must be exposed to 4 min of normal song, at a rate of six songs a minute, for about three weeks. Similar treatment after 50 days of age is ineffectual. In total isolation a song of the species type still develops, but it lacks the detail that distinguishes a dialect.

This species is highly selective: it will not imitate the songs of other species, even that of its congener, Harris's sparrow, *Z. querula.* There must be features of central nervous organization, in the development of song, which are very stable in development.

A special feature of the sounds made by birds (and other animals) is that the performer can hear

FIGURE 12-7 A pair of viduines, *Tetraenura regia* (left) watch while the prospective hosts, *Granatina granatina,* build their nest. The male viduine (above), is described as directing the attention of the female to the nest in which she will later lay her eggs. (Courtesy J. Nicolai)

FIGURE 12-8 Young viduine, *Steganura obtura*, fed by a ploceid host parent, *Pytilia phoenicoptera*. (Courtesy J. Nicolai)

them. An animal can similarly smell its own odors, but it cannot as a rule see its visible displays. Evidently, one of the factors in the development of song is the ability to hear what is sung. If a white-crowned sparrow is deafened at the time of hatching, like a chaffinch it produces an atypical song that varies from one individual to another. Deafening even at two months of normal life has the same effect, although the sensitive period for acquiring a normal song has passed. But, once the characteristic song is fully developed, deafening has little effect.

12.2.2.3 The Arizona Junco:

Junco phaeonotus, the Arizona junco, illustrates a rather different effect of isolation. The normal song is complex and divided into several sections; and it varies between individuals. Isolation does not abolish individuality but greatly reduces complexity: sometimes the song is reduced to a single "syllable" or phrase. But if a male is reared only with another of the same age, a fully complex song develops; and this song is not distinguishable (by an experimenter) from a natural one.

The most remarkable feature of the song learning of this species is observed when a male is reared alone during its first two months but is exposed regularly to the recorded song of a normal adult male. It might be expected that the young bird would imitate the adult, but such imitation hardly occurs: the young bird instead develops its own complex song. Evidently, exposure to an adult song provokes the young bird to develop complex phrases, but not the particular phrases that it hears. As Marler and Mundinger write: "The interpretation of training experiments such as these is not always as straightforward as it seems."

12.2.2.4 Indigo Birds:

The European cuckoo is a successful brood parasite that develops a song totally unlike that of any of its hosts. But some brood parasites behave quite differently: they develop songs that exactly copy those of their hosts.

The indigo birds (Viduinae) of Africa (figure 12-7) have been extensively studied by J. Nicolai and by R. B. Payne (1973, 1977). They form a subfamily of the weaver finches (Ploceidae); but instead of making elaborate nests like other weaver birds, they lay their eggs in those of fire finches, *Lagonostica,* or other species of the subfamily Estrildinae, which feed their young in an unusual way. The food has been partly digested in the crop;

the parent plunges its bill down the nestling's throat and forces the food out (figure 12-8). To survive this treatment, the nestling requires an unusual position of the tongue and a special method of breathing. In addition, as in many other species of birds, the open mouths of the nestlings of this family present complex, species-typical, colored patterns (figure 12-9); and only the species-typical pattern evokes feeding by the parents. In all these features, the parasitic viduines match the host species.

Apart from their songs, the viduines are unlike the European cuckoo in two notable respects: each viduine species often depends on a single host species; and the viduine chick does not throw out its nest mates. *Vidua chalybeata,* described by Payne, parasitizes more than one host species in different parts of its range. The young indigo birds evidently learn their songs from their foster parents. Later,

FIGURE 12-9 The distinctive pattern of the inside of the mouth of a viduine chick, *Vidua macroura.* (Courtesy J. Nicolai)

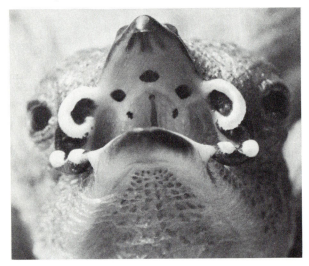

the males and females each sing similar songs; and so mating is always between birds that have been reared by foster parents of the same species. (The male sings on a fixed perch and may be visited by as many as four females in one day. There is no pairing.)

When the female lays her eggs she is attracted to nests made by birds of the same species as her foster parents. Hence the conditions of early rearing determine the selection of both mate and host. There are, however, songs on which early rearing seems to have no effect. These are complex utterances, evidently used in territorial interactions, which vary with the region: that is, they fall into dialects.

12.2.2.5 Songs as Passwords?

Not all local variation in bird song is geographical. Francisca Feekes describes how the separate colonies of a cacique each have their own variant of the species-typical song. She studied *Cacicus cela* in Surinam. The females build clusters of nests, closely packed on trees in lowland tropical forest. Males are larger than females, and brightly colored, and there are fewer of them than of females in a colony. They take no part in nest making or in the care of young, but they do sound alarm calls on the approach of a predator. The males, which sing distinctive songs, are also accurate imitators of other sounds. Songs were recorded from 27 colonies. Each colony had its own song, often two of them, and sometimes three or four. Each song has four "syllables" (figure 12-10). The first "syllable" varies little, but the others differ both in the quality of the sound and in timing. A notable feature is variation of colony songs over quite short periods. Changes coincide with the arrival of new birds, but not all such arrivals entail a change in song. Sometimes, evidently, the newcomers adjust their songs to those

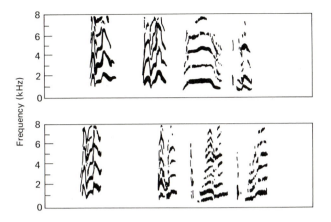

FIGURE 12-10 Sound spectrograms of two songs of *Cacicus cela,* each typical of a different colony. The first "syllable" is much the same in all colonies: it is species-typical; the rest of the song distinguishes one colony from another. The time covered (horizontal axis) is 2.4 s. (From F. Feekes, 1977)

already prevailing. One colony had a constant song for many weeks, until a new group of females began to build nests. The old song continued, but a new song was also heard, evidently from newly arrived males. The males of the colony then sang both songs, sometimes alternately, and also intermediate forms. Eventually, all males came to sing two types of song, both slightly different from the original ones.

An unexpected finding, such as this, always leads to questions on function. Feekes suggests that strange males are easily detected by their strange song—an analog of a foreign accent—and driven off. If so, this is another case of territorial singing. But, as the account above shows, strange males seem sometimes to be admitted; and it is unclear how this happens. Feekes also suggests that colony songs somehow help to keep the members of the colony together. But this suggestion is vague as well as speculative. We have, in fact, in this exam-

ple, one of an increasing number of field studies that illustrate the baffling diversity of animal social relationships.

12.2.2.6 Individual Songs: Although songs are as a rule recognizably of a particular species and no other, the preceding examples also illustrate different degrees of variation *within* species. The range of possibilities is from that of the European cuckoo or the coppersmith (10.4.2.3), with their machine-like regularity, to species in which there is individual recognition based on song (reviewed by C. G. Beer, 1970).

As Beer points out, when we come to truly "personal" songs, we are dealing not with species-typical conduct but with the varying effects of individual experience in natural conditions. Of all examples, those of the duetting species are the most remarkable (reviewed by J. M. Diamond & J. W. Terborgh; T. & B. I. Hooker; F. Nottebohm, 1972; W. H. Thorpe and others, 1972). More than 120 species, members of 32 families, sing duets: members of a mated pair sing either simultaneously or in alternate phrases; and each pair has its individual melody.

The African boubou shrike, *Laniarius aethiopicus,* is a forest-living bird that sings songs of great individuality, and is monogamous. When its songs were recorded with modern equipment, each pair proved to have its own song, of which each member usually sings part (figure 12-11): hence the songs are antiphonal duets. (Sometimes members of pairs sing in unison.) If one member of a pair flies away, the remaining member sings the full song, and this seems to recall the straying spouse. Occasionally, groups of three sing trios. The third member is then evidently an offspring of the mated pair.

It is supposed that the duets of shrikes, such as

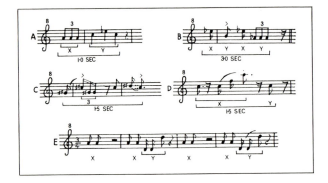

FIGURE 12-11 The songs of some birds can be accurately recorded in Western musical notation. Here are the duets of five pairs of an African shrike, *Laniarius ethiopicus.* In each case X and Y represent the two members of the pair. (After W. H. Thorpe and M. E. W. North, 1965)

Laniarius, keep the members of pairs together, in dense forest where visible signals would not do so. But, as Nottebohm points out, duetting pairs tend to countersing with duets similar to those of neighbors. Moreover, other species of several families sing duets, and not all of them live in forests. The orange-winged Amazon parrot, *Amazona amazonica,* sings duets antiphonally only when the birds are close and can see each other. Thorpe and his colleagues give the example of the white-browed robin chat, *Cossypha henglini,* of East Africa. In aviaries pairs of this species duet while perched side by side. The male sings an accelerating crescendo (it is said, as if "charged by passion"), and the female responds. Of its genus, this is the only duetting species—for no evident ecological reason. Similarly, three species of grass warblers, *Cisticola,* duet; and they live in dense vegetation; but others, in a similar environment, do not. On the other hand, the Tasmanian native hen studied by M. G. Ridpath (10.4.2.4) sings duets but lives in the open, on the ground, and is flightless.

The review by Diamond & Terborgh is concerned especially with the birds of Niugini, of which six species are known to sing duets; each belongs to a different genus, and only two species belong to the same family. Hence it might be supposed that duetting has evolved separately on five or six lines, as an adaptation to some common environmental demand. But in fact nothing of the sort is found. Of the species they studied, these authors write:

Their habitats may be tall grass, the forest floor, dense vegetation [or] the crowns of tall trees. Some live in

FIGURE 12-12 Postures of the laughing gull, *Larus atricilla,* while giving the long-call: in A, short notes are being sounded; in B, the horizontal posture is seen, as at the end of sounding a series of long notes; C, the head toss. (Reproduced by permission from C. G. Beer, Ann. N.Y. Acad. Sci. 280, 1976)

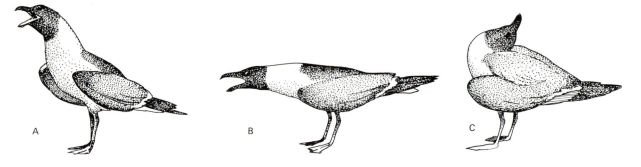

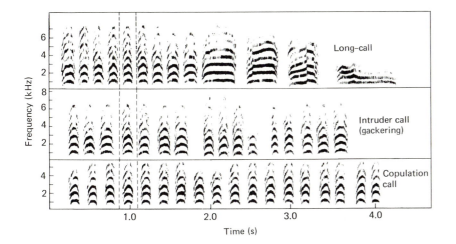

FIGURE 12-13 Sound spectrograms of the calls of laughing gulls (see figure 12-12). (From C. G. Beer 1976)

the lowlands and others in the mid-montane zones. One of the duets takes place most often on moonlit nights, another during the dawn chorus, two during presumed territorial displays, and two at any daylight hour. The singers are always in immediate visual contact in two species, . . . sometimes in visual contact in two more species, and entirely out of sight of each other in the other two.

Once again, we see how difficult it is to relate the behavioral "strategies" of species to their ecological niches.

Individual recognition is not confined to duettists. C. G. Beer (1972) describes an unusually complete study of the calls of the laughing gull, *Larus atricilla* (figures 12-12 and 12-13). This bird, like other gulls (figure 12-14), has a "long-call" which is species-typical but varies in detail

FIGURE 12-14 Lesser black-backed gull, *Larus fuscus*, during a long-call. (Photo by L. C. Shaffer from *Signals for Survival* by N. Tinbergen and H. Falkus, © Oxford University Press, 1970)

between individuals. It consists first of a series of short notes, then some long notes, and finally at least one distinct "head-toss note", and it resembles mocking laughter. The short notes vary and allow one to distinguish individuals. Variation in the other notes reflects what is happening to the bird. When mated pairs exchange long-calls, there are usually four to eight long notes; but when a long-call is given by an incubating bird as gulls fly nearby, there are usually only three long notes. The call therefore identifies the species, the individual, and—sometimes—the circumstances. Beer describes two other calls. One, "crooning", though highly variable, is not a means of individual identification. But a quite brief call, represented as "ke-hah", is also individually distinct.

Evidence of the individuality of songs or calls does not demonstrate individual recognition by the birds themselves. Conclusive evidence depends on experiments in which sounds are recorded and played to birds that might recognize them. In 10.4.2.3 evidence is given that birds learn to recognize the occupants of neighboring territories. J. B. Falls, in experiments on white-throated sparrows, *Zonotrichia albicollis,* played recordings of songs of neighbors to territorial males, and compared the response with that to recordings of strangers. A stranger's song evoked a much more vigorous response.

Such relationships are not universal. Brian Bertram studied the Indian hill mynah, *Gracula religiosa* (figure 12-15), in Assam. These grackles assemble in flocks, usually of not more than 12 birds. Like some parrots (Psittacidae), in captivity they readily imitate human speech. In Bengal they are taught to say prayers; hence perhaps follows the

FIGURE 12-15 The Indian hill mynah, *Gracula religiosa*. (Courtesy Brian Bertram)

name, *religiosa*. In nature they imitate only conspecifics, and it is not known how captivity alters their responses. The free-living birds are remarkable for their loud songs: each individual has around ten; no two individuals have the same repertoire, but neighbors of the same sex share some songs. There are song dialects: birds whose nests are separated by more than about 14 km have no songs in common. Playback experiments show birds to respond to songs by singing themselves; and this response is stronger when the song heard is familiar, that is, from a neighbor. Usually, the response is to sing the same song.

Pairs of grackles make nests in holes in trees; and there is a territory around each nest. Bertram does not discuss whether song is involved in the maintenance of territories; but the hill mynah evidently has an elaborate social system that depends on song; and the individuality of the song repertoire, which depends in part on imitation, has an important role.

B. Tschanz has illustrated a different kind of individual recognition. The guillemot, *Uria aalge,* has a "luring call" that includes a series of sound pulses, of which both the durations and the intervals between them vary between individuals. This call attracts a guillemot chick; and, if a chick is given a choice between the call of a parent and one of a strange guillemot, it moves toward the parent's call. Such discrimination is displayed by newly hatched chicks. Tschanz therefore hatched a large number of chicks in incubators, and played luring calls to them *before* hatching. Chicks were tested soon after they emerged, and duly preferred calls that had been played to them while they were still in the egg.

Here an environmental effect acts at a stage in development at which no such effect would be expected. In an earlier period, the response of chicks to luring calls would have been called "instinctive", and regarded as fixed. Tschanz has also demonstrated an interaction between the unhatched chick and the parents: shortly before hatching, as it begins to break the egg open, the chick becomes very active. The parents respond to this activity by giving their luring call.

Laughing gull chicks, studied by Beer, similarly recognize parental calls. They are fed by the parents, which regurgitate food (9.3.6). During the first few days after hatching, regurgitation is preceded merely by a crooning call from the parent, and this induces the young bird to take the food; but later, before feeding its young, the parent gives the ke-hah and long-call, and the young discriminate between calls from their parents and those from others: the latter induce a response, as if to a predator, by immobility or taking cover.

12.3 IMPRINTING

The learning of song consists of developing sequences of movements of the vocal and respiratory organs. Another example of lability in seemingly "innate" behavior is provided by the conduct toward their parents of nidifugous birds (figure 12-16) and of mammals that live in herds or flocks. According to the nursery rhyme, "Mary had a little lamb, . . . and everywhere that Mary went, that lamb was sure to go." In this case the *direction* of movement is affected—the choice of objects to which the young animal attaches itself. As the rhyme suggests, the phenomenon has been known for a long time. P. G. Kevan quotes a passage from Thomas More, translated from Latin in 1551.

They brynge up a great multytude of pulleyne, and that by a mervelous policie. For the henns do not syt upon the egges: but by kepynge them in a certayne equall heat, they brynge lyfe into them, and hatche them. The chyckens, assone as they be come owte of

FIGURE 12-16 Above, a nidicolous chick, naked and helpless in its nest; below, a nidifugous chick a few hours after hatching. (Reproduced from K. & O. von Frisch, *Animal Architecture*, 1974, by permission of Harcourt-Brace Jovanovich, New York)

the shell, followe men and women in steade of the hennes.

In the modern period the process by which a young mammal or bird becomes attached to an object has been called "imprinting" (reviewed by P. P. G. Bateson, 1971, 1973; E. H. Hess, 1973b; W. Sluckin). It has been principally studied among birds such as ducks and geese, but comparable behavior has been systematically observed among domestic dogs. Puppies, at least of some breeds, can form lasting attachments to other dogs, or to people, but only in the third to the seventh weeks after birth. Other mammals, Sluckin tells us, include buffalo calves, *Bison bison*, which have followed horses, and a zebra foal, *Equus quagga*, which followed a car.

As so often, the key word, imprinting, has been variously defined. One definition has been "the learning of parental characteristics by young animals"; but a black box is not a parent, and developing an attachment to a black box is sometimes called imprinting; hence there is some confusion here. In this book, "imprinting" means the development in early life of the tendency to follow or approach an object. The object, of course, may be a parent, and usually is; hence the term refers to the development of filial behavior. We see in 12.3.4 that there is a related phenomenon, sexual imprinting, which is distinct from imprinting as defined.

12.3.1 The Preliminary Training

One experimental method is to arrange that a bird such as a duckling, *Anas*, newly hatched from an incubator, does not see a conspecific, but has the opportunity to approach, nestle against, or follow an alternative object. The latter may be anything from a model bird that squawks, to a speechless, noiseless box. Ducklings can be induced to follow a matchbox, but also a man. Moorhen chicks, *Gallinula*, have followed a canvas hide, built to contain a man, as well as a scale model of an adult moorhen. Evidently young birds learn to approach objects that present a particular visible pattern; but for some species virtually any pattern, within wide limits, is effective. Sounds too have some influence. Adult birds with young usually cluck, quack, or otherwise make themselves heard. Such noises can increase the attractiveness of a model for ducklings. They are probably especially important for species that nest in holes: this applies to the wood duck, *Aix sponsa*, whose young run toward a calling mother even when she cannot be seen.

In properly designed experiments on imprinting, there are two stages: first the animal has a period

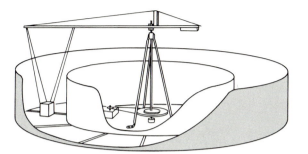

FIGURE 12-17 Diagram of apparatus in which the following response of young birds may be studied: the object on which imprinting is to be tested (a box) is carried round a runway. Part of the inner and outer walls of the runway are shown cut away. (After P. P. G. Bateson, 1973)

of training, during which it is exposed to an object. During this time, the responses of the animal to the object may be recorded, but they are not taken as firm evidence of imprinting. In the second stage the animal is tested against both the object with which it was trained and an alternative. For example, a bird trained with a box may be exposed alternately to a similar box and, say, one of a different color. Or both objects may be presented together.

The second procedure has given particularly clear results. A young bird may be trained in an apparatus (figure 12-17) in which a box can be moved round a runway. The intention is to examine how an attachment develops. The alternative objects may then be identical boxes except that one is colored yellow, the other blue. Clearly, one must control for color preference: to do this, some birds are trained on one color, some on the other. The test is then to expose birds to both colors. When this is done during a certain early period, the birds nearly always approach, nestle against, or follow the box with which they have been reared.

12.3.2 The Sensitive Period

Imprinting, like song learning, illustrates the phenomenon of the sensitive period (12.1). Figure 12-18 gives an example of the general finding that there are only a few hours or days in the life of an animal during which imprinting is easy. Experiments have been done on the onset of this period, and still more on its ending.

As we know, the sensitive period for song learning can begin before a bird is hatched (12.2.2.5). That for imprinting seems always to begin shortly after hatching, and not to depend on any special experience. Certain changes take place in the central nervous system in any bird kept in a wide range of environments. One consequence is an improvement in the ability to walk during the first hours after hatching; this may make possible a greater ability to direct movements toward particu-

FIGURE 12-18 The sensitive period for imprinting of ducklings, *Anas platyrhynchos:* of 10 birds tested at 3 to 7 h after hatching, none was imprinted or even followed an object; at the other ages, most of the birds tested at least followed; and of those that followed, a majority also became imprinted. (After G. Gottlieb, 1961)

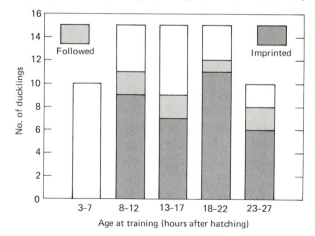

lar objects and to follow them. Another change is in the visual system. It is possible to measure the central nervous response to a flashing light, by recording from the retina and the cerebrum. The speed with which impulses reach the cerebrum increases substantially during the period from just before hatching to some hours afterwards. This, too, may contribute to the ability to respond to objects.

Such changes seem to occur with great reliability regardless of the conditions in which the animal is being reared. They are often classified as "maturation" and contrasted with "learning"; and, as might be expected, there is some evidence also for effects of the second kind. In particular, if chicks, *Gallus,* are kept without visual stimulation for a period from hatching, their ability to be imprinted may be delayed.

The beginning of the sensitive period is not sudden, but gradual. The same applies even more to the end of the period. There is a sense in which the imprinting phenomenon is an anomaly: apart from the parents, large moving objects in the environment of a young bird are likely to be dangerous; the appropriate response then is flight or concealment. In fact, in the early days of a duckling or similar bird, two opposite attitudes appear: approach and following develop first, but the second, avoidance or flight, soon becomes prominent. Even during the sensitive period for imprinting, young birds may behave in an ambivalent way toward an object: they dither between approach and withdrawal. The outcome is that, in normal development, after a few days a young bird is firmly attached to its parent or parents, but avoids other moving objects.

It might be supposed that the onset of avoidance of objects ("fear") is independent of special experience, and that it prevents further attachment.

Another possibility is that the ability to become attached to (imprinted on) an object gradually fades after a few days, and merely leaves the young bird with its newly developed avoidance response. Yet a third hypothesis is that the end of the sensitive period for imprinting depends on developing an attachment to something in the bird's environment.

There is no full account yet of the end of the imprinting period; but the third hypothesis is partly correct. Imprinting of a chick or duckling may take place at any age from about 12 h to three days. But, if a bird is imprinted on an object as early as possible, it becomes difficult to imprint it on another object, even during the later part of the period. "Sensitivity" has, then, been lost earlier than it might have been.

There are also experiments on the development of a preference for the features of the early environment. Such a preference is distinct from a tendency to approach particular objects. Chicks reared in isolation had their home cages decorated either with vertical stripes in black and white, or with horizontal stripes in yellow and red. They were tested at the age of three days, when they would normally be avoiding strange objects, by being exposed to two boxes, one with the vertical black and white stripes, the other with yellow and red horizontal stripes. The unfamiliar pattern was avoided more than the familiar. The ability to discriminate between patterns had been developed. Moreover, this development was not sudden, but gradual: the longer the exposure, the more consistent was the preference for the familiar. Evidently the development of the avoidance response depends in part on first developing an attachment to some aspect of the environment.

Of course, a natural environment rarely has the geometrical regularity of an experimenter's patterned wall. In nature, probably, the only striking pattern to which a young bird can become attached is that of a parent.

12.3.3 The Role of the Young

The young bird has so far been treated as a passive recipient of stimuli offered by the environment; but it is much more than that. If a recently hatched duckling is put in a featureless box, it moves around uttering distress calls (that is, calls which, in natural conditions, are given when a duckling is separated from its mother). If a patterned object is now put in the box, the duckling runs to it and stops calling. The stage of undirected movement is in effect a search for the missing parent. The generalized movements increase the chances of finding the mother. (In natural conditions such a search is usually not random, but directed by sounds from the parent bird.)

Such observations resemble those, described in chapter 4, in which an internal deficit, such as shortage of water, induces extra activity. The conspicuous object might then be supposed to constitute a reward: if so, it should be possible to train a young bird to develop a habit that gives it access to an object. Bateson designed a modified Skinner box with two pedals, each of which could be depressed by a chick or duckling merely by standing on it (figure 12-19). In some experiments, if the young bird stood on one of the two pedals it switched on a flashing light—a convenient form of "conspicuous object": to keep the light on, the bird had to go to the active pedal and stay there. Both chicks and ducklings quickly learned to do so. (The second pedal constituted a control: the birds were not standing on a slightly movable part of the floor just for the sake of doing so.) The conduct of these newly hatched birds therefore includes more than just the ability to follow an object.

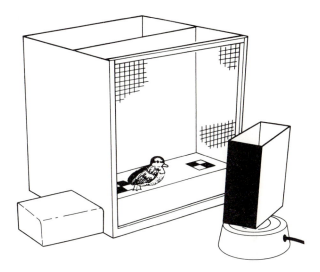

FIGURE 12-19 Cage in which young nidifugous birds can switch on a rotating flashing light by standing on the pedal on the left. Standing on the right-hand pedal has no effect, and functions as a control on the time spent on the left-hand pedal. (After P. P. G. Bateson, 1973)

Moreover, the preferences of such birds include components of remarkable subtlety. When a bird is developing an attachment to a parent (or other object), it becomes able to recognize (that is, approach) it from a variety of distances and at any angle. This is an example of object constancy. To achieve this, the bird must in some sense "learn" not just one pattern but a great variety, all corresponding to some aspect of the object on which it is imprinted. Correspondingly, the preference of a bird for a familiar object, during the imprinting period, is not for what is completely familiar: as imprinting proceeds, the tendency is increasingly for birds to prefer objects that differ slightly from what they have already experienced.

The ingenious apparatus in which this was shown includes a wheel mounted on rails (figure 12-20). The bird is put in, and the wheel moves in the di-

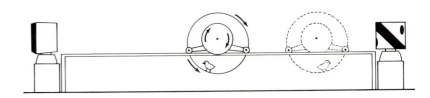

FIGURE 12-20 Apparatus for testing the relative attractiveness of two stimuli to a young nidifugous bird. At each end there is a rotating sign. When the chick runs toward one end, it moves the wheel in the opposite direction. The wheel is shown in detail below. (After P. P. G. Bateson, 1973)

rection opposite to that in which the bird is running. At each end there is a visible stimulus. As a chick approaches the end, it is attracted by the stimulus; it moves toward it, but is carried away. Hence it oscillates between the two stimuli; and the record of the movements gives a measure of their relative attractiveness. Bateson (1973) writes: "It is doubtful whether a bird could ever predict what the back of its mother is like from knowledge of the front view." In its movements, the bird "seems to be working for a slight discrepancy from the stimulation that it has already received". This presumably enables it quickly to get a composite picture of its parents' features.

12.3.4 Sexual-Imprinting

A question that has been much debated concerns the effects of imprinting in later life. There is no record of how Mary's little lamb behaved, when adult, toward other sheep; nor is anything known of its sexual behavior, or even of its sex.

We saw in 12.2.2.4 that the mating preferences of certain nest parasites depend on the song they hear in early life. It was once supposed that imprinting on an abnormal object also leads to correspondingly abnormal sexual behavior later. Hence we have the concept of *sexual-imprinting,* or the development of a sexual preference as a result of early experience. The subject of the development of sexual behavior is, of course, wider than this. We may ask a more general question: what are the factors that influence the ontogeny of mating behavior?

In experiments by J. P. Kruijt on jungle fowl (9.3.4), nine birds reared normally by their mothers were compared with 11 birds that had been in solitary confinement from the time of hatching. The isolated birds saw birds of other species flying around; they heard birds of their own and other species; and they saw and heard human beings; but they had no opportunity to become imprinted on other jungle fowl. All the birds produced sperm, and were able to ejaculate it when directly stimulated by hand massage. How did they behave when, at the age of 9 to 16 months, they encountered females of their own species?

The birds of the control group all performed normal coitus. Of the 11 isolated birds, nine completely failed; the other two succeeded, but not at first. The isolates behaved abnormally in other ways: while they were still alone, they had fits of rushing about screaming, as if they had been attacked and seized by a predator, without any outside event to provoke such an outbreak. The abnormal conduct was, no doubt, partly a consequence of the absence of imprinting during the first days after hatching; but we do not know to what extent the subsequent isolation contributed.

We now turn to less drastic experiments. Philip Guiton made a study of imprinting of the domestic fowl, which is of the same species. Sexual fixations on human beings can be induced in these birds by early experience, and the readiness to make sexual approaches to people is long-lasting; but the brown leghorn cockerels Guiton used still preferred hens when they had a choice.

M. W. Schein has described similar behavior by six domestic turkey-cocks, *Meleagris gallopavo:* three were reared with other turkeys, and so were assumed to be normal (although they also saw men from an early age); three were kept from other turkeys during their first 32 days, but not from human beings. At the age of five years, when tame to both turkeys and men, all were given the opportunity to court turkey hens; and all did so. They were also tested with a human being, and all courted him too. The crucial experiment was to give a choice between a man and a hen. The control group then chose the bird, but the others, which had been kept away from other turkeys in their first weeks, chose the man.

Sexual-imprinting has also been studied, by F. Schutz, among the ducks (Anatidae). If mallards, *Anas platyrhynchos,* are reared by adults of their own species, they pair only with conspecifics. But if drakes are reared by members of other species, their later behavior is abnormal. In the breeding season, even if they have been flocking with members of their own species, they try to pair with the females of the species on which they have been imprinted.

This bare statement implies that the process of imprinting proper is accompanied by or is identical with the development of a lasting sexual attachment. In fact, however, the two processes have quite different sensitive periods. Imprinting itself takes place soon after hatching. But Schutz has shown the sensitive period for sexual imprinting to be four to nine weeks of age. The effects of whatever happens in this period last for many years.

The mallard is sexually dimorphic: the drake is brilliantly colored, but the female is drab. And in such species, evidently, only the males display sexual imprinting. But a congener, the Chilean teal, *A. flavirostris,* is not dimorphic: the members of both sexes are drably colored (cryptic). And members of both sexes can be sexually imprinted.

Although there is a clearly defined sensitive period for sexual imprinting of ducks, it is not *essential* for mallards to have experience of their own species during that time. Schutz reared three male and three female mallards in isolation: they were deprived of both visible and audible stimulation from other birds of any kind. Yet they paired with conspecifics at the normal time.

Sexual-imprinting is not confined to precocial species. K. Immelmann (1969a,b) exchanged single eggs between zebra finches, *Taeniopyia guttata*, and Bengal finches, *Lonchura striata*. The young of these species are altricial (see figure 12-16). When the young hatched, they were reared by the foster parents. After the young birds had become independent, they were isolated until sexual maturity, when the males were tested with females of their own and their foster species. Courtship was almost always directed toward the species with which the bird had been reared. Sometimes the conspecific was attacked. The songs of fostered birds were also affected: figure 12-21 shows a sound spectrogram of the normal song of a zebra finch and the very different song of one reared by two female Bengal finches.

Another group of altricial birds, the doves, have been studied by A. Brosset. Young of four species were reared by foster parents of other species. The initial effect was to induce a response by the squabs still in the nest to the foster parents in preference to members of the young birds' own species. The response was opening the beak for food. The birds were also tested when first sexually mature, to see whether their social conduct as adults had been affected by the early rearing. Apotreptic responses were made in a normal way toward members of their own species. But sexual behavior was at first directed toward members of the species by which the birds had been reared. Here, then, is a further example of sexual-imprinting. But the abnormal behavior was not permanently "stamped in": with further experience of conspecifics, the effect was reversed, and the birds displayed normal sexual behavior toward their own kind.

12.3.5 Mammals: Imprinting and "Maternal Imprinting"

We now return to Mary's little lamb. V. H. H. & D. Sambraus have confirmed the nursery rhyme (figure 12-22): lambs, *Ovis*, can be induced to follow a human being, if they are kept away from conspecifics and have close contact with a particular person. C. G. Winfield & R. Kilgour have also observed lambs following a model ewe in a circular runway. The response is most marked at the ages of 6 to 10 days. These authors are concerned with a practical aspect: lambs, especially twins, should not be kept in conditions that encourage them to drift away from their own mother in pursuit of another. Such observations, however, test only the following-response, not imprinting itself. But other work has used the test of discriminating between two objects.

Probably, imprinting is widespread among precocial mammals. Unfortunately, the most used laboratory mammals are altricial; but guinea pigs,

FIGURE 12-21 Effect of fostering on song. Above, sound spectrogram of a zebra finch, *Taeniopygia guttata*, reared by Bengal finches, *Lonchura striata*. Below, that of a zebra finch reared by its parents. (Courtesy K. Immelmann)

FIGURE 12-22 Lamb, *Ovis*, imprinted on a human being. (Courtesy V. H. H. & D. Sambraus)

Cavia, make an exception. W. Sluckin & C. Fullerton have induced cavies aged about one week to follow a tennis ball or a striped cube. The training of some animals consisted of exposure for 2 h on each of two successive days, but others were given only two 10-min periods. The total of 20 min was just as effective as the longer period.

R. H. Porter & F. Etscorn discuss the question of "olfactory imprinting", and describe experiments on the spiny mouse, *Acomys cahirinus,* which—though a murid—is also precocial. During their first 48 h, the young were exposed for 24 h to cinnamon or cumin in the bedding in their home cage. When given a choice immediately afterward, the young mice tended to move toward the familiar odor. In further experiments mice less than 12 h old were put in a strange cage and exposed to an odor for only 1 h. When tested 24 h later, they again showed a preference for the familiar substance. The authors suggest that such acquired preferences have a survival value similar to that of the imprinting of birds.

Such phenomena may be quite widespread among the mammals. H.-M. Zippelius describes a curious feature of the family lives of shrews (Soricidae) of the genus, *Crocidura.* Members of this genus (but no others) follow their mothers in a caravan in which each holds the tail of the individual in front. Caravaning begins at the age of six or seven days, and at first can be evoked by any object. But from the eighth day it is evoked only by objects with the species odor. Experimentally, "imprinting" may be induced to the odor of another species.

G. K. Beauchamp & E. H. Hess have studied the sexual-imprinting of cavies, *Cavia cobaya.* Their findings resemble some of those on birds. If male cavies are reared with another species (in this case, with domestic chicks), as adults they still mate normally with conspecific females; but they also behave sexually toward members of the foster species. A normally reared cavy never does this. The sensitive period is evidently the first six weeks after birth.

Mammals also provide examples of the obverse of imprinting—the rapid attachment of a female exclusively to her own offspring. Such maternal-imprinting has been described by N. E. Collias. If a lamb, *Ovis,* or a kid, *Capra,* is removed from its mother at birth, it is often rejected if it is returned a few hours later: the female withdraws from its attempt to suck, and butts the infant away.

Experiments on goats have been described by P. H. Klopfer and others (1964, 1966, 1968). The period during which a female becomes attached to her kid evidently lasts only about 2 h after birth; and the first few minutes are the most crucial. If a kid is removed from its mother at the moment of birth, and returned a few hours later, it is rejected; but if it is allowed to remain with her for only 5 min, it is accepted when it is returned to her.

A goat identifies her young by its odor. If a female's olfactory sense is temporarily put out of action with cocaine, the attachment fails. Such findings have enabled Klopfer and his colleagues to foster alien young on to females. Immediately after the birth of her young, a female's olfactory sense is especially responsive; and a kid, even if not newly born, can be fostered on to her during those crucial few minutes. Such findings can be useful for stockbreeders.

Inevitably, these observations have led to speculation about human relationships; and there is indeed evidence of a process, analogous to maternal-imprinting, among human beings. S. G. Carlsson and others have examined the effects of different procedures adopted in hospital after a child has been born. They refer to earlier American work, in which the effects of a hospital routine of separating mothers from their infants for 6 h or more after birth were compared with those of allowing immediate contact between mother and infant. The mothers, who were mostly unmarried and very poor, were closely observed when the infants were about four weeks old. Those of the second group were described as behaving in a more affectionate way toward their infants while feeding them from a bottle. The observations of Carlsson and his colleagues concerned mothers in two wards of a Swedish hospital. In one ward, mothers were allowed prolonged contact with their newly born infants, in the other, they were not. Observations of the mothers' conduct were made when the infants were two to four days old. Cuddling, kissing, carressing, and

talking to the infants were recorded. The findings conform with those of the earlier study. These authors write: "The separation enforced . . . by traditional ward routine obviously reduces, at least temporarily, the affective components in mother-child interactions." Here, then, is an example of a hypothesis, based on observations of other species, tested by study of human beings, and leading to findings of practical value.

12.3.6 The Concept of Imprinting

So far, we have been mainly concerned with the "mechanism" by which birds develop social attachments (and avoidance). An obvious question to ask is: what is the survival value of these processes? It is easy to suggest an answer. Imprinting of the following response occurs in species in which the young are active early in life, and so must follow their mother or go to her at need. The young learn to recognize the mother very early. Birds are not hatched (or mammals born) with a ready-made responsiveness to their parents, for this would entail an ability to recognize the parent at any angle and in a variety of conditions. We may surmise that it is easier to evolve a learning ability than a complete ability to recognize a particular kind of object in all its aspects.

We now return to questions concerning the process of imprinting. The findings described in the preceding sections conflict with a widely propagated account, according to which imprinting is a sudden stamping in of an irreversible impression that influences not only the young bird's immediate response but also its sexual responses later. In fact, the process by which an attachment develops is gradual, and the intensity of the attachment depends on the duration of exposure to the parent or other object. As Bateson (1971) remarks: "The analogy with the formation of an imprint seems a bad one. It would be more satisfactory to liken it to the painting of a portrait in which the broad outlines are sketched first and the details are then filled in by degrees."

To continue Bateson's simile, the portrait can also be the subject of some repainting later. As we saw, a bird that has been reared exclusively with another species may later mate normally even if, on testing, it retains a preference for the species on which it was imprinted. Further, a species that depends on imprinting in early life may not display sexual-imprinting. F. Schutz, in a study of ducks (Anatidae), has described how female mallards, *Anas platyrhynchos,* can be imprinted on an inappropriate object; but such abnormal rearing has no effect on their sexual preferences later. There is, in fact, as we know, much variation among species. In the extreme case, represented by the European cuckoo, there is no evidence of any kind of imprinting whatever.

Imprinting has sometimes been described as a kind of "learning" distinct from all others. To classify it in this way could be merely a matter of convenience. Imprinting is a kind of habit formation (or "learning"), but the first systematic experiments were done by zoologists, and imprinting is rarely studied by the methods of psychologists interested in "conditioning" or related topics. (The use of a modified Skinner box is an exception.)

To classify imprinting separately from other, possibly related, phenomena could, however, have an important implication—that both at the behavioral and the physiological level imprinting is different from other processes that involve storage of information. At the behavioral level a bird or mammal certainly develops the habit of following a parent (or other object) without being rewarded for doing so by some conventional incentive such as food or even warmth. As F. V. Smith has shown, even if it is prevented from moving, a bird can become imprinted on an object. Evidently, there is storage of information when a young bird is exposed to a suitable object, merely as a result of the exposure. Such processes are sometimes called perceptual learning: something is recorded in the brain merely as a result of the stimulation falling on the exteroceptors (in imprinting, especially the eyes). The effect on behavior may be observed only later. Similar storage of information also occurs during exploratory movements (8.1.4.1); hence in this respect imprinting is not unique. Although imprinting is a distinct behavioral category, there is no good reason to treat it as fundamentally different from all others.

12.3.7 Analogs of Imprinting

In this book imprinting refers to a narrowly defined phenomenon—the process by which a young animal becomes attached to its parent. Other features of social interactions resemble imprinting in certain respects; and so we have sexual-imprinting and maternal-imprinting. In this section I describe nonsocial examples, first from feeding behavior and second from habitat selection.

G. M. Burghardt has described observations on newly hatched snapping turtles, *Chelydra serpentina.* One group was given a meal of meat, another of worms. At the age of one week, the turtles of each group received the alternative food. At the age of two weeks, the turtles were given a choice. They showed a marked tendency to prefer the food they had first received. There was, however, some tendency to prefer the worms, regardless of particular experience. Hence in this case there is evidence of an initial preference, on which is superimposed an effect of the first experience of eating.

Work by V. E. Rabinowitch on gulls of the genus, *Larus,* at first sight seems to parallel closely that on turtles. Newly hatched chicks were reared on one of three foods: chopped earthworms, pink cat food, or green cat food. When, at the age of six days, the chicks were given a choice between the familiar food and one of the others, they nearly always took the familiar food. In further experiments, however, a choice was given between two unfamiliar foods; and then sometimes a chick ate neither. That is, it did not respond to either mixture as food. The author suggests that there is a parallel in his findings to those on the search image (3.3.3). In this case there seems to be a failure to recognize the unfamiliar material as food.

A third example has been described in 4.5.2.5. Young rats are at least temporarily influenced in their preferences by their initial experiences of food.

In all these examples on feeding behavior, the animals are necessarily rewarded by ingesting the food offered. But, as we know, the imprinting process can occur even if a bird is merely exposed to a visual stimulus, in the absence of any further consequence. On the other hand, an important feature of the experiments cited is that in each case the animals were offered a choice between alternatives. In this respect, the findings from these experiments are analogous to those from the studies of imprinting described in the previous sections.

The reader will perhaps already have thought of another phenomenon, described in 7.6.1, which seems to parallel imprinting. Salmon tend to return to the stream in which they have been reared; experimentally they have been shown to discriminate the waters of that stream from those of other, similar streams.

Another example of habitat selection comes from the mammals. Some mammalian species, as we know, thrive in more than one environment. Such versatility presents a number of problems, discussed by S. C. Wecker in a study of the deer mouse, *Peromyscus maniculatus.* Members of a species with narrowly defined needs must, if they are to survive, find their way to one particular environment (compare 2.1); but those with a wider range may be faced with a choice between alternatives. The deer mice studied by Wecker (in Michigan) live both in grassland (fields) and in woods; and natural populations in one environment are to some extent segregated from those in the other. If mice are trapped and then given a choice, they usually select the environment in which they have lived. An obvious possibility is that the difference in behavior of the two populations is genetically determined. Some findings conformed with this hypothesis: offspring of mice trapped in the two environments were reared in the laboratory without experience of either environment. Later they were tested in an enclosure, of which half was field, half was woodland. The mice chose the environment from which their parents had been taken.

But in some experiments there was also evidence of an effect of rearing. The offspring of mice from a woodland stock were reared in grassland, and then given a choice of environment: they tended to choose the field environment. Hence in this case the influence of early experience overrode the response expected from mice of their genotype.

As information accumulates, we must expect further evidence of important effects of early experience. Imprinting, as defined here, may then come to be seen as one aspect of a more general phenomenon.

12.4 PRIMATES

We now come to the third major study of the ontogeny of social conduct. Nearly the whole of the present subchapter is concerned with *Macaca mu-*

latta, the rhesus monkey. There is no balanced account of the subject for the order of Primates, or even for the monkeys and apes (the Anthropoidea). The work on one species of monkey does, however, deal very thoroughly with the development of species-typical behavior, that is, of conduct of a kind which was (and sometimes still is) called instinctive or innate.

The early findings by W. A. Mason (1960, 1961a,b) and by H. F. Harlow and his group (reviewed by H. F. & M. K. Harlow; W. A. Mason, 1978), like the early speculations on imprinting, have become known to a wide public in a simplified form. Interest in them has been due in part to their possible implications for human development. They are therefore doubly important. (For reviews see J. Hanby; R. A. Hinde, 1974; G. P. Sackett & G. C. Ruppenthal.)

12.4.1 The Rhesus Monkey

12.4.1.1 The Infant Observed: When the small and appealing rhesus monkey is born it clings to its mother's fur, but its mother also holds it (figure 12-23). The infant can also climb (figure 12-24); and this helps it to find the nipple. It soon begins to explore its mother, both by looking at her and by the use of its mouth and its hands. There is much imitation of the mother from an early age: if the mother looks at something, so does the baby; if the mother manipulates an object, the baby follows suit. As the infant becomes mobile, it ventures further from its mother, but she is used as a resort when disturbed or fatigued. A wandering infant may also be recalled by its mother, notably by her looking at the infant through her legs and making a distinctive noise.

When a baby monkey is disturbed, it returns to its own mother, not to any female. Similarly, a mother usually rejects a young monkey not her own (though a mother with a very young baby may adopt another of the same age and nurse both).

There is a period of about three months of very close attachment to the mother; another three months follow during which there is greater independence, but also much resort to the mother; breast feeding ends at from six to nine months. Complete separation occurs at about one year.

The infant rhesus is equipped, evidently from birth, with reflexes that enable it to stay in a proper position and to feed. *Clinging* (already mentioned) includes a firm contraction of the flexors of the

FIGURE 12-23 Female rhesus monkey, *Macaca mulatta,* with young. (Courtesy University of Wisconsin Primate Laboratory)

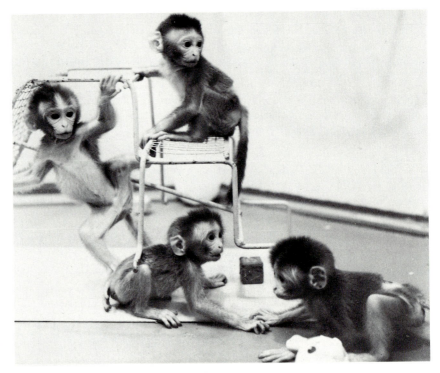

FIGURE 12-24 Group of infant rhesus monkeys. (Courtesy University of Wisconsin Primate Laboratory)

finger joints. Also associated with holding on is the *Moro reflex:* if the infant loses support, it flings its arms wide and then brings them together, and so clings with arms as well as fingers to whatever there is to grasp. Yet another is the *righting reflex* (familiar from the behavior of a cat held up and dropped): if a monkey is dropped, like a cat it falls on its feet. Two other items are related to feeding. The *rooting reflex* is turning the head from side to side and toward a source of contact on the cheek: this helps the infant to find the nipple. *Sucking* is a powerful movement of the cheek muscles which draws milk from the mammaries.

12.4.1.2 Social Deprivation: The celebrated early experiments by Mason and by Harlow and

others were on the effects of early social deprivation. In the most extreme situation young monkeys were reared for months without any contact with members of their own species. At first this procedure was called "maternal deprivation"; but, later, separation from conspecifics in general came to be emphasized: hence we may speak of social deprivation.

In some experiments, isolated infants were offered a choice between two models, one covered with cloth and soft (figure 12-25), the other, of wire. Even when the monkeys were fed on the wire, they spent most of their resting time clinging to the cloth mother. Hence the habit of resorting to the mother is not a simple consequence of being fed by her.

For a person with human feelings, this may not be surprising; but it was valuable to have it demonstrated experimentally: it disposed of the simple notion that the tendency of a young monkey to keep in contact with its mother is merely a result of its being rewarded with milk. Milk is certainly a source of attraction, but so are warmth and a rocking movement. In addition, there is a more subtle attraction, for infant monkeys distinguish their own mothers from all other monkeys.

FIGURE 12-25 Infant rhesus monkey (see previous two figures) sucks its thumb while lying on a model, cloth-covered "mother". (Courtesy University of Wisconsin Primate Laboratory)

In the experiments, the presence of an inanimate substitute mother had a considerable effect on the infant's behavior. Without one, a baby monkey, though well fed, explores little, and runs shrieking from strange objects; with one, there is a more usual amount of exploration, interrupted by resort to the mother object. Deprived monkeys are liable to sit in a corner rocking. They also sometimes inflict injury on themselves. Some go into prolonged periods of immobility, or catatonia. W. A. Mason & G. Berkson describe the use of model "mothers" that swing or otherwise move: infants reared on them do not rock themselves, and are still more exploratory than those reared on immobile models.

Observations have been made on the conduct of socially deprived monkeys later in life. (For an additional review, see S. J. Suomi and others.) Six months of isolation have a calamitous effect on social behavior, and 9 or 12 months an even greater effect. When deprived monkeys are put together in groups, they fail to form quickly a stable status system (compare 11.2.5.2): there is much violence, and deaths may result. Moreover the presence of such abnormal animals among normal macaques provokes attack, although they themselves tend to avoid most social interactions. As they grow up, however, they are liable to attack others, and in a quite abnormal way: they may attack infants of their own group, or—at the other extreme—a large male to whom normal members of the group give place.

In some experiments there has also been a severe effect on sexual conduct. Of a number of males reared on model mothers, without encounter during early life with any real monkeys, none succeeded in reproducing. Physiologically they were indistinguishable from other adult males, and they still had sexual impulses for they approached females in a sexual manner; but their subsequent behavior was not so organized that they could achieve coitus.

The isolated females, too, at first seemed unable to breed. They were, however, put with exceptionally gentle, patient, unhurried, and skilful males, and eventually some had infants. But, at least with their firstborn, they were evidently unable to behave as normal mothers: they were either indifferent to their infants, or hostile toward them. The babies are described as making desperate and pathetic efforts to approach their mothers, but were often beaten or knocked down. (It is a relief to know that only a few of these females have been studied.) Eventually the young learned to approach their mothers from behind, and to climb on their backs. The mothers sometimes groomed their young. Two of the mothers would not allow feeding, and the young had to be fed from a bottle.

When such mothers were allowed to have second infants, their "psychopathological" conduct was much less marked: evidently they had developed new habits as a result of experience with their firstborn young, and these had largely annulled the influence of abnormal rearing.

The firstborn young of these mothers, after their atypical rearing, are described as exceptionally violent toward conspecifics; they were also sexually precocious and unusually active. They were, however, not grossly abnormal, as their mothers had been.

The findings of later work have not always matched the original reports. G. W. Meier studied 10 rhesus females reared in isolation. All mated when allowed to do so, and five that were left to bear their young normally behaved in a normal maternal way. In addition, four males were reared in isolation; all mated normally, and three at least were fertile. The difference between these monkeys and those of the earlier experiments has not yet been explained. Meier's animals were in cages close together, and so could see and hear other monkeys, whereas the monkeys studied by Harlow and his colleagues were more isolated. This may have had a crucial effect on social development.

An obvious question is whether it is essential for a young monkey's social development that it should have access to a mother, as distinct from other monkeys (reviewed by J. Hanby). When young monkeys have had experience only of others of their own age, they cuddle each other a good deal, and of course they play. In these conditions their development has been said to be normal; but detailed study has shown this to be incorrect. The measure in this case was the frequency of attack on conspecifics when the monkeys were observed in social groups later in life. C. O. Anderson & W. A. Mason, however, emphasize that social deprivation influences all aspects of adult social interactions: for example, rearing only with other young results in imperfect sexual behavior later. The full complexity of normal rhesus social conduct (11.2.5.2) evidently depends on rearing both with a mother and with other young monkeys.

12.4.1.3 Rehabilitation: An important question is whether the atypical social interactions of isolates can be countered by training or experience later in life. Early attempts at such rehabilitation failed. But Suomi and others succeeded with monkeys that had been isolated for their first six months and then put with a normally reared rhesus aged three months. At that age a normal monkey does not threaten or attack even an isolate. The isolate in such an experiment tends to withdraw from the other monkey (the "therapist"); but the normal monkey approaches the isolate and clings to it. After a time, the isolate (or "patient") clings in return; and later frolicking by the normal monkey evokes similar play by the isolate. This treatment is described as leading eventually to complete rehabilitation, that is, to normal social conduct. Rehabilitation, to quote Suomi and his colleagues, "requires considerable time and effort".

Among the similarities of these findings to those on imprinting is the question of how to classify the effects of early experience on social development. There is a sensitive period, but it is even less sharply defined than that for imprinting. The first six months are the most important, but the foundations of normal conduct are evidently laid during the first year at least. Suomi and his colleagues regard the aberrant behavior of isolates as reflecting a "form of learning deficit"—that is, the development of inappropriate habits. Isolates develop atypical habits, such as clinging to themselves, sucking their own digits, and stereotyped rocking movements, instead of acquiring movements in response to external stimulation from conspecifics. Rehabilitation consists of replacing unsuitable conduct with social responses typical of the species. We saw in 7.8.2 that each species can readily acquire certain habits, but cannot develop others. The results of the experiments on rehabilitation perhaps reflect such "preparedness" in these monkeys.

12.4.1.4 Brief Separations:

The social isolation of an infant for many months could not occur in natural conditions. Such drastic experiments tell us much about developmental processes that depend on early social interactions, but nothing about how a female or her young cope with shorter partings. R. A. Hinde (1974) reviews experiments on the effects of brief separations on rhesus monkeys (see also R. W. Goy & D. A. Goldfoot). As we know, an infant rhesus at first clings tenaciously to its mother (who also holds it), then after a week or so it begins to explore its surroundings; and later it both increases its range of exploration and also plays with others of its age. But during its first year it resorts regularly to

its mother, not only for milk but as a refuge. Sleeping is always in contact with the mother.

If an infant is parted from its mother, it at once makes distinctive calls and behaves in an agitated way: there is often a period of rushing about, but this is soon followed by "depression", during which the infant moves only slowly, with a drooping attitude. Such conduct has been observed in experiments in which the mother has been removed from captive groups. When she is returned, as a rule she immediately rejoins her offspring. The young monkey clings more tenaciously to its mother than usual, and it may be a week or more before the infant returns to its normal exploratory movements.

These generalizations, though valid, must be qualified, because there is much individual variation. Some variation can be related to the infant's previous experience of mothering. Rhesus females themselves differ in their maternal behavior. Some allow their very young infants long periods of belly to belly contact, others do not—and the infants then have to work harder to remain in contact. The latter are more upset by separation than are the young that have previously experienced most security.

The importance of variation in maternal conduct appears from experiments in which the young, not the mother, is taken from the group. The main result during separation is extra activity, but on return the infant's normal behavior is soon restored. The key is evidently in the effect this procedure has on the mother. She does not suffer the combined effects of separation from her young *and* exposure to a strange environment; and so, when her infant is restored to her, her maternal conduct is hardly impaired by the separation.

An obvious question is whether brief separations influence conduct later in life. There is evidence of a long-lasting effect of a separation of only six days, at the age of six to eight months, on behavior even at two and a half years. The main effect is in a reduction in exploratory behavior, and a reluctance to approach strange objects. In other experiments, reviewed by G. P. Sackett & G. C. Ruppenthal, some infant rhesus monkeys were subjected to a series of brief separations; those of a second experimental group were taken from their usual mothers and were looked after by others. At the age of three years, members of the two experimental groups, together with controls, were observed in a social situation. Sackett & Ruppenthal write:

The multiple-mothered animals were most violent, and were dominant over the other two groups. The non-separated animals were intermediate in behavior, while the separation-controls were non-violent and low in social status. These effects were stable at three and a half years . . . Evidently, inconsistent mothering in infancy can have profound effects . . . later in life, and repeated separations from a single mother can have persistent detrimental effects on important dimensions of social behavior.

12.4.2 Species Differ

The concentration of research on the rhesus monkey leaves us in the dark about other species of Primates. G. P. Sackett and others (1976) have, however, described the effects of rearing pigtail monkeys, *Macaca nemestrina,* in complete social isolation. Unlike rhesus, infants of this species do *not* develop body rocking, self-clutching, self-injury, and greatly reduced exploration. Two further reports have now shown, in some detail, variation even among closely related species.

L. A. Rosenblum has compared captive groups of the pigtail with the bonnet monkey, *M. radiata.* The pigtail monkeys tended to space themselves out, instead of sitting in contact. In the conditions of Rosenblum's experiments, that is, in captivity,

they were also rather violent: there was even severe injury to females and young, some of whom died. In contrast, the bonnet is a contact animal, and in these experiments was peaceable.

The rearing of the young differed correspondingly. When a pigtail female gave birth, she kept away from the group; others that approached were often attacked. Female bonnets returned at once to the group after parturition, and literally made contact with them. Other monkeys were allowed to handle the newborn (but not to carry it away).

As the young began to explore, pigtail mothers restrained them vigorously; but bonnet mothers interfered only mildly. Similarly, at weaning, pigtail mothers drove off their year-old young with some vigor, but bonnets did not. At this period a female often bears a second infant. When this happened, a young pigtail (if still attached to its mother) developed habits of thumb sucking and penis sucking; and sometimes its play with other monkeys was reduced. But the arrival of an infant bonnet had little evident effect on the older infant.

If the mother were removed, the young pigtail displayed at first great agitation, followed on the second day by immobility. There was an improvement after about a week. When the female was returned, the young monkey immediately resorted to her, and clung to her with unusual tenacity for up to three further months. In these respects, the pigtail seems to resemble the rhesus. The infant bonnet deprived of its mother is described as searching around, cooing. On failure to find the mother, it attached itself to another adult; and, on return of the mother, it often disregarded her and remained attached to the foster parent.

Another such comparison, briefly described by B. Seay & N. W. Gottfried, is of the crab-eating macaque, *M. fascicularis,* and the patas monkey, *Erythrocebus patas.* (The macaque is only doubtfully distinct from *M. mulatta.*) The experimental arrangement allowed the infant monkeys to enter a play area through an aperture too small for their mothers. As a result, the mothers were kept in their separate cages, but two infants could meet and could even enter each other's cage. For rhesus infants, interactions with others of their own age are of great importance. Correspondingly, if a macaque infant aged, say, four months entered the play area, it was quickly joined by the other, although the mother was liable to interfere. In contrast, when a patas infant was approached by another, it usually returned to its home cage: there was little interaction between infants of this species. Similarly, macaque mothers allowed strange infants into their cages, but patas mothers did not.

Seay & Gottfried also describe the effects of separation from the mother on patas infants, and compare them with the effects on rhesus monkeys. As we know, rhesus monkeys respond violently to such separation. Patas infants were much less affected, though there was some reduction in their exploratory activity. There was rapid recovery on return of the mother. It would be valuable to have a more detailed, quantitative study on these lines, and still more valuable to have observations of long-term effects.

12.5 SOCIAL ONTOGENY

This chapter illustrates a central theme of modern ethology. During ontogeny, the genome, given at fertilization, interacts continually with the environment. The result is the phenotype, of which the behavior we study is a part. Adult behavior within each species may be very uniform, but this does not tell us that its patterns are irrevocably fixed. A set of examples, analyzed in great detail, is provided by bird song. Most species of birds have species-typical songs. Sometimes, the songs are exceedingly stable in development, and no treatment is known that will alter them. But the song of many species develops normally only if the young bird is in a normal environment, in which the adult song can be heard: normal song then depends on imitation. Just what features of song are labile in development, and what environmental variables influence their development, can be determined only by piecemeal analysis of the development of each species. Sometimes, imposed on the species-typical pattern, there is individuality, which allows a bird to distinguish a mate, its young, a parent, or a neighbor from other conspecifics.

A second set of examples comes from the recognition by young birds and mammals of parental characteristics. If it is exposed to such an inappropriate object during an early sensitive period, a young procosial bird or mammal can behave in a filial manner toward it. This is imprinting.

There are analogs of imprinting in the development of sexual behavior, and in recognition of young by their parents.

The last examples come from the development of Primates. The capacity to form normal relationships with members of a group, or with a mate or young, depends on conditions of rearing: fully normal conduct appears only if the young animal grows up with parents and other young. The details, however, of social ontogeny vary greatly among species.

We return to this theme in chapters 16 and 17 (especially 17.3).

13
ANALYSIS
OF COMMUNICATION

The Authors' researches confirm the opinion of all the best Manuals on Bird Watching, that the chief practical use of Birds is to teach people *how to go about with their eyes open.* How valuable that lesson is can be realised only by those who, like ourselves, have made the experiment of going about for days on end *with their eyes tightly shut.* . . . To be honest, the best Manuals make it pretty clear that Bird-watching is mostly done, contrary to expectation, *with the ears.* So perhaps the best thing to do next would be to try again and start going about *with your ears wide open.*

W. C. Sellar & R. J. Yeatman
And Now All This

13.1 THE CONCEPT

The precursors of the word "communication" referred to the ideas of community and obligation. In Latin *munis* refers to one who does his duty. *Communis,* however, means held in public, in contrast to *proprius,* one's own. *Communicare* originally meant to make something common, to divide, or to share it; and this is the origin of our word "communicate".

Today, in contrast, if communication is mentioned in a scientific context, we often think of engineering or mathematics or, in zoology, of the attempt to describe the social interactions of animals in terms of stimulus and response. Similarly, the word "inform" once had the meaning of "put into shape", or "imbue another with feeling"; but now it also means "tell"; and for an engineer, or a zoologist, information is what is communicated: as we see below, it may be defined mathematically. Engineers, then, have used words that originally described human behavior for processes that go on in wires or pipes or valves. And biologists have tried to retrieve the words, in the hope that concepts of the physical sciences will help them to describe and even perhaps to explain behavior.

In doing so, they have thrown out an important element, that of *intention.* (Compare the discussion of "threat" in 10.1.) In an encounter between two people, A may get information from B by observing B's posture or facial expression, when B does not intend that A should. B's intended message, usually conveyed in words, may be quite different; in any case, it reflects a desire to share something with B.

The passage of information, whether intended or not, depends on signals. In biology a signal is a

415

kind of stimulus. It may be defined as a small amount of energy or substance, which brings about a large change in the distribution of energy or material in a system. The definition does not require action at a distance. An important feature is the trivial character of the signal: make a slight sound, or emit a trace of an odor, and a large animal may spend much energy in taking flight. In social behavior both the source of the signal and the system influenced are animals of the same species: hence we speak of social signals.

The study of signals, or semiotic, has four components. The nature and structure of signals is *syntactics:* examples include the descriptions of bird song based on sound spectrograms, and the chemical analysis of pheromones. (2) A signal reflects the internal state of the performer; the study of this relationship is *semantics* (which in human communication is the study of meaning). Readiness to mate is an obvious example. (3) Usually, we are also interested in the effect of a signal on the recipient: this is *pragmatics*. As we know, a first step in pragmatic analysis is often to decide whether a signal causes approach or withdrawal or inhibits action. (4) Lastly, there is the question of function, in the sense of survival value. We rarely have experimental evidence on the survival value of a signal, still less on how it has evolved by natural selection; but we need a framework of hypotheses on function to make our descriptions intelligible.

Under syntactics, the definition of signal given above allows us to analyze animal communication in units of varying complexity. For one species (as we see below) an important visible signal may be a brief flash of light; for another, as described in previous chapters, it may be a pattern of colored shapes. An audible signal may be a brief sound; but it may be an elaborate melody. In each case

the experimenter has to identify, as far as he can, just what features of an animal are influencing other members of its species (pragmatic analysis). Much effort has to go into *describing* signals, and there are several ways in which they may be classified. In the next section the examples are classified by sensory modality.

13.2 THE SENSORY MODALITIES

13.2.1 Seeing

Visible signals can, obviously, act at a distance. They are always directional. Their properties are those to which photoreceptors can respond. The simplest case is a change of illumination, such as a flash of light. The other properties are movement, pattern, color, and the plane of polarization of light.

A group of beetles (Coleoptera), the fireflies (Lampyridae), mate at night, and depend on organs that produce a bright but cold glow. P. Bagnoli and others describe the neural control of the flashes produced by the "lanterns" of *Luciola lusitanica*. Flashing is controlled by volleys of impulses of which the pattern is regulated in the protocerebrum; but other parts of the brain are also involved. Hence the lanterns are neurally regulated effector organs, analogous to muscles.

J. E. Lloyd (1966, 1971) describes behavioral experiments on a number of species. The male *Photinus pyralis* flies on an erratic course, typical of its species, flashing at intervals of exactly 5.8 s. The female, on a blade of grass, flashes in reply, at the same interval but exactly 2 s later. When a male is answered by a female in accordance with the species-typical pattern, he flies toward her and repeats his own signal. Continued approach requires continuing response from the female. The final exchange of flashes usually occurs with the

FIGURE 13-1 Male great grey bowerbird, *Chlamydera nuchalis,* at his bower. Naturalists who first described these remarkable constructions believed that they had been made for the bird's own aesthetic pleasure. They are now held to attract females, and therefore to be a part of courtship. (John Warham)

male walking toward the female. The flashing pattern for each species is quite distinct, and so attempts at mating between different species do not occur. (Compare the songs of sympatric species of birds mentioned in 12.2.1.)

Another type of visible signal is a structure. Figure 13-1 shows a male bower bird, a member of the family Ptilonorhynchidae, whose elaborate and colorful constructions evidently attract females (18.4.4). A further example comes from the ghost crabs, *Ocypode.* K. E. Linsenmair describes the

sand pyramids made by *O. saratan,* and R. Barrass those of *O. ceratophthalmus.* An adult male makes a heap of sand associated with a spiral burrow (figures 13-2 and 13-3). Each new pyramid is built at least 134 cm from the nearest existing one. Hence there is a territorial effect. The females, too, are guided to the mating site—the burrow—by the pyramid.

Most visible signals studied experimentally include both pattern and movement; often color is involved as well. Examples already given range from

FIGURE 13-2 Ghost crab, *Ocypode saratan,* on burrow. (Courtesy K. E. Linsenmair)

FIGURE 13-3 Ghost crab, *Ocypode ceratophthalmus:* in the lower figure, burrowing. Compare previous figure. (From R. Barrass, 1963)

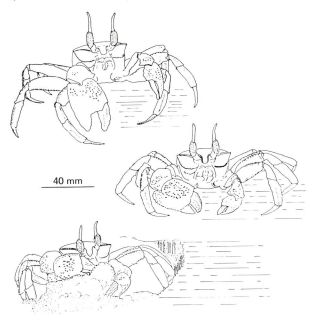

40 mm

the gaudy semaphoring of fiddler crabs (10.4.1.1) to the posturing of brilliantly colored birds (9.3). Sometimes the use of models allows the features that have a stimulating effect to be exactly determined. Many of the best examples are from brightly colored freshwater fish (9.2.1–3).

The territorial responses of the male three-spined stickleback to a patch of bright red, and its courtship of a crude but suitably bulging model, show how the role of visible patterns can be demonstrated by apparently simple experiments (9.2.1), and how one component of a display, such as color, can evoke a complex response. Experiments on another fish, *Pelmatochromis,* have analyzed a male's response to a female in relation to components of the female's highly colored appearance: a female is *attractive* by virtue of the bands of black with which she is marked; but *orientation* of the male depends on a red patch (9.2.2). Experiments on *Tilapia,* described in the same section, indicate a modest role of experience ("learning") in the development of female responsiveness to males. And in 9.2.3 I describe how components of a visible display can have an additive effect on the readiness to court or to threaten: discrimination by male Siamese fighting fish between other males and females normally depends on the structure of the fins, the position of the opercula, and the appearance of the body. Another such instance is given in the description of the responses of spiders to models (9.1.1).

We now turn to further examples. F. Alvarez and others have observed fallow deer, *Dama dama,* in southwest Spain. These animals seem to be cryptically marked, but they also sometimes make themselves conspicuous (figure 13-4). Such conduct leads to problems of explaining the behavior in terms of its function. As the figure shows, dorsally these animals are dark brown but mottled;

FIGURE 13-4   Positions of the tail of fallow deer, *Dama dama.* These animals are cryptically colored; but the rump becomes conspicuous when the tail is raised or moved. This may be an alarm signal. (Reproduced by permission from F. Alvarez et al., *Behaviour* 56, 1976)

ventrally they are pale, and so illustrate counter-shading (3.4.1). Nonetheless, they frequently raise the tail and so expose the conspicuously white ventral surface of the tail and the region around the anus. This display occurs when a deer is disturbed by a large animal such as a predator. It is therefore held to be an alarm signal. Alvarez and his colleagues point out that defecation often occurs (as a result of changes in the autonomic nervous system) when a mammal is disturbed in this way; and defecation requires raising of the tail. They suggest that the conspicuous response with the tail raised high has evolved from the original response of defecation, by an exaggeration of the movement of the tail, accompanied by changes of coloration to make the rump more visible. The hypothesis on the evolution of the display is, of course, untestable. The proposal on its function as an alarm signal, though highly plausible, as so often is not supported by experimental evidence. It is, however, compatible with the existence of such patterns among many other species (18.3.1).

We next turn to an example of a rejected hypothesis. Figure 13-5 gives examples of fish, of the family Chaetodontidae, which live in coral reefs and are superbly colored and patterned. Other coral fish, for example, some of the Pomacentridae, are similarly adorned. What is the function of these gorgeous displays? K. Z. Lorenz (1962) stated that nearly all such brilliantly colored fish hold individual territories, and that all territorial fish are conspicuous. P. R. Ehrlich and others have tested these statements by direct observation. They first point to the many small pomacentrid species that hold territories but have an unobtrusive appearance. Such species considerably reduce the scope of the hypothesis. Their own study is of 20 species of chaetodontids on the Great Barrier Reef. Few were found to be territorial, except at night (when

FIGURE 13-5 Three brilliantly patterned chaetodontid fish: at top, *Chaetodon speculum;* in middle, *C. auriga;* below, *C. trifasciatus.* (Courtesy P. R. Ehrlich)

colors would not be evident): the fish then keep apart and remain in individual coigns or crevices. Painted wood models were used to test responses to conspecific patterns; they failed to provoke apotreptic responses. Hence the hypothesis that these conspicuous patterns are territorial signals is not tenable. The patterns may be aposematic (3.5), or they may facilitate permanent pairing or help to maintain larger groups; but these proposals need to be tested by further experiment.

The next example shows how models can be used to test hypotheses based on observation in natural conditions. The signals in this case are not simply present or absent, but vary in a measurable way. The apotreptic and sexual conduct of several species of gulls (Laridae) has been recorded in great detail in the field (reviewed by N. Tinbergen, 1959). Figures 13-6 and 13-7 give examples of distinctive attitudes adopted during encounters. Such postures may be regarded as reflecting the internal state of the performer. Some writers use terms such as "aggressive upright": these seem to imply that the postures reflect an intention or an emotional state of the performer. It is not clear how such statements could be validated. They might be given a physiological content; but this has evidently not yet been achieved. The adjective "aggressive" implies that the posture is apotreptic (a threat). Labels such as "aggressive upright" are, however, given to a posture in advance of decisive evidence of function. They then, in effect, represent hypotheses on what the supposed signals do.

In the absence of formal experiment, it is sometimes possible to give evidence of correlations from close observation in natural conditions. Tinbergen gives the example of a male black-headed gull, *Larus ridibundus,* making a nest on its territory. In doing so it intermittently approaches five other gulls nearby, without disturbing them. Later, it stops nest building and approaches them with the "aggressive upright" stance. The other gulls then walk away. (The posture they adopt in doing so is called the "anxiety upright".) Such observations, made many times, can provide evidence of the existence and effects of signals.

J. G. Galusha & J. F. Stout have tested hypotheses about the postures of glaucous-winged gulls, *L. glaucescens,* observed on islands off the east coast of North America. They used models (figure 13-8) to examine how the position of the head and neck influences the conduct of an opponent. One model incorporated small motors, and so could be moved in both the vertical and the horizontal planes. In each experiment two models were put in the territory of a gull or pair of gulls, and their effects watched from a hide. The responses to the models seem to have been very similar to those observed when a real gull intruded; but, of course, the use of models allows statements on the precise effects of a particular visible stimulus. Attack was

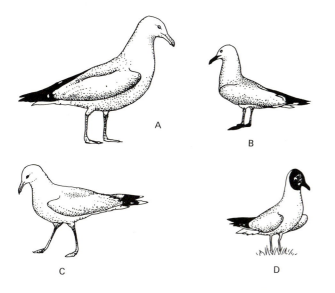

FIGURE 13-6   The upright posture of four species of gulls (Laridae): (A) Herring gull, *Larus argentatus;* (B) Hartlaub's gull, *L. novae-hollandiae;* (C) common gull, *L. canus;* (D) black-headed gull, *L. ridibundus.* These postures are commonly described as aggressive, but are related to territorial defense. (After N. Tinbergen, 1959)

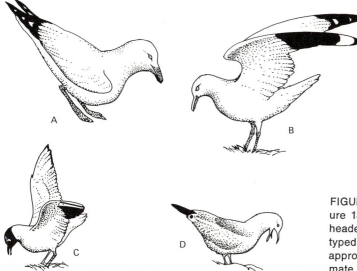

FIGURE 13-7   Choking by four species of gulls (see figure 13-6): (A) herring gull; (B) common gull; (C) black-headed gull; (D) kittiwake, *Rissa tridactyla.* This stereotyped act is performed by a male on its territory when approached by a female, that is, an actual or potential mate. (After N. Tinbergen, 1959)

FIGURE 13-8 Models used to test the responses of glaucous-winged gulls, *Larus glaucescens,* to the postures of conspecifics. (Reproduced by permission from J. G. Galusha and J. F. Stout, *Behaviour* 62, 1977, p. 223)

most frequent on models with the head and neck in a high position. The angle of the head (or bill) to the neck had little effect. A horizontal position of the model rarely provoked attack, but tended to induce withdrawal: hence it acted as a threat. These experiments illustrate the analysis of postures that form a continuum, and so are analogical. They also test hypotheses based initially on observation. One unexpected finding was the lack of significance of the head angle.

We next turn to an example of the opposed action of two visible features. The cichlid, *Haplochromis burtoni,* studied by C.-Y. Leong, is a territorial mouthbrooder (9.2.2). The male on its territory has a distinctive color pattern, of which the components vary (figure 13-9). The head has vertical black bars; and dummies with such bars provoke a high rate of attack. There is also an orange patch above the pectoral fins, and a dummy with this patch is attacked at a low rate. Both features can change in a few seconds. Males display, at the territorial boundary, with raised opercula. They may also bite an opponent. Leong used accurate models of fish as opponents, and calculated an attack rate, expressed in bites a minute, for each of a number of male fish in standard conditions. Each male was then presented with models bearing different components of the color pattern (figure 13-10). The vertical component of the head pattern increased the mean attack rate by 2.8 bites/

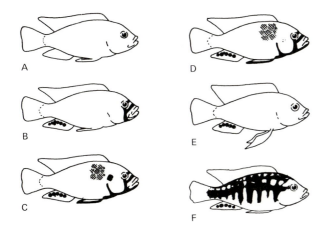

FIGURE 13-9 Color patterns of male *Haplochromis burtoni* (Cichlidae): (A) juvenile; (B) about to become territorial; (C) holding a territory; (D) spawning; (E) and (F) withdrawing from an apotreptic display by another. The hatched areas are orange colored. (After C.-Y. Leong, 1969)

min; the orange patch reduced the rate by 1.8. When both were present, the effects summed: the attack rate was 1.0 bites/min. A nonterritorial male has only the head pattern: hence, if such a male enters a territory, it is vigorously attacked. But all territorial males also have the orange patch, and encounters between neighbors are therefore less vigorous. The function of the rapid appearance and disappearance of the markings does not seem to be established.

The preceding statements apply to fish observed in captivity. R. D. Fernald & N. R. Hirata have made a study of this species in a natural environment, Lake Tanganyika. The fish were living in a remote, isolated and undisturbed pool. Only some fish had territories: nonterritorial males schooled with females and young, and resembled them in having a drab, cryptic appearance. When the schools moved into a territory (to feed) the resident male chased away the intruding males but courted the females. Females spawned only with territorial males. The most notable difference from

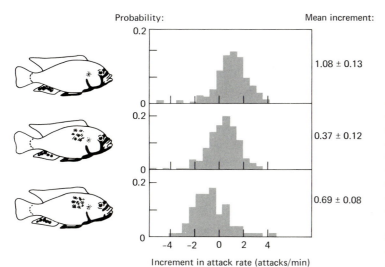

FIGURE 13-10 Effects of models with different patterns on the increment in the attack rate of male *Haplochromis burtoni*. The distributions of attack rates are similar in each case, but the means (shown on the right with their standard errors) differ. The upper model has a vertical black eye bar and no orange spots; the middle model has the eye bar and orange spots; the bottom model, no eye bar but orange spots. (After C.-Y. Leong, 1969)

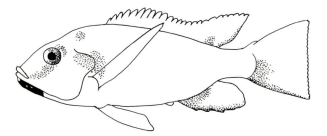

FIGURE 13-11 Sketch of the blackchin mouthbrooder, *Tilapia melanotheron,* to show the color patterns described in the text. (After G. W. Barlow, 1969)

captive fish was that few territorial males had the black eye bar; and those with such a bar were less successful in establishing territories than those without. Whether the difference is genetically or environmentally determined (or a combination of both) is not known. These findings remind us that, despite the value of observations of captive animals, they cannot give conclusive evidence on what happens in the natural environment.

Our last example in this section concerns the blackchin mouthbrooder, *Tilapia melanotheron,* studied by G. W. Barlow & R. F. Green. This is another species of which the "behavioral state", or responsiveness, is reflected in its color pattern. The colors of the sexes are similar, but the male has a yellow patch on the operculum and the female, pink. The male carries the eggs; and both sexes perform an active courtship with similar patterns of movement. Of these, bouts of quivering, each lasting less than a second, are the most prominent; and the female sometimes does more quivering than the male. The quivering, performed in such brief, discrete bursts, is a signal of the digital type. All adults are also marked with variable dark blotches (figure 13-11), and these constitute analogical signals. The smaller a fish relative to its mate, the larger and darker are the blotches. These

fish are territorial and have apotreptic displays. Barlow and Green give evidence that the blotches inhibit or modify apotreptic conduct by potential mates. Hence the visible signals of this species include both stimulating and inhibiting components.

13.2.2 Hearing

Just as we can see most visible social signals, so we can hear many audible ones. Moreover, the sound spectrograph now enables us to detect signals of too high a pitch for our ears (12.2). Sounds act at a distance, and give information about the direction of the signaler. They can also indicate the state of the signaler and—as for some species of birds—identify individuals. The subject has been extensively reviewed in collections edited by T. A. Sebeok (1968, 1977). For "ultrasounds", see G. D. Sales & D. Pye.

Like some visible signals, sounds can be effective social signals on their own. R. G. Busnel & B. Dumortier recorded the chirps made by male long-horn grasshoppers, *Ephippiger bitterensis.* A female, allowed a choice between a silent male and a loudspeaker giving male sounds, moves toward the loudspeaker. The function of the chirps exactly resembles that of the light flashes of fireflies described in the preceding section. The patterns are species-typical. Insects do not distinguish pitch: they are "tone deaf"; but they discriminate patterns based on speed of production of discrete sounds and on sound intensity. Among other insect sounds are those of the honey bee, mentioned below (13.3.2); these operate in conjunction with signals that act on other senses.

Another familiar type of call, also related to reproduction and also species-typical, is the croaking of frogs and toads (Anura) (reviewed by W. F. Blair; and by K. D. Wells). At the breeding season most species move to water bodies such as ponds, where they begin their persistent calling. The sounds of male firstcomers have been said to attract males that arrive later; but on this there seems to be little experimental evidence. The two better-established functions are in attracting a female and in maintaining a territory. The bullfrog, *Rana catesbiana,* has several distinct calls. One, given only by males, provokes calling by other males. Of three other calls, each believed to have a territorial function, one is again given only by males, another only by females, and the third by both sexes. Sometimes such calls are given by the occupier of a territory on the arrival of an intruder, and—if the intruder does not withdraw—an attack follows.

The noises of frogs are species-typical. *Hyla ewingi* and *H. verreauxi* are Australian species which, in some regions, are found together. (That is, they are sympatric.) The calls of sympatric populations of the two species are sharply distinct; but those of allopatric populations are similar (figure 13-12). The members of sympatric populations have been observed to discriminate between the sounds of their own species and those of the other (M. J. Littlejohn; Littlejohn & J. J. Loftus-Hills). Here, then, is another example of how social signals can be a means of isolating closely related sympatric species.

Human speech excepted, the best-known audible social signals are those of birds, already described in 12.2. As we know, sympatric species of much preyed-upon birds often have similar alarm calls. We assume that mutual advantage results. Other sounds, usually much more elaborate, are called songs, and are always confined to a single species: like the din made by frogs, they may help to defend a territory or to attract a mate.

But confident statements about their actual function should be made only on the evidence from experiments. The red-winged blackbird, *Agelaius phoeniceus,* has a species-typical song, sung from conspicuous perches in the breeding season. It also has a visible display, with wings spread to show red tufts (epaulets) on their leading edges.

F. W. Peek (1972a,b) gave a tranquilizer, reserpine, to territorial males in Pennsylvania, and so reduced the time they spent in their territories and the number of their displays. As expected, trespassing by conspecifics increased. Peek also obscured the epaulets of other territorial males; as a result, some of these males lost their territories altogether. Yet other males were rendered mute; and again the result was loss of territory.

The sting in this tale is due to D. G. Smith, who studied these birds in Massachusetts. He cut both hypoglossal nerves of fifteen males, and so made them sing an atypical song. Another fifteen birds had sham operations: that is, they were subjected to the same procedure, but their hypoglossal nerves were not cut. The males of both groups, experimental and control, were equally successful in maintaining territories and in breeding. This was especially surprising, because the atypical songs evoked no response by other birds; whereas the species-typical song played to a territorial male evokes apotreptic displays. This finding has still to be explained.

J. R. Krebs (1977a) describes the effects of playing the songs of great tits, *Parus major,* to other great tits. He concludes that the songs are used by potential settlers to assess whether a region is occupied by conspecifics. He also shows territory size to be positively correlated with the size of the song repertoire. Danger from predators increases with prey density. The larger the territories of a prey species, such as the great tit, the lower their density. Hence the size of the song repertoire is negatively correlated with danger from predators.

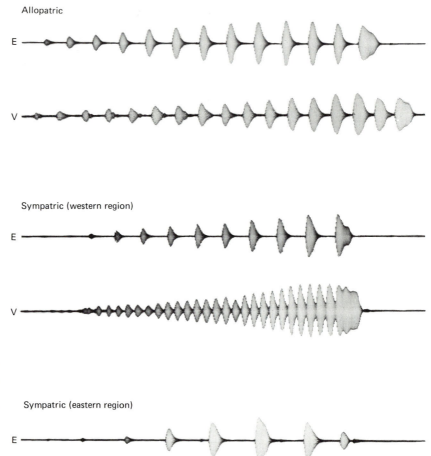

Allopatric

E

V

Sympatric (western region)

E

V

Sympatric (eastern region)

E

V

FIGURE 13-12 Oscillograms of the sounds of two species of Australian frogs, *Hyla ewingi* (E) and *H. verreauxi* (V). The two top figures, from individuals living in different regions, represent similar patterns of calling. The other two pairs of oscillograms are each from sympatric populations: in such populations, the calls of the two species are distinct, and presumably help to prevent members of different species from mating. (From M. J. Littlejohn, 1968)

Although song is often used to identify a bird's species, it may vary substantially within a species: song dialects allow birds to discriminate resident neighbors from intruders; individual songs can also keep mated pairs together and can prevent parents from feeding any but their own offspring (12.2.2.5).

Sounds studied closely include those of both young birds and young mammals. Usually they are treated as part of the repertoire of signals that attract the mother (or father) and evoke feeding or other care giving (9.3.6; 9.4.2.3). Another function is illustrated by the experiments of W. M.

Schleidt and others on turkeys, *Meleagris gallopavo.* The initial experiment was to deafen the young (poults). (Those so treated followed their mother more persistently than is normal.) Hens that had been deafened were allowed to breed; and, at hatching, they attacked their poults. In this case, evidently, the sounds made by the young birds prevent behavior by the hen that is normally directed against predators.

Among adult mammals, one group, the Cetacea, seem to make sounds rather similar to the songs of birds. R. S. Payne & S. McVay have described the "songs" of humpback whales, *Megaptera novaeangliae.* Like birds, these vast creatures use fixed sequences of sounds; but each sequence is remarkably long: the range is from 7 to 30 min. A song cycle may last for hours. The species-typical features include trains of rapidly repeated notes often alternating with longer tones; phrases in which many short notes of high and rising frequency are sounded; and further phrases of a series of lower, longer notes that tend to fall in frequency. There is, however, much variation between individuals, and this suggests the possibility of individual recognition. Unfortunately, the functions of the songs and even the sex of the singers are still a matter of speculation. Humpback whales are about 15 m long. It seems unlikely that research grants will soon be available for controlled experiments on humpbacks in captivity.

13.2.3 Smelling

13.2.3.1 Pheromones: Definition and Scope: Chemical communication is perhaps universal in the animal kingdom, but until recently it was studied only in a perfunctory way. This was partly because human beings rely much more on sight and hearing than on odor (1.1.4). Today there are, however, analytical techniques, such as gas chromatography, that enable us to detect and to analyze very small amounts of organic substances. When such substances act as social signals they are called *pheromones* (reviewed by H. H. Shorey). This definition differs from that originally proposed: P. Karlson & M. Lüscher reserved the term for *single* substances. Chemical social signals often include several substances; and the behavioral effects of such signals are often known in the absence of exact information on their chemistry. The wider definition is therefore more convenient.

Many secretions have interspecific effects; they are then called *allomones;* but here we are concerned only with social (intraspecific) interactions.

Like sounds, pheromones are effective in darkness; and they circumvent obstacles. They can act at considerable distances. On this feature there have been some exaggerations; but the male gypsy moth, *Porthetria dispar,* can certainly be attracted by the pheromone of a female at a distance of 400 m (reviewed by M. Jacobson & M. Beroza). Pheromones are also economical. The same authors give the example of a female pine sawfly, *Diprion similis,* caged in a field, which attracted 11,000 males. The amounts of material required to produce such effects are, as we see below, astonishingly small (reviewed by T. L. Payne).

Most pheromones, like visible and audible signals, have an immediate effect on the receiver; they are then called *signal* (or, sometimes, releaser) pheromones. But others alter the physiology of the receiver, and its behavior changes only much later; these are *primer* pheromones.

13.2.3.2 Some Insect Pheromones: The odorous signals of insects have been reviewed by M. C. Birch (1974) and by M. Jacobson (1970).

A celebrated example of a *sex pheromone* is

that of the silk moth, *Bombyx mori*. The female, when ready to mate, produces a single substance, *trans*-10-*cis*-12-hexadecadienol, also known as bombykol. Like those of many other moths, the males of this species have very large antennae, each with about 10,000 hair-like sensilla (figure 13-13). The receptor cells are chemoreceptors, of which the function has been studied by extremely refined electrophysiological techniques. These receptors are evidently sensitive only to bombykol; and it seems that a single molecule of this substance is enough to activate a receptor. The response of the male moth to the pheromone requires that only two hundred cells a second, in each antenna, need to be activated. Given this extraordinary sensitivity, it is hardly surprising that in the past some animal behavior has seemed to be guided by totally mysterious agencies.

Another notable sex pheromone is disparlure (*cis*-7,8-epoxy-2-methyloctadecane), secreted by the gypsy moth (mentioned in 13.2.3.1). The larvae of this species defoliate the trees of forests and orchards throughout North America. It is a native of the eastern hemisphere, but in 1869 it was rashly brought to America for silk. A calamitous population explosion occurred in 1889. M. Beroza & E. F. Knipling describe how disparlure can be used to trap males or to confuse them. The use of the pheromone also allows early detection of a possible outbreak.

There are many other examples of insect pheromones that attract males (reviewed by W. L. Roelofs & R. T. Cardé). Some consist of single substances, others of mixtures. Males, too, secrete pheromones when mating. Sometimes these signals are called aphrodisiacs; but, as M. C. Birch (1974) remarks, this is an anthropomorphism: they are often not attractants, but—when secreted just before coitus—seem to immobilize the female. They

FIGURE 13-13 Silk moth, *Bombyx mori,* with cocoon. (S. Dalton)

are *arrestants*. (One example, from the mating of cockroaches, is given in 9.1.1.) Males of night-flying species of moths (Lepidoptera) usually have eversible organs that secrete pheromones from a brushlike glandular epithelium. Birch (1970) has described the mating of the angle shades moth, *Phlogophera meticulosa* (figure 13-14). A receptive female remains still and, during some of the hours of darkness, releases a pheromone that attracts the males; while "calling" in this way, she vibrates her wings. When the male is stimulated, he flies upwind and eventually locates the female by touching her with his antennae. He then hovers close to the female and everts his two brushes for one or two seconds. Coitus follows at once and is usually successful; but males from which the brushes have been removed fail.

Birch (1974) also gives the example of the queen butterfly, *Danaus gilippus.* The male follows the female in flight, overtakes her, and—if she is receptive—makes her settle by extruding two tufts from his posterior abdomen and releasing a phero-

FIGURE 13-14 Angle shades moth, *Phlogophera meticulosa.* (S. C. Bisserôt)

mone near her antennae. The pair then couple and come to rest. Coitus lasts several hours. The "pencil" organs of the male, like the brushes of *Phlogophera,* are essential. They secrete a volatile ketone and a viscose terpenoid alcohol. The ketone is the pheromone, and the alcohol acts as an adhesive.

A sex pheromone can have more than one function. The queen substance of the honey bee, *Apis mellifera,* is an airborne pheromone that attracts males and stimulates them to coitus: males attempt coitus with models impregnated with this substance (already mentioned in 1.1.1). It also, however, attracts workers (which are sterile females), and so contributes to the cohesion of a colony and to assembly when a swarm is formed. Queen substance is therefore both a sex pheromone and an aggregation pheromone. As well, it inhibits the construction of queen cells and prevents workers from developing ovaries. The last is a priming effect. Hence this substance is both a releaser and a primer pheromone.

The *aggregation pheromones* of cockroaches are mentioned in 2.3.5. Other examples are provided by beetles (Coleoptera) of the family Scolytidae, reviewed by J. H. Borden. These insects include bark beetles and timber beetles, and are important as pests. They assemble in vast numbers and riddle trees or fallen timber with their galleries. Mass attack is believed to be necessary if the resistance of a living host is to be overcome, for trees produce deterrent quantities of resins. When adult western pine beetles, *Dendroctonus brevicomis,* emerge they fly widely. The first to attack a host tree are females, and it is not known whether these "pioneers" are attracted to trees of the appropriate species or reach them by random flight. (Other species are specially attracted to their hosts.) An aggregation pheromone is quickly produced; other beetles join the pioneers; and they too produce pheromones. Females secrete mainly a substance called brevicomin; the male aggregation pheromone, frontalin, differs chemically from that of the females. These substances not only attract other beetles but also inhibit their flight on arrival and are involved in mating. Once again, we find pheromones with multiple functions.

M. S. Blum reviews other examples of aggregation pheromones, and remarks that the mass assemblies of insects "represent a real bonanza" for predators. Correspondingly, there are substances with an opposite effect: alarm pheromones provoke dispersal and escape. Among many kinds of insects that cluster together are the aphids (figure 13-15). C. J. Kislow & L. J. Edwards describe secretions of *Myzus persicae,* which are produced on disturbance and cause the insects to stop feeding and move away: often the stimulated aphids fall from the underside of a leaf to the ground. An aphid, while responding, waves its antennae. The active substance, *trans-β*-farnesene, is secreted by species of at least three genera. Here there seems to be an analogy to the similar alarm calls of sympatric species of birds (12.2.1). But, as usual, caution is necessary: Kislow & Edwards point out that the pheromone could have a territorial or dispersive function.

The *trail pheromones* of ants are mentioned in 7.4.3. Like the more famous signals of bees (described below in 13.3.2) they are a principal means of communication among foragers (figure 13-16).

Among the eusocial insects (9.1.2) there are many examples of *alarm pheromones* (reviewed by E. O. Wilson, 1971). Ants of the species *Lasius alienus* secrete a mixture of volatile organic substances when disturbed. Some are terpenes and act at the astonishingly low concentration of only 10^9 molecules in a cubic centimeter. They induce scattering and rapid, apparently undirected running. Some substances, which we also (misleadingly) call alarm pheromones, have, however, an opposite effect: they cause assembly. Among many examples are those of termites (Isoptera). If the wall of a termite's nest is damaged, the insects nearby secrete a pheromone that attracts other members of the colony: the group that assembles then repairs the breach. Such substances are, in fact, aggregation pheromones secreted when the insects are disturbed.

13.2.3.3 Fish Odors:
Among the vertebrates I take examples from the fish and the mammals. (There are no examples from the birds, because birds seem to be exceptional in hardly using chemical communication.)

Fish of some species depend on pheromones

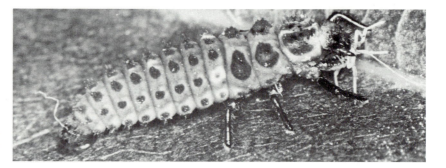

FIGURE 13-15 Beetle larva, *Coccinella septempunctata,* eating a lime aphid, *Eucallipterus tiliae.* (Courtesy A. F. G. Dixon)

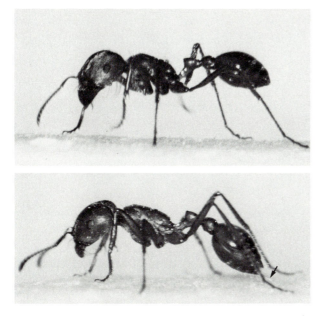

FIGURE 13-16 Harvester ant, *Pogonomyrmex mari-copa:* above, walking normally; below, a forager dragging its abdomen over the ground, with sting (shown by arrow) extruded, after it has found food. (Turid Hölldobler)

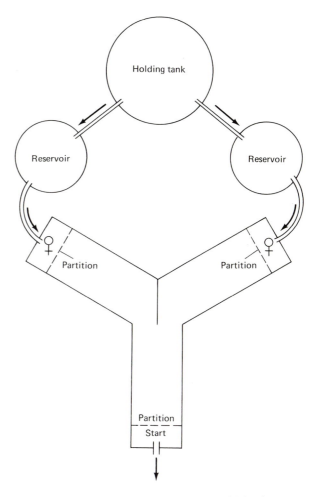

FIGURE 13-17 Diagram of Y-maze in which the responses of goldfish, *Carassius auratus,* were observed. The partitions were transparent and perforated. In each goal-arm there was a sexually inactive female to act as a visible stimulus. The test was whether a male, swimming from the compartment marked "start", could distinguish water containing the odor of an ovulating female. (After B. L. Partridge and others, 1976)

both for mating and for group behavior (reviewed by W. Pfeiffer). B. L. Partridge and others have described experiments on goldfish, *Carassius auratus.* They used a Y-maze (figure 13-17) and showed that males could distinguish, by odor alone, unovulated females from those that had ovulated. They also made some fish anosmic (unable to smell), and observed a decline in sexual activity. The female pheromone is present in the ovarian fluid: when a female has ovulated she evidently releases pheromone from the ovary and this stimulates courtship by males.

Among the most notable studies of fish pheromones are those of fright substances, also reviewed by Pfeiffer. The original work, by K. von Frisch

(1938)—more celebrated for his studies of the honey bee—arose from an accidental observation on the European minnow, *Phoxinus phoxinus.* A fish with a minor injury was put in a tank with others, and this led to vigorous swimming and scattering in all directions. When undisturbed, the fish of this species live in schools. The hypothesis was that wounded tissues release a substance that causes scattering. An initial test was to train minnows living in a lake to feed at a particular point by dropping chopped earthworms down a tube into the water. When the fish had developed this habit, substances were introduced into the water at the time of feeding; and extract of minnow tissues proved to have the expected effect. In the laboratory, worms were similarly dropped down a tube into an aquarium. The aquarium included a place in which the fish could conceal themselves. After some days, to allow for habituation, the effect of various substances on the numbers of fish at the feeding place and the numbers in the shelter were recorded. Again, tissue extracts of minnows had the expected effect.

By this means, the source of the *Schreckstoff,* or alarm substance, was shown to be injured skin, but not other tissues. Special cells in the skin, distinct from those that secrete mucus, are the source. The olfactory sense is essential for the "fright reaction": anosmic fish are unaffected. Extracts of skin alone produce the response; hence even if visual or auditory stimuli are involved, they are not essential.

13.2.3.4 Mammals:

The functions of mammalian pheromones resemble those of other groups (reviewed in the volume edited by M. C. Birch, 1974), and their importance is reflected in the array of glands that produce them. Many are modified sebaceous glands. Sometimes they are locally greatly enlarged: many deer (Cervidae) and other

FIGURE 13-18 Indian blackbuck, *Antilope cervicapra,* marks a branch with the secretion of a preorbital gland. (From F. R. Walther in T. A. Sebeok, ed., *How Animals Communicate,* 1977, by permission of Indiana Univ. Press)

Artiodactyla have large scent glands on the forehead (figure 13-18) or hind legs, and antelopes (Antelopinae) have them between the hooves. Some rodents, notably gerbils, such as *Meriones,* have conspicuous ventral (sternal) glands; other rodents, such as *Arvicola,* and also shrews, *Sorex,* have flank glands. The odors to which every newborn mammal is exposed include those from the many sebaceous glands on the nipples of the mammaries (9.4.2.3). Urine, too, is an important source of social odors. It may contain secretions of the preputial glands (figure 13-19). These discharge into the urethra and reflect, in their growth, the endocrine state of the animal.

Pheromones are involved in mating (9.4.2.1); in the interaction of parents and young; and in status and territorial relationships (chapter 10). There are also alarm pheromones. Finally, there are primer pheromones that do not immediately or directly alter behavior.

Probably in all species pheromones take part in several kinds of relationships. An example, described by T. Schultze-Westrum, is provided by *Petaurus breviceps,* a gliding phalanger of Niugini. This nocturnal, arboreal marsupial has odor-producing glands on the head, on the sternal region and feet, around the anus, and in the pouch. Groups of about six adults and their young nest together and hold territories. One or two dominant males mark the regions they occupy with secretions

FIGURE 13-19 Photomicrographs of the preputial glands of wild house mice, *Mus musculus.* Above, almost inactive gland of a subordinate male. Below, a much larger gland of a dominant animal, showing secretions pouring into a duct. (N. Call)

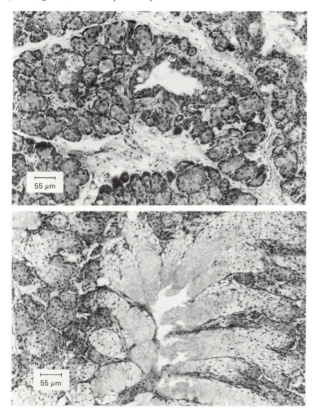

from the sternal, anal, and lateral glands and also with saliva. Dominance in this case refers to mating success; but dominant males, so defined, also perform most of the territorial displays toward neighbors. In addition, a male marks the female with which he is associated, with secretions from a gland on his head. The secretions make possible discrimination between individuals. Individual recognition exists between adult members of a group of both sexes, and also between mother and offspring. The odor of a dominant male inhibits mating, scent marking, and territorial behavior by junior males, but it provokes apotreptic displays by males of neighboring groups.

Another case of complex pheromonal signaling has been described by O. A. E. Rasa (1972, 1973). The African dwarf mongoose, *Helogale undulata,* lives in family groups of up to 12 individuals, including one reproducing pair and their young of several generations. In each group, the breeding or founding female is dominant (in the sense that she "attacks" most often), and the founding male is next in rank; but, among the young, the youngest are dominant over the others. Rasa studied scent marking by the members of a single, natural family, of which the individuals were aged from six months to six years. The main sources of pheromones are cheek and anal glands. The urine and feces of strange individuals are, however, recognized as such, and marked with the secretions of these glands. The secretions of the anal glands allow individual recognition, but those of the cheek glands have an apotreptic effect: that is, on encountering those of another individual, a mongoose performs "threat" postures; "growling threats" and "lunges" lead to the withdrawal of the other. Once again, marking is not only of objects but also of other individuals, and this is held to have a "bonding" effect within the group. Marking of objects near the nests occurs especially frequently around the time of birth of a litter; this may have a territorial function.

The scent glands and pheromones of the European rabbit, *Oryctolagus cuniculus,* have been studied both behaviorally and physiologically. As figure 13-20 shows, the weight of the inguinal glands of a male is correlated with its sexual activity; and the degree of development of the chin gland of both sexes (figure 13-21) reflects social status (10.4.1.8).

Experimental study of mammals has yielded notable examples of primer pheromones (reviewed by F. H. Bronson). In 10.5.1.1 I describe pregnancy block (the Bruce effect) induced by the odor of the urine of male rodents of several genera. This rather strange pheromonal action is suspected of being a means of regulating population growth.

Other examples come, like pregnancy block, from study of laboratory mice. One, the Lee–Boot effect, concerns the cycle of estrus. If laboratory mice, at least of some strains, have their olfactory bulbs removed, the cycle stops. Evidently the reproductive physiology of a mouse is profoundly affected by the input through the olfactory nerves. This is confirmed by experiments in which females have been kept in groups of four in the complete absence not only of males but also of their odor. The cycle of estrus then lengthens, because the females go into pseudopregnancy: that is, their reproductive tract undergoes the changes of pregnancy, but without a developing embryo. If the females are later completely isolated, their normal cycle is resumed; but if they are isolated but exposed to the odor of other females, the lengthening of the cycle and pseudopregnancy continue.

A further finding is called the Whitten effect. If a group of female mice, initially prevented from all contact with males, is exposed to a male or even its urine, the cycles shorten and become synchronized. If a male is present, matings take place; and most of these are on the third day after the male has been introduced. Like the Bruce effect, this has been described in other genera also.

Lastly, there is the Vandenbergh effect. The age at which female mice have their first estrus depends on their social environment: if an adult male is present, first estrus is 20 days earlier than it would be in the absence of males. Evidently, mice have an elaborate system of pheromones that regulate reproductive function in accordance with the

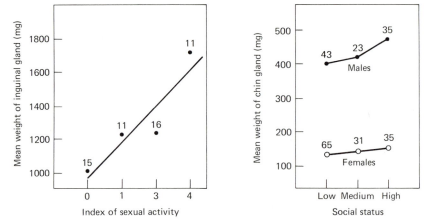

FIGURE 13-20 The sexual activity of male rabbits, *Oryctolagus cuniculus,* is positively correlated with the weight of the inguinal glands; and the social status of both sexes is related to the weight of the chin gland (see figure 13-21). The numbers give the sample size for each mean. (After R. Mykytowycz & M. L. Dudzinski, 1966)

FIGURE 13-21 European rabbit "chinning", or marking an object with the secretions of its chin gland. (Courtesy R. Mykytowycz)

social situation. Wild house mice, *Mus musculus,* often live in rather small, isolated groups (demes); hence it is possible to imagine how these pheromones could confer survival value in natural conditions.

13.2.4 Mechanical Signals

Odors, sights, and sounds can all act at a considerable distance. Another important source of social signals is the actual contact of one individual with another. The whole of the body surface of many animals is a sense organ. In earlier chapters I mention the sensilla of insects, the tactile abilities of cephalopods, and the importance of contact during the interactions of some mammals. But not all skin receptors depend on contact: the lateral line organs of fish are specialized for detecting rapid changes of water pressure; and these occur in some social interactions.

Whenever mating involves the direct transfer of sperm, tactile stimuli are likely to be important. Examples already given come from the insects as well as mammals. Even when the gametes are released into water, contact may be important, as it is for sticklebacks. Contact is also crucial for the parent–offspring relationships of mammals. And many rodents and Primates perform allogrooming during social interactions that are neither sexual nor parental.

The preceding examples are of epitreptic signals. Contact may also be apotreptic. A bite, for example, is not usually called a threat, but it falls under the definition of threat (or apotreptic behavior) used in this book: it is a social signal that tends to cause withdrawal. Claws, hoofs, and horns, like teeth, may also be used to inflict threats in this sense.

Contact signals have, however, been rather little studied, and are often enigmatic. Figure 13-22 illus-

FIGURE 13-22 Male wild rat, *Rattus norvegicus,* grooms an intruder in an interval between attacks. (Drawing by Gabriel Donald, from a photograph; from S. A. Barnett, 1975)

trates allogrooming by wild rats. I first observed this conduct during entirely peaceable interactions (1958a). It was a gentle nibbling of the fur of another rat, and therefore seemed to be epitreptic. But sometimes allogrooming is more vigorous and seems to approach biting: the animal groomed may be held down by a forefoot in intervals between attacks (that is, leaping and biting). Hence to classify this behavior adequately, more detailed observations will be needed: correlations will have to be established between different kinds of allogrooming and both physiological states and other behavior such as attack.

13.2.5 Electrical Signals

In 2.3.2 I describe the equipment of electric fish, which allows them to detect objects in the water by means of an electric field. From an anthropo-centric point of view, this is extrasensory perception; and as we know, it produces behavior that at first seems very mysterious indeed.

C. D. Hopkins has reviewed the social uses of electrical signals. The wave forms of the electrical signals of many fish are species-typical (figure 13-23). In addition, the resting discharges of some gymnotid fish, such as *Sternopygus macrurus,* differ between the sexes. A male responds to the female pattern by changing his own pattern: the resulting display is believed to be part of the male's courtship. Hopkins even gives evidence of individual recognition. At mating, either a male or a female *Sternopygus* may change the frequency of its discharge to be exactly an octave below or above that of the other. Such "duetting" is preceded by distinctive changes in the male pattern, which develop when the male comes into the breeding state: he then settles in concealment (for instance under a rock) and modifies his electrical discharges whenever a female passes nearby; the modification includes a rise in frequency and also interruptions in the discharge.

Some electrical signals seem to have the same role as aggregation pheromones. The electric eel, *Electrophorus electricus,* alters its output when it captures prey: the discharge is at exceptionally high frequency and amplitude. Nearby conspecifics approach the source of these signals. Here is an apparent analogy to the social enhancement displayed by some birds that feed in flocks (8.4.1.1).

There is also evidence for an apotreptic function. *Gymnotus carapo* has been studied in large aquaria in seminatural conditions. These fish sometimes attack and bite each other. Such conduct is accompanied and often preceded by a sharp increase in the discharge from the electric organ, followed by a rapid decrease to the resting frequency. Similarly,

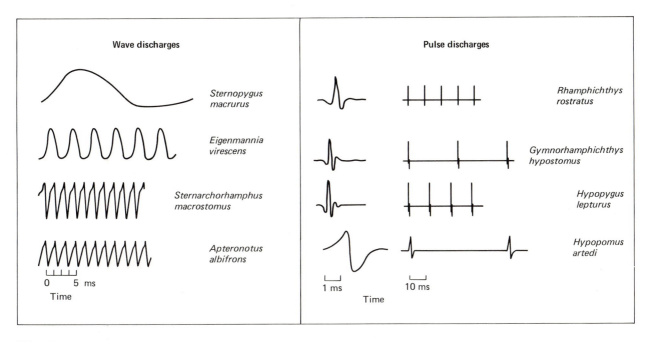

FIGURE 13-23 The electrical signals of eight species of gymnotids. To obtain oscilloscope tracings one electrode was fastened near the head and one near the tail. An upward deflection indicates that the head is positive. The wave and pulse patterns are distinct for each species, like other social signals. (After C. D. Hopkins, 1977)

several species of mormyrids accompany attack (in this case, head butting) with a rapid increase in frequency which is sometimes followed by a period of no discharge. In apotreptic interactions both fish may produce similar discharges of this sort—apparently, threats. But sometimes relationships of dominance and subordinacy are described: and then the subordinate fish either reduces the frequency of discharge or stops discharging altogether for some minutes. Prolonged cessation of discharge is evidently displayed only by subordinates (that is, fish that have been defeated), and is often accompanied by retreat. When a fish becomes electrically silent,

it is regarded as behaving in a way analogous to that of a subordinate mammal with flattened fur and drooping posture. Hence electric fish appear to possess, in their distinctive electrical discharges, an array of social signals precisely analogous to the more familiar visible, audible, and odorous displays described in preceding sections.

13.3 SIGNALS AND DISPLAYS

13.3.1 Pragmatic Questions

13.3.1.1 Identifying Signals: Descriptions of animal conduct often *presume* that certain appearances or sounds are social signals, and that they have clearly defined effects on conspecifics. In the absence of experiment, such presumptions are inevitable; but it is important that they should be recognized as such. Here is a further example.

The sexual skin of a female baboon or macaque in estrus is, to us, visually striking (figure 13-24); but it may not have the same impact on another monkey. T. E. Rowell (1967) has described receptive female baboons presenting their hindquarters to a male, only to be ignored; conversely, males sometimes make sexual advances to such a female when her sexual swelling is not visible. There is evidence of a nonvisual function for the swelling. J. Herbert & M. R. Trimble gave spayed rhesus females estradiol (an estrogenic substance). The treatment had no effect on the females' responsiveness to male advances: they did not "present" any more than did untreated controls. But the number of male advances toward them rose substantially. In contrast, giving the females testosterone made them more receptive—that is, they "presented" more; but this had no effect on the males. The obvious hypothesis was that the vagina of a receptive rhesus monkey secretes a pheromone that attracts males. H. Rahaman & M. D. Parthasarathy describe a similar finding for the bonnet macaque. R. P. Michael & E. B. Keverne (1968, 1970) accordingly tested males in a bar-pressing apparatus (6.1.2). Pressing the bar raised a barrier and gave access to a female. Estradiol was used to induce an intense redness of the sexual skin of females, but this did not enhance attractiveness to males. In contrast, vaginal secretions from receptive females had a marked effect. Evidently, the surface of the swelling helps to disseminate the odorous substance or substances. Males made temporarily anosmic were indifferent to the attractive females. Hence in this case we are at first led to as-

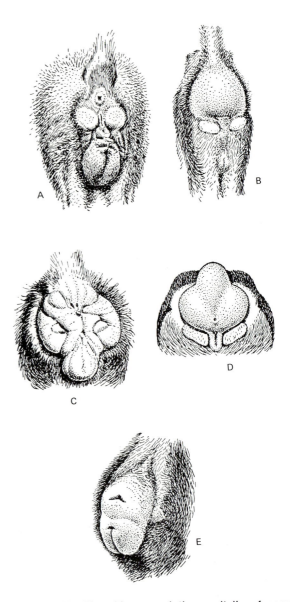

FIGURE 13-24 The skin around the genitalia of some female primates becomes swollen and conspicuous during estrus: (A) rhesus monkey, *Macaca mulatta;* (B) crab-eating monkey, *M. irus;* (C) talapoin, *Miopithecus talapoin;* (D) *Macaca maura;* (E) chimpanzee, *Pan troglodytes.* (Reproduced from W. Wickler in D. Morris, ed., *Primate Ethology,* 1967, p. 75, by permission of Weidenfeld (Publishers) Limited)

sume that the male is responding simply to a visible stimulus, but an odor proves to be a crucial component of the female's signals; and the structure that at first seems obviously to be a visible signal may be in fact a means of spreading a pheromone.

Moreover, as J. Hanby points out, the females of some species have conspicuous pink bottoms not only when they are in estrus but also after the birth of their young. Once mobile, the infant is attracted, perhaps by the bright color, and may climb on it. Hence the sexual skin of these species may be important in interactions between mother and young. Experiments are needed to identify its exact role, and to test whether exposure to a pink (and odorous) patch in early life influences conduct later on.

13.3.1.2 Probabilities and Context:

Many kinds of social interaction include several distinct signals and responses to them. Merely to describe these situations adequately demands a high degree of devotion and tenacity: a vast amount of sheer counting of incidents and postures is needed. As an example, A. W. Stokes watched blue tits, *Parus caeruleus,* at a winter feeding station. He describes visible postures and movements such as erection of the crest and fluffing of the body feathers. Both of these reduce the incidence of escape by other individuals: that is, other birds fly away more often when crest and body feathers are *not* raised. Raising the crest alone reduces escape from 37% of occasions to 3%; and raising body feathers from 34 to 5%. The percentages illustrate that there is no simple relationship between signal and response. There is also the question whether a particular signal predicts the next action by the signaler. Such an enquiry gives some indication of how a signal reflects the signaler's own internal state. Erection of the crest preceded escape by the signaler on 90% of occasions (but *absence* of erect crest still

had a 26% probability of being followed by escape). When it came to predicting attack, probabilities were surprisingly low. A number of features *tend* to precede attack; but, of these, the combination of (1) nape erect, (2) facing opponent, (3) body horizontal, (4) crest not erect, and (5) wings not raised gave only a 48% probability that attack would follow.

Other instances are given by W. J. Smith (1966, 1969). He also describes examples of signals that are given in a variety of contexts and are correspondingly difficult to interpret. The eastern kingbird, *Tyrannus tyrannus,* has a "kitter" call (figures 13-25, 13-26) which is sounded when a male touches down on a perch in his territory or when he approaches a perch and then flies off without landing. It evidently attracts females and repels rivals (and so has both epitreptic and apotreptic functions). The call also occurs when a bird approaches its mate; the mate responds with a similar cry. Moreover, a male that turns back after chasing a hawk makes the call; and a female makes a similar sound if she leaves her nest when the male is not there to take her place. Lastly, fledgling young use the call while they follow their parents; at this stage the young still get food from their parents, but their approach sometimes now evokes an apotreptic response.

Smith therefore calls the kitter sound the "locomotory hesitance vocalization". The internal states of birds making the call must be very diverse; but Smith hypothesizes that there is one thing in common to all the circumstances in which the call is made: the bird is tending to move (usually to fly), but is experiencing some "internal conflict". Such a conflict results in uncertainty about whether the bird will move or remain still; and the message supposed to be conveyed is that uncertainty.

A principal lesson from this example is the com-

FIGURE 13-25 Male eastern kingbird, *Tyrannus tyrannus,* giving the kitter call and fluttering his wings as he follows his mate to a nest under construction. (After W. J. Smith, 1966)

plexity we meet even when we try to analyze a well-defined signal that acts on only one sensory modality. The kitter call is, however, not always the same: perhaps the different forms of the call have different effects on the recipients. Such a possibility has been discussed by C. G. Beer (1976). As we know (12.2.2.5), Beer has made a detailed analysis of the long-call of the laughing gull, *Larus atricilla.* This is one of about 12 calls that a human being can identify. The long-call may be given when the bird is flying or swimming, but it is most often heard from a bird standing on the ground (figure 12-13). Moreover, Beer states: "The range of situations in which the long-call occurs covers almost all the distinguishable classes of social interactions." It has, evidently, a function in territorial conduct, courtship, and—as already described—in the care of young. Figure 13-27 shows

sound spectograms of four calls given by the same gull. Each is unequivocally (to the human ear) a long-call, and distinct from other kinds of sound made by this species; but each is different from the others. We already know that individuals of this species can be distinguished by their sounds; the figure now suggests the possibility that one individual can give different information by varying what we regard as a single call.

FIGURE 13-26 Sound spectrograms of kitter calls by eastern kingbirds: (A) a female greets her mate as she flies from the nest; (B) a male flies above a stuffed owl; (C) the same male perched after attacking the owl; (D) the same male flies to attack the owl. (From W. J. Smith, 1966)

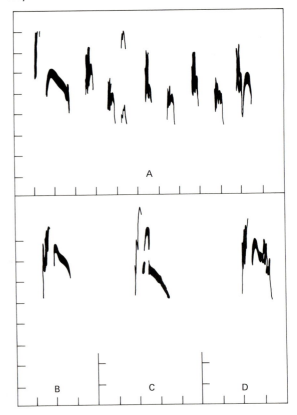

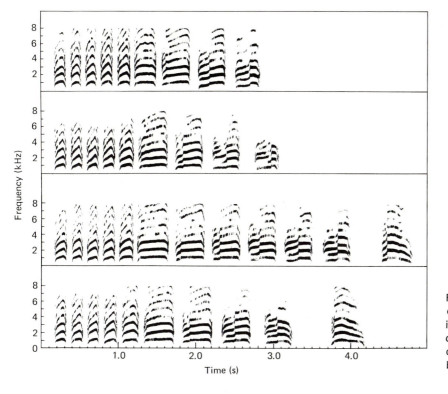

FIGURE 13-27 Sound spectrograms of four long-calls by the same laughing gull, *Larus atricilla:* each is clearly "the same" call, yet each differs from the others (From C. G. Beer, 1976)

Another finding concerns the units of which a call is made. We intuitively take the long-call as a signal; and there is experimental evidence to justify this: Beer has played recordings of such calls to gulls, and evoked appropriate responses such as calling back or beginning to leave the nest as if the mate were coming to take over. Yet, as figure 13-27 shows, the call consists of units or "notes". We have here an analog of music: a few individual notes can be arranged in a great variety of possible melodies (or cacophonies). Hence in this case the units or calls that the observer selects at first hearing can readily be broken down into smaller units for analysis.

S. T. Emlen (1972) has examined the role of the order in which notes occur (which might be called "melody") and other features of complex songs. Indigo buntings, *Passerina cyanea,* were tested by playing back the recorded song of their own species and the rather similar song of the yellow warbler, *Dendroica petechia;* in addition, the components of natural songs were rearranged and also played back. In natural conditions an intruding conspecific provokes a territory holder to a higher rate of singing, a distinctive posture, and approach. Recognition of a bird as a conspecific proved to depend not on melody but on the intervals between notes: these are remarkably constant from one individual to another.

Examination of the components of signals raises the question, asked by Beer (1977), what is a display? The term *display* is commonly used in social ethology to refer to a signal or pattern of signals (affecting any sensory modality) which acts or seems to act as a unit. The question now is how we decide on the units of study. Experiment has shown that the calls of laughing gulls, as described by Beer, are convenient units; but sometimes it is appropriate to examine the components of such patterns. The Carib grackle, *Quiscalus lugubris,* has a performance called the song-spread display, in which it makes a distinctive sound, raises and flutters the wings, rotates the tail feathers, bounces up and down, and flicks the nictitating membrane across the yellow iris. The visible display is partly illustrated in figure 13-28. R. H. Wiley recorded beak raising and wing raising by these birds in Trinidad. Both are part of the total pattern, but their intensity varies independently: beak raising occurs especially when a male is near another male, and is unaffected by the presence of females; but wing raising usually occurs when a male is near a female, and is independent of the presence of males.

The song-spread display is therefore seen as a unit because several kinds of movement are evoked at the same time; but at least two components prove to vary independently. The variation corresponds to different probabilities of further behavior by the performer: a male may follow a song-spread display either by attack or by sexual activity. Hence the level of beak raising or wing raising seem to reflect different internal states. If so, the total display can convey more information if it is analyzed in terms of its components. Whether grackles in fact interpret the performance in this way has, as far as I know, not been experimentally demonstrated.

The song-spread display is therefore a *composite signal* in two senses: (1) certain of its visible components have separate functions; and (2) it includes sounds as well as sights. Much signaling is

FIGURE 13-28 Carib grackles, *Quiscalus lugubris:* the bird on the left is performing the song-spread display. (Courtesy R. H. Wiley)

similarly composite. Chapters 9 to 12 give a number of examples: ringdoves (9.3.7.1) make both noises and gestures during courtship; many mammals (9.4) use postures, noises, odors, and contacts during an encounter with a mate or a rival. Sometimes the same message is conveyed by more than one means. In 9.4.2 I describe the features of an infant to which a female mammal responds: they include sounds, odors, and other stimuli; hence there is much redundancy, and any one can be dispensed with.

Often it is uncertain just what effect the various components of a signal system are having. Figure 13-29 illustrates an interaction between two male Australian bush rats, *Rattus fuscipes.* The postures seem to be signals; but sounds are also being ut-

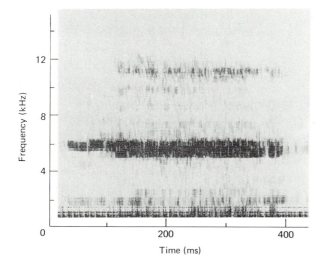

FIGURE 13-29 Above, Australian bush rats, *Rattus fuscipes,* in a clash; below, sound spectrogram of an intermediate sound, between a whistle and a scream, uttered during such encounters. The odors of the two rats were, unfortunately, not recorded. (Above: W. E. Hocking; below: S. A. Barnett & A. P. Stewart)

tered; and the two rats are certainly odorous, though the contribution of pheromones to such encounters has not yet been studied (S. A. Barnett & A. P. Stewart). D. G. Kleiman & J. F. Eisenberg review the social ethology of the dogs and cats, and give a closely similar example. They write:

When a wolf stands with its tail raised, its fur bristled, and its ears raised with the openings directed forward while its face is wrinkled in a snarl, we have no way of determining whether all of these movements or only two or three components are perceived. Nor do we know anything about what kind of information is obtained from a scent mark or a call. We [only] assume that all of these are signals . . .

The next section illustrates many of the features of complex signaling systems from one exceptional species.

13.3.2 A Special Case: The Honey Bee

Apart from man, the honey bee, *Apis mellifera,* probably has the most elaborate system of communication of all species studied. Its social interactions depend on odors, sounds, and contacts, and—to some extent—on vision. The remarkable array of sense organs and direction-finding abilities possessed by bees is mentioned in 2.2.3 (sun navigation), 2.3.1 (the use of ultraviolet and the plane of polarization of light) and 2.3.2 (response to magnetic fields). Bees also respond to gravity and to vibrations. All these play some part in their social conduct.

The discovery of the "language" of bees is usually regarded as the outstanding single finding of modern social ethology. Yet, when it was already textbook knowledge, it was questioned on the basis of both logic and experimental evidence. The resulting controversy led to further experiments of great ingenuity. The original theory has survived;

but our knowledge of bee communication has been enlarged, and our picture of the ways in which bees feed has been modified. As a result, the honey bee illustrates not only many aspects of ethology, but also important general principles of method. Excellent reviews have been published by K. von Frisch (1967), J. L. Gould (1976), M. Lindauer (1961), C. R. Ribbands, and E. O. Wilson (1971). C. D. Michener has reviewed the conduct of the family, Apidae.

13.3.2.1 Early Discoveries by Frisch:

In 2.2.3 I describe the technique developed by Frisch for training bees to feed at artificial feeding stations. An important finding concerns the social use of odors. Frisch set out a number of food sources near the experimental hive, each containing different odorous substances. If a single bee visits such a source of food, quite soon a number of other bees from her colony appear there; these recruits usually visit only sources that contain the odor of the food sampled by the pioneer bee. The latter, on return to the hive, may perform movements called the "round dance" (figure 13-30), while other bees follow and make contact with the dancer with their antennae (figure 13-31). The round dance occurs only if the food is within 40 m of the hive, or even less for some types; and it is most often observed when a source has been found of something in short supply. This may be nectar or water. If the bees are swarming, it may be a possible nest site. When food is indicated, at intervals the performing bee stops dancing and transfers some of the food in her crop to others—an example of trophallaxis (9.1.2.4).

The ability of bees to pick out the odor accompanying food might depend on odorous substances in the food itself. But in some experiments Frisch put distinctive odors on filter paper below the food

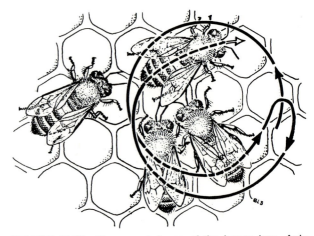

FIGURE 13-30 The round dance of the honey bee, *Apis mellifera:* the worker above is dancing in the pattern shown by the arrows, and the others are following and keeping contact with their antennae. (Reproduced from K. von Frisch: *The Social Behavior of Bees,* 1974, Fig. 15.8 and 15.11, by permission of Harvard University Press.)

at each station, so that the bees had no contact with the odorous substance. Nonetheless, recruits still assembled principally at the "correct" odor. Such an ability sounds most baffling and mysterious. The explanation is in the ability of the sensilla ("hairs") of bees to take up odors. Such odors, present in waxes on the sensilla, are detected by chemoreceptors on the antennae of other bees. These substances, then, are not pheromones, for they are not secreted by the bees; but they do convey information. A pheromone does, however, play some part in these interactions. Bees secrete, from an abdominal gland, an aggregation pheromone (13.2.3) when they are feeding. Other bees are in this way attracted to a rich source. In addition, bees are attracted by the mere sight of other bees feeding.

These findings were published in the 1920s, and have been confirmed and expanded by many workers. They show feeding by the honey bee to depend on social interactions of great complexity, in which several sensory modalities and types of signal are involved. Nonetheless, the most remarkable finding emerged two decades later; but before coming to that, let us look at some other species.

13.3.2.2 Scent Marking:

The mass of work on the honey bee and the remarkable character of its social conduct may make us forget that there are many other species of bees, some of which have been studied in detail. *Trigona postica* (described in Lindauer's book) is common in the forests of Brazil. It is regarded as a "primitive" bee. A forager, returning after a collecting flight, may settle at intervals of 2 to 3 m and mark the ground with a pheromone secreted by her mandibular gland. Some bees of this species were trained to visit a feeding table which had to be reached by flying over a lake. Lindauer describes how these bees, unable to touch down on the water, "returned to the shore, where they generously bestowed scent marks all over the feeding table and the note book and hat of the observer". But no newcomer could join the trained bees, because the latter could not guide the others without a surface on which to leave marks near the hive. Later a rope, decorated with twigs, was strung across the water. At once the twigs were marked with the pheromone, and new bees were recruited. The stingless bees (Meliponinae), to which *Trigona* belongs, can by this means guide each other to sources of food much higher or lower than the hive—for instance, at the tops of tall trees. This is presumably important in a tropical forest.

13.3.2.3 The Beeline:

So far, then, the picture of communication by bees emphasizes odors. The round dance may be interpreted as equivalent to the exclamation, "food!"; it is also a means of drawing attention to an odor. But the results of

FIGURE 13-31 A dancing honey bee, *Apis mellifera,* is surrounded by other workers, some of which are in direct contact with her through their antennae. (Courtesy Kenneth Lorenzen)

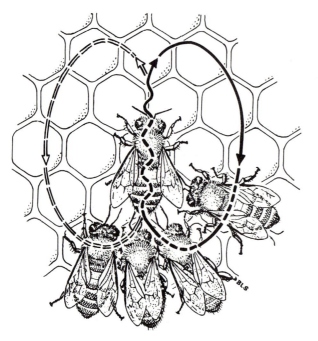

FIGURE 13-32 Waggle dance of the honey bee, *Apis mellifera:* the forager above is dancing in the pattern shown by the arrows; other workers follow her and maintain contact with their antennae (see previous two figures). (Reproduced from K. von Frisch: *The Social Behavior of Bees,* 1974, Fig. 15.8 and 15.11, by permission of Harvard University Press.)

further experiments by Frisch, reported in the 1940s, could not be explained by his early findings. The new observations concern the ability of hive bees to find sources of food at distances of substantially more than 200 m from the hive. A possible explanation was again based on response to odors. A worker, when she is about to begin foraging, makes exploratory flights during which she stores information about the topography of the hive. Such information might include the typical odors (especially of plants) in different regions of the area explored. The return of fellow workers bearing a particular odor could then give information on where to go to find a source of food.

An alternative explanation was based on a detailed study of the movements made by foragers, especially when they return after finding a new and rich distant source of food. They then perform, not a round dance, but a dance in the form of a figure eight (figure 13-32), the "waggle dance", which too attracts the attention of other workers. During the straight run the body of the dancer vibrates. At the same time, bursts of sound are produced. The crucial observations concern the relationship of measurable features of the waggle dance to the distance of the food source. Frisch found the time taken over the waggle part of the dance to be proportional to the distance. Other workers have shown the number of vibrations and the bursts of sound in each cycle to be also measures of that distance. Even a human observer can state the distance of a food source with some accuracy simply by watching a dancing bee (figures 13-33 and 13-34).

The waggle dance indicates not only distance but also direction. On a horizontal surface the dance points directly to the food, but on the more usual vertical surface of the comb the direction of the dance is indicated in the manner shown in figure 13-35. Suppose the source of food is due east from the hive, and the dance is performed at noon. In the northern hemisphere, a forager flying to the food should then fly at 90° to the left of the sun. The angle of the dancer's line of movement on the comb is, in this case, 90° to the left of the *vertical:* that is, the vertical represents the sun's direction at the time of dancing; and the angle to the vertical corresponds to the direction of the food relative to that of the sun. Dances that indicate water or a nest site similarly show both distance and direction.

Although the properties of the waggle dance are a function of the distance of the food source, the waggle dance does not, strictly speaking, measure

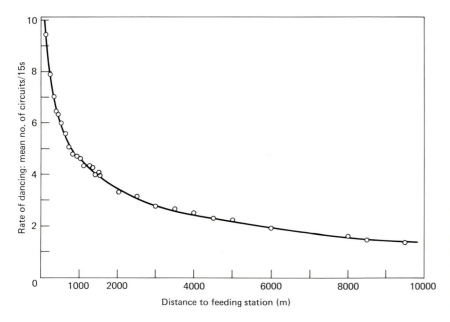

FIGURE 13-33 The relationship of the waggle dance of the honey bee (see figure 13-32) to the distance of the source of food: the more distant the food, the more time is taken over the waggle part of the dance. See also figure 13-34. (After K. von Frisch, 1967)

FIGURE 13-35 The manner in which the waggle dance of a honey bee (see previous figures) indicates direction when performed on the vertical surface of a comb: in the diagram, the direction of the food makes an angle of 45° with the direction of the sun; in the waggle dance, shown in the inset, the vertical represents the direction of the sun, and the straight run of the waggle dance is at 45° to that. (After K. Schmidt-Koenig, 1975)

FIGURE 13-34 The relationship between the time taken by a honey bee over the dance cycle and the distance of the food indicated. Each additional waggle corresponds to about 25 m, and adds about 0.08 s to the time taken. (After J. L. Gould, 1976)

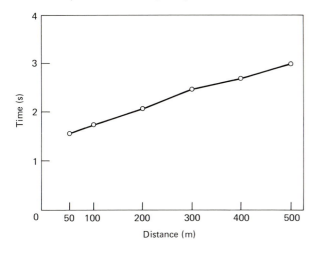

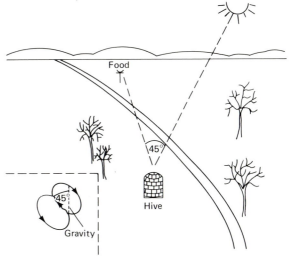

absolute distance. What seems to be measured is the work required to reach the source. For a given source, the number of waggles rises if there is a head wind. A similar effect is observed if the source is uphill. In some experiments, foragers had small weights fastened to them, like horses in a handicap race. They then indicated a greater distance than the actual one.

A remarkable finding by Martin Lindauer (1961) concerns the bees' "internal clock" (2.1.3). The direction of the sun, relative to that of a food source or a site for a new colony, is continuously changing. Sometimes, bees dance for long periods— even several hours—without a break; they then alter the orientation of their dance to correspond to the sun's movement. The ability to do this requires preliminary exposure to the sun. Bees raised in a cellar were tested after various periods of flight in sunlight. It took them five days, during which several hundred flights were made, to develop the ability. All this training was done after noon on each day; but this did not prevent the bees from later indicating the correct direction in the morning.

13.3.2.4 Controversy: During the 1960s a number of criticisms of the "bee language hypothesis" were made by A. M. Wenner (review, 1971) and his associates. Wenner emphasized the role of odor in the discovery of food sources by bees, and questioned the significance of the dances. His views were partly based on experimental findings that seemed to conflict with those of Frisch. For example, bees from an observation hive were marked and trained to collect sugar solution, flavored with clove oil, 150 m from their hive. The sugar was then removed, but some bees continued regularly to inspect the dish. When the solution was put back, there was a rapid increase in the number of visits *before* there was any dancing. This suggested

that the bees were responding to the odor or taste of the food. Accordingly, air scented with clove oil was blown through the hive, and this led to an immediate increase in foraging.

Wenner's most fundamental criticism, however, concerns the value of correlations as evidence of causal relationships. Measurable features of bee dances are undoubtedly correlated with the flights of the dancer and of other bees; but this does not prove that the dances regulate the others' movements. It may seem unlikely that such elaborate conduct could be functionless; but it is unsatisfactory to argue that certain activities are performed, *therefore* they must be useful. Other bees, such as the Meliponinae, manage very well without dancing. Moreover, these bees perform a "buzzing run" that seems to have no function. The central problem is to design a critical experiment on effects of the waggle dance on other bees. One such experiment would be to construct a model bee, of which the dances are controlled by an experimenter (figure 13-36). The model could "instruct" other bees to perform specified flights. But the technical problems of such experiments are severe (H. Esch).

Fortunately, exceedingly ingenious experiments have made the use of model bees unnecessary (reviewed by J. L. Gould, 1975, 1976). Gould himself and B. Schricker independently provided conclusive evidence of the supposed function of the waggle dance. In both cases, bees were induced to give misleading information in their dances. Schricker gave foraging bees minute quantities of an insecticide, parathion. Bees so treated perform abbreviated waggle dances: that is, they indicate shorter distances than they would if untreated. The flight distances of recruits were affected accordingly.

Gould's experiments made use of bees' three ocelli, or simple eyes. Gould covered the ocelli of dancing foragers, and so reduced the ability of bees

FIGURE 13-36 An attempt to control the foraging of honey bees by means of a model bee of which the movements are controlled by the experimenter. The object in the center is made to waggle in a manner that indicates a particular direction and distance.

to respond to the light falling on their compound eyes: the bees so treated indicated instead a direction with reference to gravity. At the same time, a light was shone into the hive. Potential recruits then responded to the light as if it were the sun. Gould predicted that bees stimulated by the dancers would fly in a direction relative to the artificial sun, and not in the direction indicated by the dancers. This was confirmed.

The role of the waggle dance is, then, not in doubt, but the controversy begun by Wenner has increased our knowledge. Some statements, formerly accepted, are now known to be wrong: for example, recruits have been said to fly quickly to a new food source (indicated by dancing), and to reach it reliably. But when individual bees were observed in the hive and followed in flight to the food, a different picture emerged. These observations were made with food sources at distances of

up to 400 m, or 57 s flying time. In the usual case, a recruit attended a dance for about six cycles, then flew out for around 6 min; on her return she again attended a dance and flew out again. This sequence was repeated several times. Even then only about half the recruits that attended the dances actually reached the food source.

More important, the part played by odors is now seen more clearly. It can also be put in a hypothetical evolutionary framework. Comparative studies suggest that communication by dancing is a recent development, superimposed on chemical communication, which is widespread among the Apidae.

All the experiments on *Apis mellifera* have been on captive bees, not on wild colonies in tropical forests. For domesticated bees, odor may be more important than for wild bees. When there are abundant sources of food near a hive, odor alone is sufficient to bring out the foragers. Such conditions are common where agriculture is practiced. Dances that indicate distant food may then be important only exceptionally. In natural forest, the distribution of food plants is quite different. As Gould (1975) says, further work is needed before we can say how important the waggle dance is in natural conditions.

The astonishment (and initial scepticism) that greeted Frisch's findings came in part from certain special features of the waggle dance. As we know, nearly all social signals, however complex in structure, are stereotyped and reflect the signaler's immediate situation. The waggle dance shares two properties with human languages but not with the signals of other species. The first is "productivity": the features of a dance can be adapted to give any one of a variety of messages; and the message may be one that a bee has never uttered before, though she may have uttered many others. A human equivalent might be: "there is a large source of food, of this odor, 500 m northwest of the hive." The second feature is "displacement": the dances of bees refer to distant things observed some time ago. There is also one very obvious difference from human languages: the dances are iconic: they have (like a map) a structural or analogical relationship to the situation they describe. The terms of human languages are not iconic but arbitrary. (I return to this subject in 15.2.)

13.4 SUMMING UP

A reader of this part is likely to be impressed by the diversity of animal conduct, but doubtful whether there are many valid generalizations on animal signals. I now attempt an orderly summing up, under four headings: (1) the description of signals, (2) the internal state they reflect, (3) their action on conspecifics, (4) their functions. A fifth aspect, the evolution of signals, is discussed in chapter 18.

1. Social signals may act on any sensory modality, including at least one (the electrical) that human beings seem not to possess. Often, social interactions involve the use of more than one sense, as when a distinctive visible pattern accompanies the release of an odor and the production of sounds.

Social signals are usually typical of a whole species, and often distinguish a species from others. Species-typical patterns are especially important when two or more similar species are sympatric. There are two major kinds of exception to this rule. First, a group of sympatric species may have common alarm signals. Second, closely related species sometimes share signals just as they share structures: for example, many species of fish threaten by raising their fins and opercula; and some of the facial expressions of Primates, such as the open mouth, are common to many species.

Signals may be digital or analogical. The simplest to study are those that are decisively on or off. Such digital signals include flashes of light and brief sounds. Many signals, in contrast, are analogical: they vary in magnitude, intensity, or duration. Although, therefore, social signals are often called "fixed action patterns", a full description often requires quantitative analysis of the signal itself and its variation (17.2.4).

2. There are many examples in preceding chapters of the correspondence between signals and the signaler's internal state. The most familiar relate to reproductive cycles, which may be seasonal or autonomous (for example, the cycle of estrus). We may also infer momentary changes of internal

state. Animals, especially vertebrates, often vacillate between approach and withdrawal, courting and threatening, and so on. Such apparent indecisiveness accompanies the fluctuations in signals mentioned in the previous paragraph.

A second kind of internal change is that accompanying habit formation; it too influences an animal's social signals. Although signals are species-typical, and fall in the now outmoded category of "instinctive" or "innate" conduct (17.1), their expression is often influenced by individual experience (chapter 12).

3. When we turn to the effects of signals (or of features that we suppose to be signals), we are likely to face questions that can be answered only by elaborate experiments. In the simplest case, a digital signal evokes a similarly digital response. Such a mechanistic relationship is implied in the concept of a "releasing" signal (17.2.4). But even a simple signal rarely evokes a response with mechanical reliability. The sources of this variation are often unknown.

The effects of a few complex signals or displays have been analyzed. Sometimes they contain components of which the actions can be recorded separately. The patches of color on a fish, or the parts of a bird's song, have been experimentally dissected. The components of a visible display may summate, or they may have distinct roles such as attraction and orientation. The effect of the notes or phrases of a song may depend on the intervals between them but not their order.

The effect of a display also depends on the internal state of the recipient; and it may depend on the context—for example, whether the performer is on its territory.

4. Signals may be classified by their functions, under the three categories of epitreptic, apotreptic, and inhibitory. Epitreptic signals include those of courtship and mating and of interactions between parents and offspring. Other signals that lead to cohesion are those that induce flocking or other assembly; yet others bring conspecifics together to a source of food. The latter may be a group of flowers, or it may be prey. In the last case the group may assemble in order to hunt. Special epitreptic relationships include those of trophallaxis or food transfer among eusocial insects, and leadership among mammals. The principal categories of apotreptic signals are those involved in territorial interactions, in status relationships within a group, and (among mammals) in weaning. Inhibitory signals include those that deter attack (or are supposed to do so); these are sometimes called "submissive" signals.

A classification orthogonal to that above may be based on *recognition*. Social signals of each of the kinds listed can make possible discrimination of species, of classes within species (sex, age group, status, and so on), and of individuals.

Lastly, many readers must wonder about the application of these findings to the human species. In the next part, therefore, we examine communication and other special features of one species, our own.

V

THE HUMAN SPECIES

More than a million years ago there originated a kind of being that survived without the usual array of standard social signals. The behavior of these human beings was, we assume, a product of natural selection; but, rather mysteriously, selection in this case led to a loss of fixed patterns of conduct and an exceptional adaptability.

At least in Western thought, our own species has usually been regarded as sharply distinct from all others. Yet to assume that human beings are a product of evolution is to imply a continuity between all the features of modern humanity and those of our animal ancestors. Hence we may ask whether ethological methods can usefully be applied to our own conduct. Is it appropriate to speak of *human ethology?*

The study of human infancy, and of adult nonverbal communication, by ethological methods, has had some success. The procedure, in such studies, is one of detailed, detached observation, accurate recording, and impersonal interpretation. An additional component of the ethological method is the *comparison* of different species. The comparative method, especially when it is applied to man, has dangers, because it is easy to draw far-reaching conclusions from superficial similarities. The next chapter therefore includes a section on the use and misuse of analogy.

Chapter 14 presents man as a Primate, and begins by examining human evolution and preagricultural life. There are, however, good grounds for saying that human ethology presents our species without its humanity. In chapter 15 I therefore attempt a statement on the fundamental differences between ourselves and all other species. Among the most important questions are those of *method*. What logical and biological principles should we use to reach valid conclusions about human beings? The reader may find two severe difficulties in thinking about such issues. First, there is little relevant, "hard" experimental or even observational evidence. Some of the information comes from what people say, not from the objective observation of behavior. This part is therefore quite unlike most of the rest of the book. Second, on some important matters we are forced to accept that we are ignorant, and that no conclusion is possible. This is a painful necessity.

Shakespeare's Hamlet called man "the paragon of animals". For Alexander Pope, man is "the glory, jest and riddle of the world". These two celebrated passages provide the next two chapter titles.

14

THE PARAGON

The aged philosopher Erdmann, . . . shook his head, declaring that he could not understand the modern men.

   "In my day, . . . we used to ask the everlasting question: 'What is man?' And you—nowadays you answer it, saying, 'He *was* an ape.' "

Lincoln Steffans
[The Autobiography]

14.1 *HOMO SAPIENS* AS A PRIMATE

14.1.1 Fossil Forms

The Primates are large-brained mammals of which most species live in trees. Their visual acuity is good; and they can grasp objects with both hands and feet. The evolution of our species within this order has been reviewed by J. B. Birdsell, by B. G. Campbell, and by D. Pilbeam (1972). Of the primate suborders, the Anthropoidea are distinguished by a reduction of the snout (and correspondingly less dependence on olfactory information), and by excellent binocular vision in bright light. Their brains are the largest, relative to body weight, in the animal kingdom. Nearly all the Anthropoidea are well equipped for movement in trees by leap-

ing; but the members of one small group (super-family), usually called the Hominoidea, when in trees move by swinging (brachiation) in the manner of a trapeze artist. The extant forms are the gibbons, *Hylobates,* and their relatives (11.2.1), the orang, *Pongo pygmaeus,* and gorilla (11.2.4.1), the chimpanzee (11.2.4.2), and the human species. Except for us, all are classified in the family Pongidae: we have the family, Hominidae, to ourselves.

Zoologically, this classification is misleading. On structural and other conventional criteria, hominids should not be put in a separate family; and recent study by a novel method has confirmed this (M.-C. King & A. C. Wilson): our macromolecules (polypeptides) differ in fewer than 1% of features from those of our nearest relatives (figure 14-1).

The fossil record of our evolution during the past 20 million years gives a clear picture in outline, but with some uncertainties (figure 14-2). This fact is obscured by the intense scrutiny given to the smallest recognizable fossil fragments, and the public excitement aroused by new discoveries. A single tooth may hit the headlines, and be given a new generic name in advance of detailed study. When authentic, such relics are often, literally, of side

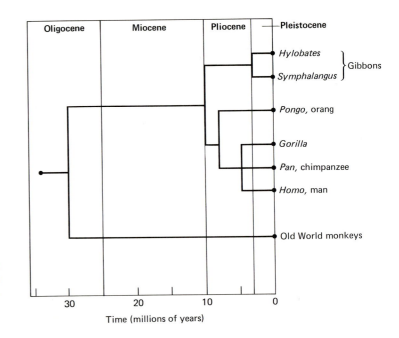

FIGURE 14-1 Diagram to show the degree of relationship, estimated from similarities of blood proteins, between our genus and those of the great apes and the gibbons. (After V. M. Sarich & A. C. Wilson, 1967)

issues. Moreover, most of our knowledge of extinct hominoids is from teeth and bits of jaws; artists nonetheless provide detailed drawings of the whole animal, including hair distribution and the shapes of lips and nose, none of which can be known. A famous example of the pitfalls of reconstruction is provided by Neanderthal man, whose bowed figure and brutal countenance for several decades regularly decorated accounts of human origins. Unfortunately, his supposed posture was based on the skeleton of a person who proved to have had vertebral osteoarthritis (W. L. Straus & A. J. E. Cave). He was as erect as we are, and for all we know he may have been quite a handsome fellow.

In the Miocene period, around 20 million years ago, apes of the fossil genus, *Dryopithecus* (and others) were widespread in Africa, Europe, and Asia. Some limb bones have been found. Evidently the dryopithecines were not structurally adapted

for life in trees but lived on the ground. Some later types (*Ramapithecus* and others) lived not in forests but on savanna. Concerning the forms that preceded man, C. J. Jolly has proposed a "new model" of human evolution. Today baboons, *Papio,* occupy an ecological niche in which there is little competition with other species; and, like ourselves and our predecessors, they are ground living. Jolly suggests that, during the Tertiary, dryopithecines began to eat largely the grass seeds available in open savanna and so, too, adopted a niche in which there was little competition. He contrasts this hypothesis with the frequent emphasis on the supposed hunting proclivities of our ancestors. He also acknowledges that the hypothesis cannot be tested.

From Miocene apes, evidently, arose on the one hand the extant apes and, on the other, various kinds of man (figure 14-3). What do we mean by "man" in this context? Definitions of species or other taxa usually depend on structure. An anatomical definition of *H. sapiens* could be based on erect posture and bipedal locomotion on an arched foot. Our species is the only living form with these features. On the other hand, it may be held that, even in a zoological context, hominids should be defined by their behavior. Hence we could assign to the family, Hominidae, only beings that depend on manufactured tools. (This would exclude chimpanzees for—even if they "manufacture" tools from sticks—they do not depend on them.) The present practice is to include, among the fossil hominids, erect forms that were also the earliest known toolmakers. These, the australopithecines, perhaps represent the next important step in human evolution.

Australopithecus is the best known generic name of a group of beings which, like the Miocene apes, were quite diverse in size and the details of structure. They lived in the late Pliocene and early Pleistocene periods (up to four million years ago), and represent more closely than any others what used to be called the missing link. From the neck down, they are hardly distinguishable from *H. sapiens*: they were fully upright, and so their hands were free for toolmaking. But the proportions of the australopithecine brain, skull, and teeth (though not the structural detail) resemble those of apes. The cranial capacity was around 500 cm³ (table 14-1), and therefore near that of a gorilla. The gorilla, however, is a much larger animal. Most

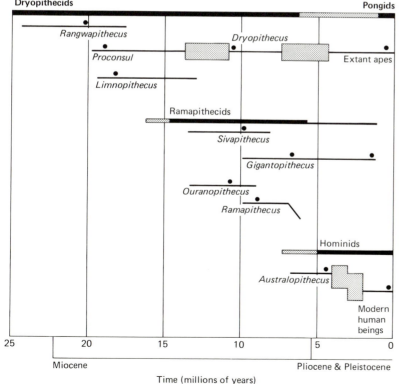

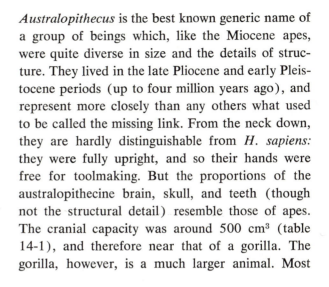

FIGURE 14-2 A current version of the evolution of the Hominoidea. The grey areas represent doubt. Even the durations of geological epochs are only approximations. (After D. Pilbeam, 1978)

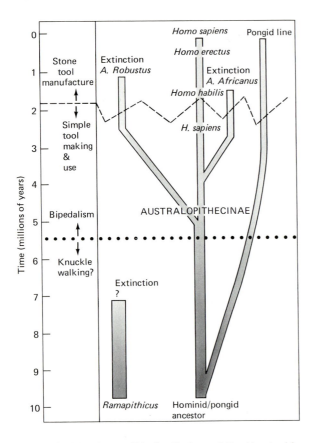

FIGURE 14-3 A possible family tree of the Hominoidea. (After J. D. Clark, 1976)

including the famous Acheulian hand axes (figure 14-4). Moreover, they had fire. The use of fire has no counterpart in the behavior of other species. It involves the use of tools (flints) and also planning ahead; and its management presumably entailed a tradition. Judging by present-day preagricultural people, such as the Eskimo, the most important use of fire was for cooking. It may also have been used in the making of tools, and it perhaps helped to keep predators away at night.

The cranial capacity of *H. erectus* was about double that of *Australopithecus;* and the ratio of brain weight to body weight of *H. sapiens* is as different from that of apes as that of apes is from mammals with the smallest brains (H. Stephan). On the time scale of evolution this change in brain size (figure 14-5) was extraordinarily rapid (J. B. S. Haldane, 1949). The continuous, rapid increase in brain size, from *Australopithecus* to *H. sapiens,* suggests selection pressure, of high intensity, for larger brains; perhaps this reflected a need for a greatly increased memory to cope with a spoken language.

Behavior must have changed greatly during this period; but, as we know, it is not possible to infer social structure from the structure or habitat even of extant species. Hence we are not justified in drawing conclusions from the fossil record about

known members of the australopithecine group had a stature of around 1.5 m, about that of present-day pygmies. Whether we should assume them to be on the direct line of human descent is uncertain (C. E. Oxnard).

In the early Pleistocene there appeared the first forms assigned to the genus, *Homo. H. erectus* is sometimes said to have evolved from australopithecine ancestors. If so, these hominids were much larger than their predecessors (David Pilbeam & S. J. Gould); and they made elaborate stone tools,

TABLE 14-1 Cranial capacities (ml) of primates

	MEAN	RANGE
Baboon (*Papio*)	200	?
Chimpanzee (*Pan*)	394	320–480
Australopithecus	508	435–600
Homo erectus	978	775–1225
Homo sapiens	1300	1000–2000

After P. V. Tobias.

FIGURE 14-4 Acheulian hand ax, from Britain, probably used for several purposes, including chopping, cutting, and digging. Such axes are found throughout Africa and much of Europe and Asia, during a period of at least a million years. (I. A. Fox)

the details of the behavior of our remote precursors. The study of stone tools, however, does provide evidence on how our ancestors lived, from about 2.5 million years ago until very recently (reviewed by J. D. Clark). Before the invention of agriculture (about 10,000 years ago), all men were gatherer-hunters. A few groups, such as the San people of the Kalahari, the aboriginal Australians, and the Eskimo have remained in that state. They

give additional clues to how our ancestors lived for some hundreds of millennia.

One clue concerns diet. I write here of gatherer-hunters, because those that have been studied recently depend more on plants than on animals for food (R. B. Lee & I. DeVore). We cannot tell whether this was the case for most preagricultural men. Once agriculture had spread widely, the most favorable regions for human life were taken over by farmers. The peoples of the Kalahari and Australian deserts and of the Arctic have adapted themselves to exceptionally hostile environments. Much the same applies to the other gatherer-hunters of recent times.

Our species probably evolved in the tropics. Meat may have been especially important in the diet of the early men who moved to colder climates. In tropical regions, plant food is plentiful at all times, but its calorigenic value (nuts ex-

FIGURE 14-5 Actual or estimated brain volumes of modern man and his possible predecessors shown against time: there was a steep increase in the last part of the period covered. (After D. Pilbeam, 1972)

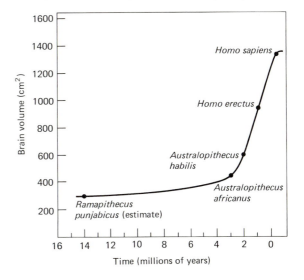

cepted) is low: venison provides about six times as many calories as the same weight of plants. In "temperate" climates, in which there are extremes of seasonal variation, plant food is hard to come by in winter, but animals are always present. The animals eaten need not be large. Aboriginal Australians eat many small lizards. A popular notion of "primitive" man, based partly on the marvelous rock paintings of dramatic pursuits and captures, is of a hunter continually in quest of and dependent on big game. Such a picture is perhaps valid for certain periods and places, but these may have been exceptional.

Statements on how early men lived must usually be surmised, but G. B. Schaller & G. R. Lowther have provided evidence of an unusual kind. These authors begin with the question of the social system of early hominids. They suggest that clues can be derived from the conduct of carnivorous mammals, which cooperate in hunting and sometimes share their food (10.3.2). Such predators also get food by scavenging, and their live prey include a high proportion of the young and the weak. Perhaps the conduct of some early *sapiens* paralleled, in certain respects, that of carnivores that hunt in groups. Schaller and Lowther spent 33 h walking 160 km across the plains of Serengeti National Park in Tanzania. At the time there were many recently born gazelles, of which they could easily have killed eight; they could also have captured a hare; and there were some dead gazelles of high nutritional value. In this period of less than two days, they calculate they could have acquired 35 kg of meat.

On another trip, during the dry season, Schaller and Lowther walked for 20 h, spread over seven days, and covered 95 km. During this period they could have eaten more than their fill from lion kills, a dead buffalo, and a sick zebra foal. They conclude that a group of hominids in such conditions could have lived by scavenging and by killing sick animals. Such an existence would involve little direct competition with other mammalian predators: wild dogs excepted, carnivorous mammals are nocturnal, whereas men—like other Primates— are active during the day. Hence our ancestors, wherever game was plentiful, may have been able to occupy an ecological niche, that of a daytime hunter, without clashing with other species.

Whether they were mainly gatherers or mainly hunters, our toolmaking ancestors lived in "savagery" for more than two million years. The world population during that time is estimated as about 10 million people—a number similar to that now crowded in great conurbations, such as Calcutta, London, New York, Sydney, and Tokyo. The few remaining gatherer-hunters, like chimpanzees in Africa, continue to live in sparse populations (10.5.2).

The most obvious difference of early hominids from the apes was in toolmaking; but there were others. There was often a home base. We know this from the discovery of many camp sites, especially those of *Homo erectus* found in southern and eastern Africa. Most are associated with streams or rivers, or with the shores of lakes or the sea. Typically, the habitat is that of dry grassland, where even today (in some protected areas) vast herds of large mammals still thrive.

The size of the groups in which early hominids lived is not known, but speculation is possible from what we know of surviving gatherer-hunters and from studying ancient camp sites. Clark suggests australopithecine groups of only 10 or 12; but much later, *Homo erectus* in favorable conditions may have lived in groups of up to 50. A feature of the lives of such people must have been a means of carrying objects over substantial distances. The

FIGURE 14-6 An aspect of social evolution: stages in the development of stone tools (compare figure 14-3). Instead of merely flaking a hand ax from a piece of rock, the core is first prepared so that a suitable, preshaped blade can be struck from it. (A) An example of such a core, with the scar left by removing a pointed flake. This "tortoise" core, from Egypt, is about 100,000 years old. (B) A pointed flake, produced in the same way as (A). (C) A Danish flint sickle blade from the Neolithic period, after the invention of farming about 10,000 years ago. (D) An elegantly pressure-flaked flint blade from the Danish Stone Age of about 4000 years ago. At that time there were also daggers and other tools of bronze. This implement may be an imitation, made by people without metal. (I. A. Fox)

camp sites are marked by accumulations of imported chunks of rock and animal remains. Such carrying is a distinctively human characteristic. The earliest handbag was an important invention.

In 8.4.2.4 I describe how imitation and tradition have led to changed behavior in primate groups. Among macaques or baboons or even chimpanzees, the scope of such change is small. A distinctive feature of early hominids, associated with their use of manufactured tools, is a continual, gradual change in their technology. The design of stone tools was progressively refined and elaborated in a manner that has no counterpart in the conduct of other species (figures 14-6 and 14-7).

In the upper Paleolithic, that is, the period that began about 200,000 years ago, we come to Neanderthal man. Despite his heavy facial bones and exceptionally large occipital region of the skull, his tools (of the Mousterian culture) were superior to those of *Homo erectus*. There are intermediates between Neanderthal and our own type; and the current hypothesis is that Neanderthal, formerly regarded as a primitive offshoot from the main human line, was in fact a form of *H. sapiens*. One notable feature of Neanderthal behavior was the habit of burying the dead with tools and sometimes animal skulls. In this way Neanderthals have bequeathed to us a remarkable number of complete, fully equipped skeletons. Today we associate formal burial of the dead with religion. It implies the existence of a culture that included concepts such as that of life after death.

About 37,000 years ago, in Western Europe, modern *Homo sapiens* replaced the Neanderthal type. Their tools were even more various and elegant than those of the Mousterian culture: bone, antler, and ivory were extensively used. With these people we begin to find drawings and paintings of animals and human beings on the walls of rocks

FIGURE 14-7 Point made by pressure-flaking glass from a beer bottle, made by Aborigines in the Kimberley area of Australia. (I. A. Fox)

and caves (André Leroi-Gourhan). Like burial of the dead, cave art may signify religious ritual; but we have no way of finding out for certain. The drawings may have been works of art in a modern sense. Certain stone tools of extraordinary delicacy seem to have had no function except as supreme examples of craftsmanship carried out for its own sake.

14.1.2 Physiological Peculiarities

The fossil record enables us to describe a series of structural changes that led to *H. sapiens*. The record of stone tools and some other remains allows tentative statements on how early erect, toolmaking Primates lived. We now turn to some further, mainly physiological, features in which *H. sapiens* differs from other Primates.

As we know, our species probably evolved in the tropics. One ground for saying this is our lack of an insulating coat of hair; we also have far more sweat glands in our skin than have other Primates. J. B. S. Haldane (1956) writes: "No other animal can swim a mile, walk twenty miles, and then climb forty feet up a tree." Human beings can do this in the tropics. Among mammals, *H. sapiens* is a rather large species, and so has a low ratio of body surface to volume; but our ability to sweat, and the absence of a heat-retaining hair cover, allow us to keep our deep body temperature near 37°C during violent exertion on a hot day.

But, although perhaps originally a tropical animal, *H. sapiens* is not specialized for any one ecological niche. Our climatic range is from the equatorial tropics to the Arctic, and from deserts at sea level to mountain regions at 5000 m. We can thrive on an exclusively plant diet, as do many millions of Hindus; but we can also live, like the Eskimo, mainly on meat. For our size, our teeth are small; and the massive canines of the male Primate have been lost. Small teeth may be related to the use of fire for cooking.

A final group of special features concerns reproduction and development (table 14-2). Some of our important characteristics are shared with the apes: births are usually single (and so make possible intense maternal care), and there is a long period of immaturity and dependence. But there are several conspicuous differences from the apes. The libido of a woman may fluctuate during the menstrual cycle, but coitus can take place at any time, even during pregnancy. There is a corresponding tendency to close and long relationships between spouses. Also close and prolonged is the relationship between mother and child. In addition, within

TABLE 14-2 Reproduction and growth of primates

	Gestation (weeks)	Age at menarche (years)	Growth ends (years)	Life span (years)
Macaque (*Macaca*)	24	2.0	7	24
Gibbon (*Hylobates*)	30	8.5	9	30
Chimpanzee (*Pan*)	33	8.8	11	35
Gorilla (*Gorilla*)	36	9.0	11	40
Man (*Homo*)	38	13.0[a]	20[a]	75[a]

[a] Very variable.
After B. G. Campbell.

the family or larger group, food is shared. Among other Primates, such sharing rarely occurs; nor is it general among the Carnivora. It is, however, a central feature of the conduct of some Canidae (3.2.6). We assume, of course, that food sharing evolved independently in the two groups.

Some writers select one or two characteristics possessed only by *H. sapiens,* and suggest that they are the essential or critical elements in human evolution. It is at least equally appropriate to suppose that we have survived by virtue of a particular *combination* of features. There are traces of many more hominoid types, both ape-like and man-like, than exist today. Two of the extant apes, the orang and the gorilla, are threatened species. In contrast, *Homo sapiens* now dominates terrestrial ecology.

14.2 QUESTIONS OF METHOD

The preceding section puts our species in its setting as a Primate. In the rest of this chapter we are concerned with the ethological scrutiny of people as they are today. Some questions of method arise.

14.2.1 Analogy

In the preceding pages, I make a number of comparisons: the human species resembles other Primates in certain respects, differs in others. Such statements are matters of fact. But comparisons are sometimes used in other ways (10.5.2; 10.6.2). The proper use of comparisons is crucial for a valid human ethology; and so we now look critically at the comparative method.

Comparisons, especially those that imply similarity, are a general feature of language. Some expressions are so familiar that we hardly think of them as figures of speech: examples are doggedly, sheepish, capricious, and vacillating. We also, as a matter of course, talk of queens in bee societies, and of soldiers in ant colonies. If we observe a bee running around in circles we say it is dancing, and so imply a similarity of its behavior to certain human antics. Anatomy provides many examples: the structural term, cloaca, is the Latin word for a drain; in the brain the hippocampus is so named for its resemblance to a kind of fish, the sea horse. The traffic is not all in one direction: we speak of the male and female parts of an electrical connection. Such usages are harmless. We do not make inferences from them: nobody expects to regulate the movements of bees by playing dance music; nor do we consult an ichthyologist if we want to know about the hippocampus.

Nonetheless, in writings in which people are compared with other animals, we find conclusions drawn on just such an inadequate basis (M. J. & H. B. Waterhouse). In the 19th century and later, in a misapplication of evolutionary theory, anthropologists based statements about human conduct on travelers' tales of apes. Accounts (not correct) of the lives of gorillas were first used to support the notion that human societies began as monoga-mous groups; later, with the arrival of new stories, human beings were said to be primarily polyga-mous. Popular writers, unabashed, continue this practice today, and pass it off as science.

It is therefore necessary to set out clearly the proper role of analogy in science. The principles were clearly stated by the Scottish philosopher, David Hume, in his *Enquiry Concerning the Human Understanding,* first published in 1748.

All our reasonings concerning matter of fact are founded on a species of Analogy, which leads us to expect from any cause the same events, which we have observed to result from similar causes. Where the causes are entirely similar, the analogy is perfect, and the inference, drawn from it, is regarded as certain and conclusive . . . But where the objects have not so exact a similarity, the analogy is less perfect, and the inference is less conclusive . . . The anatomical observations, formed upon one animal, are, by this species of reasoning, extended to all animals; and it is certain, that when the circulation of the blood, for instance, is clearly proved to have place in one creature, as a frog, or fish, it forms a strong presumption, that the same principle has place in all.

D. J. McFarland (1971) and J. Maynard Smith (1961) discuss the use of analogy in the modern context. Both comment on the use of analogies in the physical sciences in applying familiar concepts to new fields. Ohm, for example, treated the flow of electrical current as analogous to the flow of heat along a conductor. (The word "current" represents a less precise analogy with flowing water.) As McFarland writes: "Two systems [may] be said to be analogous when their behavior, defined by an equation, is identical."

There are no examples of such perfect analogies in this book. Instead, we have imperfect similarities between species. These allow us to *make hypotheses:* in 9.4.3 I give an example of a fruitful hypothesis about infant feeding, based on knowledge of mammalian milk, and in 12.3.5 there is another concerning the attitudes of mothers; in 8.1.5 I describe findings on animal exploration that have led to less conclusive, but perhaps important, observations on the curiosity of infants and young children; and in 10.5.2 I mention suppositions about crowded animals that have led to negative findings on human crowds. In each case, study of animals has led, not to a conclusion, but to *investigation* of human conduct.

An example of analogical discussion is given by N. Blurton Jones (1972). As we know (9.4.2.3), some mammalian young are carried, others are cached; the latter may be left alone for long periods. The young of the Anthropoidea are carried; but the infants in some human communities are "cached" in cots or elsewhere. Blurton Jones asks whether there is evidence of adaptation of human infants to being cached. Human milk is dilute (9.4.3); to that extent we are not adapted to caching. Another feature is the neonate's inability to maintain a steady internal temperature: effective thermoregulation in a variety of temperatures develops only after some weeks. In primitive conditions, with few or no clothes or other coverings, a neonate is kept warm by continual contact with the mother. A further factor is voiding of urine and feces: cached mammals often urinate and defecate only when stimulated by the mother. Human infants are incontinent. All these features point away from caching. Only the human infant's lack of the ability to cling suggests caching; but a woman has no fur on her body for her infant to cling to.

14.2.2 Procedures

The use of analogy is a matter of logic, but it may influence decisions on what we study, as well as the conclusions drawn from what we find. There are also questions of how we manage observation of other human beings (discussed by N. Blurton Jones, 1972; E. S. Cooper and others; R. D. Martin, 1974).

1. There is first the problem of objectivity. When we observe another species, we try to remain detached, not to think of our subjects as human, and not to change their behavior by our presence. When our subjects are people, these aims are still less easily achieved than with other species: even if we are studying infants, we are likely to feel some warmth and perhaps empathy. For this and other reasons there is sometimes a low correlation between reports by different observers. The significance of, say, what happens in an encounter between two members of a family may not be the same for two observers, even if both are ethologists (or psychologists).

2. In some writings it is urged that ethologists begin observation of a species by constructing an *ethogram,* that is, a complete catalogue of behavior patterns of the animals observed. It is usually helpful, when one begins to study a new species, to watch it informally for some time, and to familiarize oneself with its undisturbed activities. It is even useful to film the subjects, and to play back the film not only at the correct speed but also in slow motion and, sometimes, speeded up as well. But an ethogram is a different matter. (a) Whatever the subjects, a *complete* catalogue is hardly practicable. (b) Any observer, however detached and objective, begins with a frame of reference (not perhaps conscious) about behavior. (c) A catalog of behavior patterns is sometimes useful as a foundation for further study; but the items should usually be consciously selected to further some more specific inquiries. The most fruitful studies are those designed to test a hypothesis, or at least to put the

findings in a larger picture. An example, given in the next section, concerns the question whether human infants display species-typical social signals like those of animals.

3. There is often difficulty in deciding just what to record. Consider an unexpected encounter between two people walking in opposite directions. An observer may be interested in, say, the form of greeting adopted and how it is related to the degree to which the two subjects are acquainted. The behavior recorded may then be a large or "molar" unit, including the style of walking, movements of the head, and the direction of the gaze. But there are also "molecular" changes, such as a brief dilation of the pupils; and these may reflect the attitude of one person toward another (E. H. Hess & J. M. Polt).

4. Some observers *presume* that *H. sapiens* possesses species-typical signals, that is, signals universally given and understood, regardless of culture. Others, more cautious, *ask* whether this is the case. Valid generalizations about human conduct depend on investigation of people of many cultures. It is easy to presume that what is familiar to, say, behavioral scientists in Los Angeles, Moscow, or Oxford is "natural" or "normal" or even universal. But, as we see below (14.3.2), no such presumption is justified. Hence cross-cultural investigation is becoming increasingly important in the study of human conduct, despite its inconvenience and expense. In the next section we see how these principles apply to one aspect of human communication.

14.3 INFANT DEVELOPMENT AND NONVERBAL COMMUNICATION

We sometimes speak of the "languages" of bees and other animals, but this represents a misleading analogy. Of all the behavioral differences between

ourselves and other species, our principal means of communication is the clearest. As we see later, ethological methods are not appropriate for studying human languages (15.2). Attempts have, however, been made to use such methods to describe our nonverbal communication. They may be discussed under the two headings of the conduct of infants and that of adults.

In this chapter, as before, "communication" refers to any transfer of information between members of the same species: it is not reserved for *intentional* transmission. It therefore covers three kinds of situation. First, a person may emit a signal (say, a pheromone) unawares; and another may respond unconsciously. (That is, if asked, both will deny knowledge of what has happened.) Second, a person may adopt, say, a posture, without intending communication; but another may infer something from the posture. Third, there is communication in a narrower sense. A person imparts information by deliberately using a code (such as a language) shared with another. A critical reader will notice that in this paragraph I use subjective or "person" language. At the expense of simplicity, I could have made similar statements in the objective, impersonal terms used for other species; but such an exercise would be pointless.

14.3.1 Infancy

14.3.1.1 Rates of Development: Children younger than 12 months communicate (with minor exceptions) only by nonverbal means. Hence they may be regarded as particularly suitable for study of human communication without words. Human infancy was also, for several decades, regarded as a replay of part of human evolution (S. J. Gould). The original crude notion was of an ontogenetic recapitulation of phylogeny: this implied that each new evolutionary development was added to the end of the development of the previous stage: on this notion a human being at or before birth should be a primitive ape (and, indeed, an infant then has a coat of hair, the lanugo); earlier still, it should be a reptile, and so on backwards—to *Amoeba*.

But in fact, evolutionary change can occur at any stage in development. There has been a general slowing of development in human evolution so that a child remains dependent for an exceptional period; and sexual maturity is very late. In addition, there has been an alteration in the relative rates of development of certain structures. Our face resembles the face of a newborn or embryonic mammal of other species; we never develop the projecting jaws present even in an adult chimpanzee. Instead, we have a nose that accommodates the first part of the respiratory tract. Similarly, we retain an embryonic ratio of brain size to body size. Such persistence of embryonic features in the adult is *neoteny*. In our form of neoteny, developmental processes have been slowed down so that the ancestral adult structure (which included projecting jaws and so on) has not developed by the time sexual maturity is reached and growth has stopped.

If the human gestation period corresponded to the general slowing of development, it would last nearly two years (an unattractive prospect); but in fact human birth is (relative to developmental stage) premature or precocious. Hence in certain respects an infant during its first postnatal month is embryonic. Yet certain behavioral features develop early, that is, during the "embryonic" period of infancy. And it is to these that we now turn.

14.3.1.2 Stereotyped Motor Patterns:
Every infant has its own distinctive personality from soon after birth; but certain features of the conduct of infants are common to our whole species. Some resemble those of other mammals (9.4.2.3). Two

neonatal responses are highly developed and functional in other Primates, but appear to be functionless vestiges in infants. For a few days after birth, a human infant has a surprising ability to grasp an object, such as a finger: some infants at the age of a few hours can bear their own weight if they are lifted gradually while holding on. For a monkey or ape, it is essential to be able to hold on to the mother's fur. The second example is the Moro reflex. If an infant suddenly finds itself without support, it throws its arms wide and then brings them together again. This too has an obvious function for a monkey. For a human infant its only known importance is as a clinical test of central nervous function.

Two other responses, both related to feeding, are shared with other species and are of vital importance to human infants. The first is sucking (reviewed by P. H. Wolff, 1968). The powerful suction of which a baby is capable depends on the muscles and other structures of the cheeks and lips. The response is evoked by the contact of the nipple with the roof of the mouth. It can, of course, also result from presence of some other structure, such as the teat of a bottle. There is a regular rhythm, illustrated in figure 14-8. The figure also illustrates the sucking rhythms of other species, and shows that such rhythms are species-typical.

These statements apply to *nutritive sucking*. Human infants, as we all know, also indulge in *nonnutritive sucking* (figure 14-9): sucking movements occur during sleep, and objects (such as a finger or thumb) are sucked during waking hours. As the figure shows, the nonnutritive sucking of human infants has a rhythm different from that of nutritive sucking. This does not, however, apply to the nonnutritive sucking of other species.

The other stereotyped response connected with feeding is *rooting*. An infant needing milk turns its head from side to side. If, during the turning, its

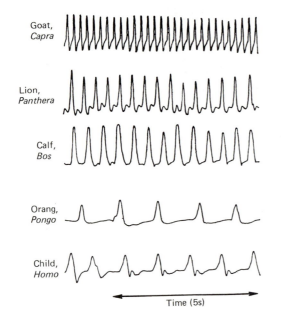

Goat,
Capra

Lion,
Panthera

Calf,
Bos

Orang,
Pongo

Child,
Homo

Time (5s)

FIGURE 14-8 The typical sucking rhythms of five species. (From P. H. Wolff, 1968)

cheek or lip is touched by an object, it turns toward the object, takes it in its mouth, and sucks. Such a series of responses obviously aids the infant in getting milk from the breast. (See also 9.4.2.3.)

The response to a mother's breast (or to the teat of a bottle) is not only to a tactile stimulus. An infant can, of course, see the breast; moreover,

FIGURE 14-9 Nonnutritive sucking: the rhythm of a four-day infant during sleep. (From P. H. Wolff, 1968)

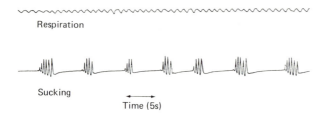

Respiration

Sucking

Time (5s)

as M. J. Russell has shown, at six weeks many babies can distinguish the odor of their mother's breast from that of a strange mother (also lactating). The source of the odor may not be the mother, but the infant: an infant may "mark" his mother with his own odor, and respond to that. On such questions much remains to be found out.

Sucking, of course, not only ensures nourishment but is a social signal: it has an effect on the mother. Other stereotyped acts of infancy function only as signals. *Crying* has been recorded in detail by P. H. Wolff (1969). Figure 14-10 illustrates distinct types of crying; as far as is known they are uttered by all young infants. The "hunger cry" is evoked not only by an empty stomach, but also by sudden loud noises. It ceases, not only when the infant is fed, but sometimes also when it is merely picked up. In some communities, such as those of gatherer-hunters, infants are carried by their mother all the time; crying is then rarely heard, unless the mother's milk fails (M. J. Konner). An accompanying factor is the infant's skin temperature: crying is more likely to occur if a baby is cold. The "angry cry" seems to occur if the "hunger cry" fails to evoke a parental response. A third sound, the "pain cry", was recorded by Wolff after infants had had blood samples drawn from the heel.

The social signals of animals elicit stereotyped responses. In particular, the cries of an infant mammal reliably attract the infant's mother; and she predictably enables the young to suck, or otherwise attends to it. The cry of a child may similarly stimulate letdown of a mother's milk. Human mothers are, however, in other respects less predictable. Wolff's observations were of American mothers. Those with their first babies were found more likely to respond as soon as crying began than were the others. Not all observers report the same findings. H. A. Moss, who also studied Amer-

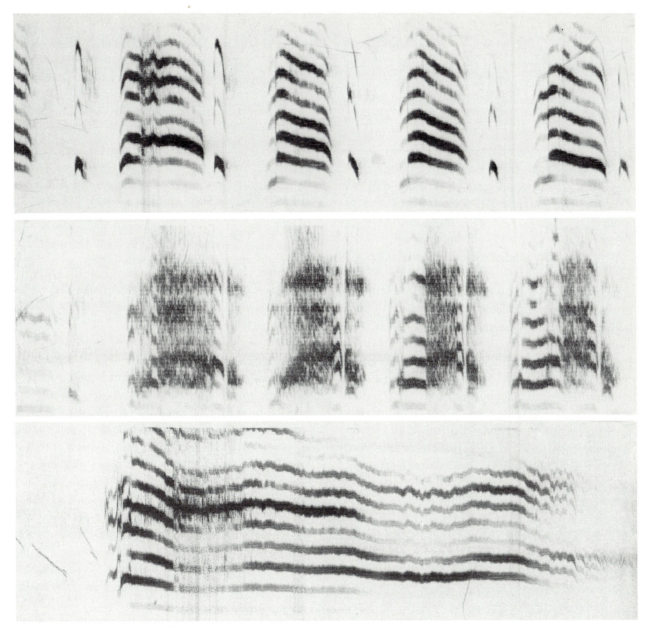

FIGURE 14-10 Sound spectrograms of three distinct and apparently universal types of crying by infants. Above, "basic" crying (by a four-day boy) with fundamental frequency of 350 to 450 Hz; such crying may result from hunger or from lack of contact with a parent. Middle, "angry" cry by four-day girl. Below, response to pain, followed by 7 s of silence during expiration. The vertical axis of each figure covers the frequency range of 0 to 7000 Hz; the horizontal axis of the two upper figures covers 4.8 s. (Spectrograms; courtesy P. H. Wolff)

ican mothers, found those with second children to respond to cries more quickly than those with first. The angry cry, in Wolff's study, evoked a more reliable response than did the hunger cry; but the most effective signal was the pain cry: in response to this "most mothers immediately rushed into the room looking worried"; moreover, even nurses "who are accustomed to such sounds by years of exposure, may betray a need to do something". It would be interesting to know more about such responses by members of both sexes and of many cultures.

The most fully studied social signal of infancy is *smiling*. The exact age at which this delightful response appears is usually stated to be around six weeks, but there is much variation among both infants and observers. From the time at which it appears, to about six months, smiling occurs reliably in response to the sight of a human face (reviewed by D. G. Freedman). Moreover, it can be evoked by a rather crude diagram; but a face-like pattern evokes an infant's attention more readily than a jumbled pattern of features (figure 14-11). Smiling is more probable if the appearance of a face is accompanied by the sound of speech—preferably that of a woman (K. S. Robson). Such an interaction is just like those we observe in other species: a visible pattern regularly evokes a clearly defined response; and the predictability is increased if the visible stimulus is accompanied by a certain kind of audible input. The ability to discriminate voices, however, as of odors, develops early. M. Mills & E. Melhuish trained babies to suck at the sound of the mother's voice, but not when they heard a stranger.

The preceding statements are deliberately "inhuman". When one comes to examine the response of a mother (or other adult) to a baby's smile, it would still be possible to give a mechanistic ac-

count; but it would sound even more absurd. John Bowlby explicitly bases his account of infancy on an ethological foundation; but he writes:

When her baby smiles and babbles a mother smiles back, "talks" to him, strokes and pats him, and perhaps picks him up. In all this each partner seems to be expressing joy in the other's presence and the effect is certainly one of prolonging their social interaction. . . .

Not only do her infant's smiles have this immediate effect . . . , but they probably exert a long-term influence on it as well. Ambrose has described the electrifying effects on a mother of seeing her baby's first social smile, and how it seems to make her thenceforward altogether more responsive to him.

Whatever kind of description of these events we prefer, we may at least conclude that an infant's smile has survival value.

After six months an infant no longer smiles indiscriminately at all faces or face-like patterns. Soon only the mother and other familiar people are welcomed. At perhaps seven months the response to a stranger may be turning away or crying. There is a superficial similarity to the change in behavior which marks the end of the imprinting period of birds (12.3.2). H. L. Rheingold & C. O. Eckerman criticize such facile comparisons. They find withdrawal from strangers, even at the ages of 6 to 12 months, far from universal. Similarly, C. M. Corter has watched infants aged 10 months during encounters with a strange woman, in the presence or absence of the mother. The stranger is described as provoking exploration rather than distress. Often, the infant looked or smiled at the stranger; but only the mother was followed about the room. As the last sentence implies, *following* is also a feature of an infant's behavior once the infant becomes mobile.

Lastly, infants make two additional kinds of sound, laughing and babbling. Both may be re-

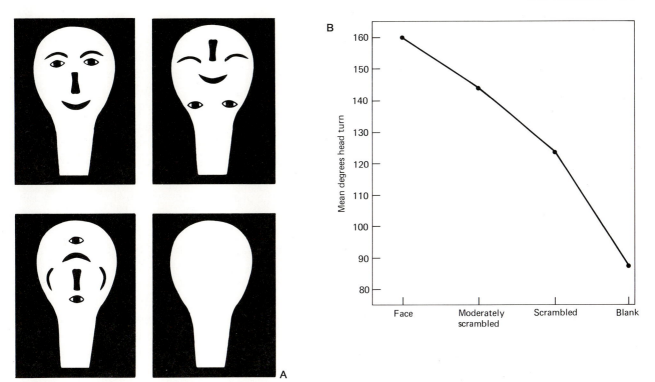

FIGURE 14-11   (A) The attention of an infant in its first months is readily captured by the sight of a human face or a face-like object, such as the diagram at top left; jumbled patterns or an empty mask are less likely to evoke a response. (B) responses (head turning) of newly born infants to the patterns shown in (A). (After D. G. Freedman, 1964)

sponses to stimulation from another person. Babbling, however, does not depend on the presence of another. It consists of a great variety of sounds, with many differences between individuals. It has no counterpart in the conduct of other species, and is regarded as a precursor of speech.

14.3.1.3 Attachment: The ethological study of the conduct of children is not confined to stereotyped acts. It covers the less specific but very important phenomena of attachment to a particular

person or to persons, and the results of separation. When an infant, at around six months, begins to distinguish its mother from other people, it also enters a period when attachment becomes important (reviewed by John Bowlby and by Michael Rutter).

It might be supposed that knowledge of human attachment arose from observation of other species, perhaps by the testing of hypotheses derived from studies of Primates (12.4). In fact, however, the initial findings were based entirely on clinical observations of human children. During this century, emphasis on the importance of childhood experience has come especially from psychoanalysis: early family relationships have been held to determine, to a large degree, many aspects of an adult's personality. In 1946, a psychoanalyst, R. A. Spitz, described the "depressed" behavior of infants aged 6 to 12 months living in a nursery. The abnormal conduct was attributed to separation from the mother. Spitz recommended therefore that such separation should be avoided; and that, if it was unavoidable, a substitute should be provided.

During the 1940s another physician, John Bowlby, also influenced by psychoanalysis, was led to his celebrated hypothesis that, if an infant or young child is deprived of maternal care for some time, there is a high probability of delinquency and inability to form satisfactory social relationships later in life. This notion has now been much qualified; but the study of human social development has, as a result, been transformed.

The psychoanalytic method was, for the most part, not to study infants or young children, but to make inferences about them from observation of adults suffering from mental illness. Now, for the first time, there were descriptions of what actually happens when a child between the ages of six months and four years is taken from its mother and its home, usually to a hospital or an orphanage. At first the child cries for long periods, and is otherwise distressed. This period of "protest" may last for several days. It is followed by a period of "despair", in which the child becomes inert; crying, if any, is subdued. In the last stage, that of "detachment", conduct is more sociable: in a hospital or children's home the nurses or other attendants now may evoke smiles. But if the mother comes on a visit, the child fails to respond to her. The original observations by Bowlby have been confirmed by independent workers, and not only in Europe and North America. B. M. Lester and others have observed "separation protest" in a study of Guatemalan infants. The pattern was the same as that in the United States, but developed earlier.

The initial account by Bowlby has, however, been qualified (M. Rutter). The sequence of protest, despair, and detachment is not universal. There are several sources of variation. If a child is already accustomed to brief separations experienced without distress, a longer separation may not evoke protest. Moreover, Bowlby originally put exclusive emphasis on *maternal* separation; but separation from the father and from siblings is also important: if a brother or sister is present in hospital, there is less distress.

The reader may not find it surprising that separation from its family makes a young child very upset. The emphasis on early *social* relationships, and the detailed investigation of the effects of separation, have nonetheless been important. The findings described above were first published during a period in which excessively simple and even mechanistic notions of infancy were prominent. Many believed that it was almost a law of nature that a child in its first months should be fed meticulously at intervals of 4 h (contrast 9.4.3). Moreover, some writers assumed that an infant's attachment to a parent or foster-parent was a consequence of receiving food and perhaps warmth. This is one instance of crude biological "models" of humanity, popular in this century (see the next chapter). We now know that the "cupboard-love" theory of attachment does not work even for macaques (12.4.1.1).

The preceding account of infancy is mainly of features that one may expect regardless of genotype (that is, of "race" and so on) or of culture. Such generalizations, when valid, are important; but on meeting a number of babies one is likely to be equally impressed by their diversity. Some are restless and demanding, others placid; some sleep most of the time, others seem (to their parents) excessively wakeful. One source of variation, studied by H. A. Moss, is their sex. In a study of American babies, the boys were found to "fuss" more than the girls. The mothers were also more responsive to their male than to their female infants. Such a difference could reflect a preference by the mothers for boys; but covariance analysis of a mass of quantitative observations showed the mothers to respond more to the boys because the boys made more fuss. It was the behavior of the infants that to some extent controlled the nurturant conduct of the mothers. There are many other examples of such interactions (M. E. Lamb; M. Lewis & L. A. Rosenblum).

Caregiving may be by several members of a family, and not only the mother. The interaction between the caregivers and the infant produces increasing diversity as the infant develops. Quite soon, the child's cries are no longer limited to those evoked by hunger, disturbance, or pain. Cries are uttered which seem to have the function only of attracting attention. (Sometimes this is oddly called "fake" crying.) Very young infants can be trained to alter their conduct for a reward. The approach of an adult, and—still more—being picked up, act as rewards. There is no stereotyped response by adults to an infant's demands. Some parents say that it is inappropriate to respond at all, on the ground that rewarding them will merely increase the demands to an intolerable level. (I have found no evidence for this.) On the other hand, some parents respond to a demand for attention from their infants as they would to a request from an adult: that is, they accede to it. Such variation illustrates our lack of stereotyped patterns of conduct (further discussed in the next chapter).

Nonetheless, objective, "inhuman" accounts of human infancy, despite their severe limitations, can be helpful. Females of other species are equipped with a repertoire of responses that enable them to look after their young untaught. Human mothers are not so equipped. They depend on "old wives tales" (which are invaluable) or on the recommendations of neighbors, nurses, physicians, or even ethologists. Certainly, they need all the help they can get.

14.3.2 Adults

We now turn to adult nonverbal communication (reviewed by P. Ekman; in a volume edited by R. A. Hinde, 1972; and by W. La Barre, 1947, 1964). Among the workers in this area, some are interested in the diversity of human conduct, others look for signals universally issued and understood. The latter, like the smiling and crying of infancy, would correspond to the species-typical signals of animals. Certainly we possess species-typical *structures* that help us to communicate without words. Our facial muscles of expression are, like those of the Anthropoidea generally, highly developed; and, unlike other species, we have the "whites" of the eyes, which enable us to observe the direction of another's gaze, and red lips, which make movements of the mouth more evident.

Although such structures are common to all human beings, an obvious feature of our nonverbal communication is its diversity. This is a matter of everyday experience. (In the English subculture in which I was reared it was customary for a host and guest to shake hands. While doing so, a woman could remain seated, but not a man. But two guests, on being introduced, were each expected merely to make a slight bow, accompanied by a muttered "How do you do?" This question, though ostensibly verbal, never evoked a reply; hence an inarticulate grunt would have served the same purpose. Such a greeting ceremony would probably be slightly strange to some readers of this book.)

A familiar example of nonverbal communication is the head nod, in which the chin moves down and up. Probably most readers use this gesture to indicate assent; but for some it represents a negative, and agreement is shown by a lateral movement in which the chin moves from side to side. Moreover, several hundred million people in India use yet another gesture (meaning "yes") in which there is a lateral nodding of the head. Yet other groups do not use head nods either for yes or for no. Further examples of gestures variously used (or rejected) include kissing (and nose rubbing), and sticking out the tongue. The last, a rude or derisive gesture in many Western cultures, is in Tibet, La Barre tells us, "a sign of polite deference". Similarly, hissing, a sign of disapproval in many Western countries, indicates deference in Japan; and among the Basuto it represents applause.

The significance of a gesture often depends on the context. A man raises his hand palm forward: he may be a priest making a ritual movement, a stranger indicating pacific intentions, or a policeman stopping traffic.

A critical reader may find the preceding paragraphs disgracefully anecdotal. In this, they reflect much currrent writing on the subject. A few systematic, experimental or quantitative studies have, however, been carried out. Often they have been designed not to study diversity but to find out whether there are signals universally given and universally responded to in all human societies. This type of investigation was founded by Charles Darwin, in this book, *On the Expression of the Emotions in Man and Animals*. A century ago, there was only anecdotal evidence available. Darwin was, however, aware of the pitfalls of anthropomorphism, and gave a number of examples, in-

FIGURE 14-12   Drawing of a baboon, *Papio,* from Darwin's *On the Expression of the Emotions* (1873). What emotion is being expressed?

cluding that shown in figure 14-12. In the caption of the drawing, we are told that the animal is "pleased by being caressed"; as Darwin remarks, "this expression would never be recognized by a stranger as one of pleasure".

When we turn to modern investigations, we should first remember that human signaling is not only by sounds or sights: contacts are certainly important and perhaps odors too. The most obvious odorous signals are cosmetic, that is, are added to increase attractiveness. Such use of scents is culturally influenced. But recent findings on the pheromones of Anthropoidea (13.2.3.4) have led to hypotheses on human pheromones (reviewed by A. Comfort). Appropriate glands are present: they include apocrine sweat glands, such as those in the axilla, associated with tufts of hair that may help to disperse secretions.

So far, little has been established; but M. K. McClintock has published evidence of a primer pheromone of women. The menstrual cycles of 135 young women, aged 17 to 22 years, living in a college dormitory, were recorded: those of roommates and close friends were found to be synchronized. In addition, some women had exceptionally long cycles while living a conventual existence; but their cycles shortened when they began to go out with men. Pheromones have not been conclusively shown to be responsible; but there is a notable similarity to the findings on pheromonal effects among mice (13.2.3.4). If pheromones are responsible, they are likely to be common to our whole species; and the effect of cosmetic scents would then be partly to disguise them—a strange phenomenon that requires more study.

The clearest evidence of species-typical signals among adults comes from experiments on the response to facial expressions. P. Ekman and others used photographs of faces expressing one of a number of emotions. People in the literate societies of Argentina, Brazil, Chile, Japan, and the United States, and in a preliterate group in Niugini, were asked to identify the emotions portrayed. Happiness and anger were usually identified correctly, but depression and fear less reliably. Such findings suggest that, as Darwin implied, some human facial expressions (and their recognition) are common to our whole species. They do not, however, tell us how the ability to recognize them develops in the individual child. There may be differences in such abilities resulting from different conditions of rearing. Certainly, it is a common experience that the features and postures of people of a strange culture are at first incomprehensible (La Barre, 1947).

In the work on facial expressions people were asked to *comment* on photographs. Hence the situation involved verbal communication, and was quite unlike that of an interaction between two animals. A nonverbal example comes from an experiment by P. C. Ellsworth and others. As we know, in apotreptic encounters a Primate sometimes *stares* at another. Accordingly, people driving cars near an American university were stared at by experimenters in a standard manner when stopped by lights at an intersection. They drove off more quickly than controls who were left unmolested. The authors do not, however, suggest any simple interpretation of their findings. In another study, Ellsworth & J. M. Carlsmith describe how eye "contact" can induce hostile behavior in one situation but not in another. Once again, we have an emphasis on the influence of context on the response made to a signal. There are indeed situations in which two individuals gaze rapturously into each other's eyes.

In general, the implication of these findings is that simple ethological procedures have little scope in the study of adult human conduct: even when language is not involved, to interpret a response one needs to know how previous experience (including verbal experience) influences the behavior observed. When a person is stared at, what—one asks—does this "mean" to that person?

The preceding examples are based on hypotheses that can be tested experimentally. The questions that may be asked, but as yet can hardly be answered, include the following. Are certain human appearances universally understood? Do some appearances evoke a uniform response? Are there in early development significant causes of variation in either the appearances (signals) or in the responses to them? An additional question is whether we share stereotyped signals with other species; if so, can anything useful be said about the evolution of human wordless communication? As an example, I. Eibl-Eibesfeldt describes an analysis of films of the conduct of Europeans, South American Indians, the San people of the Kalahari, and various Pacific groups. The record was made with cameras that photograph people at an angle to the apparent aim of the photographer. Such cameras sometimes allow filming of people unaware that their conduct is under observation.

Eibl-Eibesfeldt describes a brief action, the eyebrow flash, often observed when two acquaintances meet. Both eyebrows are raised for a fraction of a second. (Usually, this unobtrusive action is accompanied by something more obvious, such as a smile or a nod.) The interpretation of this minuscule response depends in part on the interpreter's frame of reference. A cultural anthropologist, as we shall see, would probably emphasize the differences between different communities and even individuals. Eibl-Eibesfeldt describes such differences: for example, he tells us that in Japan the eyebrow flash is considered an indecent gesture, and is therefore suppressed. He also states that, at least in some communities, very reserved people do not display it. The precise circumstances in which the movement occurs are also said to vary greatly in different communities.

Eibl-Eibesfeldt, however, is interested especially in the possible status of the eyebrow flash as a universal signal. Moreover, he writes: "By looking for . . . contexts in which eyebrow raising occurs we get hints as to its possible phylogenetic origin." He further remarks on the lifting of the eyebrows that occurs during social interactions among, for example, macaques and baboons. The effect is sometimes made conspicuous by the pallor of the upper eyelid. (He also mentions the human practice of coloring the eyelids; but this is a culturally influenced phenomenon, and may be confined to one sex.) Eibl-Eibesfeldt's suggestion is that the movement originates in a response, widespread among the Primates, that indicates surprise or attention. He supposes it to have been ritualized during evolution (18.5.4), and so to have become, in various cultures, a signal of approval, flirtatiousness, or even indignation or disapproval.

Here, then, is an attempt to interpret a brief action in terms of species-typical conduct and its evolution, and to allow, at the same time, for the extreme diversity of its roles in different communities. But trying to incorporate evolutionary concepts, such as ritualization, in the account of the "eyebrow flash" tends to obscure the authentic findings. An aspect of human nonverbal greeting has been described, apparently for the first time; and an attempt is made to classify the circumstances in which it is observed (or suppressed) in different cultures. Such studies, carried out by less anecdotal methods, could perhaps become a component in the work of cultural anthropologists.

As a rule, however, anthropologists are more likely to express doubt about the usefulness of "ethological" studies. I have already cited the work of La Barre. E. R. Leach (1972) has published a critique of, as he puts it, the belief that "the difference between non-man and man is simply one of degree, [and] that the communication systems of man are very like those of non-man only more so. Carried to extremes this thesis leads to the position that man is no more than a naked ape."

Leach states two general principles. One concerns the intrinsic character of human wordless communication. Much consists of gestures and postures that are rituals in the usual sense of the term: they are not to be confused with the evolutionary ritualization that is supposed to have produced many animal signals (18.5.4). When, for example, a man crosses himself, that may act as an indication to another; but it is not a signal that, even within a given culture, necessarily evokes a stereotyped response. The gesture contains an allusion to events that occurred in another time and place and to abstract concepts. Such religious (and other) rituals are an almost universal component of human social interactions. (They may date back to Neanderthal man.) Even when nonverbal, they have no counterpart in the conduct of other species.

The second principle concerns the context in which our nonverbal signals occur. Except in early childhood, human wordless communication is accompanied by speech, or at least depends on it. If a person points to an object and looks enquiringly at another person, the implied question is likely to be a verbal one: in such a situation words can be dispensed with only because they have been used before.

These comments illustrate the severe limitations of the study of human nonverbal communication by ethological methods. Such methods have given information of interest, especially about the conduct of infants and their parents. The subject is also a splendid source of entertainment. But, as we see in the next chapter, its scope in our attempts to understand ourselves is small.

14.4 PEOPLE AS ANIMALS

To sum up this chapter, *Homo sapiens* may be regarded zoologically as an aberrant species of the family Pongidae (the apes). The common ancestor of all the extant apes, including ourselves, probably lived in the Miocene, more than 20 million years ago. The Miocene apes, we know, had unusually large brains; we assume that, like other Primates, they had excellent binocular and color vision, that they were dexterous, and that they produced one young at a birth. They had undoubtedly evolved from arboreal forms, but were probably themselves ground living and capable of running quite quickly. From that stage certain trends led to *H. sapiens*. (1) The evolution of a bipedal, upright posture accompanied that of an arched foot fully specialized for walking, running, and jumping. (2) Correspondingly, the hands came to be used principally for manipulation. (3) Neotenic changes in rates of development led to retention of an embryonic head structure, including a still larger brain in relation to body size. (4) At some time in the Pliocene our ancestors, already fully upright but still rather small and with ape-sized brains, began making stone tools. (5) They also became homemakers, that is, they had camp sites to which they carried stones and food. (6) We infer a corresponding tendency, developing in the Pliocene or later, to monogamy. (7) At a time and by stages that we cannot know, there was a loss of stereotyped social signals, and a rapid development of extreme ontogenetic adaptability of behavior. (8) We assume that language arose during the same period, in place of wordless grunts, cries, and gestures. Nonverbal communication then became merely subsidiary: primitive man was preadapted for communicating by telephone. (9) In the late Pleistocene we find evidence of craftsmanship exercised for its own sake. Our ancestors, still dependent on gathering and hunting, also developed the arts of drawing and painting.

With the last three items we come to features of human existence that do not fit an ethological framework. We return to them in the next chapter.

15

THE RIDDLE

Don't let us forget that the causes of human actions are usually immeasurably more complex and varied than our subsequent explanations of them.

F. Dostoevsky
The Idiot

The behavioral differences between ourselves and other species are so great that to labor them may seem pointless. There are, however, at least three reasons for doing so. First, comparisons of ourselves with other animals always turn up, if only in our thoughts, when we observe animal behavior (chapter 1). Hence the clearer we are about the differences, the better. Second, comparisons can direct our attention to aspects of human existence that it is useful to discuss. Third, there is today a mass of writing on the argument from animals to man, and much of it contains logical and biological errors; I therefore try to show how these errors can be avoided.

15.1 HUMAN DIVERSITY

15.1.1 The Cultural Influence

For most animal species, and for all Primates except ourselves, it is possible to identify a quite nar-

row range of environments. The exceptions, such as houseflies and house mice, live with us. Our own species has no well-defined ecological niche. We are not obliged, by our nature, to adopt any particular habitat or diet (4.5.3); our infants can be reared in a variety of ways (9.4.2.3; 14.3.1); and our patterns of social interaction (despite a few universal signals) are bewilderingly varied. As an example, the courtship display of an animal species is highly stereotyped (chapter 9); but a person who casually attempts courtship in an unfamiliar culture is asking for trouble (La Barre, 1947). Similarly, when an animal makes something, such as a nest, the product is species-typical. The nests even of chimpanzees lack variety. But human artefacts of the most simple sort have no such uniformity: they vary both in space and in time.

These truisms are excessively general. Here is a more precise example. Many mammals make an elaborate toilet: the systematic licking and scratching of a rat or a cat are familiar. The movements are species-typical. Many people (but not all) wash regularly and otherwise care for their bodies and even those of others; but our species has no standard pattern of movements or methods of doing so. There are some superficial similarities between ourselves and other species. A lecturer who wishes to provide light relief can show pictures, side by side, of the allogrooming of two monkeys (figure 11-14) and of somebody removing lice from a friend's hair: if the postures are well chosen, there is a ludicrous similarity. But, as E. R. Leach (1972) remarks, to do this it is necessary to *select* from "the vast variety of human hair rituals". In the Trobriand Islands delousing is part of courtship: it is an accepted preliminary to coitus, as allogrooming is for baboons and macaques. But in our species, even in communities where there are plenty of body lice, delousing is not an invariable source of erotic arousal: it is not a species-typical courtship pattern.

Most anthropologists concerned with such matters discuss the *ritual* significance of cleanliness (for example, Mary Douglas): in some societies cleanliness is not next to godliness but coincides with it. The connection with hygiene or public health, if any can be discerned, is tenuous. Hence the function, too, of human cleanliness sometimes differs from that of other species.

The notion of hygiene applies not only to the body surface but also to conditions in the environment. Many species have stereotyped actions that ensure their nests or lairs are free of excreta. If one bird keeps its nest clean, we may justly predict that all others of its species will do so too. The variety of corresponding practices among different human communities is familiar: a visitor from another planet could not infer, from observing people of one culture, what is done in others. Again, cleaning practices are often rituals. An example is the spring cleaning widespread in some societies.

A similar argument applies to food habits. What people will or will not eat (also discussed by Douglas) may depend substantially on the culture in which they are reared. Nor are food habits necessarily related to nutritional or clinical needs: for example, the taboos on eating certain foods need not be related to the need to avoid parasitic infection. The rejection of horsemeat in England (reinforced by law) has no basis in dietetics or epidemiology (E. R. Leach, 1964). E. B. Tylor similarly describes variation in the use of fire and in methods of cooking among primitive peoples.

There is no animal counterpart to all this diversity within our species, or to the ritualistic function of many practices. Nor is there any animal counterpart of clothing at all, despite the attachment of seaweed to the surfaces of some crustaceans (figure 15-1). Clothes are almost universal in human communities; usually, but not always, they help to keep people warm or cool or otherwise comfortable, but they certainly have a ritual function as well.

All the features mentioned in this section are culturally influenced; but in all we see personal variation. There is cultural determination, but also individual choice.

15.1.2 The Importance of Ontogeny

The variety of human conduct makes the study of ontogeny especially important. If we wish to understand what adults do, we must examine how individuals develop. In chapter 12 I describe analyses of the development of behavior. Bird song, the conduct of young birds and mammals toward parents, and the social interactions of monkeys are all species-typical; yet they develop normally only in a certain range of environments: unusual conditions of rearing can lead to gross departures from stereotyped patterns. These examples illustrate a general and fundamental principle: the behavior we observe is part of the phenotype (16.2); even

FIGURE 15-1 *Naxia tumida,* a crustacean that clothes itself with seaweed. This species-typical behavior, presumably cryptic in function, hardly rates as an analogy to the clothing behavior of human beings. (I. A. Fox)

if we are dealing with a genetically uniform population, there may still be individual variation. When such sources of variation can be traced, often the *early* environment is especially important. In the development of human beings we have the extreme case. Our species has few stereotyped ("instinctive") behavior patterns. Correspondingly, the role of parents and others in the social and intellectual development of children is on a different scale from anything we see elsewhere. Ours is the only species of which the young are *taught* skills (8.4.3): we could appropriately call ourselves, not *Homo sapiens*—which emphasizes our rationality—but *H. docens,* the teaching hominid.

As usual, such statements about human beings can rarely be supported by formal experimental evidence; they are based on observation and, often, on familiar phenomena. Occasionally, there are accidental experiments. A. D. B. & A. M. Clarke and L. Malson reviewed studies of children reared in extreme social isolation. Such children, discovered after some years, are speechless and grossly retarded in other respects. An obvious question is whether they would have developed in this way in any environment. Perhaps such children are genetically different from normals. In a laboratory experiment there would be two groups of animals, if possible genetically similar, of which one would serve as a control. No control can exist in the human situation. There is, however, a partial answer.

Sometimes previously isolated children have been adopted and given continuous love and care by foster-parents. The result has been a sudden acceleration in intellectual and other aspects of development. There is an analogy here with physical growth: after a period in, say, infancy, during which illness has led to loss of weight, there is usually accelerated, compensatory growth, which restores the child to its expected weight. The same, to some extent, seems to apply to intellectual development after a period of deprivation.

We cannot, however, know for certain what are the lasting effects of early isolation; and in any case "early isolation" can take many forms. It is impossible to say how these children would have developed in a normal environment. E. B. Tylor describes how the Indian Emperor, Akbar Khan (1542–1605), had 12 babies reared in isolation by dumb nurses. When the children were 12 years of age, they were brought before Akbar and were found all to be speechless: they communicated by means of gestures learned from their charges. It is to be hoped that nobody will try to confirm these findings. There are other ways of studying language, and to these we now turn.

15.2 LANGUAGE

15.2.1 Origins

15.2.1.1 Evolution: We should like to know how language evolved, but we have no means of finding out (reviewed by H. B. Steklis and others). There have, however, been plenty of theories (G. W. Hewes, 1973, 1977), some of which at least give us an insight into the peculiarities of how we communicate. One group of suggestions might be called associational, onomatopaeic, or imitative. Hence there is the *bow-wow* theory; other suggested origins are imitation of sounds produced by

objects—the *ding-dong* theory; and a third is the *yo-heave-ho* theory, in which language originates from sounds made by people at work.

Such speculations make no attempt to suggest how *grammatical speech* evolved. Hewes suggests that language was originally gestural. He alludes to the linguistic abilities of chimpanzees (8.3). J. B. S. Haldane (1955) has referred to our ability to report past events, and has suggested that boasting played an important part in the evolution of language. Perhaps, then, the earliest form of propositional statement was that used by a fisherman describing his catch. The gesture involved is still familiar.

But this not entirely frivolous proposal refers to the motivation involved, not to the process by which language arose. F. R. H. Englefield has argued that language could have been an *invention*. A paleolithic genius, or family of geniuses, could have hit upon a novel mode of communication, either by gesture or by sound, and so could have enhanced their fitness and that of their children. The latter would have imitated their elders. It is hardly surprising that J. F. Kavanagh describes speculations on the evolution of language as intellectual exercises or romantic fantasies.

What we can directly observe, as usual, are the existing products of evolution. All human beings (unless their brains are severely damaged) can learn a language—gestural if they have a speech defect. The evolution of that part of the human brain especially concerned with language must have involved more than an increase in size (E. A. Drewe and others). Certainly grossly defective human beings, nanocephalic dwarfs, have brains weighing no more than those of chimpanzees aged three years or those of adult rhesus macaques; but their ability to use the spoken word is equivalent to that of a child of five years. That is, their linguistic ability is equiv-

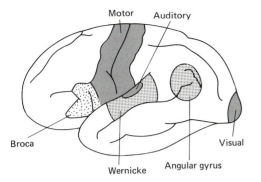

FIGURE 15-2 The human brain from the left side, to show the regions especially concerned with speech and the understanding of language: damage to these regions interferes with both.

alent or superior to that of chimpanzees (8.3). The human brain has large regions (figure 15-2) concerned with language (reviewed by B. G. Campbell; J. B. Lancaster). Our vocal apparatus is also structurally quite distinct from that of all other Primates (P. H. Lieberman and others).

The differences from other species may be regarded as genetically determined, like other interspecific differences. That does not, however, justify the statement that language is "innate" in man. First, such a proposition is empty: it adds nothing to what has already been said on language as a feature confined to our species. Second (as we see further in chapter 16), labeling a feature "innate" evades the question of how it arises and grows during individual development. It implies a fixity or predetermination, and therefore distracts attention from the all-important interaction with the environment on which development depends.

15.2.1.2 Ontogeny: The ontogeny of linguistic ability has been reviewed by R. Brown & U. Bellugi; J. S. Bruner; J. Church; J. B. Lancaster; and J. W. Torrey. At first an infant communicates feelings by nonverbal means (14.3.1). In the second year, language begins, and is then referential: words state the presence, absence, or position of people or objects: "Jill gone"; "plate on table". Quite early, however, demands can be made: "want cake". But only at three years or later does a child become able to express feelings of happiness, unhappiness, pain, and so on, in words. In the early years expressive and referential communication seem to be quite distinct, and to develop independently.

How does the use of words develop? It might be supposed that a simple answer is possible: words are learned by imitation, and the learning is encouraged and rewarded by the conduct of parents and others. Both statements are correct; but they are very incomplete. Imitation suggests an exact copying; but a child develops grammatical speech by a more complex and still inadequately analyzed process. In a language such as English, in which the order of the words is important, the earliest sentences consist of words in their proper sequence: a child does not say, "Gone Jill". (Nor, later, is there often—if ever—confusion between a Venetian blind and a blind Venetian.) The speech of one child was studied for 8 h, during which he produced 400 sentences, each of two words. Examples are "two boot", and "hear tractor". In all sentences the words were in correct sequence.

Moreover, even a quite young child can produce brief sentences that are novel: the child has not heard them before. This is most evident when the sentence does not conform to adult rules. A child is asked to *see if* his brother is in the garden; and he then says he is "seeing". Or he hears an adult use the expression "each other" and says, "They're hugging their chother". Hence a child early develops the ability to create new sentences by combining known words with grammatical patterns *inferred* from previous experience.

Such a procedure is especially notable in the use of *deictic* words (also known as indexicals). These are the words that indicate relationships (E. V. Clark). Among them are indicators of place (here, there) and personal pronouns (I, you, and so on). Such terms differ from names and many other words in having a different reference according to where the speaker is or who he is. "Here" and "there" may refer to the same place on different occasions. "That is your book" and "that is my book" may refer to the same book according to the person speaking. Some children initially use personal pronouns incorrectly, but all soon learn their proper use without systematic instruction.

The child is, however, unaware of the fact that he is using grammatical patterns. Even at the age of five, according to Torrey, a child seems unconscious of language as a phenomenon. She describes how a boy was asked to answer a question, and then to *ask* the same question. He replied, "yes", to the question, "Is John at home?"; but when urged to ask the question, he was unable to do so: all he could do was to say, "John is home." Similarly, Torrey quotes an example from much older boys. They were asked to repeat the exact words spoken by an enquirer: "I asked Alvin if he knows how to play basketball." Often the response was, "I ax Alvin do he know how to play basketball." In each case, the response is to the *meaning* of the words, but not to their form. J. Macnamara gives extensive further evidence of the prior importance of meaning.

Such findings make simple descriptions of language learning inappropriate. Speech is not acquired by a process of stimulus and response, even with the addition of straightforward imitation. And there is as yet no generally accepted set of principles for describing this process, let alone explaining it.

15.2.2 Design Features

When we turn to the speech (or, more generally, the language) of adults, we find a number of descriptions of its design features (C. F. Hockett). These may be compared with the properties of communication among other species (chapter 13). One of the most obvious differences from animal signals is, however, not a general property of language itself: although every human group has a language, languages are immensely diverse; and any person can learn any language. Moreover, it is always possible to learn a second language. (The process is different from that of learning our first language.) This is one aspect of our extreme behavioral plasticity.

These truisms apart, when one first reflects on the nature of languages, one is likely to be impressed by the *arbitrary* character of the signals. A word or sentence does not, as a rule, correspond in its own form to the characteristics of the object or event to which it refers. In most languages a few words, such as murmur and hiss, provide exceptions. The sounds of other species are, however, also arbitrary in this sense. The dances of the honey bee provide the most notable exception: these correspond in their form to the message they convey; they are iconic or analogical, like a diagram, a graph, or a map (13.3.2). The arbitrariness is not confined to sounds. Completely deaf children cannot learn to speak unless specially trained. S. Goldin-Meadow & H. Feldman studied six such children, aged 17 to 49 months, none of whom could speak much or had been trained in a standard sign language (8.3). Each had an individual system of gestural signs, evidently invented mainly by the child, not by adults.

An accompanying feature of human language is that it is *interchangeable* among individuals: anybody can say anything, however incongruous; in a language such as French a man may speak of himself as if he were a woman, and so deceive his hearers. Hence a human being can tell lies. These statements do not apply to animal communication, except perhaps that of chimpanzees (Guy Woodruff & David Premack).

A third major feature of human language is that it is *productive*. As described in the preceding section, novel sentences are continually being made from familiar units—words or phrases. Indeed, as Noam Chomsky (1967) points out, if we except clichés (such as, "it's a fine day"), it is quite rare to utter the same sentence twice: we are continually hearing new sentences; and yet we have no feeling that they are strange or difficult to understand. Bees, too, can produce novel dances at need, but their scope is by comparison trivial. Each major language has tens of thousands of words which can be assembled in millions of grammatical and meaningful sentences. There is no limit to the addition of new words. To say that the possibilities are infinite is not a mere figure of speech.

The signals of both men and bees share the phenomenon of *displacement*. We and they can both give information about objects that are no longer present. But there is a major difference between us and the bees in the ways in which we make use of this ability. Our sentences may refer to a great variety of actual *or possible* objects or events in the past *or the future*.

Next there is the difficult question of *meaning,* (sometimes referred to as "semanticity"). We saw above that attention is often given to the meaning of a sentence, but not to its form. Here are two examples from Chomsky (1967). First, two sentences, of different grammatical structure, can have the same meaning: "I expected the doctor to examine John" and "I expected John to be examined by the doctor." We are unlikely to worry about the different forms of these sentences, unless we are especially concerned with such matters as the active and passive voice of verbs. The obverse is exemplified by single sentences that have two meanings. "What disturbed John was being disregarded by everyone." In such ambiguous statements we can quickly discern two meanings: and which meaning is intended may be discoverable only by examining the context or by asking the speaker.

The preceding paragraphs exemplify the further fact that language is *reflexive:* one can talk about talk. In addition, language has an *argumentative* or critical function—a feature that K. R. Popper (1972) regards as the one most remote from anything we find in other species.

Such a list of the properties of language is rather arid when we think of what can be done by the supreme practitioners in the use of words. I therefore give three examples, each from a distinct mode of discourse.

The first concerns the use of words to convey feelings or attitudes. Such an *expressive* use is not, or need not be, referential. It is often said that we share this use with other species. We have, indeed, expressions such as, "Look out!", "I love you!", and "Go away!". These, though expressed in individual languages, have fairly close counterparts in the signals of animals. But now consider these lines of A. E. Housman (1859–1936).

> The laws of God, the laws of man,
> He may keep that will and can;

Not I: let God and man decree
Laws for themselves and not for me;
And if my ways are not as theirs
Let them mind their own affairs.
Their deeds I judge and much condemn,
Yet when did I make laws for them?

Here the poet expresses resentment or distress; but the effect of these lines depends on allusions to events and to abstract ideas. In such a case, comparisons with the outcries of other species become ludicrous.

At the other extreme, here is a passage, written in the same language and at about the same time.

Pure mathematics is the class of all propositions of the form *"p implies q,"* where *p* and *q* are propositions containing one or more variables, the same in the two propositions, and neither *p* nor *q* contains any constants except logical constants. And logical constants are all notions definable in terms of the following: Implication, the relation of a term to a class of which it is a member, the notion of *such that,* the notion of relation, and such further notions as may be involved in the general notion of propositions of the above form. In addition to these, mathematics *uses* a notion which is not a constituent of the propositions which it considers, namely the notion of truth.

Here Bertrand Russell (1872–1970) illustrates the use of language to discuss abstractions (Russell, 1903). A proposition is itself an abstraction; and Russell is concerned with classes of propositions. He also illustrates the argumentative use of language. We may say that *q* follows from *p;* or, of another proposition, that it does not follow from its premises. We are then applying the rules of logic. (Like the rules of grammar, logical principles are often intuitively understood and applied, by people who cannot state them formally.)

Lastly, here is a magnificent sentence by the linguist and anthropologist, Edward Sapir (1884–1939), which sums up much of what I have been trying to convey above.

If a man who has never seen more than a single elephant in the course of his life, nevertheless speaks without the slightest hesitation of ten elephants or a million elephants or a herd of elephants or of elephants walking two by two or three by three or of generations of elephants, it is obvious that language has the power to analyze experience into theoretically dissociable elements and to create that world of the potential intergrading with the actual which enables human beings to transcend the immediately given in their individual experiences and to join in a larger common understanding.

15.3 MODELS

We now return to the question: to what extent can the current methods of science be applied to our species? In the natural sciences we assume that the events we observe are in some sense determined: they are (we take it for granted) *caused* by earlier events. If we know enough, we can predict that certain happenings will be followed by certain others. Expose a bed bug to a source of warmth, and the insect will move toward it. Inject a stag, not in the breeding season, with testosterone, and its conduct toward females will change. Such predictions have to be expressed as probabilities, but are nonetheless causal.

Attempts have accordingly been made to apply very simple deterministic concepts to very complex human activities. Each makes use of notions from the behavioral sciences. They fall into three categories. (1) The findings of experiments on conditional reflexes and on trial-and-error behavior have been applied to the study of the human intellect and morals. (2) Observations and hypotheses on the social interactions of animals have been used to interpret human conduct. (3) The concepts of natural selection and Darwinian fitness have been applied to human behavior.

15.3.1 A "Conditioned" Species

The application to our own species of simple ideas on habit formation is associated with the work of I. P. Pavlov (5.5) and B. F. Skinner (6.1.2). Pavlov's findings on conditional reflexes had an impact far outside psychology. (A collection of his writings was published in 1957.) The general familiarity of the expression "conditioned reflex" is an index of the impact of Pavlov's concept. Moreover, in conventional textbooks of human physiology, usually addressed to medical students, it is usual to find, after the chapters on the nervous system, a simplified account of conditional reflexes. No other information is given on brain function in relation to behavior; and there is no acknowledgment that we are quite without a physiological account of human behavior, normal or abnormal.

The concept of the conditional reflex, despite its historical importance, has severe limitations, even when applied to animal behavior (5.5; 6.2). Yet Pavlov's work also influenced the writings of at least one celebrated philosopher. Bertrand Russell (1958) regarded CRs as "characteristic of human intelligence"; though in an earlier work (1927) he points to some of the limitations of CRs as explanations of how habits develop. These limitations appear also in G. B. Shaw's *The Adventures of the Black Girl in Her Search for God.* Shaw describes how his heroine meets Pavlov.

". . . If I give you a clip on the knee you will wag your ankle."

"I will also give you a clip with my knobkerry; so dont do it" said the black girl.

"For scientific purposes it is necessary to inhibit such secondary and apparently irrelevant reflexes by tying the subject down" said the professor.

As Shaw implies, an animal strapped to a table and secreting saliva (or changing its heart rate) is not adequate as a model of man, or even of how a human being learns things.

The other prominent attempt to apply "learning theory" to man is that of B. F. Skinner (1953, 1957, 1963, 1973). His experimental technique is described in 6.1.2. R. A. Boakes & M. S. Halliday remark on the attitudes of "bitter attack or impassioned defence" aroused by Skinner's views. (For criticisms see Noam Chomsky, 1959; R. S. Peters.) In his *Verbal Behavior,* Skinner writes: "the basic processes and relations which give verbal behavior its special characteristics are now fairly well understood". This assertion is unanimously rejected by those who study linguistics (15.2). He also states that his own experimental methods can be used to regulate human behavior in the same way as they regulate what a pigeon or a rat does in a Skinner box. Skinner's system is based on two components: they are (1) the "operant"—a movement that is a result of supposedly random activity, and (2) its consequences—positive or negative reinforcement (6.2). All human conduct is seen as consequences of reward and punishment. In *Beyond Freedom and Dignity,* Skinner writes: "personal attention, approval, and affection are usually reinforcing only if there has been some connection with already effective reinforcers, but they can be used when a connection is lacking. The simulated approval and affection with which parents and teachers are often urged to solve behavior problems are counterfeit."

Skinner's system is based entirely on the situation in which an animal, in confined conditions, can do little except move about restlessly, and (if a pigeon) peck a key or (if a rat) press a bar. By varying the consequences of key pecking or bar pressing, the experimenter can influence the rate at which these acts are performed. Although Skinner's animals are not, as are Pavlov's, tied down, their range of activities is severely restricted; and, still more important, what is recorded is only the output from the key or bar. Skinner systematically disregards all the phenomena of exploratory behavior (8.1): and he has nothing to say about the ability of animals (let alone people) to produce *novel* adaptive acts in response to need (8.2.4). Similarly, he ignores imitation (8.4.2).

A fundamental deficiency lies in his concept of reinforcement. In effect, positive reinforcement is defined in terms of the influence of external events on the subject's habits: whatever increases habit strength is called positively reinforcing. Consequently, we have the statement that a pianist learns to play scales smoothly because "smoothly played scales are reinforcing". This is Skinner's answer to the question, why does a pianist (try to) play scales smoothly?

In 4.5.4 I suggest a number of answers to the question: "Why is that animal eating that food?" An answer not included is, "because the food is edible". It was omitted because the word "edible" is usually defined in terms of *what is eaten*. The answer, "because it is edible", would then state that the animal is eating that food because it is eating that food. Similarly, in Skinner's system, "what is reinforcing" is equivalent to whatever is actually done. Hence Skinner's statements about reinforcement contain no objective information beyond the statement that the behavior described actually occurred: the pianist plays scales smoothly because he plays scales smoothly. This tautological statement could, however, have an additional, subjective component: the pianist plays scales smoothly because he likes to do so. This, though rather uninformative, could be important; but Skinner rejects all such subjective statements. Assertions on punishment, or aversive stimuli, are similarly vacuous: "punishable behavior can be minimized by creating circumstances in which it is not likely to occur." (For authentic uses of the concept of reinforcement see 6.2.)

Skinner explicitly rejects any fundamental difference of man from monkeys, cats, rats, or even pigeons. He states that psychologists "like other men of good will . . . want to help their fellow men", but only because "gratitude is a powerful generalized reinforcer". (In that case, surely, "good will" is an inappropriate phrase: it implies that psychologists, like other people, can to some extent choose what they do.) Skinner also refers to a critical comment on his views: "the traditional view [of our species] supports Hamlet's exclamation, 'How like a god!', [while] Pavlov, the behavioral scientist, emphasized 'How like a dog!'." For Skinner, the "behaviorist" position is "a step forward". Skinner does not, however, discuss the possibility that human beings do not like being treated as dogs. Perhaps they find it aversive.

The inadequacies of Skinner's method, even when applied to other species, are well known (8.5). The attempt to apply them to our intellectual abilities seems to reflect a desire for simple explanations of phenonmena that cannot in fact be simply explained.

15.3.2 An "Aggressive" Species

15.3.2.1 Homo pugnax: Skinner's system is an *environmental* determinism. Another kind of determinism presents human behavior as impelled by inescapable "instincts" or "drives"; usually, human depravity is emphasized. Such a pessimistic attitude has a long history (reviewed by R. J. Halliday; R. Hofstadter; A. Montagu; A. Somit).

A central theme of modern theories of this sort is fixity; human depravity is held to reflect an innate disposition laid down during evolution. At the extreme, we are represented as instinct-bound animals, not as rational beings capable of adapting themselves to circumstances. Today, these ideas are widely propagated in popular writings; and they are held to derive support not only from Darwin but from modern ethology.

Such assertions raise questions of method. To analyze them, we may take the case of *Homo sapiens* as a territorial animal. This notion is applied to a variety of social interactions, including those between states or nations and those between property-holding neighbors. It is also associated with the idea that human beings are inherently violent ("aggressive") to members of their own species. For example, N. Tinbergen (1968) writes: "In order to understand what makes us go to war, we have to recognize that man behaves like a group-territorial species." Similarly, K. Z. Lorenz (1966) states: "There cannot be any doubt . . . that intraspecific aggression is, in man, just as much of a spontaneous instinctive drive as in most other higher vertebrates."

A difficulty in dealing with these assertions (and many others like them) is that the authors make general statements, but rarely analyze them critically. Moreover, their arguments are not always consistent. For example, in the same work, Lorenz writes:

With humanity in its present . . . situation, we have good reason to consider intraspecific aggression the greatest of all dangers. We shall not improve our chances of counteracting it if we accept it as something metaphysical and inevitable.

Yet this is just the assumption that he seems to make in the passage quoted above. Similarly, despite the repeated assertion or implication of ineradicable instincts, Lorenz (1967) also proposes a cultural influence on human conduct.

[The] role played by genetic inheritance in the evolution and maintenance of phylogenetically evolved rit-

uals is, of course, taken over by tradition in cultural ritualization.

Such a statement could be used as evidence that Lorenz is not, after all, a doctrinaire "instinctivist"; but in fact there is no definitive statement of the author's views, only a wavering between contrasted attitudes.

Another extreme example of inconsistency may be quoted from E. O. Wilson (1975).

Anthropologists often discount territorial behavior as a general human attribute. This happens when the narrowest concept of the phenomenon is borrowed from zoology. . . . But . . . it is necessary to define territory more broadly, as any area occupied more or less exclusively by an animal or group of animals through overt defense or advertisement. The techniques of repulsion can be as explicit as a precipitous all-out attack or as subtle as the deposit of a chemical secretion at a scent post. Of equal importance, animals respond to their neighbors in a highly variable manner. . . . In extreme cases the scale may run from open hostility, . . . to oblique forms of advertisement or no territorial behavior at all. . . .

If these qualifications are accepted, it is reasonable to conclude that territoriality is a general trait of hunter-gatherer societies.

Wilson here seems to use the fact that some animals are not territorial, or are only "obliquely" so, as evidence for territorial conduct in human communities. (Some less extreme misuses of analogy are mentioned in 14.2.1.)

A further instance of unanalyzed assertions comes from a work in which V. C. Wynne-Edwards reviews the study of territory, and writes of the "property-holding" or "property-tenure" of many animal species (10.4). He states:

In man the primitive systems of property-tenure are *essentially the same* as those already described. Territorial claims are, or were, vested in the nation, the tribe, the family or the individual, and not infrequently in various ways in all these categories at once. [Emphasis added.]

We must now attempt a rational analysis of such assertions. If the authors quoted are right, what should we expect to find when we examine human conduct? As we know, "territory" may be defined either as an exclusively occupied region, or as a defended region. In either case, it is a truism that some people or human groups are territorial: they do occupy regions at least to the partial exclusion of others. The territories of animals are, however, regulated by stereotyped apotreptic signals; and, in a given environment, their sizes are fairly uniform. They are species-typical. If, then, people are territorial in an ethological sense, we may ask what kinds of territory they hold, by what means, and in what sorts of environment; but we find at once that these questions, valid for other species, do not apply to us.

The human species has no standard signals that regulate property holding or other such adult social interactions; we are not restricted to a narrow range of environments; and there is no typical size for the properties some of us hold. In some communities, a few individuals have vast estates, while the majority have none. In others, such discrepancies are "unthinkable". The concept of property in Western Europe is a legal one, and has changed greatly in a few centuries: it is not a single "character", handed down like an object from generation to generation (R. C. Lewontin, 1979). These commonplace statements reflect our cultural diversity. Within a single community or culture, customs, agreements, and laws regulate the holding of property. But customs and laws vary widely in time and space. So does the willingness of groups or governments to go to war.

15.3.2.2 Driven Man:
It is nonetheless argued that inherent in all people, or at least in all men, is some "instinct" or "drive" for holding territory or property, and for doing so by violent means.

Among the most notable writings on this theme are those of psychoanalysis (10.6.3). Sigmund Freud (1856–1939), the founder of this movement in psychological medicine, writes (1969): "The inclination to aggression is an original, self-subsisting instinctual disposition in man"; and Freud's theories are based on the concept of drives (*Triebe*, often translated as "instincts"), which provide energy that has to be discharged. (In 15.3.2.1, I quote K. Z. Lorenz, another physician, echoing Freud.)

A similar outlook has been expressed by writers interested in the evolutionary interpretation of man. W. D. Hamilton (1971), in a critical analysis of some aspects of natural selection, includes the following statement: "Vicious and warlike tendencies are natural in man and were formerly (at least) adaptive." He also writes:

Bringing together evidence from social anthropology, from early historical literature, from the fossil record of hominid violence and cannibalism . . . from studies of Primate behavior, and from theoretical considerations of social evolution, I find it only too easy to imagine that the genes that reared cruelty out of the Primates' aggressive drive have been favored by natural selection in the hominid lines.

A serious study of the hypothesis of an aggressive drive should have at least five components. (1) There must be exact definitions of the activities to be studied. (2) The external circumstances in which the activities occur must be closely examined. (3) There are questions on the influence of internal states. (4) We need to know what valid statements may be made both on the evolution of the activities and also on how they develop in the individual from birth onward. (5) Lastly, it is necessary to examine attitudes toward violent conduct.

1. *Definitions.* When we try to identify the activities referred to in writings on human "aggres-

sion", we find great difficulty. The notion of a drive for aggression is unsatisfactory even when applied to animals (10.6). Yet it is held that we "inherit" such a drive from our animal ancestors. In accounts of human "viciousness" (to use Hamilton's term), we find war, riot, diverse individual acts from homicide to hooliganism, and many other phenomena, including suicide, all classified together. Yet each single item in the previous sentence itself represents a heterogeneous class. "War" may include the decisions of rulers or generals; the impersonal bombing of a target or shooting down of an aircraft; the destruction of a village and its armed inhabitants; the defense of such a village; or cowering in a shell hole. In many of its aspects modern warfare involves no "aggression" in the sense of interpersonal violence. Instead, the efficient modern warrior operates weapons by remote control, and merely carries out orders in a servile manner.

At the other extreme are the types of "aggression" seen professionally by psychiatrists. Socially unacceptable violence may reflect a toxic psychosis induced by drugs, paranoid schizophrenia, depression, or other states. None has any counterpart in animal conduct (J. R. Lion & M. Penna). All are called "aggressive" because they are accompanied by a tendency to assault other people. Hence, when they are said to be cases of "aggression", they are classed together by their social effects, not the intentions or even the internal, physiological state of the actors.

If we disregard the acts of governments and armies, and also ignore pathological conduct, a large category remains; but there is no general agreement on what it includes. Here are some examples of violence: the temper tantrums of a child, the injurious initiation rites of a primitive group, the sport of boxing, infanticide, and the execution of a criminal. All these are tolerated or even encouraged in some communities; but in others the last four are regarded as barbarous.

Each of these phenomena merits separate study; but when such study is attempted, the biological frame of reference is rarely helpful. As an example, M. Dickeman has reviewed knowledge of infanticide in human communities. She rejects "facile analogies" with other species; and she is especially critical of comparisons of people with crowded laboratory rats. In some human groups, including Australian aboriginals and Eskimo, infanticide has been a regular practice. It is then "normative, culturally sanctioned behavior". Dickeman compares it with what she describes as a rarer, but also culturally accepted phenomenon: "the Aztec consumption of human sacrifices as a regular part of the upper-class diet". The latter is held to be an example of ritual; it is, however, doubtful whether the Aztecs were cannibals (W. Arens). In any case, infanticide in preagricultural (and some agricultural) societies is rational: it enables couples to rear only two or three children, and so regulates the size of the population. The modern counterpart in advanced societies is contraception, and in such societies infanticide is a crime.

2. *The Environment:* The second requirement concerns the conditions in which the behavior described actually occurs. The various kinds of action called "aggressive" have again to be examined separately. On this, there is a vast amount of information. J. H. Goldstein has reviewed knowledge on illegal violence against persons. An important feature is the variation in the incidence of crimes, such as homicide, among different communities. Large, urban Western populations might be expected to be fairly uniform in this respect, even if our whole species is not; but in fact there are vast differences: for example, New York City has about six times as many homicides for each million inhabitants as London.

There are also sometimes large differences between small, neighboring groups. J. Paddock has described antiviolent communities in Mexico. In them there is "nearly complete freedom from homicides", and an unusually low incidence of acts of interpersonal violence. Paddock's account suggests possible correlations between child-rearing practices and adult behavior. These pacific societies are marked by a relaxed method of rearing children: discipline is described as "firm and consistent but minimal"; children are accepted as part of the group, and are not the object of special attention. Paddock also observed violent communities, living in similar conditions nearby. Their children are reared quite differently. The hypothesis of a general, species-typical aggressive drive, put forward without regard to relevant information from the social sciences, gives no help in understanding such differences.

3. *The Internal States:* The hypothesis of an internal state (or drive) that makes us violent can be dealt with more briefly. (I return to the general topic of "drive" in chapter 17.) The notion is a prescientific one that turns up in some form throughout history (E. C. Wilm). As an explanation it resembles the idea of *calidum innatum,* or innate heat, which was used in the Middle Ages to account for the constancy of body temperature (E. Mendelsohn). Today we are accustomed to thinking of homeothermy (including our own) in terms of physical processes that can be measured. Much is known of the physiology and biochemistry of temperature regulation. Unfortunately, the physiology of social interactions, even those of other species, is far less developed. This leaves the field open to purely verbal, pseudoexplanations, such as the presence of an innate aggressive drive.

4. *Evolution and Development:* We now turn to questions of evolution and ontogeny. A social scientist studying a human community usually selects certain features for detailed study. The conduct chosen may be violent or at least hostile; but it may be peaceable: it may be communal hunting or agriculture, agreements on marriage, the care of children by adults or of young children by old children, education, or ceremonies of initiation. We may therefore ask why some writers should suppose "aggression" to be the special favorite of natural selection. Human beings are sociable, cooperative, and altruistic; these agreeable traits are the opposite of those that lead to violence against persons. If we attribute any one of them to natural selection, then presumably natural selection has produced them all. Here, therefore, is a paraphrase of the passage by W. D. Hamilton quoted above.

Bringing together evidence from social anthropology, from early historical literature, from the fossil record of hominid cooperative hunting and tool making . . . from studies of Primate behavior, and from theoretical considerations of social evolution, I find it easy to imagine that the genes that reared love and affection out of the Primates' cooperative drive have been favored by natural selection in the hominid lines.

Hence to say that a particular general propensity in human conduct is "phylogenetically preprogrammed" (or some such phrase) makes no useful distinction, for such a statement applies in a sense to everything we do. What is useful is to state the diverse ways in which particular kinds of conduct arise. Such statements have to be based on the study of individual development (15.1.2). The need for such a study is emphasized by the diversity of practice in human communities.

5. *Attitudes:* Lastly, there is the question of attitudes toward violence. We may ask a person what a man should do if his wife is insulted or assaulted; or what is an appropriate court sentence for assault with battery, armed robbery, or wilful homicide. We may also observe what people say and do without asking overt questions. The variety of attitudes

and opinions on such matters in modern times is familiar; and we find similar variety in all periods of which we have knowledge. E. R. Dodds describes changes among the Greeks as they passed from the archaic age of Homer (the eighth century BC) to that of Plato three centuries later. In the earlier period, what is important to a man is the esteem in which he is held by others: for this he is willing to fight and to kill or be killed. He lives in a "shame culture", and for him "saving face" is all-important. But later, conscience (in the modern sense) becomes dominant: choice of action, it is expected, will be based on what is right. Such a community is a "guilt culture". These terms are taken by Dodds from the work of social anthropologists, who find examples of both shame and guilt cultures in existing societies (for example, A. J. Marsella and others).

At the beginning, Dodds states that his book examines aspects of Greek religious experience. A reader may find such matters an incongruous intrusion in a text on ethology. But of course, that is the point. We are discussing attempts to apply notions, derived from laboratory records or observation of animals in the field, to human society in all its variety and complexity. When such attempts are made, biological concepts are found to lack explanatory power. The phenomena that we wish to understand fall outside the range of the objective behavioral sciences.

15.3.3 The Selfish Family Man

An alternative evolutionary model of *H. sapiens* has recently become prominent. We are seen as amoral creatures actuated by the need to propagate our genes: the central concept is Darwinian fitness. In biology fitness is measured by the contribution an individual makes to the next generation (chapter 18). In the past, discussions of natural selection have often been in terms of advantage to the species or, at least, to the social group. It is now argued that the notion of group advantage and group selection is an illusion, and that it is rarely possible for natural selection to act at this level (reviewed by R. D. Alexander; J. Maynard Smith, 1976; R. L. Trivers, 1971, 1972).

The argument has led to a debate, ostensibly on altruism and other moral concepts, but in fact on population genetics. In its customary meaning, the term altruism refers to a person's *intentions*. A lexical definition is: regard for others as a principle of action (reviewed by T. Nagel). By contrast (to quote J. R. Krebs & R. M. May) "in biological terms, an altruistic act . . . decreases the fitness, that is, the chances of survival and reproduction of the actor, while increasing the fitness of a conspecific." Here there is no reference to intention, but only to the *consequences* of an action. The moral concept disappears. For the biological concept of "altruism", I use the term *bioaltruism*. And I refer to workers in this field as *sociobiologists*.

The importance of distinguishing altruism (in its usual sense) from bioaltruism (as defined) may be illustrated from a passage by R. L. Trivers (1974).

One is not permitted to assume that parents who attempt to impart such virtues as responsibility, decency, honesty, and trustworthiness, generosity and self-denial are merely providing the offspring with useful information on appropriate behavior in the local culture, for all such virtues are likely to affect the amount of altruistic and egoistic behavior impinging on the parent's kin . . . socialization is a process by which parents attempt to mold each offspring in order to increase their own inclusive fitness [the chances that their genes will survive], while each offspring is selected to resist some of the molding and to attempt to mold the behavior of its parents (and siblings) in order to increase its inclusive fitness.

Much sociobiological argument is devoted to showing what actually happens *could* have resulted from a process of natural selection (18.2.3). Arguments such as those of Trivers are not based on actual observations: indeed sociobiological theorizing about human beings commonly disregards the findings of social scientists (Marshall Sahlins). Statements are made about family relationships that need to be tested against the facts. For example, Trivers "expects the parent to favor serious and useful expenditures of energy by the child (such as tending the family chickens . . .)" and "the offspring to perceive some behavior, that the parent favors, as being dull, unpleasant, moral . . .". This passage is presumably not merely a joke. It may be contrasted with the many examples, in the writings of anthropologists, of the readiness with which children in a great range of societies attempt adult tasks (J. Middleton). Trivers might respond that by doing so they increase their Darwinian (or inclusive) fitness; but of course such an argument can cover any observation: the method it exemplifies is (to repeat) to observe what happens and then to devise a *post hoc* "explanation".

Another example of sociobiological disregard of facts is the misuse of the term *kin*. In sociobiology this word refers to a close genetical relationship. But in human affairs it has a variety of meanings, often social, not biological. Similarly, the use of mother, father, sister, brother, and so on (or their equivalents in other languages) often reflect relationships and attitudes that are independent of biological (genetical) affinity (R. M. Keesing; M. Sahlins; D. M. Schneider). Hence the use of a simple word, kin, gives an impression of unity when the reference is to quite distinct sets of phenomena.

Sociobiological incoherence may be further illustrated from two comments by E. O. Wilson (1975). In a discussion of social evolution he writes: "When altruism is conceived as the mechanism by which DNA multiplies itself through a network of relatives, spirituality becomes just one more Darwinian enabling device." But elsewhere in the same work, in a review of human evolution, we find a reference to moral codes as creating "complex, intractable moral dilemmas" that are said to be "the current condition of mankind". If we face moral dilemmas (as we do), it follows that we have to make choices: we are not merely puppets jerked by Darwinian strings. The conceptual confusion illustrated here is not confined to isolated passages: it is a general feature of sociobiological writings, and arises from uncritical speculation.

We now turn to the argument on bioaltruism. It is assumed that there can be genetical variation in the tendency to be bioaltruistic. The question is then, how can bioaltruistic genes increase fitness? On any simple assumption, they should be at a disadvantage. The only important exception a priori is in parental behavior. The self-sacrifice of parents on behalf of their young can favor their own genes. This notion may be widened to include the general concept of kin selection (J. Maynard Smith, 1964): the nearer a relative, the more likely she or he is to have a given gene in common with the actor.

We return to this topic in chapter 18; here we are concerned with human applications. One of the founders of the modern, mathematical analysis of natural selection was R. A. Fisher (1958). In *The Genetical Theory of Natural Selection,* first published in 1930, he included speculations on "whether man . . . falls within the scope of a naturalistic theory of evolution". His argument is an example of the use of analogy (compare 14.2.1): he draws a parallel between the rise and fall of civilizations and the growth and death of individual organisms; and he compares human societies with those of the eusocial insects. Fisher's main proposal on man is that civilizations decline as a result of the low fertility of the most able people. (Today, nobody seems to hold such a view.) His position is therefore to some extent deterministic; but he explicitly recognizes the problems that arise from analyzing human conduct in terms of a mathematical theory of natural selection. He refers to the importance of "intellect, honor, love, generosity and saintliness"; for him, "The supreme inner arbiter of our choice in matters of right and wrong we call our conscience." And he does not regard his theory as making value judgments superfluous.

Some sociobiologists, notably E. O. Wilson (1975), seem (sometimes) to disagree. Wilson writes:

The biologist, who is concerned with questions of physiology and evolutionary history, realizes that self-knowledge is constrained . . . by the emotional control centers in the hypothalamus and limbic system of the brain. These centers flood our consciousness with all the emotions—hate, love, guilt, fear, and others—that are consulted by ethical philosophers who wish to intuit the standards of good and evil. What . . . made the hypothalamus and limbic system? They evolved by natural selection. That simple biological statement must be pursued to explain ethics and ethical philosophers . . . at all depths.

This passage seems to imply that the neurophysiology of human moral behavior is understood (which it is not); that we know how such conduct has been brought about by natural selection (which we do not); and—most important—that the study of natural selection can give a complete account of how human conduct is regulated (which it cannot). I defer further comment on all this to the end of the next section.

15.3.4 A Self-conscious Species

The models outlined in the preceding sections may be regarded as heroic attempts to solve intractable problems; or they may be regarded as examples of regrettable blindness to the scope of those problems. A neutral, and perhaps more useful attitude, is to think of them as hypotheses applied with great energy to see how far they take us in explaining phenomena such as human intellectual abilities and the opposition between the cooperative and destructive tendencies in human conduct. We have seen that they do not take us very far. None leads to any novel understanding of man.

It would be satisfactory if we could now propose a system that might solve these problems; but that is not possible. One can, however, present an account of humanity as to some extent free. Such a system answers no pressing questions, but perhaps makes easier our attempts to decide what we ought to do.

A feature of human society, evident today as never before, is a capacity to change rapidly. Such change would be impossible if individual development were not labile. Animal social behavior is species-typical, and develops very reliably. The conduct of each species of eusocial insects, for instance, remains virtually unaltered, generation after generation. Among Primates, there are minor instances of changes in food habits which have arisen, perhaps, from an ingenious "invention" and have been maintained by tradition (8.4.2.4). These may be thought of as representing a stage in our own evolution; but study of, say, potato washing by macaques or predation by baboons hardly helps us to understand human society.

Nonetheless, we speak of social *evolution*. L. L. Cavalli-Sforza compares "sociocultural" with biological evolution. In the theory of evolution by natural selection an important concept is that of fitness. In a stable environment, the typical or normal individual is usually the fittest: others, that depart from the mode, often have less chance of survival or may be infertile. Hence the selection process tends to be conservative: atypical forms are likely to survive only in a changed environment. (One way of achieving a changed environment is emigration.) Tradition, too, is often conservative, though on a much shorter time scale than that of biological evolution. And today the conservative effect of tradition is less prominent than ever before. A notable difference of social from biological evolution is in the accelerated rate of social change of the past few centuries.

Other species may display some versatility; but they are each adapted to a particular ecological niche. *Homo sapiens* is instead *adaptable* to a great range of environments. An important consequence is that most people live in conditions quite different from those in which our ancestors evolved. We still possess traits produced by natural selection acting on our gatherer-hunter forebears. Despite these traits we survive even in cities. This reflects our adaptability.

The genetical variation that allows evolutionary change by natural selection depends in the long run on mutation. The analog in social evolution (if there is one) is the development of a new idea or an invention. P. B. Medawar (1959) uses the term "exosomatic heredity" for the social process by which novel notions are transmitted. Richard Dawkins has suggested a new word, *meme,* for the social counterpart of the gene: the meme is defined as a unit of imitation. (It could also be a unit of *teaching.* See 8.4.3.) Whatever terms we use, transmission by tradition is quite different from the biological process by which genes are transmitted. There is no parallel to the distinction between genotype and phenotype. Exosomatic units are passed on, if at all, without dilution of their effect enforced by sexual reproduction.

An idea or invention can, of course, influence biological fitness. No doubt the discovery of fire, around a million years ago, favored the survival of the discoverer and his or her immediate kin. The same applies to the development of agriculture about 10,000 years ago. It was certainly followed by a vast increase in the world population. With time, the number of examples has increased exponentially: in this century alone we have, among many others, the discovery of vitamins, antibiotics, and the oral contraceptives. Even the last could, in some circumstances, increase the fitness of the users.

Determinist arguments, outlined in the previous pages, seem to imply that all these developments are an inevitable consequence of natural selection, or of other processes that are independent of human will or intention: those who believe that they have some freedom of choice must then be deluded. But nearly all adults, in practice, reject this position. This ancient debate has been recently reviewed by J. R. Lucas and by K. R. Popper (1972). We say that a person *could* have done something, but did not (J. L. Austin); or that he *ought* to take some action; and so we imply that the person has a choice. We may also say, "serves Jane right", and imply that a person has a moral responsibility for her actions. These presumptions about our conduct are among the axioms on which human society is based. The work of scientists, including sociobiologists, like that of other human beings, is founded on the presumption that we have some freedom to choose. According to S. Arieti, the only people who consistently reject the possibility that they are free to make choices are certain schizophrenics. Such people are held to be insane, and their views are rejected in all societies. This is not, in itself, evidence against determinism; but it illustrates the axiomatic character of our presumptions about the will.

Sociobiologists and other modern determinists rarely follow the example of R. A. Fisher, quoted above, and deal explicitly with these general questions. Indeed, a scientist may seem to be *obliged* to reject freedom and responsibility. His objective, whenever he goes beyond mere description, is to predict what will happen. When he tries to make correct predictions, he uses causal relationships that he or others have discovered or hypothesized. That powerful method is taken for granted as valid in most of this book. What we are now faced with is its limitations. The apparent dilemma can be resolved if we treat the scientists' method, not as all-embracing, but as a procedure employed wherever it is effective: we stop short when we come to a self-contradiction or absurdity. In all the sciences we are in any case accustomed to our predictions being only probable: we often cannot reliably predict individual events (2.3.6.2).

When we use the determinist frame of reference, we are, consciously or not, adopting a particular philosophical principle. Such a principle falls outside the natural sciences, and cannot be tested by scientific methods: it belongs, not to physics, but to metaphysics.

If we try to force all phenomena into the framework of the natural sciences (formerly called physics), we may seem to be adopting an attitude that encourages irresponsibility: if we are merely puppets jerked by genetical or evolutionary strings, we need feel no obligation to choose one mode of conduct in preference to another. We can then act merely on a whim because, even if we feel that we are making a choice, that is an illusion. If we are automata, then our belief that we (or some of us) can create something new is false: the moral principles of a Confucius, the theories of a Newton, the works of a Shakespeare or a Mozart, are comparable to the printout of an automatic typewriter programmed to respond in predetermined ways to certain inputs. But we reject that position as we go about our ordinary affairs. For those of us who are not geniuses, there are everyday examples at least of individuality. The language, dialect, and idiom we use when we speak is determined by our upbringing; but the actual words we use are our own. Indeed, there are formal arguments which demonstrate that complete determinism is logically untenable (reviewed by J. R. Lucas and by D. M. MacKay). Hence, to avoid inconsistency, we are obliged to recognize that the powerful methods of science are not all-powerful: there is much that they can predict, or hope to predict; but they should not be expected to cope with everything.

15.4 CLASSIFYING KNOWLEDGE

The preceding paragraphs imply that there is more than one kind of knowledge, and that the findings of the natural sciences constitute only one kind. If so, we should be able to design a classification of what we know about the world. When we attempt this, we have to cope with questions that have been argued by philosophers for millennia, but are usually disregarded by scientists. Bertrand Russell (1948) gives a readable, historical account of this debate.

15.4.1 Body and Mind

The customary presumption (often unacknowledged) is that we know (1) objects and events in the external world and (2) mental events, including thoughts, feelings, and intentions. The second (subjective) category we locate in our heads, but it is not directly accessible to others. (If a surgeon opens my skull, he still cannot see my thoughts.)

Such a *dualism,* though to many it is common

sense, has often been rejected. Some philosophers have said that what we talk of as events in an objective, external world are in fact known only as a result of mental processes. They therefore accept the existence only of ideas, and propose a *monism* in which there are only minds. In its extreme form, such an *idealism* has nothing to contribute to science.

An alternative kind of monism is *materialism*. (The latter word, like idealism, is used here to refer to a philosophical doctrine, and has no moral or aesthetic implications.) A scientist, when required to investigate mental events, may ask questions of his subjects; but he is quite likely to try to find out how the brain works, by using the methods he applies to other animals and even to machines. He may then treat mental events as mere epiphenomena, or byproducts of what happens in the material, objective world that is accessible to his methods; or he may reject the notion of mental events altogether.

The attitude or policy described in the previous paragraph has two components. First, it refuses to acknowledge anything not in the external world; or, at least, it consistently disregards mental events. The matter for study consists of what can in principle be observed by anybody: it is public. It may include what people say; but, at least by implication, it rules out what they think or feel. The method advocated in the first chapter of this book is monistic and materialist in this sense; and its importance and effectiveness, in the study of other species, must be recognized. It can be applied also to human affairs.

Second, the investigation of mental events by means of neurophysiology is a *reductionist* procedure. The same applies to studying overt behavior by looking for its internal, physiological causes: behavior is "reduced" to physiology. Reductionism

is a subject that sometimes arouses remarkable ire. Here we need only recognize that a materialist *and* reductionist procedure can have welcome results (see also 19.1.3). For example, the normal development of the human brain, and consequently of the human intellect, requires the presence of certain amounts of thyroid hormone in the bloodstream. The secretion of the hormone in turn depends on the presence of iodine in the food. Where there is a shortage of iodine, people are liable to develop as cretins: they are then mentally deficient. This calamity is prevented by adding iodides to table salt. The reader will be familiar with other examples of the beneficial effects of treating people as physical systems. As a result, a great deal of medicine is monistic in practice.

Another ground for a materialist program is found in what (little) we know of brain function and its relationship with our actions and our personalities (reviewed by Keith Oatley; D. E. Wooldridge). Brain damage, not necessarily extensive, can drastically alter our thoughts, abilities, and character (figure 15-3); so can small amounts of a drug that changes brain function.

15.4.2 The Question of Consciousness

Our brains, then, are material entities and can be treated as such. The undoubted successes of such treatment have had a general influence on the attitudes not only of scientists and physicians but also of others. We may trace this influence in the changing concept of consciousness (reviewed by J. Schorstein). For millennia, men have spoken of the knowledge that a man has *of himself;* the words in Latin and Greek, which correspond to our "consciousness", had this meaning. But this sort of knowledge is not easily investigated. Today, in contrast, when we say that another person is con-

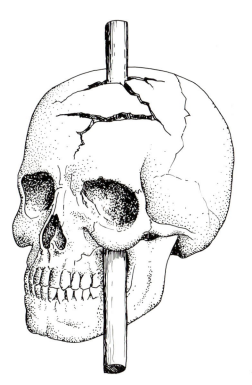

FIGURE 15-3 Drawing of the skull of a skilled worker, Phineas Gage, whose head was penetrated by an iron bar in an accident. He survived, but only as a shiftless, foul-mouthed drunkard. His friends said he was "not the same man". (After J. Schorstein, 1963)

scious, we often mean only that the person is responsive, and answers our questions, avoids pain, and accepts pleasures. This clinical or behaviorist concept can be used in describing experiments, for example, on the effects of drugs on the brains or behavior of human beings (or of animals). Hence by altering the meaning of the word "consciousness" we define a manageable region for scientific study.

But in doing so we jettison one kind of knowledge. A distinctive feature of humanity is the importance of the idea of the self (L. B. Slobodkin). Chimpanzees have perhaps a rudimentary self-consciousness (G. G. Gallup), just as they have a rudimentary linguistic ability (8.3); but there is no reason to suppose them capable of (for example) self-criticism. A person can observe the self as if it were comparable to objects or to other persons. This and our linguistic ability allow us to talk about ourselves in elaborate ways (15.2.2). We can debate what we observe, imagine future possibilities, and decide which features of human conduct we wish to promote, which to reject.

In medical practice the question whether a purely "behaviorist" attitude should be adopted may arise in an acute form. Schorstein takes the example of the surgical treatment of certain forms of insanity. In the operation called prefrontal leucotomy or lobotomy, a cut is made in the front part of the cerebrum on both sides (figure 15-4). The result has been said to be a disappearance of some of the most distressing features of the patient's behavior. Put like this, the benefit is most obviously for the people who live with or look after the patient. Unfortunately, there is also much evidence of adverse effects (reviewed by Anthony Hordern). Intellectual abilities are usually not impaired; but the patient's personality may be drastically altered. Consciousness may be retained; but conscience and the capacity for the extremes of joy and despair seem to be lost. Schorstein tells the macabre anecdote of the patient who, under local anesthesia, was asked at the moment the frontal lobe was being cut, "What is going through your mind?" "A knife", was the reply.

These operations, which for a period were done in large numbers, are now in disrepute. This is only partly because new drugs can more simply have similar effects. They are questioned because they interfere unwarrantably with the patient's personal-

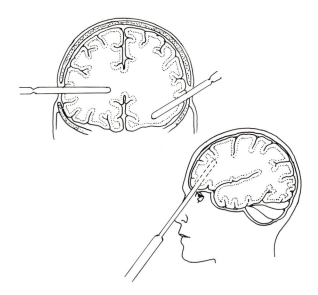

FIGURE 15-4 Diagrams to illustrate the method some-times called frontal lobotomy. Above left, a transverse section of the human brain and skull, with two leuco-tomes in place. A leucotome is a blunt knife, inserted through a small hole in the skull. The blade is moved as shown, to cut tracts between the frontal lobes and the rest of the forebrain. Below right, the method of a simpler operation: the patient is briefly anesthetized; a pick is then inserted through a hole in the orbit by a blow from a mallet and moved from side to side in the frontal lobe. The second operation could be done in 2 min. (From C. Blakemore, 1977)

ity; and the patients are usually in no state to say clearly whether they want the operation. This is a real dilemma that cannot be overcome by scientific inquiry. The solution adopted depends not only on a clinical assessment but also on the value put on preserving the patient as a person.

15.4.3 A Plural System

When such matters are brought into the open, they are likely to cause disquiet and even resentment.

The question for us now is whether there is a frame of reference in which we can incorporate all the achievements of the natural sciences, and yet allow for what is beyond their scope. We need a system that incorporates the *presumptions made by scientists, and on which the practice of science rests.* The presumptions cannot themselves be investigated by scientific methods: not even a physicist can lift himself by his own bootstraps.

An example of a usually unquestioned presumption is the use of statistical analysis to test the "significance" of experimental findings. The commonest statistical procedures are descriptions of how measurable features are distributed in the populations studied; nonetheless, they are used to validate or contravert the conclusions of experimenters. Now consider their use in justifying methods of treating diseases. It might be asked: what is the evidence that the use of such methods, with the usual carefully arranged controls, actually makes medical practice in general more effective? The immediate response could be to compare the effectiveness of treatments based on scientifically designed trials with others lacking any such basis. If the difficulties of such a comparison were overcome, the findings could then be subjected to statistical analysis. But at this point we find ourselves in a dilemma. The use of statistical analysis for such a purpose *assumes the validity of the methods we are trying to test.*

We see once again that there is more than one kind of knowledge. The presumptions made by scientists about the phenomena they study represent one kind. These presumptions are not, however, the result of private intuition, but are arrived at by a social process: they represent the agreement of a community on the principles to be adopted.

At the beginning of 15.4 I suggest that, if there

are several kinds of knowledge, then a first necessity (emphasized by the philosopher, C. I. Lewis) is to classify them. A widely cited classification is that of K. R. Popper (1972), who rejects both monism and dualism in favor of a kind of *pluralism*. His categories, or "worlds", are only three. In this he adopts a proposal made by Plato two and a half millennia ago. The main task of philosophers is, writes Popper, "to enrich our picture of the world by helping to produce imaginative and at the same time argumentative and critical theories, preferably of methodological interest". Hence Popper advocates a philosophy that should give scientists some help.

In this system, the first world is that of "physical states": it includes all material objects, inorganic or organic, and is the subject matter of natural science. The second world is that of "mental states": it includes perceptions, feelings, intentions, memories and thoughts. These are influenced by world one (as we have just seen), but we know them by introspection, not by observation. So far, then, the system resembles a conventional dualism. But the third world is that of *objective knowledge,* or "ideas in the objective sense": it includes theories and their logical relationships, arguments, and language.

A notable feature of this classification is the separation of theories, including scientific theories, (world three) from the phenomena studied by scientists (world one). In Popper's system these two worlds depend on the operation of world two as a mediator between them: a human being can perceive an object, and can also comprehend a theory or a number or an equation that refers to the object. Such comprehension is held to make possible the influence of world three on world one: our knowledge of scientific theory enables us to alter the first world. Popper argues that the third world is in some sense autonomous. But I am treating his

system only as a (possibly) convenient classification of what we know. It is not necessary to assume *autonomy*. Indeed, if one does, difficulties arise in deciding how the separate worlds interact (discussed in a volume edited by I. Lakatos & A. Musgrave).

The point of view I adopt here may be called science-centered: how do philosophers' attempts to classify or describe or analyze knowledge help scientists (and especially ethologists) in their work? More specifically, do they help us to decide on the scope of ethological concepts in our attempts to understand our own species? In asking such questions I treat scientific theories as products of people working in a community. As we see in the next chapter (16.3.2.2), arguments that we intuitively agree are self-evident are not accepted by everybody: unlettered people do not necessarily adopt logical forms that we take for granted. The readiness with which we make use of certain forms of argument is culturally influenced.

Our principal dilemma, which I have tried to outline in the preceding pages, is this. In scientific inquiry we pay attention only to the "evidence of our senses", that is (once again), to publicly observable events. "Real is what can be measured" (Max Planck). Yet in doing so, and in all our ordinary affairs, we make presumptions that fall outside the scope of science; and we often do so without being aware of them. We say we are conscious; that we choose a course of action; that we "have an idea"; or that we are applying a theory or a formula to a problem. The attempt to classify knowledge, if it does nothing else, draws attention to these tacit assumptions.

There are two reasons of the first importance why our assumptions should be made explicit. First, they have a moral significance. The frame of reference in which we work can influence our attitude to our moral obligations. Second, clarity on the principles that we apply in our inquiries, whether on man or on other species, can help us to make those inquiries more effective. In this chapter I describe widely discussed and even accepted models of humanity, and show that they have conspicuous logical and biological (let alone moral) deficiencies. Methodological inquiry cannot prevent people from putting forward such over-simple theories; nor should it do so. But acquaintance with fundamental philosophical questions could enable us to see their limitations more quickly.

These limitations are not a property of science in general. There is a danger, in subjecting supposedly rigorous theories to critical analysis, that one should seem to be derogating the scientific method. To do so can open a door to irrationalism and chaos. In the preceding pages I have tried to make clear that the methods of science, correctly applied, can be both powerful and beneficial. Alexander Pope summed it up.

> Trace science, then, with modesty thy guide;
> First strip off all her equipage of pride;
> Deduct what is but vanity or dress,
> Or learning's luxury, or idleness;
> . . .
> Then see how little the remaining sum,
> Which served the past, and must the times to
> come!

15.5 CONCLUSION

This part begins by asking whether a human ethology is possible. I now summarize what I believe can correctly be said on this question.

Statements on the evolution of the human species, and on our structure and physiology, fall in the same categories as those concerning other species. They may be based on speculation, on the fossil record, on description, or on experimental evidence. Their validity in each case is judged by the same criteria as those used in biology generally.

Man may therefore be *compared* with other species, just as we may compare a gorilla with a guinea pig or a macaque with a mandrill. Such comparisons have been, and continue to be, essential for the advance of knowledge of human physiology. Sometimes they lead to conclusions of great practical value: what we know, for example, of vitamins and hormones is derived largely from observations on other species. Much benefit has resulted from careful, critical research in which the human body has been treated as a system that conforms with the laws of physical science.

Physiology in fact rests on the physical sciences. It might be supposed that the study of human behavior could similarly rest on behavioral science or on biology generally. Much of the present chapter examines attempts to apply to human beings behavioral concepts derived from observing or experimenting on other species. These attempts have proved unsatisfying; and their defects have obliged us to digress rather widely from the conventional paths of ethology. The grounds for dissatisfaction are of five kinds.

1. Analogy is often misused (14.2.1). Suppose we see a monkey scratching another monkey. That may look very much like a person doing another's hair. We also have, perhaps, an explanation for the monkey's conduct. But that does not justify us in explaining the human behavior in the same way. At best, observation of another species can suggest a hypothesis about ourselves. And, well though that procedure works in physiology—when applied with caution—it is rarely successful in accounting for our own social interactions.

2. Other logical pitfalls concern definition. For a rational account of human conduct the kinds of behavior discussed must be clearly defined. Often, as in the debate on "aggression", no such definitions are given or even implied. A large and mixed group of phenomena are discussed as if all had the same causes. No valid conclusions can be drawn from such a muddle.

3. The concepts of human ethology, and of human beings responding automatically to reward or punishment, underestimate the scope and complexity of human actions. They represent attempts to apply to human behavior simple notions that are inadequate even for an account of animal behavior.

4. The notion of humanity driven inexorably by its evolutionary past contains two related errors. First is the belief that it is useful to describe some activities as "phylogenetically preprogrammed" or "genetically coded" and others not. Human beings have, we assume, evolved by natural selection; and, to the extent that any of our activities are a result of this evolution, then all are. Similarly, all our activities, and not only some, are influenced by our genes. Hence to state that particular features are produced by our phylogeny or our genes makes no useful distinction. The second error is the disregard of ontogeny. Suppose we are concerned with socially unacceptable violence ("aggression"), and

its opposite—for which there is no obvious name. If we wish even partly to understand them we must look, not at the unknowable past, but at their development in the individual.

5. Lastly, there is the common disregard of the implications of theories, especially determinist theories. Many writers put forward views that seem to signify that we are automata, without examining the implications of what they say. In part, this results from the presumption that the methods of the natural sciences can be applied to everything we know, and that there is only one kind of knowledge. But this notion does not stand up to critical scrutiny.

Unfortunately, to point to the limits of science can encourage a resort to irrationality. In 15.4 I therefore try to show that there are ways of looking at these questions that allow for the limitations of science and are yet rational. Any such model must satisfy three criteria: (a) it must be logical; (b) it must conform with existing knowledge; and (c) it must be morally acceptable to the people of the society in which it is used. A further inevitable feature is that the model must be incomplete: it must admit ignorance. Ethology cannot solve the problems that face us. When we look for wisdom in our dealings with each other, the Delphic exhortation still holds: know thyself.

VI

CONCEPTS

Parts II, III, and IV describe how a variety of animal species solve the problems of survival. Part V is concerned with the "strategies" of a single species, *Homo sapiens*. We now turn to some of the theories by which ethologists try to solve their own problems. (Theories of "learning" are, however, discussed in part III, and we do not return to them.) The next three chapters are on genetics, the concepts of instinct, and on the evolution of behavior—topics that are to some extent related. All are touched on earlier in the book; and some passages of these earlier chapters will perhaps be read again with more understanding when the underlying theories have been studied.

The principles of genetics, some of which are outlined in chapter 16, underlie the whole of biology. In ethology they are especially important in discussions of "instinctive" or "innate" behavior; but they are relevant whenever variation among individuals or populations is in question. J. B. S. Haldane (1946) has described the interaction of nature and nurture as one of the central problems of genetics. It is, in fact, a central matter for biology generally, and is a main theme of chapter 16.

On instinct, in chapter 17, we face questions that were already debated long before the modern period. It is now possible to state the questions more precisely than before, and to begin to answer them. To do this, we have to surrender prescientific methods of discussion, and to apply genetical and other principles that still cause much difficulty. Writings on behavior are in transition between traditional and modern concepts; there is much debate and some confusion. In an attempt to give a guide to the literature of the past three decades, I outline the recent history of ideas on instinct, as well as new research findings.

Lastly, chapter 18 deals with evolution. The role of evolutionary ideas in ethology, especially the theory of natural selection, is paradoxical. On the one hand, the evolutionary framework of biology is inescapable; on the other, statements on how behavior has evolved are inevitably speculations: they cannot be tested by direct observation. What we can observe is how existing species live now. In doing so, we assume that they are a product of a long process of evolution by natural selection; that they are consequently intricately adapted to the conditions in which they live; and that we can, by painstaking research, analyze this adaptation into its behavioral, physiological, and genetical components.

16

VARIATION
AND HEREDITY

For use almost can change the form of nature.

Shakespeare
Hamlet

Within every species that has been studied we find individual variation. Some of that variation is of genetical origin: it reflects differences in the individuals' genes. But some variation is of environmental origin: it results from differences in the conditions in which the animals live or have lived. Individual differences, then, have two sources, the genotype and the environment. Analysis of the causes of such variation is the subject matter of genetics, that is, of the *science of variation and heredity.*

We are concerned here with variation in behavior. The principles of "behavior genetics" are, however, exactly the same as those of the genetics of any other class of features, such as structural characters. Among these principles, the one that requires most emphasis is that we are concerned with *differences:* as we see further below, it is not appropriate to speak of *characteristics* as genetically or environmentally determined: *all* features are influenced both by the genes and by the environment.

16.1 SOME EXAMPLES

16.1.1 Simple Gene Substitutions

Our understanding of genetics was initially derived from simple breeding experiments. The differences studied were each "controlled" by a single gene; and so the familiar Mendelian ratios were observed. It is unusual for behavioral features to vary in this way, but an example has been described in the noises made by laboratory mice. Some mice squeak when handled; others do not. (This is presumably antipredator behavior: for the wild type it may be an alarm call.) G. D. Whitney (1969, 1973) studied eight inbred mouse strains and the results of crossing them. "Vocalization" proved to be a dominant condition: whether mice of these strains squeak or not, on being handled, evidently depends on the alleles present at a single locus.

Another example, more complex and therefore more typical, has been studied in the mating of the vinegar fly, *Drosophila melanogaster,* the species on which much of our knowledge of classical genetics is based. Margaret Bastock (1956) compared the mating of a mutant form, of which the

507

body is yellow, with the wild (normal) type. Yellow is a sex-linked recessive condition. It was already known that yellow males are less successful in competing for females than are wild males. It was hypothesized that the immediate cause of the difference was the behavior of the two types. This assumes that (as is commonly the case) the gene has a *pleiotropic* action (Hans Grüneberg): that is, different alleles at this locus, in a given environment, are responsible for two or more phenotypic differences.

Preliminary matings insured that the wild-type flies were genetically similar to the mutants except at the yellow locus (and at other loci close by). The test was to put a male and a female, aged four or five days, together in standard conditions for 1 h. Whenever a male is yellow, the percentage success is lower than when the male is of the wild type.

Courtship by the male has three components: orientation toward the female, vibration of a wing, and licking the female (figure 9-3). Yellow males proved to do less wing vibration than did wild males: the bouts of vibrating were briefer and performed at longer intervals. Difference in mating success is attributed to this difference in behavior. Control experiments were performed that largely eliminated factors such as the odor or appearance of the males.

This example illustrates some of the complexities of genetical analysis. First, it was necessary to breed for several generations to get rid of genetical variation not due to the yellow locus. Variation in the *behavioral* feature studied is, in fact, influenced by differences at many loci, not only at one. Second, variation was initially studied by recording not the presence or absence of a character but the *probability* of mating success. Third, the developmental and physiological processes, which intervene between gene action and the phenotype (that is, the observed behavior), are not known.

The honey bee, *Apis mellifera,* provides another example (W. C. Rothenbuhler). A bacterial infection, American foulbrood, attacks bee larvae and causes death, usually at the pupal stage. The infection spreads through the wax of the combs, and can produce a severe epidemic. Some strains of bees are more resistant to the infection than are others. The difference is due to a behavioral feature: the resistant bees open the cell and remove the larvae or pupae soon after death; such bees are said to be hygienic (figure 16-1).

Rothenbuhler used inbred queen bees, and inseminated them artificially, each with sperm from a single drone. When hygienic bees were crossed with bees from susceptible lines, all the offspring colonies were susceptible: the workers did not uncap the cells, and they did not remove dead larvae or pupae. Hence hygienic behavior seemed to be recessive.

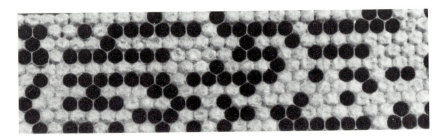

FIGURE 16-1 Comb of "hygienic" bees after infection with American foulbrood: cells with infected larvae have been uncapped and emptied. (Courtesy W. C. Rothenbuhler)

TABLE 16-1 Possible genetics of "hygienic" behavior of bees: Effect of a backcross of the F_1 double heterozygote to "hygienic" bees.

$$UuRr \quad x \quad uurr$$

$$\downarrow$$

$$UuRr \quad Uurr \quad uuRr \quad uurr$$

The two behavioral features are Uncapping and Removing. Both are evidently recessive characters. The result of the cross is 25% of each genotype. Only one type (*uurr*) is fully hygienic.

Drones of the hybrid or F_1 generation were therefore backcrossed to queens of a hygienic strain. The simplest hypothesis was that the difference in behavior depended on a single gene substitution, that is, on a single pair of alleles. If so, the backcross should have yielded 50% of each type. In fact, of 29 colonies, only 6 were hygienic; in a further 9 colonies cells with infected larvae were uncapped, but the dead larvae were not removed. Of the remainder, 6 removed dead larvae if the cells were first uncapped by the experimenter. The most probable explanation is that two pairs of alleles are involved, one responsible for the difference in uncapping the cells, and the other for removing larvae and pupae (table 16-1). As usual, however, the detailed findings do not present an entirely simple Mendelian picture. Some of the variation observed seemed to be due to differences at other loci.

16.1.2 Polygenic Effects

The preceding examples show that variation in behavioral features sometimes depends on simple genetical differences. Usually, however, genetical variation in behavior is polygenic: it depends on differences at many loci, and the variation is continuous (figure 16-2). Familiar examples of such variation are those of the body weight of, say, a mammal, or the scores made by people given tests of ability. An example from rats is given in figure 16-5.

FIGURE 16-2 Geometrical representation of Gaussian or normal distribution curves to give a visual representation of the standard deviation (SD) and the variance (see table 16-3). In each case the mean is at 0 on the horizontal scale. (After W. F. Bodmer & L. L. Cavalli-Sforza, 1976)

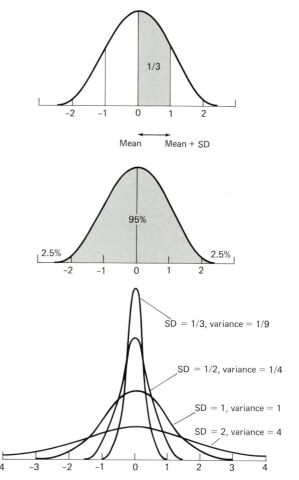

16.1.2.1 Hybridizing: Two main kinds of experiment give information on the genetics of a continuously varying character: (1) crossing two genetically distinct types, and (2) selecting for increased or diminished values over generations. The latter is, of course, the method traditionally used in the breeding of domestic plants and animals. Table 16-2a gives procedures used in quantitative analysis.

When two types are crossed, the most obvious hypothesis is that the offspring (the F₁ generation) will be intermediate between the parents. Some-

TABLE 16-2a   Dispersion about the mean.

The following gives the procedure used in the simplest possible statistical analysis of a character of which the variation is continuous. (See also figure 16-2.)

If x_i is one observation,
  n is the number of observations,
  x is the arithmetic mean,

then $$\bar{x} = \frac{\Sigma x_i}{n}.$$

When giving a mean, it is always necessary to give a measure of the scatter or dispersion about the mean, that is of variation. The measure most often used is the *variance* (σ^2):

$$\sigma^2 = \frac{\Sigma(x_i - \bar{x})^2}{n-1}.$$

That is, the deviations from the mean of each of the series of measurements are squared; these squares are summed; and the sum is divided by one less than the number of observations. When reporting calculation of a mean, it is usual to give σ, the *standard deviation* of the mean, as the measure of dispersion. Often, however, one wants a measure not only of dispersion but of the reliability of the estimate of the mean. Reliability improves with the number of observations, *n*. Hence it is common to use the *standard error of the mean* (s.e.), as a measure of reliability:

$$\text{s.e.} = \frac{\sigma}{\sqrt{n}}$$

TABLE 16-2b   Additive and dominance effects of genetical variation.

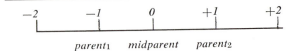

Two types, which differ in a measurable feature, are reared in the same environment, and then crossed. The offspring (F₁ generation) may be intermediate in respect of that feature (zero on the scale above); all the genotypic variance is then additive. More usually, the offspring resemble one parental type more than another: often they score near one of the parental values (-1 or $+1$); that value is then said to be dominant. Sometimes the F₁ mean value is outside the range of the parent values (for example, at -2 or $+2$). The F₁ generation is then said to display heterosis, or overdominance.

---

times, they are. The genetical variation is then said to be *additive:* each allelic difference adds or subtracts its quota of influence on the measured character. But the mean of the F₁ generation does not always coincide with the midparent value (table 16-2b). The phenomenon of *dominance* is most familiar from the effects of single allelic differences. In the preceding section I give the example of the difference of wild-type *Drosophila* from yellow: in that case the wild type is dominant; and the F₁ phenotype is not intermediate, but is indistinguishable from the homozygous wild type.

Accordingly, the variance of a measurable feature may have both additive and nonadditive components. Sometimes the mean value shown by a F₁ generation falls outside the range of the parental values (table 16-2b). There is then said to be *overdominance.* J. H. Bruell has given examples. Inbred strains of mice had been maintained by mating brothers with sisters for many generations and were each therefore genetically very uniform: that is, each must have been homozygous at nearly all loci. The strains differed genetically in many respects. Hence crossing two of them must have produced a F_1 generation heterozygous at many loci. The question was, what would be the effect of heterozygosis?

Some of the F_1 hybrids were tested for the cholesterol content of the blood serum and for hematocrit (a measure of the number of erythrocytes in a given volume of plasma). The results in each case were near the midparent value; hence for these features the genetical variation was additive. But when 31 F_1 types were given behavioral tests, the results were quite different. The tests were (1) the amount of movement during exposure for 10 min in an unfamiliar maze, and (2) the amount of running in a wheel in standard conditions (8.1.2). On both tests the hybrids scored consistently above the midparent value; and the greater the genetical difference between the parent strains, the greater was this effect.

When a hybrid scores above both its parents, it is often said to display heterosis or hybrid vigor. The phenomenon is economically important in the breeding of domestic plants and animals; hence hybrid vigor usually refers to superior growth or fertility. But in this case, we have *behavioral heterosis*.

A further effect of heterozygosis is less well-known: it often *reduces variation*. This may be seen if two inbred strains are crossed, and the variation in the resulting F_1 generation is compared with that among the members of the parent strains (I. M. Lerner). The influence of heterozygosis on features such as body weight or fertility is well established, but there are few good examples from behavioral studies. One comes from observations of F_1 mice and their parent strains in a residential maze. The hybrid mice varied less than the two inbred strains in activity, that is, in the number of

visits made to the various parts of their environment. Hence in this respect they were more predictable (S. A. Barnett & J. L. Smart). Such phenotypically uniform animals are sometimes more useful for experiments than are the developmentally more labile inbred types.

16.1.2.2 Crossing Species: It is occasionally possible to cross distinct species. In 11.2.2.1 I describe observations on baboons, *Papio,* which throw some light on the differences in the behavior of two closely related forms. Another case has been thoroughly studied by R. R. Hoy. Male crickets of the genus, *Teleogryllus,* make distinctive, species-typical sounds that attract females (compare 13.2.2). Two species, *T. commodus* and *T. oceanicus,* were crossed. The male hybrids that resulted had their own distinctive songs. The normal and hybrid songs were played to females. As expected, females of each species were attracted by the calls of conspecific males. In addition, hybrid females preferred hybrid songs. In further work, Hoy and others compared the songs of reciprocal hybrids: the hybrid song differs according to the direction of the cross (figure 16-3). Female hybrids, derived from crossing *commodus* males with *oceanicus* females, preferred the songs of males of the same parentage, and conversely. Hence it is inferred that variation in the response of the females to songs is under the same genetical control as variation in the males' songs.

Such a finding may be related to a general proposition about the evolution of social signals. Clearly, a signal is effective only if there is a standardized response to it. Both signals and responses must therefore evolve together.

16.1.2.3 Selecting: Despite the always present genetical variation, natural populations of a given

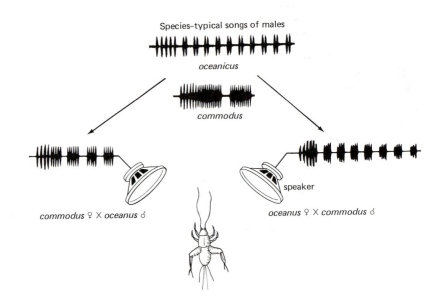

Species-typical songs of males

oceanicus

commodus

commodus ♀ X *oceanus* ♂

speaker

oceanus ♀ X *commodus* ♂

FIGURE 16-3 Male crickets, *Teleogryllus commodus* and *T. oceanicus*, have species-typical songs, represented above, center. Hybrids between the species have their own songs (also shown); and these differ according to the direction of the cross. A female is attracted to the hybrid song of males of the same parentage as her own. (After R. R. Hoy and others, 1977)

animal species often seem, superficially at least, remarkably uniform. Sometimes such uniformity has an obvious function. The members of a cryptic species (3.4.1) remain cryptic as a result of differential predation on inadequately concealed individuals. Displays such as those of courtship must not, we assume, depart much from the typical form, or their effectiveness would be reduced. The case of the yellow mutant, described above, is an example. Nonetheless, all populations that have been studied have been found to be genetically diverse (reviewed by K. Mather). An important method of revealing such variation is to test for differences of serum proteins (compare 10.4.2.1).

The existence of genetical differences makes possible selection for change over generations. Experiments on selection of behavioral features have been principally on *Drosophila* and on laboratory mice or rats; but some have been done on blowflies (5.5.3). Those on *Drosophila* have been especially concerned with orientations (2.2.2), in particular, responses to light and gravity. These are species-typical and, in natural populations, highly predictable; yet they can be altered by selection.

J. Hirsch (1963) describes experiments on the geotaxis of *Drosophila melanogaster*. His apparatus was a vertical maze (figure 16-4). The flies were introduced through a tube and were then faced with a number of choice points, at each of which they could move either up or down. They could end at the level at which they were introduced to the maze, or above or below. The extent to which they were above or below was a measure of negative or positive geotaxis. Hirsch bred from strongly positive and strongly negative flies; and he also maintained an unselected group. In this way he obtained three genetically distinct populations, differing in response to gravity.

Similarly, T. Dobzhansky & B. Spassky selected *D. pseudo-obscura* for positive and negative geo-

FIGURE 16-4 Vertical maze for experiments on the geotaxis of *Drosophila melanogaster:* the flies are introduced through the tube in the middle on the left, move through a number of choice points, and end up on the right at a level which may be the same as that at which they were introduced, above, or below; the extent to which they are above or below is a measure of negative or positive geotaxis. (Courtesy L. Ehrman)

taxis, and also for positive and negative phototaxis. Sixteen generations of selection yielded distinct populations. Such findings do more than illustrate genetical differences that influence behavior, for they also show how the genetical variation always present can have an adaptive function. Such variation makes possible a response, in a few generations, to a changed environment (compare 3.4.2). In one environment, a positive response to gravity or light may be advantageous, but in another, negative.

In experiments on selection, an experimenter may fail to measure the behavior he originally intended to study. A. W. Ewing tried to select *D. melanogaster* for high and low "spontaneous activity": he used a runway consisting of six glass funnels connected in a straight line by narrow glass tubes. The flies were put in at one end; and those that arrived first at the other end were scored as most "active"; the least active remained in the first funnel. Selection over 16 generations yielded a line that, on this definition, displayed low activity. But observation of the actual behavior revealed that what had been selected was refusal to enter the tubes: Ewing calls this claustrophobia.

By an irony, selection for a different character had previously led to a change in "activity" (reviewed by B. Burnet & K. Connolly). Aubrey Manning (1961) selected four lines of vinegar flies for 25 generations, two each for fast and slow mating, respectively. After seven generations the slow performers averaged about 80 min to complete courtship and coitus, but the mean of the fast lines was only 3 min. "General activity" was measured in an open field or arena (8.1.2), by recording the distance covered by a fly during 1 min. The slow flies were not, as might be expected, generally sluggish: on the contrary, they were more active, that is, evidently more distractible. The fast per-formers moved little in the arena and, when faced with a partner, got through mating and coitus with little delay or interruption.

Manning's experiments, like those on orienta-tions, illustrate genetical variation in a kind of spe-cies-typical behavior. In the experiments on orien-tations there were qualitative changes in response. Those on mating produced a quantitative change. The genes concerned in such a case clearly have multiple actions on the phenotype; indeed, they probably influence not only mating speed and ac-tivity, but also other features. Hence they are pleio-tropic (16.1.1). The underlying differences of physiology were, as might be expected, not iden-tified.

Another aspect of selection for mating behavior concerns the separation of species. *Drosophila per-similis* and *D. pseudo-obscura* are sibling (closely related) species of which the members sometimes interbreed. K. F. Koopman kept a mixed popula-tion of the two species for several generations; in each generation he removed the hybrids. After a time, two groups remained; and the members of each showed a much reduced propensity for hy-bridizing with the other. The mating behavior of the two groups no longer matched; hence reproduc-tive isolation was increased.

S. A. Crossley, in a similar experiment, recorded behavioral changes in detail. She used two mutant strains of *D. melanogaster*. Mixed populations were allowed to breed. The hybrid offspring of matings between the two forms could be identified by their appearance, and they were removed; hence there was strong selection against hybridizing, and for mating of like with like (homogamy). During 40 generations there was a fairly steady increase in homogamic matings, and a corresponding decline in hybridization. A control line, not subjected to selection, did not change in this way. The increased sexual isolation depended on changed mating pref-erences: the most important change was in the ten-dency of females to reject the advances of males of different genotype. (See 9.1.1 for the courtship of *Drosophila*.) Such findings support the hypothesis that reproductive isolation and the consequent for-mation of species could result from selection against behavior that allows hybridization.

We now turn to experiments on laboratory ro-dents. On them the most notable studies have concerned the ability to develop new habits ("in-telligence"), and related behavior, especially ex-ploration. R. C. Tryon used a genetically mixed stock of laboratory rats. In each generation he trained the rats to find their way through a dark maze; and he bred from two groups—the quickest to learn and the slowest. In seven generations he produced two distinct stocks (figure 16-5). On the face of it, Tryon seemed to have produced one "in-telligent" strain and one "stupid"; Tryon himself, more cautiously, used the expressions "maze-bright" and "maze-dull"; but further study showed even these apparently noncommittal terms to be mis-leading. Learning a maze involves searching it (8.1.4.1). I. Krechevsky showed the "dull" rats to be responsive to visual clues such as differences of light and dark, or black and white; this put them at a disadvantage in the dark. The apparently in-telligent rats used the clues provided by move-ment, that is, they felt their way about. In fact, as a number of workers have shown, which group of rats scores higher depends on the precise condi-tions in which they are tested (reviewed by S. A. Barnett, 1975).

In Tryon's work there was no control line on which selection was not practiced. J. C. DeFries and others, in a more elaborate research program, studied the movements of laboratory mice in an

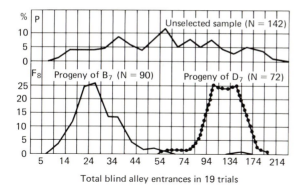

FIGURE 16-5 Selection for "intelligence": the upper graph shows the distribution of "intelligence" measured by the number of mistakes made in a maze, among 142 rats of a mixed stock; selective breeding was carried out for "maze-brightness" (B) on one line, and for "maze-dullness" (D) on the other. The result is shown in the two lower curves. (After R. C. Tryon, 1940)

open arena. Two lines were selected for high scores and two for low; there were also two control lines. Highly consistent results were achieved over 20 generations: at the end, the high lines were more than six times as "active" as the low lines. An accompanying change was in the number of fecal pellets left by the mice during testing in the arena: the low lines defecated about three times as much as the high lines. Presumably selection was acting on differences in neural function, perhaps especially on the autonomic nervous system, which controls defecation rate.

The primary effect of genetical differences is in the cellular polypeptides. In this book "gene" means "cistron": that is, a stretch of DNA that codes for a polypeptide unit of a protein. There is a big gap between polypeptide synthesis and the end result represented by behavior. Occasionally, something is known on the intervening physiology. K. Y. H. Lagerspetz and others describe observa-

tions on male laboratory mice bred respectively for high and low intensity of apotreptic conduct. The so-called "aggressive" strain had heavier testes and seminal vesicles (presumably reflecting endocrine differences). Adrenal weights did not differ, but estimates of the brain content of catecholamines (among which are the hormones of the adrenal medulla) suggested higher activity of the sympathetic nervous system of the "aggressive" mice.

16.1.2.4 Domestication: Some of the most interesting effects of selection have come from unintentional experiments. When a species is domesticated, the population of domesticated individuals changes in its genetical structure from that of the parent (wild) population. In the new environment, features disadvantageous in the wild may now favor survival. An obvious example is the response to human beings: domesticated animals usually do not flee from people, and do not attack a human being when seized or restrained. Selection to reduce savage behavior may be consciously done. But other changes may occur, over the generations, not because stockbreeders willed them, but because they were forced on the breeders by the circumstances of domestication. Many domestic animals must be tolerant of greater crowding than is the wild type. They are also likely to mature earlier, to have a simplified courtship, and to be more prone to promiscuity. Not all these features occur in all domestic species; but it easy to see how they are brought about. If there is genetical variation in these characteristics, breeding in captivity will probably reveal it.

It is quite usual for newly domesticated animals to be infertile in captivity. Variation in fertility is itself likely to be in part genetically determined. And so there is inevitable selection for certain genotypes at the expense of others.

When a species is difficult to breed in captivity, a domestic stock may originate from only one pair. R. Oeser describes the origin of a laboratory stock of the striped newt, *Triturus vittatus*. Many individuals of this species had been kept in captivity; but the first, and perhaps only, successful mating was between a male from mountains above the Black Sea and a female from near the Sea of Marmora. This pair, consequently, is the source of all the genes in the resulting stock of captive striped newts. Any rare genes possessed by either of them could be common in their descendants. Such a *founder effect* can make an isolated population differ from other populations of the same species, even in the absence of further selection.

The most important animals bred in captivity, such as cattle, sheep, camels, horses, and dogs, were first domesticated several millennia ago, and we know nothing of the details. (For comments on wild jungle fowl and our domestic varieties, see 9.3.4.) There have also been domestications of no great economic importance, as of the Siamese fighting fish (9.2.3). Their conduct differs substantially from that of the wild type.

The origins even of laboratory rats and mice, which go back only a century, are obscure. We have, however, very detailed information on the present behavioral differences of the laboratory and wild varieties of *Rattus norvegicus*—the species to which all domesticated laboratory rats belong. (For the social conduct of the wild type, see 10.5.1.) Table 16-3 summarizes some of the effects of domestication on this species (reviewed by S. A. Barnett, 1975; S. A. Barnett & others, 1979). The differences illustrate the scope of the effects of breeding in captivity; they also warn us to be cautious in drawing conclusions on what happens in nature from the study of captive varieties.

TABLE 16-3   Some behavioral differences of wild *Rattus norvegicus* from the domestic (laboratory) varieties.[a]

	Wild	Domestic
Response to strange *object* (or food) in familiar place	avoidance (= neophobia)	approach (= neophilia); if food, sampling
Response to strange *place,* starting from a familiar region	exploration (neophilic)	exploration (neophilic)
Response of adult ♂ in territory to strange adult ♂	approach: arched-back posture, jump, bite	approach: sniff, huddle[b]
Response to being attacked	flight, or collapse and death	may die
Males in artificial colonies, ♀ s also present		
mortality	high	low or nil[b]
growth	many lose weight	all grow
movement	one ♂ moves freely, the others are restricted	all move without restriction
adrenals	often hypertrophied	weights unaffected[b]

[a] See also table 16-7.
[b] There are occasional exceptions.

16.2 GENOTYPE AND ENVIRONMENT

16.2.1 The Meaning of "Inherited"

In giving the examples above, I do not use the word "inherited"; nor do I say that any *characteristics* are genetically determined, only *differences* between individuals or groups. We are now in a position to examine critically what the expression "inherited" means. This raises a fundamental question that runs through the whole of biology. It is a source of much confusion, even to biologists.

The words "inheritance" and "inherited" and their derivatives refer, in their primary use, to the passing of property from one person to another, often from parents to offspring. This is a legal and social meaning. A secondary social meaning is exemplified by the statement that one inherits one's father's name (or title); this is primarily a matter of nomenclature (though property is often involved too). Unfortunately, if white-eyed fruit flies have white-eyed offspring (instead of the normal red eyes), it is colloquial to say that the offspring inherit their eye color from their parents. But the eyes themselves are not handed on: they are separately developed in each individual. The genes, which are the principal material agents of transmission from parent to offspring, influence a complex process of development, from fertilized egg to adult animal.

The examples in the first part of this chapter are of differences in behavior which—we can be sure—correspond to differences in the animals' genes. We know this either from the effects of crossing or from the results of selection. In all such experiments, the environment is kept the same. It is convenient to say that such differences are *genetically determined*. The ambiguous word inherited is better avoided.

The expression, genetically determined, is then reserved for differences between individuals which correspond to differences in their genes. *It does not mean "influenced by genes": all characteristics are influenced by genes as well as by the environment.* This is a truism that is sometimes overlooked. Most organisms begin life as a fertilized egg, with a quota of genes derived from each parent. These influence development at every stage. At the same time, the organism is developing in an environment. The physiology of development has to be analyzed as a continual and immensely complex sequence of interactions between environment and genotype.

A major difficulty comes from the habit of some writers of saying that certain *kinds of behavior* are inherited or genetically determined (or genetically coded or some similar phrase). The behavior so described consists of species-typical action patterns, such as those of courtship and other displays. To say that these patterns are inherited is to use inherited to mean something quite different from its customary use in biology. One does not say that the possession of two eyes is inherited. This feature is certainly stable in development, but occasionally an animal of a two-eyed species has only one eye. Such cyclopia may be a result of the presence of abnormal genes: we may then properly say that the *difference from the normal type* is genetically determined. Alternatively, cyclopia could be produced by exceptional external conditions during early development: the *difference* is then environmentally determined. But, in both cases, the cyclopia is a resultant of the interactions of genotype and environment.

If all behavior and, indeed, all the characteristics of an animal are influenced by the genes, we must ask what writers are trying to distinguish, when they say that some behavior is "genetical" and some not. The actual distinction is in the *development* of the behavior (chapter 12). Some species-typical behavior is, like the possession of two eyes, exceedingly stable in development: some patterns of display, parental responses, and architectural activities seem to develop in every individual that survives; no known possible nonlethal alteration of the environment of the growing animal has much effect on the form of the behavior, once the animal reaches the stage in its life history when these activities are performed. (Of course, there is always the possibility that one day such an environmental effect will be found.)

But, as we know (chapter 12), many important species-typical activities are less stable in development than at first appears. A full understanding of variation in these (and other) activities requires analysis in terms of the genotype-environment interaction.

16.2.2 The Two Dimensions

Variation, then, depends on both genetical and environmental differences and on the interaction between them. This reiterated statement is easy to write down; but its implications can be grasped only by studying examples. In 11.2.2.1 I describe the conduct of two taxa of baboons. One would expect behavioral differences even between varieties to be genetically determined; but the differences in responses of the females toward males depend in part on the social environment, not on their different genotypes. Another example is that of habitat selection by deer mice (12.3.7): most of the differences in choice of habitat by different species seem to be determined genetically; but there is some effect of the environment in which the mice are reared.

It is now necessary to make clear two meanings of the term interaction. In ordinary speech it means simply mutual or reciprocal action. This is its meaning in the statement that ontogeny results from an interaction between genotype and environment. But in statistical analysis of findings like those in table 16-1, interaction has a technical meaning: different genotypes respond differently, and to a measurable extent, to a change of environment.

We now turn to experiments in which the influences of genotype and environment are shown quantitatively. Table 16-4 illustrates observations on inbred mice of two genotypes. The environmental variable was the amount of light. Apotreptic encounters were recorded, each between two mice of different types. By an arbitrary criterion, some encounters ended in victory for one of the mice. In bright light, mice of strain C won much more often than the other strain; but they did not do so in dim light. Hence the outcome was influenced both by genetical constitution and by the surrounding conditions; and there was interaction between the two sources of variance. Another way of putting the last point is to say that the difference between the two genotypes, in respect of the feature recorded, was evident in only one of the two environments.

In the preceding example the environmental action was direct. But often the conditions in which animals have been reared have a crucial effect on adult conduct. Table 16-5 again compares two inbred strains of mice. The environmental variable was nutrition in early life: the experimental groups had been kept short of protein during their first weeks. The most obvious feature of the table is the higher defecation rates of the mice of strain D, both controls and experimentals. This indicates a

TABLE 16-4 Number of "wins" in apotreptic encounters, each between two mice of different strains (B and C), in two environments.

		Environment	
		Bright light	Dim light
Genotype:	B	3	14
	C	27	10

The effect of the environmental variable (light) is different for the two genotypes—an example of genotype–environment interaction.

From T. W. Klein & others.

TABLE 16-5 Defecation rate, during 2 min in "open field", of two strains of laboratory mice (C and D).

		Early Environment			
		Normal[a]		Poor diet[a]	
		no. of mice	mean	no. of mice	mean
Genotype:	C	25	1.9	28	2.7
	D	30	4.0	28	3.5

[a] The control mice had been normally fed in early life; the others had been kept short of protein.
From D. A. Blizard & C. T. Randt.

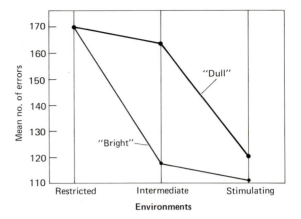

FIGURE 16-6 The experiment by R. M. Cooper & J. P. Zubeck on genotype-environment interaction. "Maze-bright" and "maze-dull" rats were reared in one of three environments—restricted, intermediate, or stimulating; and they were tested as adults in a maze. The genetical difference between them led to a marked phenotypic difference in maze performance only if they were reared in an intermediate environment. (After W. F. Bodmer & L. L. Cavalli-Sforza, 1976)

genetical influence. The environmental variable had opposite effects on the two strains: early malnourishment increased the defecation rate of the C mice, but reduced it for D. Here, then, is another example of genotype-environment interaction.

For a further example, I refer again to the rats selected for "brightness" or "dullness" (16.1.2.3 above). R. M. Cooper & J. P. Zubeck tested the effects of different conditions of rearing on their behavior. Members of each strain were reared in three environments. One (restricted) was a small cage with a minimum of furniture; a second (so-called normal) was a larger cage of conventional construction; and a third (enriched) was an enclosure with diverse objects. All rats were tested as adults for ability to learn a simple maze (figure 16-6). In the restricted environment the performance of the two types was much the same: the ability of the "bright" group was not evident. In the enriched environment there was a small difference: the "dull" rats were evidently so stimulated that they performed above expectation. The greatest difference observed was that between the groups reared in the intermediate condition.

The last example in this section concerns an effect of breeding wild rats in captivity (table 16-6;

see also table 16-3). It illustrates the problems of drawing valid conclusions in this field. The two genotypes were wild-type rats that had been trapped, and rats of the sixth to ninth generations in the laboratory. The latter must have differed genetically from the wild type (16.1.2.3). Males of both types were tested, in standard conditions, for apotreptic conduct toward male intruders. The envi-

TABLE 16-6 Apotreptic conduct (attack time, seconds) of wild *Rattus norvegicus*.

	No. of rats	Females absent	Females present
Trapped	10	37.7	73.6
Laboratory-bred[a]	7	10.2	4.8

[a] For six to nine generations.
From S. A. Barnett & R. C. Stoddart.

ronmental variable was the presence or absence of females. The table suggests not only a genetical effect, but also a genotype-environment interaction. There is, however, a methodological defect in the experimental design, which the reader will easily identify.

The nature-nurture relationship is best thought of, initially, in terms of very simple situations, such as those of tables 16-1, 16-4, and 16-5. Natural populations, however, contain a vast range of possible genotypes, and the environmental variables cannot be counted. As a result, the number of possible phenotypes is enormous. Table 16-7 gives some figures. On the system outlined in the table, if there are only three genotypes and two environments, there are 60 possible kinds of interaction. If there are 10 genotypes and 10 environments, there are 10^{144} kinds of interaction.

16.2.3 Special Environmental Effects

When it is intended to reveal genetical differences, the animals studied should, if possible, be reared and kept in identical environments. But the environmental features that can influence a developing animal are both diverse and subtle; hence they are often difficult to control. I take examples from maternal or, more generally, parental effects. Whenever animals are viviparous, or even ovoviviparous, or when there is parental care of any kind, the influence of parents on development may contribute to individual variation. Hence environmental differences may be influenced by the different parental genotypes, and environmental actions on development can reflect in part genetical variation in the parental generation.

Most of the known behavioral examples are from laboratory mammals. G. Bignami bred a

TABLE 16-7   Interactions of genotype and environment.

Suppose two populations (P_1 and P_2), genetically different, and two environments, E_1 and E_2. Members of both P_1 and P_2 are reared in each environment. Hence there are four classes of organism. A measurement is made of each individual studied. The feature measured may be of any kind: for example, mating success or maze-learning ability. For each of the four classes a mean is calculated; and each mean differs decisively from every other. It is therefore possible to array the four classes in order. In the 2×2 tables below, the class with the highest score is always in the upper left-hand cell. There are then six possible types of combination:

Type 1a	E_1	E_2		Type 1b	E_1	E_2
P_1	1	2		P_1	1	3
P_2	3	4		P_2	2	4

Type 2	E_1	E_2
P_1	1	4
P_2	2	3

Type 3	E_1	E_2
P_1	1	2
P_2	4	3

Type 4a	E_1	E_2		Type 4b	E_1	E_2
P_1	1	3		P_1	1	4
P_2	4	2		P_2	3	2

In type 1a, P_1 scores higher than P_2 in both environments; but in 1b environment E_1 is more favorable than E_2 for both genotypes. In the other combinations there are various kinds of interaction: for example, in type 4 each genotype does best in an environment to which it is adapted; one cannot say that either race or environment is superior.

From J. B. S. Haldane, 1946.

mixed stock of laboratory rats for five generations, and selected two lines, one for rapid learning to avoid a shock, the other for slow learning. He thus established two stocks that differed sharply in this respect. Reciprocal crosses were made between the two types: "low" females were mated to "high" males and "high" females to "low" males. The two hybrid classes so produced were the same genetically; they might therefore be expected to be phenotypically indistinguishable. But this expectation assumes that the environments provided by the two kinds of mother are identical, or at least that they do not have different effects on the features studied. In fact, the two groups differed: the offspring of the females of the low-avoidance strain tended to make more avoidance responses, when tested, than the offspring of females of the other type. Evidently, the two kinds of females provided environments for their growing young which differed in such a way that a behavioral difference developed.

Such a maternal effect could take place either *in utero* or in the nest. The milk supply and other conditions during the nesting phase are, of course, of crucial importance in development (9.4.2). Bignami therefore *cross-fostered* between his two stocks: that is, he exchanged litters at birth between the two types of female. And when the members of the exchanged litters reached the appropriate age, they were tested on the same problem. There was no difference between the two cross-fostered classes. Hence in this case the maternal effect must have

acted before birth. How it did so is entirely mysterious.

Table 16-8 gives another example of maternal influence. In this case the experiments were designed to distinguish between two environmental sources of variance. There were two classes of female: one had been reared with little disturbance; the other group had received extra stimulation, by regular handling, early in life. Each female reared a litter transferred at birth (fostered) *either* from a member of her own group *or* from a member of the other. This gives a 2×2 situation: two environments and two genotypes. The fostered young were tested, after weaning, by putting them in an "open field": the defecation score was then higher if the foster-mother had been handled in early life, regardless of the treatment of the true mother; hence there was an influence of the nest environment on this feature. But "activity" was influenced in a complex way by the experience of both the true mother (acting through the uterine environment) and the foster-mother.

Clearly, in genetical analysis, the environment should, if possible, be controlled for the whole of development from the stage of the fertilized egg onward. There may otherwise be unwanted sources of environmentally determined variation. But the attempt to *control* the environment may entail *simplifying* it; as a result, laboratory environments can *reduce* variation in an undesirable way. N. D. Henderson describes experiments on mice of six inbred strains and on the 30 F_1 hybrid types produced by crossing them. Mice of all genotypes were reared either in a small cage or in much larger cages containing a variety of objects (an enriched—or more natural—environment). At the age of six weeks all mice were fasted; they were then put in an enclosure in which they had to traverse a complex path

TABLE 16-8 Maternal effect on response of laboratory rats to a strange environment. (Each class had 14 to 16 rats.)

	Foster-mothers			
	Not handled		Handled	
	"activity"[a]	boluses[b]	"activity"[a]	boluses[b]
True mothers:				
not handled	47	6.4	91	12.3
handled	54	6.9	51	10.5

[a] Number of squares entered during 12 min in an "open field".
[b] Number of fecal pellets deposited in the "open field".
From V. H. Denenberg & A. E. Whimbey, 1963.

to get food. The results were as follows. (1) The inbred strains were slower to solve the problem than were the F_1 mice: hence there was behavioral heterosis. The differences between the inbred strains were also less than those between the hybrids. (2) The mice reared in the standard cages were slower than those reared in the enriched environment; this result was to be expected (8.1.4.2). (3) The most important finding for us now concerns the (genetically determined) differences between the various types of mouse: these differences were much more marked when the mice had been reared in the enriched environment. In other words, two common laboratory practices each diminished the measurable differences between mice of different genotypes: these were (a) inbreeding,

and (b) rearing in a cramped and featureless environment.

16.2.4 Heritability

16.2.4.1 Uses of the Concept: It is sometimes asked *how much* of a particular character is "due to heredity"; or the question may be put more precisely: how much of the variance is genetically determined? By itself, this question has no meaning. To see why, it is convenient to introduce the concept of *heritability* (reviewed by W. F. Bodmer & L. L. Cavalli-Sforza; and by D. S. Falconer). Figure 16-7 shows how, in a very simple case, the genetical (V_G) and environmental (V_E) components

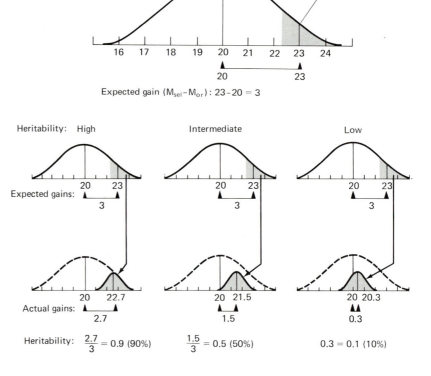

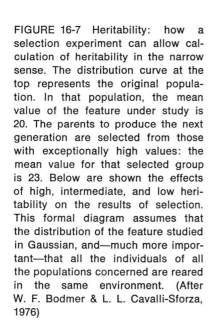

FIGURE 16-7 Heritability: how a selection experiment can allow calculation of heritability in the narrow sense. The distribution curve at the top represents the original population. In that population, the mean value of the feature under study is 20. The parents to produce the next generation are selected from those with exceptionally high values: the mean value for that selected group is 23. Below are shown the effects of high, intermediate, and low heritability on the results of selection. This formal diagram assumes that the distribution of the feature studied in Gaussian, and—much more important—that all the individuals of all the populations concerned are reared in the same environment. (After W. F. Bodmer & L. L. Cavalli-Sforza, 1976)

of the variance of a measurable feature may be calculated. If the total variance is V_T,

$$V_T = V_G + V_E \text{ and } H = \frac{V_G}{V_T},$$

where H is the heritability, or degree of genetical determination of variation in the feature measured. These statements strictly refer to a quantity called "heritability in the broad sense" (H_B). "Heritability in the narrow sense" (H_N), illustrated in the figure, is a measure only of the additive sources of genetical variation.

The two kinds of heritability have different uses. It is useful to know H_B for an existing population when one wishes to assess variation in the response to a particular treatment. In a human population it could be relevant to a program of education. H_N can, *in a constant environment,* predict the effects of differences in fertility, and so of selection, on genetical change in a population over generations.

Heritability, then, represents the *proportion* of the variance which is of genetical origin: hence, given a constant amount of genetical variation, the heritability alters with the amount of environmentally caused variation. The obverse is, of course, also true: the greater the heritability, other things equal, the less is the environmental variance. If a population consists entirely of genetically identical individuals, all variation is of environmental origin, and H = 0. If all individuals of a population could be reared in truly identical environments, then the heritability would be 100%. We now see why it is meaningless to ask simply how much of the variance of a trait is genetically determined: the answer must be that it depends on the environment. In other words, a figure for the heritability can be given only for a given population *in a specified environment.*

The preceding statements represent only the

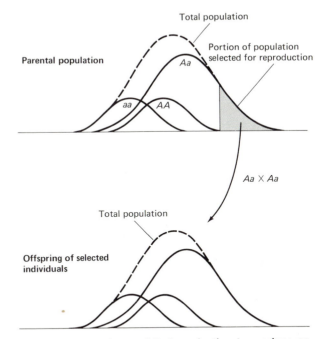

FIGURE 16-8 It is possible for selection to produce no effect, even though the population includes a genetical component of the variance in the feature selected for: the figures show the simplest possible case, that is, one in which only two alleles are involved. (After W. F. Bodmer & L. L. Cavalli-Sforza, 1976)

simplest possible situation. There are three important sources of complexity.

1. Suppose we wish to estimate the heritability of a feature by selecting for that feature. We can do so without difficulty only if the genetical sources of variance are additive. If there is overdominance (heterosis) there could, in an extreme case, be no effect of selection at all; yet there would still be variation of genetical origin. This can be illustrated from the situation in which genetical differences depend on a single pair of alleles (figure 16-8). The situation illustrated is one in which the heterozygote scores higher (or lower) than either homozygote. In such a case, selection entirely from individuals showing extreme values at one end of the

range could lead to producing the next generation entirely from heterozygotes. Assuming no differential mortality, the result would be once again equal numbers of the two kinds of homozygote and twice that number of heterozygotes; the genetical structure of the population would remain unchanged. The broad heritability, then, has two parts: the additive (V_A) represents the variance that would exist if the heterozygote were exactly intermediate between the two homozygotes. The other component (V_D) is due to dominance, and represents the heterozygotes that are not intermediate. Hence

$$V_G = V_A + V_D, \text{ and } V_T = V_A + V_D + V_E.$$

As a result of dominance, a selection experiment may produce changes, from one generation to the next, smaller than those expected. The heritability in the narrow sense (H_N) may be calculated from the difference between expected and actual change:

$$H_N = \frac{V_A}{V_T}$$

2. The preceding statements still represent a severe simplification. The second complexity is genotype-environment interaction. As we know, different genotypes respond differently to environmental changes. It is possible for two types to be indistinguishable in one environment, but quite distinct in another (16.2.2 above). In such a case, the simple equation, $V_T = V_G + V_E$, is incorrect: instead,

$$V_T = V_G + V_E + V_I$$

where V_I is the variance due to genotype-evironment interaction.

3. The last complication to be discussed here is genotype-environment correlation. This occurs when different genotypes are not randomly distributed among environments. When animals have access to a variety of environments, they commonly show a preference: they may settle in one rather than another. In the discussion above, the presumption has always been made that the different genotypes are distributed among the different environments without any such bias. This is easily arranged in the laboratory, but is perhaps rare in nature. Genotype-environment correlations may be of two kinds. First, they may be adaptive: for example, there may be genetical variation in nutritional needs or in resistance to effects of toxic substances. The selection of foods may vary correspondingly. This, in effect, represents a choice of different environments by different genotypes. Second, the biotope of a species is usually heterogeneous: some parts are more favorable, say, for breeding than others. The population of the most favorable environment may then be genetically different from that of marginal environments: "weaker" individuals "go to the wall".

Whenever anything of this kind happens, no simple formula is applicable. Instead of $V_T = V_G + V_E$, the equation would become

$$V_T = V_G + V_E + 2 (Cov_{G,E}),$$

where $Cov_{G,E}$ represents the covariance of genotypic and environmental deviations from the mean: that is, it gives an estimate of the correlation of genotype with environment, or the genotype-environment interaction.

For a more complete account of heritability, consult D. S. Falconer, a symposium edited by J. Hirsch (1967), or P. A. Parsons. For our present purposes, this concept reinforces the notion of behavior as part of the phenotype: variation in behavioral features usually has substantial genetical *and* environmental components, with the additional complexities outlined in the preceding paragraphs.

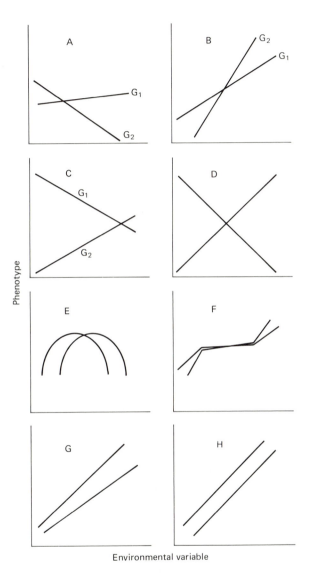

FIGURE 16-9 In each figure two genotypes are represented as varying phenotypically owing to the action of an environmental variable. The latter is represented on the horizontal axis, and may be thought of as a continuous function such as temperature. The vertical axis represents the mean phenotypic value (say, of "activity") for each temperature. The implications of studying the eight situations shown are discussed in the text. (After R. C. Lewontin, 1974)

Once again, we see that it is not appropriate to say, of any characteristic, that it is genetically determined or environmentally determined. Each characteristic develops anew in each individual; and this development depends on the continual influence of both the genotype and the environment. Some behavioral features are stable in development, others less so. It would be more convenient if we could make two sharply distinct categories, and say that some behavior is genetical (or innate or instinctive) and that other behavior is environmental (acquired or learned); but the facts do not correspond to any such simple classification.

16.2.4.2 Limitations of the Concept: The concept of heritability also illustrates the limitations of genetical analysis (R. C. Lewontin, 1974). Figure 16-9 shows a number of possible relationships between two genotypes in a continuously varying environment: the vertical axis gives a measure of a phenotypic feature, such as "activity"; the horizontal axis is the environmental variable—say, temperature. Each genotype is affected by the environment; and in each case the two genotypes respond differently to environmental change (compare table 16-7).

Figure 16-9A illustrates a simple linear relationship of phenotype with environment. Suppose the environmental variable is temperature, and the total environment of the population includes all the temperatures represented on the horizontal axis of the graph. Further suppose that the two genotypes are equally represented in the population. An investigator who took a random sample of the population (which would, of course, include both genotypes in equal numbers) would then find the behavioral variable to decline with rising temperature. At the same time, if he could distinguish the two genotypes, he would find g_1 to average higher than g_2. If, however, a more detailed analysis were made of the effect of the environment, the two genotypes would be found to score equally at a certain temperature (where the two regression lines cross). In figure 16-9B, in contrast, both genotypes give a positive regression of phenotype on the environmental variable; but the result of an investigation would again depend on the range of temperatures covered.

In figure 16-9C, there is no net effect of the environment; and in figure 16-9D there is no net effect of either genotype *or* environment.

Figures 16-9E, F illustrate differential effects of temperature on the phenotype: the two genotypes in both instances give similar phenotypes in the middle of the range of temperatures but are differentiated at the extremes.

The last two curves (figures 16-9G, H) represent presumptions often made about the relationships of genotype and environment. In particular, figure 16-9H shows a situation in which the genetical source of variation is simply additive. The reader should study these eight curves, and consider the further possibilities they offer. In each case the findings of an investigator will depend crucially on the range of environments in which the observations are made.

The last statement represents the most general limitation of the concept of heritability. The expression "heritability" itself, and some writings on the subject, may leave a reader with the impression that, if the heritability of a characteristic in a given population is 100%, then no environmental action can influence that characteristic. But, of course, as soon as the environment is changed, the heritability may change too. Such effects are further illustrated by the studies of our own species to which we now turn.

16.3 APPLICATIONS TO HUMAN POPULATIONS

Homo sapiens is highly polymorphic: that is, in any population, we find much genetical diversity. This is obvious from external characteristics, such as eye color, and from much-studied chemical features, such as the blood groups, all of which have a high heritability in any environment. Polymorphism may be regarded as a social asset. In modern human societies people have to specialize. Different types of work require different abilities and personalities. We may suppose that these differences are to some extent genetically determined. (We do not know to what extent.) Polymorphism then contributes to the adaptability of human groups.

We are also polytypic: that is, there are genetical differences between geographically separated populations. (There may also be genetical differences between groups—such as economic classes—in a single geographical region.) Hence in a genetical study of man, we may be interested in variation either within a population *or* between populations.

In some writers, this topic raises violent emotions that tend to obscure attempts at matter-of-fact analysis. Bizarre statements on the heredity of certain qualities have had wide acceptance (L. J. Kamin). R. A. Fisher (1913), who made a major contribution to the mathematical analysis of natural selection, once wrote that the upper classes contain all the finest examples of ability, beauty, and taste. This difference from the lower orders, he held, was genetically determined. Similarly, it has been confidently asserted by Europeans that people with a different skin color have a greater, genetically determined propensity than have "whites" for crimes of violence.

The obverse is to emphasize environmental

sources of variance at the expense of the genetical. Such emphasis may take one of two forms. First is the statement that variation in socially valuable qualities, such as intelligence, has no genetical component. This is an absurdity. The second is to point out that little or nothing useful can be done to alter the genetical structure of human populations; but that environmental action can and often does produce favorable effects. The second statement, which is common sense, does not contradict the general proposition that human variation has both genetical and environmental sources. For a balanced account, consult J. C. Loehlin and others.

16.3.1 Variation within Populations

16.3.1.1 Single Gene Substitutions: Our first example illustrates, once again, the inappropriateness of referring to a *characteristic* as inherited. Phenylketonuria is a condition of the kind often referred to as a hereditary disease (reviewed by D. Y.-Y. Hsia). Its incidence in Europiform populations is about 1 : 10,000–40,000. There is usually a very severe intellectual deficiency: such persons may be unable to communicate by speech. The condition is diagnosed by finding phenylpyruvic acid in the urine. Its presence is due to lack of a liver enzyme, phenylalanine hydroxylase, which in a normal person converts the amino acid phenylalanine to tyrosine. In the absence of the enzyme, phenylpyruvic acid is produced, and interferes with the development of the brain (figure 16-10).

Phenylketonuria is an autosomal recessive condition. It can therefore appear without warning among the children of normal parents; both parents are then heterozygotes. (Heterozygotes can, however, be detected: if they are given large amounts of phenylalanine, some appears in the

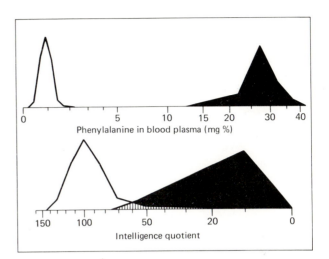

FIGURE 16-10   Phenylketonuria. Above, the distribution of concentration of phenylalanine in plasma: on left, that of the normal population; on right, that of phenylketonurics. Below, the distributions of intelligence quotient for the two populations. In each case the vertical axis represents percentages. (After L. S. Penrose, 1951)

urine.) At this point, it may reasonably be asked why the condition should not be referred to as hereditary. The answer is that such a statement disregards the environment: it implies that, *in any conditions of rearing,* people with a certain genotype will be phenylketonuric. Moreover, if it is assumed that the pathological state of a phenylketonuric is unalterable, parents and physicians who have to care for such a child may resign themselves to dealing with a permanently helpless imbecile. But if we examine the environment, we come to a different conclusion. For a phenylketonuric, phenylalanine is a poison. The condition can be diagnosed in the first weeks of life. The child can then be reared on a diet almost without phenylalanine; there is no toxic action on the developing brain, and development is normal. This outcome is a result of altering the environment, that is (in this case), the composition of the diet. (The special diet is needed only during the first six years.)

Phenylketonuria is an example of a genotype-environment interaction of which the early studies concentrated on the genetical aspects. Because the condition is very rare, the explanation sought was in the genotype of the people affected. In contrast, we may take the action of another toxic mixture, namely, milk. Although milk is essential for children, it has adverse effects on many adults. The presence of milk sugar, lactose, in food can result in a disagreeable but not fatal gastrointestinal disorder. Here, then, on the face of it, is a straightforward environmental effect: milk is toxic to adults.

There is, however, a genetical aspect. The failure of adults to digest lactose is due to the absence of an enzyme, lactase, which is present in infancy and early childhood. But some adults have a lactase and so can digest milk. Possession of a lactase is probably a dominant condition. Readers of northern European origin may find the preceding statements surprising, for adult northern Europeans usually possess a lactase. Among them, the inability to digest milk may appear—like phenylketonuria—as a rare ("hereditary") metabolic disorder; but in other populations the effect of milk is seen as analogous to that of, say, a mildly poisonous fruit.

Loehlin and his colleagues point to an instructive possible outcome. In some countries, such as the United States, school lunches are an important component in the diet of children. They usually include milk. But children of African or Asian origin, who are numerous in many American schools, may refuse the milk because of its ill effects. The result for some of them could be an inferior nutritional state, of environmental origin but imposed by a genetical difference from other children. Here is a disconcerting example of genotype-environment correlation of social importance.

Lastly, in this section, let us take, as an obviously "environmental" effect, a nutritional disease. If a human being lives for long on a diet such as the salt pork and peas formerly carried on long voyages by sail, a weakening and sometimes fatal disease, scurvy, may result. The disease is rapidly cured by ascorbic acid (vitamin C). Such an example is at the opposite end of the spectrum from phenylketonuria: there seems to be no scope here for the geneticist. But in fact there is evidence that some people (like most Primates) can synthesize ascorbic acid from other substances in food (R. Rajalakshmi and others). Hence here too there are both genetical and environmental components of the variance.

16.3.1.2 Polygenic Effects: Most socially important human characteristics vary continuously, as do stature or muscular strength: we are not divided into two groups, tall and short, like Mendel's peas. For further illustration of genetical principles, it is convenient to take, as the item measured, scores in intelligence tests. In using this example, nothing is implied on just what intelligence tests signify. There is a positive correlation between high scores in these tests and success in certain activities: for example, professors often have high scores; but this is not surprising, for the tests were designed by professors.

We first turn to the other end of the scale. Children who make low scores on these tests may be classified as mentally deficient (reviewed by L. S. Penrose, 1963). They require special schooling, and can usually make little contribution to the community. So the question may be asked, is mental deficiency "inherited"? Table 16-9 gives findings

TABLE 16-9 Mental deficiency: Parent-offspring relationships.

A group of mentally deficient (m.d.) children was studied in Suffolk, England.

Number of m.d. children:		158
Of their parents: {	percent m.d.:	6
	percent educationally subnormal:	26

A group of children was studied in Birmingham, England, all of whom had a m.d. parent.

Number of children:	345
percent m.d.:	7.5
percent backward:	18.5
percent above average:	3.0

Such findings suggest a substantial heritability of mental deficiency; but it is not possible to distinguish genetical from environmental effects. Moreover, mental deficiency (or mental retardation) is not a single condition.

From L. S. Penrose, 1963.

on the parents of mentally deficient children, and the children of mentally deficient parents. Several comments may be made. (1) The term, mental deficiency, does not refer to a homogeneous class: a physician consulted about children diagnosed as mentally deficient may find cretinism (15.4.1), severe malnutrition, various kinds of metabolic disorder, or other less clearly defined conditions. (2) Most of the children studied were reared in poverty by parents of poor education. Hence there was probably a genotype-environment correlation. Some of the children may have been in a position analogous to that of the "dull" rats reared in a restricted environment (figure 16-6). (3) Despite the undoubted genetical component, the parent–offspring correlation is weak.

More can be said when we turn to the whole range of intelligence test scores (reviewed by W. F. Bodmer & L. L. Cavalli-Sforza). When such tests were originated, some psychologists held them out as measuring general or absolute intelligence; this quality was often supposed to be innate, and to be unaffected by environmental features such as schooling. In other words, the heritability of intelligence, so measured, was believed to be at or near 100%. The implication was that the many variable environmental features which influence human development have virtually no effect on the observed variation in general "intelligence". But, as we know, this statement is not true for the problem-solving abilities of rats (16.2.2). And it is obviously unlikely to be true for human abilities of any kind. The question now is, how can we investigate the heritability of IQ rigorously?

A resemblance between parents and offspring, and between siblings, does not allow us to distinguish genetical from environmental effects. Members of a family not only tend to be similar genetically, but they also usually have similar environments. Moreover, genotype-environment correlation is likely: able parents may select, with more care than others, schooling and other aspects of their children's nurture. If the difference in ability from the general population is in part genetically determined, then such parental action will tend to increase the variance in measured intelligence. An opposite effect could also occur. If, say, a community devoted an exceptionally high proportion of educational resources to children of low attainments, the variance in measured ability could be reduced (reviewed by Robert Plomin and others).

Studies of twins (figure 16-11) suggest a high heritability of IQ. The principal ground for this conclusion is the difference between monozygotic (MZ) and dizygotic (DZ) twins: the former resemble each other in IQ more closely than do DZ twins. MZ twins are diagnosed by their concordance in such features as blood groups, for which

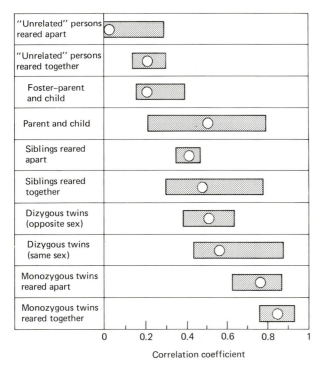

FIGURE 16-11 Correlation coefficients of the intelligence quotients of pairs of people of different relationships. Each rectangle represents the range; circles represent means. The problems of interpreting such findings are discussed in the text. (After W. F. Bodmer, 1972)

the heritability is virtually 100%. They are evidently derived from a single fertilized ovum, and so are genetically identical: in effect, they constitute a clone. DZ twins resemble ordinary brothers and sisters, except that they are born at the same time; they are derived from different ova. Differences between MZ twins should, then, be determined exclusively by the environment, and should therefore give a measure of the environmental sources of variance of the features measured. In contrast, differences between DZ twins are partly determined genetically.

There are, however, difficulties in interpreting findings on twins. (1) They represent a special, genetically distinct, minority of any population. (2) The environments of MZ twins are probably more similar than those of DZ twins. (3) All twins probably have a less favorable environment, both in utero and later, than those born singly.

Much attention has therefore been paid to children transferred soon after birth to foster parents. The question is asked: do the foster children resemble their foster parents (an environmental effect) or their biological parents (a genetical effect if we ignore the uterine environment)? When IQ is studied, the correlations with the biological parents are higher than those with foster parents. But, once again, there are problems of interpretation. For example, foster parents and children who are fostered are neither of them representative groups in the population. Moreover, fostering tends to be within social class: hence there is liable to be a genotype-environment correlation.

It is therefore hardly surprising that estimates of the heritability of IQ range rather widely. Such estimates, of course, can refer only to particular populations; and, since nearly all the research has been done in Britain or the United States, it refers to the populations of those countries. At one extreme we have estimates of around 80%. At the other, we have the statement that, on existing evidence, no heritability can be formally demonstrated. The last statement, of course, does not exclude the possibility—indeed, the probability—that there is a substantial heritability for IQ in the populations studied.

Let us suppose that the actual figure, for a given population, is somewhere between 30 and 70%. What would be the practical implications of making the estimate more accurate? R. C. Lewontin (1975) has, with good reason, suggested that such a question is trivial, and that the research required to get accurate information would not be worth the effort. All these principles, of course, apply with equal force to other socially important characteristics, ranging from moral conduct to madness. For practical purposes, the important fact is that, in every population, variation in all such features is influenced to a substantial extent by the environment; and, when the environment changes, the environmental contribution changes too. Until recently, the heritability of conditions such as phenylketonuria was 100% (or nearly); now, as a result of scientific and technical advances, it is not. We live in a rapidly changing society; hence estimates of heritability, even if they could be made accurate for a particular population at one time, are of little more than academic interest.

16.3.2 Variation between Populations

16.3.2.1 A Parable: In view of the limitations of the IQ as a measure, I do not use it in discussing differences between populations. The important genetical principles apply to any feature and any population, and can be illustrated by an imaginary example. Consider two countries, Ruritania and Kukuanaland. (These names are taken from once-celebrated works of fiction.) The Kukuanas are "black" (have much melanin in their skins), and the Ruritanians are "white" (have rather little). The character measured is called zing. Possible scores are from 0 to 100. Zing is highly valued in both communities. It is not correlated, either positively or negatively, with skin pigmentation in either population; hence skin color, though often referred to in discussions of zing, is irrelevant. The distribution of zing in each community is roughly "normal" (figure 16-2).

The estimated mean value of zing for the whole

adult population of Kukuanaland is 61; the corresponding figure for Ruritania is 55. The difference is statistically very highly "significant". Certain Kukuanas assert that the figures indicate their genetical superiority to Ruritanians. They point to the fact that investigations of zing in their own population indicate that it has quite a high heritability. Their views are, however, disputed. First, it is argued that the environments of the two populations are very different: Kukuanas live in fertile uplands of central Africa, the Ruritanians in a mountainous region of central Europe. Moreover, the two cultures, including their schools, differ greatly. Hence calculations of the heritability of zing in one population have no necessary significance for its heritability in another. No valid conclusion can be drawn, therefore, on the genetical significance of the difference between the two populations.

If some Kukuana and Ruritanian children were reared in identical environments, it might be possible to say something more decisive about the differences between them. Only a few families of each group live in the country of the other, and attend the local schools. But, of course, the children are brought up by their own parents, and so the family environment is still different for the two races. Nonetheless, when such children have been compared, their mean zing scores have proved to be about the same. But those who emphasize genetical differences refuse to accept this as useful evidence: they say, for example, that the immigrants are not representative of their respective populations.

Most geneticists and zingologists hold that no valid conclusions are possible on the relative contributions of environment and heredity in the distribution of zing within either population; the same applies even more strongly to the difference between Kukuanas and Ruritanians. Those interested in social action also point out that, although there is a "statistically significant" difference between the populations, the distributions of zing overlap to a large extent: correspondingly, both populations have a small but important minority of people with very high zing (and, of course, a corresponding group of people who are almost zingless). Hence, for practical purposes, the two populations are not very different.

A curious complexity arises when the sexes are compared. Men in Kukuanaland score rather higher than women; but the reverse is true of the Ruritanians. Geneticists say that this suggests a genotype-environment interaction; and some Kukuana women agree, for they assert that their lower mean score results from social discrimination against their sex in Kukuanaland. Hence it reflects an environmental difference from the situation in Ruritania. The debate continues.

16.3.2.2 A Cognitive Consequence of Culture:

In the preceding imaginary example, I imply that schooling can have an important influence on intellectual or cognitive development. Perhaps few will question this; but, even if so, it is still easy to underestimate the scope of environmental influences. I now, therefore, return to the real world for some examples.

P. M. Greenfield & J. S. Bruner have reviewed this subject. One of their examples concerns two preliterate societies, those of the Murray Islanders and of the Todas of India. It concerns perceptual development. Figure 16-12 illustrates the Müller–Lyer illusion. It was originally supposed that all adult human beings are subject to this illusion, in which two lines of equal length are seen as different. But the members of the two preliterate societies do not make this mistake. Evidently, this is because they are not accustomed to making three-

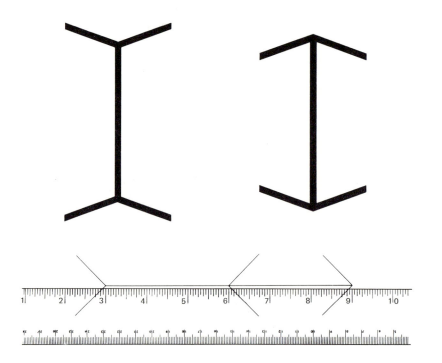

FIGURE 16-12 The Müller–Lyer illusion: two lines of equal length look different—at least, to us; but not to everybody. (From R. L. Gregory, 1970)

dimensional inferences from two-dimensional pictures. The illusion develops among such people only when they have been accustomed to interpreting pictures.

This is a rather minor example, but it has general implications: we cannot take for granted that the way in which we see things is shared by others with quite different experience. The authors cited, and S. Scribner & M. Cole more recently, discuss the role of different kinds of teaching and learning, and of the use of language, in cognitive development. Informal learning in simple societies is highly personal: it is based on imitation, identification, and helping elders in their daily tasks (compare 8.4.3). The learning that takes place is a learning of particulars, not of general principles. One result is what seems to us a deficiency in the ability to classify objects.

This deficiency has been clearly shown by A. R. Luria in a study of peasants in central Asia. Luria compared villagers carrying on a traditional mode of life with members of the same population who had moved to collective farms and had had some years of schooling. One method was to present a short list of objects, and to ask which is the item that is unlike the rest. When the unschooled peasants were given the list, bayonet, rifle, sword, and knife, a typical comment was: "There is nothing you can leave out! The bayonet is part of the gun. A man must wear the dagger on his left side and the rifle on the other." Another list was, hammer, saw, log, hatchet. Again a typical reply was: "They're all alike. The saw will saw the log and the hatchet will chop it into small pieces. If one of these things has to go, I'd throw out the hatchet. It doesn't do as good a job as the saw." Another kind of test was to present a problem in which the premises conflicted with actual experience. A man might be asked: if it took 6 h to get from here to Fergana on foot, but a bicycle were twice as slow, how long would it take on the bicycle? The answers by the preliterate farmers were consistently based on the fact that a man on a bicycle moves at least twice as quickly as one on foot. Many other examples are given in this fascinating work.

The difficulties unlettered farmers had with such questions are an example of the influence of *set* (8.2.4): their modes of thinking were not compatible with solving simple problems. But, as the authors cited above show, the difference from people in other societies is in their schooling or, more generally, in their upbringing. Environmental effects of this sort, which must be expected in all populations (A. G. J. Cryns), have important implications for the future of all groups that remain largely untouched by modern technology.

16.3.2.3 Differences between the Sexes:

The last paragraph of 16.3.2.1 reminds us that every human population includes two subpopulations, males and females. Although gender itself depends on the genotype, not all the differences between the sexes are genetically determined. Hence, once again, we face questions on nature and nurture.

Sometimes, a difference can be assigned precisely to its origin. C. C. Li gives the example of color vision. Girls are commonly described as better than boys at matching colors. The difference has been held to be environmentally determined, owing to the conventional exposure of girls to activities such as sewing. But today we know that one difference in color vision between the sexes is independent of the environment. Dichromatic deuteranopia (red-green color blindness) is a sex-linked recessive condition found in about 1.40% of European males but only 0.02% of females. Pedigrees show this difference between the sexes to be genetically determined.

As usual, features of greater social importance present greater difficulties; and, as with race differences, the subject has for long aroused violent passions. In the 16th century a Scottish religious leader, John Knox, wrote: "To promote a woman to bear superiority . . . is repugnant to nature, contrary to God, and . . . the subversion of good order and all equity and justice." There remain many who hold such views.

When we turn to rational analysis, we find that sex differences illustrate two important principles.

1. The sexes differ in the variation they display. In tests of intellectual ability, the dispersion about the mean value of males in a given population is greater than that of females in the same population. Hence there are more male idiots than female, and more at the other extreme also.

2. Of greater social importance is genotype-environment correlation. In nearly all societies it is generally *assumed* that the roles of the sexes are sharply distinct. From birth, children are reared differently according to their sex: they are clothed differently and soon are treated differently in other ways. H. Barry and others have reviewed accounts of 110 cultures. In some technologically simple communities, children are reared without distinction between the sexes; but a much more common pattern demands obedience and a nurturant and responsible attitude from girls, whereas boys are expected to be more independent, self-reliant, and ambitious. Such findings suggest that, in these aspects of personality, the differences between the sexes are culturally rather than genetically determined.

N. G. Blurton Jones (1973) describes a more detailed study of sex differences in the behavior of London children and the children of Kalahari gatherer-hunters. He criticizes accounts, supposedly quantitative, of categories such as "aggression", "dependency", and "sociability", which do not allow a critical analysis of the categories recorded. He also comments on the differences in activity and adventurousness that are supposed to exist between the sexes; these are conventionally related to the custom that women stay at home, while men go hunting. But the habits of the African women studied by Blurton Jones do not fit this picture: two or three times a week they go gathering: they travel perhaps 10 km in each direction, carrying a child and up to 14 kg of nuts on the return. Few women living in a modern city do anything comparable.

The detailed findings include a higher incidence of "agonistic" and rough and tumble behavior by boys than by girls in both populations. "Agonistic" includes expressions of hostility, and also hitting and fighting. But the *proportion* of agonistic acts performed by boys, out of the total of all acts, was the same as that for girls: the difference arose because boys *interacted* more. When epitreptic or sociable interactions were recorded, no clear sex distinction was observed.

Such findings, though important, do not allow any precise, quantitative statements on the contributions of genotype or environment to variance in the features studied. They do, however, warn us against facile presumptions.

16.4 SUMMING UP

To sum up, when we study variation in behavior what we observe is the phenotype. This is the end product of an ontogeny. Individual development is influenced by the genes (cistrons) at every stage. Cistrons determine the synthesis of polypeptides within the cell. Between that process and the behavioral phenotype is a continual immensely complex interaction with the environment. For at every stage, development is also influenced by the environment.

Hence it is always misleading to say of a phenotypic *character* that it is genetically determined, *or* that it is environmentally determined. All aspects of the phenotype depend on both nature and nurture. The statement that a particular feature has a given "heritability" can be valid only for a given environment. Calling a character "innate" or "genetically coded" may in practice mean one of two things (if it has any clear meaning at all): (1) the character is *stable in development;* (2) the *difference* from other individuals is genetically determined.

Difficulties with these principles commonly arise from two sources. First is the confusion of the bio-logical concept of genetical determination with the social meaning of inheritance. An organism inherits from its parents not characters but genes. Each character is developed anew in each individual. The second kind of difficulty arises when our knowledge of genetics is applied to human beings. A confusion may then arise with a moral issue. Most moral systems enjoin upon us respect for people different from ourselves, whether in sex, age, color, customs, or opinions. But such an attitude signifies neither a disregard of differences (however caused) nor a rejection of the possibility that differences exist.

In ethology, the correct use of genetical principles is essential for a critical analysis of the concept of instinct. We turn to this in the next chapter.

17

THE CONCEPTS
OF INSTINCT

Beware instinct; the lion will not touch the true prince.
Instinct is a great matter; I was a coward on instinct.

Shakespeare
Henry IV: Part 1

17.1 SOME TRADITIONAL NOTIONS

Writers and observers of all ages have marveled at
the precision of the complex behavior of animals:
the feeding of an insect at a flower, the construction
of a web or a nest, the flight of a gull, and much
else impress us with their elegance and apparent
skill. Such patterns have often been referred to as
instinctive behavior. We realize, or at least assume,
that the behavior is not intelligent (compare chapter 8); and that, for example, when a wasp supplies
its young with caterpillars, or when a pregnant
mouse builds a nest, these animals are not guided
by foresight. Hence, in the past, writers have attributed behavior of this sort to divine intervention.

Such explanations are now out of favor; but
some traditional concepts have persisted into our
own day, and have usually been discussed under
the heading of instinct. The meanings of instinct
and related terms fall into three main classes (reviewed by F. A. Beach, 1950; C. G. Beer, 1968).
First, a writer may refer to species-typical patterns
of behavior (that is, of movement). Examples are
given in almost every chapter of this book. Sometimes it is possible at least to surmise how the pattern fits the species to a particular niche. Second, a
writer may be concerned with the animal's internal
state. An animal runs to exhaustion in pursuit of its
prey or of a mate. A female exerts herself in caring
for her young in the face of severe difficulties. Past
writers have therefore assumed the existence of
"drives" or "instincts" that *impel* animals to achieve
certain ends (reviewed by E. C. Wilm). The Latin
word *instinguere* has given us our word, instigate,
which has much the same meaning; and it shares an
origin with "instinct". Accordingly, an 18th-century
author, H. S. Reimarus, influential in his day, listed
47 instincts. Reimarus wrote in German, and his
word, translated as instincts, is *Triebe,* or drives.
Lastly, the dictionary, like Falstaff in the epigraph
of this chapter, equates instinct with intuition or
unconscious skill. Such expressions we apply colloquially to ourselves. What is "instinctive" in this
sense may have been acquired by practice.

17.1.1 Darwin and after Darwin

In the 19th century the most notable biological writings on instinct were those of Charles Darwin (1859). In the *Origin* he writes:

An action, which we ourselves should require experience to enable us to perform, when performed by an animal, more especially by a very young one, without any experience, and when performed by many individuals in the same way, without their knowing for what purpose it is performed, is usually said to be instinctive.

But Darwin, with his usual penetration, realized that the implications of such a bare definition are not appropriate. As we know, especially from chapter 12, the kinds of behavior traditionally called instinctive are often labile in development. Correspondingly, Darwin added this to the passage quoted:

But I could show that none of these characters of instinct is universal. A little dose, as Pierre Huber expresses it, of judgment or reason often comes into play, even in animals very low in the scale of nature.

Darwin also recognized that "several distinct mental actions are commonly embraced by the term" instinct; and in *The Descent of Man* (1871), instinct in most passages refers to an internal impetus. As a result, Darwin was led to adumbrate some of the problems that would face ethologists many decades later. For example, there is the question of "conflict of drives": the "instinct of self-preservation" may lead to actions that are incompatible with the "parental instinct"; from this notion follows that of varying amounts of drive, analogous to the forces that move a machine. In *The Expression of the Emotions* (1872), Darwin refers to "nerve-force", which may be "expended in . . . violent movements".

In the absence of physiological analysis, such notions persisted into the 20th century, and were often presented in a less critical form than Darwin's. Sigmund Freud, like Reimarus, wrote of *Triebe*—again, though rather reluctantly, translated as instincts. Freud (1949) wrote:

The *aim* of an instinct is in every instance satisfaction, which can only be obtained by abolishing the condition of stimulation in the source of the instinct . . .

By the *source* of an instinct is meant that somatic process in an organ or part of the body from which there results a stimulus represented in mental life by an instinct.

In 15.3.2.2 I quote Freud on the aggressive drive, which, he supposes, is in some sense an essential component of our makeup. As we saw, this notion illustrates very well the inadequacies of the traditional concept of drive. Freud is concerned with people. Others, more recently, in applying the concept of instinct to animals, have written in a similar way. J. A. Bierens de Haan, in a much-used encyclopaedia published in 1950, asks what instinct is, and writes:

We may answer this question by describing instinct as an innate faculty of the mind, which drives an animal to perform . . . acts which are adaptive in character, but are performed without the animal knowing the relation between these acts and the end that will be attained by them. We must therefore distinguish between that faculty, the "instinct", and the acts which are the result of the working of an instinct. . . . Of instinct (and instinctive actions) we know that they are innate, and typical of the species to which the animal belongs, not of the individual animal itself.

This example illustrates the distinction between observable behavior and the words used in referring to behavior. The notion of "an innate faculty of the mind, which drives an animal" to achieve certain ends encapsulates a traditional concept of instinct. It has at least three serious defects: first, it is not a description or classification of anything observed; second, it contains no testable hypothesis (for example, about the internal springs of behavior); third, it in no sense explains anything. Nonetheless, similar ideas have appeared in more recent writings.

Also in 1950 a volume was published that marked the beginning of the modern efflorescence of ethological research. It reported a meeting at which K. Z. Lorenz gave a paper, "The comparative method of studying innate behaviour patterns". Those who heard him on that occasion (as I did) will understand, better than by reading his papers, how Lorenz has had such an influence on ethologists: the paper was immensely entertaining and stimulating. (Not all speakers at scientific conferences recognize the need to make their contributions enjoyable.) Lorenz, like Bierens de Haan, distinguishes between an "instinctive activity" and an internal source of energy or drive. The instinctive activity is species-typical and uniform; it is also said to be innate (that is, not learned), and genetically determined (or inherited). For the views of Lorenz in full, see the collection of his papers translated into English (1970, 1971).

The instinctive activity is further described as the final stage of a sequence, which begins with an internal change: the resulting state or drive impels the animal to move about until it can perform the instinctive act. The initial movements are called *appetitive behavior,* and the final performance is a *consummatory act* (terms derived from writers of an earlier period, especially Wallace Craig). The drive is said to involve the accumulation of energy (sometimes called reaction-specific energy); and the energy is discharged by performing the consummatory act. Lastly, the situation that evokes the instinctive behavior does so by activating an innate releasing mechanism (IRM).

W. H. Thorpe (1963), in an influential text first published in 1956, gives a full account of these ideas. For him, much as for Lorenz, instinctive acts

have three properties. (1) They are a form of "innate" behavior; this statement, when it has a clear meaning, refers to ontogeny: "innate" is often defined as "not learned". (2) Instinctive acts are also variously described as "inherited" or "genetically coded and therefore characteristic of the species". (3) They are internally motivated. On the last item Thorpe writes: "It is clear that energy with *some* degree of specificity, channelled in some way or another, is fundamental to the modern concept of instinct."

For critical analyses of these notions consult C. G. Beer (1964, 1968), R. C. Bolles (1967), R. A. Hinde (1970), J. S. Kennedy (1972), D. S. Lehrman (1953), A. C. A. Sevenster-Bol, P. J. B. Slater (1974), and N. Tinbergen (1969). They are still found in writings on behavior and on psychological medicine, but they are increasingly rejected by ethologists and psychologists. I now outline the main reasons for rejecting them.

17.1.2 The Modern Critique

17.1.2.1 Appetite and Consummation: First, there are inadequacies in the notions of appetitive behavior and consummatory act. Sometimes, an animal does become active, explore (at random?), encounter an object or situation, perform a stereotyped movement, and then become still: such a sequence may occur when (for instance) the animal feeds (chapter 4). This is a description that can be stated in terms of appetite and consummation. The following qualifying comments may be made.

1. Even as a description of behavior sequences impelled by a deficit, it is unsatisfactory. The end of a behavior sequence is often not a stereotyped act, but the achievement of a state. Among examples are movement to a warmer or colder place,

and taking cover when disturbed by a predator. Hence follows the notion of a consummatory *state,* that is, a specific input through external or internal sense organs that ends an activity.

2. It has, however, proved impracticable to classify movements into the distinct categories of appetitive and consummatory. A wide-ranging movement may itself be consummatory, in the sense that it ends a sequence of acts. The "reward value" of exploratory movements is discussed in 8.1.3.3. Other examples come from experiments on predatory behavior (R. H. Polsky). Seeking, pursuing, and killing prey are usually preliminaries to eating. Except when young or other conspecifics are fed, the function of these activities is therefore homeostatic. Hence, a priori, predatory behavior is appetitive, and should reflect an internal deficit (hunger). But in fact it often does not: killing prey does not depend on the predator first being deprived of food; and even when the prey are at first eaten, killing them may continue when eating has stopped. Unfortunately, these statements are based largely on observations of laboratory rats killing mice; but dogs (Canidae), cats (Felidae) of several species, and hyaenas, *Crocuta,* all sometimes kill more prey than they eat (H. Kruuk). Further, R. E. Adamec describes experiments in which domestic cats, *Felis ocreata,* were allowed to begin eating a favorite food, such as fish, and then had access to a live rat. The cats all left the food, attacked the rat, and killed it; to do this, they had to move more than one meter and jump off a shelf. The dead rat was carried back to the food tray, but not eaten: instead, the cats returned to their original meal.

The account of predatory behavior, conventional only recently, would have stated that eating is consummatory (or leads to a consummatory state); that the acts which precede eating are appetitive or variable and not consummatory; but that both eating and the preliminaries to it are impelled by a single internal source of energy, or drive. As we see, this account does not fit the facts.

17.1.2.2 Authentic Drives? Nonetheless, despite many objections, there are still references to drives in scientific writings (reviewed by R. C. Bolles, 1967; J. Gray; R. A. Hinde, 1970). The primary finding is of fluctuation in response to a given external stimulus. Fluctuation may result from deprivation, for example of food or water; there is then an intermittent deficit—for instance of blood sugar. Or the change may be rhythmic and autonomous: an example is the estrous cycle of mammals (9.4.1.2). Changes in responsiveness are relevant to the study of habit formation: the ending of an internal deficit may be rewarding (6.2.1), that is, it may induce or enhance the acquisition (learning) of a novel activity; a water-deprived (or thirsty) animal learns to go where it can drink, and so on.

To say, however, that an animal, observed to be drinking, is "exhibiting a thirst drive" is, of course, vacuous (4.5.4): it adds nothing to the statement that the animal is drinking. The concept of drive can, however, be defended on at least two grounds.

1. At the behavioral level, (a) two or more features may vary together, as if "driven" from the same source. A parturient female makes or maintains a nest, defends it, retrieves her young, and adopts a posture that allows her young to suck (9.4.2.2). (b) An activity, such as drinking, may vary as a function of one or more independent variables; these include not only the time during which the animal has been without water, but also, for example, what food it has been eating. Behavior is then as if it depended on a single process; but this process is acted on by several external agencies.

Figure 17-1 illustrates the relationships of three

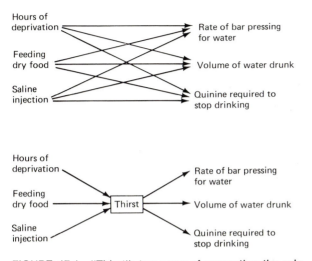

FIGURE 17-1 "Thirst": two ways of presenting the relationships between three independent variables that influence the ingestion of water, and three behavioral features, each of which could be held out as a measure of thirst. The behavioral variables, however, do not alter in unison. In the lower figure, the box labelled "thirst" represents a so-called intervening variable. See figure 17-2. (After N. E. Miller, 1959)

variables that influence water and electrolyte balance, and three measurable behavioral features that are influenced by the first three. The central box, labelled "thirst", may be regarded as an "intervening variable" with no physiological significance. An "intervening variable" is then a descriptive device, representing the relationships of the independent and dependent variables. Such descriptions have been much debated but are little used. Figure 17-2 gives actual findings. It illustrates an important principle, already discussed in 4.5.4. When, in a scientific context, we use terms such as thirst, hunger, libido, and so on, we try to measure them; but we then find that different measures, each intended to quantify the same property ("thirst" and so forth), give different results. Such findings are not compatible with the idea of a single drive or impul-

sion that determines all the kinds of behavior related to drinking (or eating or mating).

2. This argument leads inevitably to a "reductionist" procedure. Instead of an abstract description of relationships, we try to give the central box of figure 17-1 a physiological content. Some results are summarized in chapter 4. The regulation of eating and drinking by mammals is described in terms (a) of changes in blood or tissue composition, and (b), to some extent, of central nervous processes. Unitary concepts, such as hunger and thirst drives, then once again disappear. A plural analysis is necessary. The same applies to the "sex drive" of mammals (9.4.1).

17.1.2.3 Drive and Energy: The most important ground for rejecting recent theories of instinct is indeed the inadequacy of notions of drive. In

FIGURE 17-2 Three measures of "thirst" (see figure 17-1). Fasted rats were given dry food; they then received 5 ml 13.2% salt solution through a stomach tube. The left-hand columns (shaded) represent control values. The treatment reduced bar pressing, but increased the amount of water drunk; and it reduced the effect of the distastefulness of quinine. (After N. E. Miller, 1959)

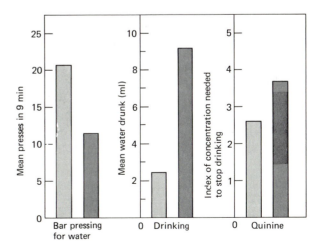

15.3.2.2 I mention the idea of "innate heat" which, before the day of scientific physiology, was supposed to explain the constant temperature of the body. In some writings expressions such as general drive, hunger drive, and so on seem to represent a similar resort to words, used as pseudoexplanations, instead of explanations or hypotheses based on observation or experiment. The words used in accounts of drive are derived from physics, especially mechanics. As C. G. Beer (1968) points out, such accounts imply the existence of a form of energy; and this energy determines whether an animal moves toward food or a mate or some other objective. Such hypothetical and mysterious energy can flow, it can be dammed up, and it can be consumed. It may also spark over and so evoke behavior of an inappropriate kind. An extreme example of mechanical analogy is provided by Lorenz (1950): the accumulation of energy is represented by the filling of a reservoir until a threshold is reached; then, given an external releasing stimulus, the machine will flush itself (that is, the animal will perform some act). Such a model or metaphor might suggest that the author is concerned with the physiology of behavior; but the model has in fact no physiological content (compare 14.2.1). And at the behavioral level it disregards an important phenomenon. There are many examples of decline in responsiveness resulting from performance of an act; but these are commonly specific to the stimulus: another stimulus may readily evoke the original response. Hence there is no exhaustion of energy, in any usual sense of the term. Examples are given in the account of habituation (5.2). Yet this model has been immensely popular, and the flushing cistern used to illustrate it has been copied in many texts. For a critical analysis, consult R. A. Hinde (1960).

Energy models, then, are at best examples of literary imagery that perhaps make writings about behavior more lively. But they may also distract attention from fruitful physiological analysis. Regular increases in responsiveness, or in the intensity with which an act is performed, do occur (chapter 4); there are also examples of threshold values, below which no response occurs. The output from a brain center may depend on the accumulation of a substance: an example is the respiratory center of the vertebrate brain stem, which discharges when the carbon dioxide in the blood reaches a certain level. (Compare the account of newt respiration in 4.2.)

17.1.2.4 Displacement Behavior:

A byproduct of "energy" models of drive is the concept of displacement behavior (reviewed by N. Tinbergen, 1952). Suppose a tern, *Sterna,* on its nest is provoked to apotreptic behavior by an intruder; the intruder flies away, and the resident immediately performs, apparently hurriedly, preening movements. To a human observer, the preening seems to be irrelevant to the situation; and it suggests that some internal source of energy, previously channeled into apotreptic conduct, has now been transferred to another behavior pattern. Close observation of behavior often suggests that, deprived of an opponent or a potential mate, an animal will resort to an alternative activity, as if it were releasing energy.

Similarly, there are many situations in which an animal is, or seems to be, stimulated to perform two incompatible responses, such as approach and withdrawal. In courtship, a potential mate is sometimes at first driven away, as if it were an intruder or rival. There seems to be a conflict between apotrepsis and courtship (chapter 9). An animal may then perform neither of the two activities that seem to the observer to be appropriate or relevant;

but instead a third, apparently incongruous act occurs. P. Sevenster (1961) gives an example from the three-spined stickleback. While it is guarding the eggs (9.2.1), the male fans them and so prevents an accumulation of carbon dioxide in the surrounding water. A male may also fan, before any eggs are laid, during courtship. Such "displacement fanning" may be attributed to the simultaneous arousal of sexual and apotreptic responses, and so to a conflict between sexual and apotreptic drives. An energy model of such behavior would state that there is a drive for courtship, one for apotrepsis, and a third for fanning; and, when the first two cancel each other out, the weak drive to fan is expressed.

The notion of displacement behavior has attracted much attention; perhaps its appeal is partly because we feel in ourselves what we call a buildup of tension, which we need to release. But the assumption that apparently substitute acts fall into a single class of displacement behavior is no longer held (reviewed by R. A. Hinde, 1960). Indeed, the whole concept of displacement behavior, like that of drive, has now been replaced by a piecemeal analysis of the interactions of behavior patterns, and of their internal causes. The reasons for rejecting the concept are of three kinds.

1. During courtship, apotrepsis, or other activity there are autonomic changes that alter the blood supply to the skin, change its secretions, and also result in raising of the hair or feathers. It is hypothesized that the resulting altered sensory input from the skin could provoke scratching or preening; another idea is that autonomic activity could induce dryness of the throat, hence "displacement" drinking. Such proposals, though speculative, point the way to physiological analysis.

2. There is also the disinhibition hypothesis. "Displacement" fanning by sticklebacks may be interpreted in this way: the cancelation of courtship and apotrepsis somehow annuls an inhibition of fanning. Similarly, J. J. A. van Iersel & A. C. A. Bol have analyzed the preening, nest building, and other stereotyped activities of terns, *Sterna*. The readiness with which each act is performed can be given a numerical value, based on the number of movements in a given period. When the values for two mutually inhibitory acts reach a certain ratio, neither is performed, but a third act is. Until that moment the third act is supposed to have been inhibited. But, despite an apparent allusion to internal states, an account in terms of disinhibition is a description of the observed behavior, including the relationships of different acts. Again, it is possible to imagine a physiological analysis; but at present none exists.

3. There is the possibility that stimulation to perform one activity can *increase* the readiness to perform others. This hypothesis applies especially to mammals, and may be related to the functioning of a part of the brain, the reticular activating system (RAS), described in 5.2.2.2. The RAS receives an input from each of the external senses (figure 5-18), and from it there is a large projection to the whole of the cerebral cortex. Whenever there is a direct input from one of the senses to a particular region of the cortex, there is also, after a delay of a few milliseconds, a further input to all cortical regions. During sleep or anesthesia an animal's cortex continues to receive specific inputs from the exteroceptors, but the diffuse projection system is silent. Responsiveness to stimuli always depends on the operation of the RAS. Hence unexpected responses to stimuli could result from a general state of arousal or responsiveness to any external change. Unfortunately, there is little good evidence on the extent to which this happens.

For all these reasons, the concept of displacement behavior is now seen to be less useful than it seemed at first.

17.1.2.5 Genetics and Phylogenetics: There are frequent references to instinct or instinctive behavior as inherited, genetically fixed, or phylogenetically preprogrammed. As we know (chapter 16), it is never appropriate to speak of a *characteristic* as genetically determined. The behavior referred to as inherited (or innate) is species-typical and develops, as a rule, with great reliability. The statement that a behavior pattern is inherited therefore represents an error of classification: the behavior is not distinguished by any genetical peculiarity but by its ontogeny: as R. A. Hinde (1959) says, it is stable in development.

The reference to phylogeny in accounts of such behavior is one way of saying that the behavior adapts the animal to a particular mode of life: the behavior is (it is assumed) a result of natural selection acting on ancestral populations; the ancestors lived in a particular environment and became adapted to it. It is an axiom of biology that most of the features of an organism—structural, behavioral, and other—have survival value: and we know that departure from the typical often reduces fitness. Hence to say that a behavior pattern is phylogenetically preprogrammed is, again, either a category error or empty. It is the former if the actual meaning concerns stability of development, or uniformity within the species; it is empty if the intention is to say something about evolution: for there is *no* category of behavior patterns, that we know of, that is *not* a product of evolution.

The reader will now understand why the terms instinct and instinctive behavior are gradually disappearing from scientific writings. They traditionally refer to notions that we have been obliged to give up. Correspondingly, the belief that statements about drives provide a valid, unifying theory of the stereotyped activities of animals has proved to be an illusion. But the behavior, of course, remains, and needs to be explained.

17.2 PATTERNS OF BEHAVIOR

At the beginning of this chapter and elsewhere I write of *patterns* of behavior. The word pattern, as used here, means a repeated set of relationships. Repetition may occur in the movements of a single animal if, for example, it develops a habit such as running along a pathway; but we are now concerned (1) with activities common to a whole taxon (usually, a species), or (2) a result of such an activity, such as a nest.

Species-typical patterns that involve behavior are of many kinds. (1) There are the stereotyped *orientations* (chapter 2): what is stereotyped is the position of the body or the direction of movement relative to some external feature. (2) Some animals display, not fixed orientations, but *habitat preferences:* given a choice, they move toward one kind of situation rather than another. (3) Some patterns seem to be autonomous, that is, independent of any special external feature: these include *rhythms* of activity. (4) Among distinctive patterns are those of *structures,* such as nests, webs, and burrows. (5) Last, and most obvious, are patterns of *movement.* Among the most-studied movements are those of courtship and territorial displays (chapters 9, 10); but the mode of locomotion and other movements are often quite distinctive. The movements that produce sounds may also be put in this category.

17.2.1 Orientations

17.2.1.1 Jacques Loeb: Chapter 2 gives plenty of examples of orientations, but there is more to say on their importance for ideas about instinct. The study of the orientations of animals was founded by Jacques Loeb (1859–1924). His book, *The Mechanistic Conception of Life,* first published in 1912, was reissued in 1964 with a historical introduction. Loeb used the expression forced movements, which reflects the mechanistic attitude he adopted toward behavior. When he began his researches, botanists had already founded the modern knowledge of the plant movements called tropisms. The growing parts of flowering plants above ground usually bend toward light (phototropism), while growing roots are influenced by gravity (geotropism). Although the detailed "mechanism" of tropisms was not known, the account of these movements was based on experiment and was objective.

In contrast, the movements of animals were commonly described or explained in terms of undefined instincts. Some animals are attracted by a light and even fly into a flame. This was held to be due to a special instinct; or it was said that the animals loved the light. Loeb (1901) rejected such expressions, and applied the principles used by botanists to the movements of animals. An animal was studied as if it were a machine constructed so that it could carry out only certain movements. Some animals are impelled to move toward light, others are forced away, just as an automatically controlled locomotive can start, stop, reverse, or change speed, but cannot leap from the rails and move off down a road.

Loeb's early work included experiments on caterpillars which, on emerging in spring, move to the tips of branches where they feed on the leaf buds. According to the view then current, these insects were moved by an instinct for self-preservation. Loeb exposed such caterpillars to light from one direction, when the only food available was in the opposite direction. They duly turned toward the light and died of starvation. For Loeb, "heliotropic" (phototactic) animals are "in reality photometric machines". Hence Loeb was ruthlessly reductionist: he held that comparative psychology would depend principally on biologists trained in physical chemistry.

Under the influence of Loeb's work, it was for some time customary to refer to animal orientations as tropisms; but this usage, based on an analogy, is inappropriate: bending movements of plants depend, not on locomotion guided by directional sense organs, but on differential growth. We can also see how much of animal behavior falls outside the scope of a system based on simple orientations. Loeb's concept of "forced movements" is an example of a brilliantly simple notion that provoked new ways of thinking and new understanding, but eventually proved to have severe limitations. Exactly the same applies to the work of Loeb's contemporary, Pavlov, on conditional reflexes (5.5).

17.2.1.2 The "Taxis Component": Attempts have been made to incorporate Loeb's conception of forced movements in accounts of complex behavior patterns (for example, by N. Tinbergen, 1951). In 2.2.2.3 I mention the gaping of nestling birds toward a parent. As we saw, a directional response of this sort does not fall in the usual definition of a taxis: it does not involve locomotion; moreover, it is a response to a particular pattern, whereas a taxis is evoked by *any* directional stimulation of a sensory modality. Hence in this book "taxis" (or "taxic") does not refer to the directional component of complex activities.

It is, however, sometimes possible to distinguish the stimuli that provoke an animal to activity from those that steer it in the right direction. In 9.2.2 I mention a chichlid fish, *Pelmatochromis subocellatus,* of which the female is brightly colored: the features of the female's appearance which stimulate a male to court are distinct from the red patch that determines the male's direction of movement.

A quite different kind of example is provided by the honey bee, when it is stimulated by an odor to fly out for food. The odor may determine the choice of plant (13.3.2.3); but the final line of flight is determined by the visible pattern presented by the flower.

In other instances the fixed pattern *is* the direction of movement. Obvious examples come from migrations, such as those of birds (2.4): the actual movements of flying are the same whether the birds are migrating or not. Small-scale movements, too, may be recognized as stereotyped only by their direction: examples include the orientation of young of mouthbrooding fish, which swim into the parent's mouth (9.2.2) and the vertical posture of a male stickleback, defending its territory against an intruder (9.2.1).

17.2.2 Habitat Preferences

Most animal species are restricted to a well-defined habitat. Some occupy a range of habitats but, given access to alternatives, tend to choose one. (See also 12.3.7.) The behavior of habitat selection has rarely been examined in detail, but it is evidently distinct from that of orientation to a specific kind of stimulus (reviewed by Linda Partridge).

J. A. Wiens reared the larvae of a frog, *Rana aurora*, in environments that provided different visible patterns: one had only vertical stripes, the other black and white squares. Later, the tadpoles were given a choice between the two. Those reared in the checked environment showed no preference; but those that had been reared on stripes, when given a choice, tended to prefer a striped environment. The sensitive period for the effect is the first 14 to 17 days in the striped environment; and if, after this, there is a period in a featureless environment, the preference is still shown. Wiens suggests that in nature these findings reflect a propensity to choose a region with plenty of vegetation; but there is some versatility in the ability to adapt to other habitats.

Other examples of habitat preference come from studies of two or more related types. V. T. Harris describes how different subspecies of deer mice, *Peromyscus maniculatus,* responded differently to artificial environments: one had the visual properties of woodland, the other, of grassland (compare 12.3.7). Each chose the laboratory environment that more closely resembled its natural habitat. Hence once again we have species-typical responses to visual patterns.

P. R. Grant has recorded similar findings, but also observed, like Wiens, some effect of early experience. Grant studied one species each of *Microtus* and *Peromyscus,* and two of *Clethrionomys.* He tested the animals in pairs in an enclosure of which half was grassland and the other half woodland; experimental pairs were of different species (or of the same species from different environments); control pairs were of the same species and previous environment. *M. pennsylvanicus,* tested with another species, always tended to occur in grassland. *P. maniculatus* occurred more often in woodland than grassland. There was no evidence of a preference by either of the species of *Clethrionomys.*

Such findings leave open the question whether early conditions of rearing influence choice of habitat. Grant therefore reared *Peromyscus* in the laboratory, and exposed them in early life to grass or to maple saplings, *Acer saccharum,* or to neither. Later, the mice were tested in the manner described above. When *Microtus* was present during the test, the *Peromyscus* previously reared with grass tended to spend more time in grassland than in woodland. Here, therefore, is evidence of an ontogenetic (environmental) effect on a difference in choice of habitat. Once again, we see that apparently fixed (instinctive) responses have some developmental lability.

17.2.3 Rhythms

Some behavior patterns occur at regular intervals (reviewed by J. Aschoff). The repetition of the activity may then depend on external changes to which the activity conforms. We have seen how the reproduction and migration of some birds depend on the seasonal changes of light intensity (2.4.2). There are also daily (circadian) rhythms that often depend on changes of illumination (2.1.3). These rhythms are species-typical, and have been called innate, or even instinctive. (There are, of course, also rhythmic activities acquired by individual animals as habits.) Not all rhythms depend on exter-

nal changes. Some are evidently independent or *endogenous*. The patterns are again species-typical.

G. P. Wells has analyzed the rhythmic movements of the lugworm, *Arenicola marina,* a polychaete much used by marine anglers as bait, and by zoologists for teaching. Worms of this group make U-shaped burrows, open at both ends, in the sand of seashores throughout the world (figure 17-3). The worms survive exposure at low tide by virtue of a blood pigment (a hemoglobin) that stores oxygen to an unusual extent: during most of this period, when the burrow is not covered by the sea, respiratory movements cease. When it is covered, the tube is kept open by regular movements of the worm: this irrigation cycle includes a burst of activity, accompanied by defecation, at intervals of about 40 min. If the worm is deprived of oxygen, there is an increase in the frequency of the movements. Clearly, the irrigation cycle has a homeostatic function; and, on the facts so far given, it appears to be analogous to the respiratory movements of newts described in 4.2.

In fact, however, the irrigation cycle continues at a steady rate over a wide range of oxygen and carbon dioxide concentrations. Moreover, the rhythm of movements is still seen if strips of the body wall, together with the ventral nerve cord, are removed and kept in constant conditions in seawater. There is evidently a *pacemaker* in the nerve cord. Similarly, defecation does not depend on a full rectum, but it too depends on the pacemaker. The neural systems responsible for such endogenous rhythms ("internal clocks") continue to function without an input from the external senses. Hence they are not reflex (5.1): they are spontaneous in a manner analogous to that of the heartbeat of a vertebrate. It is surprising to find movements with a homeostatic function which are not related to a deficit (for example, of oxygen).

FIGURE 17-3 Diagram of the burrow of a lugworm, *Arenicola marina.* Arrows show the direction of movement of water maintained by the respiratory activity of the worm; sand moves in the opposite direction. (After G. P. Wells, 1950)

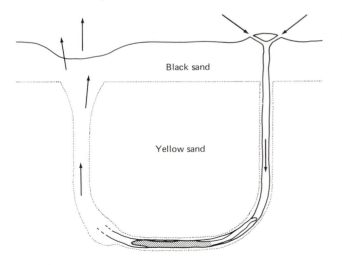

Black sand

Yellow sand

It is quite difficult even to speculate on the survival value of such a system.

As another example, the respiratory movements of the swimmerets of a crustacean, the crayfish, *Procambarus clarki,* are rhythmic. They are regulated by the abdominal ganglia. K. Ikeda & C. A. G. Wiersma describe how the rhythm originates in the fifth abdominal ganglion and spreads to the others. The first five abdominal ganglia were isolated from the rest of the central nervous system, and their afferents were also cut. They still produced a rhythmic motor output, in the same sequence and of the same duration as in the intact animal.

Sometimes there is an endogenous rhythm of the central nervous system, but normal movements depend in part on input from the periphery. Locomotion of a fish (reviewed by A. R. Blight) is typically by an undulating movement of the body, brought about by successive contractions of the myomeres; contraction on one side is accompanied by relaxation on the other. B. L. Roberts used curare in experiments on the dogfish, *Scyliorhinus canicula:* this drug (also used by surgeons) prevents contraction of the muscles but does not otherwise interfere with neural function. Roberts severed the spinal cord at the front end, to produce a "spinal" animal, that is, one in which the brain can have no influence on the skeletal muscles. He then immobilized the spinal fish with curare, and recorded the output in the ventral (motor) nerves of the cord. Since the segmental muscles were completely relaxed, the motor output could provoke no reflex response; any persistent output must therefore have been the result of the spontaneous activity of the neurons of the spinal cord. In these conditions, an intermittent output did persist; it was, however, slower than the normal rhythm; and it continued at a declining rate for only 2 h or less; in contrast, the rhythmic swimming of a spinal dog-fish not treated with curare persists for as long as 10 h.

The two preceding examples show what is meant by "endogenous" or "spontaneous": an activity so described is independent both of any rhythmic external stimulation and also of proprioceptive feedback. The spontaneous character of the behavior might suggest, to biologists of an earlier period, the existence of an internal drive or instinct; but, as with orientations, the modern means of reaching further understanding is physiological analysis. When such a reductionist method is successful, concepts such as those of instinct are replaced by statements on observed internal events, such as nerve impulses and the contractions of muscles.

17.2.4 The Structure of Movements

17.2.4.1 The "Fixed Action Pattern": Distinctive, species-typical movements have been called *fixed action patterns* (FAP). This term has been prominent in ethological writings. It is primarily a name for a familiar fact, that certain visible and audible performances form repeated units easily distinguished from others. Unfortunately, the term has not been used consistently. D. A. Dewsbury reviews the work of 10 authors, all of whom refer to FAP; no two use the same definition or criteria. Yet taxon-specific behavior patterns certainly exist: we can often identify species by their characteristic movements or sounds, or by the things they make. Here the term FAP means a "stereotyped, highly predictable, taxon-specific behavior sequence" (S. A. Barnett, 1975). This definition covers only movement patterns, and not their products (such as nests).

The definition is not very precise; but it recognizes that most writers who employ the term casually refer to the *stereotyped* character of much animal behavior (compare W. M. Schleidt, 1974). Difficulty has arisen because FAPs so defined are said to have properties in addition to stereotypy. Among them are the following: (1) the components of the pattern occur in a fixed sequence; (2) the external stimulus that provokes a FAP acts only as a "trigger": it is not required once the FAP has been set going; (3) the components of a given FAP have common internal causes not shared with any other FAP.

Such assertions may be treated as hypotheses to be tested. Before any test can be attempted, it is essential to identify the behavior pattern to be studied. In general, when an animal's behavior is newly described, it is desirable to give a minutely detailed account, with illustrations, of what is observed. It is not enough to say that an animal courted, or performed an agonistic display, or that its conduct was amicable. A full description is required, to enable another worker to repeat the observations. A report cannot be confirmed unless it is quite clear what has been reported. Moreover, two observers, separately studying the same behavior, may select different patterns, or behavioral units, for study.

17.2.4.2 Examples: I first take an example from my own experience. A male wild rat, *Rattus norvegicus,* threatens intruding adult male conspecifics (10.5.1.2). The complete apotreptic performance by a resident includes the following items: (1) tooth chattering; (2) a slow approach with raised hair, accompanied by urination and defecation; (3) adoption of a distinctive posture (figure 17-4a) and a prancing movement around the opponent; (4) leaping onto the opponent with rapid adductions of the forelimbs (figure 17-4b); (5) a brief bite; (6) rolling around or scuffling with the opponent; (7) standing on the hind limbs and patting at the opponent with the forelimbs while the opponent does the same (figure 17-4c); (8) chasing the opponent (S. A. Barnett, 1958, 1975).

All these activities may be grouped under a single heading, such as "attack"; the duration of attack may then be recorded in given conditions, such as a 15-min encounter with a stranger. This procedure implies that the several components of the conduct go together or *covary.* A further implication is therefore of a common causation. The immediate causes of such conduct are of two kinds, external and internal. The external cause is the presence of an intruder: none of the acts listed above is performed until the intruder arrives, and the direction of the various movements is determined by the intruder's position. (An additional external factor is that the performer is in a familiar region.) The internal causes probably include a certain level of androgenic hormone in the blood (10.6.3).

The complete or "ideal" sequence described above is, however, not the only possible sequence: the "threat posture" may occur after the jump and bite as well as before; and certain components, such as tooth chattering and even the jump and bite, may be absent. Moreover, each component may occur in isolation from all the others. Hence, although the different acts covary, the correlation between them is incomplete.

There are also apparently epitreptic signals. Among them is allogrooming: one rat gently nibbles at the fur of another (figure 13-22). A male may do this to a female. But sometimes, between bouts of attack, a male holds down and energetically grooms the opponent. There seem, then, to be two kinds of allogrooming, of which one is apotreptic and should be included in the list above. But there is then the question whether the two kinds can be objectively distinguished, except by

the context in which the behavior occurs. This question has not yet been answered.

The preceding account is entirely in terms of visible movements and postures, and of the tactile stimuli that result from contact between two individuals. But the encounters are accompanied by sounds from both actors and, we may be sure, also by the secretion of pheromones. The behavior we observe cannot be fully interpreted unless we know how all these kinds of social signal interact. A complete account also requires a statement of the effect of the signals on the opponent, and the countereffect of the opponent's conduct on the attacker.

One way of attempting a more detailed analysis is to select a single item, such as the threat posture, and to record its relationships to other conduct of the attacker and to the responses of the opponent. Reference, however, to this posture as if it were unequivocally identifiable on all occasions is misleading. A rat may raise itself on fully extended legs with maximally arched back; but it may also raise itself only partly; and the posture may rapidly change into one in which the animal is almost lying on its side in a position that has been loosely called submissive. These findings suggest the need for an extremely detailed quantitative analysis.

The observations on wild rats were made in the context of a physiological study of social stress, not of an analysis of FAP. Other species offer better opportunities for exact measurement of movements. Among them are lizards (Lacertilia). Figure 17-5 gives an example. J. A. Stamps & G. W.

FIGURE 17-4 Components of attack by a male wild rat, *Rattus norvegicus,* on a conspecific: above the arched-back "threat" posture; middle, leaping; below, "boxing". (Drawings by Gabriel Donald, from photographs; from S. A. Barnett, 1975)

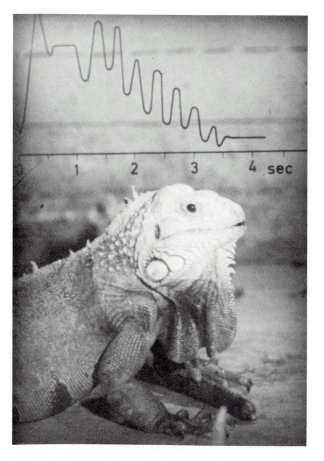

FIGURE 17-5 A South American lizard, *Iguana iguana,* with a trace of its stereotyped head nodding, directed toward another male. (Courtesy H. Distel)

Barlow describe the conduct of a West Indian lizard, *Anolis aeneus.* Their aim is explicitly to examine the concept of the FAP. A male in its cage responds to an intruder with one or more patterns of movement; and these can—it seems—be adequately studied without worrying about accompanying sounds or odors.

There are two principal displays. In one, called fan, the lizard rises on its forelegs and extends its dewlap fully; in the other, fanbob, it does the same and also moves up and down on its forelegs (push-ups). In other, less common displays there are various kinds of bobbing and degrees of extension of the dewlap. (See also 10.4.1.3.)

The authors remark that it is not always possible to suggest the functional significance of these performances. Their concern is, however, with "defining units of naturally occurring behavior", and examining whether the concept of the fixed action pattern is useful in this case. They therefore analyze the fanbob display in great detail. The two components, raising the body and extending the dewlap, were found to vary to some extent independently. (This finding resembles that, mentioned in 13.3.1.2, on the Carib grackle, *Quiscalus lugubris:* in the song-spread display of that species, the intensity of beak raising and wing raising varies independently.) Hence the two components are inferred not to have an entirely common causation. Further, the fanbob sometimes stops before the sequence of movements is completed. Lastly, the order in which the components of the fanbob are performed is not invariable: in particular, certain movements that usually take place before the final bobbing, and are therefore called introductory, may be absent, or they may occur *after* the bobbing.

T. R. Halliday (1974, 1975a,b) has described quantitatively, in great detail, the sexual behavior of the smooth newt, *Triturus vulgaris,* whose breathing I mention in 4.2. This amphibian is sexually dimorphic. The females vary in appearance, but are quite drab: dorsally they are greenish brown, but they have a pale belly. The male has a large crest; and his whole surface, including that of the crest and tail, is marked with dark spots; the head also has black stripes; and, apart from black patches, the belly is orange.

The mode of fertilization of this genus was discovered late in the 19th century, by an ingenious naturalist who had glass tanks attached to the ceiling of a room in which he could watch the behavior of newts from below. When a female or male meet and both are ready for mating, the male repeatedly presses his snout against the female. She usually moves away, and is followed; there may be a long period of pursuit, with breaks for apparent sniffing by the male. Eventually the male moves in front of the female to a "display position" (figure 17-6). The female may again swim away; but, if she stays still, the male makes distinctive movements of his conspicuous tail: in the "whip" there is a single, violent lateral movement; in the "fan" waves of contraction pass rapidly down the tail; in the "wave" (which is very variable), the male's body is also moved up and down, in a manner resembling the pushups of *Anolis*. The sequence of these performances is not constant.

After some time, the female begins to approach the male, and he retreats, still barring her way with his curved body. The female's cloaca now projects downward. The male next turns from the female and creeps away, while she follows. After creeping for 10 to 20 cm the male stops and quivers; the female now collides with his tail, which is raised. The male releases a spermatophore in front of the female, moves on and turns, again barring the female's way. The female moves forward, and pushes against the male; as a result, the spermatophore adheres to her cloaca (figure 17-7). Halliday remarks that the female seems at no time to respond directly to the spermatophore but only to the male: picking up the spermatophore, though the essential part of the proceedings, is evidently an indirect outcome of her responses to the male's performance.

The whole of this sequence may be repeated by the same pair, often three times and—very rarely—as many as seven times. The following is a table of success rates observed by Halliday:

	encounters between ♂ and ♀	courtship sequences
No. observed	47	106
No. successful	29	46

FIGURE 17-6 Fanning display by a male smooth newt, *Triturus vulgaris;* female on right. (From T. R. Halliday, 1975)

FIGURE 17-7   Smooth newts (see figure 17-6): on left the male bars the female's way after she has followed his movements; the spermatophore has just become attached to her cloaca. (Courtesy T. R. Halliday)

Despite the elaborate character of the male's conduct, mating failed in 18 out of 47 encounters. This was because the spermatophore does not become attached to the female's cloaca. In fact, the whole story of the sexual conduct of this newt, like that of the apotreptic conduct of wild rats or of lizards, illustrates very well the reason why the adjective "fixed" in "fixed action pattern" is criticized: although there is a pattern, there is much variation; and statements, both on the number and sequences of the components of the total display and also on the outcome of the encounter, must be expressed as probabilities.

Other examples are given in chapter 13. The general conclusion is clear. Displays do exist. Hence, as a name for repeated, recognizable patterns of movement and of sounds, the term fixed action pattern represents something real and obvious. But the word "fixed" should not be taken to imply an absence of significant variation. Displays vary in intensity, in the number of components they include on different occasions, and in the sequence in which the components are performed. Moreover, the components of a display may vary independently. The same statements apply, no doubt, to complex behavior patterns that are not displays (that is, are not social signals). A familiar example is self-grooming by a cat or a rat (figure 17-8).

Accordingly, accounts of FAP are beginning to include quantitative analyses of their component movements (reviewed by M. Bekoff, 1977b; W. M. Schleidt, 1974). The patterns closely studied last

FIGURE 17-8 Self-grooming by a wild rat, *Rattus norvegicus:* a complex, stereotyped behavior pattern. (Drawing by Gabriel Donald, from a photograph; from S. A. Barnett, 1975)

sumption is one of machine-like regularity: we are used to turning a switch, and so making a machine go through a programmed sequence that culminates in a fixed outcome (such as yielding a cup of coffee containing both milk and sugar).

Are FAP ever like this? Owing to lack of evidence, the question cannot be answered. A few observations have been made that suggest such an automatism. K. Z. Lorenz & N. Tinbergen (1939) describe the behavior of the greylag goose, *Anser anser,* during incubation. If an egg rolls out of the nest, the bird hooks it back with the underside of its beak (figure 17-9). If the egg rolls away when the goose has begun the pulling-in movement, the goose is said to continue as if the egg were still there. Certain stereotyped acts have been said to occur even when the appropriate stimulus is to-

from 0.1 to 10 s; most take about 1 s. Percentage coefficients of variation (table 17-1) of measured features are usually between 15 and 35. Such figures are entirely compatible with the notion of distinct patterns, but they remind us once again of the scope of biological variation. What seems not to be known is the effect of the variation on the receivers of the signals.

17.2.4.3 Stimulus Control and Reflex Chains:
In the preceding subsection I list three hypothesized properties of FAP. One is that an external stimulus merely sets the pattern going, after which the performance proceeds independently. Some patterns do occur rhythmically without special stimulation (17.2.3); but we are now concerned with those that require some external provocation. This notion is related to the concept that a *fixed* sequence of acts makes up each pattern. The pre-

TABLE 17-1 A procedure for describing fixed action patterns (FAP)

Many species-typical behavior patterns vary in amplitude or duration. A standard statistical measure of a continuously varying quantity is the *percentage coefficient of variation, V:*

$$V = \frac{100\ \sigma}{\overline{x}}$$

where σ is the standard deviation and $\overline{x}$ is the mean of a series of measurements of the behavior pattern.

Alternatively, it may be desired to express such findings as a measure of stereotypy, *S. S* could be defined as the reciprocal of *V,* but a more convenient formula is

$$S = \frac{100}{\frac{(100\ \sigma)}{\overline{x}} + 1},$$

$$\text{or}\quad S = \frac{\overline{x}}{\sigma + 0.01\ \overline{x}}.$$

When $V = 1$ (an unusually low figure), $S = 50$; when $V = 19$ (a typical figure), $S = 5$; and when $V = 39$ (a rather high figure), $S = 1$.

FIGURE 17-9 Greylag goose, *Anser anser,* retrieves an egg that has rolled from its nest. (After N. Tinbergen, 1951)

tally absent. The evidence for such *vacuum activities* is slight, and mostly anecdotal; but R. A. Hinde (1958) mentions relevant observations on 16 female canaries, *Serina canaria,* in the breeding state. The birds were observed when entirely without nest material; and they are described as going through all the motions of nest building, including movements as if searching for material, and scrabbling, pulling material into a nest pan, and wiping with the beak.

For a complex species-typical sequence that has been minutely analyzed, we return to the smooth newt. T. R. Halliday (1975) observed no vacuum activity; but he does describe stereotyped behavior directed at inappropriate objects. The sexual conduct of male newts can be induced by injecting the pituitary hormone prolactin (9.3.7; 9.4). Males so treated and isolated from females sometimes displayed toward other males, or even snails or stones.

One of Halliday's main objectives was to distinguish between (1) acts, performed by males, caused by stimuli from the female, and (2) acts that seem to depend on what the male himself has just done. He found examples of both. The dropping of a spermatophore occurs only in response to a female's contact with the male's tail. A less precise relationship is shown by the display that includes whipping and fanning of the tail (figure

17-6): this variable performance depends on the presence of a stationary female but not (evidently) on any more specific stimulation from the female. Similarly, a male stops displaying to creep away only after prolonged response of a female to his display; but there seems to be no special act by the female that induces creeping; and the duration of the interaction that precedes creeping varies greatly. These are, then, diverse examples of the control of behavior by external stimulation.

But some elements of the male's conduct appear to be independent of what the female does. The violent whipping of the tail follows after a male has moved in front of the female, regardless of the external situation. Similarly, when he has deposited a spermatophore, the male moves forward and then stops, without further provocation.

A further peculiarity of the newt's courtship is relevant to the notion, discussed above (17.1), of the consummatory act or state. The act of depositing a spermatophore might be expected to lead to a consummatory state, that is (by definition), to a long period during which no further sexual activity occurs. But, as we know, when a male first achieves such a consummation, he often immediately repeats the sequence. Moreover, as Halliday shows, repetition occurs with equal probability regardless of whether the previous sequence has achieved insemination (transfer of the spermatophore).

The one species, *Triturus vulgaris,* illustrates, then, a variety of possible relationships to be found when we scrutinize closely a particular, complex "fixed" action pattern.

17.2.4.4 Architectural Chains?
There is, however, still the possibility that some complex sequences consist of links that form an unbreakable chain. The expression, chain reflexes, has been used to refer to some behavior. Examples come

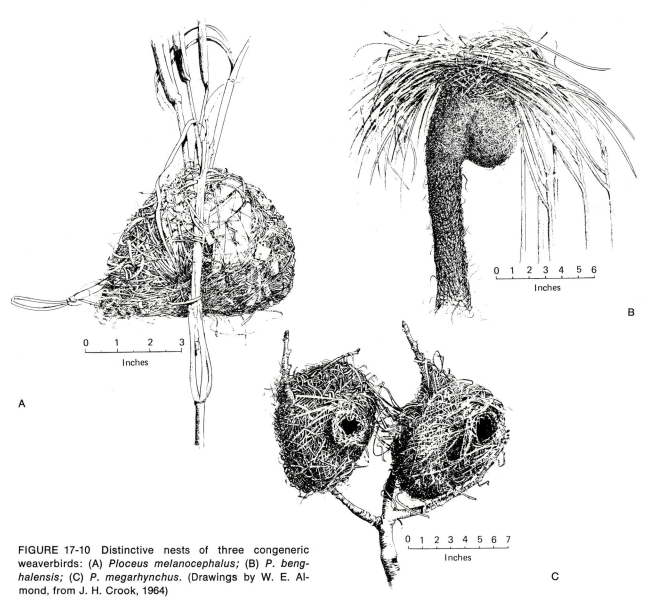

FIGURE 17-10 Distinctive nests of three congeneric weaverbirds: (A) *Ploceus melanocephalus;* (B) *P. benghalensis;* (C) *P. megarhynchus.* (Drawings by W. E. Almond, from J. H. Crook, 1964)

from the constructional activities referred to by Charles Darwin (1859) as architectural instincts.

Figures 17-10 through 22 illustrate the variety of the structures made by animals. Each is species-typical. Each, in fact, constitutes a "fixed" pattern. That is, it belongs to a class of objects distinct from other, similar classes: a spider's web is sometimes recognizable as belonging to a particular spe-

FIGURE 17-11 Two distinctive kinds of hole. Above, that of a wombat, *Vombatus vombatus,* in New South Wales; the maximum diameter is about 1.3 m. (Courtesy J. C. McIlroy) Below, that of an Indian bandicoot rat, *Bandicota bengalensis,* in a rice field in South India; the maximum diameter is about 10 cm. (S. A. Barnett)

cies and no other; the same applies to the nests of many birds, and sometimes even to burrows. Karl & Otto von Frisch have described many examples in a beautiful but incompletely documented book.

When human beings construct something—say, a tool or a shelter—there may be much variation in how they do so, even when the end products are a series of (almost) identical objects. Errors are commonly corrected, and the maker is expected to show an intelligent adaptation to varying conditions. To what extent are the constructional movements of animals similarly adaptable? On the simplest assumption, we should expect such movements to be uniform and therefore highly predictable from one occasion to another, and one individual to another.

Figure 17-12 shows a spider's web in which insects are trapped. The entangled prey is quickly wrapped and bitten. The body is then injected with digestive fluids, and the contents are sucked out.

Figure 17-13 shows how orb-web spiders build. The elaborate structure, mechanically sound though apparently flimsy, might suggest that intelligence has been at work. But the behavior of spiders is not very adaptable. Web building by spiders provides in fact excellent examples of complex end products produced by highly stereotyped behavior. The webs of members of a given species are all of the same construction, with only minor individual modifications imposed partly by the objects to which they are attached.

Another group of builders are the caddis flies (Trichoptera). The larvae live in freshwater and protect themselves with elegantly built, species-typical tubes. If the tube of a larva is removed, and suitable material is available, the larva can be studied while it constructs a new one. It first usually makes a rather crude tube; this usually takes only a few hours. Later a more elaborate structure is added, and the provisional portion is eventually

FIGURE 17-12 Web of an orb-web spider, *Metepeira crassipes,* dusted with cornflour to make it easily seen. (Courtesy H. W. Levi)

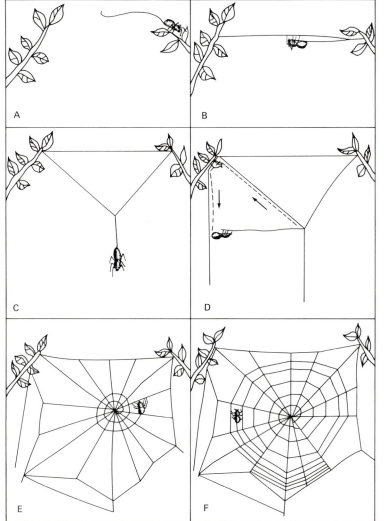

FIGURE 17-13 Web building by an orb-weaving spider; all such webs are made in the same way. (A) Wind or a convection current carries a floating line to an anchorage. (If a line fails to make a bridge, it is retrieved and eaten.) (B) The bridge is strengthened. (C) and (D) radii are made. (E) A temporary spiral is made of widely spaced lines. (F) The definitive spiral is made. (After H. W. Levi, 1978)

cut off. Figure 17-14 illustrates a species studied experimentally by Dorothy Merrill. She removed certain sensory structures from the hind ends of larvae; these included anal hooks and sensilla. As a result, there was an increase in case building, and consequently a greatly lengthened case: the larvae of one species made cases three times as long as their usual covering. The hind end of a larva is the last to be covered. Evidently, normal building ceases when stimuli are received from a newly built case which covers the posterior end.

Such an experimental analysis can give the impression that case building is mechanical and unadaptable. But G. Fankhauser & L. E. Reik re-

FIGURE 17-14 The larva and case of a caddis fly, *Ptilostomis semifasciata.* (Courtesy D. Merrill)

moved larvae of *Neuronia postica* from their cases, and offered them a variety of materials. The usual structure is of rectangular fragments of leaves or grass blades arranged in rings; but typical cases were built when the only materials available were onion skin or even cellophane; and nearly typical cases were made of paper. Some novel combinations were achieved: pine needles and sand, neither of which is used as a rule, were together made into cases. When only tinfoil, oatmeal or barley were offered, cases were still built, but they were crude.

Such observations show substantial adaptability in the use of materials. M. H. Hansell describes an example of behavior adapted to repairing damage. *Lepidostoma hirtum,* in its fifth instar, makes a tube, square in cross section, of rectangular leaf panels (figure 17-15A). The panels of one side are out of phase with those of the two adjacent sides: hence the seams that join the panels in one row are between those of the adjoining rows. The panels, however, vary to some extent in length: regularity

is not complete. This arrangement is thought to confer mechanical stability on the tube. Hansell trimmed off the ends of such tubes, so that the cut ends of the sides were level (figure 17-15B). The question was whether the larvae would restore the staggered arrangement of the panels. In fact, they did so by making some panels longer than usual. Damage was also followed by a higher rate of building. Caddis fly cases, then, represent species-typical patterns; but the behavior of the larvae that make them can be to some extent adapted to unusual circumstances.

The same applies to the structures created by the potter or mason wasps (Eumenidae). In 8.1.1.1 I mention the digger wasps that make holes in the ground. The mason wasps instead construct nests of clay, attached to trees or other objects. The female takes pellets from clay soil, first moistened (if necessary) with water brought to the site in her stomach. The pellets are carried to a building site, flattened, and made into a bottle-like structure.

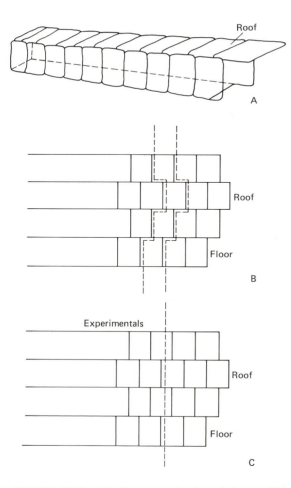

FIGURE 17-15 (A) Diagram of tube of the caddis fly, *Lepidostoma hirtum*, to show the arrangement of the panels; the front is on the right. (B) Diagram of the front of a tube to show the amount removed from the tubes of control animals: some had two rings removed, others, three. (C) as (B), but the line shows the amount of tube removed from the experimental animals. (After M. H. Hansell, 1974)

The bottle is next stocked with the paralyzed larvae of beetles (Coleoptera) or of Lepidoptera. An egg is laid; and, when the larva hatches, it has a large stock of food on which to feed.

R. W. G. Hingston describes in great detail the behavior of *Eumenes conica*, an Indian species. This solitary wasp builds groups of clay cells. Once the cells are fully stocked and the eggs are laid, each is closed with a lid; and the whole group is covered with clay. If a hole is made in a cell, the wasp may for some time continue to stock the cell; and a paralyzed larva may even fall through the gap. Eventually, when the larvae have all been put in, the wasp explores the hole and pushes any larva back that happens to be sticking out. She then gets more clay and repairs the damage. In this behavior, then, there is more than a single fixed sequence. Evidently, part of the wasp's total repertoire of behavior patterns is to investigate the whole group of cells before they are finally closed, covered, and left. If a defect is found, it is remedied.

Hingston's observations are those of a percipient naturalist, who worked before ethology existed as a distinct discipline. I now describe two studies of wasps made in the modern period, one descriptive but highly quantitative, the other experimental. Helen Spurway and others recorded nearly every visit to the nest of a female *Sceliphron madraspatanum* observed in West Bengal. The female took 14 days to build and stock a nest of 10 cells. There were about 980 visits; mud was brought on about 80% of these. Prey used to stock the cells included spiders (Araneida) and flies (Diptera). On about 10% of visits there was no load; these (exploratory?) visits included the first visit of the day, and others made after an absence of 1 h or longer. This paper is an example of minutely detailed, biometrical observation.

The second is the work of A. P. Smith, who experimented on an Australian eumenid of the genus, *Paralastor*. (When he published his observations, the species had not been named.) The nest consists of two to five underground cells; but above ground

FIGURE 17-16 An eumenid wasp, *Paralastor,* at the funnel of its underground nest. (Courtesy A. P. Smith)

The funnel is made of mud pellets in much the same way as other eumenids make their nests of clay. The "brick laying" is by a regular sequence: the wasp arrives with its pellet, and holds on to the edge of the funnel with four posterior legs. The pellet, held by the forelegs, is passed to the mandibles, and by them to the edge of the funnel. The funnel is of a standard size and shape. When it is complete, an egg is laid; and the cells are then stocked with food. The nest is sealed at ground level; and finally the funnel is destroyed. The whole process can be completed in a day.

Smith interfered with this pattern in several ways. (1) Funnels that were nearly complete were partly destroyed. The wasps rebuilt them. One wasp rebuilt its funnel seven times. (2) When some funnel stems had been built to about a height of 20 mm, the ground level was raised with a layer of 15 mm of soil. The wasps duly extended the stems to the standard height above ground level. (There is individual variation in funnel height. When a stem is damaged, the wasp rebuilds close to the original height.) (3) Holes made in the

there is also a complex funnel (figure 17-16) through which the wasp enters while stocking the nest with food for the developing larva (figure 17-17). The function of this structure is probably to keep out parasitic wasps of the family, Chrysididae.

FIGURE 17-17 Drawing of the nest, stocked with food, of *Paralastor* (see previous figure). (Courtesy A. P. Smith)

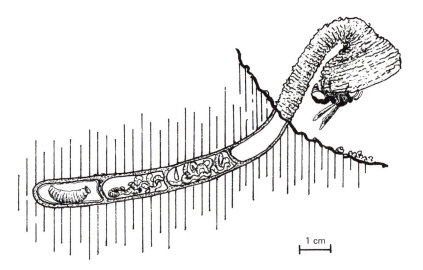

1 cm

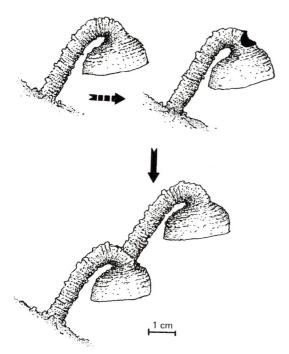

FIGURE 17-18 Funnels of *Paralastor* (see two previous figures): top left, the intact funnel; top right, with a hole in it; below, the double funnel that resulted from the wasp's response to the damage. (Courtesy A. P. Smith)

stems while funnels were under construction were quickly repaired from inside. (4) Holes were also made at the distal ends of some stems; these could not be repaired from inside, owing to the slippery inner surface of the funnels. Instead, a new funnel was made on top of the first (figures 17-18 and 17-19). (5) While the wasps were absent, Smith quickly lengthened certain funnels; hence on return a wasp was faced with a funnel at a more advanced stage than when she left. Two of the wasps on their return "examined the new 'instant' funnel briefly inside and outside and then continued construction of the funnels".

On the evidence of these experiments, building by *Paralastor* is not a "reflex chain": that is, it is not an unalterable sequence like that of a machine which, when switched on, goes through a predetermined sequence. Instead, it is a series of elaborate responses to particular situations. The responses usually occur in a standard order but, as the experiments show, they need not do so. When building has begun, the wasp's behavior is determined by the properties, at each stage, of the ex-

FIGURE 17-19 Double funnel of *Paralastor* (see previous figure) with its maker (Courtesy A. P. Smith)

isting construction. The repertoire of responses, like that of the Indian wasps studied by Hingston, includes regular inspection of the structure and the ability to repair holes. When a hole could not be repaired from inside, mud was always applied to the hole from outside. The behavior is then the same as that observed when a funnel begins to be built around the hole in the ground leading to the nest. Hence a new complete funnel is built, and a double funnel results.

As a final example of building, I take the observations of N. E. & E. C. Collias (1962) on the African village weaverbird, *Textor (Ploceus) cucullatus*. Figures 17-20 and 21 illustrate nests of such birds, and figure 17-22 shows the normal sequence of building. By damaging nests under construction, these authors found building at each stage to depend on the stimuli provided by the partly completed nest. The complete nest-building performance is, however, also influenced by practice: to some extent, weaverbirds learn to build.

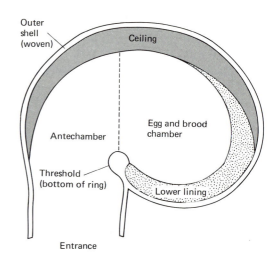

FIGURE 17-21 Diagram of the construction of the nest of a weaverbird (see figure 17-20). (After N. E. & E. C. Collias, 1962)

FIGURE 17-22 Stages in the construction of the nest of a weaverbird (see figures 17-20 and 17-21). (After N. E. & E. C. Collias, 1962)

FIGURE 17-20 Nest of a weaverbird, *Textor cucullatus*. (Courtesy N. E. Collias)

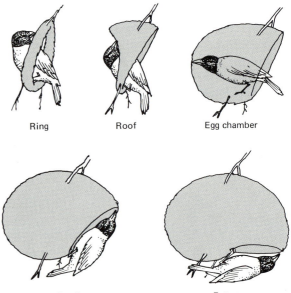

The building activities of animals have a special impact on human observers. We, too, make things; and, when we do, we can state in advance what is intended. There is a plan, perhaps only in our heads, of the final product. To what extent, and in what sense, may we say the same of animal builders? W. H. Thorpe (1963) suggests that a bird building a nest "must have some 'conception' of what the completed nest should look like"; and that even a wasp is working toward an "ideal" situation. The studies described in the preceding paragraphs do not support this notion. The behavior is often adaptable: spiders, insects, and birds may repair damage and adapt their behavior in other ways; but, at each stage of building, the behavior seems to be a response to the situation presented at the time. If *Paralastor* were working toward an idea, it would not build a double funnel (figures 17-18, 19). There is therefore no need to assume from the evidence of nest building, that wasps or even birds are capable, in any sense, of concept formation. Their behavior is, in any case, sufficiently remarkable without that.

17.2.5 The "Innate Releasing Mechanism"

A counterpart of the notion of a fixed action pattern is that of the "innate releasing mechanism" (IRM). This expression, originally used by J. von Uexküll, alludes to two aspects of "instinctive" behavior: first is the standard external stimulus, which is called a releaser; second, there is the internal organization that insures a standard response (W. M. Schleidt, 1962). Predators, for instance, may respond in a standard fashion to prey or prey-like objects (3.2.4); and there are many examples in the chapters on social conduct (part IV). The expression IRM has accordingly had much currency, yet it has almost gone out of use; and we must now see why.

1. In early writings the concept had both evolutionary and teleological components: a "releaser" was defined as "the means evolved for the sending out of key stimuli" (K. Z. Lorenz, 1935; N. Tinbergen, 1953), as if the evolutionary process somehow entailed foreknowledge of an objective. Moreover, the definition implies that a structure or activity may be called a releaser only if we know how it evolved—which is never possible (J. B. S. Haldane & H. Spurway).

2. There is next the adjective "innate". This word, when it has an intelligible meaning, refers to highly predictable behavior: the predictability arises from the stability of the behavior in individual development (17.1). The idea of behavior as innate (or inborn) is, however, misleading: behavior develops, and there are always sources of variation in the environment (chapter 12).

3. The notion of a releaser, or releasing stimulus, may be criticized on several grounds. (a) Stimuli that have specific effects on behavior are often inhibitory. In the preceding section we saw that when a nest or web is complete, the animal stops building, evidently in response to the finished structure. Similarly, a social signal may inhibit approach or prevent an animal from eating its young. (b) A specific stimulus may also have the highly predictable effect of determining the direction of movement of an animal (17.2.1), not of releasing (or inhibiting) activity. (c) The original notion of a releaser implied that certain stimuli have a single effect on the behavior of an animal; but a stimulus that evokes a particular response on one occasion may elicit another at some other time. A male honey bee, or drone, is usually fed by the workers; but in autumn he may be stung to death. A con-

specific may be attacked at one time, courted at another. An object may be eaten or used for nest building.

4. Lastly, there is the question of "mechanism". The expression IRM suggests an attempt at physiological analysis; but in fact, just as we found with the early concept of drive, there is no physiological counterpart of an IRM. The most general criticism of the IRM concept is, in fact, that it provides a seemingly convenient catch phrase, but explains nothing. Here are two examples—one of ground-living birds and one of the laughing gull—that give empirical ground for these criticisms.

The first is illustrated in figure 17-23. If a hawk flies overhead, ground-living birds run for cover.

FIGURE 17-23 Silhouettes of some of the models used to test the response of ground-living birds: + indicates that the model made birds run for cover. (After N. Tinbergen, 1951)

The figure illustrates models that evoked this response if flown over young turkeys, *Meleagris gallopavo*. But, to have this effect, they had to be moved with the short projection in front: they then simulated a hawk with its short neck. A model moved with the long projection in front more nearly resembles a goose; and to this "goose model" the young turkeys did not respond. Accordingly, a hawk-shaped object moving overhead was said to be a releaser for flight or taking cover; and the response was said to depend on an IRM.

In more detailed experiments W. M. Schleidt (1961) observed the effects not only of a hawk-shaped model but also of a circle, a long rectangle, and one resembling an aircraft. On first exposure, young turkeys responded to all models with the alarm response; but the effect was much less when the models were presented the next day. In general, there was a decline in the response in proportion to the number of presentations. This is an example of habituation (5.2). It is supposed that, in natural conditions, hawks are comparatively rare birds, and that young ground-living birds are therefore unlikely to habituate to them; but they do so to the shapes of other kinds of birds. The findings from the original experiments are explained by the unfamiliarity of the hawk-like stimulus, and not by the specific pattern that it presented. Hence there is no evidence, in this case, for a narrowly defined releasing stimulus for taking cover; and there is no ground for assuming the existence of a fixed internal "releasing mechanism". Here is a good example of the importance of studying the ontogeny of behavior in detail.

The other example is provided by the work of J. P. Hailman (1967) on the laughing gull, *Larus atricilla*. Gulls of this species have black heads and red bills. The parent bird, like the herring gull (9.3.6), regurgitates food on to the ground in response to pecking by the chick. It also moves its bill rapidly from side to side. If the chick fails to eat, the food is picked up again; and if it is still not eaten, it is economically reswallowed. (Another consequence of reswallowing is that nothing is left that might catch the eye of a predator.)

Chicks were tested after incubation. Initially they pecked at a variety of models (figure 17-24). Some laughing gull chicks were tested with herring gull models, and vice versa: each pecked just as much at models of the other species as at their own; there was, however, much individual variation. If models were kept in lateral motion to simulate the movements of a parent, more pecking occurred

FIGURE 17-24 Chicks of the laughing gull, *Larus atricilla*, were tested for their response to models of gull heads: inexperienced ("naive") chicks pecked at about an equal rate regardless of the appearance of the model; experienced chicks pecked at the highest rate when offered a model that most closely resembled the parent. Hence the species-typical pecking behavior of a chick depends in part on practice. (After J. P. Hailman, 1967)

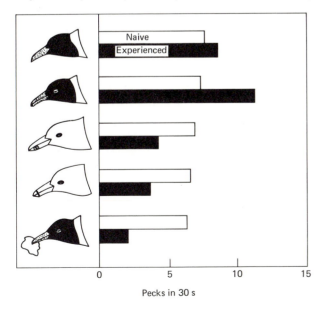

Naive
Experienced

0   5   10   15
Pecks in 30 s

than when they were kept still. Another general finding was of color preferences: chicks not only favored red (as one would expect from the color of the normal bill) but also blue.

Hailman followed the development of pecking. Accuracy improved during the first two days, and so did judgment of distance: at first, pecking movements were sometimes too vigorous and the chick fell over. In addition, the behavior became more discriminating. Chicks came to prefer the stimulus pattern associated with feeding, even when the pattern was that of another species.

Hailman regards these changes as a product of trial and error. He interprets the feeding behavior of gull chicks not as a rigidly determined fixed action pattern, as the earlier workers did, but as a product partly of experience. His observations illustrate an important principle: in natural conditions a gull chick is exposed only to a parent of its own species. The conditions in which it is reared differ very little from those of all other chicks. Hence there is little scope for variation in its responses. If the development of the behavior is merely described, it may seem to be invariable; but experiment may show that substantial variation is possible, in response to environmental differences.

In other words, the "action pattern" is "fixed" only if the conditions of rearing are fixed also. Correspondingly, once again, the notion of an *innate* releasing mechanism is seen to be misleading.

17.3 ONTOGENY AND ENVIRONMENT

17.3.1 Preformation or Epigenesis

I now enlarge on the importance of studying how behavior develops (9.4.3, chapter 12, and 16.2.2). In the beginning of modern embryology there was a debate between "preformationists" and "epigeneticists" (reviewed by Joseph Needham). The preformationists held embryological development to be an unfolding of a preexisting pattern; some early microscopists even said they could see a homunculus in each spermatozoon (F. J. Cole). Today, an epigenetic interpretation is universal among developmental biologists. Such an interpretation is not the opposite of preformationism: it does not state that what an embryo becomes depends solely on the environment—which would be obvious nonsense; instead ontogeny is seen as a process in which the growing organism is continually interacting with its environment. But in the recent history of ethology there have remained some traces of a modified preformationism.

The traditional concept of instinct implies that some behavior patterns are virtually unalterable. In modern terms, the assumption (not usually explicit) is of a fixed relationship between genotype and phenotype: if the cistrons are known, all is known. But what we *know* is that the patterns are species-typical and highly predictable. This is a description: it tells us nothing about the dynamics of development. Earlier in this chapter and in chapter 12 there are examples of species-typical behavior which, on experimental analysis, proves to be labile in development; and, as experimental studies become more diverse, more sources of lability are revealed.

Usually, lability is found by examining the differing responses of developing animals to external stimuli, such as those presented by a parent. But variation even in the internal environment can profoundly affect development. It is possible to make chimaeras, or composite animals, of which the cells come from two (or more) fertilized eggs (reviewed by Anne McLaren). If a chimaera is derived from the fusion of one female (XX) egg and one male (XY), then a "male" germ cell can develop in an ovary, and a "female" germ cell in a testis. When

this happens in amphibians, germ cells in an ovary develop into ova, *regardless of their primary sex*. Moreover, E. P. Evans and his colleagues have also described XX/XY chimaeric female mice that were fertile. Some of the cells that developed into oocytes in the ovaries of these females proved to be genetically male; that is, they carried a Y chromosome, whereas all normal oocytes carry an X chromosome. The obverse, however, is not observed: XX cells in a testis do not give rise to spermatozoa. Here once again, we have different degrees of lability in development. The differentiation of gametes is not, as has been supposed, irrevocably determined by their chromosomes. The internal environment, provided by the gonad in which the germ cell develops, evidently has a sex-determining function.

This finding illustrates the inappropriateness of a preformationist attitude. It also shows that the interaction with the environment of the developing organism begins even before fertilization.

17.3.2 Invertebrates

The invertebrates provide many examples of behavior with machine-like features, but they also illustrate some of the ways in which behavioral ontogeny is labile. Locusts usually develop into ordinary, solitary grasshoppers; but in special conditions they become gregarious and swarm. These insects have two principal modes of life; and which set of behavior patterns develops is determined largely by their early social environment (2.3.6.3).

The insects also provide analogs of imprinting. Worker ants, *Formica polyctena,* like other eusocial insects, have an elaborate system of caring for the larvae and pupae (9.1.2). For a period immediately after emergence, P. Jaisson deprived workers of access to pupae. These workers were later unable to perform their normal nursing function. For the first 15 days after emergence other workers were allowed to care for pupae only of other species. When, after this, they were given pupae of their own species, they did not care for them but ate them. Jaisson therefore describes the first 15 days after emergence as a sensitive period for the development of this behavior (12.1).

The ontogeny of feeding behavior has also been studied. Tibor Jermy and others describe experiments on the food preferences of the tobacco hornworm, *Manduca sexta,* and the corn earworm, *Heliothis zea.* Both feed on a variety of plants, and both are pests. Larvae were first fed on an artificial diet, and then on the leaves of one host species. After this they were given a choice between the plant already experienced and others known to be eaten by their species. They regularly preferred the familiar food. Such preferences were observed after only one day of "training"; and the preference persisted during periods of further feeding on an artificial diet, and after the interruption of two larval molts. Evidently, experience of a particular food induces a lasting storage of information in the central nervous system.

An interesting question is whether there is any effect of early feeding on the choice of plant made by the adult when laying eggs. Jermy and his colleagues find no evidence of such an effect. But much earlier work had brought evidence of "preimaginal conditioning" (W. H. Thorpe & F. G. W. Jones; Thorpe, 1938, 1939). An ichneumonid, *Nemeritis canescens,* lays its eggs in the larvae of the Mediterranean flour moth, *Ephestia kühniella.* (The latter is a widespread pest.) The ichneumonid detects the host larvae by odor and usually responds only to the one host species. Thorpe & Jones, however, were able experimentally to rear the ichneumonid larvae on the larvae of other species, such as the small wax moth, *Meliphora gri-*

sella. Some of the adult females, tested in an olfactometer after such treatment, then responded to the odor of wax moth larvae. A similar effect was obtained when adult ichenumonids were exposed to wax moth odor just after emergence.

The exact interpretation of these findings is uncertain. At first it seemed that a response to a hitherto ineffective odor had been induced by early exposure. But analogous experiments by Aubrey Manning (1967), on *Drosophila,* suggest an alternative. Manning tested the hypothesis of "preimaginal conditioning" by rearing the larvae of fruit flies, for eight generations, on a food mixture that contained an odorous substance, geraniol; a control line was kept on the same medium but without geraniol. The adult flies were tested, in each generation, as were Thorpe's ichneumonids, in an olfactometer. Given a choice between geraniol and no odor, 88% of the controls avoided the oil: that is, they were repelled by it. Moreover, they could not be trained to approach the odor by associating it with food reward. But the experimental flies were not repelled. Manning's interpretation is that the experimental treatment resulted in habituation to the odor. The same may apply to the ichneumonids; but this is not established. Perhaps two processes, one of induction of a response to an odor and the other of habituation, are involved. Whatever the answer, the responses of both species to odors were altered by early experience. The responses were therefore not "instinctive", in the same sense of irrevocably fixed.

17.3.3 Locomotion of Embryos

In early ethological writings, it was usual to classify all behavior patterns in two classes, the innate (or instinctive) and the learned. Such a classification implies that, if there is individual variation in behavior, then that variation must be due to "learning". But the examples of experimental analysis, given in the preceding section and elsewhere, reveal many environmental sources of variation. Hence, when we examine the ontogeny of behavior, we have to treat behavior as an embryologist does the differentiation of structures and try to examine all the environmental factors acting on the developing animal.

As an example, locomotor movements are species-typical, and develop, in ordinary conditions, with great regularity. Moreover, there is an element of "spontaneity" or "autonomy" about them: that is, movements begin without any evident external stimulation; and, as experiment has shown, some neural connections are very stable in development. Hence some features of early development seem to conform with the original concept of "innate" behavior. For reviews, consult G. Gottlieb (1976a,b), V. Hamburger (1963, 1971) and J. E. Harris.

A vertebrate embryo usually begins to move long before hatching or birth. The first movements are due to contractions of the segmental muscles (myotomes) and may occur before the muscles are innervated: that is, like the first contractions of the heart, they are *myogenic*. Embryos of the domestic fowl, *Gallus*, develop rhythmic trunk movements, but become responsive to stimulation from the sense organs only after 17 days of incubation. The functional significance of these movements has been much discussed. D. B. Brachman & L. Sokoloff prevented all such movement by chick embryos during one or two days early in development. Their methods included the use of a drug and of a poisonous substance. The result was atrophy of the muscles and a fusion or ankylosis of the limb joints, with a consequent inability to move the limbs normally. Similar changes were obtained by injuring the spinal cord. The abnormalities in the joints were shown not to be due to toxic effects or to slowing of growth. Hence in this case normal development, not only of function but of visible structure, depends on muscular contractions.

Similar movements, perhaps of similar importance functionally, are performed by other vertebrates. Early dogfish embryos, *Scyliorhinus caniculus,* display waves of myotomal contractions before they are free swimming; these contractions continue in the absence of the nerve cord (J. E. Harris & H. P. Whiting). Contractions on the two sides are at first independent; when both sides contract together the result is a movement that has been called "shrugging".

Among early studies on the movements of embryos is the much-quoted work of G. E. Coghill on the tiger salamander, *Amblystoma punctatum* (Urodela). Coghill describes the initial rhythmic contractions of the whole trunk and emphasizes that local, reflex responses appear only later. His account conflicts with an alternative view that sees reflexes developing first and coordinated movements later. It is now realized that *Amblystoma* is rather unusual and that even among the Amphibia there is much variation. A toad, *Eleutherodactylus martinicensis* (Bufonidae), is exceptional among the Anura in having no free-living larva (tadpole). Early in development, movements of the trunk, lasting 1 or 2 s, occur; but there are no fully developed swimming movements. About a day later, reflex responses, such as a single movement of the tail, can be provoked by touching the surface of the embryo (A. F. Hughes). In this case the first movements of the limbs accompany the brief movements of the trunk. This type of development is intermediate between that of *Amblystoma* and the type seen in mammals (reviewed by Hughes). In the mammalian embryos that have been studied, reflexes appear first, and more complex, coordinated movements later. In general, as V. Hamburger (1963) points out, "spontaneous" movements and local reflexes are both seen in all vertebrate embryos, and seem to be independent of each other. Usually, the "spontaneous" movements appear first.

Given a minimum of structural development, any vertebrate embryo begins to make incomplete movements. (Among them are those of the quickening of a human infant.) Superficially, it looks as though the embryo is gradually acquiring coordinated locomotor movements by practice. An alternative is that the movements of swimming or walking appear independently of practice, by a process vaguely called maturation. This hypothesis has been experimentally tested. L. Carmichael, like Coghill, used *Amblystoma punctatum*. The developing eggs were kept in water containing an anesthetic, chloretone, which prevented all movement by the hatched larvae. Ordinarily, the larvae gradually develop the ability to swim, after several stages of incomplete swimming movements. The experimental larvae were transferred to plain water at an age at which swimming is usually performed as a complete movement. As soon as they recovered from the anesthetic, they swam normally, like the controls that had been reared in plain water all the time. Here is support for the notion of maturation of swimming without practice; but Carmichael himself cautiously declined to draw any far-reaching conclusion.

17.3.4 Development of the Visual System

The notion of development as an unfolding of predetermined pattern has had some support from studies of the nervous system (reviewed by Richard Mark; J. B. Messenger, 1974; and by R. L. Meyer & R. W. Sperry). In normal animals the structural relationships between sense organs, the central nervous system, and the effector organs are uniform throughout each species. But these relationships can be altered experimentally, rather as if electronic equipment were being rewired.

The retina of the amphibian eye has a topological representation in the optic tectum of the brain: that is, there is point-for-point representation of the retina, just as there is a representation of a piece of ground on a detailed map. If the optic tract is cut, the axons distal to the cut degenerate; but the proximal portions grow out again, and normal function is restored. In some experiments the eye is rotated through 180° before regeneration occurs. Again the correct connections are restored: the axons reestablish their former relationships (figure 17-25). But the input from the eye to the brain now gives incorrect information: for exam-

FIGURE 17-25 Diagrams to illustrate the effect of inverting the eye of an amphibian: in each figure, the large arrow at the top represents an object in the animal's visual field; on the left, the representation of the arrow in the optic lobe of the brain is shown in its normal orientation. On the right, the left eye has been rotated through 180°: the nasal or front part of the eye (N) is now at the back and the temporal or rear part (T) in front. The input to the optic lobe is correspondingly inverted. The curved arrow in each figure indicates the representation of the visible object on the retina. (After Richard Mark, 1974)

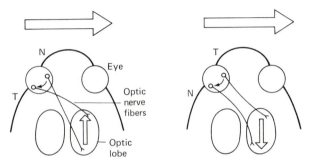

ple, light reflected by an object above the animal stimulates a region of the retina which previously received information about objects below, and the whole of the input from the eye to the brain is upside down. The movements of an animal with eyes treated in this way are correspondingly incorrect. And they remain incorrect indefinitely: the animal does not adapt its behavior to the new situation. It is, however, possible to repeat the operation, and to restore the eye to its proper position. After further regeneration of the optic tract, behavior returns to normal.

The most notable examples of different degrees of lability in development come from studies of mammals. I first mention some celebrated observations on human beings. Some people are blind, or have defective vision, owing to cataract. The condition may be present at birth. Early in this century it became possible to treat such blindness surgically, and so to restore or confer vision on a previously blind person. A number of adults have been treated (L. Ganz; R. L. Gregory & J. G. Wallace; M. von Senden; Alberto Valvo).

It might be supposed that, after recovery from the operation, a patient would immediately be able to "see"; and it had been assumed by psychologists that human beings have an "innate" ability to distinguish at least simple shapes, for instance, squares from circles. Even a quite young child can make such distinctions without effort. But in fact an adult who is blind from birth—and therefore completely without experience of seeing—after acquiring sight reports at first only a confusing mass of lights and colors. No object, however familiar by touch or odor, can be identified visually. To distinguish a square from a triangle, the subject has to learn to count the corners; and what is learned on one day is forgotten by the next—a disheartening experience for an intelligent adult. If the names of colors have

been learned, and the subject is shown an orange, the color may at once be named; but the object cannot be identified as an orange until it is touched. We readily recognize familiar objects, even when their exact appearance varies with distance and the angle at which they are seen. An adult learning to see quite lacks this *perceptual generalization*. A man who had learned to name a square, made of white cardboard, failed to identify it when the other side, painted yellow, was shown.

One implication is that in early childhood we learn gradually to recognize objects, but later forget that we have been obliged to do so. Another possibility (which does not exclude the first) is that, in the absence of use, neural structures degenerate.

These questions have been investigated by experiments on animals (reviewed by R. C. Tees). Many methods have been used to control the visual input of newborn mammals. (1) They include rearing in darkness during the first postnatal weeks, but this can undoubtedly lead to degeneration of cells in the visual area of the cerebral cortex. (2) Another method is to prevent any *patterned* input reaching the retinae, by the use of translucent head lobes or contact lenses. If chimpanzees are treated in this way for their first 18 months, there is irreversible loss of the ability to discriminate patterns. Much shorter periods result in a temporary loss; but this is rapidly restored. Similar observations have been made on macaques and rats. (3) Notable findings result from restricting kittens to certain kinds of visual input. They are prevented from seeing their own bodies by a wide, black collar round their necks. Colin Blakemore & G. F. Cooper allowed kittens, during their first five months, to see only horizontally *or* vertically striped objects. When they were put in a normal environment, the kittens were at first "visually inept": they guided themselves by touch, and were disturbed on coming to the edge of a table where they might fall. There was, however, a rapid improvement. Nonetheless, some defects were permanent. Moving objects were followed "with clumsy, jerky head movements"; judgment of distance was poor, and there were often collisions with objects.

The most remarkable observations were on the inability of these animals to respond to contours at right angles to those they had experienced during their first months. In some experiments, two kittens were observed, of which one had seen only horizontal lines, the other only vertical. They were tested with a black or a white rod. When the rod was vertical, one kitten played with it but the other ignored it; but when it was horizontal, the roles of the two kittens were reversed. Evidently the kittens were blind to contours perpendicular to those previously experienced.

Hence it is now not doubted that we to some extent "learn to see" during infancy and early childhood. The same applies to other species. In previous chapters I give other examples of the importance of complex stimulation, early in postnatal life, for the development of function (8.1.4.2; 16.2.2).

To these I add one further example of the development of behavior that depends on vision. R. C. Tees reviews the depth perception of mammals. When a young mammal becomes active, and encounters anything like a cliff, it rarely falls off. Hence we have the phenomenon called *cliff-drop aversion*. A variety of species, from mice to men, have been tested on a "visual cliff" (figure 17-26). Infant mammals (and recently hatched birds) avoid an apparent cliff on first exposure to it. This is not surprising: if one fall can be fatal, the ability to avoid it needs to develop reliably in advance of experience. Nonetheless, the development of this ability can be modified. Laboratory rats reared in

FIGURE 17-26 Brinkmanship by a young house mouse, *Mus musculus,* at a visual cliff. (I. A. Fox)

the dark for their first 20 days can still discriminate an apparent fall of 20 cm from no fall, as can controls reared in a normal amount of light. But after that age, animals reared in the light improve their discrimination of depth, while the dark-reared rats deteriorate. We know that visual experience is needed to maintain the structure of the nervous system; in this case it is thought also to enhance the discrimination both of motion and of depth.

Once again, we see the inadequacy of the simple alternatives, innate (instinctive) or acquired (learned). The development of the visual system, and of the behavior that depends on it, includes many processes, some more, some less labile in development. Only piecemeal analysis can expose the conditions necessary for normal function.

17.3.5 The Social Interactions of Eggs

In 12.2.2.5 I describe how some birds learn to distinguish the calls of their own parents before hatching. Other social interactions of unhatched birds have been observed. The work of M. A. Vince (reviewed in 1973) examines the synchronized hatching of certain species. The bobwhite quail, *Colinus virginianus,* has a large clutch; the young birds are precocial (figure 12-16); and the female leads them from the nest soon after they hatch. Hence synchrony of hatching is important. The chicks usually hatch on the 23rd day of incubation. About two days earlier the chicks begin to use their lungs for respiration, and air is admitted through a small hole in the shell. Around the same time each begins to make a clicking noise at the rate of about 80 to 150/min.

In normal conditions in a nest, with the eggs in contact, the noise can be transmitted from one to another. Some eggs were therefore put in an incubator in contact, while others were incubated in the same conditions but separated. Those in contact hatched within a few minutes of each other, but the hatching of the others was spread over periods of up to nearly 50 h. Moreover, hatching can be accelerated by exposing eggs to clicking at certain rates.

When the clutch of a precocial species is soon to hatch, the female regularly utters her attraction call, that is, the sound she makes when, later, she leads her young on the march. Among such species are various waterfowl, such as ducks (Anatidae), turkeys, *Meleagris,* and the domestic fowl, *Gallus.* Gilbert Gottlieb (1971) has described experiments on the effects of such parental stimulation on the Peking duck, a domestic variety of the mallard, *Anas platyrhynchos.* He first observed behavior during the first two days after hatching. Mobile models were used to induce the following response (12.3.1). Some of the models were silent; others gave the species-typical call. Gottlieb

also observed the effect of a call by itself. Auditory stimulation was more effective in inducing a response than was visual stimulation. There was also discrimination between the calls of different species: the conspecific call was more effective than others. Similar experiments, with similar results, were carried out on domestic fowl.

Duck embryos also respond to maternal stimulation before hatching. The incubation period is 27 days; and from the 22nd day the call of the female

FIGURE 17-27 Embryo duckling, *Anas platyrhynchos,* wired for the recording of movements in the egg before hatching. (Courtesy Gilbert Gottlieb)

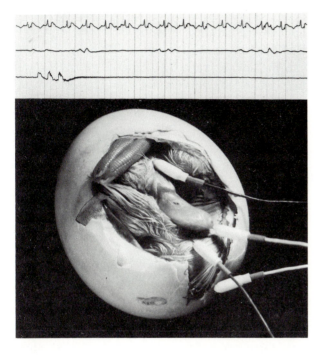

FIGURE 17-28 Embryo (see figure 17-27) wired for recording movement in the egg. Above: top trace shows heart beat; middle trace, bill clapping; bottom trace, three sounds recorded by a microphone. (Courtesy Gilbert Gottlieb)

has an effect on a distinctive movement of the embryo, bill clapping. Gottlieb recorded the responses of embryos electronically (figures 17-27, 17-28). On Days 22 and 23 of incubation the call of the female inhibits bill clapping; but for the last three days the call has an excitatory effect. The embryo is uninfluenced by the calls of other species.

The normal response of the duckling embryo to the maternal call can be accelerated or delayed by varying the amount of noise to which it is exposed from the 21st day of incubation. This finding resembles that of Vince mentioned above; and she

and her colleagues (1976) have also been able to accelerate the patterned movements of the embryos of the domestic fowl by two days by exposing them to a loud clicking noise. Lastly, Gottlieb delayed discrimination of the species-typical call by putting duck eggs in auditory isolation and preventing them from making any sounds themselves.

Hence, again, the earliest forms of social conduct, though normally highly predictable, depend—like visual abilities—on a continual interaction with specific features of the environment. It is therefore inappropriate to label them as instinctive or innate.

17.4 THE END OF INSTINCT

I now sum up the concepts of instinct.

1. First, animals display a great variety of seemingly skilled achievements. Animals find their way to habitats that suit them, cope with special dietary needs, make nests and other structures, form social groups, and care elaborately for their young. All such performances are species-typical; many consist of intricate sequences of movements that have been called fixed action patterns. The patterns are evoked, as a rule, by specific signals (social or not), which may act on any sensory modality or on several at once. They are now beginning to be analyzed in minute detail.

a. Some patterns, or some components of patterns, are autonomous: once begun, they continue without provocation. More commonly, each stage in a complex sequence depends on specific stimulation, which may be from a conspecific (in social interactions), from a structure (as in nest building), and so on. The simple notion of a releaser, or releasing stimulus, does not, however, match the complexities of the behavior. A stimulus may provoke an act, or a sequence of acts; it may determine the direction of movement; it may induce general arousal or alertness; or it may be inhibitory—that is, it may prevent any act or only certain particular acts.

b. The stereotyped patterns vary in measurable ways. The variation may be in a feature that can be counted—for example, the number of head bobs by a lizard; or there may be differences of intensity—for example, the height a threatening animal raises itself off the ground. Quantitative differences may reflect the external circumstances of the animal: examples are the nearness of a conspecific or its position in a territory. Or they may depend on the internal state of the performer (sexual maturity, stage in a sexual cycle, period of deprivation of a necessity, and so on).

2. An animal usually develops in standard, species-typical conditions: the parental behavior of a species is itself uniform and also provides uniform conditions of rearing for the young. If the conditions are altered experimentally, apparently fixed patterns often prove to have a variable development. The phenomena of imprinting, and of the learning of song by birds in early life, are the most-studied examples (chapter 12). But there are many others: they include the development of the solitary or swarming conditions of locusts (2.3.6.3) and the acquisition of food preferences by insects (17.3.2) and mammals (4.5.2.5). Lability in the development of behavior is therefore not only an artifact of the laboratory: in nature it sometimes makes animals individually adaptable to circumstances. The extreme of adaptability is that of our own species (15.1; 15.3.4). The traditional concept of innate (or instinctive) behavior implied that some acts are preformed by the evolutionary past of the species. The modern concept is that of

epigenesis: the behavioral phenotype is (like other features) a product of a development in which what is given at fertilization continually interacts with the environment. The extent to which behavior is labile, either in natural conditions or experimentally, has to be found out for each species and each behavior pattern.

3. Hence classifying the characteristics of animals into two categories, (a) genetical (inherited), and (b) environmentally determined (learned and so forth), is not appropriate. The *differences between species* are no doubt largely determined genetically; but this usually cannot be tested because species cannot interbreed (but see 11.2.2.1, 16.1.2.2). Decisive statements on the sources of variation can be made only on the evidence of experiments in which conspecifics of different genotypes are observed in different environments (16.2). Variation, quantitatively analyzed, is then seen to have three components: (a) genetical, (b) environmental, (c) interaction between the first two. Labeling some behavior patterns "genetical" represents a category error. The patterns so classified are uniform within a species because of the stability of their development (in a normal environment): they are distinguished, not by any genetical peculiarity, but by their ontogeny. Ontogenetic analysis is hampered by resort to the traditional concepts of instinctive or innate behavior.

4. The fixity of "instinct" has been attributed to ineradicable urges or drives. Statements about drives are often empty: an animal builds a nest, because it has a nest-building drive. The last six words add nothing to the previous five, *unless* "nest-building drive" can be separately defined in physiological terms. When, however, behavior can be interpreted physiologically, the need for talk about drives disappears: instead, there are state-

ments about the amount of a hormone in the blood, the output of certain neurons, or the activity of a part of the central nervous system that regulates general arousal. References to drives persist in the literature largely because we still know little of the physiology of behavior.

5. Behavior previously attributed to drives often has an evident *function:* it contributes to homeostasis by regulating osmolarity, temperature, the flow of energy through the body, and other features (chapter 4).

6. Lastly, species-typical behavior is assumed to fit a species (or the individuals of which it is composed) to a particular ecological niche: each behavior pattern may be regarded as an "adaptation" for a certain mode of life, and as a product of natural selection. This central feature of biological theory is analyzed in the next chapter.

18

EVOLUTION
AND ETHOLOGY

I know you will be sceptical about this claim that a man can find out anything about life by a journey into the past. I am aware of the stern warning about historians by Lev Tolstoi, . . . that historians are like deaf people who go on answering questions that no one has asked them.

C. M. H. Clark

Two theories of evolution are central in the biological sciences. The first states that all existing organisms have descended in the past from very different forms. This presumption—that evolution has occurred—is no longer seriously debated. The second concerns the means by which the changes of evolution are brought about. The only important attempt to answer this question is the theory of *natural selection*. This theory is usually introduced to students in their first year; yet its definition presents quite severe difficulties, and both biologists and philosophers still argue about it.

18.1 PHYLOGENY AND ORDER

18.1.1 The Evolutionary Framework

Our presumption that species have evolved (never mind how) enables us to understand or to inter-

pret otherwise incomprehensible facts. Examples are familiar from vertebrate embryology. A mammalian embryo has pharyngeal pouches and other structural arrangements, just as if it were about to develop into a fish or a tadpole; it also has a yolk sac, but no yolk. We interpret such structures as vestiges that reflect earlier evolutionary stages.

Vestigial structures are not functionless: they have a role in development, and they may differentiate into important adult organs; but the ancestral function has been lost. Similarly, it is possible to guess that certain behavior patterns reflect the evolutionary past. Here are two examples that make sense only in the context of an evolutionary interpretation.

The balloon flies (Empididae) are small insects with grasping legs and a piercing proboscis. Their principal peculiarity, the balloon, usually falls off when they are captured (E. L. Kessel). The fragile balloon-like structure is secreted by the male. That of *Hilara sartor* has no obvious function, but zoologists who first described these structures suggested that they are aeronautical surf boards. Close study suggested a more convincing hypothesis. Female empids, like the female spiders described in 9.1.1, are not only predatory but also sometimes eat males of their own species. A courting male of some species presents a dead fly to the female, and copulates while she feeds. The males of yet other species cover this bait with a gleaming secretion that in some instances forms a balloon. The balloon of yet other species contains only the dried-up remains of a fly of no nutritional value; and so finally we come to the stage of the empty balloon, which is now evidently a social signal by itself. Such a series of forms can be understood as reflecting an evolutionary sequence. If, however, all species but *H. sartor* were unknown or extinct, the balloon would be baffling indeed. No doubt there are many behavioral and other features, among the more than one million species of animals, of which the origin is likely to remain obscure because the stages that led up to them are not known.

The second example is due to W. Wickler (1962). Some cichlid fish are mouthbrooders (9.2.2): the eggs of such species require no fanning, for the respiratory movements of the parent maintain a water current over them. Moreover, the eggs are protected from predators. We are now concerned with the means by which insemination is insured. Sometimes, the male inseminates the eggs before the female takes them into her mouth. The delay before the eggs are picked up varies: the females of some species of *Tilapia* pick up the eggs very promptly. But the extreme case is that of *Haplochromis burtoni:* the female takes up the eggs immediately, before the male has released his sperm. After the female has sucked up the eggs, the male turns on one side, releases his sperm, and spreads his anal fin. The male has spots on this fin which resemble eggs (figure 18-1). The female sucks at these spots as if they were eggs, and so takes in the sperm, which fertilize the eggs in her mouth.

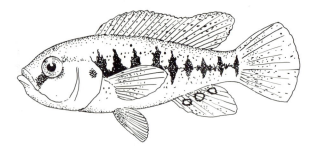

FIGURE 18-1 Egg-like spots on the anal fin of the male *Haplochromis burtoni:* the female, with eggs already in her mouth, sucks at the spots as if they were more eggs and so takes in the sperm released by the male; hence her eggs are inseminated in her mouth. (After W. Wickler, 1962)

Here, then, is another of the bizarre phenomena, found throughout the animal kingdom, of which we can at least imagine the evolutionary stages. All the females of this group respond to their eggs by picking them up, and this species-typical response is evidently evoked by anything with the visible properties of eggs. It resembles in its automatic quality the response of a parent bird that drops or injects food into the gaping mouth of a nestling: the automatic character of such conduct is shown in the response to a nest parasite such as a cuckoo (12.2.2.4); but there the inflexibility of the behavior is maladaptive. In contrast, the response of the female *H. burtoni* to a visible representation of eggs is part of normal reproductive behavior.

18.1.2 The Question of Homology

Systematic accounts of animal groups (families, orders, and so on) are said to be *natural classifications:* that is, they are held to represent evolutionary relationships (reviewed by R. A. Crowson). When our conclusions on phylogeny are based on structures, they can sometimes be tested by examination of fossils. Behavior can occasionally be inferred from the fossil record; but what we *know* about behavior always concerns existing forms. Nonetheless, as I show above, we can sometimes conveniently discuss resemblances and differences between species as if they represented the end branches of a phylogenetic tree. (For further examples, see N. Tinbergen, 1959.) As with structures, similarities may reflect a close relationship; this is evidently the case for the empid flies, which are classified by their anatomy but also resemble each other in behavior. Similarities may, however, also result from convergence. The male empids that offer a fly are behaving like certain spiders (9.1.1); but we take it for granted that the resemblance of the courtship of spiders of the genus, *Pisaura,* to that of *Empis* is due to a separate evolution. A. Petrunkevitch, in a paper published in 1926, gives another example, apparently of convergence, from within the Araneida. His paper is entitled, "The value of instinct as a taxonomic character in spiders". Spiders of the genus *Lycosa* display a form of parental care: the cocoons are carried attached to spinnerets on the abdomen. The same behavior is observed in spiders of other families, including *Bathyphantes* (Linyphiidae) and *Lithyphantes* (Theridiidae). Petrunkevitch refers to the similarities as examples of "adaptive parallelism": evidently, in each family, certain species have independently evolved the same form of parental care, perhaps as a result of occupying similar ecological niches.

In comparative anatomy a distinction is drawn between "analogous" and "homologous" structures. The conventional examples of analogs are taken from structures that have similar functions but differ in their topographical and developmental relationships: the wings of insects and of birds represent an extreme case. Homologs, in contrast, may differ in function and even in adult structure; indeed, they are interesting only when they do so. They are called homologs because their relationships with other structures, at least in embryonic development, are similar. The thyroid gland of a mammal is a two-lobed organ associated with the trachea; the endostyle of the primitive chordate, *Amphioxus,* is in the midline of the floor of the mouth. The two organs, totally dissimilar in the adult, are nonetheless described as homologs. The larva of the jawless vertebrates, such as lampreys (Petromyzontidae), has an endostyle, but this develops into a thyroid gland in the adult. Moreover, in the mammalian early embryo the thyroid begins as an anterior midline structure, and later migrates back and becomes two-lobed. Hence to say that two organs are homologous is to make a statement on a similarity of pattern, especially during development (reviewed by Alan Boyden; and by J. H. Woodger). The concept is an anatomical one: it has no necessary connection with evolution, and indeed it existed before evolution was accepted. A prominent anatomist, Richard Owen (1804–1892), in lectures first published in 1843, defined a "homologue", as "the same organ in different animals under every variety of form and function". Of course, such a definition begs the question of the meaning of "the same"; but, as we have seen, the allusion is to the structural plan.

When Darwin had provided biology with its evolutionary framework, homologs were seen also as having a common phylogeny. And Darwin himself suggested that the concept of homology could be applied to behavioral features, including those of man. In his book, *On the Expression of the Emotions in Animals and Man,* he wrote:

With mankind some expressions, such as the bristling of hair under the influence of extreme terror, or the uncovering of the teeth under that of furious rage, can hardly be understood, except on the belief that man once existed in a much lower and animal-like condition. The community of certain expressions in distinct though allied species, as in the movements of the same facial muscles during laughter by man and by various monkeys, is rendered somewhat more intelligible, if we believe in their descent from a common progenitor. He who admits on general grounds that the structure and habits of all animals have been gradually evolved, will look at the whole subject of Expression in a new and interesting light.

Some ethologists hold that the notion of homology can in fact usefully be applied to behavior (for example, F. McKinney). C. G. Beer (1974), in a critical review, gives an example from the gulls (Laridae), of which a number of species have been studied (13.2.1). In each species, during both apo-treptic behavior and courtship, one of the stereo-typed acts is turning the head to face away from the other bird (figure 18-2). Turning the head away is therefore said to be a homologous act throughout the Laridae. In contrast, similar behavior by cranes (Gruidae) and ducks (Anatidae) is not regarded as homologous to that of the gulls, but only analogous.

It is not difficult to find other examples. Figure 18-3 illustrates a posture in which a rat, *Rattus,* presents its flank to an intruder and raises itself on fully extended legs; this position, combined with raised hair, makes the animal look as large as possible. Several species of *Rattus* adopt a similar posture in similar conditions. We may guess that a common ancestor of these species also behaved in

FIGURE 18-2 Facing away by members of the family Laridae. (A) Pair of lesser black-backed gulls, *Larus fuscus,* (female on left); (B) kittiwake, *Rissa tridactyla,* on cliff; (C) common gull, *L. canus;* (D) Hartlaub's gull, *L. novae-hollandiae,* (male in foreground); (E) black-headed gull, *L. ridibundus.* (After N. Tinbergen, 1959)

this way. Hence on the grounds of pattern and of assumed phylogeny the posture in one species may be called a homolog of that in the others. On the other hand, a flank presentation on stiffened legs by a wolf or a deer, which has an apparently similar function, might be regarded as only an analog. The facial expressions of Primates, as Darwin suggested, also provide opportunities for suggesting homologies; but the bared teeth of a carnivore make perhaps only an analog of the threatening grimace of a macaque.

In each case we observe certain similarities in appearance and in the operation of muscles during the performance of certain acts. There are also similarities of function: the effects of the signals on conspecifics are sometimes much the same in different species; and similar signals may reflect similar internal states of the performers. But to bring in homology adds nothing to this account: it provides no further ordering of information; and, unlike structural homologies, it has no basis in special peculiarities of embryonic development. It may imply a presumption, which cannot be tested, about the evolution of the behavior; but such presumptions lead to no further understanding. As Beer remarks, the concept of behavioral homology is "less rigorous or precise than one is accustomed to demand in science".

18.2 NATURAL SELECTION

18.2.1 Darwin

We now turn to the means by which evolution has been brought about. In every species we find genetically determined variation. If one type is more fertile, or survives longer, than another, then its chances of leaving descendants are likely to be correspondingly greater. Natural selection in this sense has been recognized for millennia; Darwin's origi-

nality was in proposing selective elimination as an agent of *change* (J. B. S. Haldane, 1959). His theory referred to all features of all organisms. On behavior, in the *Origin,* he wrote this:

It will be universally admitted that instincts are as important as corporeal structures for the welfare of each species, under its present conditions of life. Under changed conditions of life, it is at least possible that slight modifications of instinct might be profitable to a species; and if it can be shown that instincts do vary ever so little, then I can see no difficulty in natural selection preserving and continually accumulating variations of instinct to any extent that may be profitable. It is thus, I believe, that all the most complex and wonderful instincts have originated.

As this passage shows, Darwin presented a hypothesis. In doing so, he made a major contribution not only to biology but to the way in which educated people see the world. Its importance is reflected in the many controversies it has evoked and that still continue. One source of debate is the logical status of Darwin's theory. The best-known logical difficulty is presented by the phrase, "the survival of the fittest". (This expression was not originated by Darwin.) If the expression is to have a precise meaning, we must state how fitness is measured. The test of fitness, in the theory of natural selection, is *contribution to the next generation*. In the simplest case, there are two genotypes in a uniform environment. One produces more viable offspring than the other; it is then said to be the fitter. Hence the fitness of a genotype is defined in terms of its chances of survival. Accordingly, the expression, survival of the fittest, becomes the survival of those that survive.

The theory of natural selection was indeed never rigorously stated by Darwin (or his immediate successors): instead, literary imagery was used (Edward Manier; R. M. Young). The very word selec-

FIGURE 18-3 Various forms of the arched-back "threat" posture of wild rats of the genus, *Rattus:* (A) the Australian swamp rat, *R. lutreolus;* (B) the Australian long-haired rat, *R. villosissimus,* in an intermediate posture; (C) the "roof" rat, *R. rattus,* showing an incomplete form of the posture; (D) the common, brown or

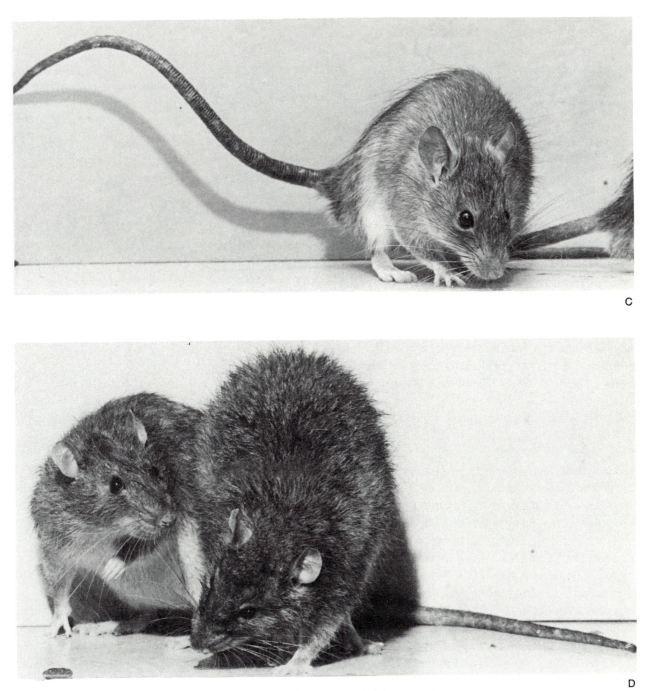

C

D

Norway rat, *R. norvegicus*. In each case, the posture is accompanied by presentation of the flank to the opponent, and raised hair. (Photos: A, B and C, I. A. Fox; D, W. E. Hocking)

tion implies a selector; it corresponds to Darwin's frequent references to the changes undergone by animals and plants under domestication, on which he wrote a lengthy treatise. But natural selection is not an agent, like a farmer choosing seed or bulls. Nonetheless Darwin, in many passages, refers to Nature (a feminine deity) as the agent of selection; sometimes she is called a power. The notion of a *struggle* for survival is also prominent in his writings; but Darwin states that this is to be regarded only as a metaphor.

Such anthropomorphic expressions are now sometimes replaced by more formal and exact statements. As an example, "natural selection is an inevitable consequence of genetical variation in fitness" (C. H. Waddington). This is a *definition* of natural selection, but makes no statement about whether natural selection actually occurs, still less whether it produces genetical changes in populations. (For discussions, see Marjorie Grene; R. H. Peters, 1976, 1978; and replies to Peters by G. L. Stebbins, and by others in the same journal.)

The neo-Darwinian hypothesis is as follows: first, there is genetical variation within species; second, this variation influences fitness; third, as a result there is sometimes change in the genetical structure of populations; and, finally, such changes are progressive, that is, not merely fluctuations.

The last item is especially important for two reasons. First, natural selection in a stable environment tends to have a stabilizing effect: individuals that differ much from the typical form of the species are often at a disadvantage (3.4.2). Many nonbehavioral examples are known. Among behavioral features the effect is particularly likely in social interactions: social signals and the responses to them have to fit with some exactness; hence signals are standardized within each species (chapter 13). L. G. Mason (1964, 1969) gives evidence from two species of insects studied in natural conditions. The males of the milkweed beetle, *Tetraopes tetraolphthalmus,* are not uniformly successful in their approaches to females. The unsuccessful males recorded by Mason varied much more in structural features than did the successful males. Similarly, a dense population of a defoliating lepidopteran, the California oak moth, *Phryganidea californica,* was studied. In such populations an exceptional amount of genetical variation may be expected. Males were caught and their wing lengths recorded. Again, intermediate forms were found to be more likely to mate than were extremes.

Second, there is the difficult concept, discussed by Grene, of "improvement": evolution by natural selection is commonly held to result in progressive changes that make organisms "better adapted" to their environments. Intuitively, this seems obvious. And sometimes improvement is measurable by the methods of physics: we can infer that, on certain evolutionary lines, fish became able to swim faster or more economically, and birds, to fly.

We therefore assume, with good reason, that each extant species is a product of a long evolutionary process of adaptation to a particular ecological niche or range of niches. A crucial question is whether, unlike Darwin, we can also now point to direct *evidence* of evolutionary change resulting from natural selection. The general answer is given in standard works, such as those of R. C. Lewontin (1974) and of J. Maynard Smith (1975). On the evolution of behavior we have some evidence, of which the celebrated example of industrial melanism is described in 3.4.2; in that case the behavior of both prey animals and predators is involved. Evolutionary theory also predicts that we should be able to produce genetical changes in experimental populations by artificial selection; such changes would be analogous to those of domestication. And in 16.1.2 I describe some findings of this sort.

Knowledge of observed and observable events is, however, distinct from what we surmise about the past. Throughout this book hypotheses that can be tested now are distinguished from statements, such as those on the past action of natural selection, that cannot. In 15.2.1.1, for example, comment is made on speculations about the evolution of human language—how it evolved and under what selection pressures. There are guesses of this kind both about minor features of social conduct and also major patterns that distinguish large groups. As an example of the latter, there is the case of bird flight. How did lizard-like animals of the Cretaceous develop into the mechanically marvelous flying creatures that we know today? The general assumption is of an initial stage of gliding. But J. H. Ostrom has proposed an alternative, based in part on a study of fossil forms. His suggestion—admittedly speculative—is of bipedal, cursorial (not tree-living) forms as forerunners of birds. Feathers are plausibly supposed to have arisen as insulation (like hair); and—this is the point—forelimbs bearing feathers became means of catching insect prey while the feathered reptile was on the run. The suggestion that the avian wing began as something like a butterfly net is likely to cause amusement; but there seems to be no means at present of deciding finally between the alternative hypotheses. We do not even know for certain what was the initial selective advantage of feathers.

18.2.2 Lamarck

In the preceding section it is suggested that there is no rational alternative to the theory of natural selection as the main cause of evolutionary change. Some readers may find that an overstatement: and in fact Darwin himself accepted another possibility. Darwin's *Origin* was a short version of a much longer work which was not published until 1975 (edited by R. C. Stauffer). In that longer survey Darwin wrote this:

My belief is, that, like corporeal structures, the mental faculties & instincts of animals in a state of nature sometimes vary slightly; & that such slight modifications are often inherited. Furthermore I cannot doubt, that an action performed many times during the life of an individual & thus rendered habitual, tends to become hereditary; but I look at this fact as of quite subordinate importance.

In this passage Darwin, as in many other writings, accepted what we now call the Lamarckian hypothesis. Indeed, in late editions of the *Origin* he went further. This was a result of his bafflement on the origin of variations. Despite the work of Gregor Mendel (1822–1884), published in 1865, the science of genetics is entirely a product of the 20th century: Darwin had to work without it.

The Lamarckian hypothesis states, in its colloquial form, that "acquired characteristics" are "inherited". Jean Baptiste de Lamarck (1744–1829) himself held that animals determine how they will live by exercising choice or will. In doing so, they exert themselves to use certain organs appropriately; and such exertion improves the performance of the organs so used, while disused organs atrophy. Such processes are, of course, familiar from observation of *individual* animals: muscles enlarge with use, deteriorate without it, and so on. Lamarck (like most people in his time and since) assumed that the effects of use and disuse are passed on to the offspring.

On this view, stereotyped behavior patterns, say,

those of nest building or web making, depend on inherited memories. Suppose that there were animals in the remote past that learned how to construct nests or webs. According to the theory, they must have undergone changes which conferred on their descendants their architectural abilities. In this way the descendants at least needed less learning by practice. Darwin himself pointed out that this could hardly hold for some of the best known of animal architects, the honey bee and other eusocial insects. What we now call the genes of bees are transmitted from generation to generation entirely by queens and drones, which do not build; nor do they forage, or perform any of the other complex acts, except mating, on which the hive depends. The traditional Lamarckian account includes the loss of such abilities from disuse; but this certainly has not happened in the millions of years during which bees must have had their present type of social organization.

Attempts have been made to test the notion of inherited memories in the laboratory. In a celebrated example, W. McDougall made rats learn to swim their way through a maze filled with water.

The training was repeated for several generations, and a progressive improvement in the rate of learning was observed. The announcement of this work created a sensation among biologists, for it seemed that the genetical transmission of an acquired habit had been demonstrated. But soon McDougall's work was given critical scrutiny (reviewed by N. L. Munn). Eventually, it was repeated by W. E. Agar and others. They, too, trained rats in a maze, generation after generation; and, like McDougall, they found a progressive improvement, at least for the first 20 generations or so. But, unlike McDougall, they also studied the performance in the maze of similar rats whose ancestors had *not* been trained; and these control rats, too, improved in just the same way, for the same number of generations. Hence, whatever was causing the improvement, it was not the training. Later, both trained and untrained groups declined in the ability to learn the maze (figure 18-4). The whole research went on for 20 years and 50 generations of rats.

With modern knowledge of the "genetic code", these findings are to be expected. Lamarckian transmission requires that an individual responds

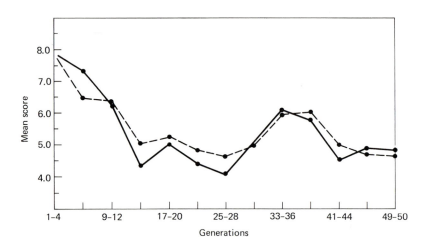

FIGURE 18-4 Test for "Lamarckian" transmission: the curves represent mean errors in swimming a maze, by generations: continuous line, laboratory rats whose parents had been trained in the maze; broken line, control rats of the same strain with untrained ancestors. Both groups improve at first; hence the change cannot be attributed to an inherited memory. (After W. E. Agar and others, 1954)

to an environmental demand by some improvement in performance; and that a change takes place in its genome which, in its offspring, produces a similar effect. On this basis, if I learn a skill, such as that of a hunter, and if my children and grandchildren do the same, my later descendants should be able to hunt without practice, or with less practice, as a result of cumulative changes in our DNA. Such a proposition is clearly untenable.

18.2.3 Modern Models

18.2.3.1 The Importance of the Individual: We now return to natural selection. Although the general theory is accepted, the particular ways in which evolutionary change occurs are still in many respects enigmatic. One means of trying to increase our understanding is to devise mathematical models: a number of presumptions are first made, preferably expressible algebraically; next their consequences are deduced; and finally actual phenomena are considered, to see whether they fit. Such methods have been used in the attempt to give an orderly account of the diversity of social systems, and are associated with the term sociobiology (15.3.3). (For reviews consult R. D. Alexander; Richard Dawkins; M. J. West Eberhard; G. C. Williams, 1966, 1975; E. O. Wilson, 1975.)

In their "selective" effects, behavioral features fall into two groups. First, there are the characteristics on which each individual depends. The homeostatic function of behavior is discussed in chapter 4: the activities of animals can often be related to the maintenance of a steady internal state. Second, reproductive behavior rarely increases the chances of the animal's survival, and may decrease them: it has survival value not for the performer, but for the offspring; it makes possible the continued existence of the replicating genotype, and of the corresponding phenotypes.

Reproductive and other social behavior has sometimes been said to be for the benefit *of the species.* We are accustomed to the idea of people working, at personal sacrifice, for the good of a group or even for the whole of mankind; but such a notion is not applicable to animals. Nonetheless, there are many examples of animal groups of which the members cooperate, for instance in the search for food, in the care of the young, and in protection against predators (part IV). That is, the members of these groups combine to produce an increase in the fitness of both themselves and others, or of their young. At the same time, some conduct is disruptive: it *decreases* the fitness of a conspecific.

There has been much debate on how these kinds of conduct evolved by natural selection (presuming that they did so). The method most used is to design simple models on paper, and to calculate what result the hypothesized relationships would produce. Consider a disruptive encounter between two individuals that must end in the retreat or death of one. One strategy is always to retreat as the opponent increases the intensity of attack. Another is to retaliate with increasing vigor. (The corresponding terms, *dove* and *hawk,* originally zoomorphisms, have now become anthropomorphisms.) The differences between the two types are genetically determined. If a population consists only of these types, the "hawks" will kill off the "doves", or will at least prevent them from breeding. But then the "hawks" will destroy each other.

In another hypothetical case, described by Richard Dawkins, a species of bird is parasitized by mites (Acarina) which cause a fatal disease. The parasites can be removed from some parts of the body only as a result of grooming by a conspecific. One possible social pattern is to groom any conspecific that needs grooming. An animal that behaves in this way is called a *sucker*. Another possible "strategy" is never to groom a conspecific, but to accept all offers of grooming. Such an individual is called a *cheat*. Now suppose a population in which both types exist, and in which the difference in behavior is again genetically determined. The cheats will do better than the suckers, and the sucker genotype will gradually disappear. After that, the population will die out owing to the mite-born disease. Yet a population consisting entirely of suckers would survive. (The inappropriate terminology, popularized by Dawkins, is used here for want of a better one. The reader must not suppose that to be generous is to be a sucker—in the ordinary senses of these terms. See 15.3.3.)

We know from studies of the real world that apotreptic behavior, though common, is rarely lethal; and that bioaltruistic behavior (such as that of "suckers") is common. In the attempt to account for this, the concept of the "evolutionarily stable strategy" (ESS) is often used (J. Maynard Smith, 1976). An ESS is a pattern of social responses; and it confers a level of biological fitness that cannot be bettered by an alternative ("mutant") pattern. The two models outlined above are not ESS; but a population entirely of "doves" or "suckers" is one.

The central problem for sociobiologists is whether natural selection can produce bioaltruistic behavior and, if so, in what circumstances. At first sight, the answer seems to be "no", *except* when the beneficiaries are offspring. An animal that acts to its own disadvantage is seemingly weighed out of the race; and, if its difference from others in this respect is genetically determined, then its genotype, and hence its bioaltruistic behavioral phenotype, must disappear. There is, however, much more to be said.

18.2.3.2 Group Selection:

It may seem that bioaltruistic conduct could evolve by *group selection*. Suppose that a species is divided into small groups (demes), with little breeding between them; then the chances of *group* survival might be enhanced by the presence of bioaltruistic individuals. The groups must be small, so that genotypes which (in a given environment) engender bioaltruistic conduct can become established as a result of chance fluctuations in gene frequencies. This process is called *genetic drift*.

For interdemic selection to take place, demes must in certain respects resemble individual animals: they must not only differ in genetical composition but also show differential survival as a result; and the surviving demes must be capable of splitting or sending out "propagules" and so producing more demes (J. Maynard Smith, 1976). Whether these requirements are actually met in nature has been much debated. Most discussions of the subject are purely theoretical, but M. J. Wade (1976, 1977, 1978) has published an experimental study of the flour beetle, *Tribolium castaneum*. 192 genetically heterogeneous populations were studied, each initially of 16 adults, in standard conditions. There were four treatments: (1) group selection for high population density after 37 days; (2) group selection for low density after the same period; (3) no group selection, but instead individual selection within populations determined by the number of adults; (4) simulated random extinction by use of a table of random numbers. Group selection in both directions had a clear effect after only four or five generations. In further experiments some degree of migration between groups did not prevent this effect.

The subject is likely to remain controversial for some time (see M. J. Wade, 1978); but most model builders in the 1970s have regarded group selection as unlikely. There is, however, one exception. The human species, including our ancestors for a period that cannot be estimated, may have survived partly by virtue of the bioaltruistic conduct of members of small groups. This notion conforms with anthropological findings: there are human groups in which the importance of "blood" ties is explicitly rejected (15.3.3). Hypotheses on how we or other species evolved cannot be tested; but, as Wade shows, it is possible to provide empirical evidence on some aspects of group selection in animal populations. When more such experiments have been done, discussions on this question will perhaps become more profitable.

18.2.3.3 Kin Selection:

The previous passage disregards the fact that members of a deme are likely to be closely related. We now therefore examine the concept of *kin selection*. This is an extension of the principle, stated above, that parental care has survival value. Parental conduct may reduce the parents' chances of survival; but if, as a result, the probability of survival of the offspring is sufficiently increased, then—as the theory of natural selection states—such conduct will be favored. We also know that elaborate parental care is widespread in the animal kingdom. Hence so far we have only decided that what actually happens is also theoretically possible—no doubt, a reassuring conclusion. The same comment applies to much theorizing in this field. J. Maynard Smith (1978) has put the point less harshly: "I believe that the main role of models in evolutionary biology is to help us to see whether, in particular cases, the proposed causes (. . . selection pressures) are sufficient to account for the observed results."

The survival value of parental care arises from the presence in the offspring of the parents' genes. Consider the famous example of the plovers (Charadriidae): if a hawk approaches the nest, the bird runs along the ground, with a wing trailing as if injured, and so (presumably) distracts the predator (figure 18-5). Such a *distraction display* is assumed to reduce the chances of survival of the parent only slightly, but greatly to increase those of the nestlings. Now suppose that only some plovers behave in this way; and that the difference from the others is genetically determined. Injury feigning will then spread through the population, because the offspring of the birds that perform this act will be

FIGURE 18-5 Golden plover, *Pluvialis apricarius,* runs along the ground dragging its wing, on the approach of a predator: an example of a distraction display.

more likely than others to have the same genotype.

By the same principle, conduct that favors the survival of other relatives has survival value (reviewed by W. D. Hamilton, 1972): the closer the relationship, the greater the probability of sharing a given genotype (table 18-1). Hence bioaltruistic behavior, it is held, can evolve if the beneficiaries are close kin of the actor. Such an effect would presumably be aided if animals could discriminate between their close kin and others; and, as we know, at least some birds and mammals can distinguish

their own offspring (chapters 9, 13). But, in the absence of such discrimination, bioaltruism could still have survival value: a parental response to any conspecific young could favor the parents' kin, because in any ordinary situation it is likely to be evoked by their own young.

The same principle holds for bioaltruistic conduct toward any conspecific. Examples come from the many birds that live in groups of which only some members breed, while others help the breeders (reviewed by J. L. Brown, 1978; J. T. Emlen).

TABLE 18-1   Kin selection and inclusive fitness

The coefficient of genetical relationship between two individuals, *r*, may be simply calculated if we assume no inbreeding, and that (as is usual among animals) the species is diploid: $r = \Sigma \left(\frac{1}{2}\right)^L$ where L is the number of generations that separate the individuals. In the diagrams below, the individuals whose relationship is calculated are represented as solid circles.

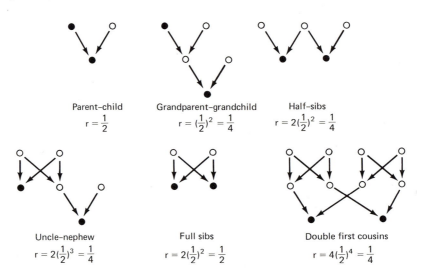

Parent–child
$r = \frac{1}{2}$

Grandparent–grandchild
$r = \left(\frac{1}{2}\right)^2 = \frac{1}{4}$

Half–sibs
$r = 2\left(\frac{1}{2}\right)^2 = \frac{1}{4}$

Uncle–nephew
$r = 2\left(\frac{1}{2}\right)^3 = \frac{1}{4}$

Full sibs
$r = 2\left(\frac{1}{2}\right)^2 = \frac{1}{2}$

Double first cousins
$r = 4\left(\frac{1}{2}\right)^4 = \frac{1}{4}$

Aid to conspecifics is held to have survival value if the beneficiaries are likely to carry the same genes as the actor. The probability of genetical similarity is a function of *r*. Suppose an animal behaves in such a way that its own life is endangered, but there is a net gain for its genotype. The genotype which, in a given environment, produces aid-giving behavior, is then said to have a greater *inclusive fitness* than other genotypes.

Diagram from J. L. Brown, 1975.

TABLE 18-2 Helpers and fertility: Mean numbers fledged annually by groups of Florida scrub jays, *Aphelocoma coerulescens.*

Breeding pairs:	Without Helpers	With Helpers
Inexperienced	1.03 (37)	2.06 (18)
Experienced	1.62 (45)	2.20 (81)

Numbers in parentheses are sample sizes.
From J. T. Emlen, 1978, after G. E. Woolfenden.

The groups of the Florida scrub jay, *Aphelocoma coerulescens,* studied by G. E. Woolfenden, consist of a breeding pair and their offspring from previous years. The nonbreeders help to maintain territories, which are permanent; they are also responsible for about 30% of the feeding of the nestlings; and they take part in mobbing predators, such as hawks. The most usual number of such helpers is two, but there may be as many as six. Reproductive success is improved by the presence of helpers (table 18-2).

A human observer is likely to find such groups of birds an agreeable sight. Moreover, there is an objective, neo-darwinian interpretation of their social "strategy" in terms of kin selection. But not all breeding groups fit this picture. S. L. Vehrencamp describes the communal nesting of anis, *Crotophaga sulcirostris.* The groups consist of up to four monogamous pairs. There is a single, communal clutch of eggs; and the birds of both sexes incubate and feed the young. During the early stages of laying, females roll the eggs of other females out of the nest; but at a certain point this "competitive" behavior stops. The amount of parental care provided by each bird is positively correlated with the number of eggs of that bird in the clutch. The *causal* relationships of this strange situation seem not to be established. But evidently, in this case, we have an initial "antisocial" phase in which each female performs disruptive acts; but this suddenly gives place to bioaltruistic behavior.

A further strange example of disruptive behavior is provided by some genera of salamanders, including *Amblystoma* (S. J. Arnold). I describe the mating of a member of this group in 17.2.4. Males of some species may behave as if they were females, and induce other males to deposit a spermatophore and so waste it. The males of other species cover the spermatophores of rival males with their own; they are therefore evidently spared the exertions of courtship, at the expense of a rival. As a contribution to sociobiological terminology, I propose that this should be called *caddish behavior.*

We now return to bioaltruism. A much-discussed case is that of alarm calls. To make a noise on approach of a predator seems likely to reduce the fitness of the caller, but such an action may increase that of conspecifics in earshot. The reader who recalls 12.2.1 may question this statement on two grounds. First, it may be asked whether there is evidence from observation of such an effect; in fact, there is not. Second, alarm calls are difficult to locate; hence it might be argued that making an alarm call does *not* impair the alarmist's chance of survival. But these objections can be countered. Alarm calls may be supposed to have their special properties because, in the past, they were more easily located and therefore it *was* dangerous to utter them. On these assumptions, alarm calling should have survival value only if many of the neighboring conspecifics that benefit from them are, say, first cousins.

P. W. Sherman has examined an actual example. He studied ground squirrels, *Spermophilus beldingi,* which give a distinctive call on the approach of mammalian predators, such as weasels, *Mustela frenata.* Calls are made mostly by females, especially those that had borne young. Moreover, females were more likely to call if they had surviving relatives in their group. Sherman concludes that the alarm calls of this species mainly influence close relatives of the caller. He refers to the effect he hypothesises as *nepotism*.

The principle of kin selection applies to other kinds of cooperation. In territorial interactions, and in relationships of dominance and subordinacy, the conduct of the actors is usually cooperative, even when apotreptic (10.1). Often it appears to be bioaltruistic. Suppose an actual clash between two conspecifics; usually, in such an encounter, when one animal shows obvious superiority, the other withdraws; in doing so, the loser may give a signal (of "submission"), but in any case its altered conduct tends to inhibit pursuit and further injurious attack. The restraint of the victor is then seemingly bioaltruistic, because there may be further encounters with the loser in which the victor has once again to exert itself. As we know, apotreptic conduct in general is typically formal rather than lethal: animals with powerful means of injuring others (teeth, claws, horns, stings, and so on) may perform elaborate species-typical sequences that end in the parting of two unwounded antagonists.

18.2.3.4 Reciprocity: Much ingenuity has been devoted to the theoretical possibilities in this field. As an example, there is the notion of *reciprocal bioaltruism* (R. L. Trivers, 1971). The proposals concerning kin selection and allied phenomena begin (as we saw above) with a theoretical question: how can natural selection account for conduct apparently disadvantageous to the actor? Animals tend to display mutual tolerance, or even to aid conspecifics, regardless of the closeness of their relationship. (Of course, all members of the same species are kin; but the relationship must often be very remote.) Such tolerance often appears to be bioaltruistic. Now suppose that an animal slightly endangers itself, and in doing so greatly improves the chances of survival of another. This could have survival value for the actor, if there were a high probability of the beneficiary returning the "favor" on some later occasion. Trivers suggests that there could be selection for such conduct in stable groups of long-lived animals capable of individual recognition.

C. Packer describes conduct by baboons, *Papio anubis,* which—he believes—corresponds to Triver's hypothesis. These animals, observed for eight years in Tanzania, are often involved in clashes and may wound each other; but fatal injury was seen only once. When a male is involved in an apotreptic interaction with another, he may "solicit help" from a third: the gesture is repeatedly and rapidly to turn the head from the third male to the opponent. Packer observed such acts on 140 occasions; on 97, the result was a temporary coalition (11.2.5.2) between the first male and another. The aid provided in such coalitions sometimes enabled a male to annex a female in estrus. Hence it conferred a form of dominance on the male that had solicited help. Packer observed a total of 18 males. Those that most often gave aid also most often received it; and there was a tendency to solicit aid from a favorite partner. Such observations at least conform with the hypothesis of reciprocal bioaltruism.

Another example of an empirical study, with some speculative interpretation, is that of J. D. & S. H. Ligon. Twenty-four flocks of green wood-hoopoes, *Phoeniculus purpureus* (figure 18-6) were watched in Kenya for several years. Most birds were marked and, after long periods of observation, kinship and social status were identified. Flocks included up to 16 birds, but each contained only a single breeding pair. Other members helped in the care of young (9.3.5). The helpers appeared to

FIGURE 18-6 Green wood-hoopoes, *Phoeniculus purpureus*, at their nest. The young are fed not only by their parents, but also by helpers. (Courtesy Sandra H. Ligon)

exert themselves to feed the young: there were many examples of a helper taking food from another bird and giving it to nestlings. The authors suggest that the result is the achievement of "personal ties" with the young birds; and that the young later help the helpers when the latter themselves breed. Moreover, this conduct is said to occur even when the interaction is between "unrelated" birds—that is, birds from quite different families. Members of flocks are, of course, often kin; but the authors suggest that helping has no necessary connection with kinship, and falls within the definition of reciprocal bioaltruism.

The two preceding examples show that evolutionary models can lead ethologists to make, or at least to interpret, their observations in new ways. But such studies of actual relationships, relevant to the models, are unusual. The success of the models is judged mainly by their ability to suggest how what is known to happen can have resulted from natural selection. Consider the case of the Tasmanian native hen, *Tribonyx mortierii* (10.4.2.4). J. Maynard Smith & M. G. Ridpath have discussed wife sharing by the males of this species. Often, permanent breeding groups consist of one female and two males. But a male that shares a female with another male produces on average only 50% of the young. It should therefore be to his advantage to drive out the other male. Certainly, apotreptic behavior occurs (figure 18-7). The suggested explanation is that the two males in each of these *ménages à trois* are brothers. Hence we have here a special case of kin selection. Not all, however, can be explained. In this species there are more males than females. Presumably this unusual sex ratio preceded wife sharing, but how it arose is not

FIGURE 18-7 Two male Tasmanian native hens, *Tribonyx mortierii,* in apotreptic postures. (Courtesy M. G. Ridpath)

known; the authors can only make a few suggestions.

A further, much-cited example is that of eusociality among the Hymenoptera. The eusocial condition (9.1.2) has evidently arisen on a number of occasions among the ants, bees, and wasps. W. D. Hamilton (1972) suggests that these insects, owing to their peculiar mode of sex determination, are especially likely to evolve a system in which females become helpers instead of breeding for themselves. The males of all Hymenoptera, including those of the solitary species, arise from unfertilized eggs: hence they are haploid, that is, they possess only one set of chromosomes. The females arise in the usual way from fertilized eggs, and so are diploid. In an ordinary diploid species, a female is equally kin with her sisters and her daughters:

$r = \frac{1}{2}$ (table 18-1). But in a haplodiploid species, a female is genetically more closely kin to her sisters than to her daughters: $r = \frac{3}{4}$ (figure 18-8). Hence for a female Hymenopteran there is greater survival value—in terms of replication of her genotype—in helping her sisters to reproduce than in producing more daughters herself.

This argument has been further elaborated by R. L. Trivers & H. Hare. They discuss the question of the number of brothers that the females ought to produce. Full brothers share only a quarter of their genes with their sisters. They conclude that the appropriate ratio of females to males is 3 : 1; and they state that just this ratio is actually found in many species of Hymenoptera in which there is only one breeding female (queen) in each colony. Unfortunately, R. D. Alexander & P. W. Sherman

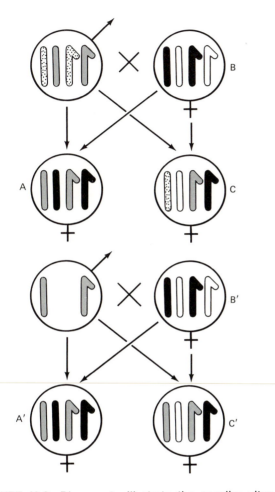

FIGURE 18-8 Diagram to illustrate the peculiar situation in a haplodiploid species. Each circle represents an individual with its complete set of chromosomes. Above, the situation in an ordinary diploid species: female (A) has half her genes in common with her mother (B) and, like her sister (C), she has half her genes from each parent. Below, the situation of a haplodiploid species. Female (A') has half her genes in common with her mother (B'), but, in common with her sister (C'), she has all her father's genes and, on average, half her mother's. Hence sisters are more closely "kin" than are mothers and daughters. (From J. Maynard Smith, 1975)

have revealed facts that do not fit these proposals. Among them is the phenomenon, frequent among the eusocial Hymenoptera, of multiple matings by females; to the extent that this happens, many of the females reared by workers are *not* full sisters. Moreover, according to Alexander & Sherman, the actual ratios of males to females, in both the solitary and the eusocial Hymenoptera, are exceedingly variable and often do not fit the hypothesis. Alexander & Sherman also consider the termites, which do not have a haplodiploid system of sex determination. (They therefore do not fit the hypothesis about the origin of eusociality.) On the basis of the sociobiological models, termites should have equal numbers of the two sexes; but in fact they seem to have a rather higher proportion of females. Some people nonetheless still emphasize the value of Hamilton's model, as a neo-darwinian explanation of eusociality; others emphasize the exceptions and therefore the limitations of the model. Which attitude one adopts is at present a matter of personal preference.

Models of increasing ingenuity will no doubt be designed; but there is greater need of more information on what actually happens in nature, and of more experiments that give reproducible results.

18.3 NICHES OF EXTANT SPECIES

Most accounts of behavior in this book are based on direct observation and experimental analysis; but in many writings statements on the evolution of the behavior observed are prominent. The preceding section illustrates some of the difficulties of analyzing the ways in which natural selection operates. But statements on evolution and behavior rarely attempt the precision of sociobiological models. Instead they "suggest (though no more than that) the selection pressures that have in the past moulded the species to what it is now" (Tinbergen, 1965). That is, they try to relate species-typical behavior to ecological niche; and of course they are inevitably restricted to findings on extant species.

18.3.1 Some Examples of "Adaptation"

In 3.4–6 I describe concealing, warning, and startling patterns. The theory of natural selection implies that such features may be expected to have survival value. Experiments have shown that cryptic patterns do indeed help to conceal; that conspicuous (aposematic) adornment does sometimes protect animals against attack; and that appearances (deimatic) that startle us also startle predators. Hence the experimental findings at least conform with the theory. They do not, however, constitute a proof: the experiments sufficiently prove only the effects of the patterns now; the events in the past, which led to the evolution of the patterns, have to be surmised.

The patterns may be described as "adaptations" for concealment and so on. The term "adaptation" in biology has two distinct and useful meanings, both of which refer to processes. (1) All complex organisms are capable of *ontogenetic adaptation:* organs that have much use commonly do not wear out, like the parts of a machine; instead they become more effective, sometimes by enlargement (muscles, kidneys, and many others). Habit formation comes under the heading of ontogenetic adaptation. (2) In this chapter we are concerned with *phylogenetic adaptation*—the process by which the genetical makeup of populations alters as a result of natural selection.

We assume that all the behavior (and other features) we observe are influenced by this process; but we are not thereby told just what is the role of any particular characteristic. And when we try to find out, we often encounter severe difficulties. As examples, here are four studies, each of predator–prey interactions.

The first concerns rabbits and their relatives (Lagomorpha), gazelles (Gazellinae), and other mammals that raise their tails as they move away from a predator. The effect is to expose a conspicuous patch of white fur (figure 18-9). This has often been assumed to be an alarm signal (13.2.1); if so, it presumably alerts conspecifics at the cost of some danger to the signaler, and is therefore perhaps a case of bioaltruism. N. Smythe proposes instead that the tail flash is a "pursuit invitation" signal: the predator is held to be encouraged to embark on a chase when the prey is alert to the danger; there is then perhaps a briefer contact with the predator; or the predator may be tired out by speed or agility, with a minimum disturbance of normal activity, such as feeding. (See also P. H. Harvey & P. J. Greenwood.) Another act that could have the same function is "stotting" by antelopes (figure

FIGURE 18-9 Pronghorn antelopes, *Antilocapra americana,* with the white rump patch showing. This display occurs on the approach of a predator. Is it a warning signal? (After W. Etkin, 1964)

FIGURE 18-10 Stotting by a young female Thomson's gazelle, *Gazella thomsoni:* the movement consists of a distinctive and conspicuous leaping, enjoyable to watch and, one might suppose, liable to attract the attention of any predator nearby. (After F. R. Walther, 1977)

18-10). If Smythe is right, conspicuous behavior can both sound the alarm *and* favor the survival of the actor. We might call this the *sporting hypothesis,* and compare it with the similarly imaginative Beau Geste hypothesis described below (18.6).

Smythe also compares the tail flash with the curious phenomenon of *mobbing.* Small birds collect around a predator such as a hawk or an owl and fly toward it while uttering alarm calls. Such behavior is the opposite of flight or concealment; but it is supposed to enhance the survival of the performers

by preventing the predator from picking out and seizing a single victim. Smythe's hypothesis shows that commonly accepted functions for well-known behavior are often mere presumptions; that alternative proposals are often, with ingenuity, possible; and that deciding between the alternatives may be difficult. The tail flash could have any of the following functions: (a) warning; (b) assembling the herd; (c) pursuit invitation; (d) "submission" to another member of the group (D. H. Hirth & D. R. McCullough). And its role could differ from species to species.

The second case is reviewed by M. Edmunds, and concerns the eye stripe of certain birds, reptiles, and frogs. The eye is often concealed by disruptive markings (figure 18-11), of which the stripe appears to be one example. But the birds with eye stripes are also those that feed on quickly moving prey. It has therefore been proposed that the stripe acts as a sighting line between eye and beak, and so aids in prey capture. Clearly, in such instances, the stripes could have a double function. But the sighting function cannot exist where, as in some frogs, the line does not run from eye to mouth; and for them Edmunds remarks that it must have a camouflaging function. In the absence of experiment, such a decisive statement—though of a kind often made—seems rash.

The third example arises from experiments designed to test a hypothesis. W. A. Montevecchi investigated the function of the pigment in the eggs of

FIGURE 18-11 Head of a snake to show how markings can obscure the presence of an eye. (Reproduced from H. B. Cott, *Looking at Animals: A Zoologist in Africa,* 1975, p. 163, by permission of Collins Publishers, London)

birds. He exposed eggs, either in their normal state or artificially painted in various colors (figure 18-12), to predation by crows, *Corvus* (compare 3.3.2.2). When the crows were allowed plenty of time to hunt, eggs of the laughing gull, *Larus atricilla,* did not benefit from being camouflaged. But, in other conditions, eggs of the quail, *Coturnix coturnix,* did benefit. These statements concern only the supposed cryptic value of pigmentation. But dark coloring of eggs may be disadvantageous. Montevecchi found pigmented eggs to be more susceptible to overheating by the sun. The color of the eggs of birds may therefore reflect not merely the need for protection from predators but also the effects of sunlight. The importance of these two factors must depend on the position and other features of the nest, and so presumably on the species.

The fourth case is also experimental. N. Tinbergen and others (1962) investigated what they describe as a seemingly trivial act, performed by black-headed gulls, *Larus ridibundus:* these birds, after their young have hatched, remove the broken egg shell. Removal takes only a few seconds. What, the authors ask, is the survival value of such an act? These eggs, too, are cryptically colored. Experiments showed the presence of shell fragments, with their jagged edges and white inner surface, to increase the likelihood of predation by other species of birds. Hence there is strong evidence that the behavior has an antipredator function.

But, unlike some other birds that nest on the ground, the black-headed gull removes the broken shell only after a delay of an hour or two. A possible explanation comes from the predatory behavior of black-headed gulls themselves: they are liable to attack chicks that have just hatched and are therefore wet, but not dry ones. Delay is therefore perhaps a compromise: the danger to the chick immediately after hatching may be greater if the parent leaves the nest to dispose of egg shells than if the parent protects the chick from the occupants of neighboring territories close by. Moreover, there are alternative functions for removing broken shells. The fragments could conceivably endanger the chick by allowing the growth of pathogenic bacteria, or by cutting it with their sharp edges; they might also obstruct the parents when brooding. These and yet other effects cannot be ruled out.

D. J. McFarland (1976) discusses this and analogous cases, and writes:

Experiments on the survival value of behaviour, which are necessarily conducted in somewhat artificial conditions, can never reveal the exact way in which natural selection operates. This is because, in the complex natural situation, it is the overall effect of selection that is important. In nature there are many conflicting pressures, so that the design effected by natural selection is inevitably a compromise.

FIGURE 18-12 Eggs of the Japanese quail, *Corturnix coturnix:* these eggs are cryptically colored; in an experiment, some were painted white. (Courtesy W. A. Montevecchi)

The last example in this section is a study of 516 species of birds, carried out by R. R. Baker and G. A. Parker with the aid of a computer. Their title is "The Evolution of Bird Coloration"; but what they ask is whether there are correlations of the color patterns of existing species with reproductive or ecological patterns. Their findings conflict with common presumptions (including those with which they began their work). They find no clear evidence of an effect of sexual selection on coloration. That is, the gaudy coloring often possessed by males but not females could not be shown to play a significant part in attracting a mate. (It may, however, have a secondary role in courtship.) Their main general conclusion is that color patterns are principally related to the risk of predation. Some birds are distasteful to predators, and so their bright colors are perhaps aposematic (3.5). A second possibility is of conspicuous colors and patterns helping to distract predators from females and young (18.2.3.3). Other and more detailed hypotheses are put forward, and could be tested. This study illustrates once again the hazards of "evolutionary" interpretations. To many people it seems obvious that gaudy coloring must have social functions—in mating or territorial defense and so on. But good evidence for this presumption rarely exists. This study also shows, on a massive scale, how it is possible to establish correlations between species-typical features and ecological niche. Such correlations suggest hypotheses that can be tested by experiment.

18.3.2 The Comparative Method

The preceding examples suggest the importance of comparative studies. They may take several forms. (1) A species with a distinctive niche may be compared with others, closely related, with different behavior. I give examples in the succeeding paragraphs. (2) A widespread phenomenon, such as the presence of conspicuous features or conduct in only one sex, may be analyzed. (See 18.4.3–4 below, on sexual selection.) (3) Social signals may be individually scrutinized and suggestions made on their nonsocial origins in the past (18.5).

All these concern social interactions because they have been most studied; but comparative descriptions of nonsocial behavior, such as locomotor patterns or feeding (or—as we see below—antipredator behavior) are also possible. Janet Kear made an experimental study of seven partly sympatric species of British finches (Fringillidae); all are seed eaters, and remove the husk before swallowing the seed. The different species have different sizes of beak; and the adults, given a choice, tend to select the size of seed that they can readily husk and that allows them to ingest the maximum weight of food in a given time. Hence in this respect feeding behavior is species-typical. But the adult phenotype is a product of a complex development. Young birds, inevitably, take smaller seeds than do adults. Moreover, they come to eat larger seeds by a process of habit formation: they learn to cope with the larger seeds by practice.

Other factors in the choice of seeds are illustrated in experiments by M. F. Willson on eight species of finches studied in Illinois. There was the expected relationship between beak size and size of seeds chosen; but there was no evidence that choice maximized calorie intake (compare 4.5.2.2). In natural conditions the most advantageous feeding pattern may be one that maximizes intake of seeds or, more generally, quantity of food by weight.

Some studies have illustrated not only adaptation to particular foods or modes of life but also adaptability to different modes. In another study of food habits, E. E. Werner & D. J. Hall describe experiments on sunfish (Centrarchidae). Three congeners are sympatric in North American coastal waters, but the overlap of their habitats is not complete. The green sunfish, *Lepomis cyanellus,* tends to live in shallow, inshore waters; the blue gill, *L. macrochirus,* and the pumpkinseed, *L. gibbosus,* live further out; and the latter is a bottom-living form, but the blue gill is not. These fish were experimentally reared in standard ponds with water plants. Some ponds were stocked with all three species, others with only one. When the species were together, each had a distinct pattern of feeding which corresponded to the type of habitat normally occupied. But when alone, the members of each species spread out into the other habitats, and each tended to eat the same variety of foods. In the absence of competition with other species, the fish grew more rapidly than when they were competing. Hence in some conditions behavioral plasticity enables these fish to adopt several ecological niches instead of only one. (See also 11.2.5.)

Other comparative studies have emphasized the convergence of separate species toward a common pattern, related to a similar mode of life. Gulls (Laridae) usually nest on flat ground (9.3.6); but some nest on cliffs (figure 18-13). The kittiwake, *Rissa tridactyla,* studied by Esther Cullen, nests only on narrow ledges overlooking the sea. The need to hold on is met by exceptionally well-developed claws and muscles in the foot. Cullen describes also a set of distinctive behavioral features which, she holds, are related to cliff dwelling. An advantage of these precarious nest sites is evidently the absence of predators: kittiwakes are much less preyed upon than are ground-dwelling gulls. Accordingly, some behavior patterns seem to have been lost during evolution of the cliff-dwelling habit: the alarm call, frequently heard from other gulls on the approach of a predator, is rarely heard

FIGURE 18-13   Seabirds often nest in colonies. Above, the petrel, *Fulmarus glacialis,* occupies a cliff, where predation is rare. Below, the tern, *Sterna hirundo,* nests on flat ground; a predator is being mobbed. (Reproduced from D. Lack, *Ecological Adaptations for Breeding Birds,* 1968, by permission of Methuen & Co., Ltd., London)

from kittiwakes; and, unlike other gulls, kittikawes do not attack predators. When the chicks hatch, other gulls (as described in the previous section) carry the broken shells away from the nests, but kittiwakes do not. The chicks themselves, unlike those of other species, are not cryptically colored.

Most gull chicks run away from danger. Kittiwake chicks have nowhere to run: they remain immobile; and if approached by a strange adult they turn their heads away, so exposing a distinctive black neck band. This, perhaps, inhibits attack by conspecifics. The nest itself is more elaborate than that of other gulls: it is a hollowed out platform of mud collected elsewhere and trampled down. When the parents return to the nest with food, they do not utter a food call; and experiment has shown that they do not distinguish their own chicks from others. The last features are clearly related to the fact that their chicks are always to be found in their nest.

Cullen describes yet other features of social conduct which seem to be related to cliff dwelling. If she is right, other cliff-dwelling birds should behave in similar ways. J. P. Hailman (1965) therefore made observations on the Galapagos swallow-tailed gull, *Larus furcatus*. This species is believed to have evolved the cliff-dwelling habit independently of the kittiwake; resemblances should therefore be a result of convergence. Among similarities to the kittiwake are that the chicks stay in the nest for an exceptionally long period; they face always toward the cliff wall and remain immobile; and they do not run if threatened. Hailman gives other examples of similarity between the two species, which conform with expectation.

To establish a correlation, it would of course be convenient if there were yet more species that could be studied in this way. The most general principle illustrated by these studies of gulls is, once again, that what we know of behavior nearly always concerns existing forms. Given minutely detailed observations on many species, we can hope to establish correlations between behavior and ecological niche. These correlations we interpret in the framework of evolution by natural selection; such interpretations make a convenient frame of reference. The same applies to other kinds of comparative studies described in the succeeding sections.

18.4 STRATEGIES OF REPRODUCTION

18.4.1 The Number of Spouses

In chapter 9 we saw something of the diverse mating systems in the animal kingdom. For an orderly general account of such variety, we first need to classify them (table 18-3). To explain them we begin, once again, by seeking correlations: are particular mating systems correlated with particular types of environment or ecological niche? If so, we could be led to hypotheses about the survival value of the systems (see T. H. Clutton-Brock & P. H. Harvey, 1978).

Table 18-3 classifies the kinds of mating system possible with two sexes, each separate from the other. Usually, a species has only one system. Some are capable of more than one, but the only major

TABLE 18-3 Types of mating systems

Promiscuity[a]	The sexes meet briefly, for coitus only.
Polygamy	There are prolonged associations with more than one partner of the opposite sex, either simultaneously or in succession (serial polygamy).
Polygyny:	one male mates with more than one female.
Polyandry:	one female mates with more than one male.
Monogamy	There is prolonged association with only one partner of the opposite sex, which may be seasonal or perennial.

[a] Also called polybrachygamy.

exception is the human species, in which all systems listed in the table are found. The table omits parthenogenesis, hermaphroditism, and sex change; and—with one exception in the next paragraph—they are omitted from this account.

When we try to explain mating systems, we meet difficulties that may be illustrated from the work of D. R. Robertson on *Labroides dimidiatus*. This is a cleaner fish, that is, a species that feeds on ectoparasites of other fish. Each individual begins life as a female, but some become male later on. Robertson observed groups of these fish for two years on the Great Barrier Reef off the east coast of Australia. Each group consists of a male with up to six mature and some immature females. If a male dies, the "dominant" (oldest) female of the group rapidly changes sex: conduct toward other females alters in a few hours, and the whole change takes only two to four days.

There are other such protogynous hermaphrodites with more females than males, but not very many. What is the function (survival value) of such a system? Any discussion of this topic must be speculative. Robertson bases a suggestion on the fact that each male fertilizes the eggs of a number of females. Of all the members of a group, his genotype therefore contributes the most to later generations. But, it may be supposed, the senior female that ends up as a male is the best adapted to the immediate environment. Such a system is then economical in its production of males, and also perhaps allows rapid genetical adaptation to environmental demands.

If these suppositions are correct, it may reasonably be asked why such systems are so rare. To answer it, we should have to speculate further on the advantages of alternatives. Unfortunately, there is no good ground on which to base a comparison between the system of *Labroides* and more conventional ones such as those described in 9.2.

Much has, however, been written on the relative advantages of the modes of life listed in table 18-3. One question is what can lead to the close association of one male with one or several females, or of one female with one or several males. What is the (biological) objection to promiscuity? Any discussion that is not purely abstract must deal with animal groups of which we have extensive knowledge. Hence many hypotheses (reviewed by R. K. Selander) have been based on the habits of birds. Most birds (probably more than 90%) are monogamous: they are neither promiscuous nor polygamous—and, a moralist might say, an example to us all. But, since we assume evolution by natural selection, we cannot suppose birds to be moved by ethical principles: we may ask instead in what circumstances monogamy can enhance fitness.

Monogamy, it is suggested, is advantageous when there is scarcity of food or of some other essential, such as nesting sites, during the breeding season. If both parents combine to feed the young, or to defend their territory, in such conditions the chances of their young surviving are—it is supposed—enhanced; and this advantage outweighs loss of the male's opportunity to fertilize the eggs of several females.

Is it possible to give evidence for these presumptions? A study has been made of the weaverbirds (Ploceidae), reviewed by J. H. Crook & P. A. Butterfield, and by D. Lack (1968). Among the subfamily, Ploceinae, some species live in forests and eat mostly insects. Nests are solitary, and monogamous pairs are formed. Other species live in open grasslands and eat mostly seeds. The sexes are dissimilar, for only the male is brightly colored (in the breeding season). Nests are in groups, and mating is usually polygynous. It is suggested that forest isolation and monogamy reflect a relative scarcity of food, while the mass nesting and polygyny of the graminivorous savanna birds occur where there is food in excess. Unfortunately, there is no general correlation of this kind: most other tropical graminivorous species are monogamous. And when we turn to other families, we find more anomalies. Among the sandpipers (Scolopacidae), care of young is usually by only one parent; the young are nidifugous (figure 12-16) and feed themselves soon after hatching. Polygyny would then be expected, but most sandpipers are monogamous. The same applies to many species of ducks (Anatinae). Still more surprising is what we find among the nest parasites. Four families of birds include many species, like the cuckoo, of which the young are reared by other species. Among them, there are no obvious advantages of either monogamy or polygamy. The members of two families, the Viduinae (figures 12-7 to 9) and the Indicatoridae, are indeed promiscuous; but the parasitic cowbirds (Icteridae) and cuckoos (Cuculidae) are monogamous.

Attempts have been made to preserve the theory of monogamy with subsidiary hypotheses. Lack suggests that in some (northern) climates, where the breeding season is short, it may be advantageous for birds to arrive at their nest site already paired. Such an explanation perhaps fits the facts about sandpipers and ducks, but does not help at all with the cuckoos.

When we turn to polygyny, we find similar ingenuity with hypotheses, and similar problems. Polygyny is held to have evolved when a species has access to more than enough food during the breeding season. Both in North America and in Africa there is a concentration of polygynous species of birds in marshlands; and in these environments there is much local variation in food availability. G. H. Orians suggests that in these conditions it is advantageous for females to choose males —even males already mated—that occupy the territories in which there is most food. If he is right, we should expect females of polygynous species often to select males that are already mated, even when unmated males are available. In addition, the reproductive performance of females should not be diminished by having to share a male with other females. R. K. Selander gives examples of species that satisfy these predictions. Unfortunately, however, some studies have failed to reveal expected correlations: for example, about 5% of European passerine (perching) birds are polygynous; and the food habits and niches of these species do not fit the hypothesis.

Similar difficulties are encountered in studies of special features of mating systems. In 12.2.2.5 I give the example of duetting by mated pairs. Many species of birds sing duets, but it has not been possible to relate this clearly to any ecological niche. The behavior may have several functions which differ with species; but we do not know what these functions are.

In general, we may suspect the existence of many factors, some not identified, that help to determine the survival value of the different mating systems. Among birds we find weak correlations of mating patterns with ecological niche. Perhaps such correlations do reflect the workings of natural selection. But much more information, about many species, is needed for a convincing account.

18.4.2 The Number of Offspring

Table 18-2 gives only one possible classification of reproductive systems. Figure 18-14 illustrates another (reviewed by H. S. Horn; S. C. Stearns, 1976, 1977). It refers to two extreme kinds of reproductive "strategy". (1) A high rate of increase (r) may be advantageous; vast numbers of eggs may then be produced (as by many aquatic species); or, among mammals, there may be large and frequent litters (as among many species of rodents). (2) Some species, notably of mammals and birds,

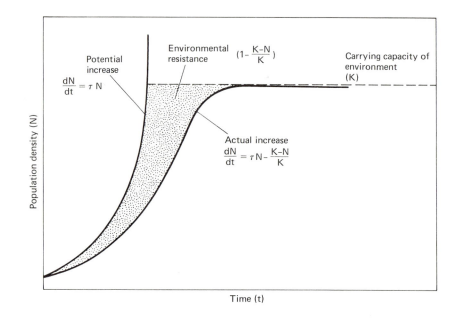

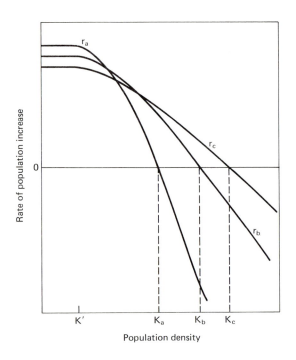

FIGURE 18-14 Above, the theoretical relationships between potential rate of increase of a population, the carrying capacity of the environment, and the growth of a population from a point much below the maximum. Below, the relationship between r and K selection. The curves represent the rates of increase of three competing genotypes (a, b, c). Below the critical population density, K', each population grows at its maximum rate (r_a, r_b, r_c). As density increases, the rates of increase decline, but to different extents. Each achieves a growth rate of zero at a different population density: K_a, K_b, and K_c represent the carrying capacities for the three genotypes. Given the relationships shown, genotype (a) will be most successful if the environment fluctuates so greatly that populations are always growing (r selection); but in a stable environment genotype c will be most successful (K selection). (Lower figure after M. Gadgil & W. H. Bossert, 1970)

reproduce at a low rate: instead of selection for high fertility, there is then supposed to be K selection, that is, selection especially for increased efficiency in making use of food and other resources. Such selection increases K, or the carrying capacity of the environment.

It is suggested (for example by E. R. Pianka; and by N. G. Hairston and others) that these alternative patterns can be correlated with environmental features. In unstable environments populations are likely to fluctuate widely. Such populations grow at a rate related to their density (compare 10.4.3), but usually decline catastrophically before the maximum is reached. Animals with these characteristics may be expected to be small, to reproduce early and only once, to have a short lifespan, to display little or no parental care or complex social structure, and to have good means of dispersal. These are some of the supposed correlates of r selection. Stable environments allow, it is held, the evolution of species with the opposite features; and these reflect K selection. But, as Pianka remarks, we cannot exclude other causes of the two "strategies": even "historic accidents" cannot be ruled out.

One difference between the two kinds of life history is sometimes described by an analogy with economics. Animals of the first type are said to *invest* little in each offspring: they can therefore afford to produce many young. Animals subject to K selection invest much in each young one; hence it is appropriate that they should safeguard their investment by prolonged parental care.

The references to r and K selection represent, then, hypotheses on how selection works in different environments. Like the discussions on mating patterns (outlined in the previous subsection), they are statements on how natural selection might operate given certain presumptions. They also provide a starting point for a classification of reproductive types. The value of this method needs to be tested by further ecological study of many species. Only by such study can we hope to establish reliable correlations between patterns of social conduct and ecological niche. But even such correlations are only a beginning. A critical test of an evolutionary hypothesis is to transfer populations from one kind of habitat to another, and to see whether changes in life histories, predicted by the hypothesis, actually occur. Unfortunately, as Stearns (1977) remarks, "Placing evolutionary interpretations at risk has not been popular. Evolution moves slowly and biologists are impatient."

18.4.3 Intrasexual Selection

The most-debated general question on mating is that of sexual selection. The question arises from the marked secondary differences that sometimes distinguish the sexes. The proposed answer dates back to Charles Darwin (1871). The males of many species of mammals and birds are more conspicuous than the females. (Occasionally the situation is reversed.) It is supposed that such sexual dimorphism is relevant to the chances of mating in two ways (reviewed by T. R. Halliday, 1978). The first is *intrasexual selection*. Males are often polygynous; if they compete for females among themselves, they may be aided by signals or weapons that deter rivals. Even monogamous males might be aided in this way, if there were (for example) competition for breeding places at the beginning of the season. Such competition could also be between females, such as those of the jaçanas described in 9.3.5. The second is *epigamic* (intersexual) *selection*. In this case members of one sex (usually the males) are held to compete for the attention of the members of the other.

Unfortunately, in practice, we often see marked sexual dimorphism without knowing whether its role is intrasexual or epigamic. There is no decisive evidence from natural populations that females select some types of male in preference to others *and, in doing so, increase their fertility*. There are, however, some further relevant examples from nature.

N. B. Davies & T. R. Halliday (1977) observed the mating of toads, *Bufo bufo,* in a pond in England. The females were usually larger than the males. Mating was confined to a breeding season of a few weeks. Only a minority of males were seen to pair. A male that did so mounted a female, grasped her firmly with his forelegs, and was carried in this position (amplexus), sometimes for many days. In experiments, two males, of which one was about 10 mm longer than the other, were put in a tank with a female. One of the males quickly seized the female; the other then tried to dislodge the first, and was repelled by kicks. Sometimes, a male in amplexus was dislodged, but only by a larger male.

So far, we have a case of intrasexual selection. But these authors show female fertility to depend on the female having a male of suitable size: release of sperm evidently depends on stimulation from the eggs as they are shed; and such stimulation is most effective only if the male is of the right size. These authors suggest that females can influ-

FIGURE 18-15 Red deer stag, *Cervus elaphus,* aged 11 years, in his winter coat. (Copyright Fiona Guinness)

FIGURE 18-16 Red deer stags (see figure 18-15): on right, a stag one day after casting his antlers, in an apotreptic encounter with a subordinate; status depends in part on the possession of antlers, but is not lost immediately on shedding them. (Courtesy G. A. Lincoln)

ence their own fertility: the hypothesis is that, if a female is mounted by a male of inappropriate size, she moves toward other, unmated males; and one of these may displace the male in occupation. If so, there is also an element of epigamic selection.

An apparent example of intrasexual selection is seen in the red deer, *Cervus elaphus* (figure 18-15), studied experimentally by G. A. Lincoln. Stags are polygynous: in the breeding season (rut) they assemble a "harem" of as many as 20 hinds, and drive away other males. Such groups are kept together by the action of the stag. Lincoln studied these handsome animals on the Scottish island of

Rhum, where there was a population of about 1600. He observed the effects of loss of antlers, either by accident or by experimental amputation, on the conduct of stags. One effect was a decline in status. Lincoln left a pile of maize at which the animals fed; some stags were able to displace others at this feeding point: that is, in this sense, they were dominant. Dominance was lost with the antlers. Moreover, stags deprived of antlers had no access to hinds during the rutting season.

To a human observer, antlers look like weapons, and they are indeed used in locking heads during a clash. But Lincoln gives evidence that they are equally significant as visual signals. Other signals, important during the rut, probably include the conspicuous mane, the thick neck, and the dark body. Stags also rear up (figure 18-16), roar, and thrash at plants with their antlers. Hinds display none of these appearances or activities.

So far, we seem to have here a particularly clear example of intrasexual selection. But there are two flaws. First, a few stags (hummels) fail to grow antlers. Nonetheless, they sometimes succeed in breeding. Lincoln believes that, unlike stags that lose their antlers, hummels adapt their conduct to their condition and make sufficiently effective use of displays in which the antlers are not involved. Secondly, Lincoln & F. E. Guinness, in a detailed account of conduct during the rut, describe how hinds move freely in the region in which the stags space themselves out for the breeding season. They suggest that the hinds to some extent select a stag— that is, the stags' displays are at least partly epigamic. Their findings conflict with earlier statements that the hinds are passive and subservient to the stags. (This may be true once an association has been formed.) Such findings, based on critical research, remind us again how easy it is to make glib (and often anthropomorphic) interpretations of animal conduct on inadequate evidence.

Another type of question concerns the evolution of such dimorphism. Madhav Gadgil discusses both red deer and also insect species of which the males are of two distinct types. Each species has structures apparently used in competing for females. Gadgil suggests that the difference between the two male forms is always genetically determined; and that the forms represent alternative "strategies". One is to develop powerful or conspicuous struc-

FIGURE 18-17 Stag beetles, *Cervus lucanus,* in coitus. (S. C. Bisserôt)

FIGURE 18-18 Four male ruffs, *Philomachus pugnax,* in their lek, each with his distinctive plumage. One drab female is shown. (Reproduced from D. Lack, *Ecological Adaptations for Breeding in Birds,* 1968, by permission of Methuen and Co., Ltd., London)

tures, such as the antlers of deer or the enormous horns of beetles such as *Cervus lucanus* (figure 18-17); these may be supposed to enhance reproductive success, but at a cost in energy needed to develop and carry them. The alternative is to economize on energy, at the cost of inferiority in epigamic or intrasexual effectiveness. An obvious question is whether such speculations can point the way to further study. At present, as we know, they show only how what is the case *could* have happened. Perhaps they will eventually lead to quantitative study of the contrasted male types.

18.4.4 Epigamic Selection

For a notable example of apparently purely epigamic selection, we may turn to the ruff, *Philomachus pugnax* (figure 18-18). In the breeding season groups of males assemble in small areas, called leks, where many of the males occupy modest territories and display to visiting females. As the figure shows, the females have slender, elegant figures, but no striking plumage. The males in contrast are visually bizarre. When a female is ready for coitus, she crouches in front of a male. It is assumed that this act is influenced by the male's total

display—not only his ruff but also the quivering of his spread wings, shuddering, and bowing. Despite the need for caution in interpreting conduct not tested by experiment, we may perhaps accept this as a genuine epigamic display. It is, however, exceptional: in no other species of bird is there so much individual variation. Moreover, as so often, there is a complication. A. J. Hogan-Warburg describes two types of male: only about 60% have territories, and these are the ones with the most varied plumage; the others, called satellite males, have white ruffs (presumably more conspicuous at a distance). The satellites nip in and copulate while an occupier is defending his territory. It would be interesting to know the genetics of this remarkable polymorphism.

There are, however, many examples of gorgeous coloring and conspicuous displays apparently associated with courtship. When, rarely, a species is polyandrous, the female is the gaudy one; but usually it is the male. The most celebrated example is the peacock, *Pavo cristatus* (figure 18-19). Peafowl are common in the north of India, where they may be seen in wooded land near farms. They are also kept in captivity. W. P. Pycraft describes how the polygynous males gather in an arena or lek in

FIGURE 18-19 The display of the peacock, *Pavo cristatus.* (American Museum of Natural History)

the breeding season, and there display to females. They do so not only by spreading their notorious tail feathers but also by rattling the plumes and quivering the wings. If all goes well, the female, after a time, squats in front of the male and allows him to mount. Since females have no gorgeous tail feathers, we may presume that this extraordinary structure is of significance only in courtship. If so, the fantastic decoration is a product of selection resulting from the preferences of the female.

There is, however, no experimental evidence of the effects of the peacock's display. The need for such evidence is exemplified in a report, cited by Margaret Bastock (1967), that albino peacocks successfully court hens despite their lack of gaudy coloring. These birds, observed in the Lahore zoo, are described as displaying with exceptional vigor and persistence.

From the wealth of possible examples, here is one more, even stranger than the previous two. The bowerbirds (Ptilonorhynchidae) of Australia and Niugini have been studied by A. J. Marshall. These fairly large birds are not themselves conspicuous, but they construct signals that are (figure 13-1): their bowers resemble nests built on the ground; some are painted (for instance with fruit pulp); others are decorated with objects such as orchids, fruits, and pebbles. The spotted bowerbird, *Chlamydera maculata,* uses any bright or light-colored object that it can carry. Bleached bones, shells, and fruits are assembled in considerable numbers. If a visitor to the habitat of this species loses his car keys, surgical instruments, tableware, or—as in one instance—his glass eye kept in a cup over night, he should search the nearest bower.

In the past, writers have supposed that bowers were made for the maker's pleasure; that they displayed a highly developed aesthetic sense; and that they had nothing to do with breeding. In fact, the bowers are made by males in the breeding season, and are the sites at which they perform displays. No systematic experiments have been done on the effects on females; but each type of bower is characteristic of the species that makes it, just like the more familiar kinds of courtship. It is generally assumed that here, too, we have examples of epigamic display. Bowerbirds, however, differ from ruffs and peacocks in being solitary when breeding. Other solitary species with magnificent displays include the birds of paradise, whose plumage (described by E. T. Gilliard) rivals that of the peacock.

One of many questions about sex and selection concerns monogamous species. It is easy to see how both intrasexual and epigamic selection could occur among promiscuous or polygamous animals; but when a species is monogamous it would be expected that virtually all adults mate. Yet, as we know, most birds are monogamous; and among them are many species of which the males are

gaudy and perform elaborate territorial or courtship displays. A possible but speculative answer has already been given—David Lack's suggestion of an advantage from *early* mating.

There is, however, a more general question: we must often be uncertain whether apparently epigamic courtship displays do in fact influence female choice. As Margaret Bastock (1967) remarks, epigamic selection depends on females being initially coy and unwilling to mate. But coyness may reflect, not choosiness in adopting a partner, but physiological unreadiness. Stimulation from the male is, for some species, essential for a female's normal reproductive performance (9.3.7). Epigamic selection still seems a plausible hypothesis for many species; but an elaborate courtship may not be anything to do with female choice. The precise scope of epigamic selection remains to be found out.

18.5 ORIGINS OF SIGNALS

The phenomena of sexual selection represent special cases of social signaling. In accounts of other types of social signals a number of proposals have been made on how the signals evolved: the signals are held to be derived from movements or other features with a nonsocial function.

18.5.1 Autonomic and Protective Responses

Some visible, odorous, or audible features have obvious nonsocial functions, yet could give information to conspecifics. R. J. Andrew (1973) reviews the possibility that processes regulated by the autonomic nervous system act as social signals.

The autonomic (or visceral motor) nervous system of birds and mammals regulates body temperature, the distribution of blood to the skeletal muscles and viscera, and other processes, especially those related to homeostasis. When an animal is disturbed, autonomic changes take place that prepare it for "fight or flight". These include cooling processes, such as panting (which may be accompanied by sounds), and an increase of the blood supply to the skin (as in blushing). The primary response to disturbance may, however, not be vigorous action but immobility. If so, there may be changes that tend to conserve heat, such as raising of feathers or hair. Disturbance may also result in sweating, urination, and defecation, and the consequent release of odors. In 13.2.1 there is a possible example from the supposed alarm signal of deer, *Dama dama*.

There are also nonautonomic responses to disturbance: birds and mammals may give a brief gasp, flatten their external ears (if any), and close their eyes. The primary function of the last two seems to be protection; but the facial expression of many mammals, under attack by a conspecific or during hesitant approach to a possible mate, includes these features (figure 10-38): they seem to have become social signals.

Further examples come from buntings of the genus, *Emberiza* (R. J. Andrew, 1956). These birds, like mammals, respond visibly to a rise in internal temperature: they not only pant, but also flatten their feathers and so reduce surface insulation; and by raising their wings they increase the area over which heat is lost. Such acts are performed after the vigorous or prolonged flying that occurs when a bird is fleeing from, or pursuing, another. But, after a male has chased a female, although both have exerted themselves to a similar extent, only the male performs cooling responses. Similar conduct is seen after a male has attacked a female. The apparent cooling response is supposed to have become a social signal and to indicate a particular state of the performer.

Another example is the conduct of a domestic cat faced with an opponent (10.6.1). The physiological basis of this pattern has been extensively studied: it includes a much increased activity of the autonomic nervous system. Such internal changes, as we know, take place in *anticipation* of the need for vigorous action; and they have a straightforward homeostatic function. But the visible consequences also seem to act as a signal.

The signaling role of visible, audible, or odorous changes brought about by the autonomic nervous system has still to be clearly demonstrated. At present, for a number of species of birds and mammals, we have a plausible notion that could be tested by experiment.

18.5.2 The "Displacement" Hypothesis

A second hypothetical source of social signals is the conduct sometimes called displacement behavior (17.1.2.4). Suppose a male bird is performing a stereotyped activity such as mating; suppose also that its partner flees before coitus is completed. Thus frustrated, the bird turns abruptly to an alternative activity, such as preening. In another type of situation two opposed responses are simultaneously evoked: for example, the approach of a potential mate can evoke *either* courtship *or* rapid withdrawal. Sometimes, neither response is seen, but instead a third is performed. Possible alternatives include eating, drinking, preening, and others that seem (to a human observer) irrelevant to the circumstances. Such conduct has been classified under the one category of displacement behavior, on the ground that it represents a "buildup of drive" or of "central excitation" that has to "overflow" or be expressed in some kind of behavior.

The original concept of displacement behavior is now largely discarded (17.1.2.4). Nonetheless, birds and mammals do break off from certain social interactions; these movements are held to be social signals derived from "displacement preening". Similarly, snapping movements of the beak of a heron during courtship look like incomplete feeding movements, and so are regarded as derived from "displacement feeding". And that of grass pulling by a herring gull is held to be "displacement nest building".

18.5.3 Intention Movements

The last supposed source of displays may be illustrated by what happens when a bird is about to fly away: it crouches and raises its tail feathers before springing off. Sometimes these preliminary movements are performed, but the bird remains where it is. Other movements precede biting or striking at an opponent; and these, too, may occur without actual biting or striking. Such an act has been called an intention movement, but this term can be criticized: to speak of "intention" seems to imply a statement about an animal's feelings, or at least about its internal state; but what we observe is overt behavior. Hence a phrase such as "preparatory movement" might be more appropriate.

Movements that resemble the preliminaries to moving away, biting, and other acts are common during the social encounters of birds and mammals. Certain signals are therefore held to have originated with them.

18.5.4 Ritualization

Two general propositions apply to all these evolutionary hypotheses. First, if they are correct, then social situations must evoke (or have evoked) the various kinds of primary response—autonomic, protective, "displaced", or "intention". Second, during evolution such responses have become social signals, by a natural-selection process influencing both

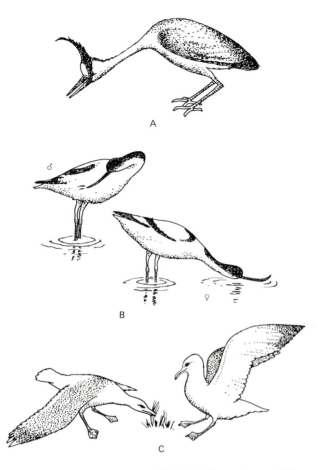

FIGURE 18-20 Displays by birds that have been attributed to ritualization of displacement behavior. (A) Male heron, *Ardea ardea*, snapping (a food-catching movement) during courtship. (B) Male avocet, *Recurvirostra avosetta*, makes preening movements during courtship. (C) Territorial herring gull, *Larus argentatus*, pulling grass (a nest-building movement) during an apotreptic display. (After N. Tinbergen, 1952)

activities unexpectedly, and do something else. It is believed that the alternative activities, whatever their causes, have in evolution been transformed into social signals. A group of examples is illustrated in figure 18-20: some species of birds make perfunctory movements as if preening during social

the response to the signal and the signal itself. The response to an appearance, such as raised hair or feathers, or to some other feature, could be acquired during the responder's lifetime: it could be a matter of habit formation (chapter 12). But often this seems not to be necessary: most species-typical responses to social signals appear to be stable in development (chapter 17).

The presumed effect of natural selection on the signal itself is called *ritualization* (reviewed by A. D. Blest, 1966), by analogy with human ceremonies that have only a symbolic function. (Examples include the formal consumption of fragments of food or mouthfuls of wine of negligible nutritive value and the flourishing of swords or other obsolete weapons.) The analogy is remote, for human ceremonies vary from group to group and change quickly in historical time, whereas the social signals of animals usually apply to a whole species, and remain the same from one generation to the next.

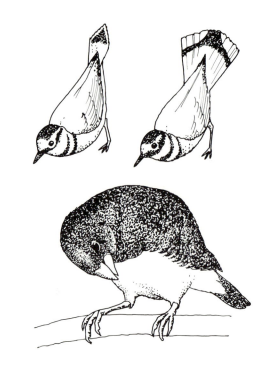

FIGURE 18-22 Visual displays believed to be derived from reproductive behavior. Above, scraping by the kill-deer, *Charadrius vociferus*, which is held to originate in nest building. Below, display by a finch, *Spermestes bicolor*, perhaps evolved from the movements of feeding the young. (Reproduced from J. P. Hailman in T. Sebeok, ed., *How Animals Communicate*, 1977, by permission of Indiana University Press)

FIGURE 18-21 Two displays believed to be a result of ritualization. Left, an apotreptic posture of the chamois, *Rupicapra rupicapra,* perhaps derived from the movements of fighting. On right, marabou stork, *Leptoptilos crumeniferus,* erect and gaping—a posture possibly derived from escape behavior. (Reproduced from J. P. Hailman in T. Sebeok, ed., *How Animals Communicate*, 1977, by permission of Indiana University Press)

Ritualization may then be defined as the modification, during evolution, of a behavior pattern, so that it becomes a social signal. Most displays that are believed to have evolved in this way are now signals and nothing else. Visible movements often expose some striking color or pattern (figures 18-21 and 18-22); and these must be supposed to have evolved in parallel with the changes in behavior.

The definition above fits the customary use of the term ritualization; but a reader may object to it, on the ground that we can only guess how a social signal has evolved. Hence, when using the term, we should, strictly speaking, always refer to "supposed ritualization". But in practice, it is usual to call any harmless apotreptic conduct ritualized. For instance, Peter Weygoldt uses the word in his account of the encounters of male whip spiders (10.4.1.1). But what is known is only that these elaborate interactions occur. To say that they are ritualized represents a presumption that they have evolved from acts of violence. In such a context, the notion of ritualization draws attention to the existence of a large class of social interactions, those that tend to separate the actors without direct harm to either.

The preceding paragraphs may seem to imply doubt about the validity of hypotheses on the evolution of displays. But the actual intention is, once again, to point to a distinction between statements about the evolution of behavior, and those about either the causes (internal or external) or the effects of conduct that can be observed here and now. Statements on what we can observe directly can be tested by experiment; those on past events cannot.

Nonetheless, some of the peculiarities of animal signals make sense only in the context of their derivation from other behavior with a different function. In this they resemble certain familiar features in the structural development of vertebrates (18.1). The hypotheses on the *functions* of signals, discussed in the next section, are—like the behavioral examples above—speculative but are more open to rigorous test.

18.6 FUNCTIONS OF SIGNALS

As information accrues on diverse species, correlations begin to emerge between the features of certain kinds of signals and their functions. Here follow three examples of such correlations, each interpreted in terms of the hypothetical effects of selection acting in the past.

1. One of the features of the songs of some birds and of cetaceans is their complexity (12.2.1; 13.2.2). To some extent this can be explained, or at least understood, as insuring that each individual responds only to the signals of conspecifics; and when there is individual recognition, still more complexity is appropriate. But for some groups these explanations are not satisfying. An example is the family of wrens (Troglodytidae), of which nine species have been studied by D. E. Kroodsma (1977b). The wrens are small, unobtrusive birds, of which the sexes are similar; but the male's singing is often astonishingly elaborate: one species has more than 100 types of song. These performances are held to be an audible counterpart of a peacock's feathers, a ruff's plumage, or a bowerbird's bower: that is, they have an epigamic function. If so, there should be some correlation between song virtuosity and polygyny; and this is what Kroodsma finds. Here is at least some evidence for sounds as epigamic characters, to go with that on the visible signals already discussed.

2. Some of the most persistent singing is territorial rather than erotic. In 10.4.2.3 I describe repetitive sounds of astonishing persistence. Such sounds are heard not only from some birds but from frogs (Anura), cicadas (Hemiptera, Cicadidae), and others. Moreover, many birds other than wrens sing several distinct variations on the species-typical theme, and change at short intervals from one to another; and often they are monogamous. Hence it may be doubted whether their function is epigamic. J. R. Krebs (1977b) has therefore made an ingenious suggestion, called the "Beau Geste hypothesis". The name comes from a once-celebrated novel of adventure by P. C. Wren, in which Our Hero finds himself the sole survivor in a fort in the

North African desert. Under attack, he rushes from embrasure to embrasure, fires off a shot from each, and so gives the enemy the impression that the defending population is much larger than one.

The hypothesis has been debated by P. J. B. Slater (1978), by Catherine Rechten, and by Krebs (1978) himself. An important feature of this apparently frivolous idea is that it could be tested by experiments in which recorded songs are played to birds in various situations. As usual, alternative hypotheses exist. For example, variety of songs could reduce the likelihood of habituation in the hearers (D. E. Kroodsma, 1978a).

3. The last speculation concerns principally apotreptic sounds. E. S. Morton points out that these signals, among birds and mammals, are usually of low pitch and harsh; in contrast, epitreptic signals are likely to be high pitched and to consist of pure tones. Morton suggests that it is advantageous for a threatened animal to withdraw only if there is a substantial probability of its being worsted should the encounter come to an actual clash. Defeat is likely to be correlated with the size and hence the strength of the opponent; and the larger the individual, the lower the pitch of the sounds of low frequency. On this argument, then, the deeper and harsher a sound, the more appropriate it is—from the point of view of survival—for a threatened individual to avoid its opponent.

We might call this the double-bass hypothesis. It receives some support from observations by N. B. Davies & T. R. Halliday (1978), whose work on toads, *Bufo bufo,* is mentioned above (18.4.3). As we know, only some males mate; and a male in amplexus may be displaced by another. In experiments, mated males were silenced by rubber bands passed through the mouth and round the back of the head. This prevented croaking; but there was no evidence that it affected other behavior. Re-corded croaks were then played during attempts by an unmated male to displace the one in amplexus. The larger the male, the deeper its croak. Hence it was possible to provide a small male with a deep croak and a large male with one of higher pitch. There was a clear tendency for attacks to be more frequent and to last longer if the croaks indicated that the defender was smaller than the attacker. (There were, however, other factors. The authors suggest that the strength of the defensive kicks may have had some influence on the outcome.)

We should not be dazzled by the ingenuity of the hypotheses described in this section. As the preceding example implies, what we know, or can find out, is whether, in the interactions of existing forms, the hypothesized correlations actually exist. If they do, then we may think of the relationships as if they had been produced by the natural-selection processes suggested; but we can rarely test any such presumption experimentally.

18.7 SUMMING UP

By accepting the fact of evolution, we acquire a means of ordering the immense diversity of species and of behavior. But the usual concept of evolution includes that of natural selection: indeed, until Darwin announced his theory, even the fact of evolution was not accepted. Yet Darwin's theory remained for decades only a hypothesis, based on no direct evidence. In 1892 G. J. Romanes referred to attempts to apply the principle dogmatically "in every case where it is *logically possible* that the principle has come into play." He also wrote: "the term natural selection thus becomes a magic word, or Sesame, at the utterance of which every closed door is supposed to be immediately opened. . . . Such a blind faith, indeed, I hold to be highly inimical, not only to the progress of biological science, but even to the true interests of the natural selection theory itself."

Today we are still faced with such problems. The principle of natural selection, taken by itself, is a tautology: *if* in a population there is genetical variation in fitness, *then* different genotypes will contribute differently to the next generation. Hence fitness is defined in terms of reproductive success. The primary effect of natural selection so defined has often been demonstrated: it is to preserve the existing state of affairs; that is, selection is stabilizing. The important Darwinian concept is that natural selection is also an agent of change; and that the changes it produces are not merely fluctuations. They are, indeed, commonly held to be irreversible.

Unlike Darwin, we know that all natural populations vary genetically, and that this variation entails genetically determined differences in fitness. We have some examples of genetical change in natural populations, related to the adaptation of these populations to environmental changes. And artificial selection has produced genetical change in the laboratory populations of the expected kinds. Among this evidence there are examples of genetically determined changes in behavior.

There have also been attempts to analyze the natural selection process in detail, especially in relation to social interactions. Hypotheses or models have been constructed, based on sets of presumptions about animal conduct; and the consequences of these presumptions have been stated—though not always with general agreement. The hypotheses have given us useful classifications, especially of mating patterns and reproductive "strategies". They also represent attempts to find rules, of high generality, about the relationships of social patterns with conditions of life; but to test inferences, based on the hypotheses, much field work and many experiments are needed.

Such studies increasingly reveal the surprising and fascinating diversity of life histories and behavior. They also make clear some of the problems of method that we face. As knowledge increases, we may hope to expose correlations between patterns of behavior and ecological relationships. The axiom is that each species is, as a result of natural selection, intricately adapted to its environment and mode of life (niche). On this basis we are encouraged to look for order in all the variety we see around us.

19

THE CONCEPTS
OF BEHAVIOR

It may be that some future philosophy will be based on differences as our common-sense philosophy of today is based on similarities. . . . If so, we do not know how these problems will appear to our descendants.

J. B. S. Haldane (1959)

The modern science of behavior has an unfamiliar look, for several reasons. Like other disciplines, it has its own language; and this language is rapidly changing. The disinclination to use such long-established words as instinct, which come easily off the tongues of most people, makes immediate comprehension harder, although it improves rigor. And technical terms such as conditioned reflex, which have come into general use during this century, often have a special sense in science different from that of colloquial usage. Moreover, ethological research is becoming more physiological. Students of behavior have to know more about the brain, the sense organs, the endocrine glands, and other systems than ever before. But, more important than these obvious changes, there are presumptions—often unstated—on how we should investigate behavior. We now examine some of the theoretical principles, already mentioned in earlier chapters, which emerge from current attempts to study be-

havior scientifically. In the behavioral sciences we face, more obviously than in most others, fundamental questions of method.

19.1 OBJECTIVITY

19.1.1 Behaviorism and Awareness

One of the sources of modern ethology is the method of treating behavior as something produced by a mechanism. Some of the clearest examples come from the study of orientations (chapter 2), of which the pioneer was Jacques Loeb (1918) (17.2.1.1). Loeb's contemporary, I. P. Pavlov (1928, 1957), a physiologist, tried to analyze the "higher mental processes" responsible for "learning" in a similar way (5.5; 15.3.1). A third prominent worker, whose name appears in all histories of behavioral science, is J. B. Watson (1878–1958); he advocated a science of behavior based entirely on observing overt movements (including speech). Like the methods of Loeb and Pavlov, this procedure, *behaviorism,* rejects mental events as topics of study (Watson 1930). Notions such as consciousness, will, desire, intention, and so on are discarded as objects of scientific enquiry, on the ground that they do not refer to observable, quantifiable events. Modern ethologists retain an element of behaviorism in their work, in the sense that they try to be objective: they usually avoid statements that attribute human feelings, thoughts, or abilities to other species, because doing so can lead to error or at least to assumptions that cannot be tested (chapter 1).

For some purposes such a policy is essential. If one is studying the settlement of the larvae of oysters, *Ostrea,* it does not help to "explain" their behavior by a will to settle, or by an adhesive drive: that would be like attributing the movement of a steam engine to an *élan locomotif.* But the principle of strict objectivity is difficult to apply, especially if it is interpreted as requiring us to restrict our descriptions of behavior to the actual movements observed. There are at least two causes of difficulty.

1. Our language is against such a method: in colloquial speech it is natural to say that a larva *wants* to settle. Hence we have to use strange ways of speaking if we wish to avoid bogus explanations and unjustified assumptions on what causes behavior. At the same time, it may seem absurd to refuse to say, for example, that a chimpanzee behaved affectionately or angrily; or that it (or he, or she) was frightened. But if, in scientific communication, such expressions are allowed about chimpanzees, it becomes unclear where the line should be drawn: at what level in the animal kingdom should we refuse to employ anthropomorphic and mentalistic language? In this book objective language is generally used for all species except our own. The intention is to write clearly about what is observed (or observable). It is then possible to describe not only what has been seen, but also what can be seen again. On such matters there can be general agreement among those who have the opportunity to record the phenomena for themselves. Such a method does not, of course, exclude physiological findings.

2. An extreme behaviorist position requires that we describe only movements. But in practice it is often impossible to make sense of behavior by doing only that. If we see a bird flapping its wings, pointing its beak upward, and uttering cries, we may call this activity courtship or territorial defense, according to the circumstances and our interpretation of the behavior. But in doing so, we incorporate in our description allusions to the function of the behavior observed, or to its goal.

One aspect of the goal-directedness of behavior is that the animal may seem conscious, or aware of the end toward which it is working. To what extent are we justified in speaking of the awareness of animals? This question has been asked by D. R. Griffin (1976). He does not, however, propose any usable criteria by which we can distinguish awareness from its absence. In practice, we think of an animal as aware when we feel we can identify, from its behavior, thoughts or emotions that we too experience. Such a presumption, of course, need not accompany the finding that an activity is goal-directed. But by making it, we may be helped to form hypotheses that can be tested objectively. If we adopt this method, we need not make a firm decision on whether animals are conscious of what they are doing. It may sometimes be convenient, especially when beginning on a problem, to speak *as if* one's subjects are conscious; but afterwards one should try to present findings that can be checked by other workers, regardless of whether these others have empathy for the animals they study.

The principle of objectivity applies also to the question whether animals are in any sense free to choose what they do. Part V discusses the axiom that human beings have freedom of choice. When animals seem to behave in a "voluntary" way, ethologists rarely speak of them as if they were human: that is, we do not say that animals have a "will of their own": instead we treat them as if the behavior was impelled from within, and not forced on the animal by conditions outside it. The implication is that the causes of such behavior may then be sought—for example, in the brain. In most scientific contexts, to attribute the behavior to the animal's will would be a purely verbal, pseudoexplanation: it would give the phenomenon a name, but would not relate it to other observable events, such as measurable changes in the nervous system.

Nonetheless, it is not necessary to brush off the whole concept of voluntary behavior, or even the idea of mind (compare Gregory Razran, 1971). It is more useful to ask what real features distinguish the behavior colloquially called voluntary. The simplest many-celled animals are "reflex" systems (chapter 5): at almost all times they *reflect,* in their behavior, the immediate input from the external senses. In a discussion on the evolution of mind, D. O. Hebb (1965) calls such animals sense-dominated automata. A jellyfish or a marine larva (chapter 2), if it reacts at all, responds with the same kind of act however often a stimulus is presented. As brains become larger, so behavior becomes more adaptable: the input from the senses is combined, by means we do not know, with the results of *previous* inputs and activity. Hence there is increasing ability to vary the response to a given situation. Moreover, much of the brain of the most complex animals seems organized for autonomous function: one part excites another, without waiting for any special information from the external senses. Hebb identifies the central activity with thought, and equates mind or consciousness with freedom

from the dominance of the senses, combined with a capacity to store and reorganize information from outside (compare chapter 8). Hebb's own comment on these equations is, "Maybe such theory is nonsense."

Accordingly, I leave open the question whether other species possess the freedom of choice of which we are aware in ourselves—or, indeed, whether a statement about an animal's freedom of choice can be given a useful meaning. It seems hardly necessary to worry about this at present. There is plenty to do in the way of objective, probabilistic study, even of chimpanzees. Chapters 8 and 11 give examples of successful research on apes without resort to subjective interpretations or presumptions about freedom.

19.1.2 Function and Teleology

Another aspect of goal-directed behavior is that we are liable to speak as though the behavior can be *explained* by its end. Such explanations are said to be *teleological,* and are commonplace in human affairs: we often say we intend to do something, because of the end we shall thereby achieve; and we also explain the actions of others by their ends. But few writers now accept teleological explanations of animal behavior as useful (reviewed by Marjorie Grene. 1974; J. L. Mackie). We do not say that future events determine what is happening now.

1. Animal behavior is often goal-directed, in the sense that the behavior tends to put the animal in certain kinds of place or to insure the achievement of a given internal state. Such a state is a reference value or *Sollwert* (2.2.2.1; 4.1; 4.3). Often we can see that achieving such a state has survival value. But, when we say all this, we do not imply a conscious intention on the part of an animal. A di-

rected movement may be an orientation of one of the kinds described in chapter 2; or it may be something more complex, as in many social interactions. Often, it is the result of habit formation. Goal-directed activities of these kinds are explained, in the first place, by the immediate situation of the animal and by its current internal state. They may also be partly explained by the earlier experiences of the animal. These causes are in the past. For such activities some people use the term *teleonomic* (C. S. Pittendrigh, 1958).

2. In the second place we explain behavior patterns (and other features) by their functions, that is, by their contribution to survival. Such explanations are quite distinct from those based on behavioral interactions or on physiology. They still, however, refer to (hypothetical) past events (during the evolution of the species): there is no explanation in terms of what the animal intends.

The preceding comments use the notion of cause in a conventional way. But some writers (for example, N. Tinbergen, 1963) not only reject teleology (as most of us do) but distinguish the "causation" of behavior both from effects acting early in development and also from those of past evolution. Hence "causation", in this usage, refers only to what is acting on the animal when it is observed. But the usual meaning of causation includes everything relevant that has happened in the past. There seems to be little point in defining causation so narrowly.

19.1.3 Physiology and Reductionism

Another question of method concerns reductionism. In biology one may try to explain the activities of a whole organism by its physiology or even its chemistry. This statement will perhaps be received by most readers as a truism; but some people reject it; and, at the other extreme, some state that an organism is *nothing but* the molecules or even the ultimate particles (electrons and so on) that compose it (reviewed by Marjorie Grene, 1974; P. B. Medawar, 1974).

In practice (as already shown in 15.4.1) reduction is sometimes useful, sometimes not. Consider a physician taking a patient's blood pressure. The procedure he adopts is an application of mechanics: he is treating the heart as a pump. Indeed, the discovery that the heart pumps the blood around the body was one of the most important single findings in physiology and medicine. To interpret what he observes, the physician may be concerned with the state of the patient's blood vessels. There may be pathological changes in the walls of the arteries. Such changes may usefully be investigated chemically. In principle, treating the blood vessels as a chemical system can help in preventing or treating cardiovascular disease. On the other hand, blood pressure is notoriously influenced by emotional state. The last statement could be expanded in at least two ways. First, it could lead to a behavioristic analysis: it might be useful to make objective, impersonal assertions on the effects of environmental variables on a patient's blood pressure. Second, the patient could (and—most people would say—should) be treated as a person with feelings. The last two procedures are nonreductionist.

We may now turn to more general statements. To reject reduction altogether would be to throw out a large part of behavioral science. Most of the nonsocial components of behavior have a homeostatic function (chapter 4); they can hardly be seriously studied without physiology. And social conduct too can also sometimes be analyzed physiologically: examples are given in 9.3.7, 9.4.1, and 10.5. The next important advances in ethology are quite likely to come from further physiological analysis, perhaps of the relationship between central nervous function and overt behavior. But we are not therefore obliged to jettison concepts concerning the whole organism. Medawar gives, as examples of "distinctive notions of biology at the organism level", heredity, infection, immunity, and sexuality. In ethology we have orientation, habit formation, exploration, territory, and social status, among others. An exploring animal, for example, is a chemical system. But a pure reductionist, who states that it is *only* a chemical system, is involved in a self-contradiction: he states that exploring can be reduced entirely to physics and chemistry; but if so, there is no exploring animal to be explained. K. R. Popper (1974) gives the analogy of the man who draws a detailed map of the room in which he is working, and tries to include the map itself. Whenever he adds a new line to the map, he creates a new object to be drawn . . . Unfortunately, this analogy may not be convincing. As Grene (1974) writes:

To think anti-reductively demands thinking in terms of hierarchical systems, of levels of reality and the like; but we don't know any longer how to think in that way—and to be told, even to *know,* that the contrary position is absurd does not in itself allow us to embrace wholeheartedly what ought to be the more reasonable alternative. For anti-reductivism is "reasonable" only in the perverse sense that its negation is self-contradictory, not in the more substantive sense of fitting smoothly into a *Weltanschauung* in which . . . we can feel at home.

The study of overt behavior by observation, experimental analysis of overt behavior patterns and the physiology of behavior are all exemplified in nearly every chapter of this book. All are necessary components of ethology; and all may appear in a single investigation; but each may be separately pursued. Some workers are enthralled by watching and recording what animals do, but have little liking or talent for designing experiments. Some are happy only if designing experiments on behavior. Yet others are dissatisfied unless they can attempt physiological analysis. Rejection of any of these methods is merely stultifying. The science of behavior is difficult enough, without unnecessary restrictions on the means we use to enlarge it.

19.1.4 Habit Formation and Cognition

Reduction must not be confused with simplification. For example, the feeding behavior of mammals is, at the behavioral level, very diverse. Suppose we try to explain it physiologically; we might, in principle, then establish rules that apply to all mammals. Finding regularities of high generality, or laws, is one of the objectives of research. But the regulation of feeding is very complicated (4.5.2); and the laws that describe it are unlikely to be simple.

Statements on "learning theory" have often combined attempts at both generality and extremes of simplicity, when in fact what we know of habit formation and related phenomena is bewilderingly complex (part III). Two simple concepts dominated research on "learning" until recently—those of the conditional reflex (CR) and of trial-and-error (instrumental or operant conditioning). The first we associate especially with I. P. Pavlov (5.5), the second with E. L. Thorndike (1898, 1911) and B. F. Skinner (6.1.2; 6.2).

Pavlov's original objective was physiological analysis of "higher mental processes"; but his primary achievement was to establish regularities in the effects of reinforcement (and its absence) on autonomically regulated responses such as salivation (5.5). In doing so he used concepts, such as that of extinction, which are now components of all accounts of habit formation. He also introduced the notion of the orienting reflex (OR). His findings have often been interpreted in an extremely simple way: a stimulus such as food in the mouth induces a response such as salivation; another stimulation, such as a sound, at first evokes only the OR, but later, salivation. A machine can be made to respond like this. Pavlov himself made observations that showed, quite dramatically, the inadequacy of such a mechanistic interpretation. First, the preliminary training of a dog, before it will reliably display CRs, is prolonged and elaborate: it cannot be explained in terms of CRs. Second, more important, by requiring his subjects to make difficult discriminations, Pavlov evoked "experimental neurosis", in which behavior is severely disrupted. Such findings reflect the immense complexity of the internal processes involved in even such an apparently simple response as salivary or gastric secretion (5.5.1.4).

The most obvious limitation of CRs is that the experimental conditions in which they are observed allow hardly any behavior. The other popular method, that of the problem box, allows the animal to move but ignores all its movements except those that activate a device and provide reinforcement. Usually, the movement recorded is pressing a bar. Behavior is then presented as a set of response rates that vary with the outcome of bar pressing: that is, all the behavior that is acknowledged depends on the "schedules of reinforcement" provided by the environment. And the environment is, of course, the experimenter and his special equipment. There is little connection between such a "cumulative record" of instrumental movements, on the one hand, and an account of an animal moving around a natural environment, on the other. The most obvious defect in the former is the disregard of exploratory behavior and the accompanying storage of information (8.1.4).

Historically there is a curious anomaly. During the first half of this century, the equipment most used by experimental psychologists was not the problem box but the maze (reviewed by N. L. Munn). A maze allows much more attention to behavior than does a closed problem box; indeed, to an observer unbiased by presumptions about reinforcement and stimulus-response relationships, it forces attention to apparently spontaneous movements; and the study of activity in mazes did eventually lead to fundamentally important findings on the causes and effects of exploratory movements (6.1.1, 8.1.3–4). But this happened only after a long period during which the problem box dominated experimental psychology and profoundly influenced the outlook of psychologists.

During this period quite different ideas about "learning" were separately put forward. These ideas were, and are, incompatible with stimulus-response concepts of behavior, and with the notion that all storage of information in the central nervous system depends on reinforcement: if a single word is required to name them, one may say that they concern *cognition* (8.2.4). In particular, apes were described as sometimes solving problems, not by trial and error, but instantaneously, by using information previously acquired on a number of separate occasions. This has been called insight behavior. Much more recently, the remarkable "linguistic" capacity of chimpanzees has been revealed (8.3).

A separate development resulted from study of the effects of injury to the brain of mammals. As early as 1929, K. S. Lashley (1890–1958) was critical of stimulus-response concepts and of interpretations of central nervous function in terms of the reflex arc. In early experiments, cerebellar lesions were made in rats that had learned to run a maze quickly and without error. When tested again, such rats still ran the maze without error, although they could not walk or run normally. Similarly, if an animal has learned a pathway on foot, it can swim the same route if the paths are now flooded. Such phenomena cannot be interpreted in simple stimulus-response terms. We see here again the phenomena of goal-directedness: an animal can achieve an end by variable means (Lashley, 1950).

Most such work has been on mammals—mainly laboratory rodents and Primates (reviewed by R. L. Isaacson). But some of the abilities observed in them have also been found among the invertebrates. In 8.1.1.1 I describe some remarkable achievements of wasps. It is hardly surprising that ethologists hesitate to use terms such as "cognition": to say that wasps have cognitive abilities sounds like saying that they can think things out; and ethologists dedicated to objective interpretation are reluctant to say that wasps can think. On the other hand, it is now sometimes said that computers can think, and the expression "artificial intelligence" has entered the vocabulary. Some people may therefore conclude that wasps should be equated with the more thoughtful kinds of computers.

In preceding sections I emphasize the value both of concepts derived from objective study of behavior, and also of the physiological analysis of behavior ("reductionism"). On the other hand, reasons are given for hesitating to attribute awareness or consciousness to animals; teleology is rejected; and severe reservations are made about applying the notion of intention to animal behavior. But none of this justifies us in ignoring the complexities of storage of information in the central nervous system, or of the corresponding adaptability of behavior (chapter 8).

19.2 EVOLUTION AND EPIGENESIS

19.2.1 The Neo-Darwinian Paradigm

Objective description, experimental analysis, and physiological interpretation of behavior can all lead to repeatable observations and to testable hypotheses. The other principal foundation of ethology, the theory of evolution by natural selection, has a different role (chapter 18). It provides a frame of reference, or paradigm, for ordering our findings. The prominence of evolutionary accounts of animal behavior is attributable partly to the conventional training of zoologists of the first half of this century: comparative anatomy, based on the idea of homology (18.1.2), was central, and was presented as a study of phylogeny. The resulting systematic knowledge of the animal kingdom made a basis for all zoology. It also led to occasional debates that were enjoyable at the time but not conspicuously fruitful in the long run: for example, there was much argument on whether the Chordata had arisen from primitive Echinodermata. The relevant observations of existing forms, together with a few dubious fossil fragments, did not give much to go on. The reader may speculate on whether current discussions of the phylogeny of behavior patterns will be regarded in the same light a few decades hence.

Whatever the answer, the principal use of the evolutionary framework today is to help us to describe the vast variety of existing animal behavior patterns, and to relate these patterns to mode of life or ecological niche. Attempts are now being made to show how natural selection can have produced the forms we see today (chapter 18). But the resulting models are not merely speculative exercises: they also have implications for the population genetics of existing species; that is, they can lead to hypotheses testable by study of extant forms. Such studies do not, however, in themselves, logically require an evolutionary framework. We can, and do, investigate the ecology and reproductive "strategies" of animal species that have different habitats, social systems, and feeding habits; and we can try to establish how these are related.

Such study requires detailed information, on many aspects of the lives of many species, which is only now beginning to be acquired; but at least the information, unlike the evolutionary processes that led to present species, is accessible; and it can be analyzed without making any evolutionary presumptions.

In biology, the theory of natural selection apart, theories of high generality come from reductionist studies at the level of cells or of biochemistry. The outstanding example of a unitary theory is that concerning the material of heredity. Those who, like many ethologists, investigate whole organisms must continue to struggle with heterogeneous material. Ethology provides as yet no grand synthesis, but—as I fear this book shows very clearly—remains a fragmented subject. Unifying principles come from other branches of biological science.

19.2.2 The Intractable Principle of Interactionism

One such principle, for ethology perhaps the most important, concerns the ontogeny of behavior. When modern ethology was founded, the emphasis on phylogeny led to some extremes of simplification. Behavior patterns were treated as if they were structures: their predictability was overemphasized, as in the notion of fixed action patterns (17.2.4.1.). The patterns were said to be innate, genetically coded, or phylogenetically preprogrammed. It is now coming to be realized that such terms are inappropriate. In particular, the ontogeny of behavior was neglected.

Hence the early account is now being replaced by another, conceptually much more difficult, which incorporates our knowledge both of genetics and of ontogeny. (See especially chapters 12, 16, 17.)

Each unit or pattern of behavior undergoes a development in each individual. The final product in the adult may be remarkably uniform throughout a species, but abnormal conditions of rearing may produce quite exceptional phenotypes. The extent of the developmental lability of each pattern can be decided only by experiment on that pattern. Moreover, there are different kinds of lability. Locusts with their two phases (2.3.6.3) and eusocial insects with their castes (9.1.2), give examples of the way in which behavior can be switched from one developmental path to another. Another much-studied category is that in which sensitive periods early in development are important, as in imprinting (12.3). But the most general kinds of lability come from the adaptability to circumstances of individual behavior—usually discussed under the heading of learning. Many apparently fixed behavior patterns incorporate an adaptive component, that is, some element of habituation or habit formation. The obverse also holds: different species have different capacities for adapting their behavior to circumstances (7.8).

What is given at fertilization is not an already existing organization but only a genome; and even the individual cells of a many-celled animal develop in an environment and are specifically influenced by it. This is the principle of epigenesis (17.3.1). The principle is applied in genetical studies of differences among individuals of the same species (16.2): such studies sometimes enable us to distinguish between the genetical and environmental components of the observed (phenotypic) variation.

Genetical variation between individuals and ontogenetic lability combine to make both populations and individuals responsive to changing environmental demands. "Adaptation" may accordingly be phylogenetic (a property of populations) or ontogenetic (individual) (18.3.1). The two kinds of variation oblige biologists to face problems of method and interpretation which have no counterparts in the physical sciences.

19.3 ORDER AND DIVERSITY

In the physical sciences the trend is toward reduction of phenomena to a few laws or principles. The variety of mixtures and substances we see around us is reduced first to a small number of elements, later to a smaller number of ultimate particles. In the process, chemistry and physics become, to some extent, fused into a single discipline. The search for unifying principles is traditionally that of the "natural philosopher": it may be contrasted with that of the "natural historian", whose concern is with variety. Both are represented in the biological sciences, and the same person may bring together the two extreme attitudes in teaching and even in research.

In biology, reductionists, however enthusiastic, are obliged to face diversity. Sometimes, they can make use of it. Suppose two species or varieties differ in, say, their behavioral responses to a drug. Then a biochemical comparison of the two types might reveal enzymic features corresponding to the behavioral differences.

One consequence of variety is the importance of classification. The science of biological classification, or taxonomy, was not long ago associated with the accumulation of dead bodies or fragments in museums, and with sterile debates on whether such material should be divided into more or fewer species. Today, the classification of organisms involves biochemistry, immunology, genetics, and special mathematics (R. A. Crowson). But the importance of classifying phenomena is much wider than this. Much of the work even of philosophers consists of classifying concepts, propositions, words, and other items; such work requires exceptional penetration and judgment. When successful, it can influence the ways in which scientists and others see the world, and so can help to determine what they do (15.4).

A general principle of method, advocated in this book, is that all means should be used in the attempt to find out more about behavior. Ethology is a hospitable subject. It can accommodate the interests of many kinds of scientists, from those interested in the physics of sense organs to the modern counterparts of the old-fashioned naturalist. But, unlike the products of philosophy, the findings of scientists are almost always about details. The questions asked are rarely grand ones, such as "what is learning?", but are highly specific. For example, given a drug that makes an animal better able to develop useful habits, on what chemical system in the nerve cells does the drug act?

Such a method is unpretentious, though it occasionally produces momentous results. Even when it does not, it is continuously revealing new, beautiful, and surprising facts. We may assume that nothing is inexplicable; but nearly everything remains unexplained.

GLOSSARY

It will be proved to thy face, that thou hast men about thee, that usually talk of a noun, and a verb, and such abominable words, as no Christian ear can endure to hear.

Shakespeare
Henry IV, Part 2

In this book I have (I hope) defined all the terms that I find useful, and that have a special meaning in ethology. These definitions are *stipulative:* they state what the words mean when they are used in this book (and also how I recommend others to use them). Stipulative definitions are statements of a writer's intention: they can be convenient or inconvenient, but can never properly be said to be wrong.

Another important kind of definition is *lexical*. In a dictionary most definitions are statements on how words have been used, and are now being used. Hence lexical definitions can be correct or incorrect. Most of the words in this book, as in all other writings, are used with their lexical meanings; but there are important exceptions. An example is "threat". Technical terms, or jargon, are indeed inevitable; but they do not justify obscure writing. According to one of Oscar Wilde's characters, to be intelligible is to be found out. This is a risk any writer of a scientific text should be willing to accept.

Most of the words listed below are special terms in ethology. Some technical terms, used only in single passages, have been omitted, but are defined where they occur. For them, the reader should consult the index.

The symbol ▲ marks terms which are used in this book, if at all, only in discussing the writings of other authors. It implies that their use is not recommended.

Aggression ▲   A word with many meanings, and a source of much confusion (10.6; 15.3.2).

Agonistic behavior ▲   *Apotreptic behavior* and the conduct associated with it and the responses to it. A useful term only if the actions covered are precisely specified (10.1).

Allele   Two or more genes are alleles of each other when they occupy the same position (*locus*) on homologous chromosomes and produce different effects on a given developmental process.

Allogrooming   Tending the body surface of a *conspecific*.

Allopatric [of species] Occupying different geographical regions. Contrast *sympatric*.

Altricial young Mammals or birds born or hatched in a helpless condition; hence initially confined to a nest or lair. Compare with *precocial young* (9.4.2).

Altruism Concern for others as a principle of conduct. In its primary use, not an ethological term. See *bioaltruism* (15.3.3; 18.2.3).

Amplitude Magnitude or extent (of a stimulus).

Anemotaxis *Taxis* influenced by air movement. Usually results in a movement upwind (2.3.3).

Anthropomorphism Description or explanation of animal behavior as if the animals were human.

Aposematism Conspicuous appearance associated with aversive taste or poisonous composition (3.5).

Apotreptic behavior Conduct that tends to cause withdrawal by a *conspecific*. This term has the same meaning as *threat*, as threat is often used in ethology.

Appetitive behavior ▲ Variable behavior impelled by an internal deficit and ended by its abolition (17.1.2.1).

Aversive stimulus Stimulus that causes withdrawal or avoidance.

Bait-shyness Refusal of food previously accepted, after eating it has been followed by illness. Must not be confused with *neophobia* (4.5.2.4).

Bioaltruism Behavior that decreases the fitness (chances of survival and reproduction) of the actor but increases the fitness of a *conspecific*. *Altruism* is sometimes used with this meaning.

Biotope The special localities, within a habitat, occupied by a given species.

Caste Type of *eusocial insect* structurally and behaviorally distinct from others of its species.

Chemotaxis *Taxis* that depends on stimulation by a substance or mixture of substances.

Circadian rhythm A cycle of behavioral or physiological changes recurring about every 24 h.

Classical conditioning Formation of a *conditional reflex*.

Cognition Internal processes, involving information stored on two or more occasions, which regulate behavior (8.2.4; 19.1.4).

Cognitive processes See *cognition*.

Communication Transfer of information between *conspecifics*. Has many other meanings, some much wider (13.1).

Conditional reflex (CR) A response, elicited by a previously indifferent stimulus (CS), as a result of repeated application of the CS at about the time of application of an existing (*unconditional*) stimulus for a similar act. The latter is the *unconditional response* (or reflex). In a mammal the response is usually mediated by the autonomic nervous system, but may be a tendon reflex. The CS is "indifferent" only with respect to the activity to be studied: it must arouse attention from the first. See *orienting response*. (5.5)

Conditional (conditioned) stimulus See *conditional reflex*.

Conditioned reflex ▲ See conditional reflex.

Congener Member of the same genus.

Conspecific Member of the same species.

Consummatory act ▲ Stereotyped behavior pattern that comes after *appetitive behavior* and ends an "instinctive" behavior sequence (17.1).

Consummatory state ▲ Bodily state of which the achievement ends an activity. The state, or *reference value*, may be a temperature, a chemical feature such as a blood sugar level, and so on (17.1).

Cooperation Behavioral interaction of two or more conspecifics that tends to increase the *fitness* of the actors or of other conspecifics (10.1).

Critical period ▲ See *sensitive period*.

Crypsis Resembling the background. A means of protection from predators (3.4).

Deimatic effects Changes of appearance, usually sudden, which deter predators (3.6).

Deme Small population partly or completely isolated from others of the same species.

Deutero-learning Development of ability to solve problems as a result of diverse experience, especially in early life (8.1.4.2).

Discrimination Responding to a stimulus, S_1, but not to a similar stimulus, S_2. Discrimination is the obverse *of generalization* (5.5.1.1; 6.1.1).

Displacement behavior ▲ (17.1.2.4; 18.5.2).

Display Imprecise term referring to a *social signal* or pattern of signals, especially visible ones (13.3.1.2).

Disruptive behavior Behavior that tends to reduce the *fitness* of a conspecific (10.1).

Dominance Often ambiguous term referring to an animal's having prior access to food, a place, or a mate among members of its own group. The exact meaning of dominance should be stated in any report in which it is used. Dominance should be distinguished from an animal's superiority resulting from its being on its own *territory*. Dominance should also be distinguished from being a *leader* (10.1; 11.3).

Dominance hierarchy ▲ See *status system*.

Dominant See *dominance*.

Drive ▲ An internal state causing altered activity; often accompanied by an epithet, as in "hunger drive" (4.5.4; 17.1.2).

Dymantic ▲ See *deimatic effects*.

Eccritic Preferred.

Entrainment Synchronization of a biological rhythm, such as that of sleep, with an environmental sequence, such as that of night and day. (See *Zeitgeber*.) (2.1.3)

Epigamic selection Selection for features that increase the chances of mating by attracting members of the opposite sex (18.4.4).

Epitreptic behavior Behavior that tends to cause the approach of a conspecific. Obverse of *apotreptic behavior*.

Ethology The science of animal behavior. Includes the scientific investigation of behavior by all means and by all kinds of people.

Eusocial insect Species of insect in which there is cooperation in care of young, reproductive division of labor, and the presence of at least two generations in the colony (9.1.2; 13.3.2).

Exploratory behavior An imprecise term referring to apparently unrewarded movements about an animal's living space (8.1).

Exploratory learning Inferred storage of information in the brain leading to superior habit formation after apparently unrewarded experience of a situation (8.1.4.1).

External inhibition Interference with a response by a novel external stimulus (5.5.1.3).

Extinction Decline in performance of a habit as a result of its repeated evocation without subsequent

reinforcement (6.2.1.4). Pavlov's original term for this phenomenon was *internal inhibition* (5.5.1.3).

Feedback Transfer of output to input, in such a way as to modify the input. (In positive feedback the input is facilitated. In negative feedback the input is reduced.) (4.1)

Feedforward Change that anticipates need.

Fitness Proportion of the next generation contributed by an organism's offspring (18.2).

Fixed action pattern Stereotyped, highly predictable, taxon-typical behavior sequence (17.2.4.1).

Generalization Responding to a stimulus, S_2, in the same way as to a similar stimulus S_1. The obverse of *discrimination* (6.2.2).

Geotaxis *Taxis* evoked by gravity.

Habit Pattern of response individually developed as a result of *reward* or *punishment*.

Habituation Decline in performance of an act as a result of changes in the nervous system due to repetition of a stimulus which evokes the act (5.2–4).

Harem Group of adult females associated and mating with a single male.

Home range An imprecise term referring to the whole region visited by an animal during a specified period. Home range should be distinguished from *territory* (11.4.1).

Homeostasis Maintaining a steady internal state (4.1).

Homeotherm Animal of which the deep body temperature is kept steady despite a varying external temperature.

Homolog An organ with a structure or set of relationships, especially during embryonic development, resembling those of a different organ of another species. The similarity of pattern is assumed to be due to common descent of the two organisms. A much-debated concept in comparative anatomy. Not a useful term in ethology (18.1.2).

Imitation The performance of a novel action as a result of observing the action performed by another (8.4.2).

Imprinting Development during an early *sensitive period* of the tendency to follow or otherwise to approach an object, usually a *conspecific* (12.3).

Inhibition A neural process that prevents or reduces

the activity of an effector organ. (Has other meanings.)

Innate behavior ▲   (17.1).

Innate releasing mechanism (IRM) ▲   (17.2.5).

Insight behavior   Imprecise term referring to a sudden adaptive change in behavior (8.2.4).

Instinct ▲   (chapter 17).

Instinctive behavior ▲   (chapter 17).

Instrumental conditioning ▲   *Trial-and-error behavior* (chapters 6, 7).

Intention movement   Incomplete movement preliminary to performance of a complete pattern. The importance, if any, of this concept is that some such movements are said to have undergone *ritualization* during evolution, and to have become *social signals* (18.5.3).

Internal inhibition ▲   Synonym of *extinction* (5.5.1.3).

Intersexual selection   Synonym of *epigamic selection*.

Intrasexual selection   Selection for features that enhance the ability to compete for mates with members of the same sex (18.4.3).

IRM   *Innate releasing mechanism*.

Kinesis   Undirected movement of which the velocity or rate (or degree) of turning varies with the intensity of a particular type of stimulation (2.2.4).

Klinokinesis   *Kinesis* in which the rate or degree of turning depends on the intensity of stimulation (2.2.4.2).

Klinotaxis   *Taxis* dependent on lateral deviations of body or part of body and comparison and equalization of stimulation on the two sides (2.2.2.1).

Latency   Interval between stimulus and response.

Latent learning ▲   *Exploratory learning*.

Leader   Animal that goes ahead of its group or otherwise determines direction of the group's movement. Leadership should not be confused with *dominance* (10.1).

Learning set   The ability to solve a class of problems. Distinct from the ability to solve a particular problem; see *deutero-learning* (8.1.4; 8.2).

Lek   Communal mating ground.

Light-compass orientation   Movement at a temporarily fixed angle to a source of light, usually from the side (2.2.3).

Locus   The position occupied by a gene or one of its *alleles* on a chromosome. Homologous chromosomes have identical loci in the same linear order.

Maternal imprinting   Attachment of female to her young resulting from the presence of the young shortly after birth. Compare *imprinting* (12.3.7).

Migration   The movement of a population from one region to another, and its subsequent return (2.4).

Motivation ▲   The fluctuating internal states that determine what kinds of behavior and what intensity of activity can be evoked. (See *drive*.) (17.1.2)

Negative reinforcer   *Punishment*.

Neophilia   Approaching unfamiliar, in preference to familiar, objects or places (8.1.3).

Neophobia   The avoidance of unfamiliar objects in a familiar environment. Not to be confused with *bait-shyness* (1.1.3).

New-object reaction   *Neophobia*.

Niche   The mode of life or role of a species in relation to the ecosystem of which it is part.

Operant ▲   Action that leads to reinforcement, positive or negative (6.1.2).

Operant conditioning ▲   *Trial-and-error behavior* (chapters 6, 7).

Orientation   Position or direction of movement in relation to a source of stimulation or to a destination.

Orienting response (OR)   Movement evoked by a novel stimulus. The classical example is the pricking of the ears and turning of the head of a dog exposed to a sudden noise (5.2.2.2; 5.5.1).

Orthokinesis   Kinesis in which the velocity of movement depends on the intensity of stimulation (2.2.4.1).

Pair bond ▲   Refers to a prolonged association between a male and a female (9.3.7.1).

Peck-dominance ▲   Feature of a *status system* in which animal A behaves apotreptically more often toward animal B, than does B toward A. Contrast *peck-right*.

Peck order ▲   *Status system*.

Peck-right ▲   Feature of a *status system* in which animal A behaves apotreptically toward animal B, but B never toward animal A. Contrast *peck-dominance*.

Pheromone   Odor that acts as a *social signal* (13.2.3.1).

Photonegative Moving away from light or toward dark.

Photopositive Moving toward light or away from dark.

Phototaxis *Taxis* evoked by light.

Piloerection Raising or bristling of the hair.

Play Imprecise term referring as a rule to behavior which resembles that of adults but is incomplete and erratic. In particular, behavior called social play appears to be unrelated to any special internal need, consists of incomplete or distorted adult patterns, and has no specific outcome (8.4.2.6).

Pleiotropic (of a gene) Influencing more than one phenotypic feature.

Poikilotherm An animal of which the deep body temperature depends on the outside temperature (2.3.4). Contrast *homeotherm*.

Polyandry Mating by a female with more than one male during the same breeding season. The males usually take part in the rearing of the young.

Polybrachygamy Promiscuity, or mating with two or more others during the same breeding season.

Polyethism Division of labor among *eusocial insects* (9.1.2).

Polygamy *Polyandry* or *polygyny*.

Polygyny Mating by a male with more than one female in a given breeding season.

Positive reinforcer *Reward* (6.2.1.1).

Precocial young Young that are mobile very shortly after birth or hatching. Contrast *altricial young* (9.4.2.3).

Primer pheromone A *pheromone* with a slowly acting physiological effect. Contrast *releaser pheromone* (13.2.3).

Promiscuity *Polybrachygamy*.

Protohabituation Change in the behavior of Protozoa which resembles *habituation* (5.4.1).

Pseudoconditioning *Sensitization* that simulates a specific effect of training (5.3.2).

Punishment Response-contingent *aversive stimulus* (6.2.4).

Queen Fertile female of species of *eusocial insect*. Compare *worker* (9.1.2; 13.3.2).

Reductionism Presumption that a complex system can be fully understood by analyzing it in terms of simpler constituents or concepts (19.1.3).

Reference value A state (or goal) which behavior (or physiological processes) tends to achieve. Synonym of *Sollwert* (chapter 4).

Reflex A response that is an immediate and simple reaction to stimulation, is highly predictable, is performed always by the same muscles, and is consistently related to a particular kind of stimulation (5.1.3).

Reinforcement The operation of a *reward,* or of removal of a *punishment* (6.2).

Releaser ▲ A standard external stimulus which evokes a standard response.

Reward A stimulus which strengthens the response that evokes it (6.2.1).

Ritualization The hypothetical modification of a behavior pattern during evolution, so that it becomes a *social signal*. Not to be confused with the rituals of human conduct (18.5.4).

Search(ing) image Hypothetical representation in the central nervous system of a class of objects (especially prey) which enhances responsiveness to such objects (3.3.3).

Sensitive period A period in an animal's life, usually early, when a particular kind of habit is easily acquired, or when it is easy to evoke a particular kind of behavior. Synonym of *critical period* (12.1).

Sensitization Persistent increase in responsiveness owing to repeated stimulation. The obverse of *habituation* (5.3).

Sexual imprinting Process analogous to *imprinting* by which experience in early life influences the objects toward which the adult is sexually responsive (12.3.4).

Sexual selection Selection for features that enhance the ability to compete for a mate. See also *intrasexual* and *epigamic* selection.

Signal A small change in distribution of energy or matter which induces a much larger change. A signal may or may not act at a distance (13.1).

Social behavior Interactions between *conspecifics*.

Social signal Any property of an animal which acts as a *signal* and has a distinctive influence on a *conspecific* (13).

Social stress Imprecise term referring to adverse physiologica! effects of social interactions (10.5).

Sociobiology The interpretation of social interactions in terms of presumptions about the action of natural selection. Sometimes used in a wider sense that almost coincides with the whole of social ethology.

Sollwert *Reference value.*

Startle display See *deimatic effects* (3.6).

Status system Relationships of *dominance* and *subordinacy* within a group of *conspecifics*. Synonym of dominance hierarchy and, sometimes, of peck order (10.1; 11.3).

Stimulus An event (usually a *signal*) that excites any of an animal's receptors.

Stress ▲ Physiological response to adverse environmental agencies.

Stressor ▲ Adverse environmental agency.

Subordinacy The obverse of *dominance* (11.3).

Subordinate An individual that displays *subordinacy*. The obverse of *dominant*.

Symbiosis Association of members of two or more species to their mutual advantage. (Sometimes used for all associations of different species, whatever the precise relationship.)

Sympatric [of species] Occupying the same geographical region. Contrast *allopatric*.

Taxis Movement directly to or from a single source of stimulation (2.2.2).

Teaching Behavior that tends to alter the behavior of a *conspecific* (pupil), and tends to be persisted in until the pupil achieves a certain standard of performance. This is an objective, ethological definition, used especially for comparing animal with human behavior (8.4.3).

Teleology Explanation of an event by its outcome. The most usual kind of such explanation is where an action is undertaken on the basis of prediction of its result. Such actions are performed only by human beings. See also *teleonomy*. (19.1.2)

Teleonomy ▲ Explanation of an action in terms of its outcome, but based on the attribution to the action of causes operating in the past. Contrast *teleology*. (19.1.2)

Telotaxis *Taxis* not dependent on symmetrical stimulation (2.2.2.3).

Territory A region occupied by an individual, pair, or larger group to the exclusion of other *conspecifics*. The term is restricted by many authors to defended regions (10.4; 11.4.1).

Thermotaxis *Taxis* in response to a source of heat (2.3.4).

Threat *Apotreptic behavior.*

Transverse orientation Orientation (not necessarily movement) at an angle (which may be only temporarily fixed) to the direction of a stimulus (2.2.3).

Trial-and-error behavior Gradually acquiring a habit, partly as a result of elimination of unnecessary movements (chapters 6, 7).

Tropotaxis Taxis dependent on simultaneous comparison of stimulation intensity on the two sides (2.2.2.2).

Unconditional response See *conditional reflex*.

Warning coloration *Aposematism.*

Worker Infertile member of colony of *eusocial insects*. See also *queen* (9.1.2; 13.3.2).

Zeitgeber An environmental agency that regulates the timing of a biological rhythm. (See *entrainment*.) (2.1.3)

Zoomorphism Explaining what people do by reference to animal behavior.

Zugunruhe Restlessness (of a bird) at the season of migration (2.4.2).

REFERENCES

Some of the titles of papers have been shortened. The following special abbreviations are used for three journals cited frequently:

AB   *Animal Behaviour*
JCPP   *Journal of Comparative and Physiological Psychology*
ZTP   *Zeitschrift für Tierpsychologie*

Ackerknecht E. H. 1958 In *The History and Philosophy of Knowledge of the Brain and its Functions.* Oxford: Blackwell. Contributions of Gall and the phrenologists to knowledge of brain function.

Ademec R. E. 1976 *Behav. Biol.* **18**, 263–272. The interaction of hunger and preying in the domestic cat.

Adler H. E. 1955 *J. Genet. Psychol.* **86**, 159–177. Observational learning in cats.

Adler L. L., Adler H. E. 1977 *Dev. Psychobiol.* **10**, 267–271. Observational learning in the dog.

Agar W. E. et al. 1954 *J. Exp. Biol.* **31**, 308–321. Test of McDougall's Lamarckian experiment on the training of rats.

Alcock J. 1969 *Ibis* **111**, 308–321. Observational learning in three species of birds.

Aleksiuk M. 1976 *J. Therm. Biol.* **1**, 153–156. Metabolic and behavioural adjustments to temperature change in the red-sided garter snake.

Alexander R. D. 1974 *Annu. Rev. Ecol. Syst.* **5**, 325–383. The evolution of social behavior.

Alexander R. D., Sherman P. W. 1977 *Science* **196**, 494–500. Local mate competition and parental investment in social insects.

Alloway T. M. 1973 In Corning W. C., Dyal J. A., Willows A. O. D. (ed.) *Invertebrate Learning.* New York & London: Plenum. Learning in insects.

Altmann S. A. 1962 *Ann. N.Y. Acad. Sci.* **102**, 338–435. The sociobiology of rhesus monkeys.

Alvarez F., Braza F., Norzagaray A. 1976 *Behaviour* **56**, 298–308. The use of the rump patch in the fallow deer.

Anderson B. et al. 1977 *Aggr. Behav.* **3**, 33–46. Effects of short-term crowding on aggression in captive groups of pigtail monkeys.

Anderson C. O., Mason W. A. 1974 *JCPP* **87**, 681–690. Early experience and complexity of social organization in groups of young rhesus monkeys.

Andersson B. 1978 *Physiol. Rev.* **58**, 582–603. Regulation of water intake.

Andersson M. & Erlinge S. 1977 *Oikos* **29**, 591–597. Influence of predation on rodent populations.

Andrew R. J. 1956 *Br. J. Anim. Behav.* **4**, 41–45. Some remarks on behaviour in conflict situations.

Andrew R. J. 1957 *Behaviour* **10**, 255–308. The aggressive and courtship behaviour of certain Emberizines.

Andrew R. J. 1973 *Behaviour* **51**, 135–165. Arousal and the causation of behaviour.

Andy O. J., Stephan H. 1974 In Holloway R. L. (ed.) *Primate Aggression, Territoriality, and Xenophobia.* New York & London: Academic. Comparative primate neuroanatomy of structures relating to aggressive behavior.

Angst W., Thommen D. 1977 *Folia Primatol.* **27**, 198–229. Infant killing in monkeys and apes.

Applewhite P. B. 1968 *Nature (London)* **217**, 287–288. Non-local nature of habituation in a rotifer and protozoan.

Applewhite P. B., Gardner F. T. 1973 *Behav. Biol.* **9**, 245–250. Tube-escape behavior of paramecia.

Applewhite P. B., Morowitz H. J. 1966 *Yale J. Biol. Med.* **39**, 90–105. The Micrometazoa as model systems for studying the physiology of memory.

Aranda L. C. et al. 1968 *Physiol. Behav.* **3**, 753–756. The influence of the four first anterior ganglia on learned behavior in *Lumbricus terrestris*.

Archer J. 1973 *AB* **21**, 205–235. Tests for emotionality in rats and mice.

Arens W. 1979 *The Man-eating Myth.* New York: Oxford University Press.

Arieti S. 1972 *The Will to be Human.* New York: Quadrangle.

Armitage K. B. 1974 *J. Zool.* **172**, 233–265. Male behaviour and territoriality in the yellow-bellied marmot.

Arnold S. J. 1976 *ZTP* **42**, 247–300. Sexual behavior, sexual interference and sexual defense in salamanders.

Aronson L. R. 1951 *Am. Mus. Novit.* **1486**, 1–22. Orientation and jumping behavior in the gobiid fish *Bathygobius soporator*.

Aronson L. R. 1971 *Ann. N. Y. Acad. Sci.* **188**, 378–393. Further studies on orientation and jumping behavior in the gobiid fish, *Bathygobius soporator*.

Aschoff J. 1960 *Cold Spring Harbor Symp. Quant. Biol.* **25**, 11–28. Exogenous and endogenous components in circadian rhythms.

Austin J. L. 1956 *Proc. Br. Acad.* **17**, 109–132. Ifs and cans.

Babkin B. P. 1951 Pavlov: A Biography. London: Gollancz.

Baerends G. P. 1941 *Jur. Tijd. Entomol.* **84**, 71–275. Fortpflanzungsverhalten und Orientierung der Grabwespe.

Baerends G. P. 1957 In Brown M. E. (ed.) *The Physiology of Fishes.* Vol. 2: *Behavior.* New York: Academic. Behavior: the ethological analysis of fish behavior.

Baerends G. P., Baerends-Van Roon J. M. 1950 *Behaviour Suppl.* **1**, 1–242. The ethology of cichlid fishes.

Bagnoli P. et al. 1976 *JCPP* **108**, 133–156. Neural mechanisms underlying spontaneous flashing in the firefly *Luciola lusitanica*.

Baker R. R., Parker G. A. 1979 *Philos. Trans. R. Soc. Ser. B* **287**, 63–130. The evolution of bird coloration.

Baldwin B. A., Ingram D. L. 1968 *Physiol. Behav.* **3**, 409–415. Behavioral thermoregulation in the pig.

Baldwin J. D. 1968 *Folia Primatol.* **9**, 281–314. The social behavior of adult male squirrel monkeys.

Baldwin J. D. 1971 *Folia Primatol.* **14**, 23–50. The social organization of a semifree-ranging troop of squirrel monkeys.

Bandura A. 1977 *Social Learning Theory.* Englewood Cliffs, N.J.: Prentice-Hall.

Banks J. H., Miller R. E., Ogawa N. 1966 *J. Genet. Psychol.* **108**, 199–211. Discriminated autonomic and instrumental responses during avoidance conditioning in the rhesus monkey.

Barfield, R. J. 1971 *J. Endocrinol.* **49**, 305–310. Gonadotrophic hormone secretion in the female ring dove in response to visual and auditory stimulation by the male.

Barlow G. W. 1977 In Sebeok T. A. (ed.) *How Animals Communicate.* Bloomington & London: Indiana University Press. Modal action patterns.

Barlow G. W., Green R. F. 1969 *Commun. Biol.* **4**, 71–78. Effect of relative size of mate on color patterns in a mouthbreeding cichlid fish.

Barnett S. A. 1956 *Behaviour* **9**, 24–43. The feeding of wild and laboratory rats.

Barnett S. A. 1958a *Proc. Zool. Soc. London* **130**, 107–152. Social behaviour in wild rats.

Barnett S. A. 1958b *J. Psychosom. Res.* **3**, 1–11. "Social stress" in wild rats. 1. The adrenal cortex.

Barnett S. A. 1964 In Carthy J. D., Duddington C. L. (ed.) *Viewpoints in Biology,* 3. London: Butterworths. Social stress.

Barnett S. A. 1975 *The Rat: A Study in Behavior.* Chicago: University of Chicago Press. (2nd edn.)

Barnett S. A. 1977 *Aggr. Behav.* **3**, 209–229. The instinct to teach: Altruism or aggression?

Barnett S. A., Cowan P. E. 1976 *Interdiscip. Sci. Rev.* **1**, 43–62. Activity, exploration, curiosity and fear.

Barnett S. A., Dickson R. G., Hocking W. E. 1979 *Aggr. Behav.* **5**, 105–119. The social interactions of wild and domestic "Norway" rats.

Barnett S. A., Evans C. S., Stoddart R. C. 1968 *J. Zool.* **154**, 391–396. Influence of females on conflict among wild rats.

Barnett S. A., McEwan I. M. 1973 *Physiol. Behav.* **10**, 741–746. Movements of virgin, pregnant and lactating mice in a residential maze.

Barnett S. A., Mount L. E. 1967 In Rose A. S. (ed.) *Thermobiology.* London: Academic. Resistance to cold in mammals.

Barnett S. A., Smart J. L. 1970 *Q. J. Exp. Psychol.* **22**, 494–502. Activity of inbred and F_1 mice in a residential maze.

Barnett S. A., Stewart A. P. 1975 *Aust. J. Zool.* **23**, 103–112. Audible signals during intolerant behaviour of *Rattus fuscipes.*

Barnett S. A., Stoddart R. C. 1969 *J. Mammal.* **50**, 321–325. Effects of breeding in captivity on conflict among wild rats.

Barrass R. 1963 *J. Anim. Ecol.* **32**, 73–85. The burrows of *Ocypode ceratophthalmus.*

Barry H., Bacon M. K., Child I. L. 1957 *J. Abnorm. Soc. Psychol.* **55**, 327–332. A cross-cultural survey of some sex differences in socialization.

Bartoshuk A. K. 1962 *Percept. Mot. Skills* **15**, 15–27. Human neonatal cardiac acceleration to sound.

Bastian J. 1966 In Busnel R.-G. (ed.) *Les Systèmes Sonar Animaux: Biologie et Bionique.* Tome II. France: Laboratoire de Physiologie Acoustique. The transmission of arbitrary environmental information between bottlenose dolphins.

Bastock M. 1956 *Evolution* **10**, 421–439. A gene mutation which changes a behavior pattern.

Bastock M. 1967 *Courtship: A Zoological Study.* London: Heinemann Educational.

Bastock M., Manning A. 1955 *Behaviour* **8**, 85–111. The courtship of *Drosophila melanogaster.*

Bates B. C. 1970 *Primates* **11**, 271–284. Territorial behavior in primates.

Bates H. W. 1862 *Trans. Linn. Soc. Lond.* **23**, 495–566. Contributions to an insect fauna of the Amazon Valley.

Bateson G. 1942 In *Science, Philosophy & Religion.* New York: Second Symposium. Social planning and the concept of "deutero-learning".

Bateson P. P. G. 1971 In Moltz H. (ed.) *Ontogeny of Vertebrate Behavior.* New York: Academic. Imprinting.

Bateson P. P. G. 1973 In Hinde R. A., Stevenson-Hinde J. (ed.) *Constraints on Learning.* London: Academic. Internal influences on early learning in birds.

Batzli G. O., Getz L. L., Hurley S. S. 1977 *J. Mammal.* **58**, 583–591. Suppression of growth and reproduction of microtine rodents by social factors.

Baylor E. R., Smith F. E. 1957 In Scheer B. T. (ed.) *Recent Advances in Invertebrate Physiology.* Eugene: University of Oregon. Diurnal migration of plankton crustaceans.

Beach F. A. 1940 *J. Comp. Psychol.* **29**, 193–245. Effects of cortical lesions and the copulatory behavior of male rats.

Beach F. A. 1950 *Am. Psychol.* **5**, 115–124. The Snark was a Boojum.

Beach F. A. 1974 *Biol. Reprod.* **10**, 2–18. Behavioral endocrinology and the study of reproduction.

Beach F. A., Jaynes J. 1956a *J. Mammal.* **37**, 177–180. Maternal retrieving in rats. 1. Recognition of young.

Beach F. A., Jaynes J. 1956b *Behaviour* **10**, 104–125. Maternal retrieving in rats. 3. Sensory cues in the lactating female's response.

Beauchamp G. K., Hess E. H. 1971 *ZTP* **28**, 69–76. The effects of cross-species rearing on the social and sexual preferences of guinea pigs.

Beck B. B. 1974 *J. Hum. Evol.* **3**, 509–516. Baboons, chimpanzees, and tools.

Beer C. G. 1963 *Tuatara* **11**, 170–177. The zoologist's approach to behaviour.

Beer C. G. 1964 *Tuatara* **12**, 16–39. The zoologist's approach to behaviour.

Beer C. G. 1968 *Sci. Psychoanal.* **12**, 198–213. Ethology on the couch.

Beer C. G. 1970 *Adv. Study Behav.* **3**, 27–74. Individual recognition of voice in the social behavior of birds.

Beer C. G. 1972 *Proc. XV Int. Ornithol. Congr.*, 339–356. Individual recognition of voice and its development in birds.

Beer C. G. 1974 In White N. F. (ed.) *Ethology and Psychiatry*. Toronto: University of Toronto. Comparative ethology and the evolution of behaviour.

Beer C. G. 1976 *Ann. N.Y. Acad. Sci.* **280**, 413–432. The communication behavior of gulls.

Beer C. G. 1977 *Am. Zool.* **17**, 155–165. What is a display?

Bekoff M. 1976 In Bateson P. P. G., Klopfer P. H. (ed.) *Perspectives in Ethology*. Vol 2. New York: Plenum. Animal play: Problems and perspectives.

Bekoff M. 1977a *Am. Nat.* **111**, 715–732. Mammalian dispersal and the ontogeny of individual behavioral phenotypes.

Bekoff M. 1977b In Hazlett B. A. (ed.) *Quantitative Methods in the Study of Animal Behavior*. New York: Academic. Quantitative studies of three areas of ethology.

Bell R. W. 1974 *Dev. Psychobiol.* **7**, 39–42. Ultrasounds in small rodents.

Bell S. M., Ainsworth M. D. S. 1972 *Child Dev.* **43**, 1171–1190. Infant crying and maternal responsiveness.

Bell W. J., Burk T., Sams G. R. 1973 *Behav. Biol.* **9**, 251–255. Cockroach aggregation pheromone.

Bellisle F. 1979 *Neurosci. Biobehav. Rev.* **3**, 163–169. Human feeding behavior.

Ben Shaul D. M. 1962 In Jarvis C., Morris D. (ed.) *Inter Zoo Year Book*. Vol. 4. London: Hutchinson. The composition of the milk of wild animals.

Berlyne D. E. 1960 *Conflict, Arousal, and Curiosity*. New York: McGraw-Hill.

Berlyne D. E. 1969 In Tapp J. T. (ed.) *Reinforcement and Behavior*. London: Academic. The reward-value of indifferent stimulation.

Bernal J. F., Richards M. P. M. 1973 In Barnett S. A. (ed.) *Ethology and Development*. London: Heinemann Medical. What can the zoologists tell us about human development?

Bernays E. A., Chapman R. F. 1974 In Browne L. B. (ed.) *Experimental Analysis of Insect Behaviour*. Berlin: Springer-Verlag. The regulation of food intake by acridids.

Bernstein I. S. 1964 *Folia Primatol.* **2**, 50–63. The integration of rhesus monkeys introduced to a group.

Bernstein I. S. 1966 *Tulane Stud. Zool.* **13**, 49–54. Analysis of a key role in a capuchin group.

Bernstein I. S. 1970 In Rosenblum L. A. (ed.) *Primate Behavior—Developments in Field and Laboratory Research*. New York: Academic. Primate status hierarchies.

Bernstein I. S., Gordon T. P. 1974 *Am. Sci.* **62**, 304–311. Aggression in primate societies.

Beroza M., Knipling E. F. 1972 *Science*, **177**, 19–27. Gypsy moth control with the sex attractant pheromone.

Berry K. H. 1974 *Univ. Calif., Berkeley, Publs. Zool.* **101**, 1–60. The ecology and social behavior of the chuckwalla.

Berthold P. 1975 In Farner D. S., King J. R., Parkes K. C. (ed.) *Avian Biology*. Vol. 5. New York: Academic. Migration: Control and metabolic physiology.

Bertram B. 1970 *Anim. Behav. Monog.* **3**, 79–192. The vocal behaviour of the Indian hill mynah.

Bertram B. C. R. 1975 *J. Zool.* **177**, 463–482. Social factors influencing reproduction in wild lions.

Beswick D. G. 1970 In Day H. I., Berlyne D. E., Hunt D. E. (ed.) *Intrinsic Motivation: A New Direction in Education*. Toronto: Holt, Rinehart & Winston. Individual differences in curiosity.

Beukema J. J. 1968 *Behaviour* **31**, 1–126. Predation by the three-spined stickleback.

Beusekom G. van 1948 *Behaviour* **1**, 195–225. Some experiments on optical orientation in *Philanthus triangulum*.

Bidder G. P. 1930 *Nature* (*London*) **125**, 783–786. Cataclasms in evolution.

Bider J. R., Thibault P., Sarrazin R. 1968 *Mammalia* **32**, 137–163. Schémes dynamiques spatio-temporels de l'activité de *Procyon lotor*.

Bierens de Haan J. A. 1950 In *Chambers Encyclopaedia*. Vol. 7. Instinct.

Bignami G. 1965 *AB* **13**, 221–227. Selection for high rates and low rates of avoidance conditioning.

Birch H. G. 1945 *J. Comp. Psychol.* **38**, 367–383. The relation of previous experience to insightful problem-solving.

Birch M. C. 1970 *AB* **18**, 310–316. Pre-courtship use of abdominal brushes by the nocturnal moth, *Phlogophora meticulosa*.

Birch M. C. (ed.) 1974 *Pheromones*. Amsterdam: North-Holland.

Birdsell J. B. 1972 *Human Evolution*. Chicago: Rand McNally.

Bishop J. A., Cook L. M., Muggleton J. 1978 *Philos. Trans. R. Soc. Ser. B* **281**, 489–514. The response of two species of moths to industrialization.

Bitterman M. E. 1968 In Ingle D. (ed.) *The Central Nervous System and Fish Behavior*. Chicago: University of Chicago Press. Learning in fish.

Bitterman M. E. 1975 *Science* **188**, 699–709. The comparative analysis of learning.

Bitterman M. E., Schoel W. M. 1970 *Annu. Rev. Psychol.* **21**, 367–436. Instrumental learning in animals.

Blair W. F. 1968 In Sebeok T. A. (ed.) *Animal Communication*. Bloomington: Indiana University Press. Amphibians and reptiles.

Blakemore C. 1977 *Mechanics of the Mind*. Cambridge: Cambridge University Press.

Blakemore C., Cooper G. F. 1970 *Nature* (*London*) **228**, 477–478. Development of the brain depends on the visual environment.

Blest A. D. 1957 *Behaviour* **11**, 210–256. The function of eyespot patterns in the Lepidoptera.

Blest A. D. 1966 In Thorpe W. H., Zangwill O. L. (ed.) *Current Problems in Animal Behaviour*. Cambridge: Cambridge University Press. The concept of "ritualisation."

Blight A. R. 1977 *Biol. Rev.* **52**, 181–218. The muscular control of vertebrate swimming movements.

Blizard D. A., Randt C. T. 1974 *Nature* (*London*) **251**, 705–707. Genotype interaction with undernutrition and external environment in early life.

Blodgett H. C. 1929 *Univ. Calif. Berkeley, Publ. Psychol.* **4**, 113–134. The effect of reward upon maze performance.

Blum M. S. 1974 In Birch M. C. (ed.) *Pheromones*. Amsterdam: North-Holland. Pheromonal bases of social manifestations in insects.

Blurton-Jones N. (ed.) 1972 *Ethological Studies of Child Behaviour*. Cambridge: Cambridge University Press.

Blurton-Jones N. G. 1973 In Michael R. P., Crook J. H. (ed.) *Comparative Ecology and Behaviour of Primates*. London: Academic. Sex differences in behaviour of London and bushman children.

Boakes R. A., Halliday M. S. 1970 In Borger R., Cioffi F. (ed.) *Explanation in the Behavioural Sciences*. Cambridge: Cambridge University Press. The Skinnerian analysis of behaviour.

Bodmer W. F. 1972 In Richardson K., Spears D. (ed.) Race, Culture and Intelligence. Harmondsworth: Penguin. Race and IQ.

Bodmer W. F., Cavalli-Sforza L. L. 1976 *Genetics, Evolution, and Man*. San Francisco: Freeman.

Boer P. J. den 1961 *Arch. Neerl. Zool.* **14**, 283–409. Activity patterns in the woodlouse.

Bolles R. C. 1962 *JCPP* **55**, 230–234. The readiness to eat and drink.

Bolles R. C. 1967 *Theory of Motivation*. New York: Harper and Row.

Bolwig N. 1946 *Dan. Naturhistor. Foren.* **109**, 81–217. Sense organs of house fly larvae.

Booth D. A. 1976 In Silverstone T. (ed.) *Appetite*

and Food Intake. Life Sciences Research Report **2.** West Berlin: Dahlem Konferenzen. Feeding control.

Booth D. A., Simson P. C. 1971 *Q. J. Exp. Psychol.* **23,** 135–145. Food preferences acquired by association with variations in amino acid nutrition.

Borden J. H. 1974 In Birch M. C. (ed.) *Pheromones.* Amsterdam: North-Holland. Aggregation pheromones in the Scolytidae.

Bouissou M.-F. 1975 *ZTP* **38,** 419–435. Établissement des rélations de dominance-soumission chez les bovins domestiques.

Bourne P. G. 1971 In Eleftheriou B. E., Scott J. P. (ed.) *The Physiology of Aggression and Defeat.* New York: Plenum. Adrenal function in two combat situations.

Bovet-Nitti F. 1968 In Bovet D., Bovet-Nitti F., Oliverio A. (ed.) *Recent Advances on Learning and Retention.* Roma: Accademia Nazionale dei Lincei. L'acquisizione e la retenzione del comportamento di fuga nella "shuttle box".

Bowlby J. 1969 *Attachment and Loss.* Vol. 1. London: Hogarth.

Boycott B. B., Young, J. Z. 1955 *Proc. R. Soc. London Ser. B* **143,** 449–480. A memory system in *Octopus vulgaris.*

Boyden A. 1973 *Perspectives in Zoology.* Oxford: Pergamon.

Brady J. 1971 In Menaker M. (ed.) *Biochronometry.* Washington, D.C.: National Academy of Sciences. The search for an insect clock.

Braemer W., Braemer H. 1958 *Limnol. Oceanogr.* **3,** 362–372. Orientation of fish to gravity.

Brattstrom B. H. 1978 In Greenberg N., MacLean P. D. (ed.) *Behavior and Neurology of Lizards.* Rockville, Md.: National Institute of Mental Health. Learning in lizards.

Brawn V. M. 1961 *Behaviour* **18,** 107–147. Aggressive behaviour in the cod.

Breznak J. A. 1975 *Symp. Soc. Exp. Biol.* **29,** 559–580. Symbiotic relationships between termites and their intestinal microbiota.

Brian A. D. 1949 *Scot. Nat.* **61,** 144–155. Dominance in the great tit.

Brian M. V. 1965 *Symp. Zool. Soc. London* **14,** 13–38. Caste differentiation in social insects.

Brian M. V. 1977 *Ants.* London: Collins.

Brian M. V. 1979 *Soc. Insects* **1,** 121–122. Caste differentiation and division of labor.

Brian M. V., Abbott A. 1977 *AB* **25,** 1047–1055. The control of food flow in a society of *Myrmica rubra.*

Bristowe W. S. 1958 *The World of Spiders.* London: Collins.

Broadhurst P. L. 1960 In Eysenck H. J. (ed.) *Handbook of Abnormal Psychology.* London: Pitman. Abnormal animal behaviour.

Bronson F. H. 1974 In Birch M. C. (ed.) *Pheromones.* Amsterdam: North-Holland. Pheromonal influences on reproductive activities in rodents.

Brookshire K. H. 1976 In Masterton R. B. et al. (ed.) *Evolution of Brain and Behavior in Vertebrates.* Hillsdale, N.J.: Erlbaum. Vertebrate learning: Evolutionary divergences.

Brosset A. 1971 *ZTP* **20,** 279–300. L' "imprinting" chez les Columbidés.

Brower J. V. Z. 1958a *Evolution* **12,** 32–37. Mimicry in some North American butterflies. Part I.

Brower J. V. Z. 1958b *Evolution* **12,** 123–136. Mimicry in some North American butterflies. Part II.

Brower J. V. Z. 1958c *Evolution* **12,** 273–285. Mimicry in some North American butterflies. Part III.

Brown J. L. 1964 *Univ. Calif. Berkeley Publ. Zool.* **60,** 223–328. Agonistic behavior in the Steller's jay.

Brown J. L. 1970 *AB* **18,** 366–378. Cooperative breeding and altruistic behaviour in the Mexican jay.

Brown J. L. 1972 *AB* **20,** 395–403. Communal feeding of nestlings in the Mexican jay.

Brown J. L. 1975 *The Evolution of Behavior.* Fig. 9.4, p. 204. New York: Norton.

Brown J. L. 1978 *Annu. Rev. Ecol. Syst.* **9,** 123–155. Avian communal breeding systems.

Brown R., Bellugi U. 1964 In Lenneberg E. H. (ed.) *New Directions in the Study of Language.* Cambridge, Mass.: M.I.T. Press. The child's acquisition of syntax.

Bruce H. M. 1961. *J. Reprod. Fertil.* **2,** 138–142. The pregnancy-block induced in mice by strange males.

Bruce H. M. 1967 In Wolstenholme G. E. W., O'Connor M. (ed.) *The Effects of External Stimuli on Reproduction*. London: Churchill Livingstone. Effects of olfactory stimuli on reproduction.

Bruch H. 1969 *J. Nerv. Ment. Dis.* **149**, 91–114. Hunger and instinct.

Bruell J. H. 1964 *Am. Zool.* **4**, 125–138. Behavioral and physiological characters of mice and the problem of heterosis.

Bruner J., Tauc L. 1966 *Symp. Soc. Exp. Biol.* **20**, 457–475. Long-lasting phenomena in the molluscan nervous system.

Bruner J. S. 1974–5 *Cognition* **3**, 255–287. From communication to language.

Bruner J. S., Jolly A., Sylva K. (ed.) 1976 *Play–Its Role in Development and Evolution*. Harmondsworth: Penguin.

Bryan J. S., Krasne F. B. 1977 *J. Physiol.* **271**, 351–368. Protection from habituation of the crayfish lateral giant fibre escape response.

Buchsbaum R. 1976 *Animals without Backbones*. Chicago: University of Chicago Press.

Buffon G. L. 1802 *Histoire naturelle*. Paris. (Translated by William Smellie as *A Natural History*, Kelly, London, 1866.)

Bullock T. H., Horridge G. A. 1965 *Structure and Function in the Nervous Systems of Invertebrates*. San Francisco: Freeman.

Bünning E. 1973 *The Physiological Clock*. Berlin: Springer-Verlag. (3rd edn.)

Burgess A., Dean R. F. A. 1962 *Malnutrition and Food Habits*. London: Tavistock.

Burghardt G. M. 1967 *Psychon. Sci.* **7**, 383–384. The primacy effect of the first feeding experience in the snapping turtle.

Burkhardt D. 1967 In Burkhardt D., Schleidt W., Altner H. (ed.) *Signals in the Animal World*. London: Allen & Unwin. The nerve as an electro-chemical conduction path.

Burnet B., Connolly K. 1974 In Abeelen J. H. F. van (ed.) *The Genetics of Behaviour*. Amsterdam: North-Holland. Activity and sexual behaviour in *Drosophila melanogaster*.

Burt W. H. 1949 *J. Mammal.* **30**, 25–27. Territoriality.

Busnel R. G., Dumortier B. 1954 *C.R. Soc. Biol.* **148**, 1751–1754. Caractères du signal du sifflet de Galton provoquant la phonotaxie de la ♀ *d'Ephippiger bitterensis*.

Buss I. O., Smith N. S. 1966 *J. Wildl. Manage.* **30**, 375–388. Reproduction and breeding of the African elephant.

Bustard H. R. 1970 *Ecology* **51**, 724–728. The natural regulation of numbers in *Gehyra variegata*.

Butler C. G. 1949 *The Honeybee*. Oxford: Clarendon Press.

Butler R. A. 1965 In Schrier A. M., Harlow H. F., Stollnitz F. (ed.) *Behavior of Nonhuman Primates*. London: Academic. Investigative behavior.

Caldwell R. L., Dingle H. 1976 *Evolution* **31**, 220–223. Variation in agonistic behavior between populations of the stomatopod, *Haptosquilla glyptocercus*.

Calhoun J. B. 1961 *Trans. N.Y. Acad. Sci.* **23**, 437–444. Social organization in a single population of domesticated rats.

Campbell B. G. 1967 *Human Evolution: An Introduction to Man's Adaptations*. London: Heinemann Educational.

Campbell R. G., Hashim S. A., Itallie B. van 1971 *New Engl. J. Med.* **285**, 1402–1407. Studies of food-intake regulation in man.

Carlsson S. G. et al. 1978 *Dev. Psychobiol.* **11**, 143–150. Effects of amount of contact between mother and child on the mother's nursing behavior.

Carmichael L. 1927 *Psychol. Rev.* **34**, 34–47. Development of behavior in vertebrates removed from external stimulation.

Carpenter C. R. 1964 *Naturalistic Behavior of Non-Human Primates*. University Park, Pa.: Pennsylvania State University Press.

Carpenter C. R. 1965 In DeVore I. (ed.) *Primate Behavior*. New York: Holt, Rinehart & Winston. The howlers of Barro Colorado Island.

Carrick R. 1963 *Proc. XIIIth Int. Ornithol. Congr.* 740–753. Territory in the Australian magpie.

Carrick R. 1972 In *Population Ecology of Migratory Birds: A Symposium*. U.S. Department of the Interior Wildlife Research Report 2. Population ecology of the Australian black-backed magpie, royal penguin, and silver gull.

Castilla J. C. 1972 *Mar. Biol.* **12**, 222–228. Responses of *Asterias rubens* to bivalve prey.

Cavalli-Sforza L. L. 1971 In Hodson F. R., Kendall D. G., Tautu P. (ed.) *Mathematics in the Archaeological and Historical Sciences.* Edinburgh: Edinburgh University Press. Similarities and dissimilarities of sociocultural and biological evolution.

Cesnola A. P. di 1904 *Biometrika* **3**, 58–59. The protective value of colour in *Mantis religiosa.*

Charles G. H. 1961 *J. Exp. Biol.* **38**, 189–202. The orientation of *Littorina* species to polarized light.

Chen C.-S. 1967 *Nature (London)* **214**, 15–17. Can rats count?

Cheng M.-F. 1976 *Nature (London)* **263**, 148–149. Interaction of lighting and other environmental variables on activity of hypothalamo-hypophyseal-gonadal system.

Chiszar D. et al. 1976 *Anim. Learn. Behav.* **4**, 273–278. Investigatory behavior in the plains garter snake.

Chitty D. 1960 *Can. J. Zool.* **38**, 99–113. Population processes in the vole.

Chitty D. 1967 *Proc. Ecol. Soc. Aust.* **2**, 51–78. The natural selection of self-regulatory behaviour in animal populations.

Chitty D. 1977 In Stonehouse B., Perrins C. (ed.) *Evolutionary Ecology.* Baltimore: University Park Press. Natural selection and the regulation of density.

Chitty D., Southern H. N. (ed.) 1954 *The Control of Rats and Mice.* (3 Vols.) Oxford: Clarendon Press.

Chivers D. J. 1969 *Folia Primatol.* **10**, 48–102. Daily behaviour and spacing of howling monkey groups.

Chomsky N. 1959 *Language* **35**, 26–58. Verbal behavior.

Chomsky N. 1967 In Darley F. L. (ed.) *Brain Mechanisms Underlying Speech and Language.* New York: Grune & Stratton. The general properties of language.

Christian J. J., Lloyd J. A., Davis D. E. 1965 *Recent Prog. Horm. Res.* **21**, 501–578. The role of endocrines in the self-regulation of mammalian populations.

Church J. 1971 In Moltz H. (ed.) *The Ontogeny of Vertebrate Behavior.* New York: Academic. The ontogeny of language.

Church R. M. 1963 *Psychol. Rev.* **70**, 369–402. The varied effects of punishment.

Ciba Foundation 1972 *Physiology, Emotion & Psychosomatic Illness.* Amsterdam: Ciba Foundation Symposium & Associated Scientific Publishers.

Clark E. V. 1978 In Bruner J. S., Garton A. (ed.) *Human Growth and Development.* Oxford: Clarendon Press. From gesture to word: On deixis.

Clark J. D. 1976 In Isaac G. L., McCown E. R. (ed.) *Human Origins.* New York: Benjamin. African origins of man.

Clark R. B. 1959 *Br. J. Anim. Behav.* **7**, 85–90. The tubicolous habit and the fighting reactions of *Nereis pelagica.*

Clarke A. M., Clarke A. D. B. 1976 *Early Experience: Myth and Evidence.* London: Open Books.

Clarke T. A. 1970 *Ecol. Monogr.* **40**, 189–212. Territorial behavior and population dynamics of the garibaldi.

Clutton-Brock T. H., Harvey P. H. 1976 In Bateson P. P. G., Hinde R. A. (ed.) *Growing Points in Ethology.* Cambridge: Cambridge University Press. Evolutionary rules and primate societies.

Clutton-Brock T. H., Harvey P. H. (ed.) 1978 *Readings in Sociobiology.* Reading: Freeman.

Clyne D. 1967 *Aust. Zool.* **14**, 189–197. The construction of the net and sperm-web of a cribellate spider.

Coelho A. M., Bramblett C. A., Quick L. B. 1977 *Am. J. Phys. Anthropol.* **46**, 253–264. Social organization and food resource availability in primates.

Coghill G. E. 1929 *Anatomy and the Problem of Behavior.* Cambridge: Cambridge University Press.

Cole F. J. 1930 *Early Theories of Sexual Generation.* Oxford: Clarendon Press.

Collias N. E. 1956 *Ecology* **37**, 228–239. Socialization in sheep and goats.

Collias N. E., Collias E. C. 1962 *Auk* **79**, 568–595. Nest building in a weaverbird.

Collias N. E., Collias E. C. 1967 *Condor* **69**, 360–386. Red jungle fowl in north-central India.

Comfort A. 1974 In Birch M. C. (ed.) *Pheromones*. Amsterdam: North-Holland. The likelihood of human pheromones.

Connolly K. 1969 In Wolff P. H., MacKeith R. (ed.) *Planning for Better Learning*. London: Heinemann. Sensory-motor co-ordination.

Cook A. et al. 1969 *AB* **17**, 330–339. The homing habit of the limpet.

Cook S. B. 1969 *AB* **17**, 679–682. Homing in the limpet *Siphonaria normalis*.

Cooper E. S. et al. 1974 *Bull. Br. Psychol. Soc.* **27**, 3–7. Direct observation?

Cooper R. M., Zubeck J. P. 1958 *Can. J. Psychol.* **12**, 159–164. Effects of enriched and restricted early environments on the learning ability of bright and dull rats.

Copeland M. 1918 *J. Exp. Zool.* **25**, 177–227. Olfactory reactions of the marine snails *Alectrion obsoleta* and *Busycon canaliculatum*.

Corning W. C., Kelly S. 1973 In Corning W. C., Dyal J. A., Willows A. O. D. (ed.) *Invertebrate Learning*. Vol 1. New York & London: Plenum. The turbellarians.

Corning W. C., VonBurg R. 1973 In Corning W. C., Dyal J. A., Willows A. O. D. (ed.) *Invertebrate Learning*. Vol 1. New York & London: Plenum. Protozoa.

Corter C. M. 1973 *Child Dev.* **44**, 705–713. The mother's and a stranger's control over the behavior of infants.

Cott H. B. 1940 *Adaptive Coloration in Animals*. London: Methuen.

Cott H. B. 1975 *Looking at Animals: A Zoologist in Africa*. London: Collins.

Courtney P. A., Fenton M. B. 1976 *J. Appl. Ecol.* **13**, 413–422. The effects of a small rural garbage dump on populations of small mammals.

Craig W. 1918 *Biol. Bull.* (*Woods Hole, Mass.*) **34**, 91–107. Appetites and aversions as constituents of instincts.

Crane J. 1941 *Zoologica* N.Y. **26**, 145–208. Crabs of the genus *Uca*.

Crane J. 1975 *Fiddler Crabs of the World*. Princeton, N.J.: Princeton University Press.

Crawford M. P. 1939 *Psychol. Bull.* **36**, 407–446. The social psychology of the vertebrates.

Crespi L. P. 1942 *Am. J. Psychol.* **55**, 467–517. Quantitative variation of incentive and performance.

Crisp D. J. 1976 In Newell R. C. (ed.) *Adaptation to Environment: Essays on the Physiology of Marine Animals*. London: Butterworths. Settlement responses in marine organisms.

Croll N. A. 1970 *The Behaviour of Nematodes*. London: Arnold.

Crook J. H. 1964 *Proc. Zool. Soc. London* **142**, 217–255. Nest construction and repair behaviour of weaver birds.

Crook J. H., Butterfield P. A. 1970 In Crook J. H. (ed.) *Social Behaviour in Birds and Mammals*. London: Academic. Gender role in the social system of Quelea.

Crossley S. A. 1975 *Evolution* **28**, 631–647. Changes in mating behavior produced by selection for ethological isolation between mutants of *Drosophila melanogaster*.

Crowson R. A. 1970 *Classification and Biology*. London: Heinemann.

Croze H. 1970 *Searching Image in Carrion Crows*. Berlin: Parey.

Cryns A. G. J. 1962 *J. Soc. Psychol.* **57**, 283–301. A critical survey of cross-cultural intelligence in Africa.

Cullen E. 1957 *Ibis* **99**, 275–302. Adaptations in the kittiwake to cliff-nesting.

Curio E. 1976 *The Ethology of Predation*. Berlin: Springer-Verlag.

Curtis H. 1969 *The Marvellous Animals*. London: Heinemann Educational.

Dainton B. H. 1954 *J. Exp. Biol.* **31**, 188–197. The activity of slugs.

Dansky J. L., Silverman I. W. 1973 *Dev. Psychol.* **9**, 38–43. Effects of play on associative fluency.

Darby C. L., Riopelle A. J. 1959 *JCPP* **52**, 94–98.

Darchen R. 1955 *ZTP* **12**, 1–11. Stimuli nouveaux et tendance exploratrice chez *Blatella germanica*. Observational learning in the rhesus monkey.

Darling F. F. 1937 *A Herd of Red Deer*. London: Oxford University Press.

Darwin C. 1859 *On the Origin of Species*. London: Murray.

Darwin C. 1873 *On The Expression of the Emotions in Man and Animals*. London: Murray.

Darwin C. 1875 *The Variation of Animals and Plants under Domestication*. (2 vols.) London: Murray.

Darwin C. 1901 *The Descent of Man and Selection in Relation to Sex*. London: Murray. (2nd edn.)

Datta L. G. 1962 *Am. J. Psychol.* **75**, 531–553. Learning in *Lumbricus terrestris*.

Davenport J. W. 1976 In Walsh R. N., Greenough W. T. (ed.) *Environments as Therapy for Brain Dysfunction*. New York: Plenum. Environmental therapy in hypothyroid and other disadvantaged animal populations.

Davies N. B. 1977 *AB* **25**, 1016–1033. Prey selection and the search strategy of the spotted flycatcher.

Davies N. B. 1978 In Krebs J. R., Davies N. B. (ed.) *Behavioural Ecology: An Evolutionary Approach*. Oxford: Blackwell Scientific. Ecological questions about territorial behaviour.

Davies N. B., Halliday T. R. 1977 *Nature* (*London*) **269**, 56–58. Optimal mate selection in the toad *Bufo bufo*.

Davies N. B., Halliday T. R. 1978 *Nature* (*London*) **274**, 683–685. Deep croaks and fighting assessment in toads *Bufo bufo*.

Davis C. M. 1928 *Am. J. Dis. Child.* **36**, 651–679. Self selection of diet by newly weaned infants.

Davis C. M. 1939 *Can. Med. Assoc. J.* **41**, 257–261. The self-selection of diets by young children.

Davis D. E. 1953. *Q. Rev. Biol.* **28**, 373–401. Rat populations.

Davis J. M. 1973 In Bateson P. P. G., Klopfer P. H. (ed.) *Perspectives in Ethology*. New York: Plenum. Imitation.

Davis W. J. 1976 In Rosenzweig M. R., Bennett E. L. (ed.) *Neural Mechanisms of Learning and Memory*. Cambridge: M.I.T. Press. Plasticity in the invertebrates.

Dawkins M. 1971a *AB* **19**, 566–574. Perceptual changes in chicks: The "search image" concept.

Dawkins M. 1971b *AB* **19**, 575–582. Shifts of "attention" in chicks during feeding.

Dawkins M. 1977 *AB* **25**, 1034–1046. Do hens suffer in battery cages?

Dawkins R. 1976 *The Selfish Gene*. London: Oxford University Press.

Daykin P. N., Kellogg F. E., Wright R. H. 1965 *Can. Entomol.* **97**, 239–263. Host-finding and repulsion of *Aëdes aegypti*.

Deag J. M. 1977 *AB* **25**, 465–474. Aggression and submission in monkey societies.

DeFries J. C., Hegmann J. P., Halcomb R. A. 1974 *Behav. Biol.* **11**, 481–495. Response to 20 generations of selection for open-field activity in mice.

Deiker T. E., Hoffeld D. R. 1973 *AB* **21**, 607–612. Threat behaviour in *Cichlasoma nigrofasciatum*.

Delgado J. M. R., Roberts W. W., Miller N. E. 1954 *Am. J. Physiol.* **179**, 587–593. Learning motivated by electrical stimulation of the brain.

Denenberg V. H., Whimbey A. E. 1963 *Science* **142**, 1192–1193. Behavior of adult rats modified by experiences their mothers had as infants.

Denton E. J. 1970 *Philos. Trans. R. Soc. London, Ser. B* **258**, 285–313. Reflecting surfaces in some marine animals.

De Ruiter L. 1952 *Behaviour* **4**, 222–232. The camouflage of stick caterpillars.

Dethier V. G. 1976 *The Hungry Fly*. Cambridge: Harvard University Press.

DeVore I. (ed.) 1965 *Primate Behavior*. New York: Holt, Rinehart & Winston.

DeVore I., Washburn S. L. 1963 In Howell F. C., Bourlière F. (ed.) *African Ecology and Human Evolution*. New York: Wenner-Gren Foundation. Baboon ecology and human evolution.

Dewsbury D. A. *AB* **26**, 310–311. What is (was?) the "fixed action pattern"?

Diamond J. M., Terborgh J. W. 1968 *Auk* **85**, 62–82. Dual singing by New Guinea birds.

Dickeman M. 1975 *Annu. Rev. Ecol. Syst.* **6**, 15–37. Demographic consequences of infanticide.

Diebschlag E. 1940 *Z. Vgl. Physiol.* **27**, 67–104. Über den Lernvorgang bei der Haustaube.

Dingle H. 1969 *AB* **17**, 561–575. A statistical and information analysis of aggressive communication in the mantis shrimp.

Dingle H. 1972 In Winn H. E., Olla B. L. (ed.) *Behavior of Marine Animals.* New York: Plenum. Aggressive behavior in stomatopods and information theory.

Dobzhansky Th., Spassky B. 1967 *Proc. R. Soc. London, Ser. B* **168**, 27–47. Effects of selection and migration on geotactic and phototactic behaviour of *Drosophila.*

Dodds E. R. 1963 *The Greeks and the Irrational.* Cambridge: Cambridge University Press.

Dorst J. 1962 *The Migration of Birds.* London: Heinemann.

Douglas M. 1966 *Purity and Danger.* Harmondsworth: Penguin.

Drachman D. B., Sokoloff L. 1966 *Dev. Biol.* **14**, 401–420. The role of movement in embryonic joint development.

Draper P. 1973 *Science* **182**, 301–303. Crowding among hunter-gatherers.

Drees O. 1952 *ZTP* **9**, 171–207. Die angeborenen Verhaltensweisen bei Springspinnen.

Drewe E. A. et al. 1970 *Cortex* **6**, 129–163. Neuropsychological research on man and monkey.

Duelli P., Wehner R. 1973 *J. Comp. Physiol.* **86**, 37–53. Polarized light orientation in *Cataglyphis bicolor.*

Dunford C. 1977 *AB* **25**, 885–906. Social system of round-tailed ground squirrels.

Dunning D. C. 1968 *ZTP* **25**, 129–138. Warning sounds of moths.

Durnin J. V. G. A. 1961 *J. Physiol.* **156**, 294–306. The relationship between expenditure and intake of calories.

Durnin J. V. G. A., Passmore R. 1967 *Energy, Work and Leisure.* London: Heinemann Educational.

Dyal J. A. 1973 In Corning W. C., Dyal J. A., Willows A. O. D. (ed.) *Invertebrate Learning.* Vol. 1. New York: Plenum. Behavior modification in annelids.

Dyal J. A., Corning W. C. 1973 In Corning W. C., Dyal J. A., Willows A. O. D. (ed.) *Invertebrate Learning.* Vol. 1. New York: Plenum. Invertebrate learning and behavior taxonomies.

Eastment A. M., Hughes R. N. 1968 *Percept. Mot. Skills* **26**, 935–938. Reactions of ferret-polecat hybrids to complexity and change.

Edmunds M. 1974 *Defence in Animals.* Harlow, Essex: Longman.

Ehrlich P. R. et al. 1977 *J. Zool.,* **183**, 213–228. The behaviour of chaetodontid fishes with special reference to Lorenz's "poster colouration" hypothesis.

Eibl–Eibesfeldt I. 1972 In Hinde R. A. (ed.) *Non-Verbal Communication.* Cambridge: Cambridge University Press. Similarities and differences between cultures in expressive movements.

Eisenberg J. F., McKay G. M., Jainudeen M. R. 1971 *Behaviour* **38–39**, 193–225. Reproductive behavior of the Asiatic elephant.

Eisenstein E. M., Osborn D., Blair H. J. 1973 In Perez-Miravete A. (ed.) *Behaviour of Micro-Organisms.* London: Plenum. Behavior modification in Protozoa.

Eisenstein E. M., Peretz B. 1973 In Peeke H. V. S., Herz M. J. (ed.) *Habituation.* Vol. II: *Physiological Substrates.* New York: Academic. Comparative aspects of habituation.

Ekman P. (ed.) 1973 *Darwin and Facial Expression.* New York: Academic.

Ekman P., Sorenson E. R., Friesen W. V. 1969 *Science* **164**, 86–88. Pan-cultural elements in facial displays.

Ellefson J. O. 1968 In Jay P. C. (ed.) *Primates: Studies in Adaptation and Variability.* New York: Holt, Rinehart & Winston. Territorial behavior in the common white-handed gibbon.

Elliott M. H. 1928 *Univ. Calif. Berkeley Publ. Psychol.* **4**, 19–30. The effect of change of reward on maze performance.

Ellis P. E. 1970 *Proc. Int. Study Conf. Cur. Fut. Prob. Acridol.*, London, 63–77. Phase variation in locusts.

Ellsworth P., Carlsmith J. M. 1973 *J. Pers. Soc. Psychol.* **28**, 280–292. Eye contact and gaze aversion in an aggressive encounter.

Ellsworth P. C., Carlsmith J. M., Henson A. 1972 *J. Pers. Soc. Psychol.* **21**, 302–311. The stare as a stimulus to flight.

Elton C. 1942 *Voles, Mice and Lemmings.* Oxford: Clarendon Press.

Emlen J. T. 1978 *Am. Nat.* **112**, 265–286. Density anomalies and regulatory mechanisms in land bird populations.

Emlen S. T. 1967 *Auk* **84**, 309–342. Migratory orientation in the indigo bunting.

Emlen S. T. 1970 *AB* **18**, 215–224. The influence of magnetic information on the orientation of the indigo bunting.

Emlen S. T. 1975 In Farner D. S., King J. R., Parkes K. C. (ed.) *Avian Biology.* Vol. 5. New York: Academic. Migration: Orientation and navigation.

Emlen S. T., Emlen J. T. 1966 *Auk* **83**, 361–367. A technique for recording migratory orientation of captive birds.

Engen T., Lipsitt L. P. 1965 *JCPP* **59**, 312–316. Decrement and recovery of responses to olfactory stimuli in the human neonate.

Englefield F. R. H. 1977 *Language. Its Origin and its Relation to Thought.* London: Elek/Pemberton.

Epstein A. N., Milestone R. 1968 *Science* **160**, 895–896. Showering as a coolant for rats.

Erber J. 1975 *J. Comp. Physiol.* **99**, 243–255. The dynamics of learning in the honey bee.

Esch H. 1964 *Z. Vgl. Physiol.* **48**, 534–546. Beiträge zum Problem der Entfernungsweisung in den Schwänzeltänzen der Honigbiene.

Espmark Y. 1964 *AB* **12**, 159–163. Rutting behaviour in reindeer.

Estes R. D., Goddard J. 1967 *J. Wildl. Manage.* **31**, 52–70. Hunting behavior of the African wild dog.

Etkin W. (ed.) 1964 *Social Behavior and Organization among Vertebrates.* Chicago: University of Chicago Press.

Evans E. P., Ford C. E., Lyon M. F. 1977 *Nature (London)* **267**, 430–431. The capacity of the XY germ cell to become an oocyte.

Evans S. M. 1966a *AB* **14**, 102–106. Non-associative avoidance learning in nereid polychaetes.

Evans S. M. 1966b *AB* **14**, 107–119. Non-associative behavioural modifications in *Nereis diversicolor.*

Evans S. M. 1969a *Biol. Bull. (Woods Hole Mass.)* **137**, 95–104. Habituation in *Nereis diversicolor.*

Evans S. M. 1969b *Biol. Bull. (Woods Hole Mass.)* **137**, 105–117. Habituation in intact and decerebrate worms.

Evans W. E., Bastian J. 1969 In Andersen H. T. (ed.) *The Biology of Marine Mammals.* New York: Academic. Marine mammal communication.

Ewer D. W., Bursell E. 1951 *Behaviour* **3**, 40–47. The classification of elementary behaviour patterns.

Ewer R. F. 1963 *ZTP* **20**, 570–607. The behaviour of the meerkat.

Ewer R. F. 1968 *Ethology of Mammals.* London: Logos.

Ewert J.-P. 1976 In Fite K. V. (ed.) *The Amphibian Visual System.* New York: Academic. The visual system of the toad.

Ewing A. W. 1963 *AB* **11**, 369–378. Attempts to select for spontaneous activity in *Drosophila melanogaster.*

Factor R. M., Waldron I. 1973 *Nature (London)* **243**, 381–384. Population densities and human health.

Fagen R. M. 1976 In Bateson P. P. G., Klopfer P. H. (ed.) *Perspectives in Ethology.* Vol. 2. New York: Plenum. Exercise, play and physical training in animals.

Falconer D. S. 1960 *Introduction to Quantitative Genetics.* Edinburgh: Oliver & Boyd.

Falls J. B. 1969 In Hinde R. A. (ed.) *Bird Vocalizations.* Cambridge: Cambridge University Press. Territorial song in the white-throated sparrow.

Fankhauser G., Reik L. E. 1935 *Physiol. Zool.* **8**, 337–359. Case-building of the caddis-fly larva, *Neuronia postica.*

Farkas S. R., Shorey H. H. 1974 In Birch M. C. (ed.)

Pheromones. Amsterdam: North-Holland. Orientation to a distant pheromone source.

Farkas S. R., Shorey H. H. 1976 *AB* **24**, 686–689. Anemotaxis and odour-trail following by *Helix aspersa.*

Farner D. S., Lewis R. A. 1971 *Photophysiology* **6**, 325–370. Photoperiodism and reproductive cycles in birds.

Feather B. W. 1965 *Psychol. Bull.* **63**, 425–441. Semantic generalization of classically conditioned responses.

Feekes F. 1977 *Ardea* **65**, 197–202. Colony-specific song in *Cacicus cela.*

Fernald R. D., Hirata N. R. 1977 *AB* **25**, 964–975. Field study of *Haplochromis burtoni.*

Ferster C. B., Skinner B. F. 1957 *Schedules of Reinforcement.* New York: Appleton-Century-Crofts.

File S. E., Wardill A. G. 1975a *Psychopharmacologia* **44**, 53–59. Head-dipping as a measure of exploration.

File S. E., Wardill A. G. 1975b *Psychopharmacologia* **44**, 47–51. The reliability of the hole-board apparatus.

Finger F. W. 1972 In Myers R. D. (ed.) *Methods in Psychobiology.* Vol. 2. New York: Academic. Measuring behavioral activity.

Fisher E. M. 1939 *J. Mammal.* **20**, 21–36. Habits of the southern sea otter.

Fisher R. A. 1913 *Eugen. Rev.* **5**, 309–315. Some hopes of a eugenist.

Fisher R. A. 1930 *The Genetical Theory of Natural Selection.* Oxford: Clarendon Press.

Fisler G. F. 1965 *Univ. Calif. Berkeley Publ. Zool.* **77**, 1–108. Adaptations and speciation in harvest mice.

Fitzgerald B. M. 1977 *J. Anim. Ecol.* **46**, 367–397. Weasel predation on a cyclic population of the montane vole.

Fitzgerald T. K. (ed.) 1977 *Nutrition and Anthropology in Action.* Assen, Netherlands: Van Gorcum.

Fitzsimons J. T. 1972 *Physiol. Rev.* **52**, 468–561. Thirst.

Flint P. 1965 *AB* **13**, 187–193. The effect of sensory deprivation on the behaviour of Nereis.

Ford E. B. 1975 *Ecological Genetics.* London: Chapman & Hall.

Ford H. A. 1971 *Heredity* **27**, 227–236. The degree of mimetic protection gained by new partial mimics.

Fouts R. S., Rigby R. L. 1977 In Sebeok T. A. (ed.) *How Animals Communicate.* Bloomington: Indiana University Press. Man-chimpanzee communication.

Fox M. W. 1973 *Behaviour* **47**, 290–301. Social dynamics of captive wolf packs.

Fraenkel G. S., Gunn D. L. 1961 *The Orientation of Animals.* New York: Dover Publications. (2nd edn.) [Originally published in 1940.]

Fraser D., Waddell M. S. 1974 *Lab. Pract.* **23**, 58–59. The importance of social and self-grooming for the control of ectoparasitic mites.

Free J. B. 1965 *Symp. Zool. Soc. London* **14**, 39–59. The allocation of duties among worker honeybees.

Freedman D. G. 1964 *J. Child. Psychol. Psychiat.* **5**, 171–184. Smiling in blind infants.

Freedman J. L. 1975 *Crowding and Behavior.* New York: Viking.

Freedman J. L. 1978 In Krames L., Pliner P., Alloway T. (ed.) *Aggression, Dominance, and Individual Spacing.* New York: Plenum. The effects of high density on human behavior and emotions.

Freedman J. L. et al. 1972 *J. Exp. Soc. Psychol.* **8**, 528–548. Crowding and human aggressiveness.

Freeland W. J. 1976 *Biotropica* **8**, 12–24. Pathogens and the evolution of primate sociality.

Freud S. 1949 *Instincts and their Vicissitudes.* London: Hogarth.

Freud S. 1969 *Civilization and Its Discontents.* London: Hogarth. [First published in 1930.]

Friedman M. I., Stricker E. M. 1976 *Psychol. Rev.* **83**, 409–431. The physiological psychology of hunger.

Frisch K. von 1938 *Naturwissenschaften* **26**, 601–606. Zur Psychologie des Fisch-Schwarmes.

Frisch K. von 1967 *The Dance Language and Orientation of Bees.* Cambridge: Harvard University Press.

Frisch K. von, Frisch O. von 1974 *Animal Architecture.* New York: Harcourt Brace Jovanovich.

Frith H. J. 1962 *The Mallee-Fowl*. Sydney: Angus & Robertson.

Fry C. H. 1972 *Living Bird* **11**, 75–112. The biology of African bee-eaters.

Gadgil M. 1972 *Am. Nat.* **106**, 574–580. Male dimorphism as a consequence of sexual selection.

Gadgil M., Bossert W. H. 1970 *Am. Nat.* **104**, 1–24. Life historical consequences of natural selection.

Galef B. G. 1976 In Rosenblatt J. S. et al. (ed.) *Advances in the Study of Behavior*. Vol. 6. New York: Academic. Social transmission of acquired behavior.

Gallup G. G. 1970 *Science* **167**, 86–87. Chimpanzees: Self-recognition.

Galusha J. G., Stout J. F. 1977 *Behaviour* **62**, 222–235. Aggressive communication by *Larus glaucescens*.

Ganz L. 1968 In Newton G., Levine S. (ed.) *Early Experience and Behavior*. Springfield, Ill.: Thomas. Generalization behavior in the stimulus-deprived organism.

Garb J. L., Stunkard A. J. 1974 *Am. J. Psychiat.* **131**, 1204–1207. Taste aversions in man.

Garcia J., Hankins W. G., Rusiniak K. W. 1974 *Science* **185**, 824–831. Behavioral regulation of the milieu interne.

Garcia J., Koelling R. A. 1967 *Radia. Res. Suppl.* **7**, 439–450. Aversions induced by X-rays, toxins and drugs.

Gardner B. T., Gardner R. A. 1971 In Schrier A. M., Stollnitz F. (ed.) *Behavior of Nonhuman Primates*. New York: Academic. Two-way communication with an infant chimpanzee.

Gartlan J. S. 1968 *Folia Primatol.* **8**, 89–120. Structure and function in primate society.

Gartlan J. S. 1973 In Menzel E. W. (ed.) *Precultural Primate Behavior*. Vol. 1. *Symp. IVth Int. Congr. Primat.*, Basel: Karger. Variations in the group organization of primates.

Gass C. L., Angehr G., Centa J. 1976 *Can. J. Zool.* **54**, 2046–2054. Regulation of food supply by territoriality in the rufous hummingbird.

Geist, V. 1978 In Krames L., Pliner P., Alloway T. (eds) *Aggression, Dominance, and Individual Spacing*. New York: Plenum. On weapons, combat, and ecology.

Gelber B. 1952 *JCPP* **45**, 58–65. The behavior of *Paramecium aurelia*.

Gibb J. A. 1977 In Stonehouse B., Perrins C. (ed.) *Evolutionary Ecology*. Baltimore: University Park Press. Factors affecting population density in the wild rabbit.

Gibson J. J. 1966 *The Senses Considered as Perceptual Systems*. Boston: Houghton Mifflin.

Gillett S. D. 1973 *AB* **21**, 599–606. Aggregation behaviour in adults of the desert locust.

Gillett S. D. 1975 *AB* **23**, 494–503. Changes in the social behaviour of the desert locust in response to the gregarizing pheromone.

Gilliard E. T. 1969 *Birds of Paradise and Bower Birds*. London: Weidenfeld & Nicolson.

Gleitman H., Rozin P. 1971 In Hoar W. S., Randall D. J. (ed.) *Fish Physiology*. Vol. 4. New York: Academic. Learning and memory.

Goldin-Meadow S., Feldman H. 1977 *Science* **197**, 401–403. The development of language-like communication without a language model.

Goldman L., Swanson H. 1975 *ZTP* **37**, 225–236. Population control in confined colonies of golden hamsters.

Goldstein J. H. 1975 *Aggression and Crimes of Violence*. New York: Oxford University Press.

Goldstein, S. R. 1975 *AB* **23**, 179–185. The establishment of a stable community of Siamese fighting fish.

Gonzalez R. C., Gentry G. V., Bitterman M. E. 1954 *JCPP* **47**, 385–388. Relational discrimination of intermediate size in the chimpanzee.

Gottlieb G. 1961 *JCPP* **54**, 422–427. Developmental age as a baseline for determination of the critical period in imprinting.

Gottlieb G. 1971 *Development of Species Identification in Birds*. Chicago: University of Chicago Press.

Gottlieb G. 1976a *Psychol. Rev.* **83**, 215–234. Conceptions of prenatal development.

Gottlieb G. 1976b In Gottlieb G. (ed.) *Neural and Behavioral Specificity*. New York: Academic. The roles of experience in the development of behavior and the nervous system.

Gould J. L. 1975 *Science* **189**, 685–693. Honey bee recruitment: The dance-language controversy.

Gould J. L. 1976 *Q. Rev. Biol.* **51**, 211–244. The dance-language controversy.

Gould J. L., Kirschvink J. L., Deffeyes K. S. 1978 *Science* **201**, 1026–1028. Bees have magnetic remanence.

Gould S. J. 1977 *Ontogeny and Phylogeny*. Cambridge: Harvard University Press.

Gould S. J., Lewontin R. C. 1979 *Proc. R. Soc. London Ser. B* **205**, 581–598. The spandrels of San Marco and the Panglossian paradigm: a critique of the adaptationist programme.

Goy R. W., Goldfoot D. A. 1974 In Schmitt F. O., Worden F. G. (ed.) *The Neurosciences*. Cambridge: M.I.T. Press. Development of sexual behavior in the male rhesus monkey.

Grant P. R. 1970 *AB* **18**, 411–426. Experimental studies of competitive interaction in a two-species system.

Gray J. 1953 *How Animals Move*. Cambridge: Cambridge University Press.

Green C. D. 1966 *Ann. Appl. Biol.* **58**, 327–339. Orientation of male *Heterodera rostochiensis* and *H. schachtii* to their females.

Green S. 1975 *ZTP* **38**, 304–314. Dialects in Japanese monkeys.

Greenfield P. M., Bruner J. S. 1966 *Int. J. Psychol.* **1**, 89–107. Culture and cognitive growth.

Gregory R. L. 1970 *The Intelligent Eye*. London: Weidenfeld & Nicolson.

Gregory R. L., Wallace J. G. 1963 *Exp. Psychol. Soc. Monogr.* **2**, 1–46. Recovery from early blindness.

Grene M. 1974 *The Understanding of Nature*. Dordrecht, Holland: Reidel.

Grene M. 1978 In Gregory M. S., Silvers A., Sutch D. (ed.) *Sociobiology and Human Nature*. San Francisco: Jossey-Bass. Sociobiology and the human mind.

Grether W. F. 1938 *J. Comp. Psychol.* **25**, 91–96. Pseudo-conditioning without paired stimulation.

Grice G. R. 1948 *J. Exp. Psychol.* **38**, 1–16. The relation of secondary reinforcement to delayed reward.

Griffin D. R. 1958 *Listening in the Dark*. New Haven: Yale University Press.

Griffin D. R. 1965 *Bird Migration*. London: Heinemann.

Griffin D. R. 1976 *The Question of Animal Awareness*. New York: Rockefeller University Press.

Griffiths M. 1965 *Comp. Biochem. Physiol.* **16**, 383–392. Rate of growth and intake of milk in a suckling echidna.

Griffiths W. J., Harmon C. T. 1954 *Jpn. Psychol. Res.* **1**, 9-20. Self-selection of diet in wild and domesticated Norway rats.

Gross C. G. 1968 In Weiskrantz L. (ed.) *Analysis of Behavioral Change*. New York: Harper & Row. General activity.

Grüneberg H. 1963 *The Pathology of Development*. Oxford: Blackwell.

Guiton P. 1961 *AB* **9**, 167–177. The influence of imprinting on the behaviour of the brown leghorn cock.

Gunn D. L. 1975 *AB* **23**, 409–412. The meaning of the term "klinokinesis".

Gwynn A. M. 1968. *Aust. Bird Bander* **6**, 71–75. The migration of the Arctic tern.

Haartman L. von 1951 *Acta Zool. Fenn.* **67**, 1–57. Der Trauerfliegenschnäpper.

Hailman J. P. 1965 *Wilson Bull.* **77**, 346–362. Cliff-nesting adaptations of the Galapagos Swallow-tailed Gull.

Hailman J. P. 1967 *Behaviour Suppl.* **15**, 1–159. The ontogeny of an instinct.

Hailman J. P. 1977 In Sebeok T. A. (ed.) *How Animals Communicate*. Bloomington: Indiana University Press. Communication by reflected light.

Hainsworth F. R., Stricker E. M. 1970 In Hardy J. D., Gagge A. P., Stolwijk J. A. J. (ed.) *Physiological and Behavioral Temperature Regulation*. Springfield, Ill.: Thomas. Salivary cooling by rats.

Hairston N. G., Tinkle D. W., Wilbur H. M. 1970 *J. Wildl. Manage.* **34**, 681–690. Natural selection and population growth.

Halberg F. 1960 *Perspect. Biol. Med.* **3**, 491–527. The 24-hour scale: A time dimension of adaptive functional organization.

Haldane J. B. S. 1946 *Ann. Eugen.* **13**, 197–205. The interaction of nature and nurture.

Haldane J. B. S. 1949 *Ric. Sci.* 68–76. Disease and evolution.

Haldane J. B. S. 1955 *Sci. Prog.* (*London*) **43**, 385–401. Animal communication and the origin of human language.

Haldane J. B. S. 1956 *J. R. Anthrop. Inst.* **86**, 1–14. The argument from animals to men.

Haldane J. B. S. 1959 In Bell P. R. (ed.) *Darwin's Biological Work.* Cambridge: Cambridge University Press. Natural selection.

Haldane J. B. S. 1963 *Penguin Science Survey B,* 224–238. Life and mind as physical realities.

Haldane J. B. S., Spurway H. 1954 *Insectes Soc.* **1**, 247–283. A statistical analysis of communication in *Apis mellifera.*

Hall B. 1975 *Lancet* (i), 779–781. Changing composition of human milk and early development of an appetite control.

Hall K. R. L., DeVore I. 1965 In DeVore I. (ed.) *Primate Behavior: Field Studies of Monkeys and Apes.* New York: Holt, Rinehart & Winston. Baboon social behavior.

Hall K. R. L., Schaller G. B. 1964 *J. Mammal.* **45**, 287–298. Tool-using behavior of the California sea otter.

Halliday R. J. 1971 *Victorian Stud.* **14**, 389–405. Social Darwinism.

Halliday T. R. 1974 *J. Herpetol.* **8**, 277–292. Sexual behaviour of the smooth newt.

Halliday T. R. 1975a *Zool. J. Linn. Soc.* **56**, 291–300. The biological significance of certain morphological characters in the smooth newt and the palmate newt.

Halliday T. R. 1975b *AB* **23**, 291–322. Sexual behaviour in the smooth newt.

Halliday T. R. 1978 In Krebs J. R., Davies N. B. (ed.) *Behavioural Ecology: An Evolutionary Approach.* Oxford: Blackwell Scientific. Sexual selection and mate choice.

Halliday T. R., Sweatman H. P. A. 1976 *AB* **24**, 551–561. To breathe or not to breathe; the newt's problem.

Hamburger V. 1963 *Q. Rev. Biol.* **38**, 342–365. Some aspects of the embryology of behavior.

Hamburger V. 1971 In Tobach E., Aronson L. R., Shaw E. (ed.) *The Biopsychology of Development.* New York: Academic. Development of embryonic motility.

Hamilton T. C. 1975 *Adv. Behav. Biol.* **13**, 111–130. Behavioral plasticity in protozoans.

Hamilton W. D. 1971 In Eisenberg J. F., Dillon W. S. (ed.) *Man and Beast: Comparative Social Behavior.* Washington: Smithsonian Institution. Selection of selfish and altruistic behavior in some extreme models.

Hamilton W. D. 1972 *Annu. Rev. Ecol. Syst.* **3**, 193–232. Altruism and related phenomena.

Hanby J. 1976 In Bateson P. P. G., Klopfer P. H. (ed.) *Perspectives in Ethology.* Vol. 2. New York: Plenum. Sociosexual development in primates.

Hansell M. H. 1974 *AB* **22**, 133–143. Regulation of building unit size in the house building of the caddis larva *Lepidostoma hirtum.*

Haralson J. V., Bitterman M. E. 1950 *Am. J. Psychol.* **63**, 250–256. A lever-depression apparatus for the study of learning in fish.

Haralson J. V., Groff C. I., Haralson S. J. 1975 *Physiol. Behav.* **15**, 455–460. Classical conditioning in the sea anemone, *Cribrina xanthogrammica.*

Harding R. S. O. 1977 *Am. J. Phys. Anthropol.* **47**, 349–354. Patterns of movement in open country baboons.

Hardy A. C. 1956 *The Open Sea.* London: Collins.

Harlow H. F. 1949 *Psychol. Rev.* **56**, 51–65. The formation of learning sets.

Harlow H. F., Blazek N. C., McClearn G. E. 1956 *JCPP* **49**, 444–448. Manipulatory motivation in the infant rhesus monkey.

Harlow H. F., Harlow M. K. 1965 In Schrier A. M., Harlow H. F., Stollnitz F. (ed.) *Behavior of Nonhuman Primates.* London: Academic. The affectional systems.

Harlow H. F., Harlow M. K., Meyer D. R. 1950 *J. Exp. Psychol.* **40**, 228–234. Learning motivated by a manipulation drive.

Harriman A. E. 1974 *J. Gen. Psychol.* **90**, 53–61. Self-selection of diet by Southern Plains wood rats.

Harris G. W. 1964 *Endocrinology* **75**, 627–648. Sex hormones, brain development and brain function.

Harris J. E. 1962 *Br. J. Obstet. Gynaecol.* **69**, 818–821. Early embryonic movements.

Harris J. E., Whiting H. P. 1954 *J. Exp. Biol.* **31**, 501–524. The locomotory system of the dogfish embryo.

Harris L. J. et al. 1933 *Proc. R. Soc. London Ser. B* **113**, 161–190. Appetite and choice of diet.

Harris V. T. 1952 *Contrib. Lab. Vertebr. Biol. Univ. Mich.* **56**, 1–53. Habitat selection by prairie and forest races of the deermouse.

Harris W. V. 1961 *Termites, Their Recognition and Control.* Bristol: Longmans.

Hart B. L. 1974 *Psychol. Bull.* **81**, 383–400. Gonadal androgen and sociosexual behavior of male mammals.

Hartup W. W., Coates B. In Hoppe R. A., Milton G. A., Simmel E. C. (ed.) *Early Experiences and the Processes of Socialization.* New York: Academic. Imitation in childhood socialization.

Harvey P. H., Greenwood P. J. 1978 In Krebs J. R., Davies N. B. (ed.) *Behavioural Ecology: An Evolutionary Approach.* Oxford: Blackwell Scientific. Anti-predator defence strategies.

Hasler A. D. 1971 In Hoar W. S., Randall D. J. (ed.) *Fish Physiology.* Vol. 6. New York: Academic. Orientation and fish migration.

Hassell M. P. 1976 In May R. M. (ed.) *Theoretical Ecology: Principles and Applications.* Philadelphia: Saunders. Arthropod predator-prey systems.

Hayes K. J., Hayes C. 1952 *JCPP* **45**, 450–459. Imitation in a home-raised chimpanzee.

Hayward J. S. 1965 *Can. J. Zool.* **43**, 341–350. Microclimate temperature and its adaptive significance in *Peromyscus.*

Healey M. C. 1967 *Ecology* **48**, 377–392. Aggression and self-regulation of population size.

Hebb D. O. 1949 *The Organization of Behavior.* New York: Wiley.

Hebb D. O. 1955 *Am. J. Psychiat.* **111**, 826–831. The mammal and his environment.

Hebb D. O. 1956 *Can. J. Psychol.* **10**, 165–166. The distinction between "classical" and "instrumental".

Hebb D. O. 1958 *A Textbook of Psychology.* Philadelphia: Saunders.

Hebb D. O. 1965 *Proc. R. Soc. London, Ser. B* **161**, 376–383. The evolution of mind.

Hebb D. O., Williams K. 1946 *J. Gen. Psychol.* **34**, 59–65. A method of rating animal intelligence.

Hedgecock E. M., Russell R. L. 1975 *Proc. Nat. Acad. Sci. U.S.A.* **72**, 4061–4065. Normal and mutant thermotaxis in *Caenorhabditis elegans.*

Hediger H. 1950 *Wild Animals in Captivity.* London: Butterworths.

Heiligenberg W. 1974 *Adv. Study Behav.* **5**, 173–200. Processes governing behavioral states of readiness.

Heiligenberg W., Kramer U. 1972 *J. Comp. Physiol.* **77**, 332–340. Aggressiveness as a function of external stimulation.

Henderson N. D. 1970 *JCPP* **72**, 505–511. Genetic influences on the behavior of mice can be obscured by laboratory rearing.

Herbert J., Trimble M. R. 1967 *Nature (London)* **216**, 165–166. Effect of oestradiol and testosterone on the sexual receptivity and attractiveness of the female rhesus monkey.

Hess E. H. 1973 *Imprinting: Early Experience and the Developmental Psychobiology of Attachment.* New York: Van Nostrand Reinhold.

Hess E. H., Polt J. M. 1960 *Science* **132**, 349–350. Pupil size related to interest value of visual stimuli.

Hewes G. W. 1973 *Curr. Anthropol.* **14**, 5–24. Primate communication and the gestural origin of language.

Hewes G. W. 1977 In Rumbaugh D. M. (ed.) *Language Learning by a Chimpanzee.* New York: Academic. Language origin theories.

Hicks V. C., Carr H. A. 1912 *J. Anim. Behav.* **2**, 98–125. Human reactions in a maze.

Hinde R., Smith D. C. 1974 *Biol. J. Linn. Soc.* **6**, 349–356. "Chloroplast symbiosis".

Hinde R. A. 1958 *Proc. Zool. Soc. London* **131**, 1–48. The nest-building of domesticated canaries.

Hinde R. A. 1959 *Biol. Rev.* **34**, 85–128. Behaviour and speciation in lower vertebrates.

Hinde R. A. 1960 *Symp. Soc. Exp. Biol.* **14**, 199–213. Energy models of motivation.

Hinde R. A. (ed.) 1969 *Bird Vocalizations*. Cambridge: Cambridge University Press.

Hinde R. A. 1970 *Animal Behaviour*. New York: McGraw-Hill.

Hinde R. A. (ed.) 1972 *Non-Verbal Communication*. Cambridge: Cambridge University Press.

Hinde R. A. 1974 *Biological Bases of Human Social Behaviour*. New York: McGraw-Hill.

Hinde R. A., Fisher J. 1951 *Br. Birds* **44**, 393–396. The opening of milk bottles by birds.

Hinde R. A., Stevenson-Hinde J. (ed.) 1973 *Constraints on Learning*. London: Academic.

Hingston R. W. G. 1928 *Problems of Instinct and Intelligence*. London: Arnold.

Hirsch J. 1963 *Science* **142**, 1436–1442. Behavior genetics and individuality.

Hirsch J. (ed.) 1967 *Behavior-Genetic Analysis*. New York: McGraw-Hill.

Hirsch J., McCauley L. A. 1977 *AB* **25**, 784–785. Classical conditioning in the blowfly.

Hirth D. H., McCullough D. R. 1977 *Am. Nat.* **111**, 31–42. Evolution of alarm signals in ungulates.

Hobbes T. 1946 *Leviathan*. Oxford: Blackwell. [First published in 1651.]

Hockett C. F. 1960 In Lanyon W. E., Tavolga W. N. (ed.) *Animal Sounds and Communication*. Washington D.C.: American Institute of Biological Sciences. Logical considerations in the study of animal communication.

Hofstadter R. 1955 *Social Darwinism in American Thought*. New York: Braziller.

Hogan J. A., Roper T. J. 1978 In Rosenblatt J. S. et al. (ed.) *Advances in the Study of Behavior*. New York: Academic. The properties of reinforcers.

Hogan-Warburg A. J. 1966 *Ardea* **54**, 109–229. Social behavior of the ruff.

Hokanson J. E. 1970 In Megargee E. I., Hokanson J. E. (ed.) *The Dynamics of Aggression*. New York: Harper. Psychophysiological evaluation of the catharsis hypothesis.

Hokanson J. E., Willers K. R., Koropsak E. 1968 *J. Pers.* **36**, 386–404. The modification of autonomic responses during aggressive interchange.

Hölldobler B. 1969 *Science* **166**, 757–758. Host finding by odor in *Atemeles pubicollis*.

Hölldobler B. 1970 *Z. Vgl. Physiol.* **66**, 215–250. Zur Physiologie der Gast-Wirt-Beziehungen bei Ameisen.

Holling C. S. 1966 *Mem. Entomol. Soc. Can.* **48**, 1–86. The response of invertebrate predators to prey density.

Holloway R. L. (ed.) 1974 *Primate Aggression, Territoriality, and Xenophobia*. New York: Academic.

Holmes W. 1940 *Proc. Zool. Soc. London* **110**, 17–35. The colour changes and colour patterns of *Sepia officinalis*.

Holst D. von 1969 *Z. Vgl. Physiol.* **63**, 1–58. Sozialer Stress bei Tupajas.

Holst E. von 1950 *Symp. Soc. Exp. Biol.* **4**, 143–172. Quantitative Messung von Stimmungen im Verhalten der Fische.

Holsworth W. N. 1967 *Aust. J. Zool.* **15**, 29–64. Population dynamics of the quokka.

Hoogland R., Morris D., Tinbergen N. 1957 *Behaviour* **10**, 205–236. The spines of sticklebacks as means of defence.

Hooker T., Hooker B. I. 1969 In Hinde R. A. (ed.) *Bird Vocalizations*. Cambridge: Cambridge University Press. Duetting.

Hopkins C. D. 1977 In Sebeok T. A. (ed.) *How Animals Communicate*. Bloomington: Indiana University Press. Electric communication.

Hordern A. 1968 In Joyce C. R. B. (ed.) Psychopharmacology: Dimensions and Perspectives. London: Tavistock. Psychopharmacology: Some historical considerations.

Horn G. 1970 In Horn G., Hinde R. A. (ed.) *Short-term Changes in Neural Activity and Behaviour*. Cambridge: Cambridge University Press. Changes in neuronal activity and behaviour.

Horn G., Hill R. M. 1964 *Nature* (*London*) **202**, 296–298. Habituation of the response to sensory stimuli of neurones in the brain stem of rabbits.

Horn H. S. 1978 In Krebs J. R., Davies N. B. (ed.) *Behavioural Ecology: An Evolutionary Approach.* Oxford: Blackwell Scientific. Optimal tactics of reproduction and life-history.

Hornocker M. G. 1969 *J. Wildl. Manage.* **33**, 457–464. Territoriality in mountain lions.

Horridge G. A. 1959 *Proc. R. Soc. London, Ser. B* **150**, 245–262. The rapid responses of *Nereis* and *Harmothoë.*

Howard E. 1920 *Territory in Bird Life.* London: Murray.

Hoy R. R. 1974 *Am. Zool.* **14**, 1067–1080. Genetic control of acoustic behavior in crickets.

Hoy R. R., Hahn J., Paul R. C. 1977 *Science* **195**, 82–83. Hybrid cricket auditory behavior.

Hsia D. Y.-Y. 1967 In Hirsch J. (ed.) *Behavior-Genetic Analysis.* New York: McGraw-Hill. The hereditary metabolic diseases.

Hughes A. F. 1965 *Proc. Zool. Soc. London* **144**, 153–161. The development of behaviour in *Eleutherodactylus martinicensis.*

Hughes R. N. 1965 *JCPP* **60**, 149–150. Spontaneous alternation and response to stimulus change in the ferret.

Hullo A. 1948 *Behaviour* **1**, 297–310. Role des tendances motrices et des données sensorielles dans l'apprentissage du labyrinthe par les blattes.

Humphrey N. K., Keeble G. R. 1974 *Nature (London)* **251**, 500–502. The reaction of monkeys to "fearsome" pictures.

Hytten F. E. 1954 *Br. Med. J.* (i), 175–182. Clinical and chemical studies in human lactation.

Iersel J. J. A. van 1958 *Arch. Neerl. Zool.* **13**, 383–400. Territorial behaviour of the male three-spined stickleback.

Iersel J. J. A. van, Assem J. van den 1965 *Anim. Behav. Suppl.* **1**, 145–162. Orientation in the digger-wasp.

Iersel J. J. A. van, Bol A. C. A. 1958 *Behaviour* **13**, 1–88. Preening of two tern species.

Ikeda K., Wiersma C. A. G. 1964 *Comp. Biochem. Physiol.* **12**, 107–115. Autogenic rhythmicity in the abdominal ganglia of the crayfish.

Imanishi K. 1957 *Primates* **1**, 1–29. Enculturation in the subhuman society of *Macaca fuscata.*

Imanishi K. 1960 *Curr. Anthropol.* **1**, 393–407. Social organization of primates in their natural habitat.

Immelmann K. 1969a In Hinde R. A. (ed.) *Bird Vocalizations.* Cambridge: Cambridge University Press. Song development in estrildid finches.

Immelmann K. 1969b *ZTP* **26**, 677–691. Über den Einfluss frühkindlicher Erfahrungen auf die geschlechtliche Objektfixierung bei Estrildiden.

Ingram J. C. 1977 *AB* **25**, 811–827. Interactions between parents and infants in the common marmoset.

Isaacson R. L. 1976 In Rosenzweig M. R., Bennett E. L. (ed.) *Neural Mechanisms of Learning and Memory.* Cambridge: M.I.T. Press. Experimental brain lesions and memory.

Iversen S. D. 1973 In Deutsch J. A. (ed.) *The Physiological Basis of Memory.* New York: Academic. Brain lesions and memory in animals.

Jackson R. R. 1978 *J. Arachnol.* **5**, 185–230. Alternative mating tactics of the jumping spider.

Jacobson M. 1974 In Rockstein M. (ed.) *The Physiology of Insects.* Vol. 3. New York: Academic. Insect pheromones.

Jacobson M., Beroza M. 1963 *Science* **140**, 1367–1373. Chemical insect attractants.

Jaisson P. 1975 *Behaviour* **52**, 1–37. L'ontogénèse des comportements de soins aux cocons chez la jeune fourmi rousse.

Jander R. 1963 *Annu. Rev. Entomol.* **8**, 95–114. Insect orientation.

Jay P. 1965 In DeVore I. (ed.) *Primate Behavior.* New York: Holt, Rinehart & Winston. The common langur of north India.

Jelliffe D. B., Jelliffe E. F. P. 1971 *W. H. O. Chron.* **25**, 537–540. The uniqueness of human milk.

Jenni D. A. 1974 *Am. Zool.* **14**, 129–144. Evolution of polyandry in birds.

Jenni D. A., Collier G. 1972 *Auk* **89**, 743–765. Polyandry in the American Jaçana.

Jennings H. S. 1906 *Behavior of the Lower Organisms.* Bloomington: Indiana University Press.

Jensen D. D. 1967 In Corning W. C., Ratner S. C. (ed.) *Chemistry of Learning.* New York: Plenum. The phylogeny of learning.

Jermy T., Hanson F. E., Dethier V. G. 1968 *Entomol.*

Exp. Appl. **11**, 211–230. Induction of specific food preference in lepidopterous larvae.

Jolly A. 1966 *Science* **153**, 501–506. Lemur social behavior and primate intelligence.

Jolly C. J. 1970 *Man* **5**, 5–26. The seed-eaters.

Jouventin P., Pasteur G., Cambefort J. P. 1977 *Evolution* **31**, 214–218. Observational learning of baboons.

Kaada B. 1967 In Clemente C. D., Lindsley D. B. (ed.) *Aggression and Defense.* Los Angeles: University of California Press. Brain mechanisms related to aggressive behavior.

Kagan J. 1976 *Am. Sci.* **64**, 186–196. Emergent themes in human development.

Kagan J., Tulkin S. R. 1971 In Schaffer H. R. (ed.) *The Origins of Human Social Relations.* London: Academic. Social class differences in child rearing.

Kaiser H. 1969 *Verh. Zool. Bot. Ges. Wien* **26**, 79–85. Regulation der Individuendichte am Paarungsplatz bei der Libelle.

Kalmijin A. J. 1971 *J. Exp. Biol.* **55**, 371–383. The electric sense of sharks and rays.

Kamin L. J. 1974 *The Science and Politics of I.Q.* Hillside, N.J.: Erlbaum.

Kandel E. R. 1976 *Cellular Basis of Behavior.* San Francisco: Freeman.

Karlson P., Lüscher M. 1959 *Nature (London)* **183**, 55–56. "Pheromones".

Katz D. 1953 *Animals and Men.* Harmondsworth: Penguin.

Kaufmann J. H. 1962 *Univ. Calif. Berkeley Publ. Zool.* **60**, 95–222. Ecology and social behavior of the coati.

Kaufmann J. H. 1967 In Altmann S. A. (ed.) *Social Communication among Primates.* Chicago: University of Chicago Press. Social relations of adult rhesus monkeys.

Kaufmann J. H. 1974 *AB* **22**, 281–369. Social ethology of the whiptail wallaby.

Kavanagh J. F. 1971 In Hellmuth J. (ed.) *Exceptional Infant.* Vol. 2. New York: Brunner/Mazel. The genesis and pathogenesis of speech and language.

Kavanau J. L. 1967 *Science* **155**, 1623–1639. Behavior of captive white-footed mice.

Kawai M. 1965 *Primates* **6**, 1–30. Newly-acquired pre-cultural behavior of Japanese monkeys.

Kawamura S. 1959 *Primates* **2**, 43–60. Sub-culture propagation among Japanese macaques.

Kear J. 1962 *Proc. Zool. Soc. London* **138**, 163–204. Food selection in finches.

Keesing R. M. 1972 In Beining P. (ed.) *Kinship Studies in the Morgan Centennial Year.* Washington DC: Anthropological Society of Washington. The lure of kinship.

Keeton W. T. 1974 In Lehrman D. S. et al. (ed.) *Advances in the Study of Behavior.* Vol. 3. New York: Academic. Homing in birds.

Kellogg W. N., Kellogg L. A. 1933 *The Ape and the Child.* New York: McGraw-Hill.

Kemp F. D. 1969 *AB* **17**, 446–451. Thermoregulatory behaviour in the lizard *Dipsosaurus dorsalis.*

Kemp G. A., Keith L. B. 1970 *Ecology* **51**, 763–779. Red squirrel populations.

Kennedy D., Evoy W. H., Hanawalt J. T. 1966 *Science* **154**, 917–919. Release of coordinated behavior in crayfish by single central neurons.

Kennedy J. S. 1972 *J. Aust. Entomol. Soc.* **11**, 168–176. The emergence of behaviour.

Kennedy J. S. 1974 In Browne L. B. (ed.) *Experimental Analysis of Insect Behaviour.* Berlin: Springer-Verlag. Changes of responsiveness in the patterning of behavioural sequences.

Kessel E. L. 1955 *Syst. Zool.* **4**, 97–104. The mating of balloon flies.

Kettlewell H. B. D. 1973 *The Evolution of Melanism.* Oxford: Clarendon Press.

Kevan P. G. 1976 *AB* **24**, 16–17. Sir Thomas More on imprinting.

Kilgour R., Scott T. H. 1959 *Proc. N.Z. Soc. Anim. Prod.* **19**, 36–43. Leadership in dairy cows.

Kimble D. P., Ray R. S. 1965 *AB* **13**, 530–533. Reflex habituation and potentiation in *Rana pipens.*

Kimble G. A. 1961 *Hilgard and Marquis' Conditioning and Learning.* New York: Appleton-Century-Crofts.

Kimble G. A. (ed.) 1967 *Foundations of Conditioning and Learning.* New York: Appleton-Century-Crofts.

King J. A. 1955 *Contrib. Lab. Vertebr. Biol. Univ. Mich.* **67**, 1–123. Social behavior in a black-tailed prairiedog town.

King J. A. 1973 *Annu. Rev. Ecol. Syst.* **4**, 117–138. The ecology of aggressive behavior.

King M.-C., Wilson A. C. 1975 *Science* **188**, 107–116. Evolution at two levels in humans and chimpanzees.

Kish G. B. 1955 *JCPP* **48**, 261–264. Learning when the onset of illumination is used as reinforcing stimulus.

Kislow C. J., Edwards L. J. 1972 *Nature (London)* **235**, 108–109. Repellent odour in aphids.

Kleerekoper H. et al. 1974 *AB* **22**, 124–132. Exploratory behaviour of goldfish.

Kleiman D. G. 1977 *Q. Rev. Biol.* **52**, 39–69. Monogamy in mammals.

Kleiman D. G., Eisenberg J. F. 1973 *AB* **21**, 637–659. Comparisons of canid and felid social systems.

Klein T. W., Howard J., DeFries J. C. 1970 *Psychon. Sci.* **19**, 177–178. Agonistic behavior in mice: strain differences.

Kling J. W., Stevenson J. G. 1970 In Horn G., Hinde R. A. (ed.) *Short-term Changes in Neural Activity and Behaviour.* Cambridge: Cambridge University Press. Habituation and extinction.

Klopfer P. H. 1959 *Behaviour* **14**, 282–299. Social interactions in discrimination learning.

Klopfer P. H., Adams D. K., Klopfer M. S. 1964 *Proc. Nat. Acad. Sci. U.S.A.* **52**, 911–914. Maternal "imprinting" in goats.

Klopfer P. H., Gamble J. 1966 *ZTP* **23**, 588–592. Maternal "imprinting" in goats: The role of chemical senses.

Klopfer P. H., Klopfer M. S. 1968 *ZTP* **25**, 862–866. Maternal "imprinting" in goats: Fostering of alien young.

Koch A. L., Carr A., Ehrenfeld D. W. 1969. *J. Theor. Biol.* **22**, 163–179. The migration of the green turtle to Ascension Island.

Koford C. B. 1957 *Ecol. Monogr.* **27**, 153–219. The vicuna and the puna.

Kohler I. 1962 *J. Genet. Psychol.* **100**, 331–335. Pavlov and his dog.

Köhler W. 1925 *The Mentality of Apes.* New York: Harcourt Brace.

Kohn M. 1951 *JCPP* **44**, 412–421. Satiation of hunger.

Konishi M. 1973. *Am. Sci.* **61**, 414–424. How the owl tracks its prey.

Konner M. J. 1972 In Blurton Jones N. (ed.) *Ethological Studies of Child Behaviour.* Cambridge: Cambridge University Press. The developmental ethology of a foraging people.

Koopman K. F. 1950 *Evolution* **4**, 135–148. Natural selection for reproductive isolation.

Kortlandt A. 1967 In Starck D., Schneider R., Kuhn H.-J. (ed.) *Neue Ergebnisse der Primatologie.* Stuttgart: Gustav Fischer. Experimentation with chimpanzees in the wild.

Kovach J. K., Kling A. 1967 *AB* **15**, 91–101. Neonate sucking behaviour in the kitten.

Kramer G. 1951 *Proc. Int. Ornithol. Cong. (Uppsala, 1950)* **10**, 269–280. Eine neue Methode zur Erforschung der Zugorientierung.

Krasne F. B. 1976 In Rosenzweig M. R., Bennett E. L. (ed.) *Neural Mechanisms of Learning and Memory.* Cambridge: M.I.T. Press. Invertebrate systems as a means of gaining insight into learning and memory.

Krebs C. J. 1966 *Ecol. Monogr.* **36**, 239–273. Fluctuating populations of *Microtus californicus.*

Krebs C. J. 1978 In Krames L., Pliner P., Alloway T. (ed.) *Aggression, Dominance, and Individual Spacing.* New York: Plenum. Aggression, dispersal, and cyclic changes in populations of small rodents.

Krebs C. J. et al. 1973 *Science* **179**, 35–41. Population cycles in small rodents.

Krebs C. J., Myers J. H. 1974 In MacFadyen A. (ed.) *Advances in Ecological Research.* Vol. 8. London: Academic. Population cycles in small mammals.

Krebs J. R. 1971 *Ecology* **52**, 2–22. Territory and breeding density in the great tit.

Krebs J. R. 1977a In Stonehouse B., Perrins C. (ed.) *Evolutionary Ecology.* Baltimore: University Park Press. Song and territory in the great tit.

Krebs J. R. 1977b *AB* **25**, 475–478. Song repertoires: The Beau Geste hypothesis.

Krebs J. R. 1978 *AB* **26**, 304–305. Beau Geste and song repetition.

Krebs J. R., MacRoberts M. H., Cullen J. M. 1972 *Ibis* **114**, 507–530. Flocking and feeding in the great tit.

Krebs J. R., May R. M. 1976 *Nature (London)* **260**, 9–10. Social insects and the evolution of altruism.

Krebs J. R., Ryan J. C., Charnov E. L. 1974 *AB* **22**, 953–964. Hunting by expectation or optimal foraging?

Krechevsky I. 1937 *J. Comp. Psychol.* **23**, 139–159. Brain mechanisms and variability.

Kreidl A. 1893 *Stud. Biol. Akad. Wiss. Math. Nat. Kl. Wien.* **102**, 149–174. Weitere Beiträge zur Physiologie des Ohrlabyrinthes.

Kroodsma D. E. 1977a *AB* **25**, 390–399. Song development in the song sparrow.

Kroodsma D. E. 1977b *Am. Nat.* **111**, 995–1008. Song organization among North American wrens.

Kroodsma D. E. 1978a *Nature (London)* **274**, 681–683. Continuity and versatility in bird song.

Kroodsma D. E. 1978b In Burghardt G. M., Bekoff M. (ed.) *The Development of Behavior: Comparative and Evolutionary Aspects.* New York: Garland. Aspects of learning in the ontogeny of bird song.

Kruijt J. P. 1964 *Ontogeny of Social Behaviour in Burmese Red Junglefowl.* Leiden: Brill.

Kruschinski L. W. et al. 1963 *ZTP* **20**, 474–486. Vergleichende physiologisch-morphologische Erforschung komplizierter Verhaltensformen von Vögeln.

Kruuk H. 1972 *J. Zool.* **166**, 233–244. Surplus killing by carnivores.

Kuffler S. W., Nicholls J. G. 1976 *From Neuron to Brain.* Sunderland, Mass.: Sinauer.

Kühme W. 1965 *ZTP* **22**, 495–541. Freilandstudien zur Soziologie des Hyänenhundes.

Kummer H. 1957 *Beih. Schweiz. Z. Psychol. Anwend.* **33**, 1–91. Soziales Verhalten einer Mantelpavian-Gruppe.

Kummer H. 1971 *Primate Societies.* Chicago: Aldine.

Kummer H., Götz W., Angst W. 1974 *Behaviour* **48**, 62–87. Triadic differentiation in baboons.

Kuo Z. Y. 1930 *J. Comp. Psychol.* **11**, 1–35. The genesis of the cat's behavior toward the rat.

LaBarre W. 1947 *J. Pers.* **16**, 49–68. The cultural basis of emotions and gestures.

LaBarre W. 1964 In Sebeok T. A., Hayes A. S., Bateson M. C. (ed.) *Approaches to Semiotics.* The Hague: Mouton. Paralinguistics, kinesics, and cultural anthropology.

Lack D. 1943 *The Life of the Robin.* Harmondsworth: Penguin.

Lack D. 1968 *Ecological Adaptations for Breeding in Birds.* London: Methuen.

Lade B. I., Thorpe W. H. 1964 *Nature (London)* **202**, 366–368. Dove songs as innately coded patterns of specific behaviour.

Lagerspetz K. Y. H., Tirri R., Lagerspetz K. M. J. 1968 *Scand. J. Psychol.* **9**, 157–160. Neurochemical and endocrinological studies of mice bred for aggressiveness.

Lakatos I., Musgrave A. (ed.) 1970 *Criticism and the Growth of Knowledge.* Cambridge: Cambridge University Press.

Lamb M. E. 1977 *Hum. Dev.* **20**, 65–85. The infant social world.

Lancaster J. B. 1968 In Jay P. C. (ed.) *Primates: Studies in Adaptation and Variability.* New York: Holt, Rinehart & Winston. Primate communication and the emergence of human language.

Landenberger D. E. 1966 *AB* **14**, 414–418. Learning in the Pacific starfish.

Lanyon W. E. 1957 *Publ. Nuttall Ornithol. Club* **1**, 1–67. The comparative biology of the meadowlarks (*Sturnella*) in Wisconsin.

Lanyon W. E. 1960 In Lanyon W. E., Tavolga W. N. (ed.) *Animal Sounds and Communication.* Washington: American Institute of Biological Sciences. The ontogeny of vocalizations in birds.

Larsson K. 1962 *J. Exp. Zool.* **151**, 167–176. Mating behavior in male rats. 1. Effects of lesions in the dorsolateral and median cortex.

Larsson K. 1964 *J. Exp. Zool.* **155**, 203–214. Mating

behavior in male rats. 2. Effects of lesions in the frontal lobes.

Lashley K. S. 1929 *Brain Mechanisms and Intelligence*. Chicago: University of Chicago Press.

Lashley K. S. 1934 In Murchison C. (ed.) *Handbook of General Experimental Psychology*. Worcester: Clark University Press. Nervous mechanisms in learning.

Lashley K. S. 1950 *Symp. Soc. Exp. Biol.* **4**, 454–482. In search of the engram.

Laverack M. S. 1968 *Symp. Zool. Soc. London* **23**, 299–326. On superficial receptors.

Lawick-Goodall J. van 1968 *Anim. Behav. Monogr.* **1**, 161–311. The behaviour of free living chimpanzees.

Lawick-Goodall J. van 1970 In Lehrman D. S., Hinde R. A., Shaw E. (ed.) *Advances in the Study of Behavior*. New York: Academic. Tool-using in primates.

Lawick-Goodall J. van 1973 In Menzel E. W. (ed.) *Symposium of the IVth International Congress of Primatology*. Vol. 1: *Precultural Primate Behavior*. Basel: Karger. Cultural elements in a chimpanzee community.

Laws R. M., Parker I. S. C. 1968 *Symp. Zool. Soc. London* **21**, 319–359. Elephant populations in East Africa.

Leach E. R. 1964 In Lenneberg E. H. (ed.) *New Directions in the Study of Language*. Cambridge: M.I.T. Press. Anthropological aspects of language.

Leach E. R. 1972 In Hinde R. A. (ed.) *Non-Verbal Communication*. Cambridge: Cambridge University Press. The influence of cultural context on nonverbal communication in man.

Le Boef B. J. 1974 *Am. Zool.* **14**, 163–176. Male-male competition and reproductive success in elephant seals.

Lee R. B., DeVore I. 1968 *Man the Hunter*. Chicago: Aldine.

Lees A. D. 1948 *J. Exp. Biol.* **25**, 145–207. The sensory physiology of the sheep tick.

Lees D. R., Creed E. R. 1975 *J. Anim. Ecol.* **44**, 67–83. Industrial melanism in *Biston betularia*.

Lehr E. 1967 *ZTP* **24**, 208–244. Experimentelle Untersuchungen an Affen und Halbaffen über Generalisation von Insekten-und Blütenabbildungen.

Lehrman D. S. 1953 *Q. Rev. Biol.* **28**, 337–363. Konrad Lorenz's theory of instinctive behavior.

Lehrman D. S. 1955 *Behaviour* **7**, 241–286. Parental feeding behaviour in the ring dove.

Lehrman D. S. 1961 In Young W. C. (ed.) *Sex and Internal Secretion*. Baltimore: Williams & Wilkins. Hormonal regulation of parental behavior.

Lehrman D. S. 1964 In Etkin W. (ed.) *Social Behavior & Organization among Vertebrates*. Chicago: University of Chicago Press. Behavior cycles in reproduction.

Lehrman D. S., Brody P. N., Wortis R. P. 1961 *Endocrinology* **68**, 507–516. The mate and nesting material as stimuli for incubation in the ring dove.

Le Magnen J. 1959. *C. R. Acad. Sci.* **249**, 2400–2402. Un phénomène d'appétit provisionnel.

Le Maho Y. 1977 *Am. Sci.* **65**, 680–693. The emperor penguin.

Leong C.-Y. 1969 *Z. Vgl. Physiol.* **65**, 29–50. The attack readiness of *Haplochromis burtoni*.

Lerner I. M. 1954 *Genetic Homeostasis*. Edinburgh: Oliver & Boyd.

Leroi-Gourhan A. 1968 *The Art of Prehistoric Man in Western Europe*. London: Thames & Hudson.

Lester B. M. et al. 1974 *Dev. Psychol.* **10**, 79–85. Separation protest in Guatemalan infants.

Lett B. T. 1973 *Learn. Motiv.* **4**, 237–246. Delayed reward learning.

Lett B. T. 1975 *Learn. Motiv.* **6**, 80–90. Long delay learning.

Lettvin J. Y. et al. 1959 *Proc. Inst. Radio Electron. Eng. Aust.* **47**, 1940–1951. What the frog's eye tells the frog's brain.

Leuthold W., Leuthold B. M. 1975 *ZTP* **39**, 75–84. Parturition in the African elephant.

Levi H. W. 1978 *Am. Sci.* **66**, 734–742. Orb-weaving spiders and their webs.

Levi L. (ed.) 1975 *Society, Stress and Disease*. Vol 2. London: Oxford University Press.

Lewis C. I. 1956 *Mind and the World-Order*. New York: Dover. [Originally published in 1929.]

Lewis M., Rosenblum L. A. (ed.) 1974 *The Effect of the Infant on Its Caregiver.* New York: Wiley.

Lewontin R. C. 1974 *Am. J. Hum. Genet.* **26**, 400–411. The analysis of variance and the analysis of causes.

Lewontin R. C. 1975 *Annu. Rev. Genet.* **9**, 387–405. Genetic aspects of intelligence.

Lewontin R. C. 1979 *Behav. Sci.* **24**, 5–14. Sociobiology as an adaptationist program.

Leyhausen P. 1956 *ZTP* **2**. Verhaltensstudien an Katzen.

Li C. C. 1971 In Cancro M. D. (ed.) *Intelligence: Genetic and Environmental Influences.* New York: Grune & Stratton. A genetic model for human intelligence.

Liddell H. S. 1956 *Emotional Hazards in Animals and Man.* Springfield, Ill.: Thomas.

Lidicker W. Z. 1966 *Ecol. Monogr.* **36**, 27–50. A feral house mouse population.

Lieberman P. H., Klatt D. H., Wilson W. H. 1969 *Science* **164**, 1185–1187. Vocal tract limitations on the vowel reportoires of primates.

Ligon J. D., Ligon S. H. 1978 *Nature (London)* **276**, 496–498. Communal breeding in green woodhoopoes.

Lincoln G. A. 1972 *J. Exp. Zool.* **182**, 233–250. Antlers in the behaviour of red deer.

Lincoln G. A., Guinness F. E. 1973 *J. Reprod. Fertil. Suppl.* **19**, 475–489. The sexual significance of the rut in red deer.

Lindauer M. 1961 *Communication among Social Bees.* Cambridge: Harvard University Press.

Lindauer M., Martin H. 1972 In *Animal Orientation and Navigation.* Washington: Symposium NASA SP-262 U.S. Govt. Magnetic effect on dancing bees.

Lindburg D. G. 1971 In Rosenblum L. A. (ed.) *Primate Behavior* **2**. New York: Academic. The rhesus monkey in North India.

Linden E. 1974 *Apes, Men, and Language.* New York: Penguin.

Linsenmair K. E. 1967 *ZTP* **24**, 404–456. Konstruktion und Signalfunktion der Sandpyramide der Reiterkrabbe.

Lion J. R., Penna M. 1974 In Whalen R. E. (ed.) *The Neuropsychology of Aggression.* New York: Plenum. Human aggression.

Lisk R. D. 1962 *Am. J. Physiol.* **203**, 493–496. Estradiol and sexual receptivity.

Lisk R. D. 1971 *AB* **19**, 606–610. Oestrogen and progesterone synergism and maternal nest-building.

Lissmann H. W., Machin K. E. 1958 *J. Exp. Biol.* **35**, 451–486. Object location in *Gymnarchus niloticus.*

Littlejohn M. J. 1968 *Aust. Zool.* **15**, 259–264. Frog calls and the species problem.

Littlejohn M. J., Loftus-Hills J. J. 1968 *Evolution* **22**, 659–663. Premating isolation in the *Hyla ewingi* complex.

Livesey P. J. 1966 *Aust. J. Psychol.* **18**, 71–79. The rat, rabbit and cat in the Hebb-Williams test of intelligence.

Livesey P. J. 1967 *Aust. J. Psychol.* **19**, 55–62. The Hebb-Williams elevated pathway test.

Lloyd J. E. 1966 *Misc. Publ. Mus. Zool. Univ. Mich.* **130**, 1–95. The flash communication system in fireflies.

Lloyd J. E. 1971 *Annu. Rev. Entomol.* **16**, 97–122. Bioluminescent communication in insects.

Loeb J. 1901 *Comparative Physiology of the Brain.* London: Murray.

Loeb J. 1918 *Forced Movements, Tropisms, and Animal Conduct.* Philadelphia: Lippincott.

Loeb J. 1964 *The Mechanistic Conception of Life.* Cambridge: Harvard University Press. [First published in 1912.]

Loehlin J. C., Lindzey G., Spuhler J. N. 1975 *Race Differences in Intelligence.* San Francisco: Freeman.

Lorenz K. Z. 1935 *J. Ornithol.* **83**, 137–213; 289–413. Der Kumpan in der Umwelt des Vogels.

Lorenz K. Z. 1950 *Symp. Soc. Exp. Biol.* **4**, 211–268. Innate behaviour patterns.

Lorenz K. Z. 1952 *King Solomon's Ring.* London: Methuen.

Lorenz K. Z. 1962 *Proc. R. Inst. G. B.* **39**, 282–296. The function of colour in coral reef fishes.

Lorenz K. Z. 1966 *On Aggression.* London: Methuen.

Lorenz K. Z. 1967 *Philos. Trans. R. Soc. London Ser.*

B **251**, 278–284. The psycho-social evolution of human culture.

Lorenz K. Z. 1970 *Studies in Animal and Human Behaviour.* Vol. I. London: Methuen.

Lorenz K. Z. 1971 *Studies in Animal and Human Behaviour.* Vol. II. London: Methuen.

Lorenz K. Z., Tinbergen N. 1939 *ZTP* **2**, 1–29. Der Eirollbewegung der Graugans.

Lott D., Scholz S. D., Lehrman D. S. 1967 *AB* **15**, 433–437. Exteroceptive stimulation of the reproductive system of the female ring dove.

Lucas J. R. 1970 *The Freedom of the Will.* Oxford: Clarendon Press.

Luco J. V. 1971 In Kao F. F., Koizumi K., Vassale M. (ed.) *Research in Physiology.* Bologna: Aulo Gaggi. Memory in insects.

Lukowiak K., Jacklet J. W. 1972 *Science* **178**, 1306–1308. Habituation and dishabituation.

Luria A. R. 1976 *Cognitive Development.* Cambridge: Harvard University Press.

Lüscher V. 1964 *Insectes Soc.* **6**, 79–90. Die spezifische Wirkung männlicher und weiblicher Ersatzgeschlechtstiere auf die Entstehung von Ersatzgeschlechtstieren bei *Kalotermes flavicollis.*

Lüscher M. 1969 *Proc. 6th Cong. Int. Union Study Soc. Insects,* 165–170. Die Bedeutung des Juvenilhormons für die Differenzierung der Soldaten bei *Kalotermes flavicollis.*

Mackay D. A., Underwood A. J. 1977 *Oecologia (Berlin)* **30**, 215–237. Homing in the intertidal limpet *Cellana tramoserica.*

MacKay D. M. 1960 *Mind* **69**, 31–40. The logical indeterminacy of a free choice.

Mackie G. O. 1964 *Proc. R. Soc. London Ser. B* **159**, 366–391. Locomotion in a siphonophore colony.

Mackie J. L. 1966 *Philos. Rev.* **75**, 441–466. The direction of causation.

Macnamara J. 1972 *Psychol. Rev.* **79**, 1–13. Language learning in infants.

Magnus D. 1958 *ZTP* **15**, 398–426. Untersuchungen zur Bionomie und Ethologie des Kaisermantels.

Maier N. R. F., Schneirla T. C. 1935 *Principles of Animal Psychology.* New York: McGraw-Hill.

Maller O. 1967 In Kare M. R., Maller O. (ed.) *The Chemical Senses and Nutrition.* Baltimore: Johns Hopkins University Press. Specific appetite.

Mallory F. F., Clulow F. V. 1977 *Can. J. Zool.* **55**, 1–17. Evidence of pregnancy failure in the wild meadow vole.

Malson L. 1972 *Wolf Children and the Problem of Human Nature.* New York: Monthly Review Press.

Manciaux M., Debry G., Comoy J. 1968 *Arch. Fr. Pediatr.* **25**, 103–110. Le comportement alimentaire du jeune enfant.

Manier E. 1978 *The Young Darwin and his Cultural Circle.* Dordrecht, Holland: Reidel.

Manning A. 1961 *AB* **9**, 82–99. Selection for mating speed in *Drosophila melanogaster.*

Manning A. 1967 *Nature (London)* **216**, 338–340. "Pre-imaginal conditioning" in *Drosophila.*

Mark R. F. 1974 *Memory and Nerve Cell Connections.* Oxford: Clarendon Press.

Markl H., Lindauer M. 1965 In Rockstein M. (ed.) *The Physiology of Insecta.* New York: Academic. Physiology of insect behavior.

Marler P. 1957 *Behaviour* **11**, 13–39. The signals of birds.

Marler P. 1959 In Bell P. R. (ed.) *Darwin's Biological Work.* Cambridge: Cambridge University Press. Animal communication.

Marler P. 1965 In DeVore I. (ed.) *Primate Behavior: Field Studies of Monkeys and Apes.* New York: Holt, Rinehart & Winston. Communication in monkeys and apes.

Marler P. 1974 In Krames L., Pliner P., Alloway T. (ed.) *Advances in the Study of Communication and Affect.* Vol. 1: *Nonverbal Communication.* New York: Plenum. Animal communication.

Marler P., Mundinger P. 1971 In Moltz H. (ed.) *The Ontogeny of Vertebrate Behavior.* New York: Academic. Vocal learning in birds.

Marsella A. J., Murray M. D., Golden C. 1974 *J. Cross Cult. Psychol.* **5**, 312–328. Shame.

Marshall A. J. 1954 *Bower-Birds.* Oxford: Clarendon Press.

Martin G. M., Bellingham W. P., Storlien L. H. 1977

Physiol. Behav. **18**, 415–420. Effects of color experience on chickens' formation of aversions.

Martin R. D. 1966 *Science* **152**, 1403–1404. Tree shrews: Unique reproductive mechanism.

Martin R. D. 1974 In Broughton W. B. (ed.) *The Biology of Brains.* London: Institute of Biology. The biological basis of human behaviour.

Mason L. G. 1964 *Evolution* **18**, 492–497. Stabilizing selection for mating fitness.

Mason L. G. 1969 *Evolution* **23**, 55–58. Mating selection in the California oak moth.

Mason W. A. 1960 *JCPP* **53**, 582–589. The effects of social restriction on rhesus monkeys. 1. Free social behavior.

Mason W. A. 1961a *JCPP* **54**, 287–290. The effects of social restriction on rhesus monkeys. 2. Gregariousness.

Mason W. A. 1961b *JCPP* **54**, 694–699. The effects of social restriction on rhesus monkeys. 3. Dominance.

Mason W. A. 1971 *Primate Behav.* **2**, 107–137. Social organization in *Saimiri* and *Callicebus*.

Mason W. A. 1976 In Masterton R. B. et al. (ed.) *Evolution of Brain and Behavior in Vertebrates.* Hillsdale, N.J.: Erlbaum. Primate social behavior.

Mason W. A. 1978 In Burghardt G. M., Bekoff M. (ed.) *The Development of Behavior: Comparative and Evolutionary Aspects.* New York: Garland. Social experience and primate cognitive development.

Mason W. A., Berkson G. 1975 *Dev. Psychobiol.* **8**, 197–211. The development of rocking in rhesus monkeys.

Mason W. A., Hollis J. H. 1962 *AB* **10**, 211–221. Communication between young rhesus monkeys.

Mather K. 1970 *Symp. Zool. Soc. London* **26**, 27–39. The nature and significance of variation in wild populations.

Matthews G. V. T. 1968 *Bird Navigation.* Cambridge: Cambridge University Press.

Maynard Smith J. 1961 In Banton M. (ed.) *Darwinism and the Study of Society.* London: Tavistock. Evolution and history.

Maynard Smith J. 1964 *Nature* **201**, 1145–1147. Group selection and kin selection.

Maynard Smith J. 1975 *The Theory of Evolution.* Harmondsworth: Penguin. (3rd edn.)

Maynard Smith J. 1976 *Q. Rev. Biol.* **51**, 277–283. Group selection.

Maynard Smith J. 1978 *AB* **26**, 632–633. In defence of models.

Maynard Smith J., Price G. R. 1973 *Nature (London)* **246**, 15–18. The logic of animal conflict.

Maynard Smith J., Ridpath M. G. 1972 *Am. Nat.* **106**, 447–452. Wife sharing in the Tasmanian native hen.

McCarthy J. D., Galle O. R., Zimmern W. 1975 *Am. Behav. Sci.* **18**, 771–791. Population density, social structure, and interpersonal violence.

McClintock M. K. 1971 *Nature (London)* **229**, 244–245. Menstrual synchrony and suppression.

McCosker J. E. 1977 *Science* **197**, 400–401. Fright posture of the plesiopid fish *Calloplesiops altivelis*.

McDougall W. 1938 *Br. J. Psychol.* **28**, 321–345. Fourth report on a Lamarckian experiment.

McFarland D. J. 1971 *Feedback Mechanisms in Animal Behaviour.* London: Academic.

McFarland D. J. 1974 In McFarland D. (ed.) *Motivational Control Systems Analysis.* London: Academic. Experimental investigation of motivational state.

McFarland D. J. 1976 In Bateson P. P. G., Hinde R. A. (ed.) *Growing Points in Ethology.* Cambridge: Cambridge University Press. The temporal organisation of behaviour.

McGinitie G. E., McGinitie N. 1968 *Natural History of Marine Animals.* New York: McGraw-Hill. (2nd edn.)

McGrew W. C. 1974 *J. Hum. Evol.* **3**, 501–508. Tool use by wild chimpanzees.

McGrew W. C., Tutin C. E. G., Midgett P. S. 1975 *ZTP* **37**, 145–162. Tool use in captive chimpanzees.

McGuire T. R., Hirsch J. 1977 *Proc. Natl. Acad. Sci. U.S.A.* **74**, 5193–5197. Behavior-genetic analysis of *Phormia regina*.

McKenna J. J. 1978 *Am. J. Phys. Anthropol.* **48**, 503–

510. Biosocial functions of grooming among *Presbytis entellus*.

McKinney F. 1978 In Rosenblatt J. S. et al. *Advances in the Study of Behavior*. New York: Academic. Social behavior in closely related species of birds.

McLaren A. 1976 *Mammalian Chimaeras*. Cambridge: Cambridge University Press.

McNab B. K. 1963 *Am. Nat.* **97**, 133–140. Bioenergetics and the determination of home range size.

Meadows P. S., Campbell J. I. 1972 *Adv. Mar. Biol.* **10**, 271–382. Habitat selection by aquatic invertebrates.

Mech L. D. 1960 *The Wolf*. New York: American Museum of Natural History.

Medawar P. B. 1959 *The Future of Man*. London: Methuen.

Medawar P. B. 1974 In Ayala F. J., Dobzhansky T. (ed.) *Studies in the Philosophy of Biology*. London: Macmillan. A geometric model of reduction and emergence.

Meier A. H. 1973 *Am. Sci.* **61**, 184–187. Daily hormone rhythms in the white-throated sparrow.

Meier G. W. 1965 *AB* **13**, 228–231. The effects of social isolation during rearing.

Mendelsohn E. 1964 *Heat and Life*. Cambridge: Harvard University Press.

Menzel E. W. 1971 *Folia Primatol.* **15**, 220–232. Communication about the environment in young chimpanzees.

Menzel E. W., Halperin S. 1975 *Science* **189**, 652–654. Objective communication between chimpanzees.

Menzel R., Erber J., Masuhr T. 1974 In Browne L. B. (ed.) *Experimental Analysis of Insect Behaviour*. Berlin: Springer-Verlag. Learning and memory in the honeybee.

Merrill D. 1965 *J. Exp. Zool.* **158**, 123–132. Casebuilding in caddis-worms.

Messenger J. B. 1973 *AB* **21**, 801–826. Learning in the cuttlefish.

Messenger J. B. 1974 In Broughton W. B. (ed.) *The Biology of Brains*. London: Institute of Biology. Information configurations in central nervous systems.

Messenger J. B. 1977 *Symp. Zool. Soc. London* **38**, 347–376. Prey-capture and learning in the cuttlefish.

Meyer D. L., Platt C., Distel H.-J. 1976 *J. Comp. Physiol.* **110**, 323–331. Postural control mechanisms in the upside-down catfish.

Meyer R. L., Sperry R. W. 1976 In Gottlieb G. (ed.) *Neural and Behavioral Specificity*. New York: Academic. Retinotectal specificity.

Meyerriecks A. J. 1960 *Publ. Nuttall Ornithol. Club* **2**, 1–158. Breeding behavior of North American herons.

Meyers B. 1971 In Moltz H. (ed.) *The Ontogeny of Vertebrate Behavior*. New York: Academic. Early experience and problem-solving.

Michael R. P., Keverne E. B. 1968 *Nature (London)* **218**, 746–749. Pheromones in the communication of sexual status.

Michael R. P., Keverne E. B. 1970 *Nature (London)* **225**, 84–85. Primate sex pheromones of vaginal origin.

Michener C. D. 1974 *The Social Behavior of the Bees*. Cambridge: Harvard University Press.

Michener G. L. 1973 *J. Mammal.* **54**, 1001–1003. Intraspecific aggression in ground squirrels.

Middleton J. (ed.) 1970 *From Child to Adult*. New York: Natural History Press.

Miller N. E. 1955 *Ann. N.Y. Acad. Sci.* **63**, 141–143. Food consumption as a measure of hunger.

Miller N. E. 1959 In Koch E. (ed.) *Psychology: A Study of a Science*. Vol. 2: *General Systematic Formulations. Learning, and Special Processes*. New York: McGraw-Hill. Liberalization of basic S-R concepts.

Miller N. E. 1961 *Ann. N.Y. Acad. Sci.* **92**, 830–839. Integration of neurophysiological and behavioral research.

Miller N. E. 1967 *Proc. Am. Philos. Soc.* **111**, 315–325. Laws of learning relevant to its biological basis.

Miller N. E. 1969 *Science* **163**, 434–445. Learning of visceral and glandular responses.

Miller N. E., Dollard J. 1945 *Social Learning and Imitation*. London: Routledge.

Millikan G. C., Bowman R. I. 1967 *Living Bird* **6**, 23–41. Galapagos tool-using finches.

Mills M., Melhuish E. 1974 *Nature* (*London*) **252**, 123–124. Recognition of mother's voice in early infancy.

Milton K., May M. L. 1976 *Nature* (*London*) **259**, 459–462. Body weight, diet and home range area in primates.

Modha M. L. 1967 *East Afr. Wildl. J.* **5**, 74–95. The ecology of the Nile crocodile.

Mogenson G. J. 1978 In Veale W. L., Lederis K. (ed.) *Current Studies of Hypothalamic Function.* Vol. 2. Basel: Karger. Neural mechanisms for the control of food and water intakes.

Monfort-Braham N. 1975 *ZTP* **39**, 332–364. La structure sociale du topi.

Monfort-Braham N., Ruwet J.-C. 1967 *Ann. Soc. R. Zool. Belg.* **97**, 131–159. Les déclencheurs dans le comportement sexuel du *Pelmatochromis subocellatus.*

Montagu A. 1976 *The Nature of Human Aggression.* London: Oxford University Press.

Montevecchi W. A. 1976 *Behaviour* **58**, 26–39. The adaptive significance of avian eggshell pigmentation.

Moore B. R. 1973 In Hinde R. A., Stevenson-Hinde J. (ed.) *Constraints on Learning.* London: Academic. Pavlovian reactions in instrumental learning.

Morrell G. M., Turner J. R. G. 1970 *Behaviour* **36**, 116–130. The response of wild birds to artificial prey.

Morris R. L., Erickson C. J. 1971 *AB* **19**, 398–406. Pair bond maintenance in the ring dove.

Morrison S. D. 1968 *J. Physiol.* **197**, 305–323. The energy expended by rats on spontaneous activity.

Morton E. S. 1977 *Am. Nat.* **3**, 855–869. Motivation-structural rules in some bird and mammal sounds.

Moss H. A. 1974 In Krames L., Pliner P., Alloway T. (ed.) *Advances in the Study of Communication and Affect.* Vol. 1: *Nonverbal Communication.* New York: Plenum. Communication in mother-infant interaction.

Mostler G. 1935 *Z. Morphol. Oekol. Tiere* **29**, 381–454. Beobachtungen zur Frage der Wespenmimikry.

Mount L. E. 1960 *J. Agric. Sci.* **55**, 101–105. The influence of huddling and body size on the metabolic rate of the young pig.

Mourier H. 1965 *Vidensk. Medd. Dan. Naturhis. Foren. Khobenhavn* **128**, 221-231. The behaviour of house flies towards "new objects".

Mowrer O. H. 1960 *Learning Theory and the Symbolic Process.* New York: Wiley.

Moyer K. E. 1976 *The Psychobiology of Aggression.* New York: Harper.

Mpitsos G. J., Collins S. D. 1975 *Science* **188**, 954–957. Rapid aversive conditioning in *Pleurobranchaea.*

Mpitsos G. J., Davis W. J. 1973 *Science* **180**, 317–320. Classical and avoidance conditioning in *Pleurobranchaea.*

Mrosovsky N., Powley T. L. 1977 *Behav. Biol.* **20**, 205–223. Set points for body weight and fat.

Muckensturm B. 1965 *C. R. Acad. Sci.* **260**, 3183–3184. Possibilités inattendues de manipulation chez l'Épinoche.

Muenzinger K. F. 1934 *J. Comp. Psychol.* **17**, 267–277. Electric shock for correct response in visual discrimination.

Mulligan J. A. 1966 *Univ. Calif. Berkeley Publ. Zool.* **81**, 1–76. Singing in the song sparrow.

Munn N. L. 1950 *Handbook of Psychological Research on the Rat.* New York: Houghton Mifflin.

Myers W. A. 1970 *J. Exp. Anal. Behav.* **14**, 225–235. Observational learning in monkeys.

Myhre K., Hammel H. T. 1969 *Am. J. Physiol.* **217**, 1490–1495. Behavioral regulation of internal temperature in *Tiliqua scincoides.*

Mykytowycz R., Dudzinski M. L. 1966 *CSIRO Wildl. Res.* **11**, 31–47. Odoriferous and other glands in relation to social status and sexual activity in the rabbit.

Mykytowycz R., Fullagar P. J. 1973 *J. Reprod. Fertil. Suppl.* **19**, 503–522. Effect of social environment on reproduction in the rabbit.

Myrberg A. A. 1976 In Burkhardt D., Schleidt W., Altner H. (ed.) *Signals in the Animal World.* London: Allen & Unwin. Electric location by fishes.

Nagel T. 1970 *The Possibility of Altruism.* Oxford: Clarendon Press.

Nagel U. 1971 *Proc. 3rd Int. Congr. Primat. Zurich 1970,* **3**, 48–57. Social organization in a baboon hybrid zone.

Nagel U., Kummer H. 1974 In Holloway R. L. (ed.) *Primate Aggression, Territoriality, and Xenophobia.* New York: Academic. Cercopithecoid aggressive behavior.

Needham J. 1934 *A History of Embryology.* Cambridge: Cambridge University Press.

Nelson M. C. 1971 *JCPP* **77**, 353–368. Classical conditioning in the blowfly.

Newell G. E. 1958 *J. Mar. Biol. Assoc. U.K.* **37**, 241–266. The behaviour of *Littorina littorea.*

Nicholas W. L. 1975 *The Biology of Free-living Nematodes.* Oxford: Clarendon.

Nicholls M. F., Kimble G. A. 1964 *J. Exp. Psychol.* **67**, 400–402. Effect of instructions upon eyelid conditioning.

Nichols D. 1962 *Echinoderms.* London: Hutchinson.

Nicholson A. J. 1934 *Bull. Entomol. Res.* **25**, 85–99. The influence of temperature on the activity of sheep-blowflies.

Nicolai J. 1964 *ZTP* **21**, 129–204. Der Brutparasitismus der Viduinae.

Noirot E. 1964 *JCPP* **57**, 97–99. Changes in responsiveness to young in the mouse.

Noirot E. 1972 *Dev. Psychobiol.* **5**, 371–387. Ultrasounds and maternal behavior.

Norton-Griffiths M. 1967 *Ibis* **109**, 412–424. The feeding behaviour of the oystercatcher.

Norton-Griffiths M. 1969 *Behaviour* **34**, 55–114. Parental feeding in the oystercatcher.

Nottebohm F. 1972 *Am. Nat.* **106**, 116–140. The origins of vocal learning.

Oatley K. 1972 *Brain Mechanisms and Mind.* London: Thames & Hudson.

Oeser R. 1951 *Aquar. Terrar. Z.* **4**, 103–106. Haltung und Zucht des *Triturus vittatus.*

Ogilvie D. M., Stinson R. H. 1966 *Can. J. Zool.* **44**, 511–517. Temperature selection by laboratory mice.

O'Kelly L. I. et al. 1966 *JCPP* **61**, 194–197. Water regulation in the rat.

Okon E. E. 1972 *J. Zool.* **168**, 139–148. Ultrasound production in infant rodents.

Olds J. 1958 In Harlow H. F., Woolsey C. N. (ed.) *Biological and Biochemical Bases of Behavior.* Madison: University of Wisconsin Press. Adaptive functions of paleocortical and related structures.

Olds J. 1977 *Drives and Reinforcements: Behavioral Studies of Hypothalamic Functions.* New York: Raven.

Olds J. A., Milner P. 1954 *JCPP* **47**, 419–427. Reinforcement produced by electrical stimulation of rat brain.

Orians G. H. 1969 *Am. Nat.* **103**, 589–603. The evolution of mating systems.

Orr R. T. 1970 *Animals in Migration.* London: Collier-Macmillan.

Ostrom J. H. 1979 *Am. Sci.* **67**, 46–56. Bird flight: How did it begin?

Oswald M., Erwin J. 1976 *Nature (London)* **262**, 686–687. Control of intragroup aggression by male pigtail monkeys.

Ounsted M., Sleigh G. 1975 *Lancet* (i), 1393–1397. The infant's self-regulation of food intake.

Owen R. 1855 *Lectures on the Comparative Anatomy and Physiology of the Invertebrate Animals.* London: Longmans. (2nd edn.)

Owen-Smith R. N. 1975 *ZTP* **38**, 337–384. The social ethology of the white rhinoceros.

Oxnard C. E. 1975 *Nature (London)* **258**, 389–395. The place of the autralopithecines in human evolution: grounds for doubt?

Packer C. 1977 *Nature (London)* **265**, 441–443. Reciprocal altruism in *Papio anubis.*

Paddock J. 1975 *Aggr. Behav.* **1**, 217–233. Antiviolent and "normal" communities.

Palmer J. D. 1976 *An Introduction to Biological Rhythms.* New York: Academic.

Pantin C. F. A. 1965 *Am. Zool.* **5**, 581–589. The coelenterate behavior machine.

Pardi L. 1960 *Cold Spring Harbor Symp. Quant. Biol.* **25**, 395–401. The solar orientation of littoral amphipods.

Parsons P. A. 1967 *The Genetic Analysis of Behaviour.* London: Methuen.

Partridge B. L., Liley N. R., Stacey N. E. 1976 *AB* **24**, 291–299. Pheromones in the sexual behaviour of goldfish.

Partridge L. 1978 In Krebs J. R., Davies N. B. (ed.) *Behavioural Ecology: An Evolutionary Approach.* Oxford: Blackwell Scientific. Habitat selection.

Passmore J. 1974 *Man's Responsibility for Nature.* London: Duckworth.

Patterson F. G. 1978 *Brain Lang.* **5**, 72–97. The gestures of a gorilla.

Paulian P. 1964 *Mammalia Suppl.* **28**, 1–146. Contribution à l'étude de l'otarie de l'Ile Amsterdam.

Pavlov I. P. 1928 *Lectures on Conditioned Reflexes.* London: Lawrence & Wishart.

Pavlov I. P. 1957 *Experimental Psychology and Other Essays.* New York: Philosophical Library.

Payne R. B. 1973 *Ornithol. Monogr. Am. Ornithol. Union* **11**, 1–333. Behavior, mimetic songs and song dialects of the parasitic indigobirds.

Payne R. B. 1977 *Annu. Rev. Ecol. Syst.* **8**, 1–28. Brood parasitism in birds.

Payne R. S. 1971 *J. Exp. Biol.* **54**, 535–573. Acoustic location of prey by barn owls.

Payne R. S., McVay S. 1971 *Science* **173**, 585–597. Songs of humpback whales.

Payne T. L. 1974 In Birch M. C. (ed.) *Pheromones.* Amsterdam: North-Holland. Pheromone perception.

Peck J. W. 1978a *JCPP* **92**, 555–570. Rats defend different body weights depending on palatability and accessibility of food.

Peck J. W. 1978b *Physiol. Behav.* **21**, 599–607. Rats drinking quinine- or caffeine-adulterated water defend lean body weights against caloric and osmotic stress.

Peek F. W. 1972a *AB* **20**, 112–118. The territorial function of vocal and visual display in the male red-winged blackbird.

Peek F. W. 1972b *AB* **20**, 119–122. Territory maintenance in the male red-winged blackbird.

Peeke H. V. S., Peeke S. C. 1973 In Peeke H. V. S., Herz M. J. (ed.) *Habituation.* Vol 1: *Behavioral Studies.* New York: Academic. Habituation in fish.

Pelkwijk J. J. ter, Tinbergen N. 1937 *ZTP* **1**, 193–204. Eine reizbiologische Analyse einiger Verhaltensweisen von *Gasterosteus aculeatus.*

Penrose L. S. 1951 *Ann. Eugen.* **16**, 134–141. Pleiotropic effects in phenylketonuria.

Penrose L. S. 1963 *The Biology of Mental Defect.* London: Sidgwick & Jackson.

Perdeck A. C. 1958 *Ardea* **46**, 1–37. Orientation in migrating starlings and chaffinches.

Peters R. H. 1976 *Am. Nat.* **110**, 1–12. Tautology in evolution and ecology.

Peters R. H. 1978 *Am. Nat.* **112**, 759–762. Predictable problems with tautology in evolution and ecology.

Peters R. S. 1974 *Psychology and Ethical Development.* London: Allen & Unwin.

Petrunkevitch A. 1926 *Biol. Bull.* **50**, 427–432. Instinct as a taxonomic character in spiders.

Pettersson M. 1956 *Nature (London)* **177**, 709–710. Diffusion of a new habit among greenfinches.

Pfeiffer W. 1974 In Birch M. C. (ed.) *Pheromones.* Amsterdam: North-Holland. Pheromones in fish and amphibia.

Pianka E. R. 1970 *Am. Nat.* 104, 592–597. On *r*- and *K*-selection.

Pilbeam D. 1972 *The Ascent of Man.* New York: Macmillan.

Pilbeam D. 1978 *Discovery* **13**, 2–9. Rethinking human origins.

Pilbeam D., Gould S. J. 1974 *Science* **186**, 892–901. Size and scaling in human evolution.

Pilleri G., Knuckey J. 1969 *ZTP* **26**, 48–72. Behavior patterns of Delphinidae.

Pittendrigh C. S. 1958 In Roe A., Simpson G. G. (ed.) *Behavior and Evolution.* New Haven: Yale University Press. Adaptation, natural selection, and behavior.

Planck M. 1960 *A Survey of Physical Theory.* New York: Dover. (Originally published in 1925.)

Plomin R., DeFries J. C., Loehlin J. C. 1977 *Psychol. Bull.* **84**, 309–322. Genotype-environment interaction and correlation in human behavior.

Plotnik R. J., Tallarico R. B. 1966 *Psychon. Sci.* **5**, 195–196. Object-quality learning-set formation in the young chicken.

Poirier F. E. 1969 *Folia Primatol.* **11**, 119–133. Behavioral flexibility and intertroop variation among Nilgiri langurs.

Polsky R. H. 1975 *Behav. Biol.* **13**, 81–93. Hunger, prey feeding, and predatory aggression.

Pooley A. C. 1977 *J. Zool.* **182**, 17–26. Nest opening response of the Nile crocodile.

Popper K. R. 1972 *Objective Knowledge: An Evolutionary Approach.* Oxford: Clarendon Press.

Popper K. R. 1974 In Ayala F. J., Dobhansky T. (ed.) *Studies in the Philosophy of Biology.* London: Macmillan. Scientific reduction.

Porter R. H., Etscorn F. 1974 *Nature* (*London*) **250**, 732–733. Olfactory imprinting in *Acomys cahirinus.*

Portmann A. 1961 *Animals as Social Beings.* London: Hutchinson.

Portmann A. 1967 *Animal Forms and Patterns.* New York: Schocken.

Poulter T. C. 1968 In Sebeok T. A. (ed.) *Animal Communication.* Bloomington: Indiana University Press. Marine mammals.

Powers W. T. 1973 *Behavior: The Control of Perception.* Chicago: Aldine.

Prechtl H. F. R. 1958 *Behaviour* **13**, 212–242. The directed head turning response of the human baby.

Premack D. 1965 *Nebr. Symp. Motiv.* **13**, 123–188. Reinforcement theory.

Premack D. 1969 In Tapp J. T. (ed.) *Reinforcement and Behavior.* New York: Academic. Some boundary conditions of contrast.

Premack D. 1976 *Intelligence in Ape and Man.* Hillsdale, N.J.: Erlbaum.

Prosser C. L. (ed.) 1973 *Comparative Animal Physiology.* Philadelphia: Saunders.

Prosser C. L., Hunter W. S. 1936 *Am. J. Physiol.* **117**, 609–618. The extinction of startle responses.

Prychodko W. 1958 *Ecology* **39**, 500–503. Effect of aggregation of laboratory mice on food intake at different temperatures.

Pycraft W. P. 1914 *The Courtship of Animals.* London: Hutchinson.

Quastler H. 1958 In Yockey H. P., Platzman R. L., Quastler H. (ed.) *Symposium on Information Theory in Biology* (Gatlinburg, Tennessee, October 29–31, 1956). London: Pergamon. A primer on information theory.

Quine D. A., Cullen J. M. 1964 *Ibis* **106**, 145–173. The pecking response of young arctic terns.

Rabinowitch V. E. 1968 *AB* **16**, 425–428. The development of food preferences in gull chicks.

Rahaman H., Parthasarathy M. D. 1971 *Commun. Behav. Biol.* **6**, 97–104. Olfactory signals in the mating of bonnet monkeys.

Rajalakshmi R., Deodhar A. D., Ramakrishnan C. V. 1965 *Acta Paediatr. Scand.* **54**, 375–382. Vitamin C secretion during lactation.

Rasa O. A. E. 1969 *ZTP* **26**, 825–845. Territoriality and dominance in *Pomacentrus jenkinsi.*

Rasa O. A. E. 1972 *J. Mammal.* **53**, 181–185. Social organization in dwarf mongooses.

Rasa O. A. E. 1973 *ZTP* **32**, 293–318. Marking behaviour in the African dwarf mongoose.

Raskin D. C. 1972 In Black A. H., Prokasy W. F. (ed.) *Classical Conditioning II: Current Research and Theory.* New York: Appleton-Century-Crofts. Orienting and defensive reflexes and conditioning.

Ratner S. C., Gilpin A. R. 1974 *JCPP* **86**, 911–918. Habituation of normal and decerebrate earthworms.

Ratner S. C., Miller K. R. 1959 *JCPP* **52**, 102–105. Classical conditioning in earthworms.

Razran G. 1961 *Psychol. Rev.* **68**, 81–147. Interoceptive conditioning, semantic conditioning, and the orienting reflex.

Razran G. 1971 *Mind in Evolution.* Boston: Houghton Mifflin.

Rechten C. 1978 *AB* **26**, 305. Interspecific mimicry in birdsong.

Reese W. G., Dykman R. A. 1960 *Physiol. Rev.* **40**, 250–265. Conditional cardiovascular reflexes.

Regal P. J. 1966 *Copeia* **3**, 588–590. Thermophilic response following feeding in reptiles.

Regal P. J. 1967 *Science* **155**, 1551–1553. Voluntary hypothermia in reptiles.

Reichardt W., Poggio T. 1976 *Q. Rev. Biophys.* **9**, 311–375. Visual control of orientation behaviour in the fly.

Reimarus H. S. 1762 *Allgemeine Betrachtungen über die Triebe der Tiere*. Hamburg.

Reis D. J. 1974 In Frazier S. H. (ed.) "Aggression". *Res. Publ. Ass. Nerv. Ment. Dis.* **52**. Baltimore: Williams & Wilkins. Central neurotransmitters in aggression.

Reiter L. W., Macphail R. C. 1979 *Neurobehav. Toxicol.* **1**, 53–66. Motor activity: methods with potential use in toxicity testing.

Rensch B. 1956 *Am. Nat.* **90**, 81–95. Increase of learning capability with increase of brain size.

Rensch B., Altevogt R. 1953 *ZTP* **10**, 119–134. Visuelles Lernvermögen eines Indischen Elefanten.

Rettenmeyer C. W. 1970 *Annu. Rev. Entomol.* **15**, 43–74. Insect mimicry.

Reyniers J. A., Ervin R. F. 1946 *Lobund Rep.* (i), 1–84.

Reynierse J. H. 1968 *AB* **16**, 480–484. Effects of temperature on earthworm behaviour.

Reynolds V. 1967 *The Apes*. New York: Dutton.

Reynolds V. 1976 *The Biology of Human Action*. Reading: Freeman.

Rheingold H. L. (ed.) 1963 *Maternal Behavior in Mammals*. London: Wiley.

Rheingold H. L., Eckerman C. O. 1973 In Reese H. W. (ed.) *Advances in Child Development and Behavior*. Vol 8. New York: Academic. Fear of the stranger.

Ribbands C. R. 1953 *Behaviour and Social Life of Honeybees*. London: Bee Research Association.

Richards M. P. M. 1967 In McLaren A. (ed.) *Advances in Reproductive Physiology*. Vol. 2. London: Logos. Maternal behaviour in rodents and lagomorphs.

Richards O. W. 1953 *The Social Insects*. London: Macdonald.

Ridpath M. G. 1972a *CSIRO Wildl. Res.* **17**, 1–51. The Tasmanian native hen. I. Patterns of behaviour.

Ridpath M. G. 1972b *CSIRO Wildl. Res.* **17**, 53–90. The Tasmanian native hen. II. The individual, the group, and the population.

Riege W. H., Cherkin A. 1971 *Science* **172**, 966–968. Learning in the goldfish.

Rilling S., Mittelstaedt H., Roeder K. D. 1959 *Behaviour* **14**, 164–184. Prey recognition in the praying mantis.

Riopelle A. J., Hill C. W. 1973 In Dewsbury D. A., Rethlingshafer D. A. (ed.) *Comparative Psychology: A Modern Survey*. New York: McGraw-Hill. Complex processes.

Roberts B. L. 1969 *J. Mar. Biol. Assoc. U.K.* **49**, 33–49. Spontaneous rhythms in the motoneurons of spinal dogfish.

Roberts N. L. 1955 *Proc. R. Zool. Soc. N.S.W.*, 24–33. The Australian netting spider.

Roberts S. K., Skopik S. D., Driskill R. J. 1971 In Menaker M. (ed.) *Biochronometry*. Washington, D.C.: National Academy of Sciences. Circadian rhythms in cockroaches.

Roberts T. D. M. 1967 *Neurophysiology of Postural Mechanisms*. London: Butterworths.

Roberts W. W., Mooney R. D., Martin J. R. 1974 *JCPP* **86**, 693–699. Thermoregulatory behaviors of laboratory rodents.

Robertson A. 1973 In Howe G. M., Loraine J. A. (ed.) *Environmental Medicine*. London: Heinemann Medical. Urbanization, stress and mental health.

Robertson C. M., Sale P. F. 1975 *Behaviour* **54**, 1–25. Sexual discrimination in the Siamese fighting fish.

Robertson D. R. 1972 *Science* **177**, 1007–1009. Sex reversal in a coral-reef fish.

Robins C. R., Phillips C., Phillips F. 1959 *Zoologica* **44**, 77–84. Behavior of the blennioid fish *Chaenopsis ocellata*.

Robinson I. 1975 *The New Grammarians' Funeral*. Cambridge: Cambridge University Press.

Robson K. S. 1967 *J. Child Psychol. Psychiat.* **8**, 13–25. Eye-to-eye contact in maternal-infant attachment.

Roelofs W. L., Cardé R. T. 1974 In Birch M. C. (ed.) *Pheromones*. Amsterdam: North-Holland. Sex pheromones in the reproductive isolation of lepidopterous species.

Romanes G. J. 1892-7 *Darwin, and after Darwin*. London: Longmans.

Ronald K. 1960 *Can. J. Zool.* **38**, 623–642. The effects of physical stimuli on the larval stage of *Terranova decipiens*.

Rose R. M. 1969 In Bourne P. G. (ed.) *The Psychology and Physiology of Stress*. New York: Academic. Androgen excretion in stress.

Rose R. M., Bernstein I. S., Gordon T. P. 1975 *Psychosom. Med.* **37**, 50–60. Consequences of social conflict on plasma testosterone levels in rhesus monkeys.

Rose S. P. R. 1975 In Ebling F. J. (ed.) *Racial Variation in Man*. London: Blackwell. Scientific racism and ideology.

Rosenblatt J. S., Aronson L. R. 1958 *AB* **6**, 171–182. The influence of experience on the behavioural effects of androgen.

Rosenblum L. A. 1971 In Schaffer M. R. (ed.) *The Origins of Human Social Relations*. London: Academic. Infant attachment in monkeys.

Ross H. S. 1974 *J. Exp. Child Psychol.* **17**, 436–451. The influence of novelty and complexity on exploratory behavior in 12-month-old infants.

Roth G. 1976 *J. Comp. Physiol.* **109**, 47–58. The prey catching behavior of *Hydromantes italicus*.

Roth L. M., Dateo G. P. 1966 *J. Insect Physiol.* **12**, 255–265. A sex pheromone produced by males of the cockroach *Nauphoeta cinerea*.

Roth L. M., Willis E. R. 1952 *Am. Midl. Nat.* **47**, 66–129. A study of cockroach behavior.

Rothenbuhler W. C. 1967 In Hirsch J. (ed.) *Behavior-Genetic Analysis*. New York: McGraw-Hill. Genetic and evolutionary considerations of social behavior of honeybees.

Routtenberg A., Kuznesof A. W. 1967 *JCPP* **64**, 414–421. Self-starvation of rats living in activity wheels.

Rovner J. S. 1967 *AB* **15**, 273–281. Acoustic communication in a lycosid spider.

Rowell T. E. 1966 *AB* **14**, 430–443. The organization of a captive baboon group.

Rowell T. E. 1967 *AB* **15**, 499–509. A comparison of the behaviour of a wild and a caged baboon group.

Rowell T. E. 1974 *Behav. Biol.* **11**, 131–154. Social dominance.

Royama T. 1970 *J. Anim. Ecol.* 39, 619–668. The hunting behaviour and selection of food by the great tit.

Rozin P. 1976 In Rosenblatt J. S. et al. (ed.) *Advances in the Study of Behavior*. Vol. 6. New York: Academic. The selection of foods.

Rozin P. N., Mayer J. 1961 *Science* **134**, 942–943. Thermoregulatory behavior in the goldfish.

Rumbaugh D. M. 1965 In Rosenblum L. A., Cooper R. W. (ed.) *The Squirrel Monkey*. New York: Academic. The learning and sensory capacities of the squirrel monkey.

Rumbaugh D. M. 1970 In Rosenblum L.A. (ed.) *Primate Behavior—Developments in Field and Laboratory Research*. New York: Academic. Learning skills of anthropoids.

Rumbaugh D. M. (ed.) 1977 *Language Learning by a Chimpanzee: The Lana Project*. New York: Academic.

Rushforth N. B. 1973 In Corning W. C., Dyal J. A., Willows A. O. D. (ed.) *Invertebrate Learning*. Vol. 1. New York: Plenum. Behavioral modifications in coelenterates.

Russell B. 1903 *The Principles of Mathematics*. London: Allen & Unwin.

Russell B. 1927 *An Outline of Philosophy*. London: Allen & Unwin.

Russell B. 1948 *Human Knowledge: Its Scope and Limits*. London: Allen & Unwin.

Russell B. 1958 *Portraits from Memory and Other Essays*. London: Allen & Unwin.

Russell M. J. 1976 *Nature (London)* **260**, 520–522. Human olfactory communication.

Rust M. K., Burk T., Bell W. J. 1976 *AB* **24**, 52–67. Pheromone-stimulated locomotory and orientation responses in the American cockroach.

Rutter M. 1972 *Maternal Deprivation Reassessed*. Harmondsworth: Penguin.

Ryan J. 1973 In Hinde R. A., Stevenson-Hinde J. (ed.) *Constraints on Learning*. London: Academic. Interpretation and imitation in early language development.

Sackett G. P. et al. 1976 In Walsh R. N., Greenough

W. T. (ed.) *Environments as Therapy for Brain Dysfunction.* New York: Plenum. The effects of total social isolation on rhesus and pigtail macaques.

Sackett G. P., Ruppenthal G. C. 1973 In Barnett S. A. (ed.) *Ethology and Development.* London: Heinemann Medical. Development of monkeys after varied experiences during infancy.

Sade D. S. 1972 In Tuttle R. (ed.) *The Functional and Evolutionary Biology of Primates.* Chicago: Aldine. A longitudinal study of social behavior of rhesus monkeys.

Sahlins M. 1977 *The Use and Abuse of Biology.* London: Tavistock.

Sales G. D., Pye D. 1974 *Ultrasonic Communication by Animals.* London: Chapman & Hall.

Salmon M. 1965 *Zoologica* **50**, 123–150. Waving display and sound production in the courtship of *Uca pugilator*.

Salmon M. 1971 *Physiol. Zool.* **44**, 210–224. Signal characteristics and acoustic detection by fiddler crabs.

Salmon M., Atsaides S. P. 1968 *Am. Zool.* **8**, 623–639. Visual and acoustical signalling during courtship by fiddler crabs.

Salt G. W. 1967 *Ecol. Monogr.* **37**, 113–144. Predation in an experimental protozoan population.

Saltzman I. J. 1949 *JCPP* **42**, 161–173. Secondary reinforcement.

Sambraus V. H. H., Sambraus D. 1975 *ZTP* **38**, 1–17. Prägung von Nutztieren auf Menschen.

Sanders G. D. 1975 In Corning W. C., Dyal J. A., Willows A. O. D. (ed.) *Invertebrate Learning.* Vol. 3. New York: Plenum. The cephalopods.

Sapir E. 1957 *Culture, Language and Personality.* Berkeley: University of California Press.

Sargent T. D. 1968 *Science* **159**, 100–101. Cryptic moths: Effects on background selection of painting the circumocular scales.

Sargent T. D. 1969 *AB* **17**, 670–672. Behavioural adaptations of cryptic moths.

Sarich V. M., Wilson, A. C. 1967 *Science* **158**, 1200–1202. Immunological time scale for hominid evolution.

Sawyer C. H. 1962 *Proc. Int. Union Physiol. Sci.* **1**, 642–649. Gonadal hormone feed-back and sexual behavior.

Sayers G., Sayers M. A. 1948 *Recent Prog. Horm. Res.* **2**, 81–115. The pituitary-adrenal system.

Scaife M. 1976 *AB* **24**, 200–206. The response to eye-like shapes by birds.

Schaller G. B. 1963 *The Mountain Gorilla.* Chicago: University of Chicago Press.

Schaller G. B. 1972 *The Serengeti Lion.* Chicago: University of Chicago Press.

Schaller G. B., Lowther G. R. 1969 *Southwest. J. Anthropol.* **25**, 307–341. The relevance of carnivore behavior to the study of early hominids.

Schein M. W. 1963 *ZTP* **20**, 462–467. The irreversibility of imprinting.

Schein M. W., Fohrman M. H. 1955 *Br. J. Anim. Behav.* **3**, 45–55. Dominance in a herd of cattle.

Scheltema R. S. 1974 *Thalassia Jugosl.* **10**, 263–296. Larval settlement of marine invertebrates.

Schenkel R. 1947 *Behaviour* **1**, 81–129. Ausdrucksstudien an Wolfen.

Schenkel R. 1966 *Symp. Zool. Soc. London* **18**, 11–22. Play, exploration and territoriality in the wild lion.

Schenkel R. 1967 *Am. Zool.* **7**, 319–329. Submission in the wolf and dog.

Schenkel R., Schenkel-Hulliger L. 1969a *Ecology and Behavior of the Black Rhinoceros (Diceros bicornis L.)* Hamburg: Parey.

Schenkel R., Schenkel-Hulliger L. 1969b *Acta Trop.* **26**, 97–135. The Javan rhinoceros: Ecology and behaviour.

Schiller P. H. 1957 In Schiller C. H. (ed.) *Instinctive Behaviour.* London: Methuen. Innate motor action as a basis of learning.

Schjelderup-Ebbe T. 1922 *Z. Psychol.* **88**, 226–252. Beiträge zur Sozialpsychologie des Haushuhns.

Schleidt W. M. 1961 *ZTP* **18**, 534–560. Reaktionen von Truthühnern auf fliegende Raubvögel.

Schleidt W. M. 1962 *ZTP* **19**, 697–722. Die historische Entwicklung der Begriffe "Angeborenes auslösendes Schema" und "Angeborener Auslösemechanismus".

Schleidt W. M. 1974 *ZTP* **36**, 184–211. How "fixed" is the fixed action pattern?

Schleidt W. M., Schleidt M., Magg M. 1960 *Behaviour* **16**, 254–260. Störung der Mutter-Kind-Beziehung bei Truthühnern durch Gehörverlust.

Schmidt-Koenig K. 1975 *Migration and Homing in Animals*. Berlin: Springer-Verlag.

Schneider D. M. 1972 In Reining P. (ed.) *Kinship Studies in the Morgan Centennial Year*. Washington D.C.: Anthropological Society of Washington. What is kinship all about?

Schneirla T. C. 1953 In Roeder K. D. (ed.) *Insect Physiology*. New York: Wiley. Insect behavior.

Schneirla T. C. 1956 *Smithsonian Report 1955*, 379–406. The army ants.

Schneirla T. C. 1966 *Q. Rev. Biol.* **41**, 283–302. Behavioral development and comparative psychology.

Schneirla T. C. 1971 *Army Ants: A Study in Social Organization*. San Francisco: Freeman.

Schoener T. W. 1968 *Ecology* **49**, 123–141. Sizes of feeding territories among birds.

Schöne H. 1952 *Verh. Dtsch. Zool. Ges.* **12**, 157–162. Die statische Gleichgewichtsorientierung dekapoder Crustaceen.

Schöne H. 1954 *Z. Vgl. Physiol.* **36**, 241–260. Statozystenfunktion und statische Lageorientierung bei Dekapoden Krebsen.

Schöne H. 1957 *Z. Vgl. Physiol.* **39**, 235–240. Kurssteuerung Mittels der Statocysten.

Schorstein J. 1963 *Penguin Science Survey B*, 202–223. The present state of consciousness.

Schricker B. 1974 *Apidologie* **5**, 149–175. Der Einfluss subletaler Dosen von Parathion auf die Entfernungsweisung bei der Honigbiene.

Schultz D. P. 1965 *Sensory Restriction Effects on Behavior*. New York: Academic Press.

Schultze-Westrum T. 1965 *Z. Vgl. Physiol.* **50**, 151–220. Innerartliche Verständigung durch Düfte beim Gleitbeutler.

Schuster R. H. 1976 *Science* **192**, 1240–1242. Lekking behavior in Kafue lechwe.

Schusterman R. J. 1963 *JCPP* **56**, 96–100. Two-choice behavior of children and chimpanzees.

Schusterman R. J. 1964 *JCPP* **58**, 153–156. Successive discrimination-reversal training and multiple discrimination training in one-trial learning by chimpanzees.

Schutz F. 1965 *ZTP* **22**, 50–103. Sexuelle Prägung bei Anatiden.

Scott J. P., Fredericson E. 1951 *Physiol. Zool.* **24**, 273–309. Fighting in mice and rats.

Scribner S., Cole M. 1973 *Science* **182**, 553–559. Cognitive consequences of formal and informal education.

Seay B., Gottfried N. W. 1975 *J. Gen. Psychol.* **92**, 5–17. A phylogenetic perspective for social behavior in primates.

Sebeok T. A. (ed.) 1968 *Animal Communication*. Bloomington: Indiana University Press.

Sebeok T. A. (ed.) 1977 *How Animals Communicate*. Bloomington: Indiana University Press.

Selander R. K. 1972 In *Sexual Selection and the Descent of Man 1871–1971*. Chicago: Aldine. Sexual selection and dimorphism in birds.

Seligman M. E. P. 1970 *Psychol. Rev.* **77**, 406–418. Generality of laws of learning.

Semal-Van Gansen P. 1952 *Acad. R. Belg. Cl. Sci.* **38**, 718–735. Le système de l'hydre.

Senden M. von 1960 *Space and Sight*. London: Methuen. [Originally published in 1932.]

Serban G. (ed.) 1975 *Nutrition and Mental Functions*. New York: Plenum.

Sevenster P. 1961 *Behaviour Suppl.* **9**, 1–170. A causal analysis of a displacement activity.

Sevenster P. 1968 In Ingle D. (ed.) *The Central Nervous System and Fish Behavior*. Chicago: University of Chicago Press. Motivation and learning in sticklebacks.

Sevenster-Bol A. C. A. 1962 *Arch. Neerl. Zool.* **15**, 175–236. Drive reduction after a consummatory act.

Sharman G. B., Calaby J. H. 1964 *CSIRO Wildl. Res.* **9**, 58–85. Reproductive behaviour in the red kangaroo.

Sharpless S., Jasper H. H. 1956 *Brain* **79**, 655–680. Habituation of the arousal reaction.

Sheldon M. H. 1968 In Weiskrantz L. (ed.) *Analysis of Behavioral Change*. New York: Harper. Learning.

Sherman P. W. 1977 *Science* **197**, 1246–1253. Nepotism and the evolution of alarm calls.

Shettleworth S. J. 1975 *J. Exp. Psychol.* **104**, 56–87. Reinforcement and the organization of behavior.

Shorey H. H. 1976 *Animal Communication by Pheromones*. New York: Academic.

Sidman M. 1956 *Ann. N.Y. Acad. Sci.* **65**, 282–302. Drug-behavior interaction.

Siebenaler J. B., Caldwell D. K. 1956 *J. Mammal.* **37**, 126–128. Cooperation among adult dolphins.

Siegel S. et al. 1968 *J. Exp. Psychol.* **78**, 171–174. Generalization gradients following classical conditioning.

Simon C. A. 1975 *Ecology* **56**, 993–998. The influence of food abundance on territory size in *Sceloporus jarrovi*.

Simonds P. E. 1965 In DeVore I. (ed.) *Primate Behavior: Field Studies of Monkeys and Apes*. New York: Holt, Rinehart & Winston. The bonnet macaque in South India.

Simoons F. J. 1961 *Eat Not This Flesh*. Madison: University of Wisconsin Press.

Simpson M. J. A. 1968 *Anim. Behav. Monogr.* **1**, 1–73. The display of the Siamese fighting fish.

Skard Ø. 1950 *Acta Psychol.* **7**, 89–109. A comparison of human and animal learning.

Skinner B. F. 1953 *Science and Human Behavior*. New York: Macmillan.

Skinner B. F. 1957 *Verbal Behavior*. New York: Appleton-Century-Crofts.

Skinner B. F. 1963 In Marx M. H. (ed.) *Theories in Contemporary Psychology*. New York: Macmillan. The flight from the laboratory.

Skinner B. F. 1973 *Beyond Freedom and Dignity*. Harmondsworth: Penguin.

Slater P. J. B. 1974 In Broughton W. B. (ed.) *The Biology of Brains*. London: Institute of Biology. A reassessment of ethology.

Slater P. J. B. 1978 *AB* **26**, 304. Beau Geste has problems.

Slobodkin L. B. 1978 In Bateson P. P. G., Klopfer P. H. (ed.) *Perspectives in Ethology* Vol. 3. New York: Plenum. Is history a consequence of evolution?

Slotnick B. M., Katz H. M. 1974 *Science* **185**, 796–798. Olfactory learning-set formation.

Sluckin W. 1965 *Imprinting and Early Learning*. London: Methuen.

Sluckin W., Fullerton C. 1969 *Psychon. Sci.* **17**, 179–180. Attachments of infant guinea pigs.

Smith A. P. 1978 *AB* **26**, 232–240. Nest construction in the mud wasp *Paralastor*.

Smith C. C. 1968 *Ecol. Monogr.* **38**, 31–63. Social organization in *Tamiasciurus*.

Smith D. G. 1976 *Behaviour* **56**, 136–156. The function of red-winged blackbird song.

Smith F. V. 1962 *Symp. Zool. Soc. London* **8**, 171–191. Perceptual aspects of imprinting.

Smith J. N. M. 1974a *Behaviour* **48**, 276–302. Food searching of thrushes. I. Description and analysis of search paths.

Smith J. N. M. 1974b *Behaviour* **49**, 1–61. Food searching of thrushes. II. The adaptiveness of the search patterns.

Smith J. N. M., Dawkins R. 1971 *AB* **19**, 695–706. The hunting behaviour of great tits.

Smith W. J. 1966 *Publ. Nuttall Ornithol. Club* **6**, 1–250. Communication in the genus *Tyrannus*.

Smith W. J. 1969 *Science* **165**, 145–150. Messages of vertebrate communication.

Smith W. J. 1977 In Sebeok T. A. (ed.) *How Animals Communicate*. Bloomington: Indiana University Press. Communication in birds.

Smith W. J. et al. 1973 *Behaviour* **46**, 12–220. Behavior of a captive population of black-tailed prairie dogs.

Smythe N. 1970 *Am. Nat.* **104**, 491–494. "Pursuit invitation" signals.

Snowdon C. T. 1969 *JCPP* **69**, 91–100. The control of meal parameters with oral and intragastric feeding.

Snowdon C. T. 1970 *JCPP* **71**, 68–76. Gastrointestinal sensory and motor control of food intake.

Snyder R. L. 1961 *Proc. Nat. Acad. Sci. U.S.A.* **47**,

449–455. Mechanisms that regulate population growth.

Somit A. 1972 *Br. P. Pol. Sci.* **2**, 209–238. Biopolitics.

Southern H. N. 1970 *J. Zool.* **162**, 197–285. The natural control of a population of tawny owls.

Southwick C. H. 1966 *Behaviour* **18**, 182–209. Intragroup agonistic behavior in rhesus monkeys.

Southwick C. H. 1969 In Garattini S., Sigg E. B. (ed.) *Aggressive Behaviour*. Amsterdam: Excerpta Medica Foundation. Aggressive behaviour of rhesus monkeys in natural and captive groups.

Southwick C. H., Beg M. A., Siddiqi M. R. 1965 In DeVore I. (ed.) *Primate Behavior*. New York: Holt. Rhesus monkeys in North India.

Southwick C. H., Siddiqi M. F., Farooqui M. Y., Pal B. C. 1974 In Holloway R. L. (ed.) *Primate Aggression, Territoriality, and Xenophobia*. New York: Academic. Xenophobia among free-ranging rhesus groups.

Southwick C. H., Siddiqi M. F., Farooqui M. Y., Pal B. C. 1976 *AB* **24**, 11–15. Effects of artificial feeding on aggressive behaviour of rhesus monkeys.

Spiegel T. A. 1973 *JCPP* **84**, 24–37. Caloric regulation of food intake in man.

Spillett J. J. 1968 *The Ecology of the Lesser Bandicoot Rat in Calcutta*. Bombay: Natural History Society.

Spitz R. A. 1946 *Psychoanal. Study Child* **2**, 313–342. Anaclitic depression.

Spradbery J. P. 1973 *Wasps*. London: Sidgwick & Jackson.

Spurway H., Dronamraju K. R., Jayakar S. D. 1964 *J. Bombay Nat. Hist. Soc.* **61**, 1–26. One nest of *Sceliphron madraspatanum*.

Spurway H., Haldane J. B. S. 1953 *Behaviour* **6**, 8–34. The comparative ethology of vertebrate breathing.

Stamps J. A. 1973 *Copeia* **2**, 264–272. Displays and social organization in female *Anolis aeneus*.

Stamps J. A., Barlow G. W. 1973 *Behaviour* **47**, 67–94. Variation and stereotypy in the displays of *Anolis aeneus*.

Starr M. P. 1975 *Symp. Soc. Exp. Biol.* **29**, 1–20. Classifying organismic associations.

Starzl T. E., Taylor C. W., Magoun H. W. 1951 *J.*

Neurophysiol. **14**, 479–496. Collateral afferent excitation of reticular formation of brain stem.

Stauffer R. C. (ed.) 1975 *Charles Darwin's Natural Selection*. Cambridge: Cambridge University Press.

Stearns S. C. 1976 *Q. Rev. Biol.* **51**, 2–47. Life-history tactics.

Stearns S. C. 1977 *Annu. Rev. Ecol. Syst.* **8**, 145–171. The evolution of life history traits: A critique of the theory and a review of the data.

Stebbins G. L. 1977 *Am. Nat.* **111**, 386–390. In defense of evolution: Tautology or theory?

Steklis H. B., Harnad S. R., Lancaster J. (ed.) 1976 *Origins and Evolution of Language and Speech*. New York: New York Academy of Sciences (*Ann. N.Y. Acad. Sci.* **280**).

Stephan H. 1972 In Tuttle R. (ed.) *The Functional and Evolutionary Biology of Primates*. Chicago: Aldine. Evolution of primate brains.

Sternburg J. G., Waldbauer G. P., Jeffords M. R. 1977 *Science* **195**, 681–683. Batesian mimicry.

Stevenson J. G. 1967 *AB* **15**, 427–432. Reinforcing effects of chaffinch song.

Steward C. C., Atwood C. E. 1963 *Can. J. Zool.* **41**, 577–594. The sensory organs of the mosquito antenna.

Steward R. C. 1967 *J. Zool.* **183**, 47–62. Industrial melanism in moths.

Stimson J. 1970 *Ecology* **51**, 113–118. Territorial behavior of the owl limpet.

Stimson J. 1973 *Ecology* **54**, 1020–1030. Territory in the ecology of the intertidal limpet *Lottia gigantea*.

Stinson R. H., Fisher K. C. 1953 *Can. J. Zool.* **31**, 404–416. Temperature selection in deer mice.

Stokes A. W. 1962 *Behaviour* **19**, 118–138. Agonistic behaviour among blue tits at a winter feeding station.

Stratton L. O., Coleman W. P. 1973 *JCPP* **83**, 7–12. Maze learning and orientation in the fire ant.

Straus W. L., Cave A. J. E. 1957 *Q. Rev. Biol.* **32**, 348–363. The posture of Neanderthal man.

Strecker R. L., Emlen J. T. 1953 *Ecology* **34**, 375–385. Regulatory mechanisms in house-mouse populations.

Struhsaker T. T. 1967 *Behaviour* **29**, 83–121. Social structure among vervet monkeys.

Strum S. C. 1975 *Science* **187**, 755–757. Primate predation: The development of a tradition in a troop of baboons.

Sugiyama Y. 1967 In Altmann S. A. (ed.) *Social Communication among Primates*. Chicago: University of Chicago Press. Social organization of Hanuman langurs.

Sund P. N. 1958 *Q. J. Microsc. Sci.* **99**, 401–420. The muscular anatomy and swimming of *Stomphia coccinea*.

Suomi S. J., Harlow H. R., Novak M. A. 1974 *J. Hum. Evol.* **3**, 527–534. Reversal of social deficits produced by isolation rearing in monkeys.

Sutherland N. S. 1969 *JCPP* **67**, 160–176. Shape discrimination in rat, octopus, and goldfish.

Sutherland N. S., Mackintosh J., Mackintosh N. J. 1963 *AB* **11**, 106–110. The visual discrimination of reduplication patterns by octopus.

Swan H. 1974 *Thermoregulation and Bioenergetics*. New York: American Elsevier.

Swanson H. H., Lockley M. R. 1978 *AB* **4**, 57–89. Population growth and social structure of confined colonies of Mongolian gerbils.

Sylva K., Bruner J. S., Genova P. 1976 In Bruner J. S., Jolly A., Sylva K. (ed.) *Play—Its Role in Development and Evolution*. Harmondsworth: Penguin. The role of play in the problem-solving of children 3–5 years old.

Taggart N. 1962 *Br. J. Nutr.* **16**, 223–235. Diet, activity and body-weight.

Tavolga M. C., Essapian F. S. 1957 *Zoologica* **42**, 11–31. The behavior of the bottle nosed dolphin.

Tavolga W. N. 1960 In Lanyon W. E., Tavolga W. N. (ed.) *Animal Sounds & Communication*. Washington: American Institute of Biological Sciences. Sound production and underwater communication in fishes.

Tayler C. K., Saayman G. S. 1973 *Behaviour* **44**, 286–298. Imitative behaviour by bottlenose dophins.

Tees R. C. 1976 In Gottlieb G. (ed.) *Neural and Behavioral Specificity*. New York: Academic. Perceptual development in mammals.

Teitelbaum P. 1955 *JCPP* **48**, 156–163. Sensory control of hypothalamic hyperphagia.

Teleki G. 1975 *J. Hum. Evol.* **4**, 125–184. Primate subsistence patterns: collector-predators and gatherer-hunters.

Terman C. R. 1973 *J. Reprod. Fertil. Suppl.* **19**, 457–463. Reproductive inhibition in asymptotic populations of prairie deermice.

Terrace H. S. et al. 1979 *Science* **206**, 891–902. Can an ape create a sentence?

Thomas G. 1974 *AB* **22**, 941–952. The influence of encountering a food object on searching behavior in *Gasterosteus aculeatus*.

Thompson W. R., Heron W. 1954 *Can. J. Psychol.* **8**, 17–31. The effects of restricting early experience on the problem-solving capacity of dogs.

Thorndike E. L. 1898 *Psychol. Rev. Monogr. Suppl.* **2**, no. 8. Animal intelligence: An experimental study.

Thorndike E. L. 1911 *Animal Intelligence: Experimental Studies*. Darien, Conn.: Hafner.

Thorpe W. H. 1938 *Proc. R. Soc. London Ser. B* **126**, 370–397. Olfactory conditioning in a parasitic insect.

Thorpe W. H. 1939 *Proc. R. Soc. London Ser. B* **127**, 424–433. Pre-imaginal conditioning in insects.

Thorpe W. H. 1950 *Behaviour* **13**, 257–263. Detour experiments with *Ammophila pubescens*.

Thorpe W. H. 1951 *Bull. Anim. Behav.* **9**, 34–40. The definition of terms used in animal behaviour studies.

Thorpe W. H. 1961 *Bird-Song*. Cambridge: Cambridge University Press.

Thorpe W. H. 1963 *Learning and Instinct in Animals*. London: Methuen.

Thorpe W. H., et al. 1972 *Behaviour Suppl.* **18**, 1–197. Duetting and antiphonal song in birds.

Thorpe W. H., Jones F. G. W. 1938 *Proc. R. Soc. London, Ser. B* **124**, 56–81. Olfactory conditioning in a parasitic insect.

Thorpe W. H., North M. E. W. 1965 *Nature (Lon-*

don) **208**, 219–222. Vocal imitation: With special reference to the antiphonal singing of birds.

Timms A. M., Keenleyside M. H. A. 1975 *ZTP* **39**, 8–23. The reproductive behaviour of *Aequidens paraguayensis*.

Tinbergen L. 1960 *Arch. Neerl. Zool.* **13**, 265–379. The natural control of insects in pinewoods.

Tinbergen N. 1951 *The Study of Instinct.* Oxford: Clarendon.

Tinbergen N. 1952 *Q. Rev. Biol.* **27**, 1–32. "Derived" activities.

Tinbergen N. 1953 *The Herring Gull's World.* London: Collins.

Tinbergen N. 1959 *Behaviour* **15**, 1–70. Comparative studies of the behaviour of gulls.

Tinbergen N. 1963 *ZTP* **20**, 410–433. Aims and methods of ethology.

Tinbergen N. 1965 In Moore J. A. (ed.) *Ideas in Modern Biology.* New York: Natural History Press. Behavior and natural selection.

Tinbergen N. 1968 *Science* **160**, 1411–1418. On war and peace in animals and man.

Tinbergen N. 1969 In Harré R. (ed.) *Scientific Thought.* Oxford: Clarendon. Ethology.

Tinbergen N. et al. 1962 *Behaviour* **19**, 74–117. Egg shell removal by the black-headed gull (*Larus ridibundus* L.).

Tinbergen N., Kruyt W. 1938 *Z. Vgl. Physiol.* **25**, 292–334. Über die Orientierung des Bienenwolfes.

Tinbergen N., Kuenen D. J. 1939 *ZTP* **3**, 37–60. Die auslösenden und die richtunggebenden Reitzsituationen der Sperrbewegung von jungen Drosseln.

Tinbergen N., Perdeck A. C. 1950 *Behaviour* **3**, 1–38. The begging response in the newly-hatched herring gull.

To L. P., Tamarin R. H. 1977 *Ecology* **58**, 928–934. The relation of population density and adrenal gland weight in cycling and noncycling voles.

Tobias P. V. 1963 *Nature* **197**, 743–746. Cranial capacity of *Zinjanthropus* and other Australopithecines.

Torrey J. W. 1976 In Petrinovich L., McGaugh J. L. (ed.) *Knowing, Thinking and Believing.* New York: Plenum. The psychology of linguistic knowledge.

Tredgold R. F., Soddy K. 1956 *Tredgold's Text-book of Mental Deficiency.* London: Baillière, Tindall and Cox.

Trivers R. L. 1971 *Q. Rev. Biol.* **46**, 35–57. The evolution of reciprocal altruism.

Trivers R. L. 1972 In Campbell B. (ed.) *Sexual Selection and the Descent of Man 1871–1971.* Chicago: Aldine. Parental investment and sexual selection.

Trivers R. L. 1974 *Am. Zool.* **14**, 249–264. Parent-offspring conflict.

Trivers R. L., Hare H. 1976 *Science* **191**, 249–263. Haplodiploidy and the evolution of the social insects.

Tryon R. C. 1940 *Yearb. Nat. Soc. Stud. Educ.* **39**, 111–119. Genetic differences in maze-learning ability.

Tsang Y.-C. 1934 *Comp. Psychol. Monogr.* **10**, 1–56. The function of the visual areas of the cortex in learning.

Tschanz B. 1968 *ZTP* **25**, 244–245. Die Entstehung der persönlichen Beziehung zwischen Jungvogel und Eltern.

Tsumori A. 1967 In Altman S. A. (ed.) *Social Communication among Primates.* Chicago: University of Chicago Press. Newly acquired behavior and social interactions of Japanese monkeys.

Turner E. R. A. 1965 *Behaviour* **24**, 1–46. Social feeding in birds.

Tylor E. B. 1964 *Researches into the Early History of Mankind and the Development of Civilization.* Chicago: University of Chicago Press.

Uexküll J. von 1957 In Schiller C. H. (ed.) *Instinctive Behaviour.* London: Methuen. [Originally published in 1934.]

Ulrich R. E., Hutchinson R. R., Azrin N. H. 1965 *Psychol. Rec.* **15**, 111–126. Pain-elicited aggression.

Uvarov B. P. 1966 *Grasshoppers and Locusts. A Handbook of General Acridology.* Vol. 1. Cambridge: Cambridge University Press.

Vale H., Sundberg H., Ursin H. 1976 *Physiol. Behav.* **16**, 337–341. Habituation of orienting and motor responses.

Vale J. R., Vale C. A., Harley J. P. 1971 *Commun. Behav. Biol.* **6**, 209–221. Interaction of genotype and population number with regard to aggressive behavior, social grooming, and adrenal and gonadal weight.

Valenstein E. S. V., Riss W. R., Young W. C. 1955 *JCPP* **48**, 397–403. Experiential and genetic factors in sexual behavior in the male guinea pig.

Valvo A. 1971 *Sight Restoration after Long-term Blindness: The Problems and Behavior Patterns of Visual Rehabilitation.* New York: American Foundation for the Blind.

Vehrencamp S. L. 1977 *Science* **197**, 403–405. Fecundity and parental effort in communally nesting anis.

Vernon J. A. 1963 *Inside the Black Room.* London: Souvenir Press.

Verplanck W. S. 1954 In Elliott R. M. (ed.) *Modern Learning Theory.* New York: Appleton-Century-Crofts. Burrhus F. Skinner.

Vince M. A. 1958 *AB* **6**, 53–59. "String-pulling" in birds.

Vince M. A. 1973 In Gottlieb G. (ed.) *Studies on the Development of Behavior and the Nervous System.* Vol. 1: *Behavioral Embryology.* New York: Academic. Environmental effects on the activity and development of the avian embryo.

Vince M. A., Reader M., Tolhurst B. 1976 *JCPP* **90**, 221–230. Effects of stimulation of embryonic activity in the chick.

Vowles D. M. 1965 *Br. J. Psychol.* **56**, 15–31. Maze learning and visual discrimination in the wood ant.

Waddington C. H. 1939 *An Introduction to Modern Genetics.* London: Allen & Unwin.

Wade M. J. 1976 *Proc. Natl. Acad. Sci. U.S.A.* **73**, 4604–4607. Group selection among laboratory populations of *Tribolium.*

Wade M. J. 1977 *Evolution* **31**, 134–153. An experimental study of group selection.

Wade M. J. 1978 *Q. Rev. Biol.* **53**, 101–114. Models of group selection.

Walcher D. N., Kretchmer N., Barnett H. L. 1976 *Food, Man and Society.* New York: Plenum.

Walcott C., Gould J. L., Kirschvink J. L. 1979 *Science* **205**, 1027–1029. Pigeons have magnets.

Walker E. L., et al. 1955 *JCPP* **48**, 19–23. Choice alternation.

Walsh R. N., Cummins R. A. 1976 *Psychol. Bull,* **83**, 482–504. The open-field test.

Walther F. 1958 *ZTP* **15**, 340–380. Zum Kampf- und Paarungsverhalten einiger Antilopen.

Walther F. R. 1977 In Sebeok T. A. (ed.) *How Animals Communicate.* Bloomington: Indiana University Press. Artiodactyla.

Ward S. 1973 *Proc. Natl. Acad. Sci. U.S.A.* **70**, 817–821. Chemotaxis by the nematode *Caenorhabditis elegans.*

Warren J. M. 1973 In Dewsbury D. A., Rethlingshafer D. A. (ed.) *Comparative Psychology: A Modern Survey.* New York: McGraw-Hill. Learning in vertebrates.

Warren J. M. 1974 *J. Hum. Evol.* **3**, 445–454. Possibly unique characteristics of learning by primates.

Warren J. M. 1976 In Masterton R. B. et al. (ed.) *Evolution of Brain and Behavior in Vertebrates.* Hillsdale, N.J.: Erlbaum. Tool use in mammals.

Waterhouse M. J., Waterhouse H. B. 1973 In Michael R. P., Crook J. H. (ed.) *Comparative Ecology and Behaviour of Primates.* London: Academic. Primate ethology and human social behaviour.

Watson A. 1977 In Stonehouse B., Perrins C. (ed.) *Evolutionary Ecology.* Baltimore: University Park Press. Population limitation and territorial behavior in Scottish red grouse.

Watson A., Moss R. 1971 In Esser A. H. (ed.) *Behavior and Environment. The Use of Space by Animals and Men.* New York: Plenum. Spacing as affected by territorial behavior, habitat and nutrition in red grouse.

Watson J. B. 1930 *Behaviorism.* Chicago: University of Chicago Press.

Webb S. D., Collette J. 1975 *Am. Behav. Sci.* **18**, 750–770. Urban ecological and household correlates of stress-alleviative drug use.

Wecker S. C. 1963 *Ecol. Monogr.* **33**, 307–325. The role of early experience in habitat selection by the prairie deer mouse.

Weinstock S. 1954 *JCPP* **47**, 318–322. Resistance to extinction of a running response.

Weisler A., McCall R. B. 1976 *Am. Psychol.* **31**, 492–508. Exploration and play.

Weiss B. 1957 *JCPP* **50**, 481–485. Thermal behavior of the subnourished and pantothenic-acid-deprived rat.

Weiss B. A., Schneirla T. C. 1967 *Behaviour* **28**, 269–279. Inter-situational transfer in *Formica schaufussi*.

Weiss K. 1953 *ZTP* **10**, 29–44. Versuche mit Bienen und Wespen in farbigen Labyrinthen.

Wells G. P. 1950 *Symp. Soc. Exp. Biol.* **4**, 127–142. Spontaneous activity cycles in polychaete worms.

Wells K. D. 1977 *AB* **25**, 666–693. The social behaviour of anuran amphibians.

Wells M. J. 1958 *Behaviour* **13**, 96–111. Reactions to *Mysis* by newly hatched *Sepia*.

Wells M. J. 1962 *Brain and Behaviour in Cephalopods.* London: Heinemann Educational.

Wells M. J. 1968 In Salánki J. (ed.) *Neurobiology of Invertebrates.* New York: Plenum. Sensitization and the evolution of associative learning.

Wells M. J. 1974 In Bellairs R., Gray E. G. (ed.) *Essays on the Nervous System.* Oxford: Clarendon Press. A location for learning.

Wells M. J. 1975 In Usherwood P. N. R., Newth D. R. (ed.) *"Simple" Nervous Systems.* London: Edward Arnold. Evolution and associative learning.

Wells M. J. 1978 *Octopus.* London: Chapman & Hall.

Wells M. J., Buckley K. L. 1972 *AB* **20**, 345–355. Snails and trails.

Wells M. J., Wells J. 1957 *J. Exp. Biol.* **34**, 131–142. The function of the brain of octopus in tactile discrimination.

Wells M. J., Wells J. 1971 *AB* **19**, 305–312. Conditioning and sensitization in snails.

Wells P. H. 1967 In Corning W. C., Ratner S. C. (ed.) *Chemistry of Learning.* New York: Plenum. Training flatworms in a maze.

Wenner A. M. 1971 *The Bee Language Controversy.* Boulder, Colo.: Educational Programs Improvement Corporation.

Wenner A. M., Johnson D. L. 1966 *AB* **14**, 149–155. Simple conditioning in honey bees.

Werner E. E., Hall D. J. 1976 *Science* **191**, 404–406. Niche shifts in sunfishes.

Wessenberg H., Antipa G. 1970 *J. Protozool.* **17**, 250–270. Capture and ingestion of *Paramecium* by *Didinium nasutum*.

West Eberhard M. J. 1975 *Q. Rev. Biol.* **50**, 1–33. The evolution of social behavior by kin selection.

Westerman R. A. 1963 *Science* **140**, 676–677. Somatic inheritance of habituation of responses to light in planarians.

Weygoldt P. 1974 *ZTP* **34**, 217–223. Kampf und Paarung bei der Geisselspinne.

Weygoldt P. 1977 In Sebeok T. A. (ed.) *How Animals Communicate.* Bloomington: Indiana University Press. Communication in crustaceans and arachnids.

Whalen R. E., Beach F. A., Kuehn R. E. 1961 *Endocrinology* **69**, 373–380. Effects of exogenous androgen on sexually responsive and unresponsive male rats.

Whistler H. 1963 *Popular Handbook of Indian Birds.* Edinburgh: Oliver & Boyd.

White B. L., Held R., Castle P. 1967 In Hellmuth J. (ed.) *Exceptional Infant.* Vol 1. New York: Brunner/Mazel. Observations on the development of visually-directed reaching.

Whitford W. G., Hutchison V. H. 1963 *Biol. Bull.* **124**, 344–354. Cutaneous and pulmonary gas exchange in the spotted salamander.

Whitford W. G., Hutchison V. H. 1965 *Physiol. Zool.* **38**, 228–242. Gas exchange in salamanders.

Whitney G. D. 1969 *J. Hered.* **60**, 337–340. Vocalization of mice: a single genetic unit effect.

Whitney G. D. 1973 *Behav. Genet.* **3**, 57–64. Vocalization of mice influenced by a single gene.

Wickens D. D., Miles R. C. 1954 *JCPP* **47**, 315–317. Extinction changes during a series of reinforcement-extinction sessions.

Wickler W. 1962 *ZTP* **19**, 129–164. Ei-Attrappen und Maulbrüten bei afrikanischen Cichliden.

Wickler W. 1967 In Morris D. (ed.) *Primate Ethology.* London: Weidenfeld & Nicolson. Socio-sexual signals and their intra-specific imitation among primates.

Wiens J. A. 1970 *Copeia* **3**, 543–548. Effects of early experience on substrate pattern selection in *Rana aurora* tadpoles.

Wiepkema P. R. 1971 *Behaviour* **39**, 266–273. Positive feedbacks at work during feeding.

Wigglesworth V. B. 1941 *Parasitology* **33**, 67–109. The sensory physiology of the human louse.

Wigglesworth V. B., Gillett J. D. 1934a *J. Exp. Biol.* **11**, 120–139. The function of the antennae in *Rhodnius prolixus*.

Wigglesworth V. B., Gillett J. D. 1934b *J. Exp. Biol.* **11**, 408. The function of the antennae in *Rhodnius prolixus:* Confirmatory experiments.

Wilcoxon H. C., Dragoin W. B., Dral P. A. 1971 *Science* **171**, 826–828. Illness-induced aversions in rat and quail.

Wiley R. H. 1973 *Behaviour* **47**, 129–152. The strut display of male sage grouse.

Wiley R. H., Wiley M. S. 1977 *Behaviour* **62**, 10–34. Recognition of neighbors' duets by stripe-backed wrens.

Wilkins L., Richter C. P. 1940. *J. Am. Med. Assoc.* **114**, 866–868. A great craving for salt by a child with cortico-adrenal insufficiency.

Williams G. C. 1957 *Univ. Calif. Berkeley Publ. Zool.* **59**, 249–284. Homing of California rocky shore fishes.

Williams G. C. 1966 *Adaptation and Natural Selection.* Princeton: Princeton University Press.

Williams G. C. 1975 *Sex and Evolution.* Princeton: Princeton University Press.

Willows A. O. D. 1973 In Corning W. C., Dyal J. A., Willows A. O. D. (ed.) *Invertebrate Learning.* Vol. 2. New York: Plenum. Learning in gastropod mollusks.

Willows A. O. D., Corning W. C. 1975 In Corning W. C., Dyal J. A., Willows A. O. D. (ed.) *Invertebrate Learning.* Vol. 3. New York: Plenum. The echinoderms.

Willson M. F. 1971 *Condor* **73**, 415–429. Seed selection in some North American finches.

Wilm E. C. 1925 *The Theories of Instinct.* New Haven: Yale University Press.

Wilson C. C. 1972 *Folia Primatol.* **18**, 256–275. Spatial factors and the behavior of nonhuman primates.

Wilson D. P. 1952 *Ann. Inst. Oceanogr.* **27**, 49–156. The influence of the substratum on the metamorphosis of the larvae of marine animals.

Wilson E. O. 1971 *The Insect Societies.* Cambridge: Harvard University Press.

Wilson E. O. 1975 *Sociobiology.* Cambridge: Harvard University Press.

Wilson E. O., Bossert W. H. 1963 *Recent Prog. Horm. Res.* **19**, 673–716. Chemical communication among animals.

Wilson R. C. et al. 1976 *Behav. Biol.* **17**, 495–506. Open-field behavior in muroid rodents.

Wiltschko W., Wiltschko R. 1975 *ZTP* **37**, 337–355. The interaction of stars and magnetic field in the orientation of night migrating birds.

Wiltschko W., Wiltschko R. 1976 *J. Comp. Physiol.* **109**, 91–99. Interrelation of magnetic compass and star orientation in night-migrating birds.

Windecker W. 1939 *Z. Morphol. Oekol. Tiere* **35**, 84–138. Euchelia (Hypocrita) jacobaeae und das Schutztrachtenproblem.

Winfield C. G., Kilgour R. 1976 *Appl. Anim. Ethol.* **2**, 235–243. Following behaviour in young lambs.

Winick M., Jaroslow A., Winer E. 1978 *Growth* **42**, 391–397. Foster placement, malnutrition and environment.

Winick M., Meyer K. K., Harris R. C. 1975 *Science* **190**, 1173–1175. Malnutrition and environmental enrichment by early adoption.

Wodinsky J., Bitterman M. E. 1953 *Am. J. Psychol.* **66**, 137–140. The solution of oddity problems by the rat.

Wolf E. 1926 *Z. Vgl. Physiol.* **3**, 615–691. Über das Heimkehrvermögen der Bienen.

Wolf E. 1927 *Z. Vgl. Physiol.* **4**, 221–254. Über das Heimkehrvermögen der Bienen.

Wolff P. H. 1968 *Brain Behav. Evol.* **1**, 354–367. Sucking patterns of infant mammals.

Wolff P. H. 1969 In Wolff P. H., Keith R. M. (ed.) *Planning for Better Learning. Clinics in Developmental Medicine* **33**. London: Heinemann. What we must and must not teach our young children.

Woodruff G., Premack D. 1979 *Cognition* **7**, 333–362. Intentional communication in the chimpanzee: the development of deception.

Woodger J. H. 1945 In Le Gros Clark W. E., Medawar P. B. (ed.) *Essays on Growth and Form.* Oxford: Clarendon Press. On biological transformations.

Wood-Gush D. G. M. 1971 *The Behaviour of the Domestic Fowl.* London: Heinemann Educational.

Wooldridge D. E. 1963 *The Machinery of the Brain.* New York: McGraw-Hill.

Woolfenden G. E. 1975 *Auk* **92**, 1–15. Florida scrub jay helpers at the nest.

Wootton R. J. 1972a *Behaviour* **41**, 232–241. The behaviour of the male three-spined stickleback in a natural situation.

Wootton R. J. 1972b *Can. J. Zool.* **50**, 537–541. Changes in the aggression of the male three-spined stickleback after fertilization of eggs.

Wrangham R. W. 1974 *AB* **22**, 83–93. Artificial feeding of chimpanzees and baboons in their natural habitat.

Wright R. H. 1976 *Colloq. Int. C.N.R.S.* **265**, 61–71. The olfactory transmission of information.

Wyers E. J., Peeke H. V. S., Herz M. J. 1973 In Peeke H. V. S., Herz M. J. (ed.) *Habituation.* Vol. 1: *Behavioral Studies.* New York: Academic. Behavioral habituation in invertebrates.

Wynne-Edwards V. C. 1962 *Animal Dispersion.* Edinburgh: Oliver & Boyd.

Yamaguchi S., Myers R. E. 1972 *Brain Res.* **37**, 109–114. Failure of discriminative vocal conditioning in rhesus monkey.

Yeaton R. I. 1972 *J. Mammal* **73**, 139–147. Social organization in Richardson's ground squirrel.

Yerkes R. M. 1912 *J. Anim. Behav.* **2**, 332–352. The intelligence of earthworms.

Yerkes R. M., Tomilin M. I. 1935 *J. Comp. Psychol.* **20**, 321–359. Mother-infant relations in chimpanzee.

Yoshiba K. 1968 In Jay P. C. (ed.) *Primates: Studies in Adaptation and Variability.* New York: Holt, Rinehart & Winston. Local and intertroop variability in social behavior of Indian langurs.

Young J. Z. 1964 *A Model of the Brain.* Oxford: Clarendon Press.

Young J. Z. 1975 *The Life of Mammals.* Oxford: Clarendon Press.

Young R. E. 1976 *Science* **191**, 1046–1047. Bioluminescent countershading in midwater animals.

Young R. E., Roper C. F. E. 1977 *Fish. Bull.* **75**, 239–252. Intensity regulation of bioluminescence during countershading.

Young R. M. 1970 In Symondson A. (ed.) *The Victorian Crisis of Faith.* London: S.P.C.K. The impact of Darwin on conventional thought.

Young W. C. 1961 In Young W. C. (ed.) *Sex and Internal Secretions.* Vol. II. Baltimore: Williams & Wilkins. The hormones and mating behavior.

Young W. C. 1965 In Beach F. A. (ed.) *Sex and Behavior.* New York: Wiley 1965. The organization of sexual behavior by hormonal action.

Zener K. 1937 *Am. J. Psychol.* **50**, 384–403. Behavior accompanying conditioned salivary secretion.

Zimmerman B. J., Rosenthal T. L. 1974 *Psychol. Bull.* **81**, 29–42. Observational learning of rule-governed behavior by children.

Zippelius H. M. 1972 *ZTP* **30**, 205–320. Die Karawanenbildung bei Feld- und Hausspitzmaus.

Zucker R. S., Kennedy D., Selverston A. I. 1971 *Science* **173**, 645–650. Neuronal circuit mediating escape responses in crayfish.

Zuckerman S. 1932 *The Social Life of Monkeys and Apes.* London: Kegan Paul.

INDEX OF AUTHORS

SUBJECT INDEX

Italic numbers refer to sections within chapters.